Computerized Accounting with
QUICKBOOKS® PRO 2003

Kathleen Villani
Queensborough Community College

James B. Rosa
Queensborough Community College

EMCParadigm
PUBLISHING

DEDICATION

In loving memory of Ray Waszak

With love and thanks to our parents...
 Elizabeth and Raymond Villani
 Livia and Bruno Rosa

And to our families...
 Harry, Kristin, Jennifer, and Lynnann Whitbeck
 Renee, Raina, and Olivia Rosa

Developmental Editor	James Patterson
Cover Designer	Leslie Anderson
Testing	Desiree Faulkner
Indexing	Donald Glassman
Desktop Production	Leslie Anderson

Publishing Team—George Provol, Publisher; Janice Johnson, Director of Product Development; Lori Landwer, Marketing Manager; Shelley Clubb, Electronic Design and Production Manager.

Registered Trademarks—QuickBooks® Pro and QuickBooks Basic® are registered trademarks of Intuit, Inc. Windows, Microsoft Word, and Microsoft Excel are registered trademarks of Microsoft Corporation in the United States and other countries.

Library of Congress Cataloging-in-Publication Data
 Villani, Kathleen.
 Computerized accounting with QuickBooks Pro 2003 : for use with Quickbooks 2003 and
 Quickbooks Pro 2003 / Kathleen Villani, James B. Rosa.
 p. cm.
 Includes index.
 ISBN 0-7638-1952-2
 1. Quickbooks. 2. Small business—Accounting—Computer Programs. 3. Small business—
 Finance—Computer Programs. I. Title: Quickbooks Pro 2003. II Rosa, James B. III. Title

 HF5679 .V534 2004
 657'.9042'02855369—dc21

 2003048767

Text and CD: ISBN 0-7638-1952-2
Order Number:01603

©2004 by Paradigm Publishing Inc.
 Published by EMCParadigm
 875 Montreal Way
 St. Paul, MN 55102

 (800) 535-6865
 E-mail: educate@emcp.com
 Web Site: www.emcp.com

Contents

Preface

QuickBooks Pro Edition 2003 is one of the most popular general ledger software packages used by small and medium sized businesses. The program allows you to maintain a general ledger; track vendor, customer, and inventory activities; process payroll for company employees; prepare bank reconciliation; track time for employees and jobs; and so on.

QUICKBOOKS BASIC AND QUICKBOOKS PRO

This text was developed using QuickBooks Pro. Intuit, the maker of QuickBooks Pro, also offers a version of this product called QuickBooks Basic. QuickBooks Pro offers a few features, such as allowing for multiple users and exporting data to other software packages, that are not offered in QuickBooks Basic. The few additional features included in QuickBooks Pro are noted in the text. Essentially, the capabilities in QuickBooks Pro and QuickBooks Basic are identical, except where noted.

ABOUT THIS TEXT

Computerized Accounting with QuickBooks Pro Edition 2003 teaches both the accountant and non-accountant student how to use QuickBooks Pro Edition 2003. Each chapter contains a tutorial of the procedural steps needed to process accounting data along with illustrations of accounting concepts. QuickBooks Pro steps are fully explained and reinforced with several guided exercises; a company called Kristin Raina Interior Designs is used to illustrate the topics of each chapter. The topics presented in each chapter build on the topics covered in the previous chapters. Beginning with chapter 2, there are two case problems that review the topics of that chapter.

This text is organized to follow the four levels of operation in QuickBooks Pro: New Company Setup, Lists, Activities, and Reports. The New Company Setup is more effectively learned when someone *understands* the basic operations of the QuickBooks Pro software. Therefore, chapters 1 - 5 present how to *use* QuickBooks Pro following a normal business flow. Chapter 1 introduces you to some basic steps in moving around the QuickBooks Pro software and opening company files. Chapter 2 illustrates when bills are received and subsequently paid, or when bills are paid immediately. Chapter 3 illustrates when a company earns revenue and creates a bill for a customer and subsequently collects the money, or when the cash is received immediately for services rendered. Chapter 4 presents the use of the general journal. Chapter 5 presents the purchase and sale of inventory items.

After the basic QuickBooks Pro operations are mastered, the New Company Setup level of operation is explained. Chapters 6 and 7 illustrate the New Company Setup process using the EasyStep Interview, and chapter 8 illustrates the New Company Setup process with the alternative method — Skip EasyStep Interview. Chapter 9 moves onto the setup and processing of payroll transactions. Throughout these chapters, many reports, including the financial statements, will be viewed and printed. Upon completion of chapters 1 - 9, the reader will have a thorough understanding of the New Company Setup, Lists, Activities, and Reports levels of operation.

The remainder of the book presents a variety of topics. Chapter 10 illustrates QuickBooks Pro banking features.

Chapter 11 presents the capabilities of job accounting and time-tracking. Chapter 12 presents more advanced features available in QuickBooks Pro such as customizing the appearance and default settings of reports, customizing activity windows and invoices, viewing graphs, exporting information into Microsoft Excel and Word, and memorizing transactions.

ABOUT THE SOFTWARE

QuickBooks Pro Edition 2003 or QuickBooks Basic Edition 2003 must be loaded on a computer running Windows 98 or Windows NT 4.0 or higher in order for you to use this book. It is assumed the reader is familiar with using a personal computer and understands some basic Windows terminology. At times, specific Windows operating procedures are explained when they would enhance the operation of QuickBooks Pro.

QuickBooks Pro or QuickBooks Basic can be purchased in retail stores or directly from Intuit (1-888-2-Intuit or 1-888-246-8848). Education Paks, purchased directly from Intuit (1-800-446-8848), are available for schools that wish to load the software on several computers in a computer laboratory. Education Paks are available for groups of 10, 25, or 50 workstations.

THE COMPANY FILES CD

Included with the text is a CD that contains the company starter files for the sample company used throughout the text. Each company file contains the opening balances for the chapter sample problem and the two end-of-chapter cases so you can follow the material and complete the problems correctly. You will be instructed to make a backup copy of the files onto a floppy disk, your hard drive, or a designated network directory, and store the original CD in a safe place.

There are company files for each chapter except chapters 6 and 8. In these two chapters, you will be instructed on how to create a new company file.

SUPPLEMENTS FOR INSTRUCTORS

This text comes with the following supplements: an Instructor's Guide on CD-ROM, Test Bank, and Web course management files in both WebCT and Blackboard platforms.

The **Instructor's Guide** includes the following information for each chapter:
- Overview
- Sample syllabi
- Chapter objectives
- Guidelines for the instructor on key software items
- Lecture notes
- Procedure reviews
- Solutions to the key concepts, procedure checks, and case problems

The **Test Bank** on IRC for this text includes test questions, quizzes, and tests that correspond to each chapter of the book. Instructors can add, edit, and delete items in the Test Bank as desired.

The **Class Connection** course management tool provides customizable Web pages in WebCT and Blackboard platforms. Using this tool, instructors can provide a syllabus, assignments, quizzes and study aids, and other course materials online, hold e-discussions and group conferences, send and receive email and assignments from students, and manage grades electronically.

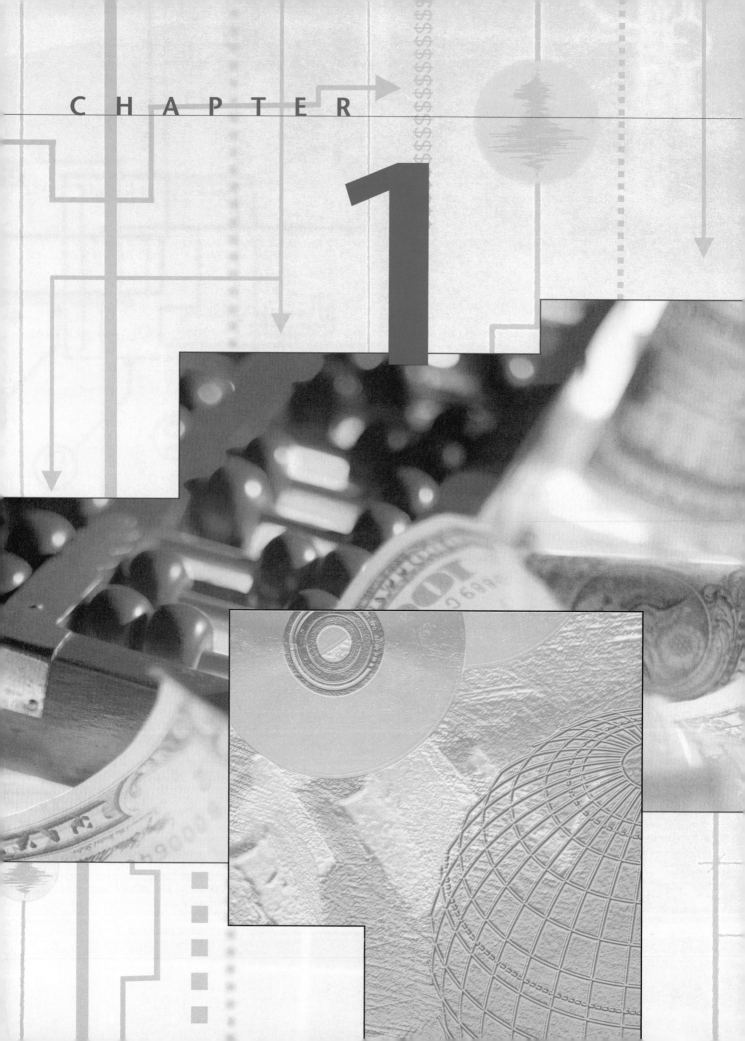

Introduction to

QUICKBOOKS PRO
2003

CHAPTER OBJECTIVES

- Describe the differences and similarities between computerized and manual accounting

- Identify the four levels of operation within QuickBooks Pro

- Open QuickBooks Pro

- Open a company file

- Make a backup copy of a company file

- Restore a backup copy of a company file

INTRODUCTION

Accounting for the financial activity of any company involves repetitive recording of day-to-day business activities. Recording common business activities such as paying bills, purchasing merchandise, selling merchandise, and paying payroll involves repeating the same steps over and over again. Many of these activities can occur several times in the course of one day requiring much repetitive recording.

With the introduction of mainframe computers, certain processes such as payroll became very simple to perform on computers. Companies appeared that used mainframe computers to process payrolls for local businesses. Eventually other accounting activities were processed by mainframe computers, such as maintaining the general ledger and journals. As personal computers became more common, several computerized accounting software packages became available that enabled the processing of all routine business activities from paying bills, to buying and selling merchandise, to paying payroll—all without the user needing a mainframe computer.

With a computerized accounting software package, as business activities are recorded, all necessary reports from the general ledger, to the journals, to the payroll reports, and the **financial statements** are instantly prepared. This makes them available on a more timely basis. Also, with accounting software, if an error is noticed it can be easily corrected, and a revised report immediately printed.

Originally only people trained in accounting commonly used accounting software. But as more people began to use personal computers, business owners and non-accounting people started to record business activities on their own using accounting software.

QuickBooks® Basic Edition 2003 and *QuickBooks® Pro Edition 2003* are examples of accounting software packages used to record all types of business and accounting activities and prepare a variety of reports, including financial statements. However, unlike many accounting software products, they are designed with the non-accountant in mind. Many of the data entry windows are described in everyday, non-accounting terms. However, behind the scenes, QuickBooks Basic and QuickBooks Pro use traditional accounting procedures to record, summarize, and report financial information. Therefore, a basic understanding of accounting terms and procedures allows you to operate the software more efficiently. Throughout the text, accounting terms and concepts are displayed in the margins that describe the accounting going on behind the scenes in QuickBooks Basic and QuickBooks Pro.

Note: Because QuickBooks Pro allows for multiple users and has some features that QuickBooks Basic does not, this text was developed using QuickBooks Pro. Except where noted, the capabilities described in QuickBooks Pro are also available in QuickBooks Basic using the same procedures.

ACCOUNTING WITH QUICKBOOKS PRO VERSUS MANUAL AND OTHER COMPUTERIZED ACCOUNTING SYSTEMS

In accounting, every **transaction** that involves money must be recorded. In a manual accounting system, all transactions are recorded chronologically in a **journal.** At the end of the month, these transactions are posted (rewritten)

---

accounting The process of recording, summarizing, and presenting the financial information of a company in the form of financial statements.

financial statements Summaries of the financial information of a company. The most common are the income statement and the balance sheet.

transaction A monetary business event or activity.

journal The document where transactions are originally recorded chronologically. At the end of the month, transactions in the general journal are posted (rewritten) to the general ledger.

general ledger The document where transactions are summarized by account.

trial balance A report containing all the general ledger account names, their debit and credit balances, and the total debits and credits.

special journals Journals such as the purchases journal, cash payments journal, sales journal, and cash receipts journal. These journals can be used instead of the general journal to chronologically record similar transactions. At the end of the month, transactions in the special journals are posted (rewritten) to the general ledger.

in a book called the general ledger. The **general ledger** summarizes the information by descriptive names, called accounts. Examples of accounts are Cash, Accounts Receivable, and Inventory (assets); Accounts Payable and Notes Payable (liabilities); Capital and Drawings, and Stock and Retained Earnings (equity); Fees Earned and Sales (revenue); and Rent, Insurance, Salaries, and Depreciation (expenses). After routine transactions and any necessary adjustments are recorded in the journal and posted to the general ledger, a **trial balance** is prepared to confirm that the general ledger is in balance, and then the financial statements are prepared.

To facilitate the recording of so many transactions in a manual accounting system, several journals are used with similar transactions recorded in each journal. Typically, a purchases journal is used to record purchases of merchandise on account; a sales journal is used to record sales of merchandise on account; a cash receipts journal is used to record collections of sales on account, cash sales, or any other cash receipt activity; and a cash payments journal is used to record payment of purchases on account, cash purchases, or any other cash payment activity. These journals are often referred to as **special journals.** Any transaction that is not appropriately recorded in a special journal is recorded in the general journal. Month-end adjusting journal entries and fiscal year-end closing entries are recorded in the general journal.

Many computerized accounting software packages follow the procedures used in a manual accounting system. Transactions are recorded in special journals and the general journal as appropriate, and transactions from the journals are then posted to the general ledger. Users of other accounting software packages need to analyze the transaction, determine the correct journal to record the transaction, enter the data, view the journal entry for correctness, and then post the journal entry to the general ledger.

QuickBooks Pro, on the other hand, is designed for the non-accountant as well as the accountant. QuickBooks Pro does not do its recording in special journals; instead, it identifies transactions by business function: vendors, customers, employees, and banking. The language used in recording transactions is common business language: enter bills, pay bills, create invoices, receive payments, and so on. The user enters the transaction based on the nature of the activity. Then, behind the scenes, the software updates the appropriate reports and financial statements based on the activity entered into the system.

FOUR LEVELS OF OPERATION

Although much of the accounting is conducted behind the scenes in QuickBooks Pro, an understanding of the accounting concepts used by the software will help you determine how to record financial information correctly. The operations conducted by QuickBooks Pro can be classified into four levels: New Company Setup, Lists, Activities, and Reports. (See figure 1–1.)

NEW COMPANY SETUP: The first level of operation is creating and setting up a new company file with the background information for the new company. This involves recording the company name, address, identification numbers, fiscal periods, type of business, accounts, and balances.

LISTS: The second level of operation is recording background information in Lists. These Lists include Chart of Accounts, Item, Price Level, Customer:Job, Vendor, Employee, Payroll Item, and so on. Information is initially recorded in Lists as part of New Company Setup, but can be revised by adding, deleting, or editing information.

The Lists in QuickBooks Pro function in a way similar to that of a database. Certain information is stored on these Lists, and as business activities involving any item on the Lists are processed, the information can simply be recalled and plugged into the windows rather than requiring you to re-key the data.

ACTIVITIES: The third level of operation is recording daily business activity in QuickBooks Pro. This is where the majority of the routine accounting work is processed. Activities are identified with common language such as enter bills, write checks, create invoices, receive payments, and so on. In addition, the information in Lists is frequently used to eliminate repetitive keying of data.

REPORTS: At certain times, it is necessary to display and print a variety of reports and financial statements based on information entered into QuickBooks Pro. The fourth level of operation is using QuickBooks Pro to display and print an assortment of Reports, such as financial statements, including the income statement and balance sheet, as well as the reports related to each activity, such as vendor, customer:job, inventory, and payroll reports.

Information that appears on the Reports is gathered during other operations within QuickBooks Pro. As data is entered in the New Company Setup, Lists, and Activities levels of operation, the information is simultaneously recorded in the Reports level. QuickBooks Pro provides for simple as well as more elaborate reporting. All of the Reports can be customized according to the user's needs.

FIGURE 1-1
Four Levels of Operation in QuickBooks Pro

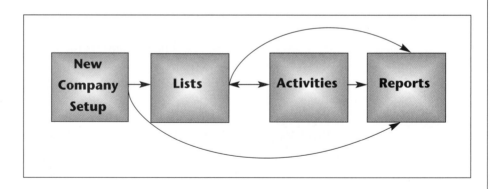

INSTALLING THE COMPANY FILES NEEDED FOR THIS TEXT

QuickBooks Pro must be installed on your computer in order for you to use this book. Enclosed with the text is a company files CD that contains the company files you will use to learn the topics presented in each chapter and do the two case problems at the end of the chapters. There are company files for all chapters except chapters 6 and 8, where you will learn how to create a new company file.

Throughout the text, you will be called on to open and use the company files provided on the CD. Rather than opening the files directly from the CD, it may be more convenient for you to install the company files onto your hard drive. By default, QuickBooks Pro stores company files in the path: C:\Program Files\Intuit\QuickBooks Pro. You or your instructor can also install them on some other hard drive or network directory. This book will assume the subfolder QuickBooks Pro is used to store the company files. If you use a different subfolder, you must adjust the instructions accordingly.

To install the company files CD onto the hard drive—
1. Insert the company files CD into the CD-ROM drive.
2. Click the *Start* button on the Windows Taskbar.
3. At the Start Menu, right click.
4. At the short-cut menu, click *Explore*.
5. In the Exploring window on the left side, click the CD-ROM drive.
6. In the Exploring window on the right side, double-click *QB2003Files*.
7. Confirm with your instructor that the folder shown in the Unzip to folder text box is the desired location for your company files. If you want to extract the company files to another folder, click <u>B</u>rowse, and then find the correct folder location.
8. If the folder shown in the Unzip to <u>f</u>older text box is correct, click <u>U</u>nzip.

OPENING QUICKBOOKS PRO

To open QuickBooks Pro—
1. Click *Start* on the Windows desktop Taskbar.
2. At the Start menu, click *All Programs*.
3. At the All Programs menu, click *QuickBooks Pro*.
4. At the QuickBooks Pro menu, click *QuickBooks Pro*. (See figure 1–2.)

FIGURE 1-2
Start, All Programs, and QuickBooks Pro Menus

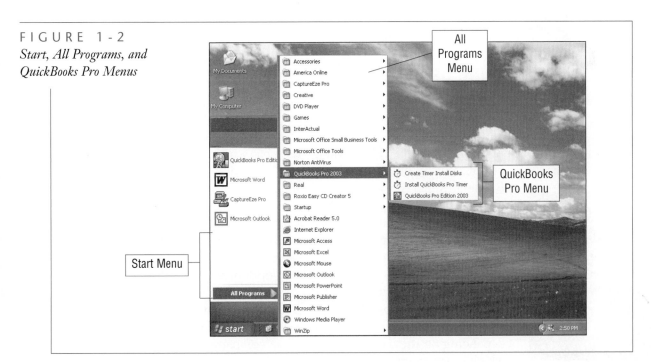

When QuickBooks Pro is opened, the QuickBooks Pro main window appears. The first time you open QuickBooks Pro on your computer, a window will also appear titled *Welcome to QuickBooks Pro Edition 2003*. In this window, you have four choices: Crea<u>t</u>e a new company, O<u>p</u>en an existing company, Convert from <u>Q</u>uicken, or Open a <u>s</u>ample file.

If QuickBooks Pro has previously been used on your computer, a window will appear titled *No Company Open*. (See figure 1-3.) In the No Company Open window, all company files previously opened will be listed where you can select a company name and click the Op<u>en</u> button. Notice under the box listing the company files that the Location path is indicated. This path will be useful later on as you begin to open several different company files. You also have four additional choices: Crea<u>t</u>e a new company, O<u>p</u>en an existing company, Restore a bac<u>k</u>up file, or Open a <u>s</u>ample file.

Note: If a company file was previously used on this computer, the company file may automatically be opened. In this case click on <u>F</u>ile, then <u>C</u>lose Company and you should see a window as in figure 1-3

FIGURE 1-3
*QuickBooks Pro
Main Window with
No Company File
Open Message*

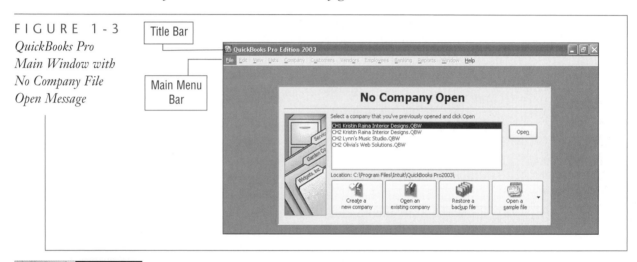

In chapters 1–5, 7, and 9–12, you will open an existing company from the company files provided on the CD. In chapters 6 and 8, you will learn how to create a new company file.

USING DROP-DOWN MENUS AND DIALOG BOXES

Regardless of whether a company is open or not, notice the QuickBooks Pro main window shown in figure 1-3. Along the top is the QuickBooks Pro Title bar, which will include a company name when a company file is open. Below the Title bar is the Main Menu bar which includes the menu choices of <u>F</u>ile, <u>E</u>dit, <u>V</u>iew, <u>L</u>ists, <u>C</u>ompany, C<u>u</u>stomers, Vend<u>o</u>rs, Emplo<u>y</u>ees, <u>B</u>anking, <u>R</u>eports, <u>W</u>indow, and <u>H</u>elp. When no company is open, only the menus <u>F</u>ile and <u>H</u>elp are active and can be chosen. You can choose a menu by clicking the menu name with the mouse or by pressing the Alt key and the underlined letter from the menu name on the keyboard. (In Windows XP, you must press the Alt key to see the underlined letter in the menu name. In this text, we will show menu options with the short-cut key underlines for users who are using an operating system prior to Windows XP.) Whenever you choose a menu, a drop-down menu appears that lists additional choices or commands. Choices on the menus will vary at times depending on the data entered into the company file and depending on which of the open windows is active.

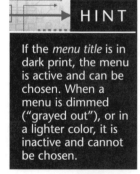

HINT

If the *menu title* is in dark print, the menu is active and can be chosen. When a menu is dimmed ("grayed out"), or in a lighter color, it is inactive and cannot be chosen.

HINT

If the *command* is in dark print, the command is active and can be chosen. If the command is dimmed ("grayed out"), it is inactive and cannot be chosen.

FIGURE 1-4
File Menu

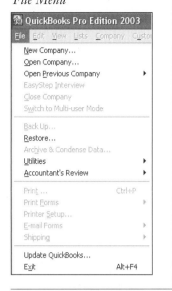

On the Main Menu bar, click <u>F</u>ile. The <u>F</u>ile drop-down menu appears displaying commands or choices. (See figure 1–4.)

When you choose a command that is followed by ellipses (…), a window, called a dialog box, will appear. Additional information must be entered in the dialog box for the command to be processed. Included in dialog boxes are command buttons (such as <u>O</u>pen, Cancel, OK). The active command button will have a slightly darker line around it. You may activate a command button by clicking the button. If the button is active (has the dark line around it), you can also activate the command by pressing the Enter key.

When you choose a command on the drop-down menu followed by an arrow, an additional drop-down menu, called a submenu, will appear listing additional commands or choices.

OPENING A COMPANY FILE

The sample company file that came with this textbook, Kristin Raina Interior Designs, will be used to illustrate the topics in each chapter.

HINT

To select is to highlight something by clicking once. To choose is to activate a command, sometimes with one click, sometimes by double-clicking.

To open Kristin Raina Interior Designs—

1. At the *Welcome to QuickBooks Pro Edition 2003* window or at the *No Company Open* window, click on the O<u>p</u>en an existing company button.

Note: You can also click on <u>F</u>ile on the Main Menu bar, then click on <u>O</u>pen Company.

The Open a Company dialog box appears. Most likely, the subfolder *QuickBooks Pro* will appear in the Look <u>i</u>n text box. QuickBooks Pro automatically assigns the extension .QBW to each company file.

2. In the Open a Company dialog box in the Look <u>i</u>n text box, choose *QuickBooks Pro*, or whatever subfolder contains the company files.
3. Select the company *CH1 Kristin Raina Interior Designs.QBW*.

When you select a company name, the name also appears in the File <u>n</u>ame text box. (See figure 1–5.)

4. Click <u>O</u>pen.

FIGURE 1-5
Open a Company Dialog Box with CH1 Kristin Raina Interior Designs Company File Selected

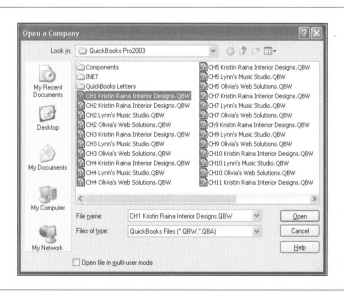

Once a company file is open, the main window of QuickBooks Pro changes. (See figure 1-6.)

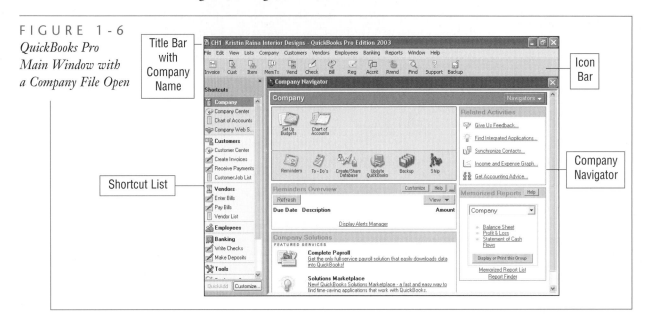

Note: If a window appears titled Automatic Update – Privacy Information, click the X to close the window. If a window appears titled Getting Started, click the X to close the window.

The company name, CH1 Kristin Raina Interior Designs, is now displayed in the title bar. Under the Main Menu bar is the Icon bar. Along the left is the Shortcut List and covering the remainder of the screen is the Company Navigator. The Icon bar, Shortcut List, and Company Navigator are additional methods that can be used to access information in QuickBooks Pro as an alternative to using the Main Menu bar. In this text, only the Main Menu bar is used. The Icon bar, Shortcut List, and Company Navigator will be closed allowing more screen space for the windows.

To close the Icon bar:
1. At the Main Menu bar, click View.
2. At the View menu, click Icon Bar to remove the check mark.

To close the Shortcut List:
1. Click on the X above the word Shortcuts.

To close the Company Navigator:
1. Click on the X.

Note: There may be variations to these windows depending on which operating system is installed on your computer. Instead of a Shortcut List, you may have an Open Windows List. If so, close the Open Windows List in the same manner as the Shortcut List. If you receive a message on Closing the Open Window List, check the box Do not display this message in the future, then click Yes.

MULTI-USER AND SINGLE-USER MODE

Intuit, the maker of QuickBooks Pro, also offers a software product called QuickBooks Basic. QuickBooks Basic operates in much the same way as QuickBooks Pro, but there are a few differences. The major difference between the two is that QuickBooks Pro is designed so that many people can use one company file at the same time. Assume a business has three bookkeepers, each with their own computer on their desk. When using QuickBooks Pro, each bookkeeper can access the company records at the same time on their own computer. This is referred to as running the software in **multi-user mode**. Multi-user mode allows each bookkeeper to do his or her work individually, but, at the same time, all information entered individually updates the company file as a whole. QuickBooks Pro allows for up to five users at one time. A company file in QuickBooks Basic, on the other hand, can only be accessed and changed by one user at a time. In other words, QuickBooks Basic can only run a company file in **single-user mode**.

multi-user mode A setting in QuickBooks Pro which allows up to five users to access a company file at the same time, each on their own individual computer. Not available in QuickBooks Basic.

single-user mode A setting avaiblable in QuickBooks Pro, and the only setting in QuickBooks Basic, which allows only one user at a time to access a company file.

In the computer laboratory environment, you will use QuickBooks Pro in single-user mode because each user is using the company files individually; your work is not connected to anyone else's work. When QuickBooks Pro is in single-user mode, the menu choice in the File menu is Switch to Multi-user Mode; when in multi-user mode, the menu choice is Switch to Single-user Mode. Because you should be working in single-user mode, the menu choice should be Switch to Multi-user Mode.

If QuickBooks Basic, not QuickBooks Pro, is installed on your computer, the multi-user mode option is not displayed. As stated earlier, the actual use of QuickBooks Basic and QuickBooks Pro and all the windows displayed are the same. Throughout the text, the name QuickBooks Pro will be used.

BACKING UP A COMPANY FILE

In business, it is advisable to make backup copies of records on a regular basis and store the backup copies in a safe place, separate from the business location. In the event of damage to a company's computer and/or files, the backup copies can be used to restore the lost or damaged data.

WHY BACKING UP A FILE IS IMPORTANT

In this text, you will use the Back Up command for two purposes. First, Back Up will be used to make a copy of the original company file. The original company file can then be preserved intact for others to use, while the backup copy can be restored for you to use for the practice exercises.

Second, as in business, you will use the Back Up command to make backup copies of the exercise company files on floppy disks or on a network directory. In the event your copy is deleted from the hard drive you are working on, you will have a backup copy. This will also be helpful in the event you will be using a different computer each time in the computer lab.

NAMING BACKUP FILES

Two types of names are used in QuickBooks Pro to identify a company file—the file name and the company name. When your backup copy is made and restored, it is recommended you include your name, or your initials, as part of the company *file* name, to distinguish your individual copy of the file from those of other students. In the restored copy (your exercise copy), the *company name* will also be changed to include your name, or your initials, to further identify the exercise copy of the company file as your copy.

In each chapter, the original company file will be preceded with the prefix CH1, CH2, and so on, which represents the chapter number. The backup copies will be assigned the prefix EX1, EX2, and so on. EX stands for exercise and is the prefix that will be used to identify the company file as a backup copy exercise file.

QuickBooks Pro automatically assigns the extension .QBB to a backup copy and condenses the file. The condensed backup copy cannot be used for work; they are strictly for use as stored copies.

Backup copies can be made to the QuickBooks Pro subfolder, a subfolder of your choice, or to a floppy disk. It is recommended that you create your own subfolder on the hard drive, using Windows Explorer, and use your subfolder to store your backup copy of the company file. The instructions below assume you have created your own individual subfolder.

To make a backup copy of the CH1 Kristin Raina Interior Designs company file—

1. Click <u>F</u>ile, then click <u>B</u>ack Up. The QuickBooks Backup dialog box appears. (See figure 1-7).

FIGURE 1-7
QuickBooks Back Up Dialog Box

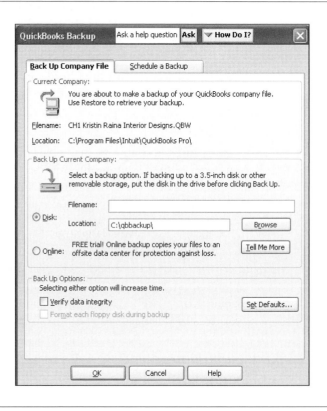

2. The <u>D</u>isk option should be selected.
3. In the Filename text box, key **EX1 [Your Name] Kristin Raina Interior Designs**.

4. Next to the Location text box, click the Browse button. The Back Up Company to dialog box appears.
5. In the Save in text box, choose your subfolder, a network directory designated by your instructor, or a floppy drive. (See figure 1-8).

FIGURE 1-8
Back Up Company to Dialog Box

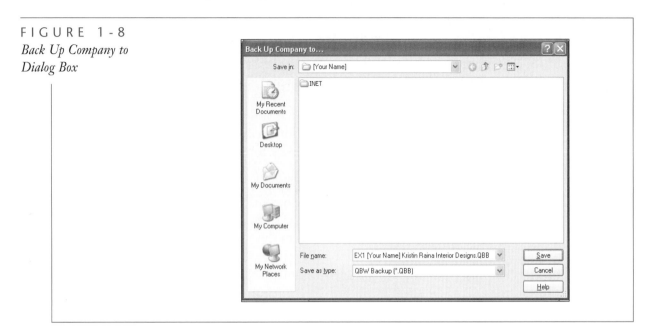

6. Click Save.
7. You return to the QuickBooks Backup dialog box. (See figure 1-9).

FIGURE 1-9
QuickBooks Back Up Dialog Box – Complete

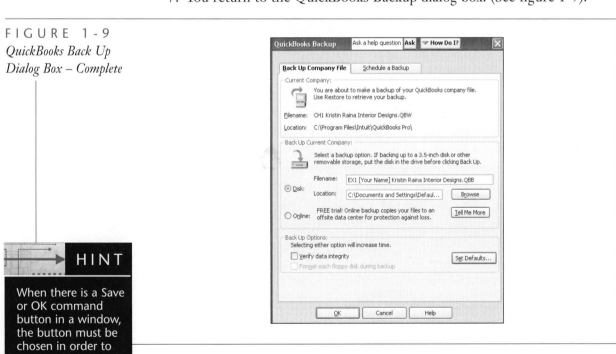

HINT

When there is a Save or OK command button in a window, the button must be chosen in order to save the changes. If you exit out of the window by clicking the X (the Close button), all changes will be lost.

Note: Notice on the QuickBooks Backup dialog box there is a command button Set Defaults which allows you to establish the default location for your backup files.

8. Click OK. A message appears stating *Your data has been backed up successfully.*
9. Click OK.

Note, however, that the *original company file is still open*. To work on the backup copy of the company file that you just created, you must restore the backup copy.

RESTORING A COMPANY FILE

You use the Restore command to open a backup copy of a company file. Recall that backup copies are automatically assigned the extension .QBB and that they are condensed copies of a company file. QuickBooks Pro gives the restore copy a .QBW extension, which denotes the working copies of the company file. If you are using floppy disks to store your backup copies of company files, it is recommended that you use the hard drive for the exercises and use the floppy disks only for back up. Using floppy disks for the exercises is very slow and all your work for one company file may not fit on one floppy disk.

Restoring a backup file is a two-step process. In the first step you determine which backup copy you wish to restore *from*; in the second step you determine which company file you wish to restore *to*. In business, the backup company file would be restored to the original company file name. In this book, however, the intent is to retain the original company file intact for others to use, so the backup company will *not* be restored to the original company file name, but rather to your exercise company file name.

To restore the backup copy of the company file—
1. Click <u>F</u>ile, and then click <u>R</u>estore. The Restore Company Backup dialog box appears. (See figure 1-10.)

FIGURE 1-10
Restore Company Back Up Dialog Box

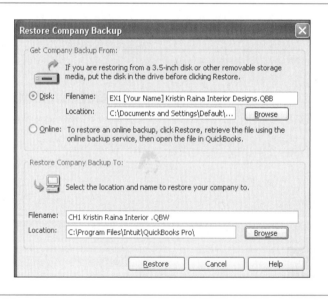

2. In the Get Company Backup From section, the <u>D</u>isk option should be selected.
3. Click the <u>B</u>rowse button. The Restore From dialog box appears.
4. In the Look <u>i</u>n text box, choose the location where you saved your backup copy.
5. Select the company file *EX1 [Your Name] Kristin Raina Interior Designs Company. QBB*. The prefix EX and your name or initials will be used for the restore copies as well as the backup copies. (See figure 1-11.)

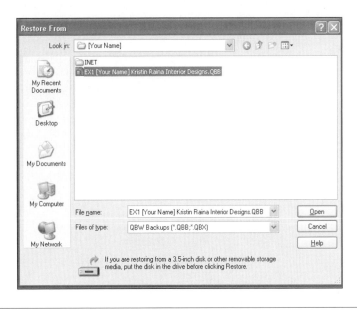

6. Click Open. You return to the Restore Company Backup dialog box.
7. In the Restore Company Backup To section, click the Browse button. The Restore To dialog box appears.
8. In the Save in text box, choose the subfolder where you will be opening and working on your copies of the company files.
9. In the File name text box, key **EX1 [Your Name] Kristin Raina Interior Designs**. (See figure 1-12).

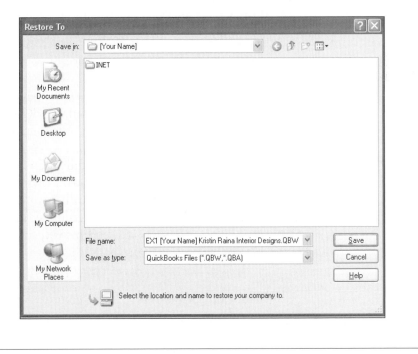

10. If the information is correct, click <u>S</u>ave. You return to the Restore Company Backup dialog box. (See figure 1-13).

FIGURE 1-13

*Restore Company
Back Up Dialog Box –
Complete*

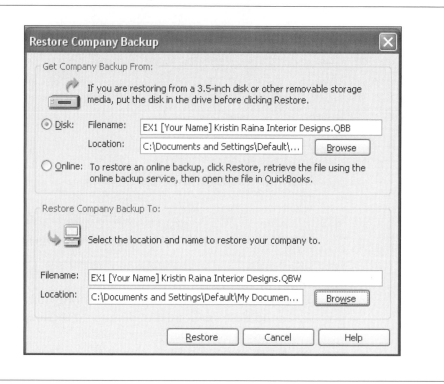

11. If the information is correct, click <u>R</u>estore.
12. A message stating *Your data has been restored successfully* should appear. Click OK at the message.
13. If the Company Navigator window appears, click the X to close it.

If you use a file name that already exists, a warning appears indicating that this company file exists, and asking you if you want to replace it. If you click <u>Y</u>es and then click <u>R</u>estore, a second warning will appear that you are about to overwrite an existing file. If this is what you want to do, click <u>Y</u>es and then you must key **yes** in the box, and click OK. If the name shown is not the correct file name, click <u>N</u>o and enter the correct file name in the Restore To dialog box.

After your backup copy is successfully restored, your exercise copy of the company file appears in the QuickBooks Pro window, but the Title bar indicates the original company file name. Before you begin working, you should change the company name in the Company Information window to match your exercise company file name. This will then further identify this company file as your individual company file.

To change the company name—
1. Click <u>C</u>ompany on the Main Menu bar, and then click Compan<u>y</u> Information.

2. At the Company Information window, in the Company <u>N</u>ame text box, change the company name to: **EX1 [Your Name] Kristin Raina Interior Designs**. (See figure 1–14.)

FIGURE 1-14
*Company Information
Window*

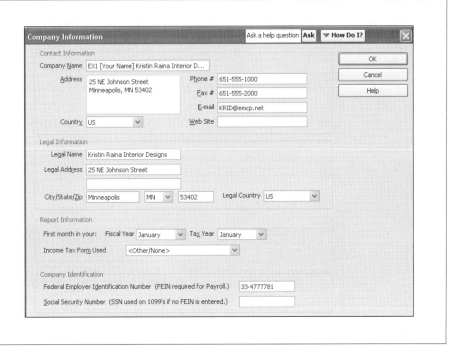

3. If the information is correct, click OK.

The company name is changed in the Title bar. This company name will now appear in the heading of the reports. The name in the Title bar comes from the Company Information window. The name of the company file in the Open a Company dialog box is based on the file name typed in the Back Up and Restore dialog boxes. Be careful to type the *same* name in both places. This will help you to more easily keep track of your files.

EXITING QUICKBOOKS PRO

Most work is automatically saved in QuickBooks Pro when the correct command button is chosen. At the end of a session, it is recommended that you use the Back Up command to save your work onto a floppy disk or a network directory designated by your instructor. However, it is not necessary to make a backup copy of the exercise file for this session. To exit QuickBooks Pro, click the X (Close button) on the QuickBooks Pro Title bar, or click <u>F</u>ile and then E<u>x</u>it.

HINT

The *file name* appears in the Open a Company, Back Up, and Restore dialog boxes, and Windows Explorer. The *company name* appears in the Title bar of QuickBooks Pro and the reports.

QuickBooks Pro Edition 2003 is one of several business software products offered by Intuit, Inc. In addition to QuickBooks Pro and QuickBooks Basic, Intuit offers Quicken, a personal finance software, and TurboTax, a tax preparation software. Their Web site offers a review of all their products, in addition to support services and order processing. You can find them at www.intuit.com.

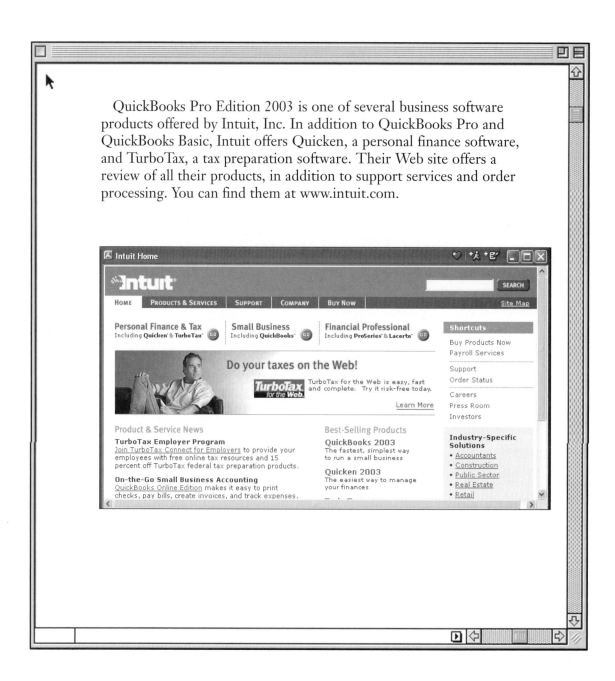

P R O G R E S S
Check

PROCEDURE REVIEW

To open a company file—
1. Open QuickBooks Pro.
2. At the *Welcome to QuickBooks Pro Edition 2003* window or at the *No Company Open* window, click on the Open an existing company button, or click File, and then click Open Company.
3. In the Open a Company dialog box in the Look in text box, choose *QuickBooks Pro*, or the subfolder containing the company files for this course.
4. Select the company *CH# Company Name.QBW*.
5. Click Open.

To make a backup copy of a company file—
1. Click File, then click Back Up.
2. In the QuickBooks Backup dialog box, the Disk option should be selected.
3. In the Filename text box, key **EX1 [Your Name] Kristin Raina Interior Designs**.
4. Next to the Location text box, click the Browse button.
5. At the Back Up Company to dialog box, in the Save in text box, choose your subfolder, a network directory designated by your instructor, or a floppy drive.
6. Click Save.
7. In the QuickBooks Backup dialog box, click OK.
8. At the *Your data has been backed up successfully* message, click OK.

To restore the backup copy of the company file—
1. Click File, and then click Restore.
2. At the Restore Company Backup dialog box, in the Get Company Backup From section, the Disk option should be selected.
3. Click the Browse button.
4. At the Restore From dialog box, in the Look in text box, choose the location where you saved your backup copy.
5. Select the company file *EX1 [Your Name] Kristin Raina Interior Designs Company. QBB*.
6. Click Open.
7. At the Restore Company Backup dialog box, in the Restore Company Backup To section, click the Browse button.
8. At the Restore To dialog box, in the Save in text box, choose the sub-folder where you will be opening and working on your copies of the company files.
9. In the File name text box, key **EX1 [Your Name] Kristin Raina Interior Designs**.
10. Click Save.
11. In the Restore Company Backup dialog box, click Restore.

12. At the *Your data has been restored successfully* message, click OK.
13. If the Company Navigator window appears, click the X to close it.

To change the company name—
1. Click Company, and then click Company Information.
2. In the Company Information dialog box at the Company Name text box, key **EX# [Your Name] Company Name**.
3. Click OK.

KEY CONCEPTS

Select the letter of the item that best matches each definition.

a. Company Name   f. Reports
b. Ellipses   g. New Company Setup
c. Activities   h. Main Menu Bar
d. QuickBooks Pro   i. Back Up
e. File Name   j. Lists

_____ 1. A software package used to record business and accounting activities, designed with the non-accountant in mind.
_____ 2. The level of operation that creates a new company file.
_____ 3. The level of operation that records background information.
_____ 4. The level of operation where most routine work is processed.
_____ 5. The level of operation where information can be displayed and printed.
_____ 6. Follows a command on a menu and means additional information must be entered in a second window called a dialog box.
_____ 7. The name that appears in the Title bar of QuickBooks Pro. The source is the Company Information window.
_____ 8. The part of the QuickBooks Pro window where the File, Edit, View, Lists, Company, Customers, Vendors, Employees, Banking, Reports, Window, and Help menus are displayed.
_____ 9. The name indicated in the Back Up and Restore windows.
_____ 10. Command used to make a copy of the original company file.

PROCEDURE CHECK

1. List the steps for opening a company file called Mary's Marathon Track Club that is stored in the QuickBooks Pro subfolder on the hard drive.
2. Assume you are instructed to work on a company file named CH1 Hercules Body Building Equipment. List the steps to make a backup copy called EX1 [Your Name] Hercules Body Building Equipment and then restore the backup copy. Assume the company file is stored in the QuickBooks Pro subfolder and backed up and restored in the [Your Name] subfolder. If you backed up the file to a floppy disk, how would the steps be different? The same?

Ch. 1   Nicole Stradling

Key Concepts
1) d
2) g
3) i
4) c
5) l
6) b
7) a
8) h
9) e
10) f

Procedure Check
1) a. Open Quickbooks Pro.

   b. At the No Co. Open window, click on the Open an existing company button.

   c. In the Look In text box, choose the subfolder that contains the file. (in the hard drive)

   d. Select the company called Mary's Marathon Track Club.

   e. Click Open.

2) a. Click File then click Back Up.

   b. When the dialog box comes up, the Disk option should be selected.

   c. In the Filename text box, key Ex1 [Nicole] Hercules Body Building Equipment.

   d. Click the Browse button.

   e. At the Back Up Co. dialog box, in the Save In text box, choose your subfolder.

f. Click Save.

g. In the Back Up dialog box, press OK.

h. When it's been saved properly, press OK.

If you put the backup file on a floppy, you would have to put the disk in, & save it to the floppy instead of the subfolder. The rest of the procedures would be the same.

3) In the first step, you determine which back up copy you wish to restore from, then you determine which company file you wish to restore it to.

4) With a computer, you can get your work done so much faster than on paper. QuickBooks & Peachtree make the life of an accountant a lot easier.

3. Assume you are working on a company file previously backed up and restored as EX1 [Your Name] Lynette's Boutique but are unable to finish the work today. When you return the next day to complete the work, explain how you would open the company file assuming no additional backup copy was made.

 4. Discuss the advantages of using a computerized accounting software package instead of using non-computerized accounting methods. Discuss the specific advantages of using QuickBooks Pro.

2

VENDORS

Enter Bills, Pay Bills, and Write Checks

CHAPTER OBJECTIVES

- Identify the system default accounts for vendors

- Update the Vendor List

- Record purchases on account in the Enter Bills window

- Process credit memos in the Enter Bills window

- Record payments of accounts payable in the Pay Bills window

- Record cash purchases in the Write Checks window

- Display and print vendor-related reports

INTRODUCTION

vendor Someone from whom the company buys goods or services, either on account or for cash.

QuickBooks Pro allows you to track all vendor transactions. A **vendor** is someone from whom the company buys goods or services, either on account or for cash. You should establish a file for each vendor prior to entering transactions for that vendor. The collection of all the vendor files comprises the *Vendor List* (Lists).

Once a vendor file is established, transactions (Activities) such as receiving a bill from a vendor, paying that bill, or writing a check for a cash purchase can be entered in the *Enter Bills*, *Pay Bills*, and *Write Checks* windows. As transactions are recorded in the activities windows, QuickBooks Pro will simultaneously update the Vendor List and any related reports (Reports) with the information about the transactions for the particular vendor.

In this chapter, you will record and pay bills received by our sample company, Kristin Raina Interior Designs, for non-inventory purchases of goods and services, such as operating expenses and assets acquisitions. In addition, you will write checks for cash purchases when bills have not been previously received or entered.

QUICKBOOKS PRO VERSUS MANUAL ACCOUNTING: VENDOR TRANSACTIONS

purchases journal A journal used to record all purchases of goods on account; can be in a single-column or multi-column format.

In a manual accounting system, all purchases of goods on account are recorded in a multi-column **purchases journal.** At the conclusion of the month, the totals are posted to the asset, expense, and liability (Accounts Payable) accounts affected by the transactions. As each purchase transaction is recorded, the appropriate vendor's account in the accounts payable subsidiary ledger is updated for the new liability on a daily basis. Payments for open accounts payable balances and payments for cash purchases of goods/services are recorded in a multi-column **cash payments journal.** As is done with the purchases journal, monthly totals are posted to the general ledger accounts while payment information is recorded daily in the vendor's subsidiary ledger record.

cash payments journal A journal used to record all cash payment activities including payment of accounts payable.

In QuickBooks Pro, the Vendor List serves as the accounts payable subsidiary ledger for the company. The Vendor List includes all companies and individuals from whom the company buys goods and services. Relevant information, such as name, address, contact, credit limit, and so on, is entered at the time the vendor's file is created on the Vendor List.

When the company receives a bill for goods or services, the bill is recorded in the Enter Bills window. The Enter Bills window is equivalent to the multi-column purchases journal. QuickBooks Pro automatically updates the **Chart of Accounts List** and general ledger and at the same time updates the vendor's file on the Vendor List for the new liability. When the bill is to be paid, you enter the transaction in the Pay Bills window. The Pay Bills window is equivalent to the part of the cash payments journal that records payment of open accounts payable. This transaction also updates the Chart of Accounts List and general ledger and at the same time updates the vendor's file on the Vendor List for the payment of the liability.

Chart of Accounts List A list of all accounts a business uses.

For a check written for a bill not previously entered, you use the Write Checks window. This is equivalent to the part of the cash payments journal that records payment for cash purchases of goods/services. Again, the Chart of Accounts List, general ledger, and the vendor's file on the Vendor List will be simultaneously updated.

SYSTEM DEFAULT ACCOUNTS

To process transactions expeditiously and organize data for reporting, QuickBooks Pro establishes specific general ledger accounts as default accounts in each activity window. When you enter transactions, QuickBooks Pro automatically increases or decreases certain account balances depending on the nature of the transaction. For example, when you enter a vendor invoice in the Enter Bills window, QuickBooks Pro automatically increases (credits) the Accounts Payable account because the Enter Bills window is used to record purchases on account. When you write a check in the Pay Bills window, QuickBooks Pro automatically decreases (debits) the Accounts Payable account. Therefore, you do not have to enter the account number or name for these default accounts because they have been pre-established by QuickBooks Pro.

Throughout the text, we will identify the default accounts for each type of transaction, such as vendor, customer, inventory, and payroll.

CHAPTER PROBLEM

In this chapter, you will enter and track vendor transactions for Kristin Raina Interior Designs, a sole proprietorship providing interior decorating and design services to both residential and commercial clients. The owner of the business, Kristin Raina, began operations on January 1, 2004, by investing $50,000 in the business. During January Kristin Raina devoted most of her time to organizing the business, securing office space, and buying assets. Beginning February 1, 2004, she wishes to begin tracking vendor transactions. Information for several vendors has been entered in the Vendor List. This information, along with February 1, 2004, beginning balances, is contained in the company file CH2 Kristin Raina Interior Designs.

Begin by opening the company file—
1. Open QuickBooks Pro.
2. At the *No Company Open* window, click on the Open an existing company button or click File, and then click Open Company.
3. At the Open a Company dialog box in the Look in text box, choose the *QuickBooks Pro* subfolder, or the subfolder containing the company files.
4. Select the company *CH2 Kristin Raina Interior Designs.QBW* and click Open.
5. If the Company Navigator window appears, click the X to close it.

Next, make a backup copy of the company file—
1. Click File, then click Back Up.
2. In the QuickBooks Backup dialog box, the Disk option should be selected.
3. In the Filename text box, key **EX2 [Your Name] Kristin Raina Interior Designs**.
4. Next to the Location text box, click the Browse button.
5. At the Back Up Company to dialog box, in the Save in text box, choose your subfolder, a network directory designated by your instructor, or a floppy drive.
6. Click Save.
7. In the QuickBooks Backup dialog box, click OK.
8. At the *Your data has been backed up successfully.* message, click OK.

HINT

In Windows XP, you must press the Alt key to see the underlined letter in the menu name. In this text, we will show menu options with the shortcut key underlines for users who are using an operating system prior to Windows XP.

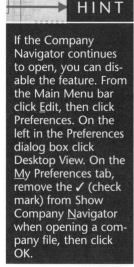
Now restore the backup copy of the company file—
1. Click File, and then click Restore.
2. At the Restore Company Backup dialog box, in the Get Company Backup From section, the Disk option should be selected.
3. Click the Browse button.
4. At the Restore From dialog box, in the Look in text box, choose the location where you saved your backup copy.
5. Select the company file *EX2 [Your Name] Kristin Raina Interior Designs Company.QBB* and click Open.
6. At the Restore Company Backup dialog box, in the Restore Company Backup To section, click the Browse button.
7. At the Restore To dialog box, in the Save in text box, choose the sub-folder where you will be opening and working on your copies of the company files.
8. In the File name text box, key **EX2 [Your Name] Kristin Raina Interior Designs** and click Save.
9. In the Restore Company Backup dialog box, click Restore.
10. At the *Your data has been restored successfully.* message, click OK.
11. If the Company Navigator window appears, click the X to close it.

The backup copy has been restored, but the company name still reads CH2 Kristin Raina Interior Designs.

Change the company name—
1. Click Company, and then click Company Information.
2. Change the company name to **EX2 [Your Name] Kristin Raina Interior Designs**.
3. Click OK.

LISTS: THE VENDOR LIST

The Vendor List contains a file for each vendor with which the company does business. For example, the utility company that supplies electricity, the company that provides advertising, and the company from which the business's equipment is purchased are all vendors. The Vendor List contains important information on each vendor, such as company name, address, contact person, type of vendor, terms, credit limit, tax ID, and current balance owed. All vendors the company does business with should be included in the Vendor List.

You should enter the information for each vendor in the Vendor List prior to recording transactions. However, if you inadvertently omit a vendor, you can add that vendor during the Activities level of operation with a minimum of disruption.

You will need to periodically revise the Vendor List to add new vendors, delete vendors no longer used in the business, or to make modifications as background information on vendors changes. These adjustments to the vendor files in the Vendor List are referred to as *updating* the Vendor List, and are part of the second level of operation in QuickBooks Pro.

Kristin Raina has entered information for existing and anticipated vendors in the Vendor List of her company file.

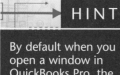

To review the Vendor List—
1. Click <u>R</u>eports, and then click <u>L</u>ist.
2. At the List submenu, click Ven<u>d</u>or Contact List. A list of vendors with their respective opening balances is displayed. (See figure 2–1.)

FIGURE 2-1
Vendor Contact List

Most of the reports provide a drill-down feature. When reviewing a report, QuickBooks Pro, like many computerized accounting programs, allows you to "drill down" from a report to the original window where data has been entered. You then have the opportunity to review the information and make corrections if necessary.

To view a specific vendor file—
1. Move the mouse pointer to the vendor *Jeter Janitorial Services*.

   Notice that the mouse pointer turns into a magnifying glass with a Z in the center called the zoom glass.

2. With the zoom glass over *Jeter Janitorial Services*, double-click the mouse button. This drills you down to the Edit Vendor window. (See figure 2–2.)

FIGURE 2-2
Vendor File – Jeter Janitorial Services

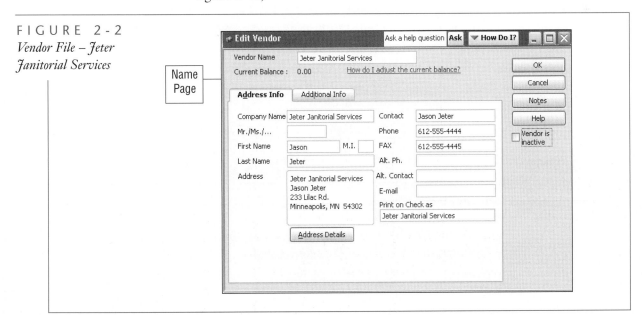

The vendor's file contains three parts:

NAME **P**AGE	This portion displays the vendor's name, current balance, and four command buttons: OK, Cancel, No<u>t</u>es, and Help. The No<u>t</u>es command button is used to add notes about the vendor.
A<u>D</u>DRESS **I**NFO **T**AB	This tab allows you to enter the vendor's company name, address, contact person, telephone and fax numbers, and e-mail address. The <u>A</u>ddress Details button can be used to edit address information.
ADD<u>I</u>TIONAL **I**NFO **T**AB	This tab allows you to enter information such as the vendor's account number, credit limit, and tax ID along with the ability to create customized fields.

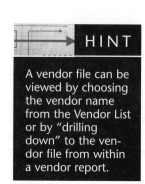

A vendor file can be viewed by choosing the vendor name from the Vendor List or by "drilling down" to the vendor file from within a vendor report.

3. Close the Edit Vendor window.
4. Close the *Vendor Contact List* report.

ADDING A VENDOR

Kristin Raina has just hired a new accountant who will provide accounting services each month for the business. She wishes to add this vendor to the Vendor List by creating a vendor file.

To add a new vendor—
1. Click <u>L</u>ists, and then click <u>V</u>endor List.

   The Vendor List window appears. (See figure 2–3.) All List windows have three drop-down menu buttons on the bottom of the window. The first menu button represents the name of the List, in this case Ven<u>d</u>or. The second menu button is Ac<u>t</u>ivities, and the third menu button is Re<u>p</u>orts. These menu buttons are short cuts you can use instead of using the Main Menu bar drop-down menus to access commands.

FIGURE 2-3
Vendor List Window

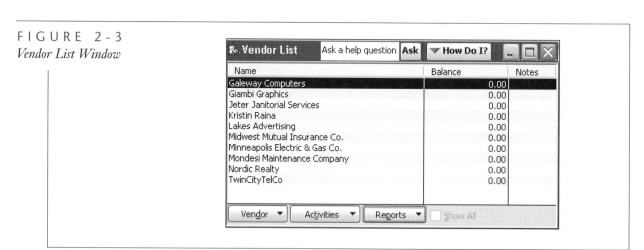

2. At the Vendor List window, click the Ven<u>d</u>or menu button. A drop-down menu appears. (See figure 2–4.)

FIGURE 2-4
Vendor Menu

3. Click New. The New Vendor window appears. (See figure 2–5.)

FIGURE 2-5
New Vendor Window

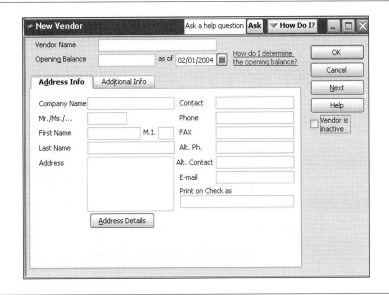

4. Enter the data below on the Name Page and the Address Info tab. (The Address Details button can be used to enter the address, but it isn't necessary.)

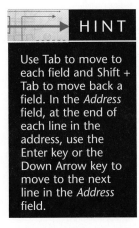

HINT

Use Tab to move to each field and Shift + Tab to move back a field. In the *Address* field, at the end of each line in the address, use the Enter key or the Down Arrow key to move to the next line in the *Address* field.

NAME PAGE

Vendor Name:	**[Your Name] Accounting Service**
Opening Balance:	**0 as of February 1, 2004**

ADDRESS INFO

Company Name:	**[Your Name] Accounting Service**
First Name:	**[Your first name]**
Last Name:	**[Your last name]**
Address:	**One Main Plaza**
	St. Paul, MN 53602
Contact:	**[Your name]**
Phone:	**651-555-2222**
Fax:	**651-555-2223**
E-mail:	**[Your initials]@emcp.net.**
Print on Check as:	**[Your Name] Accounting Service**

Your New Vendor window should look similar to figure 2–6.

FIGURE 2-6
*New Vendor Window
- Name Page and
Address Info Tab
Complete*

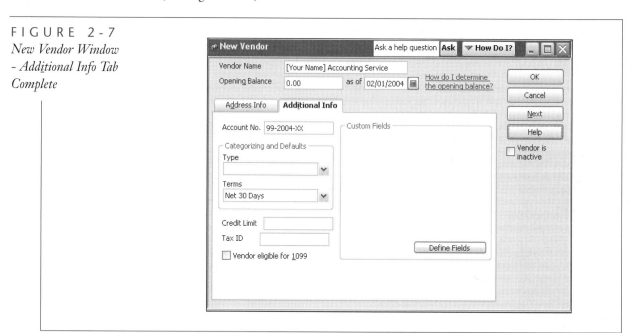

5. Click the Additional Info tab and complete the information below.

ADDITIONAL INFO		
Account No.	=	**99-2004-XX**
Terms	=	**Net 30 Days**

(See figure 2–7.)

FIGURE 2-7
*New Vendor Window
- Additional Info Tab
Complete*

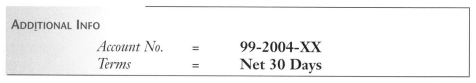

6. If the information is correct, click OK.
7. Click the X (Close button) to close the Vendor List window.

DELETING A VENDOR

Kristin Raina wishes to delete Lakes Advertising from the Vendor List because the company has ceased to operate.

To delete a vendor—

1. Click Lists, and then click Vendor List.
2. At the Vendor List window, select (highlight) *Lakes Advertising* but do not open the file. (See figure 2–8.)

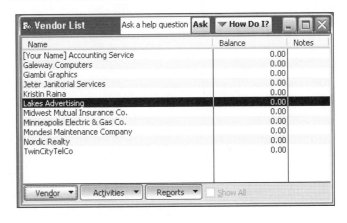

FIGURE 2-8
Vendor List – Lakes Advertising Selected

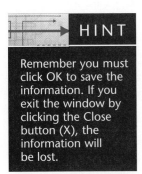
3. Click the Vendor menu button.
4. At the Vendor menu, click Delete.
5. The Delete Vendor warning appears. Click OK. The vendor file will be deleted.
6. Close the Vendor List window.

QuickBooks Pro cannot delete a vendor who has a balance or a vendor who has been part of a transaction for the fiscal period. If a vendor will no longer be used but there has been activity to the file for the period, you can place a check in the *Vendor is inactive* box. The vendor's name is no longer displayed in the reports, but the vendor information is retained in QuickBooks Pro and can be accessed as needed.

EDITING A VENDOR

Kristin Raina needs to edit the file for Minneapolis Electric & Gas Co. because the billing address has changed.

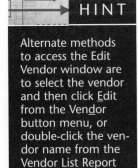
To edit a vendor file—

1. Open the Vendor List and double-click *Minneapolis Electric & Gas Co.* This will open the vendor file in the edit mode. (See figure 2–9.)

FIGURE 2-9

Edit Vendor Window

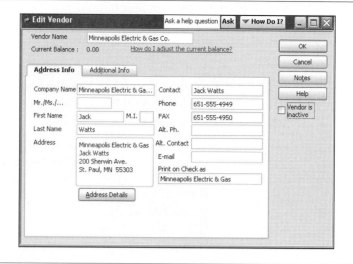

2. Since this is an edit of an address, click <u>A</u>ddress Details. The Edit Address Information window will appear. (See figure 2–10.)

FIGURE 2-10

*Edit Address
Information Window*

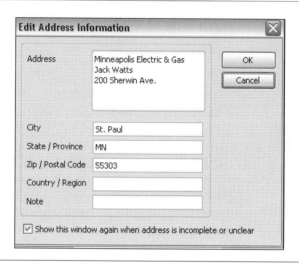

3. At the *Address* field, delete the current street address and in its place key **150 Douglas Ave.** Then click OK. **(**See figure 2–11.)

FIGURE 2-11

*Edit Vendor Window –
Complete*

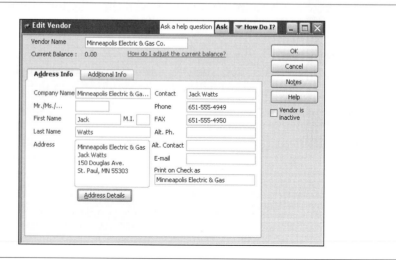

4. If the information is correct, click OK.
5. Close the Vendor List window.

PRACTICE *exercise*

Add the following vendor—
ADDRESS INFO

NAME PAGE

Vendor Name:	**Williams Office Supply Company**
Opening Balance:	**0 as of February 1, 2004**

ADDRESS INFO

Company Name:	**Williams Office Supply Company**
First Name:	**Bernard**
Last Name:	**Williams**
Address:	**15 Grand Ave S.**
	Minneapolis, MN 55404
Contact:	**Bernard Williams**
Phone:	**612-555-2240**
FAX:	**612-555-2241**
E-mail:	**Wilsup@emcp.net**
Print on Check as:	**Williams Office Supply Company**

ADDITIONAL INFO

Account No.:	**55-8988**
Terms:	**Net 30 Days**

Delete the following vendor—
Mondesi Maintenance Company

Edit the following vendor—
New phone/fax for Giambi Graphics:

Phone:	**612-555-0002**
FAX:	**612-555-0003**

QuickCheck: The updated Vendor Contact List appears in figure 2–12.

FIGURE 2-12
*Updated Vendor
Contact List*

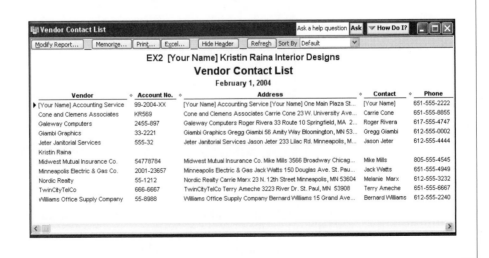

THE ENTER BILLS WINDOW

In QuickBooks Pro, the Enter Bills window is used to record **purchases on account.** This window allows you to identify the vendor sending the bill, the invoice date, due date, terms of payment, and nature of purchase (expense, asset, or item). QuickBooks Pro uses the default Accounts Payable account from the Chart of Accounts to post all open bill liabilities. Certain recurring bills can be set up to be recorded automatically as they become due. In addition, you can use this window to record credit memos.

purchase on account
When a company receives a bill for goods or services from a vendor but plans to pay it at a later date.

QuickBooks Pro records a transaction that is a purchase on account as follows:

Asset/Expense/Drawings	XXX		
Accounts Payable			XXX

At the same time, QuickBooks Pro updates the vendor's file on the Vendor List to reflect the new liability.

Recall from chapter 1 that the third level of operation in QuickBooks Pro is Activities. In this case, the Activity is the recording of purchases on account in the Enter Bills window. Accounts Payable is the default general ledger posting account. All transactions entered in this window will result in a credit to the Accounts Payable account. The *Account* field in this window is used to indicate the asset, expense, or drawings account to be debited.

The QuickBooks Pro Enter Bills window appears in figure 2–13.

FIGURE 2-13
Enter Bills Window —
Expenses Tab

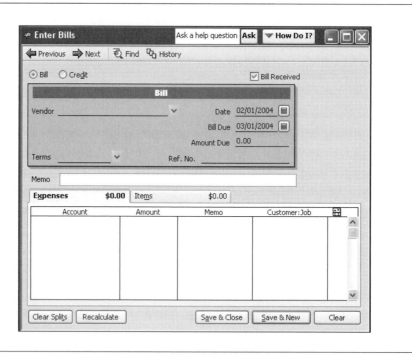

The Enter Bills window has two tabs: Expenses and Items. The Expenses tab should be the active tab. The Items tab is used for inventory items, which will be covered in a later chapter.

The Enter Bills window allows you to select a vendor from the Vendor List, enter a bill reference number, indicate whether the bill is a credit card charge, and indicate the item of expense purchased. Most of the data fields are self-explanatory but take special note of the following fields:

PREVIOUS/NEXT ARROWS	Used to move from current transaction to previous or next transaction. The current transaction will be saved before moving to the previous/next window.
FIND	Used to search for previously recorded bills by vendor, date range, amount, and reference number.
BILL/CREDIT OPTION BUTTONS	If the transaction is a bill received from a vendor, click the Bill button. If it is a credit memo from a vendor, click the Credit button.
BILL RECEIVED	Indicates that the bill has been received for this expense or item. If unchecked, the expense or item was received but the bill will follow at later date.
EXPENSES/ITEMS TABS	For non-item purchases, such as expenses, non-inventory assets, and so on, click Expenses. If this is a purchase of an item, such as inventory, click the Items tab.
CLEAR SPLITS BUTTON	Used to erase entries on the Expenses tab.
RECALCULATE BUTTON	Used to add up multiple entries on the Expenses and Items tabs to fill the *Amount Due* field.
SAVE & CLOSE BUTTON	Used to save (post) the transaction and close the window.
SAVE & NEW BUTTON	Used to save (post) the transaction and clear the window for a new transaction.
CLEAR BUTTON	Used to clear the entire screen if errors are made.

ENTERING A BILL

On February 2, 2004, Kristin Raina received a bill for utilities services from Minneapolis Electric & Gas Co. in the amount of $350, Ref. No. 125-55. The bill is due March 3, 2004, terms **Net 30 Days.**

Net 30 Days Full payment of an invoice within 30 days of the invoice date is requested.

To enter a bill—
1. Click Vendors, and then click Enter Bills.
2. Click the Bill option and the Bill Received box, if necessary.
3. To display the Vendor drop-down list, click the down arrow in the *Vendor* field and then click *Minneapolis Electric & Gas Co.*
4. At the *Date* field, choose *02/02/2004.* (Click the calendar icon, click through the months to find February 2004, and then click 2.)
5. At the *Bill Due* field, choose *03/03/2004.*
6. At the *Amount Due* field, key **350.**

7. At the *Terms* field click *Net 30 Days*, if necessary.
8. At the *Ref. No.* field, key **125-55**.
9. At the Expenses tab in the *Account* field, click the first line to display the drop-down list arrow. At the account drop-down list, click *6500 Utilities Expense*. (See figure 2–14.)
10. If the information is correct, click Save & Close.

FIGURE 2-14
Enter Bills Window Completed

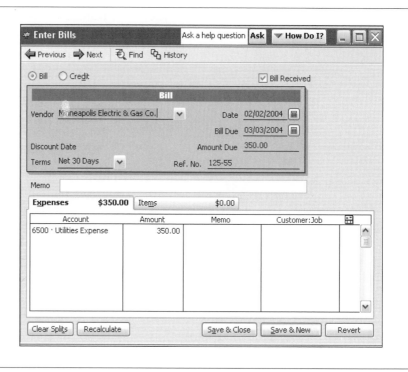

Recall that Save & Close will save the information and close the window. The Next arrow will save the information and then clear the fields for the next transaction. The Previous arrow will display the window for the previous transaction. Since this is the first transaction, the Previous arrow cannot yet be used.

ACCOUNTING
c o n c e p t

For a purchase of an expense on account the general ledger posting is as follows:

6500 Utilities Exp		2010 Accts Payable	
Dr	Cr	Dr	Cr
350			350

In addition, the Vendor File (sub-ledger) for Minneapolis Electric & Gas Co. will reflect the new liability.

Minn Electric & Gas	
Dr	Cr
	350

UPDATING A LIST WHILE IN AN ACTIVITIES WINDOW
On February 2, 2004, Kristin Raina received a bill for prepaid advertising services from Cone and Clemens Associates in the amount of $600, Invoice No. X-145. The bill is due March 3, 2004, terms Net 30 Days. Cone and Clemens Associates is a new vendor.

To update the Vendor List from the Enter Bills window—
1. Click Vendors, and then click Enter Bills.
2. At the Vendor drop-down list, click < Add New >.

The New Vendor window appears. This is the same window that appears when choosing New from the Vendor menu button in the Vendor List window.

3. Enter the information for the new vendor listed below.

4. Click OK to save the information. You will exit the New Vendor window and the new vendor is now listed in the *Vendor* field.
5. Complete the remaining fields of the Enter Bills window.
6. On the E̲xpenses tab, click the account *1410 Prepaid Advertising*.

   You use the E̲xpenses tab to indicate which account should be debited. The account can be an asset, expense, or drawings account. Remember when using this window that by default Accounts Payable is the account credited. (See figure 2–15.)

7. If the information is correct, click S̲ave & New.

FIGURE 2-15
Enter Bills Window Completed

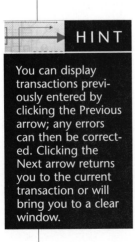

HINT

You can display transactions previously entered by clicking the Previous arrow; any errors can then be corrected. Clicking the Next arrow returns you to the current transaction or will bring you to a clear window.

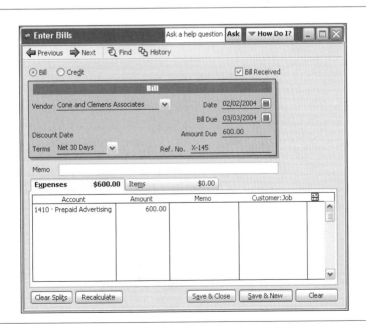

CORRECTION OF ERRORS

There are several ways to correct an error in a recorded transaction. One way is to open the window that contains the transaction and use the Previous button to view it. You can then make the necessary correction and save the transaction by choosing Next, Previous, or the Save buttons. As an alternative to correcting an error in a transaction, you can delete the transaction by clicking Edit on the Main Menu bar, clicking Delete Bill, and then reentering the transaction correctly.

Assume on February 2, 2004 that Kristin Raina inadvertently records a Prepaid Advertising amount for $300, realizes the correct amount is $600, and then further realizes that the invoice had already been recorded. The bill is from Cone and Clemens Associates, Invoice No. X-145, due March 3, 2004, terms Net 30 Days.

To record an erroneous transaction, make corrections, and then delete the transaction—

1. Click Vendors, and then click Enter Bills (if necessary).
2. At the Vendor drop-down list, click *Cone and Clemens Associates.*
3. Enter information in the *Date, Bill Due, Terms, Ref. No.,* and *Account* fields.
4. In the *Amount Due* field, key **300**.
5. Click Save & New.
6. You will receive a warning that the Reference No. has already been used. That should indicate to you that you are incorrectly recording an invoice for the second time. For now, ignore the warning and click Keep Number. The transaction is recorded.
7. Click the Previous arrow.

FIGURE 2-16
Edit Menu

Edit	
Undo Typing	Ctrl+Z
Revert	
Cut	Ctrl+X
Copy	Ctrl+C
Paste	Ctrl+V
New Bill	Ctrl+N
Delete Bill	Ctrl+D
Memorize Bill	Ctrl+M
Void Bill	
Copy Bill	Ctrl+O
Go To Transfer	Ctrl+G
Transaction History...	Ctrl+H
Show List	Ctrl+L
Use Register	Ctrl+R
Notepad	
Change Account Color...	
Use Calculator	
Find Bills...	Ctrl+F
Advanced Find...	
Preferences...	

Upon reviewing the transaction, you realize the correct amount should have been $600.

8. In the *Amount Due* and *Amount* fields, change the amount to **600** and click Save & New.
9. A message appears saying *You have changed the transaction. Do you want to record your changes?* Click Yes.

The corrected transaction is then saved with the new amount. But you now realize that this transaction is a duplicate transaction and you wish to delete the transaction completely.

10. Click Previous to view the transaction.
11. Click Edit on the Main Menu bar. (See figure 2–16.)

In QuickBooks Pro, when a window is open, there are different choices on the Edit menu relevant to that open window. In the case of the Enter Bills window, one choice is Delete Bill. This will delete the entire second transaction.

12. Click Delete Bill.
13. You will receive the message *Are you sure you want to delete this transaction?* Click OK. The duplicate transaction is deleted.

PRACTICE *exercise*

Record the following transactions in the Enter Bills window—

FEB. 3 Received bill from Nordic Realty for February rent, $800. Invoice No. F-12. Due date February 13, 2004 (charge to Rent Expense Account No. 6400).

FEB. 5 Received bill from Williams Office Supply Company for purchase of office supplies, $475. Invoice No. K-222. Due date March 6, 2004 (charge to Office Supplies Account No. 1305).

FEB. 9 Received bill from Midwest Mutual Insurance Co. for one-year insurance policy, $2,400. Invoice No. 01-21. Due date March 10, 2004 (charge to Prepaid Insurance Account No. 1420).

FEB. 12 Received bill from Galeway Computers for a new computer, $3,600. Invoice No. 556588. Due date March 13, 2004 (charge to Computers Account No. 1800).

FEB. 23 Received bill from [Your Name] Accounting Service for accounting service, $300. Invoice No. Feb04. Due date March 24, 2004 (charge to Accounting Expense Account No. 6020).

PROCESSING A CREDIT MEMO

Credit memo A reduction of Accounts Payable as a result of a return or an allowance by a vendor.

QuickBooks Pro allows you to process **credit memos** from vendors using the Enter Bills window. The resulting credit will reduce the balance owed to that vendor.

On February 25, 2004, Kristin Raina returned $75 of damaged office supplies to Williams Office Supply Company for credit, using credit memo CM-245.

To record a vendor credit—

1. Click Ven**d**ors, and then click Enter **B**ills.
2. At the Vendor drop-down list, click *Williams Office Supply Company*.
3. Click the Cre**d**it option button. When this button is chosen, the default entry is a debit to Accounts Payable.
4. Enter the appropriate information in the *Date, Credit Amount,* and *Ref. No.* fields.
5. At the *Memo* field, key **Return damaged office supplies**.
6. At the E**x**penses tab in the *Account* field, click *1305 Office Supplies*. (See figure 2–17.) If the information is correct, click S**a**ve & Close.

FIGURE 2-17
Credit Memo Completed

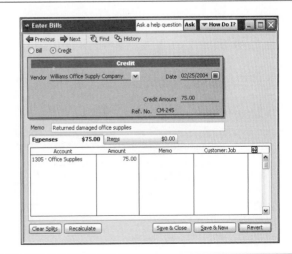

For a return of office supplies for credit, the general ledger posting is as follows:

2010 Accts Payable		1305 Office Supplies	
Dr	Cr	Dr	Cr
75			75

In addition, the vendor file for Williams Office Supply Company will reflect the reduced liability amount:

Williams Office Supply Co.	
Dr	Cr
CM 75	Bill 475
	Bal 400

ACTIVITIES: THE PAY BILLS WINDOW

Payment on account
Payment of an outstanding accounts payable.

In QuickBooks Pro, the Pay Bills window is used to record the **payment on account.** These are the bills previously recorded in the Enter Bills window. This window displays all open bills as of a selected date. Bills can be paid in full or a partial payment can be made. Payment can be in the form of check, credit card, or online payment. In addition, several bills can be paid at one time.

The Pay Bills window is designed only for payments of existing bills. The default accounts are Accounts Payable and Cash. The transaction is recorded as follows:

		Accounts Payable		XXX			
		Cash				XXX	

At the same time, the vendor's file on the Vendor List will also be updated to reflect the payment. The QuickBooks Pro Pay Bills window appears in figure 2–18.

FIGURE 2-18
Pay Bills Window

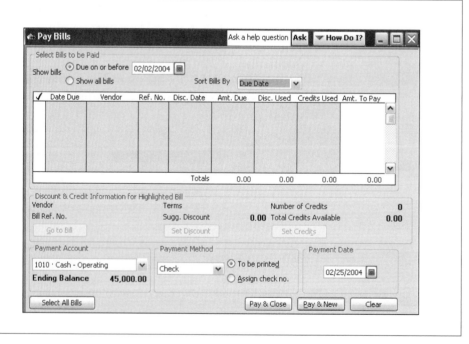

This window allows you to select a bill or bills to be paid, pay all or part of each bill, and designate checks to be printed by the computer. Note the following fields:

SHOW BILLS	Displays all bills or bills due by a certain date.
SORT BILLS BY	Lists bills by due date, vendor amount, or discount date.
GO TO BILL BUTTON	Allows you to view selected bill in the Enter Bills window.
SET DISCOUNT/ SET CREDITS BUTTONS	Used to activate any discount or credit for bill selected for payment.
PAYMENT ACCOUNT	Lists accounts from which this payment can made.
PAYEMENT METHOD	Lists methods of payment. If the To be printed option button is selected a check number starting with 1 will be assigned to each check in sequence. When the Assign check no. option is chosen, a new dialog box appears where a check number can be assigned.
PAYMENT DATE	Indicates the date of payment that will appear on the payment check and on all reports.

If you make an error in this window, and have chosen Pay & Close or Pay & New, you cannot correct the error in this window. However, you can correct the error in the Write Checks window, as will be explained later.

Activities identified as purchases on account were recorded in the Enter Bills window. Subsequently, Activities identified as payment of the outstanding accounts payable (previously recorded in the Enter Bills window) are then recorded in the Pay Bills window. Accounts Payable and Cash are the default general ledger posting accounts. All transactions entered in this window will result in a debit to the Accounts Payable account and a credit to the Cash account.

PAYING A BILL IN FULL

On February 10, 2004, Kristin Raina wishes to pay the bill from Nordic Realty Corp. for the rent bill received on February 3, 2004, (Check No. 1). Do not print the check.

To pay a bill—
1. Click Vendors, and then click Pay Bills.
2. At the Show bills options, click *Show all bills*.
3. At the *Payment Account* field, click *1010 Cash-Operating*.
4. At the *Payment Method* field choose *Check* and then *Assign check no.*
5. At the *Payment Date* field, choose *02/10/2004*.
6. From the listing, choose the bill from *Nordic Realty* by clicking in the ✓ field to place a check mark. (See figure 2–19.)

FIGURE 2-19
Pay Bills Window –
Vendor Bill Selected

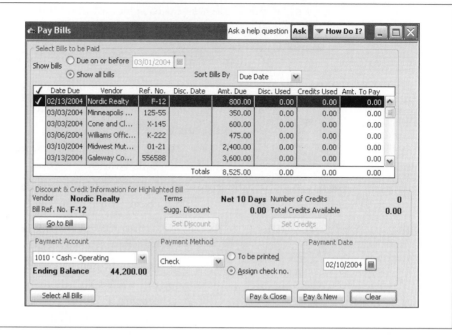

7. Click Pay & Close. The Assign Check Numbers window will appear.
8. Click the *Assign the appropriate check number next to each bill payment check* option.
9. At the *Check No.*, key **1**. (See Figure 2-20.)

FIGURE 2-20
Assign Check No. Window

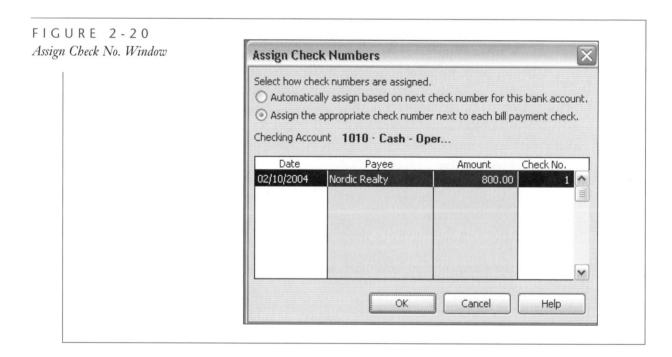

10. Click OK.

ACCOUNTING
c o n c e p t

For a payment of an existing Accounts Payable, the general ledger posting is as follows:

2010 Accts Payable		1010 Cash-Operating	
Dr	Cr	Dr	Cr
800			800

In addition, the Vendor File (subledger) for Nordic Realty Corp. will reflect the payment:

Nordic Realty Corp.	
Dr	Cr
Pay. 800	800 Bill
	0

Even though a check is not printed, for accounts payable and general ledger purposes, the bill is now considered paid. The vendor balance owed has been reduced along with the cash balance. Each time you click Pay & Close in this window, the Assign Check Number dialog box appears. After assigning the first check number, you can either use the foregoing procedure and indicate a check number, or you can click the *Automatically assign based on next check number for this bank account.* option button. Subsequent check numbers will be assigned in sequence. You will not see a check number in this window but you will see the check number for these transactions in the Write Checks window and reports.

MAKING A PARTIAL PAYMENT OF A BILL

QuickBooks Pro allows a partial payment to be made toward an outstanding bill. On February 23, 2004, Kristin Raina wishes to make a partial payment of $200 toward the Cone and Clemens Associates outstanding bill of $600 (Check No. 2).

To make a partial payment—

1. Click Ven**d**ors menu, and then **P**ay Bills.
2. Click the Show all bills option to display all bills.
3. At the *Payment Method* field choose Check and the **A**ssign check no. should be selected.
4. At the *Payment Date* field,, set the payment date for *02/23/2004*.
5. In the *Amt. To Pay* field on the line for the Cone and Clemens Associates bill, key **200**.

When you move to another field, the bill will automatically be checked for payment. (See figure 2–21.)

FIGURE 2-21
Pay Bills Window — Partial Payment

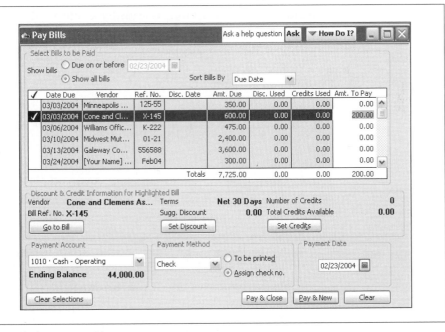

6. Click Pay & Close.
7. At the Assign Check Numbers window, click the Automatically assign based on next check number for this bank account option.
8. Click OK.

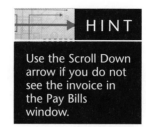

HINT

Use the Scroll Down arrow if you do not see the invoice in the Pay Bills window.

PRACTICE exercise

Record the following transactions in the Pay Bills window—

FEB. 25   Paid [Your Name] Accounting Services bill in full (Check No. 3).

FEB. 26   Made a partial payment of $1,000 toward Galeway Computers bill of $3,600 (Check No. 4).

ACTIVITIES: THE WRITE CHECKS WINDOW

Cash purchase
Payment of any bill or item other than accounts payable.

In QuickBooks Pro, the Write Checks window is used to record **cash purchases** that have not been previously entered into the system. The Write Checks window is useful for companies that usually pay on account but occasionally receive bills and remit payments immediately, or for companies that do not purchase goods or services on account and therefore do not need to track vendor data. Accounts Payable is not used, which allows for the recording of a cash purchase in one step. The data fields in this window are similar to that of the Enter Bills window—payee (vendor name), date, expense, asset, or item purchased.

The Write Checks window is used for all cash purchases. The default account is Cash. The transaction is recorded as follows:

	Asset/Expense/Drawing	XXX		
	Cash			XXX

A transaction entered in this window will not be tracked through the *Accounts Payable* or *Vendor* reports.

Activities identified as cash purchases are recorded in the Write Checks window. In this window, the Cash account is the default credit posting account because all transactions result in a cash payment by check. All transactions entered in this window will result in a credit to the Cash account. The account field in this window is used to indicate the asset, expense, or drawings account to be debited.

On February 27, 2004, Kristin Raina receives a bill for $125 for monthly janitorial services from Jeter Janitorial Services. She pays it with Check No. 5.

To write a check—

1. Click <u>B</u>anking, and then click <u>W</u>rite Checks.
2. At the *Bank Account* field make sure *1010 Cash-Operating* is displayed, the To be printe<u>d</u> box is not checked, and the Check No. is 5.
3. At the *Date* field, choose *02/27/2004*.
4. At the Pay to the Order of drop-down list, click *Jeter Janitorial Services*.
5. At the *$* field, key **125**.
6. At the E<u>x</u>penses tab in the *Account* field, click *6300 Janitorial Expenses*. (See figure 2–22.)

FIGURE 2-22
*Write Checks Window
Completed*

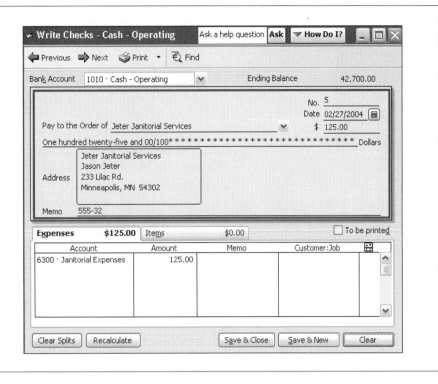

7. If the information is correct, click Save & New. Even though a check is not printed, the bill is now considered paid.

If you click Previous at this time, you will see the payments recorded in this window as well as the payments recorded in the Pay Bills window. Activities recorded in the Pay Bills window are actually checks written that subsequently appear in the Write Checks window, in addition to the checks written in the Write Checks window. The payments are recorded in check number sequence. Remember, since checks are not being printed, the program automatically assigns the next check number. Any errors recorded in the Pay Bills window cannot be corrected in the Pay Bills window, but they can be corrected in the Write Checks window.

To see an example of this, click the Previous arrow several times. Each time, notice that the payments include those entered in both the Write Checks and Pay Bills windows. As you scroll through the windows, notice the window is different for payments made in the Write Checks and Pay Bills windows. Notice also that the check numbers are in sequence.

ACCOUNTING
concept

For a cash payment of an expense the general ledger posting will be as follows:

6300 Janitorial Expenses
Dr	Cr
125	

1010 Cash-Operating
Dr	Cr
	125

The vendor file is unaffected because payment was made immediately.

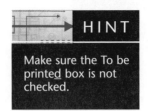

Record the following transactions in the Write Checks window:

FEB. 27   Received bill from Giambi Graphics for design supplies, $200. Pay immediately with Check No. 6 (charge to Design Supplies Account No. 1300).

FEB. 27   Received bill from TwinCityTelCo for telephone service for February, $275. Pay immediately with Check No. 7 (charge to Telephone Expense Account No. 6450).

FEB. 27   The owner, Kristin Raina, withdrew $400 for personal use. Pay immediately with Check No. 8 (charge to Kristin Raina, Drawings Account No. 3020).

REPORTS: VENDOR AND FINANCIAL REPORTS

Reports, the fourth level of operation in QuickBooks Pro, reflect the information and activities recorded in the various Lists and Activities windows. QuickBooks Pro can display and print a variety of reports, many of which should be printed on a monthly basis.

VENDOR REPORTS FROM THE REPORTS MENU

The Accounts Payable and vendor-related reports help a company manage its liability payments, ensure timely and correct remittances, control cash flow, and retain an accurate record of all vendor-related transactions. Among these reports are the *Unpaid Bills* report and the *Vendor Balance Detail* report.

Unpaid Bills Report

The *Unpaid Bills* report lists all unpaid bills for each vendor at a specific date. The report will list each open bill (with date and invoice number) for a vendor, along with any credit memos applied. The report may be customized to show all vendors or only those with outstanding bills.

To view and print the *Unpaid Bills* report—
1. Click <u>R</u>eports, and then click <u>V</u>endors & Payables.
2. At the Vendors & Payables submenu, click <u>U</u>npaid Bills Detail.
3. At the Date calendar, choose *02/29/2004*, and then click Refre<u>s</u>h on the command line. The *Unpaid Bills Detail* report displays. (See figure 2–23.)

Along the top of the *Unpaid Bills Detail* report window are several buttons (<u>M</u>odify Report, Memori<u>z</u>e, Prin<u>t</u>, and so on). This row of buttons is called the command line. Notice the diamond shape before each of the title headings in the report text. If you wish to change the size of a column, you can click and drag the diamond in either direction.

FIGURE 2-23

*Unpaid Bills Detail
Report*

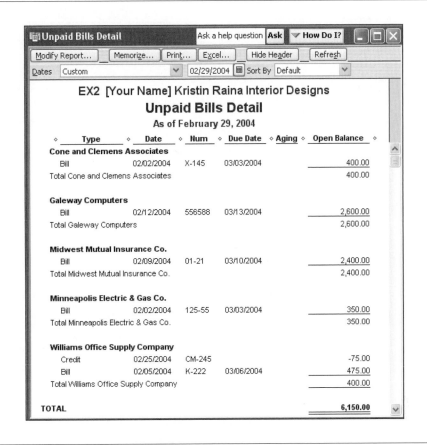

Type	Date	Num	Due Date	Aging	Open Balance
Cone and Clemens Associates					
Bill	02/02/2004	X-145	03/03/2004		400.00
Total Cone and Clemens Associates					400.00
Galeway Computers					
Bill	02/12/2004	556588	03/13/2004		2,600.00
Total Galeway Computers					2,600.00
Midwest Mutual Insurance Co.					
Bill	02/09/2004	01-21	03/10/2004		2,400.00
Total Midwest Mutual Insurance Co.					2,400.00
Minneapolis Electric & Gas Co.					
Bill	02/02/2004	125-55	03/03/2004		350.00
Total Minneapolis Electric & Gas Co.					350.00
Williams Office Supply Company					
Credit	02/25/2004	CM-245			-75.00
Bill	02/05/2004	K-222	03/06/2004		475.00
Total Williams Office Supply Company					400.00
TOTAL					**6,150.00**

4. To print the report, click Print on the command line.

   If you receive a message about Printing Features, place a check mark in the box to the left of Do not display this message in the future and click OK. The Print Reports dialog box appears. (See figure 2–24.) At the Print Reports dialog box, settings, fonts, and margins can be changed. The orientation of the report may also be changed. There is a Preview button if you wish to preview the report before printing. At this time, do not change any settings other than the orientation. For most reports, the portrait orientation is fine, but for some wider reports, the landscape orientation may be more useful.

5. At the Print Reports dialog box, choose Portrait in the Orientation section, then click Print.
6. Close the report.

   If you receive a message about Memorize Report, place a check mark in the box to the left of Do not display this message in the future and click No.

FIGURE 2-24
*Print Reports Dialog
Box*

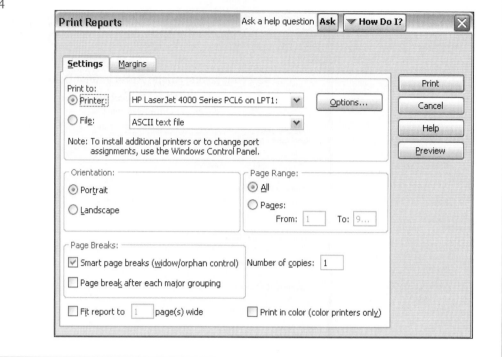

Vendor Balance Detail Report

The *Vendor Balance Detail* report displays all transactions for each vendor with the remaining balance owed. This report is similar to an accounts payable subsidiary ledger in a manual system. The report shows all vendor-related transactions, that is, all bills, payments, and credit memos for each vendor, in chronological order.

To view and print the *Vendor Balance Detail* report—
1. Click Reports, and then click Vendors & Payables.
2. At the Vendors & Payables submenu, click Vendor Balance Detail.
3. Click the Print button on the command line.
4. At the Print Reports dialog box, choose Portrait orientation and click Print. Your printout should look like figure 2–25.
5. Close the report.

FIGURE 2-25
Vendor Balance Detail Report

EX2 [Your Name] Kristin Raina Interior Designs
Vendor Balance Detail
All Transactions

Accrual Basis

Type	Date	Num	Account	Amount	Balance
[Your Name] Accounting Service					
Bill	02/23/2004	Feb.04	2010 · Accounts Payable	300.00	300.00
Bill Pmt -Check	02/25/2004	3	2010 · Accounts Payable	-300.00	0.00
Total [Your Name] Accounting Service				0.00	0.00
Cone and Clemens Associates					
Bill	02/02/2004	X-145	2010 · Accounts Payable	600.00	600.00
Bill Pmt -Check	02/23/2004	2	2010 · Accounts Payable	-200.00	400.00
Total Cone and Clemens Associates				400.00	400.00
Galeway Computers					
Bill	02/12/2004	556588	2010 · Accounts Payable	3,600.00	3,600.00
Bill Pmt -Check	02/26/2004	4	2010 · Accounts Payable	-1,000.00	2,600.00
Total Galeway Computers				2,600.00	2,600.00
Midwest Mutual Insurance Co.					
Bill	02/09/2004	01-21	2010 · Accounts Payable	2,400.00	2,400.00
Total Midwest Mutual Insurance Co.				2,400.00	2,400.00
Minneapolis Electric & Gas Co.					
Bill	02/02/2004	125-55	2010 · Accounts Payable	350.00	350.00
Total Minneapolis Electric & Gas Co.				350.00	350.00
Nordic Realty					
Bill	02/03/2004	F-12	2010 · Accounts Payable	800.00	800.00
Bill Pmt -Check	02/10/2004	1	2010 · Accounts Payable	-800.00	0.00
Total Nordic Realty				0.00	0.00
Williams Office Supply Company					
Bill	02/05/2004	K-222	2010 · Accounts Payable	475.00	475.00
Credit	02/25/2004	CM-245	2010 · Accounts Payable	-75.00	400.00
Total Williams Office Supply Company				400.00	400.00
TOTAL				6,150.00	6,150.00

VENDOR REPORTS FROM THE LISTS MENU

QuickBooks Pro allows you to view and print several vendor reports from the Lists windows. Once a list is accessed, a reports list is available when choosing the Reports menu button in the List window. Reports for one vendor only or for all vendors can be printed. An example of a vendor report you can access from the Vendor List window is the *Transaction List by Vendor* report.

To view and print a Vendor List report such as *Transaction List by Vendor*—

1. Click Lists, and then click Vendor List. The Vendor List window is displayed.
2. Click the Reports menu button. The Reports drop-down menu that appears contains a menu of available reports. (See figure 2–26.)
3. Click Reports on All Vendors.
4. At the Reports on All Vendors submenu, click Transaction List by Vendor.
5. At the *From* and *To* fields, choose *02/01/2004* and *02/29/2004* and then click Refresh on the command line. The report for that period displays.
6. To print the report, click the Print button on the command line.
7. In the Print Reports dialog box, choose Landscape orientation and click Print. Your report should look like figure 2–27.

FIGURE 2-26
Vendor List – Reports Button Menu

FIGURE 2-27

Transaction List by Vendor Report

EX2 [Your Name] Kristin Raina Interior Designs
Transaction List by Vendor
February 2004

Type	Date	Num	Memo	Account	Clr	Split	Amount
[Your Name] Accounting Service							
Bill	02/23/2004	Feb.04		2010 · Accounts Payable		6020 · Accounting Expense	-300.00
Bill Pmt -Check	02/25/2004	3	99-2004-XX	1010 · Cash - Operating		2010 · Accounts Payable	-300.00
Cone and Clemens Associates							
Bill	02/02/2004	X-145		2010 · Accounts Payable		1410 · Prepaid Advertising	-600.00
Bill Pmt -Check	02/23/2004	2	KR569	1010 · Cash - Operating		2010 · Accounts Payable	-200.00
Galeway Computers							
Bill	02/12/2004	556588		2010 · Accounts Payable		1800 · Computers	-3,600.00
Bill Pmt -Check	02/26/2004	4	2455-897	1010 · Cash - Operating		2010 · Accounts Payable	-1,000.00
Giambi Graphics							
Check	02/27/2004	6	33-2221	1010 · Cash - Operating		1300 · Design Supplies	-200.00
Jeter Janitorial Services							
Check	02/27/2004	5	555-32	1010 · Cash - Operating		6300 · Janitorial Expenses	-125.00
Kristin Raina							
Check	02/27/2004	8		1010 · Cash - Operating		3020 · Kristin Raina, Drawin...	-400.00
Midwest Mutual Insurance Co.							
Bill	02/09/2004	01-21		2010 · Accounts Payable		1420 · Prepaid Insurance	-2,400.00
Minneapolis Electric & Gas Co.							
Bill	02/02/2004	125-55		2010 · Accounts Payable		6500 · Utilities Expense	-350.00
Nordic Realty							
Bill	02/03/2004	F-12		2010 · Accounts Payable		6400 · Rent Expense	-800.00
Bill Pmt -Check	02/10/2004	1	55-1212	1010 · Cash - Operating		2010 · Accounts Payable	-800.00
TwinCityTelCo							
Check	02/27/2004	7	666-6667	1010 · Cash - Operating		6450 · Telephone Expense	-275.00
Williams Office Supply Company							
Bill	02/05/2004	K-222		2010 · Accounts Payable		1305 · Office Supplies	-475.00
Credit	02/25/2004	CM-245	Return damaged ...	2010 · Accounts Payable		1305 · Office Supplies	75.00

8. Close the report and the Vendor List window.

The *Transaction List by Vendor* report displays the general ledger account posting for each transaction. In addition, this report includes transactions that were entered through the Write Checks window and do not appear on the above *Unpaid Bills Detail* and *Vendor Balance (A/P)* reports.

The *Unpaid Bills Detail* report and *Vendor Balance Detail* report displayed from the Reports menu above can also be accessed from the Vendor List window by clicking the Reports menu button, clicking Reports on All Vendors, and then clicking A/P Reports on the submenu.

DRILLING DOWN TO A TRANSACTION WINDOW

Previously you used the drill-down feature to view the Edit Vendor window from the Vendor List. While viewing reports, it is frequently helpful to see the originating transaction or document that gave rise to the report figures. The drill-down feature allows you to quickly move from a report to the related transaction windows and back to the report again. If the transaction is incorrect, you can edit or remove the transaction at that time. Any changes to the transactions are automatically reflected in subsequent reports.

When Kristin Raina reviewed the *Unpaid Bills* report she discovered that the bill from Minneapolis Electric & Gas Co. was entered incorrectly at $350, while the correct amount was $450.

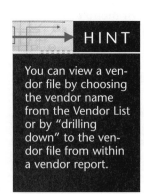

HINT

You can view a vendor file by choosing the vendor name from the Vendor List or by "drilling down" to the vendor file from within a vendor report.

To drill down from a report and correct an error—

1. Click Reports, and then click Vendors & Payables.
2. At the Vendors & Payables submenu, click Unpaid Bills Detail.
3. Set the date for *02/29/2004* and click Refresh on the command bar.
4. Place the mouse pointer over the Minneapolis Electric & Gas Co. bill until it changes into a zoom glass and double-click. The original bill entry will appear. (See figure 2–28.)

FIGURE 2-28

Minneapolis Electric & Gas Bill Transaction

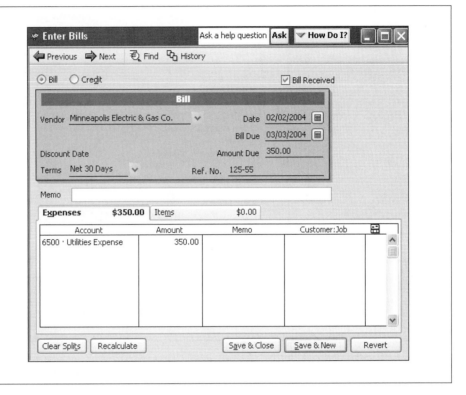

5. In the *Amount Due* field, change the amount to **450**.
6. After completing the change, click Save & Close.
7. At the Recording Transaction window, click Yes.
8. If the Report needs to be refreshed window appears, click Yes.

   You will be returned to the report with the corrected figure in place. (See figure 2–29.)

9. To print the corrected report, click Print on the command line.
10. At the Print Reports dialog box, choose Landscape orientation, and then click Print.
11. Close the report.

FIGURE 2-29
Corrected Unpaid Bills Report

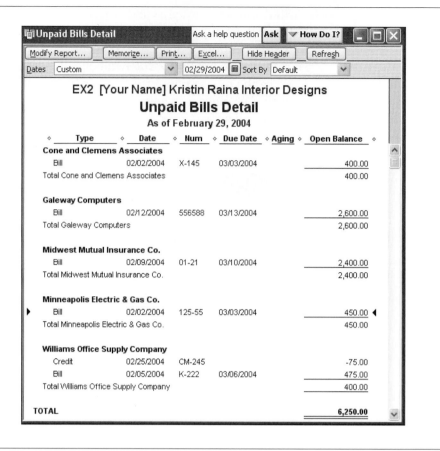

OTHER REPORTS

As activities are entered in the windows, behind-the-scenes accounting activity is recorded in general journal format, posted to the general ledger, and flowed into the financial statements. QuickBooks Pro can display and print these standard accounting reports, such as the *Journal* report. The *Journal* report displays, in general journal format, all transactions recorded during a specified period of time.

To view and print the *Journal* report—
1. At the Reports menu, click Accountant & Taxes.
2. At the Accountant & Taxes submenu, click Journal.
3. At the *From* and *To* fields, choose *02/01/2004* and *02/29/2004*, and then click Refresh on the command line. The *Journal* report is displayed.
4. To print the report, click the Print button on the command line.
5. At the Print Reports dialog box, choose Landscape orientation and Print. (See figure 2–30.)
6. Close the report.

EX2 [Your Name] Kristin Raina Interior Designs
Journal
February 2004

Trans #	Type	Date	Num	Name	Memo	Account	Debit	Credit
3	Bill	02/02/2004	125-55	Minneapolis Electric & Gas Co.		2010 · Accounts Payable		450.00
				Minneapolis Electric & Gas Co.		6500 · Utilities Expense	450.00	
							450.00	450.00
4	Bill	02/02/2004	X-145	Cone and Clemens Associates		2010 · Accounts Payable		600.00
				Cone and Clemens Associates		1410 · Prepaid Advertising	600.00	
							600.00	600.00
6	Bill	02/03/2004	F-12	Nordic Realty		2010 · Accounts Payable		800.00
				Nordic Realty		6400 · Rent Expense	800.00	
							800.00	800.00
7	Bill	02/05/2004	K-222	Williams Office Supply Company		2010 · Accounts Payable		475.00
				Williams Office Supply Company		1305 · Office Supplies	475.00	
							475.00	475.00
8	Bill	02/09/2004	01-21	Midwest Mutual Insurance Co.		2010 · Accounts Payable		2,400.00
				Midwest Mutual Insurance Co.		1420 · Prepaid Insurance	2,400.00	
							2,400.00	2,400.00
9	Bill	02/12/2004	556588	Galeway Computers		2010 · Accounts Payable		3,600.00
				Galeway Computers		1800 · Computers	3,600.00	
							3,600.00	3,600.00
10	Bill	02/23/2004	Feb.04	[Your Name] Accounting Service		2010 · Accounts Payable		300.00
				[Your Name] Accounting Service		6020 · Accounting Expense	300.00	
							300.00	300.00
11	Credit	02/25/2004	CM-245	Williams Office Supply Company	Return damaged ...	2010 · Accounts Payable	75.00	
				Williams Office Supply Company	Return damaged ...	1305 · Office Supplies		75.00
							75.00	75.00
12	Bill Pmt -Check	02/10/2004	1	Nordic Realty	55-1212	1010 · Cash - Operating		800.00
				Nordic Realty	55-1212	2010 · Accounts Payable	800.00	
							800.00	800.00
13	Bill Pmt -Check	02/23/2004	2	Cone and Clemens Associates	KR569	1010 · Cash - Operating		200.00
				Cone and Clemens Associates	KR569	2010 · Accounts Payable	200.00	
							200.00	200.00
14	Bill Pmt -Check	02/25/2004	3	[Your Name] Accounting Service	99-2004-XX	1010 · Cash - Operating		300.00
				[Your Name] Accounting Service	99-2004-XX	2010 · Accounts Payable	300.00	
							300.00	300.00
15	Bill Pmt -Check	02/26/2004	4	Galeway Computers	2455-897	1010 · Cash - Operating		1,000.00
				Galeway Computers	2455-897	2010 · Accounts Payable	1,000.00	
							1,000.00	1,000.00
16	Check	02/27/2004	5	Jeter Janitorial Services	555-32	1010 · Cash - Operating		125.00
				Jeter Janitorial Services	555-32	6300 · Janitorial Expenses	125.00	
							125.00	125.00
17	Check	02/27/2004	6	Giambi Graphics	33-2221	1010 · Cash - Operating		200.00
				Giambi Graphics	33-2221	1300 · Design Supplies	200.00	
							200.00	200.00
18	Check	02/27/2004	7	TwinCityTelCo	666-6667	1010 · Cash - Operating		275.00
				TwinCityTelCo	666-6667	6450 · Telephone Expense	275.00	
							275.00	275.00
19	Check	02/27/2004	8	Kristin Raina		1010 · Cash - Operating		400.00
				Kristin Raina		3020 · Kristin Raina, Drawings	400.00	
							400.00	400.00
TOTAL							**12,000.00**	**12,000.00**

QuickBooks Pro automatically assigns transaction numbers (Trans #). You cannot change them. Notice in figure 2–30 that there is no transaction number 5. This was the transaction that was deleted earlier in the chapter. The software deletes the transaction, but will move to the next transaction number for the next transaction. When comparing your work to the solutions, do not be concerned if you have different transaction numbers as long as you have the correct journal entries.

The Type column in figure 2–30 indicates the window where the activity was recorded. The Bill type entries represent the transactions entered in the Enter Bills window. Notice that each of these transactions has a credit to

Accounts Payable because this is the default for that account. The Credit type entry represents the credit memo entered in the Enter Bills window. Recall that when the credit memo option is chosen, the default account becomes a debit to Accounts Payable. The Bill Pmt – Check type entries represent the transactions entered in the Pay Bills window. All of these transactions are a debit to Accounts Payable and a credit to Cash, which are the default accounts for this window. The Check type entries are from the Write Checks window, which all have a credit to Cash because that is the default account for this window.

EXITING QUICKBOOKS PRO

Once you have completed this session, you should make a backup copy of your exercise company file to a floppy disk or network directory using the back up procedures explained in chapter 1. When you back up to a floppy disk, be sure to change the Save in text box to the location where you keep your backup files, and carefully type in the correct file name.

After making a backup copy of the company file, exit QuickBooks Pro and return to the Windows desktop by clicking File and then Exit.

INTERNET
Resources

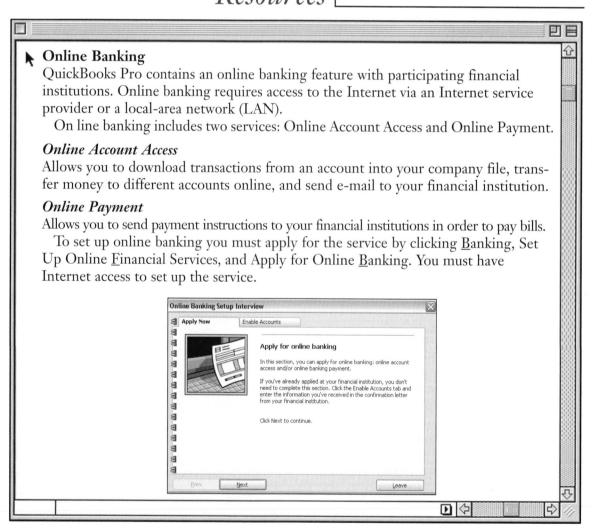

Online Banking
QuickBooks Pro contains an online banking feature with participating financial institutions. Online banking requires access to the Internet via an Internet service provider or a local-area network (LAN).

On line banking includes two services: Online Account Access and Online Payment.

Online Account Access
Allows you to download transactions from an account into your company file, transfer money to different accounts online, and send e-mail to your financial institution.

Online Payment
Allows you to send payment instructions to your financial institutions in order to pay bills.

To set up online banking you must apply for the service by clicking Banking, Set Up Online Financial Services, and Apply for Online Banking. You must have Internet access to set up the service.

P R O G R E S S *Check*

PROCEDURE REVIEW

To add a vendor—
1. Click Lists, and then click Vendor List.
2. At the Vendor List window, click the Vendor menu button.
3. At the Vendor menu, click New.
4. Enter the background data for the vendor.
5. Click OK.
6. Close the Vendor List window.

To delete a vendor—
1. Click Lists, and then click Vendor List.
2. At the Vendor List window, select the vendor you wish to delete.
3. Click the Vendor menu button.
4. At the Vendor menu, click Delete.
5. Click OK at the warning.
6. Close the Vendor List window.
   You cannot delete a vendor who has a balance or who was used in a transaction during the period.

To edit a vendor—
1. Click Lists, and then click Vendor List.
2. At the Vendor List window, select the vendor you wish to edit and then click the Vendor menu button, or double-click the vendor name.
3. At the Vendor menu, click Edit.
4. Change the appropriate information.
5. Click OK.
6. Close the Vendor List.

To enter a bill—
1. Click Vendors, and then click Enter Bills.
2. Click the Bill option.
3. At the Vendor drop-down list, click the vendor name.
4. Enter the bill date in the *Date* field.
5. Enter the due date in the *Bill Due* field.
6. Enter the amount in the *Amount Due* field.
7. Select the terms in the *Terms* field.
8. Enter the invoice number in the *Ref. No.* field.
9. Select the account to be debited in the Expenses tab.
10. Click Save & Close.

To update the Vendor List while in an Activity window—
1. Click Vendors, and then click Enter Bills.
2. At the Vendor drop-down list, click < Add New >.
3. Follow the procedures to add a vendor.
4. Click OK.

To process a credit memo—
1. Click Vendors, and then click Enter Bills.
2. Click the Credit option button.
3. Follow the procedures for entering a bill.

To pay a bill—
1. Click Vendors, and then click Pay Bills.
2. Click Show all bills.
3. At the *Payment Account* field, choose the appropriate cash account.
4. At the *Payment Method* field choose Check and Assign check no. should be selected.
5. Enter the payment date in the *Payment Date* field.
6. Choose the bill to be paid by clicking in the ✓ field to the left of the bill.
7. Click Pay & Close. The Assign Check Number window will appear.
8. Click the *Assign the appropriate check number next to each bill payment check* option.
9. Enter the check number.
10. Click OK.

To write a check—
1. Click Banking, and then click Write Checks.
2. At the *Bank Account* field, choose the appropriate account.
3. Enter the check date in the *Date* field.
4. Choose the payee from the Pay to the Order of drop-down list.
5. At the *$* field enter the amount of the check.
6. At the Expenses tab, choose the account to be debited.
7. Click Save & Close.

To view and print vendor reports from the Reports menu—
1. Click Reports, and then click Vendors & Payables.
2. At the Vendors & Payables submenu, choose a report.
3. Indicate the appropriate dates for the report, and then click Refresh.
4. Click Print on the command line.
5. At the Print Reports dialog box, review the settings, then click Print.
6. Close the report.

To view and print vendor reports from the Lists menu—
1. Click Lists, and then click Vendor List.
2. Click the Reports menu button.
3. Click Reports on All Vendors.
4. Choose a report.
5. Indicate the appropriate dates for the report, and then click Refresh.
6. Click Print on the command line.
7. At the Print Reports dialog box, review the settings, then click Print.
8. Close the report and the Vendor List window.

KEY CONCEPTS

Select the letter of the item that best matches each definition.

a. *Journal* report
b. Write Checks window
c. System Default account
d. Vendor List
e. *Unpaid Bills* report
f. Credit Memo
g. Pay Bills window
h. Vendor
i. Enter Bills window
j. *Transactions List by Vendor* report

_____ 1. Someone from whom the business buys goods or services.

_____ 2. Contains a file for all vendors with whom the company does business.

_____ 3. A report that lists all unpaid vendor bills at a specific date.

_____ 4. Processed through the Enter Bills window to reflect a reduction of the vendor's liability due to a credit for return or allowance.

_____ 5. Activity window used to record vendor bills to be paid at a later date.

_____ 6. Activities displayed in general journal format for a specified period of time.

_____ 7. Report from the Vendor List that displays the general ledger account posting for the transaction.

_____ 8. A pre-identified general ledger account that will increase or decrease automatically depending on the type of transaction entered.

_____ 9. Activity window used to record cash purchase of goods or services from a vendor.

_____ 10. Activity window used to pay bills previously entered in the Enter Bills window.

PROCEDURE CHECK

1. Your company has changed its telephone carrier. Describe the steps to add the new vendor to the system.
2. Upper management requests a list of all businesses from whom the company buys goods or services. How would you use QuickBooks Pro to quickly produce this information?
3. You receive a batch of bills that must be paid immediately. You do not need to maintain an Accounts Payable record of these payments. How would you use QuickBooks Pro to expeditiously enter these payments into the system and write the appropriate payment checks?

4. A vendor calls your company to complain that a bill forwarded 45 days ago remains unpaid. How would you use QuickBooks Pro to verify this complaint?

5. You wish to view all the bills received from a vendor and all payments to that vendor. How would you use QuickBooks Pro to obtain the required information?

6. Compare and contrast a manual accounting system with a computerized accounting system for processing vendor transactions including how the accounts payable subsidiary ledger compares to the Vendor List.

CASE PROBLEMS

CASE PROBLEM 1

On April 4, 2004, Lynn Garcia began her business, called Lynn's Music Studio, as a music instructor by depositing $10,000 cash in a bank account in the business name. She also contributed a piano and some guitars. The musical instruments have an outstanding note balance of $2,000, which will now be assumed by the business. The cash, musical instruments, note payable, and capital have all been recorded in the opening balances of the books. Lynn anticipates spending the beginning of the month setting up her studio and expects to provide piano and guitar lessons later in the month. Record the transactions listed below for the month of April.

1. Open the company file CH2 Lynn's Music Studio.QBW.
2. Make a backup copy of the company file LMS2 [Your Name] Lynn's Music Studio.
3. Restore the backup copy of the company file. In both the Restore From and Restore To windows use the file name LMS2 [Your Name] Lynn's Music Studio.
4. Change the company name to LMS2 [Your Name] Lynn's Music Studio.
5. Add the following vendors to the Vendor List:

Vendor Name:	**Pioneer Phone**
Opening Balance:	**0 as of April 1, 2004**
Company Name:	**Pioneer Phone**
Address:	**1000 Route 6**
	Carbondale, PA 18407
Contact:	**Customer Service**
Phone:	**570-555-6000**
FAX:	**570-555-6500**
E-mail:	**pioph@emcp.net**
Terms:	**Net 15 Days**

Vendor Name:	**Steamtown Electric**
Opening Balance:	**0 as of April 1, 2004**
Company Name:	**Steamtown Electric**
Address:	**150 Vine Lane**
	Scranton, PA 18501
Contact:	**Customer Service**
Phone:	**570-555-2500**
FAX:	**570-555-3000**
E-mail:	**steam@emcp.net**
Terms:	**Net 15 Days**

Delete the following vendor:
   Universal Electric
Edit the following vendor:
   Mutual Insurance Company telephone number: **570-555-5600**

6. Using the appropriate window, record the following transactions for April 2004.

Apr. 2	Received bill for rent for the month of April from Viewhill Realty Management, $600, paid immediately, Check No. 1. Do not print check.
Apr. 2	Received a bill for a one-year insurance policy on account from Mutual Insurance Company, $1,200, Invoice No. 4010102, Net 30 Days.
Apr. 5	Purchased furniture on account from Mills Family Furniture, $2,500, Invoice No. 1257, Net 30 Days.
Apr. 6	Purchased a computer system on account from Computer Town, $3,000, Invoice No. X234, Net 30 Days.
Apr. 9	Purchased music supplies on account from Strings, Sheets, & Such, $500, Invoice No. 1290, Net 15 Days.
Apr. 9	Received bill for tuning of piano and guitars from Tune Tones, $100, paid immediately, Check No. 2. Tune Tones is a new vendor:

Vendor Name:	**Tune Tones**
Opening Balance:	**0 as of April 1, 2004**
Company Name:	**Tune Tones**
First Name:	**Tony**
Last Name:	**Tune**
Address:	**500 Monroe Ave.**
	Dunmore, PA 18512
Contact:	**Tony Tune**
Phone:	**570-555-1111**
FAX:	**570-555-2222**
E-mail:	**TUNE@emcp.net**
Terms:	**Net 30 Days**

Apr. 9	Purchased office supplies on account from Paper, Clips, and More, $400, Invoice No. 01-1599, Net 30 Days.
Apr. 12	Received the telephone bill from Pioneer Phone, $50, Invoice No. pp401, Net 15 Days.
Apr. 13	Received utilities bill from Steamtown Electric, $70, Invoice No. SE401, Net 15 Days.
Apr. 20	Paid in full Strings, Sheets, & Such, Invoice No. 1290 (Check No. 3). Do not print check.
Apr. 23	Received a credit memo from Paper, Clips, and More, $50, Invoice No. CM250, for office supplies returned.
Apr. 26	Paid in full Pioneer Phone, Invoice No. pp401 (Check No. 4).
Apr. 27	Paid in full Steamtown Electric, Invoice No. SE401 (Check No. 5).
Apr. 30	Made a partial payment of $1,000 to Mills Family Furniture (Check No. 6).
Apr. 30	Made a partial payment of $1,000 to Computer Town (Check No. 7).
Apr. 30	The owner, Lynn Garcia, withdrew $1,000, for personal use. (Check No. 8).

7. Display and print the following reports for April 1, 2004, to April 30, 2004:

   a. *Unpaid Bills Detail*
   b. *Vendor Balance Detail*
   c. *Transaction List by Vendor*
   d. *Journal*

CASE PROBLEM 2

On June 1, 2004, Olivia Chen began her business as an Internet consultant and Web page designer, Olivia's Web Solutions, by depositing $25,000 cash in a bank account in the business name. She also contributed a computer system. The computer has an outstanding note balance of $2,500 that will be assumed by the business. The cash, computer, note payable, and capital have all been recorded in the opening balances of the books. Olivia anticipates spending the beginning of the month setting up her office and expects to provide Web design and Internet consulting services later in the month. You will record the transactions listed below for the month of June.

1. Open the company file CH2 Olivia's Web Solutions.QBW.
2. Make a backup copy of the company file OWS2 [Your Name]Olivia's Web Solutions.

3. Restore the backup copy of the company file. In both the Restore From and Restore To windows use the file name OWS2 [Your Name] Olivia's Web Solutions.

4. Change the company name to OWS2 [Your Name] Olivia's Web Solutions.

5. Add the following vendors to the Vendor List:

Vendor Name:	**Comet Computer Supplies**
Opening Balance:	**0 as of June 1, 2004**
Company Name:	**Comet Computer Supplies**
Address:	**657 Motor Parkway**
	Center Island, NY 11488
Contact:	**Customer Service**
Phone:	**631-555-4444**
FAX:	**631-555-4455**
E-mail:	**CometCs@emcp.net**
Terms:	**Net 15 Days**

Vendor Name:	**Chrbet Advertising**
Opening Balance:	**0 as of June 1, 2004**
Company Name:	**Chrbet Advertising**
Address:	**201 East 10 Street**
	New York, NY 10012
Contact:	**Chris Chrbet**
Phone:	**212-555-8777**
FAX:	**212-555-8778**
E-mail:	**Cadv@emcp.net**
Terms:	**Net 30 Days**

Delete the following vendor:
  Johnson Ad Agency
Edit the address for Martin Computer Repairs:
  366 North Franklin Street
  Garden City, NY 11568

6. Using the appropriate window, record the following transactions for June 2004.

Jun. 1   Received bill for rent for the month of June from ARC Management, $800, paid immediately. Check No. 1. Do not print check.

Jun. 4   Received a one-year insurance policy on account from Eastern Mutual Insurance, $1,800, Invoice No. 87775, Net 30 Days.

Jun. 4   Purchased software on account from Netsoft Development Co., $3,600, Invoice No.38745, Net 30 Days.

Jun. 7   Purchased office furniture on account from Lewis Furniture Co., $3,200, Invoice No. O9887, Net 30 Days.

Jun. 8   Purchased six months of advertising services on account from Chrbet Advertising, $1,200, Invoice No. O-989, Net 30 Days.

Jun. 11   Purchased computer supplies on account from Comet Computer Supplies, $600, Invoice No. 56355, Net 15 Days.

Jun. 14   Received bill for online Internet services, from Systems Service, $150, paid immediately (Check No. 2). Systems Service is a new vendor:

Vendor Name:	**Systems Service**
Opening Balance:	**0 as of June 1, 2004**
Company Name:	**Systems Service**
First Name:	**Jeremy**
Last Name:	**Jones**
Address:	**36 Sunrise Lane**
	Hempstead, NY 11004
Contact:	**Jeremy Jones**
Phone:	**516-555-2525**
FAX:	**516-555-2526**
E-mail:	**Sysser@emcp.net**
Terms:	**Net 30 Days**

Jun. 15   Purchased office supplies on account from Office Plus, $450, Invoice No. 3665, Net 30 Days.

Jun. 18   Received the telephone bill from Eastel, $350, Invoice No. 6-2568, Net 30 Days.

Jun. 21   Received utilities bill from LI Power Company, $125, Invoice No. OWS-23556, Net 15 Days.

Jun. 21   Returned office supplies to Office Plus for a $75 credit, CM789.

Jun. 21   Paid in full Eastern Mutual Insurance, Invoice No. 87775 (Check No. 3). Do not print check.

Jun. 25   Paid in full Comet Computer Supplies, Invoice No. 56355 (Check No. 4).

Jun. 28   Paid in full LI Power Company, Invoice No. OWS-23556 (Check No. 5).

Jun. 30   Made a partial payment of $2,000 to Netsoft Development Co. (Check No. 6).

Jun. 30   Made a partial payment of $1,500 to Lewis Furniture Co. (Check No. 7).

Jun. 30   The owner, Olivia Chen, withdrew $500, for personal use. (Check No. 8.)

7. Display and print the following reports for June 1, 2004, to June 30, 2004:

    a. *Unpaid Bills Detail*
    b. *Vendor Balance Detail*
    c. *Transaction List by Vendor*
    d. *Journal*

CHAPTER

3

CUSTOMERS

Create Invoices, Receive Payments, Enter Sales Receipts, and Make Deposits

CHAPTER OBJECTIVES

- Identify the system default accounts for customers

- Update the Customer:Job List

- Record sales on account in the Create Invoices window

- Record collections of accounts receivable in the Receive Payments window

- Record cash sales in the Enter Sales Receipts window

- Record deposits in the Make Deposits window

- Display and print customer-related reports

INTRODUCTION

customer A person or business that the company sells goods or services to, either on account or for cash.

QuickBooks Pro allows you to track all customer transactions. A **customer** is a person or business that the company sells goods or services to, either on account or for cash. A file for each customer should be established prior to entering transactions for a particular customer. The collection of all the customer files comprises the *Customer:Job List* (Lists).

Once a customer file is established, transactions (Activities) such as creating an invoice for a customer, receiving payment from that customer, or making a cash sale can be entered in the *Create Invoices*, *Receive Payments*, *Enter Sales Receipts*, and *Make Deposits* windows. As transactions are recorded in these activities windows, QuickBooks Pro will simultaneously update the Customer:Job List and any related reports (Reports) with the information about the transactions for the particular customer.

In this chapter, our sample company, Kristin Raina Interior Designs, will create invoices for design and decorating services, receive payments for invoices, make cash sales, and deposit funds.

QUICKBOOKS PRO VERSUS MANUAL ACCOUNTING: CUSTOMER TRANSACTIONS

sales journal A journal used to record all sales of goods on account; can be in single-column or multi-column format.

In a manual accounting system, all sales of goods on account are recorded in a multi-column **sales journal.** At the conclusion of the month, the totals are posted to the accounts receivable and revenue accounts affected by the transactions. As each sales transaction is recorded, the appropriate customer's account in the accounts receivable subsidiary ledger is updated for the new receivable on a daily basis. Collections of open accounts receivable balances and cash sale of goods/services are recorded in a multi-column **cash receipts journal.** As was done with the sales journal, monthly totals are posted to the general ledger accounts while payment information is recorded daily in the customer's subsidiary ledger record.

cash receipts journal A journal used to record all cash receipt activities including collection of accounts receivable.

In QuickBooks Pro, the Customer:Job List serves as the accounts receivable subsidiary ledger for the company. The Customer:Job List includes all companies and individuals to whom the company sells goods and services. Relevant information, such as name, address, contact, credit limit, and so on, is entered at the time the customer's file is created on the Customer:Job List.

When the company creates an invoice for goods or services, the invoice is created in the Create Invoices window. The Create Invoices window is equivalent to the multi-column sales journal. This transaction will update the Chart of Accounts List and general ledger while at the same time updating the customer's file on the Customer:Job List for the new receivable. When the customer pays the invoice, the company enters this transaction in the Receive Payments window. The Receive Payments window is equivalent to the part of the cash receipts journal that records collection of open accounts receivable. QuickBooks Pro automatically updates the Chart of Accounts List and general ledger while at the same time updating the customer's file on the Customer:Job List for the payment of the receivable.

To record a check received for an invoice not previously entered, the Enter Sales Receipts window is used. This window is equivalent to the remainder of the cash receipts journal, which records all cash receipts other than collection of accounts receivable. Again, the Chart of Accounts List and general ledger and the customer's file on the Customer:Job List will be simultaneously updated.

SYSTEM DEFAULT ACCOUNTS

As we saw in chapter 2, in order to process transactions expeditiously and organize data for reporting, QuickBooks Pro establishes specific general ledger accounts as default accounts in each window. When you enter transactions, QuickBooks Pro automatically increases or decreases certain account balances depending on the nature of the transaction.

For example, for vendors, when you enter a transaction in the Enter Bills window, QuickBooks Pro automatically increases (credits) the Accounts Payable account, and when you pay the bills in the Pay Bills window, QuickBooks Pro automatically decreases (debits) the Accounts Payable account. Similarly, for customers, when you enter a transaction in the Create Invoices window, QuickBooks Pro automatically increases (debits) the Accounts Receivable account because the Create Invoices window is used to record sales on account. When you record a collection of accounts receivable in the Receive Payments window, QuickBooks Pro automatically decreases (credits) the Accounts Receivable account. Therefore, you do not have to enter the account number or name for these default accounts because they have been pre-established by QuickBooks Pro.

CHAPTER PROBLEM

In this chapter, you will enter and track customer transactions for Kristin Raina Interior Designs. Kristin Raina provides interior design and decorating services both on account and for cash. Customers and clients remit payment for invoices; these funds are periodically deposited in the company checking account. Information for several customers has been entered in the Customer:Job List. This information, along with February 1, 2004, beginning balances and vendor activity from chapter 2, are contained in the company file CH3 Kristin Raina Interior Designs.

Begin by opening the company file—
1. Open QuickBooks Pro.
2. At the *No Company Open* window, click on the Open an existing company button or click File, and then click Open Company.
3. At the Open a Company dialog box in the Look in text box, choose the *QuickBooks Pro* subfolder or the subfolder containing the company files.
4. Select the company file *CH3 Kristin Raina Interior Designs.QBW*, and then click Open.
5. If the Company Navigator window appears, click the X to close it.

Next, make a backup copy of the company file—
1. Click File, then click Back Up.
2. In the QuickBooks Backup dialog box, the Disk option should be selected.
3. In the Filename text box, key **EX3 [Your Name] Kristin Raina Interior Designs**.
4. Next to the Location text box, click the Browse button.
5. At the Back Up Company to dialog box, in the Save in text box, choose your subfolder, a network directory designated by your instructor, or a floppy drive.

6. Click Save.
7. In the QuickBooks Backup dialog box, click OK.
8. At the *Your data has been backed up successfully* message, click OK.

Now restore the backup copy of the company file—
1. Click File, and then click Restore.
2. At the Restore Company Backup dialog box, in the Get Company Backup From section, the Disk option should be selected.
3. Click the Browse button.
4. At the Restore From dialog box, in the Look in text box, choose the location where you saved your backup copy.
5. Select the company file *EX3 [Your Name] Kristin Raina Interior Designs. QBB* and click Open.
6. At the Restore Company Backup dialog box, in the Restore Company Backup To section, click the Browse button.
7. At the Restore To dialog box, in the Save in text box, choose the sub-folder where you will be opening and working on your copies of the company files.
8. In the File name text box, key **EX3 [Your Name] Kristin Raina Interior Designs** and click Save.
9. In the Restore Company Backup dialog box, click Restore.
10. At the *Your data has been restored successfully* message, click OK.
11. If the Company Navigator window appears, click the X to close it.

The backup copy has been restored, but the company name still reads CH3 Kristin Raina Interior Designs.

Change the company name—
1. Click Company, and then click Company Information.
2. Change the company name to: **EX3 [Your Name] Kristin Raina Interior Designs**.
3. Click OK.

THE CUSTOMER:JOB LIST

The Customer:Job List contains a file for each customer to whom the company sells goods or services. Each file contains important information, such as company name, address, contact person, type of customer, terms, credit limit, preferred payment method, and current balance owed. You should include all customers the company does business with in the Customer:Job List.

Recall from chapter 1 that the second level of operation in QuickBooks Pro is recording background information on Lists. Lists are revised periodically when new customers are added, customers not used in the business are deleted, and modifications are made as background information on a customer changes. These adjustments to the customer files are referred to as updating the Customer:Job List.

As previously stated, the Customer:Job List contains a file for each customer with which the company does business. You should try to enter the information for each customer in the Customer:Job List prior to recording transactions. However, if you inadvertently omit a customer, you can add that customer during the Activities level of operation with a minimum of disruption.

Kristin Raina has entered information for existing and anticipated customers in the Customer:Job List.

To review the Customer:Job List—
1. Click Reports, and then click List.
2. At the List submenu, click Customer Contact List. A list of customers is displayed. (See figure 3–1.)

FIGURE 3-1

Customer Contact List

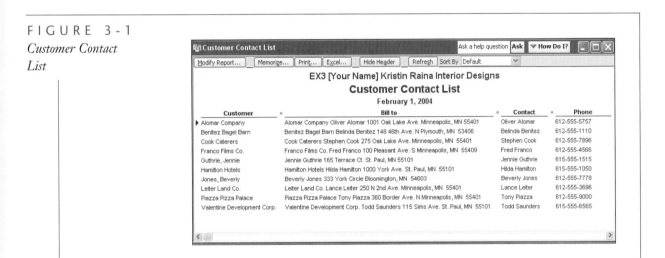

To view a specific customer file—
1. Place the zoom glass over the customer *Alomar Company*.
2. Double-click the mouse button. The Edit Customer window with the Alomar Company customer file is displayed. (See figure 3–2.)

FIGURE 3-2

Customer File —
Alomar Company

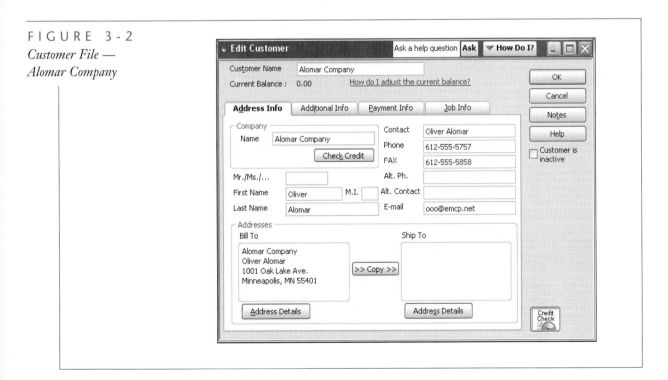

The customer file contains five parts:

NAME PAGE	This portion displays the customer's name, current balance, and four command buttons: OK, Cancel, Notes, and Help. The Notes command button is used to add notes about the customer.
ADDRESS INFO tab	This tab allows you to enter the customer's company name, billing and shipping address, contact person, telephone and fax numbers, and e-mail address. The Address Details button can be used to edit address information.
ADDITIONAL INFO tab	This tab allows you to enter information such as customer type, terms, preferred send method, and resale number along with the ability to create customized fields.
PAYMENT INFO tab	This tab allows you to enter a customer account number, credit limit, preferred payment method, and credit card information.
JOB INFO tab	This tab allows you to enter information, such as job status and start and end dates for a job for this customer.

FIGURE 3-3
Customer:Job Menu

3. Close the Edit Customer window.
4. Close the Customer Contact List Report.

ADDING A CUSTOMER

Kristin Raina has just been hired by a new client, Maria Ordonez, to provide interior decorating services for Ordonez' new residence.

To add a new customer—

1. Click Lists, and then click Customer:Job List.
2. At the Customer:Job List window, click the Customer:Job button. A drop-down menu appears. (See figure 3–3.)
3. At the Customer:Job menu, click New. The New Customer window appears. (See figure 3–4.)

FIGURE 3-4
New Customer Window

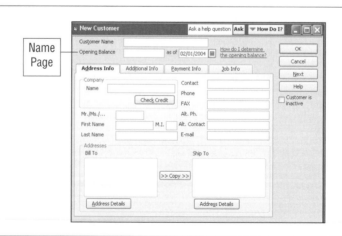

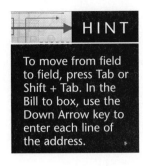

HINT

To move from field to field, press Tab or Shift + Tab. In the Bill to box, use the Down Arrow key to enter each line of the address.

4. Enter the data below on the Name Page and Address Info tab.

NAME PAGE		
	Customer Name:	**Ordonez, Maria**
	Opening Balance:	**0 as of February 1, 2004**
ADDRESS INFO		
	First Name:	**Maria**
	Last Name:	**Ordonez**
	Bill To:	**210 NE Lowry Ave.**
		Minneapolis, MN 54204
	Contact:	**Maria Ordonez**
	Phone:	**612-555-9999**
	FAX:	**612-555-9998**
	E-mail:	**MO@emcp.net**

(See figure 3–5.)

FIGURE 3-5
New Customer Window — Name Page and Address Info Tab Complete

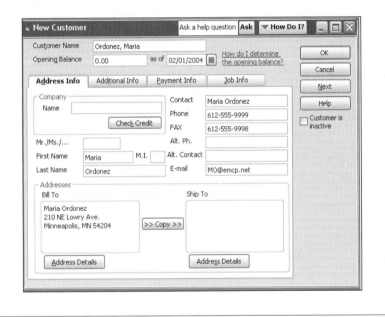

5. Click the Additional Info tab and complete the information below.

ADDITIONAL INFO		
	Type:	**Residential**
	Terms:	**Net 30 Days**
	Preferred Send Method:	**None**

(See figure 3–6.)

FIGURE 3-6

New Customer
Window —
Additional Info Tab
Completed

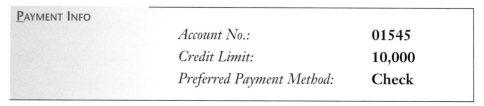

6. Click the Payment Info tab and complete the information below.

PAYMENT INFO

Account No.:	**01545**
Credit Limit:	**10,000**
Preferred Payment Method:	**Check**

(See Figure 3-7.)

FIGURE 3-7

New Customer
Window — Payment
Info Completed

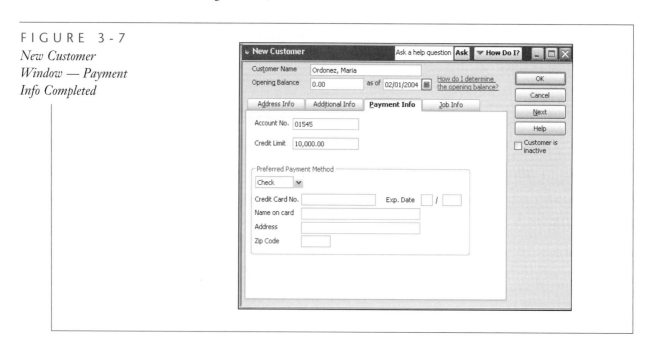

7. If the information is correct, click OK.
8. Close the Customer:Job List.

DELETING A CUSTOMER

Kristin Raina wishes to delete Valentine Development Corp. from the Customer:Job List because the company has gone out of business.

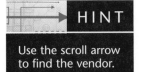

HINT

Use the scroll arrow to find the vendor.

To delete a customer—

1. Click Lists, and then click Customer:Job List.
2. At the Customer:Job List, select (highlight) *Valentine Development Corp.* but do not open the file. (See figure 3–8.)

FIGURE 3-8
Customer: Job List — Valentine Development Corp. Selected

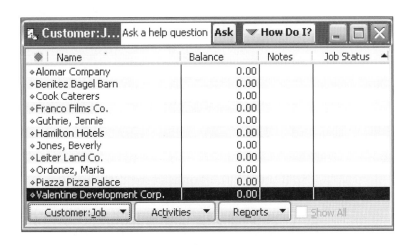

3. Click the Customer:Job menu button.
4. At the Customer:Job menu, click Delete. Click OK at the Delete Customer:Job dialog box. The customer file is now deleted.
5. Close the Customer:Job List window.

A customer with a balance or a customer who has been part of a transaction for the current accounting period cannot be deleted, but can be marked inactive. The customer's name is no longer displayed in the reports but the information is retained in QuickBooks Pro and can be accessed if needed.

HINT

Other ways to access the Edit Customer window are to select the customer, click the Customer:Job button and then click Edit, or to double-click the customer name in the Customer:Job List Report.

EDITING A CUSTOMER

Kristin Raina needs to edit the file for Piazza Pizza Palace because the contact person has changed.

To edit a customer file—

1. Open the Customer:Job List, and double-click *Piazza Pizza Palace*. This will open the customer file in edit mode.
2. At the *Contact* field, delete the current name and key **Mikey Piazza**. (See figure 3–9.)

FIGURE 3-9
*Edit Customer
Window — Piazza
Pizza Palace*

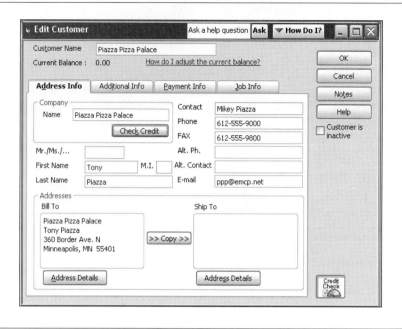

3. If the information is correct, click OK.
4. Close the Customer:Job List window.

PRACTICE *exercise*

Add the following customer—

NAME PAGE

Customer Name:	**Burnitz Bakery Company**
Opening Balance:	**0 as of February 1, 2004**

ADDRESS INFO

Company Name:	**Burnitz Bakery Company**
First Name:	**Barry**
Last Name:	**Burnitz**
Address:	**18 N Grand Ave.**
	Minneapolis, MN 55403
Contact:	**Barry Burnitz**
Phone:	**612-555-2240**
FAX:	**612-555-2241**
E-mail:	**BBC@emcp.net**

ADDITIONAL INFO

Type:	**Commercial**
Terms:	**Net 30 Days**
Preferred Send Method:	**E-mail**

PAYMENT INFO

Account:	**R1825**
Credit Limit:	**10,000**
Preferred Payment Method:	**Check**

Delete the following customer—
Leiter Land Company

Edit the following customer—
New phone/fax for Benitez Bagel Barn:
Phone: 612-555-1233
Fax: 612-555-1234

QuickCheck: The updated Customer Contact List appears in figure 3–10.

FIGURE 3-10
Updated Customer
Contact List

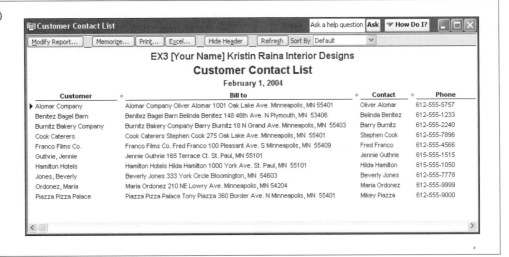

ACTIVITIES: THE CREATE INVOICES WINDOW

sale on account A sale
on account occurs
when a company sells
goods or services to a
customer but does not
receive payment until a
future date.

Recall from chapter 1 that the third level of operation in QuickBooks Pro is Activities. In QuickBooks Pro, Activities identified as **sales on account** are recorded in the Create Invoices window (figure 3–11). Accounts Receivable is the default general ledger posting account. All transactions entered in this window will result in a debit to the Accounts Receivable account. The account to be credited, usually a revenue account, is determined based on the item chosen.

QuickBooks Pro records a sales-on-account transaction as follows:

		Accounts Receivable			XXX					
		Revenue							XXX	

At the same time, QuickBooks Pro updates the customer's file on the Customer:Job List to reflect the new receivable.

In the Create Invoices window, you can identify the customer who will be invoiced, the invoice date and number, terms of payment, and items sold or services provided. You can print the invoice from this window or by clicking File and then Print Forms. You can change the invoice format based on the type of sale.

FIGURE 3-11
Create Invoices Window

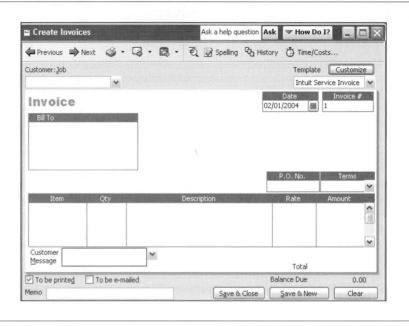

The Create Invoices window allows you to select a customer from the Customer:Job List and create an invoice with an invoice number, description of services provided or product sold, and terms given. In addition, several different invoice formats are available that you can use depending on the nature of the sale. Most of the data fields are self-explanatory but take special note of the following fields:

TEMPLATE	QuickBooks Pro allows for three types of invoice formats: product, professional, and service. Choose the one that best describes the items sold. For this chapter, Service Invoice will be used. In addition, you can customize or download additional formats.
ITEM	Used to indicate item of service or inventory sold. Choose from the drop-down list. Once an item is selected, the description and rate will be filled in automatically based on data entered in the Item List.
HISTORY BUTTON	Indicates if there are any payments against this invoice.
	Allows you to print this invoice immediately rather than using the Print Forms submenu of the File menu.

The Previous and Next arrows, and the Save & Close, Save & New, and Clear buttons, all have the same function in this window as in the Enter Bills window.

ITEMS

Kristin Raina Interior Designs has established two service revenue items in the Item List, Decorating and Design. Decorating Services represent interior decorating consulting and are billed at a rate of $50 per hour. Design Services represent interior design work on specific projects and are billed at a rate of $60 per hour.

To view items—

1. Click Lists, and then click Item List. The Item List appears. (See figure 3–12.)

FIGURE 3-12
Item List Window

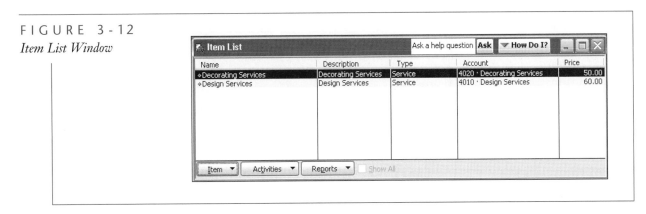

2. To view the data for the Decorating Services item, double-click the item. The Edit Item window will appear. (See figure 3–13.)

FIGURE 3-13
*Edit Item Window —
Decorating Services*

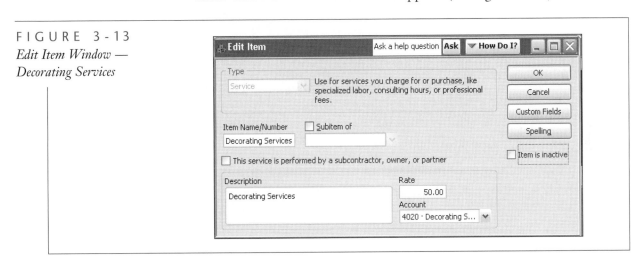

Decorating is indicated as a service item (rather than inventory or payroll). The window also contains a description, rate per unit (hour), and default general ledger posting account. QuickBooks Pro uses this data when you create an invoice for a customer for this service.

3. Close the Edit Item and Item List windows.

CREATING AN INVOICE

On February 2, 2004, Kristin Raina provided 12 hours of decorating services on account to Beverly Jones.

HINT

In the event a new customer needs to be added while in the Create Invoices window, click < Add New > from the Customer:Job drop-down list.

To create an invoice—

1. Click Customers, and then click Create Invoices.
2. At the Customer:Job drop-down list, click *Jones, Beverly*.
3. At the *Template* field, accept the default choice, *Intuit Service Invoice*.
4. At the *Date* field, choose *02/02/2004*.
5. At the *Invoice #* field, key **1001.**
6. At the *Terms* drop-down list, accept the default choice, *Net 30 Days*.
7. At the Item drop-down list, click *Decorating Services*. The data from the decorating file in the Item List will complete the *Description* and *Rate* fields. (See figure 3–14.)

FIGURE 3-14
Create Invoices Window — Partially Completed

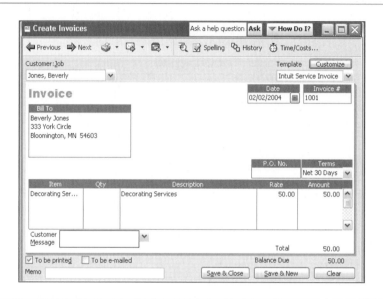

8. At the *Qty* field, key **12.**

   When you move to the next field, the Amount box will be completed based on the hourly rate times the hours invoiced.

9. The To be printed and To be e-mailed boxes should not have a check mark in it. (See figure 3–15.)

FIGURE 3-15
Create Invoices Window — Completed

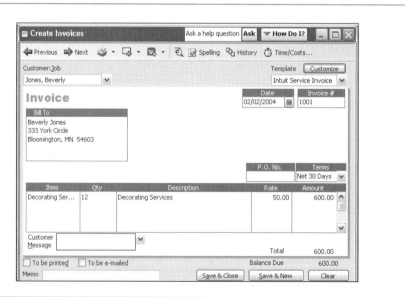

As stated earlier, the default account to debit in the Create Invoices window is Accounts Receivable. An account to be credited is not indicated in this window. The item for Decorating Services in the Item List indicated the revenue account that should be credited when entering this item in an activity window. Once you choose the Decorating Services item in the Create Invoices window, QuickBooks Pro knows from the Item List to credit the revenue account Decorating Services for this transaction.

10. If the information is correct, click Save & Close.

ACCOUNTING *concept*

For a sale of decorating services on account the general ledger posting is as follows:

In addition, the Customer File (subledger) for Beverly Jones will reflect the new receivable:

1200 Accts. Rec.	
Dr	Cr
600	

4020 Decor. Serv.	
Dr	Cr
	600

Jones, Beverly	
Dr	Cr
600	

PRACTICE *exercise*

Record the following transactions in the Create Invoices window:

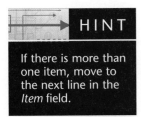

FEB. 5   Provided 16 hours of design services to Jennie Guthrie on account. Invoice No. 1002. *QuickCheck:* 960

FEB. 12   Provided 8 hours of decorating services and 16 hours of design services to Cook Caterers. Invoice No. 1003. *QuickCheck:* 1360

FEB. 18   Provided 24 hours of design services to Franco Films Co. Invoice No. 1004. *QuickCheck:* 1440

FEB. 23   Provided 24 hrs of decorating services to Burnitz Bakery Company. Invoice No. 1005. *QuickCheck:* 1200

FEB. 25   Provided 6 hours of decorating services and 15 hours of design services to Cook Caterers. Invoice No. 1006. *QuickCheck:* 1200

ACTIVITIES: THE RECEIVE PAYMENTS WINDOW

In QuickBooks Pro, the Receive Payments window is used to record the **collection of accounts receivable** 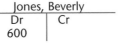 from customers previously invoiced in the Create Invoices window. This window displays all open invoices for a specific customer. Payment can be in the form of cash, check, or credit card. In addition, customer credit memos can be recorded.

collection of accounts receivable Collection of accounts receivable occurs when a customer pays part or all of their outstanding balance due the company; sometimes referred to as payment of accounts receivable.

The Receive Payments window is designed only for collection of existing invoices. The default accounts are Accounts Receivable and Cash or Undeposited Funds (discussed later in this chapter). The transaction is recorded as follows:

	Cash (or Undeposited Funds)	XXX	
	Accounts Receivable		XXX

At the same time, the customer's file on the Customer:Job List is updated to reflect the payment. The QuickBooks Pro Receive Payments window appears in figure 3–16.

FIGURE 3-16
*Receive Payments
Window*

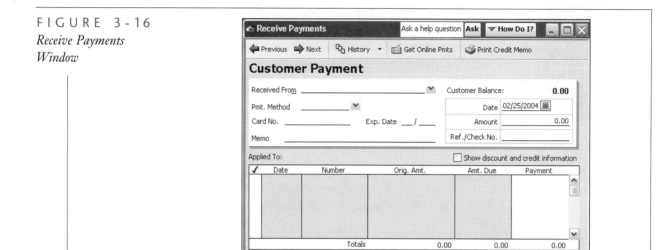

Once a customer is identified, a list of open invoices will be displayed. Note the following fields:

CUSTOMER BALANCE AND AMT. DUE	Indicates the balance owed by this customer for all open invoices.
PMT. (PAYMENT) METHOD	Indicates whether customer is paying invoice by check, cash, or credit card.
SHOW DISCOUNT AND CREDIT INFORMATION	A check in this box will display all discounts and credit against open invoices.
SET DISCOUNT BUTTON	Used to apply a discount for an early payment.
SET CREDITS BUTTON	Used to display and apply unused credits from a customer.
AUTO APPLY/ CLEAR PAYMENTS BUTTON	Auto Apply is the default button. If no invoice has been selected, Auto Apply will automatically apply payment to the oldest invoice. When a payment is applied, the button switches to Clear Payments, which allows you to erase all fields of information.
GO TO BUTTON	Used to drill down to original invoices.
GROUP WITH OTHER UNDEPOSITED FUNDS/ DEPOSIT TO	If the company deposits receipts in a separate transaction, click the Group with other undeposited funds button. If the Deposit To button is clicked, the receipts will be posted to the Cash account immediately.

Activities identified as sale on account were recorded in the Create Invoices window. Subsequently, Activities identified as collection of an outstanding accounts receivable (previously recorded in the Create Invoices window) are now recorded in the Receive Payments window. Cash or Undeposited Funds and Accounts Receivable are the default general ledger posting accounts. All transactions entered in this window will result in a debit to the Cash or Undeposited Funds account and a credit to the Accounts Receivable account.

RECEIVING A PAYMENT IN FULL

On February 12, 2004, Kristin Raina receives a $600 payment from Beverly Jones for Invoice No. 1001, her check No. 6544.

To record a receipt of payment—
1. Click Customers, and then click Receive Payments.
2. At the Received From drop-down list, click *Jones, Beverly*. All open invoices for Beverly Jones will be displayed. (See figure 3–17.)

FIGURE 3-17
Receive Payments Window — Beverly Jones

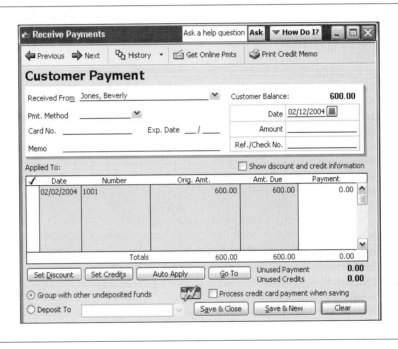

3. At the Pmt. Method drop-down list, click *Check*.
4. At the *Date* field, choose *02/12/2004*.
5. At the *Amount* field, key **600**.

   Once the amount is entered and you move to the next field, a check mark will appear next to open invoice No. 1001 indicating the $600 payment will be applied to that invoice automatically (since this is the only open invoice).

6. At the *Ref./Check No.* field, key **6544**.
7. Click the *Group with other undeposited funds* button. The transaction is now ready for posting. (See figure 3–18.)

FIGURE 3-18
Receive Payments Window — Completed

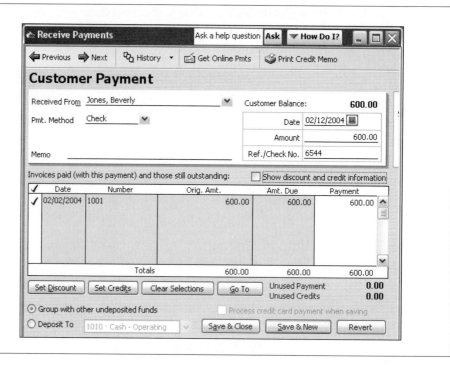

8. Click S̲ave & Close.

S̲ave & Close returns you to the main window. If you wish to remain in the Receive Payments window after posting, click the S̲ave & New button or the Next arrow. This posts the transaction and clears the window for the next entry.

ACCOUNTING
c o n c e p t

For a payment of an existing Accounts Receivable the general ledger posting is as follows:

In addition, the Customer File (subledger) for Beverly Jones will reflect the payment:

1250 Undeposited Funds		1200 Accts Rec		Beverly Jones	
Dr	Cr	Dr	Cr	Dr	Cr
600			600	Inv 600	Pay. 600
				0	

ENTERING A PARTIAL PAYMENT OF AN INVOICE

The Receive Payments window allows you to record partial payments of open invoices. On February 20, Franco Films remits $500 toward their open invoice No. 1004 in the amount of $1,440. Their Check No. 1255. No discount allowed.

To record a partial payment of an invoice—

1. Click C̲ustomers, and then click Receive P̲ayments.
2. At the Received Fro̲m drop-down list, click *Franco Films Co.* The open invoice will be displayed along with the unpaid amount of $1,440 in the *Customer Balance* field.

3. At the Pmt. Method drop-down list, click *Check*.
4. At the *Date* field, choose *02/20/2004*.
5. At the *Amount* field, key **500**.

When you move to the next field, the amount appears in the *Payment* field in the Applied To display.

6. At the *Ref./Check No.* field, key **1255**.
7. Click the Group with other undeposited funds button. The transaction is ready for posting. (See figure 3–19.)

FIGURE 3-19
Receive Payments Window — Partial Payment

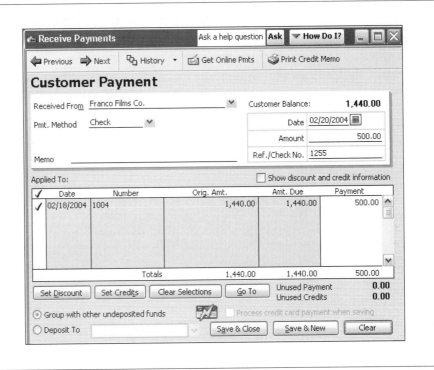

8. Click S<u>a</u>ve & Close.

RECEIVING PAYMENT FOR MORE THAN ONE INVOICE

QuickBooks Pro allows you to record a payment of several invoices at the same time. On February 26, 2004, Cook Caterers remits $2,560 in full payment of Invoices No. 1003 and 1006. Their check No. 655.

To record payment of more than one invoice—
1. Click C<u>u</u>stomers, and then click Receive Pa<u>y</u>ments.
2. At the Received Fro<u>m</u> drop-down list, click *Cook Caterers.* All open invoices are displayed. (See figure 3–20.)

FIGURE 3-20

*Receive Payments
Window — Invoices
Displayed*

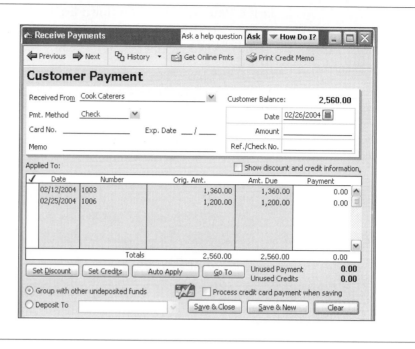

3. At the *Date* field, choose *02/26/2004*.
4. At the *Amount* field, key **2560**. When you move to the next field, the amount will be applied to the two invoices. (See figure 3–21.)

FIGURE 3-21

*Receive Payments
Window — Payment
Applied*

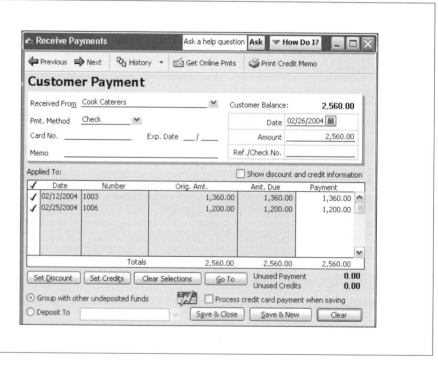

5. Complete the *Pmt. Method* and *Ref./Check No.* fields, and click the Group with other undeposited funds button. (See figure 3–22.)

FIGURE 3-22
*Receive Payments
Window — Complete*

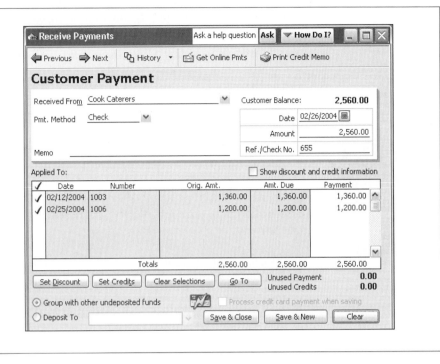

6. If the information is correct, click Save & Close.

PRACTICE *exercise*

Record the following transactions in the Receive Payments window:

FEB. 27   Received $960 from Jennie Guthrie in full payment of Invoice No. 1002, her check No. 674.

FEB. 27   Received $600 from Burnitz Bakery Company in partial payment of Invoice No. 1005. Their check No. 12458.

ACTIVITIES: THE ENTER SALES RECEIPTS WINDOW

In QuickBooks Pro, you use the Enter Sales Receipts window to record sales where payment is received immediately. Since you do not use Accounts Receivable, this window allows you to record a **cash sale** in one step. The data fields in this window are similar to those of the Create Invoices window: customer, date, item sold, service provided, and so on.

cash sale A sale for which payment is received immediately.

The Enter Sales Receipts window is used for all cash sales of goods and services. The default account is Cash or Undeposited Funds. The transaction is recorded as follows:

		Cash (or Undeposited Funds)		XXX		
		Revenue			XXX	

A transaction entered in this window will not be tracked through the Accounts Receivable or Customer reports.

Activities identified as cash sales are recorded in the Enter Sales Receipts window. In this window, the Cash account is the default debit posting account because all transactions result in a cash receipt. All transactions entered in this window will result in a debit to the Cash account. The account to be credited is based on the item selected. As in the Create Invoices window, when an item is selected, QuickBooks Pro uses the information from the Item List to determine which account should be credited.

On February 26, Kristin Raina provided 8 hours of design services to Hamilton Hotels on Invoice No. 1007. Hamilton Hotels issued Check No. 25546 in full payment.

HINT

After entering the quantity, you must move to another field for the amount to be computed.

To record a cash sale—
1. Click C̲ustomers, and then click Enter S̲ales Receipts.

If you receive a message about Merchant Account Service, place a check mark in the box to the left of Do not display this message in the future and click No.

2. At the Customer:J̲ob drop-down list, click *Hamilton Hotels*.
3. Enter the appropriate date and key **1007** in the *Sale No.* field. The To be printe̲d box should not be checked.
4. Complete the balance of the window in the same manner as an invoice. (See figure 3–23.)

FIGURE 3-23
*Enter Sales Receipts
Window — Completed*

ACCOUNTING
concept

For a cash sale the general ledger posting is as follows:

1250 Undeposited Funds		4010 Design Serv.	
Dr	Cr	Dr	Cr
480			480

5. If the information is correct, click S̲ave & Close.

The customer file is unaffected because the payment was received at point of sale.

THE MAKE DEPOSITS WINDOW

In most accounting textbooks, it is usually assumed that when cash is received it is immediately posted to a Cash account. However, many businesses post to the Cash account only when funds are actually deposited in the checking account, which may be several days after the funds are received. For these businesses, the receipt of funds is posted to a current asset account titled "Undeposited Funds" until a deposit is made. At that point, a second transaction is recorded to show the undeposited funds transferred to the Cash-Operating account. Debits to the Cash-Operating account should coincide with deposits recorded on the bank statement. This allows the company to more easily track deposits during the month-end bank reconciliation process.

When the Undeposited Funds account is utilized, cash receipts are recorded as follows:

		Undeposited Funds		XXX		
		Accounts Receivable/Revenue			XXX	

This entry results from activities entered in the Receive Payments and Enter Sales Receipts windows.

When funds previously received and recorded in the Receive Payments or Sales Receipts windows are subsequently deposited in the bank, the Make Deposits window is used. The default accounts are Cash and Undeposited Funds. The transaction is recorded as follows:

		Cash		XXX		
		Undeposited Funds			XXX	

Activities identified as a deposit of funds are recorded in the Make Deposits window. In this window, Cash and Undeposited Funds are the default general ledger posting accounts. All transactions entered in this window will result in a debit to the Cash account and a credit to the Undeposited Funds account.

In this chapter, Kristin Raina will deposit all receipts at one time at month-end. In a real-world setting, deposits are made more frequently depending on collection volume. This window allows you to deposit each receipt individually, deposit several receipts, or deposit all receipts at one time. On February 27, Kristin Raina deposits all collections for the month.

To deposit all receipts collected and previously recorded as Undeposited Funds—
1. Click Banking, and then click Make Deposits. The Payments to Deposit window is displayed showing all undeposited receipts. (See figure 3–24.)

FIGURE 3-24
*Payments to Deposit
Window*

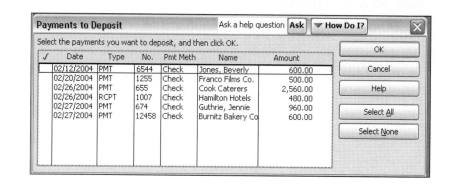

2. Since all receipts will be deposited, click Select <u>A</u>ll. All receipts will be check-marked for deposit. (See figure 3–25.)

FIGURE 3-25
*Payments to Deposit
Window — All Receipts
Selected*

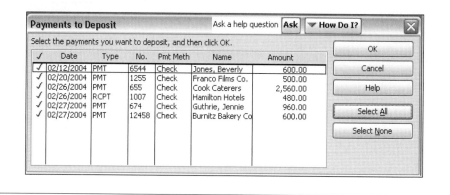

3. If the information is correct, click OK. You will be forwarded to the Make Deposits window.
4. In the <u>D</u>eposit To drop-down list, click *1010 Cash - Operating.*
5. At the *Date* field, choose *02/27/2004.* (See figure 3-26.)

FIGURE 3-26
*Make Deposits Window
— Complete*

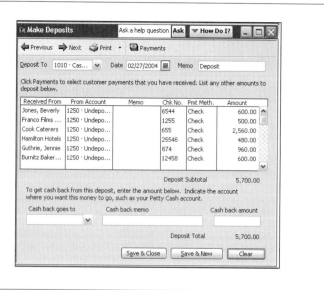

HINT

If you make an error on the deposit, use the Previous arrow to display the deposit, click Edit, and then click Delete Deposit.

6. If the information is correct, click S**a**ve & Close.

ACCOUNTING
c o n c e p t

The deposit of receipts as a separate transaction is recorded as follows:

1010 Cash - Operating		1250 Undeposited Funds	
Dr	Cr	Dr	Cr
5,700			5,700

REPORTS: CUSTOMER AND FINANCIAL REPORTS

Recall from chapter 1 that Reports, the fourth level of operation, display the information and activities recorded in the various Lists and Activities windows. QuickBooks Pro can display and print a variety of reports concerning customers, many of which should be printed at the end of the month.

CUSTOMER REPORTS FROM THE REPORTS MENU

The Accounts Receivable and customer-related reports help the company to manage its collections, control cash flow, and retain an accurate record of all customer-related transactions. Among these reports are the *Open Invoices* report and the *Customer Balance Detail* report.

Open Invoices Report

The *Open Invoices* report lists all unpaid invoices for each customer at a specific date. The report will list each open invoice, with date and invoice number, for a customer, along with the terms and due date. The report may be customized to show all customers or only those with outstanding bills.

To view and print the *Open Invoices* report—
1. Click Reports, and then click Customers & Receivables.
2. At the Customers & Receivables submenu, click Open Invoices.
3. At the *Date* field, choose *02/29/2004.*
4. Click Refresh on the command line. The report will be displayed. (See figure 3–27.)

FIGURE 3 - 27
Open Invoices Report

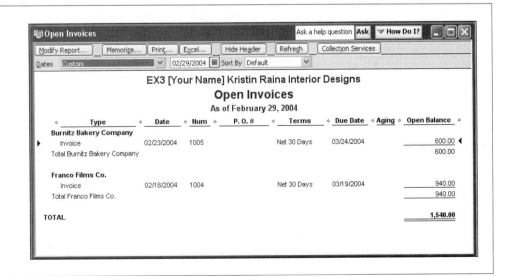

5. To print the report, click Print on the command line.
6. At the Print Reports dialog box, choose Portrait orientation, and then click Print.
7. Close the report.

Customer Balance Detail Report

The *Customer Balance Detail* report displays all transactions for each customer with the remaining balance owed. This report is similar to an accounts receivable subsidiary ledger in a manual accounting system.

To view and print the *Customer Balance Detail* report—
1. Click Reports, and then click Customer & Receivables.
2. At the Customers & Receivables submenu, click Customer Balance Detail.

The report will show all invoices, payments, and credit memos for each customer in chronological order.

3. To print the report, click Print on the command line.
4. At the Print Reports dialog box, choose Landscape orientation, and then click Print. Your printout should look like figure 3–28.
5. Close the report.

HINT

Click and drag on the diamond between the titles with your mouse to change the width of a column.

FIGURE 3-28

Customer Balance Detail Report

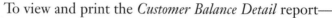

EX3 [Your Name] Kristin Raina Interior Designs
Customer Balance Detail
All Transactions

Accrual Basis

Type	Date	Num	Account	Amount	Balance
Burnitz Bakery Company					
Invoice	02/23/2004	1005	1200 · Accounts Receivable	1,200.00	1,200.00
Payment	02/27/2004	12458	1200 · Accounts Receivable	-600.00	600.00
Total Burnitz Bakery Company				600.00	600.00
Cook Caterers					
Invoice	02/12/2004	1003	1200 · Accounts Receivable	1,360.00	1,360.00
Invoice	02/25/2004	1006	1200 · Accounts Receivable	1,200.00	2,560.00
Payment	02/26/2004	655	1200 · Accounts Receivable	-2,560.00	0.00
Total Cook Caterers				0.00	0.00
Franco Films Co.					
Invoice	02/18/2004	1004	1200 · Accounts Receivable	1,440.00	1,440.00
Payment	02/20/2004	1255	1200 · Accounts Receivable	-500.00	940.00
Total Franco Films Co.				940.00	940.00
Guthrie, Jennie					
Invoice	02/05/2004	1002	1200 · Accounts Receivable	960.00	960.00
Payment	02/27/2004	674	1200 · Accounts Receivable	-960.00	0.00
Total Guthrie, Jennie				0.00	0.00
Jones, Beverly					
Invoice	02/02/2004	1001	1200 · Accounts Receivable	600.00	600.00
Payment	02/12/2004	6544	1200 · Accounts Receivable	-600.00	0.00
Total Jones, Beverly				0.00	0.00
TOTAL				1,540.00	1,540.00

CUSTOMER REPORTS FROM THE LISTS MENU

QuickBooks Pro allows you to view and print several customer reports directly from the Lists menu. Once you access the Customer:Job List, click the Reports button in the Customer:Job Lists window. Reports can be printed for one customer only or for all customers. One such report is the *Transaction List by Customer* report.

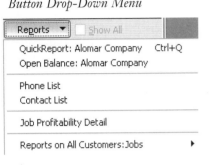

FIGURE 3-29

Customer:Job List — Reports Button Drop-Down Menu

To view and print a Customer List report such as *Transaction List by Customer*—

1. Click Lists, and then click Customer:Job List. The Customer:Job List window is displayed.
2. Click the Reports menu button on the Customer:Job List window. The Reports drop-down menu contains a menu of available reports. (See figure 3–29.)
3. Click Reports on All Customers:Jobs.
4. At the Reports on All Customer:Job submenu, click Transactions by Customer.
5. At the *From* and *To* fields, choose *01/01/2004* to *02/29/2004*.
6. Click Refresh on the command line. The report for that period will be displayed. (See figure 3–30.)

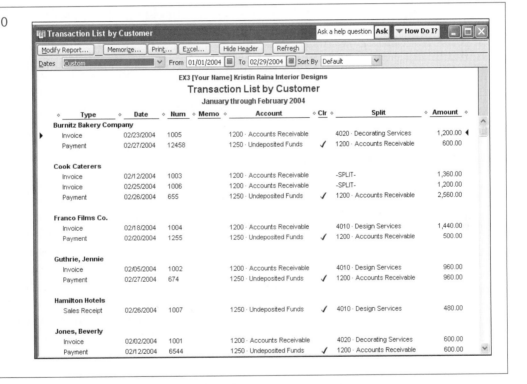

FIGURE 3-30

Transaction List by Customer Report

7. To print the report, click the Print button on the command line.
8. In the Print Reports dialog box, choose Landscape orientation and click Print.
9. Close the report and the Customer:Job List window.

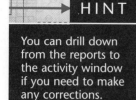

HINT

You can drill down from the reports to the activity window if you need to make any corrections.

HINT

Transaction numbers are assigned by QuickBooks Pro and cannot be changed. So do not be surprised if your transaction numbers differ from those shown in Quick-Books Pro because you deleted transactions. The important thing is to make sure that the journal entries themselves are correct.

The *Transaction List by Customer* report displays the general ledger account posting for each transaction. In addition, transactions that were entered through the Enter Cash Sales window, which do not appear on Open Invoices and Customer Balance Detail reports above, will be included in this report.

The *Open Invoices* report and *Customer Balance Detail* report displayed from the Reports menu above can also be accessed from the Customer:Job List window by clicking the Report menu button, clicking Reports on All Customers:Jobs, and then clicking A/R Reports.

OTHER REPORTS

As activities are entered in the windows, behind-the-scenes accounting activity is recorded in general journal format, posted to the general ledger, and flowed into the financial statements. You can display and print standard accounting reports showing this activity, such as the *Journal* report. The *Journal* report displays, in general journal format, all transactions recorded during a specified period of time.

To view and print the *Journal* report—
1. Click Reports, and then click Accountant & Taxes.
2. At the Accountant & Taxes submenu, click Journal.
3. At the *From* and *To* fields, choose *02/01/2004* to *02/29/2004*.
4. Click Refresh on the command line. The *Journal* report is displayed.
5. To print the report, click Print on the command line.
6. At the Print Reports dialog box, choose the Landscape orientation and click Print. Your printout should look like figure 3–31.
7. Close the report.

Notice on your printout that all activity for February is displayed in the order in which it was entered. The earlier transactions are the vendor activities recorded in chapter 2. The later transactions are the customer activities recorded in this chapter. Scroll down to the transactions for this chapter and look in the Type column. This indicates the window where the activity was recorded. The Invoice type is from the Create Invoices window. Each of these transactions has a debit to Accounts Receivable because this is the default for that account. The Payment type is from the Receive Payments window. All of these transactions are a debit to Undeposited Funds and a credit to Accounts Receivable, which are the default accounts for these windows. The Sales Receipt type is from the Enter Sales Receipts window, which all have a debit to Undeposited Funds because that is the default account for this window. The Deposit type is from the Make Deposits window. This transaction by default is a debit to Cash and a credit to Undeposited Funds.

EXITING QUICKBOOKS PRO

Upon completing this session, make a backup copy of your practice exercise company file to a floppy disk using the Back Up command. Be sure to change the Save in text box to the A drive and carefully key in the correct file name.

FIGURE 3-31

Journal Report — Partial

EX3 [Your Name] Kristin Raina Interior Designs
Journal
February 2004

Trans #	Type	Date	Num	Name	Memo	Account	Debit	Credit
20	Invoice	02/02/2004	1001	Jones, Beverly		1200 · Accounts Receivable	600.00	
				Jones, Beverly	Decorating Services	4020 · Decorating Services		600.00
							600.00	600.00
21	Invoice	02/05/2004	1002	Guthrie, Jennie		1200 · Accounts Receivable	960.00	
				Guthrie, Jennie	Design Services	4010 · Design Services		960.00
							960.00	960.00
22	Invoice	02/12/2004	1003	Cook Caterers		1200 · Accounts Receivable	1,360.00	
				Cook Caterers	Decorating Services	4020 · Decorating Services		400.00
				Cook Caterers	Design Services	4010 · Design Services		960.00
							1,360.00	1,360.00
23	Invoice	02/18/2004	1004	Franco Films Co.		1200 · Accounts Receivable	1,440.00	
				Franco Films Co.	Design Services	4010 · Design Services		1,440.00
							1,440.00	1,440.00
24	Invoice	02/23/2004	1005	Burnitz Bakery Company		1200 · Accounts Receivable	1,200.00	
				Burnitz Bakery Company	Decorating Services	4020 · Decorating Services		1,200.00
							1,200.00	1,200.00
25	Invoice	02/25/2004	1006	Cook Caterers		1200 · Accounts Receivable	1,200.00	
				Cook Caterers	Decorating Services	4020 · Decorating Services		300.00
				Cook Caterers	Design Services	4010 · Design Services		900.00
							1,200.00	1,200.00
26	Payment	02/12/2004	6544	Jones, Beverly		1250 · Undeposited Funds	600.00	
				Jones, Beverly		1200 · Accounts Receivable		600.00
							600.00	600.00
27	Payment	02/20/2004	1255	Franco Films Co.		1250 · Undeposited Funds	500.00	
				Franco Films Co.		1200 · Accounts Receivable		500.00
							500.00	500.00
28	Payment	02/26/2004	655	Cook Caterers		1250 · Undeposited Funds	2,560.00	
				Cook Caterers		1200 · Accounts Receivable		2,560.00
							2,560.00	2,560.00
29	Payment	02/27/2004	674	Guthrie, Jennie		1250 · Undeposited Funds	960.00	
				Guthrie, Jennie		1200 · Accounts Receivable		960.00
							960.00	960.00
30	Payment	02/27/2004	12458	Burnitz Bakery Company		1250 · Undeposited Funds	600.00	
				Burnitz Bakery Company		1200 · Accounts Receivable		600.00
							600.00	600.00
31	Sales Receipt	02/26/2004	1007	Hamilton Hotels		1250 · Undeposited Funds	480.00	
				Hamilton Hotels	Design Services	4010 · Design Services		480.00
							480.00	480.00
32	Deposit	02/27/2004			Deposit	1010 · Cash - Operating	5,700.00	
				Jones, Beverly	Deposit	1250 · Undeposited Funds		600.00
				Franco Films Co.	Deposit	1250 · Undeposited Funds		500.00
				Cook Caterers	Deposit	1250 · Undeposited Funds		2,560.00
				Hamilton Hotels	Deposit	1250 · Undeposited Funds		480.00
				Guthrie, Jennie	Deposit	1250 · Undeposited Funds		960.00
				Burnitz Bakery Company	Deposit	1250 · Undeposited Funds		600.00
							5,700.00	5,700.00
TOTAL							**30,160.00**	**30,160.00**

Quickbooks Pro has teamed up with Dun & Bradstreet to allow users to obtain up-to-date credit information of your business customers. This subscription service allows you to do credit monitoring online through several detail screens.

Dun & Bradstreet (D&B)

Dun & Bradstreet is the world's leading provider of business-to-business credit, marketing, purchasing, and receivables management information. Their database covers more than 57 million businesses in 200 countries. It contains hundreds of millions of pieces of data from trade styles to financial statements.

Dun & Bradstreet conducts millions of on-site and telephone interviews to gather business information on all industries, both in the United States and internationally.

Through the use of the D&B D-U-N-S® number, a company can register with D&B and establish a financial file so that they can obtain vital business and financial information on vendors and customers and, in turn, vendors and customers can obtain financial information on the registered company. Many companies will not sell goods on account to a potential customer who does not have a D-U-N-S number or whose D-U-N-S number file contains negative or incomplete data.

Dun & Bradstreet can be reached at www.dnb.com.

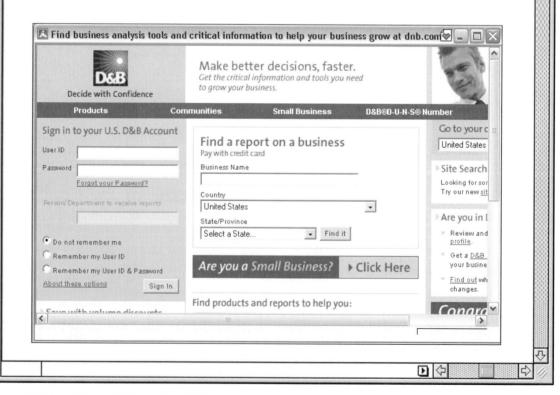

P R O G R E S S
Check

PROCEDURE REVIEW

To add a customer—
1. Click Lists, and then click Customer:Job List.
2. At the Customer:Job List window, click the Customer:Job menu button.
3. At the Customer:Job menu, click New.
4. Enter the background data for the customer.
5. Click OK.
6. Close the Customer:Job List window.

To delete a customer—
1. Click Lists, and then click Customer:Job List.
2. At the Customer:Job List window, select the customer you wish to delete.
3. Click the Customer:Job menu button.
4. At the Customer:Job menu, click Delete.
5. Click OK at the warning.
6. Close the Customer:Job List window.
   You cannot delete a customer who has a balance or who was used in a transaction during the current accounting period.

To edit a customer—
1. Click Lists, and then click Customer:Job List.
2. At the Customer:Job List window, select the customer you wish to edit.
3. Click the Customer:Job menu button.
4. At the Customer:Job menu, click Edit.
   (You can also double-click the customer name to enter the Edit window.)
5. Change the appropriate information.
6. Click OK.
7. Close the Customer:Job List window.

To create an invoice—
1. Click Customers, and then click Create Invoices.
2. At the Customer:Job drop-down list, click the customer name.
3. At the *Template* field, accept *Intuit Service Invoice*.
4. Enter the invoice date in the *Date* field.
5. Enter the invoice number in the *Invoice #* field.
6. Select the terms in the *Terms* drop-down list.
7. Select the appropriate item(s) at the Item drop-down list.
8. Enter the quantity.
9. Make sure the To be printed and To be-e-mailed boxes are not checked.
10. Click Save & Close.

To receive a payment—
1. Click Customers, and then click Receive Payments.
2. At the Received From drop-down list, click the customer name.
3. At the Pmt. Method drop-down list, click *Check*.
4. Enter the payment date in the *Date* field.

5. Enter the amount in the *Amount* field.
6. Enter the check number in the *Ref./Check No.* field.
7. Click Group with other undeposited funds.
8. Click S̲ave & Close.

To enter a cash sale—
1. Click C̲ustomers, and then click Enter S̲ales Receipts.
2. At the Customer:J̲ob drop-down list, click the customer name.
3. Complete the balance of the window in the same manner as an invoice.
4. Click S̲ave and Close.

To make a deposit—
1. Click B̲anking, and then click Make D̲eposits.
2. At the Payments to Deposit window, click Select A̲ll to deposit all receipts.
3. Click OK.
4. At the Make Deposits window in the *Deposit To* field, accept or choose *1010 Cash - Operating* account.
5. Enter the deposit date in the *Date* field.
6. Click S̲ave & Close.

To view and print customer reports from the R̲eports menu—
1. Click R̲eports, and then click C̲ustomers & Receivables.
2. At the Customers & Receivables submenu, choose a report.
3. Choose the appropriate dates for the report, and then click Refre̲sh.
4. Click Prin̲t on the command line.
5. At the Print Reports dialog box, review the settings, then click Print.
6. Close the report.

To view and print customer reports from the L̲ists menu—
1. Click L̲ists, and then click Customer:J̲ob List.
2. Click the Rep̲orts menu button.
3. Click R̲eports on All Customers:Jobs.
4. Choose a report.
5. Choose the appropriate dates for the report, and then click Refre̲sh.
6. Click Prin̲t on the command line.
7. At the Print Reports dialog box, review the settings, then click Print.
8. Close the report.

KEY CONCEPTS

Select the letter of the item that best matches each definition.

a. Customer:Job List
b. Receive Payments window
c. Cash Sales
d. Create Invoices window
e. Customer:Job List – Reports Menu button

f. Customer
g. Undeposited Funds
h. Enter Sales Receipts window
i. Deposit Funds window
j. *Customer Balance Detail* report

_____ 1. Contains a file for all customers with which the company does business.
_____ 2. A report that displays all transactions for a customer.

_____ 3. Window used to deposit funds collected.

_____ 4. A person or business that the company provides services for or sells a product to.

_____ 5. Window used to record the payment of invoices.

_____ 6. Sales where payment is received immediately.

_____ 7. Window used to record sales on account.

_____ 8. Collections not yet deposited in the bank.

_____ 9. Used to access a report that includes the Enter Sales Receipts window in addition to the Create Invoices and Receive Payments windows.

_____ 10. Window used to record sales for cash.

PROCEDURE CHECK

1. Your company has obtained a new major client. Describe the steps to add the new client to the system.

2. Your company has the type of business that makes cash sales to many customers and rarely tracks accounts receivable. How would you use QuickBooks Pro to record your sales?

3. Your business wishes to track all the deposits made to the bank in order to facilitate the month-end bank reconciliation process. How would you record collection of funds in order to accomplish this?

4. You wish to determine the oldest unpaid invoices. How would you use QuickBooks Pro to obtain that information?

5. Upper management requests a report of revenue generated by each customer. How would you use QuickBooks Pro to develop this information?

6. Compare and contrast a manual accounting system with a computerized accounting system for processing customer transactions. Include how the accounts receivable subsidiary ledger compares to the Customer:Job List.

CASE PROBLEMS

CASE PROBLEM 1

On April 1, 2004, Lynn Garcia began her business of Lynn's Music Studio. Lynn began by depositing $10,000 cash in a bank account in the business name. She also contributed a piano and some guitars. The musical instruments have an outstanding note balance of $2,000 that has been assumed by the business. The cash, musical instruments, note payable, and capital have all been recorded in the opening balances of the books. For the first part of the month, Lynn set up her studio. She has now begun providing piano and guitar lessons. Piano lessons are billed at $35 per hour and guitar lessons are billed at $30 per hour. You will record the transactions listed below for the month of April. The company file for this chapter includes the beginning information for Lynn's Music Studio along with the transactions recorded in chapter 2.

1. Open the company file CH3 Lynn's Music Studio.QBW.

2. Make a backup copy of the company file and name it LMS3 [Your Name] Lynn's Music Studio.

3. Restore the backup copy of the company file. In both the Restore From and Restore To windows use the file name LMS3 [Your Name] Lynn's Music Studio.

4. Change the company name to LMS3 [Your Name] Lynn's Music Studio.

5. Add the following customer to the Customer:Job List:

Customer Name:	**Musical Youth Group**
Opening Balance:	**0 as of April 1, 2004**
Company Name:	**Musical Youth Group**
First Name:	**Dana**
Last Name:	**Thompson**
Address:	**550 Marion Lane**
	Scranton, PA 18504
Contact:	**Dana Thompson**
Phone:	**570-555-6642**
FAX:	**570-555-6700**
E-mail:	**myg@emcp.net**
Type:	**group**
Terms:	**Net 30 Days**
Credit Limit:	**20,000**

Delete the following customer:
    Rivera Family

6. Using the appropriate window, record the following transactions for April 2004:

Apr. 9   Provided 15 hours guitar lessons and 10 hours piano lessons on account to Jefferson High School, Invoice No. 2001, Net 10 Days.

Apr. 12   Provided 3 hours piano lessons to the Schroeder Family, Invoice No. 2002. Received payment immediately, Check No. 478.

Apr. 13   Provided 12 hours piano lessons to Highland School, Invoice No. 2003, Net 30 Days.

Apr. 16   Provided 8 hours guitar lessons and 5 hours piano lessons to Twin Lakes Elementary School, Invoice No. 2004, Net 30 Days.

Apr. 16   Provided 6 hours guitar lessons to the Patterson Family, Invoice No. 2005. Received payment immediately, Check No. 208.

Apr. 20   Provided 5 hours guitar lessons and 7 hours piano lessons to Mulligan Residence, Invoice No. 2006, Net 30 Days.

Apr. 20   Received payment in full from Jefferson High School for Invoice No. 2001, Check No. 28759.

Apr. 23   Provided 5 hours of piano lessons to Douglaston Senior Center, Invoice No. 2007, Net 30 Days. Douglaston Senior Center is a new client:

Customer Name:	**Douglaston Senior Center**
Opening Balance:	**0 as of April 1, 2004**
Company Name:	**Douglaston Senior Center**
First Name:	**Herbie**
Last Name:	**Richardson**
Address:	**574 S Beech Street**
	Scranton, PA 18506
Contact:	**Herbie Richardson**
Phone:	**570-555-7748**
FAX:	**570-555-8800**
E-mail:	**DSC@emcp.net**
Type:	**group**
Terms:	**Net 30 Days**
Credit Limit:	**25,000**

Apr. 23   Provided 10 hours guitar lessons and 10 hours piano lessons to the Musical Youth Group, Invoice No. 2008. Received payment immediately, Check No. 578.

Apr. 26   Provided 15 hours guitar lessons and 10 hours piano lessons on account to Jefferson High School, Invoice No. 2009, Net 10 Days.

Apr. 26   Received payment in full from Highland School for Invoice No. 2003, Check No. 75281.

Apr. 27   Provided 2 hours guitar lessons for the Patel Family, Invoice No. 2010. Received payment immediately, Check No. 629.

Apr. 30   Provided 8 hours guitar lessons and 5 hours piano lessons to Twin Lakes Elementary School, Invoice No. 2011, Net 30 Days.

Apr. 30   Received partial payment of $145 from Mulligan Residence for Invoice No. 2006, Check No. 715.

Apr. 30   Deposited all receipts for the month.

7. Display and print the following reports for April 1, 2004, to April 30, 2004:
   a. *Open Invoices*
   b. *Customer Balance Detail*
   c. *Transaction List by Customer*
   d. *Journal*

CASE PROBLEM 2

On June 1, 2004, Olivia Chen began her business Olivia's Web Solutions. Olivia began by depositing $25,000 cash in a bank account in the business name. She also contributed a computer. The computer has an outstanding note balance of $2,500 that has now been assumed by the business. The cash, computer, note payable, and capital have all been recorded in the opening balances of the books. For the first part of the month, Olivia set up her office. She has now begun providing Web design and Internet consulting services to individuals and small businesses. The Web Page Design Services are billed at $125 per hour and the Internet Consulting Services at

$100 per hour. You will record the transactions listed below for the month of June. The company file includes the beginning information for Olivia's Web Solutions along with the transactions recorded in chapter 2.

1. Open the company file CH3 Olivia's Web Solutions.QBW.
2. Make a backup copy of the company file and name it OWS3 [Your Name] Olivia's Web Solutions.
3. Restore the backup copy of the company file. In both the Restore From and Restore To windows use the file name: OWS3 [Your Name] Olivia's Web Solutions.
4. Change the company name to: OWS3 [Your Name] Olivia's Web Solutions.
5. Add the following customer to the Customer:Job List:

Customer Name:	**Thrifty Stores**
Opening Balance:	**0 as of June 1, 2004**
Company Name:	**Thrifty Stores**
First Name:	**William**
Last Name:	**Way**
Address:	**23 Boston Ave.**
	Bronx, NY 11693
Contact:	**William Way**
Phone:	**718-555-2445**
FAX:	**718-555-2446**
E-mail:	**Thrifty@emcp.net**
Type:	**Commercial**
Terms:	**Net 30 Days**
Credit Limit:	**25,000**

Delete the following customer:
Printers Group

6. Using the appropriate window, record the following transactions for June 2004:

Jun. 11   Provided 8 hours of Internet Consulting Services and 10 hours of Web Page Design Services on account to Long Island Water Works, Invoice No. 1001, Net 30 Days.

Jun. 14   Provided 8 hours of Web Page Design Services on account to Sehorn & Smith, Invoice No. 1002, Net 30 Days.

Jun. 15   Provided 8 hours of Web Page Design Services on account to the Scheider Family, Invoice No. 1003.

Jun. 17   Provided 4 hours of Internet Consulting Services and 8 hours of Web Page Design Services on account to Miguel's Restaurant, Invoice No. 1004, Net 30 Days.

Jun. 18   Provided 4 hours of Internet Consulting Services to the Singh Family, Invoice No. 1005. Received payment immediately, Check No. 687.

Jun. 21   Provided 8 hours of Web Page Design Services on account to Breathe Easy, Invoice No. 1006, Net 30 Days.

Jun. 25	Received payment in full from Long Island Water Works for Invoice No. 1001, Check No. 124554.
Jun. 25	Provided 12 hours of Web Page Design Services on account to Thrifty Stores, Invoice No. 1007, Net 30 Days.
Jun. 28	Provided 8 hours of Internet Consulting Services on account to Artie's Auto Repair, Invoice 1008, Net 30 Days. Artie's Auto Repair is a new client:

Customer Name:	**Artie's Auto Repair**
Opening Balance:	**0 as of June 1, 2004**
Company Name:	**Artie's Auto Repair**
First Name:	**Leon**
Last Name:	**Artie**
Address:	**32 West 11th Street**
	New Hyde Park, NY 11523
Contact:	**Leon Artie**
Phone:	**516-555-1221**
FAX:	**516-555-1231**
E-mail:	**ArtieAuto@emcp.net**
Type:	**Commercial**
Terms:	**Net 30 Days**
Credit Limit:	**25,000**

Jun. 28	Received payment in full from Sehorn & Smith for Invoice No. 1002, Check No. 3656.
Jun. 29	Provided 12 hours of Internet Consulting Services on account to South Shore School District, Invoice No. 1009, Net 30 Days.
Jun. 29	Received payment in full from Miguel's Restaurant for Invoice No. 1004, Check No. 3269.
Jun. 30	Provided 8 hours of Internet Consulting Services on account to Sehorn & Smith, Invoice No. 1010, Net 30 Days.
Jun. 30	Received partial payment of $250 from Breathe Easy for Invoice No. 1006, Check No. 1455.
Jun. 30	Deposited all receipts for the month.

7. Display and print the following reports for June 1, 2004, to June 30, 2004:

a. *Open Invoices*
b. *Customer Balance Detail*
c. *Transaction List by Customer*
d. *Journal*

CHAPTER

4

PERIOD-END PROCEDURES

General Journal Entry

CHAPTER OBJECTIVES

- Update the Chart of Accounts List

- Record adjustments in the General Journal Entry window

- View the effect of period-end adjustments on the trial balance

- Display and print period-end reports

- Change the reports display using the Modify Report button

- Display and print financial statements

INTRODUCTION

general journal In a manual accounting system, the book in which transactions are initially recorded.

QuickBooks Pro allows you to record journal entries in general journal format. As seen in chapters 2 and 3, QuickBooks Pro records daily activities in windows such as Enter Bills, Pay Bills, Write Checks, Create Invoices, Receive Payments, and so on. However, behind the scenes, QuickBooks Pro also records the activities in general journal format using debits and credits. The accounts used to record the activities come from the *Chart of Accounts* (Lists).

generally accepted accounting principles (GAAP) Principles used to prepare the financial statements of a company. They consist of both formal accounting regulations and procedures mandated by regulatory agencies, and of traditionally used accounting procedures.

At times, some account balances (Activities) will need to be adjusted based on information that does not appear in the daily activities so that the financial statements can be properly prepared in accordance with generally accepted accounting principles. These adjustments to the accounts are called adjusting journal entries and are recorded in the *General Journal Entry* window. As you record the daily activities and adjusting journal entries, QuickBooks Pro simultaneously updates the accounting records and financial statements (Reports).

adjusting journal entries Adjustments made to accounts at certain periods of time, such as the end of the month or the end of the fiscal year, to bring the balances up to date.

In this chapter, our sample company, Kristin Raina Interior Designs, will make the necessary adjusting journal entries for February, the end of the first month of operations.

QUICKBOOKS PRO VERSUS MANUAL ACCOUNTING: GENERAL JOURNAL ENTRIES

debit Dollar amount recorded in the *left* column of an account. Depending on the account, it either increases or decreases the balance in the account.

In a manual accounting system, the general journal is the document in which transactions are initially recorded. For each transaction, the dollar value of at least one account must be recorded as a debit amount and the dollar value of at least one account must be recorded as a credit amount. The total dollar value of debits must equal the total dollar value of credits. Companies have the option of recording all transactions exclusively in the general journal or, alternatively, for frequent similar transactions, in special journals. In either case, at month-end, the transactions from all journals are posted to the general ledger.

credit Dollar amount recorded in the *right* column of an account. Depending on the account, it either increases or decreases the balance in the account.

Periodically, certain adjustments that are not daily business activities must be made to the accounts to update the balances. These adjustments, called adjusting journal entries, are always recorded in the general journal. They are then posted to the general ledger to update the balances in the accounts. The adjusted balances are used to prepare the financial statements. These adjusting journal entries must always be made on the date the financial statement is prepared, but can be recorded more often. Most large companies typically prepare the adjusting journal entries on a monthly basis.

special journals The purchases journal, cash payments journal, sales journal, and cash receipts journal.

QuickBooks Pro does not follow the format of the special journals for daily transactions. Instead, all activities are recorded in the different windows depending on the nature of the activity. Behind the scenes, QuickBooks Pro records the activity in general journal format as seen in the *Journal* report. However, for adjusting journal entries, QuickBooks Pro uses the General Journal Entry window in a manner similar to that of a manual accounting system. As information entered in each of the windows, including the General Journal Entry window, is saved, the general ledger balances, the Chart of Accounts List balances, and the financial statements are simultaneously updated. Because of the ease of updating balances in a computerized accounting system, even small companies can now record adjusting journal entries on a monthly basis.

CHAPTER PROBLEM

In this chapter, you will record the adjusting journal entries for the end of the first month of business, February 29, 2004, for Kristin Raina Interior Designs. The February 1, 2004, beginning balances, along with all vendor and customer activities for the month of February illustrated in chapters 2 and 3, are contained in the company file CH4 Kristin Raina Interior Designs.

Begin by opening the company file—
1. Open QuickBooks Pro.
2. At the *No Company Open* window, click on the Open an existing company button or click File, and then click Open Company.
3. At the Open a Company dialog box in the Look in text box, choose the *QuickBooks Pro* subfolder or the subfolder containing the company files.
4. Select the company, *CH4 Kristin Raina Interior Designs.QBW*, and click Open.
5. If the Company Navigator window appears, click the X to close it.

Next, make a backup copy of the company file—
1. Click File, then click Back Up.
2. In the QuickBooks Backup dialog box, the Disk option should be selected.
3. In the Filename text box, key **EX4 [Your Name] Kristin Raina Interior Designs**.
4. Next to the Location text box, click the Browse button.
5. At the Back Up Company to dialog box, in the Save in text box, choose your subfolder, a network directory designated by your instructor, or a floppy drive.
6. Click Save.
7. In the QuickBooks Backup dialog box, click OK.
8. At the *Your data has been backed up successfully* message, click OK.

Now restore the backup copy of the company file—
1. Click File, and then click Restore.
2. At the Restore Company Backup dialog box, in the Get Company Backup From section, the Disk option should be selected.
3. Click the Browse button.
4. At the Restore From dialog box, in the Look in text box, choose the location where you saved your backup copy.
5. Select the company file *EX4 [Your Name] Kristin Raina Interior Designs Company.QBB* and click Open.
6. At the Restore Company Backup dialog box, in the Restore Company Backup To section, click the Browse button.
7. At the Restore To dialog box, in the Save in text box, choose the subfolder where you will be opening and working on your copies of the company files.
8. In the File name text box, key **EX4 [Your Name] Kristin Raina Interior Designs** and click Save.
9. In the Restore Company Backup dialog box, click Restore.
10. At the *Your data has been restored successfully* message, click OK.
11. If the Company Navigator window appears, click the X to close it.

The backup copy has been restored, but the company name still reads CH4 Kristin Raina Interior Designs.

Change the company name—
1. Click Company, and then click Company Information.
2. Change the company name to **EX4 [Your Name] Kristin Raina Interior Designs**.
3. Click OK.

LISTS: THE CHART OF ACCOUNTS LIST

Recall from chapter 1 that the second level of operation in QuickBooks Pro is recording background information on Lists. Lists need to be revised periodically when new accounts need to be added, accounts not used in the business need to be deleted, or modifications need to be made to an account. When you make these revisions to the accounts, you are updating the Chart of Accounts List.

The Chart of Accounts List is the list of accounts a company uses as it conducts its business. In a manual accounting system all of the individual accounts are placed together in a book called the general ledger. Each account in the general ledger shows all the increases and decreases in the account, reflected as debits and credits, and the balance in each account. In computerized accounting systems, a general ledger is also maintained showing the increases, decreases (debits and credits), and the balance for each account. In addition, the Chart of Accounts List displays the balance next to each account name. Because of this, the Chart of Accounts List has become synonymous with the general ledger in computerized systems although it indicates only the balance, not all of the detail activity.

In QuickBooks Pro, the Chart of Accounts List consists of the account number, name, type, and balance. The account numbers are optional but are used in this text. The name you assign an account is the name that appears in the windows and reports. The balance is determined by the original amount entered (if any) when the account is first created, and then subsequently adjusted by activities entered in the windows.

The account types are used by the software to determine where to place the account name and balance on the financial statements and to establish the system default accounts.

The account types consist of—

Assets:
  Bank
  Accounts Receivable
  Other Current Asset
  Fixed Asset
  Other Asset

Liabilities:
  Accounts Payable
  Credit Card
  Other Current Liability
  Long Term Liability

Equity:
  Equity

Income and Expenses:
> Income
> Cost of Goods Sold
> Expense
> Other Income
> Other Expense

As was seen in chapters 2 and 3, QuickBooks Pro identifies certain accounts as system default accounts and uses them to identify the transactions recorded in the windows. For example, the Accounts Payable account type is used to identify the Accounts Payable liability account when transactions are recorded in the Enter Bills window. The Accounts Receivable account type is used to identify the Accounts Receivable asset account when transactions are recorded in the Create Invoices window. When QuickBooks Pro looks for an account, it looks for the account type, not the account name.

Kristin Raina previously entered information to establish the Chart of Accounts List that was then used for the February activities recorded in chapters 2 and 3.

To review the Chart of Accounts List—
1. Click <u>R</u>eports, and then click <u>L</u>ist.
2. At the List submenu, click <u>A</u>ccount Listing. The Account Listing is displayed. (See figure 4–1.)

FIGURE 4-1
Account Listing

EX4 [Your Name] Kristin Raina Interior Designs
Account Listing
February 29, 2004

Account	Type	Balance Total	Description	Accnt. #	Tax Line
1010 · Cash - Operating	Bank	47,400.00		1010	<Unassigned>
1200 · Accounts Receivable	Accounts Receivable	1,540.00		1200	<Unassigned>
1250 · Undeposited Funds	Other Current Asset	0.00		1250	<Unassigned>
1300 · Design Supplies	Other Current Asset	200.00		1300	<Unassigned>
1305 · Office Supplies	Other Current Asset	400.00		1305	<Unassigned>
1410 · Prepaid Advertising	Other Current Asset	600.00		1410	<Unassigned>
1420 · Prepaid Insurance	Other Current Asset	2,400.00		1420	<Unassigned>
1700 · Furniture and Fixtures	Fixed Asset	12,000.00		1700	<Unassigned>
1700 · Furniture and Fixtures:1750 · Accum. Dep., Furniture and Fix	Fixed Asset	0.00		1750	<Unassigned>
1800 · Computers	Fixed Asset	3,600.00		1800	<Unassigned>
1800 · Computers:1850 · Accum. Dep., Computers	Fixed Asset	0.00		1850	<Unassigned>
2010 · Accounts Payable	Accounts Payable	6,250.00		2010	<Unassigned>
2020 · Notes Payable	Other Current Liability	7,000.00		2020	<Unassigned>
2030 · Interest Payable	Other Current Liability	0.00		2030	<Unassigned>
3010 · Kristin Raina, Capital	Equity	50,000.00		3010	<Unassigned>
3020 · Kristin Raina, Drawings	Equity	-400.00		3020	<Unassigned>
3900 · Retained Earnings	Equity			3900	<Unassigned>
4010 · Design Services	Income			4010	<Unassigned>
4020 · Decorating Services	Income			4020	<Unassigned>
6020 · Accounting Expense	Expense			6020	<Unassigned>
6030 · Administrative Expense	Expense			6030	<Unassigned>
6175 · Deprec. Exp., Furniture	Expense			6175	<Unassigned>
6200 · Insurance Expense	Expense			6200	<Unassigned>
6300 · Janitorial Expenses	Expense			6300	<Unassigned>
6350 · Promotion Expense	Expense			6350	<Unassigned>
6400 · Rent Expense	Expense			6400	<Unassigned>
6450 · Telephone Expense	Expense			6450	<Unassigned>
6500 · Utilities Expense	Expense			6500	<Unassigned>

In QuickBooks Pro, the account balances that flow into the financial statements are based on the account type. If you want to subtotal two or more accounts, you can identify an account as a *subaccount*. Subaccounts show a subtotal amount on the financial statements in addition to the regular total amounts. When an account is identified as a subaccount, the account it is a subaccount of is called the *parent* account.

In Kristin Raina's Chart of Accounts List, the accumulated depreciation accounts were marked as subaccounts of the related asset account. This was done in order to see the accumulated depreciation account as a deduction from the cost of an asset on the financial statements.

Review the Account Listing in figure 4–1. Look at the *1700 Furniture and Fixtures* account. The account below it is *1700 Furniture and Fixtures:1750 - Accum. Dep., Furniture and Fix.* This means account 1750 is a subaccount of 1700. Account 1700 is a parent account because it has a subaccount. Notice the same setup with accounts 1800 and 1850 on the Account Listing.

To view a specific account—
1. With the Account Listing open, place the zoom glass over the *Cash - Operating* account.
2. Choose *Cash - Operating* by double-clicking the mouse. The Edit Account window for Cash - Operating is displayed. (See figure 4–2.)

FIGURE 4-2
Edit Account Window

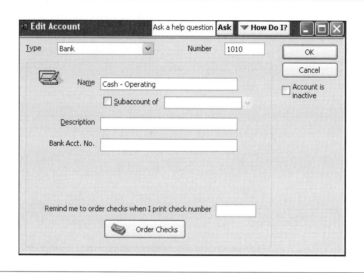

An account contains the following parts:

TYPE	Use the drop-down list to display and choose the account type. QuickBooks Pro uses the account type for system default accounts in windows and for placement on financial statements.
NUMBER	An account number is optional. Account numbers will be used in this text and have been established in the company files.
NAME	Fill in an account name of your choice. The software uses the account type for necessary identification (default accounts and placement on financial statements), not the account name. The name keyed in this field appears in the windows and on reports.
SUBACCOUNT OF	Accounts can be identified as subaccounts of another account. To activate this field, click the mouse to place a check mark in the box. Once this box is activated, use the drop-down list to determine which account this will become a subaccount of.
DESCRIPTION	This field is optional. A description entered here will appear on certain reports.
BANK ACCT. NO.	This field is optional. It is listed as reference for the user.

3. Close the Edit Account window.
4. At the *Account Listing* report double-click *1850 - Accum. Dep., Computers.* At the Edit Account window, notice how this account is marked as a subaccount of 1800 - Computers. Close the Edit Account window.
5. Close the *Account Listing* report window.

ADDING AN ACCOUNT

In preparation for recording month-end adjusting journal entries, Kristin Raina has determined that she needs to add an Advertising Expense account to the Chart of Accounts List.

To add a new account—
1. Click **L**ists, and then click Chart of **A**ccounts.
2. At the Chart of Accounts window, click the **A**ccount menu button.
3. At the Account menu, click New. The New Account window appears. (See figure 4–3.)

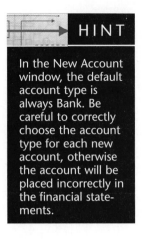
FIGURE 4-3
New Account Window

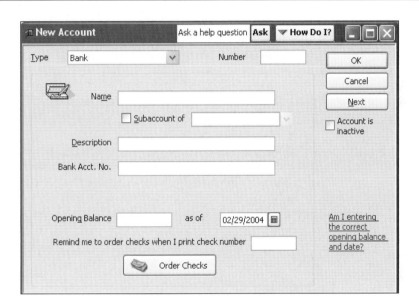

4. At the **T**ype drop-down list, click *Expense*.
5. Enter the data below for the account number and name.

Number:	**6050**
*Na**m**e:*	**Advertising Expense**

(See figure 4–4.)

FIGURE 4-4
New Account
Window Complete

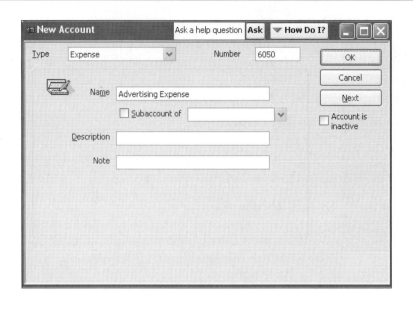

6. If the information is correct, click OK.
7. Close the Chart of Accounts window.

DELETING AN ACCOUNT

Kristin Raina has decided the Promotion Expense account is not necessary and it should be deleted.

To delete an account—
1. Click Lists, and then click Chart of Accounts.
2. At the Chart of Accounts window, select (highlight) *6350 Promotion Expense*.
3. Click the Account menu button.
4. At the Account menu, click Delete.
5. The Delete Account warning appears. Click OK. The account will be deleted.
6. Close the Chart of Accounts window.

An account with a balance cannot be deleted. It can instead be marked inactive and will no longer appear in reports.

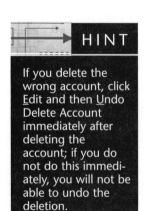

HINT

If you delete the wrong account, click Edit and then Undo Delete Account immediately after deleting the account; if you do not do this immediately, you will not be able to undo the deletion.

EDITING AN ACCOUNT

Kristin Raina decides to change the account name Furniture and Fixtures to just Furniture.

To edit an account—
1. Open the Chart of Accounts List, and select the *1700 Furniture and Fixtures* account.
2. At the Chart of Accounts window, click the Account menu button.
3. At the Account menu, click Edit. The Edit Account window appears.
4. At the *Name* field, delete the part of the name *and Fixtures*.
   (See figure 4–5.)

FIGURE 4-5

Edit Furniture
Account Complete

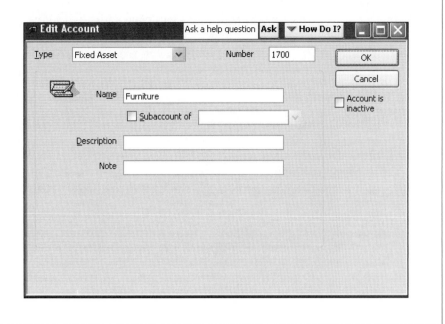

5. If the information is correct, click OK.
6. Close the Chart of Accounts window.

PRACTICE *exercise*

Add the following accounts:

Type:	**Expense**
Number:	**6325**
Name:	**Office Supplies Expense**
Type :	**Other Expense**
Number:	**7000**
Name:	**Interest Expense**

Delete the following account:

6030 Administrative Expenses

Edit the following account:

Change the name of account 1750 to *Accum. Dep., Furniture*

QuickCheck: The updated Chart of Accounts List appears in figure 4–6.

FIGURE 4-6
Updated Chart of
Accounts List

EX4 [Your Name] Kristin Raina Interior Designs
Account Listing
February 29, 2004

Account	Type	Balance Total	Description	Accnt. #	Tax Line
1010 · Cash - Operating	Bank	47,400.00		1010	<Unassigned>
1200 · Accounts Receivable	Accounts Receivable	1,540.00		1200	<Unassigned>
1250 · Undeposited Funds	Other Current Asset	0.00		1250	<Unassigned>
1300 · Design Supplies	Other Current Asset	200.00		1300	<Unassigned>
1305 · Office Supplies	Other Current Asset	400.00		1305	<Unassigned>
1410 · Prepaid Advertising	Other Current Asset	600.00		1410	<Unassigned>
1420 · Prepaid Insurance	Other Current Asset	2,400.00		1420	<Unassigned>
1700 · Furniture	Fixed Asset	12,000.00		1700	<Unassigned>
1700 · Furniture:1750 · Accum. Dep., Furniture	Fixed Asset	0.00		1750	<Unassigned>
1800 · Computers	Fixed Asset	3,600.00		1800	<Unassigned>
1800 · Computers:1850 · Accum. Dep., Computers	Fixed Asset	0.00		1850	<Unassigned>
2010 · Accounts Payable	Accounts Payable	6,250.00		2010	<Unassigned>
2020 · Notes Payable	Other Current Liability	7,000.00		2020	<Unassigned>
2030 · Interest Payable	Other Current Liability	0.00		2030	<Unassigned>
3010 · Kristin Raina, Capital	Equity	50,000.00		3010	<Unassigned>
3020 · Kristin Raina, Drawings	Equity	-400.00		3020	<Unassigned>
3900 · Retained Earnings	Equity			3900	<Unassigned>
4010 · Design Services	Income			4010	<Unassigned>
4020 · Decorating Services	Income			4020	<Unassigned>
6020 · Accounting Expense	Expense			6020	<Unassigned>
6050 · Advertising Expense	Expense			6050	<Unassigned>
6175 · Deprec. Exp., Furniture	Expense			6175	<Unassigned>
6200 · Insurance Expense	Expense			6200	<Unassigned>
6300 · Janitorial Expenses	Expense			6300	<Unassigned>
6325 · Office Supplies Expense	Expense			6325	<Unassigned>
6400 · Rent Expense	Expense			6400	<Unassigned>
6450 · Telephone Expense	Expense			6450	<Unassigned>
6500 · Utilities Expense	Expense			6500	<Unassigned>
7000 · Interest Expense	Other Expense			7000	<Unassigned>

REPORTS: THE TRIAL BALANCE

trial balance A report containing all the general ledger account names, their respective debit or credit balances, and the total debits and total credits.

In a manual accounting system, as journal entries are recorded and posted to the general ledger, errors can occur when posting to the general ledger or when doing arithmetic computations. The trial balance is used to verify that the total debits equal the total credits, which means the general ledger is in balance. In a computerized system, on the other hand, there is less chance of the accounts being out of balance because the postings to the general ledger and arithmetic computations occur automatically.

But a trial balance is still useful. It allows you to view the accounts and their debit or credit balances without having to look at all the detail in the general ledger. It is often useful to review the trial balance prior to making adjusting journal entries.

To view and print the trial balance—
1. Click Reports, and then click Accountant & Taxes.
2. At the Accountant & Taxes submenu, click Trial Balance.
3. At the *From* and *To* fields, choose *01/01/2004* and *02/29/2004*, and then click the mouse in the screen. The trial balance is displayed. (See figure 4–7.)

FIGURE 4-7
Trial Balance Report

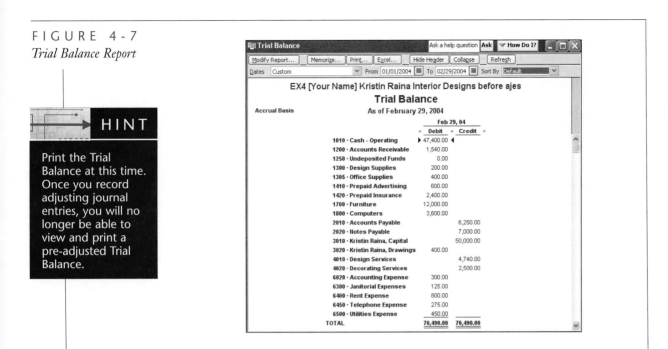

4. To print the report, click the Print button on the command line.
5. At the Print Reports dialog box, check the settings, then click Print.
6. Close the report.

 **THE GENERAL JOURNAL ENTRY WINDOW**

You usually need to enter adjusting journal entries before preparing financial statements in order to adjust account balances based on accounting rules. In QuickBooks Pro, adjusting journal entries are recorded in the General Journal Entry window. This window is set up similar to that for a manual accounting system. It lists the account and amount of the debit entry, the account and amount of the credit entry, and an explanation.

The QuickBooks Pro General Journal Entry window appears in figure 4–8.

FIGURE 4-8
*General Journal Entry
Window*

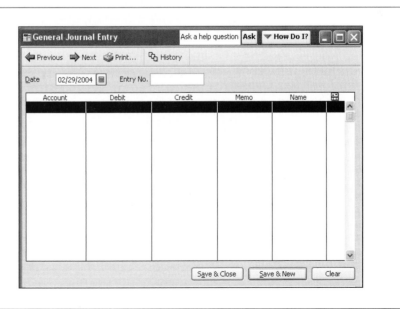

HINT

Use the Scroll arrow in the drop-down list to find the account.

HINT

In the event a new account needs to be added while in the General Journal Entry window, click < *Add New* > from the account drop-down list. This opens the New Account window and allows you to add the new account to the list without exiting the General Journal Entry window.

As you recall from chapter 1, the third level of operation in QuickBooks Pro is Activities. Activities identified as adjustments to account balances are entered in the General Journal Entry window. There are not any default accounts in this window because each adjusting journal entry will be different. The account to debit and the account to credit must be indicated. Adjusting journal entries are usually dated the last day of the month.

The first adjusting journal entry Kristin Raina makes on Feburary 29, 2004, is to record (debit) Advertising Expense and reduce (credit) the Prepaid Advertising account for one month of service. The prepaid advertising was originally purchased on February 1 for $600 and represents a six-month prepayment. One month of Advertising Expense is $100 ($600/6 months).

To record a journal entry—

1. Click <u>C</u>ompany, and then click Make Journal Entry. The General Journal Entry window appears.

   A message may appear about assigning numbers to journal entries. As you know, QuickBooks Pro automatically assigns a Transaction No. to each transaction recorded in each of the windows. You cannot change the Transaction No. In the event that a transaction is deleted, that transaction number is also deleted; the next transaction would then be assigned the next number in sequence. QuickBooks Pro allows the user to assign journal entry numbers to each transaction. In this book, journal entry numbers are used for the adjusting journal entries. Once you start a sequence of numbers in the General Journal Entry window, QuickBooks Pro will automatically assign the next adjusting journal entry number in sequence but you can edit or delete the automatically assigned journal entry number. If you receive the message box, place a check mark in the box to the left of Do not display this message in the future, and click OK.

2. Choose *02/29/2004* in the <u>D</u>ate field.
3. In the *Entry No.* field, key **AJE1**.
4. In the first line of the *Account* field, click the down-pointing arrow and then click *6050 Advertising Expense*.
5. In the *Debit* field, key **100**.
6. Move to the second line in the *Account* field, click the down-pointing arrow, and then click *1410 Prepaid Advertising*.
7. In the *Credit* field, *100* should appear; if it does not, key **100**.
8. In the *Memo* field, key **To record one month advertising expense.** (See figure 4–9.) The *Memo* field is optional; you do not have to enter an explanation.
9. If the entry is correct, click S<u>a</u>ve & Close.

FIGURE 4-9
*General Journal Entry
Window Completed*

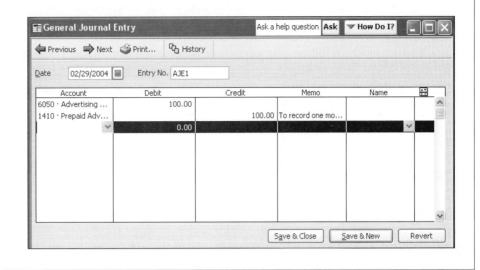

As in the other windows, the Previous and Next arrows can be used to view previous and subsequent journal entries. Choosing one of the arrows saves the entry. The <u>S</u>ave & New button can be used when entering more than one journal entry.

ACCOUNTING
c o n c e p t

For this adjusting journal entry, the general ledger posting is as follows:

6050 Advertising Exp.			1410 Prepaid Advertising		
Dr	Cr			Dr	Cr
100			Bill	600	100 Adj.
			Bal	500	

In all journal entries the total dollar value of debits must equal the total dollar value of credits. In the General Journal Entry window, if you attempt to save an entry that is not in balance, a warning window appears that gives you the opportunity to correct the journal entry. If the journal entry is not corrected, you will not be able to save it.

PRACTICE *exercise*

Record the following adjusting journal entries in the General Journal Entry window:

FEB. 29   Record one month of insurance expense. The insurance was purchased for $2,400 in February and recorded as Prepaid Insurance. It is a one-year policy effective February 1. *QuickCheck:* 200

FEB. 29   Record the depreciation expense on the Furniture of $100 per month.

FEB. 29   Record the depreciation expense on the Computer of $60 per month. Add the new account *6185 Deprec. Exp., Computers* while in the General Journal Entry window.

FEB. 29   Record one month of interest expense on the note payable of $50. (Credit Interest Payable.)

FEB. 29   The Office Supplies on hand totaled $250. Refer to the Office Supplies account on the Trial Balance to determine the amount of the adjustment. *QuickCheck:* 150

PERIOD-END AND FINANCIAL REPORTS

Reports, the fourth level of operation in QuickBooks Pro, reflect the Activities and adjustments recorded in the windows, and the information compiled in the Lists. When you complete the adjusting journal entries, you should display and print the period-end accounting reports and the financial reports.

ACCOUNTING REPORTS

The period-end accounting reports consist of the *Journal*, the *General Ledger*, and the *Adjusted Trial Balance* reports. These reports should be printed at the end of each month.

Journal Report

In the previous chapters, the *Journal* report was printed for the entire month. However, it is not necessary to reprint all the journal entries when you wish to view only the adjusting journal entries. All reports can be customized to modify the appearance of the report or the fields of information to be displayed. In this case, we will customize the report using the Filter feature which will display only the general journal entries in the Journal report.

To view and print only the adjusting journal entries in the Journal report—
1. Click <u>R</u>eports, and then click <u>A</u>ccountant & Taxes.
2. At the Accountant & Taxes submenu, click <u>J</u>ournal.
3. At the *From* and *To* fields, choose *02/01/2004* and *02/29/2004* and then click Refre<u>s</u>h on the reports command line.

   All transactions for February, from all windows are displayed. Scroll to the bottom of the entries. Notice the account type General Journal. These are the adjusting journal entries entered in the General Journal Entry window.

4. Click <u>M</u>odify Report on the command line. The Modify Report: Journal dialog box appears.
5. Click the <u>F</u>ilters tab.
6. In the *Filter* field, click *Transaction Type*. The box to the right of the *Filter* field changes to Transaction Type.
7. From the Transaction Type drop-down list, click *Journal*. (See figure 4–10.)

FIGURE 4-10
*Modify Report: Journal,
Filters Tab Completed*

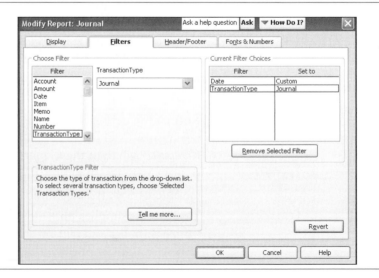

8. Click OK. Only the journal entries recorded in the General Journal Entry window are displayed.
9. To print the report, click Print on the command line.
10. At the Print Reports dialog box, check the settings, and then click Print. (See figure 4–11.)

FIGURE 4-11

Journal Report –
Adjusting Journal
Entries

EX4 [Your Name] Kristin Raina Interior Designs
Journal
February 2004

Trans #	Type	Date	Num	Name	Memo	Account	Debit	Credit
33	General Journal	02/29/2004	AJE1			6050 · Advertising Expense	100.00	
					To record on...	1410 · Prepaid Advertising		100.00
							100.00	100.00
34	General Journal	02/29/2004	AJE2			6200 · Insurance Expense	200.00	
						1420 · Prepaid Insurance		200.00
							200.00	200.00
35	General Journal	02/29/2004	AJE3			6175 · Deprec. Exp., Furniture	100.00	
						1750 · Accum. Dep., Furniture		100.00
							100.00	100.00
36	General Journal	02/29/2004	AJE4			6185 · Deprec. Exp., Computers	60.00	
						1850 · Accum. Dep., Computers		60.00
							60.00	60.00
37	General Journal	02/29/2004	AJE5			7000 · Interest Expense	50.00	
						2030 · Interest Payable		50.00
							50.00	50.00
38	General Journal	02/29/2004	AJE6			6325 · Office Supplies Expense	150.00	
						1305 · Office Supplies		150.00
							150.00	150.00
TOTAL							**660.00**	**660.00**

11. Close the report.

General Ledger Report

All transactions recorded in any of the windows are posted to the general ledger. The *General Ledger* report displays all activity to each account and lists the balance after each activity.

To view and print the *General Ledger* report—
1. Click Reports, and then click Accountant & Taxes.
2. At the Accountant & Taxes submenu, click General Ledger.
3. At the *From* and *To* fields, choose *02/01/2004* and *02/29/2004* and then click Refresh on the command line. The general ledger is displayed. (See figure 4–12.)

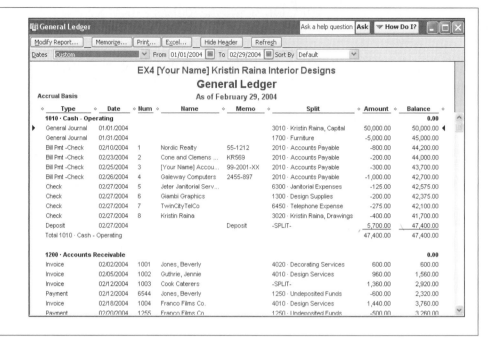

FIGURE 4-12
General Ledger Report

Look at the activity in the Cash – Operating account. Each increase and decrease to the account is shown with a balance after each activity. QuickBooks Pro does not use debits and credits in the general ledger. Instead, each account is displayed showing the increase or decrease activity and the balance in the account after each activity.

4. To print the report, click Print on the command line.
5. At the Print Reports dialog box, check the settings, and then click Print.
6. Close the report.

HINT

Once you record the adjusting journal entries, you can no longer create a pre-adjusted trial balance.

Adjusted Trial Balance Report

The trial balance of February 29, 2004 (figure 4–7), was reviewed prior to preparing the adjusting journal entries. Typically, the trial balance is printed again after the adjusting journal entries have been recorded. The second trial balance is referred to as the *Adjusted Trial Balance* report. To distinguish between the two printed trial balances, you will modify the report by changing the name in the heading of the second trial balance to *Adjusted Trial Balance*.

To view and print the *Adjusted Trial Balance* report—

1. Click Reports, and then click Accountant & Taxes.
2. At the Accountant & Taxes submenu, click Trial Balance.
3. At the *From* and *To* fields, choose *01/01/2004* and *02/29/2004* and click Refresh on the command line. The trial balance is displayed. Notice that the heading includes the default heading Trial Balance. You will use the Modify Report button on the command line to change the heading.
4. Click Modify Report on the command line. The Modify Report dialog box appears.
5. Click the Header/Footer tab.

6. In the *Report Title* field, key the word **Adjusted** before *Trial Balance*. (See figure 4–13.)

FIGURE 4-13
Modify Report: Trial Balance, Header/Footer Tab Completed

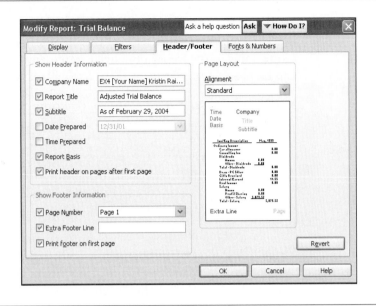

7. If the information is correct, click OK. The trial balance heading now displays as *Adjusted Trial Balance*.
8. To print the report, click Print on the command line.
9. At the Print Reports dialog box, check the settings, and then click Print. Your printout should look like figure 4–14.

FIGURE 4-14
Adjusted Trial Balance Report

EX4 [Your Name] Kristin Raina Interior Designs
Adjusted Trial Balance
As of February 29, 2004

Accrual Basis

	Feb 29, 04	
	Debit	Credit
1010 · Cash - Operating	47,400.00	
1200 · Accounts Receivable	1,540.00	
1250 · Undeposited Funds	0.00	
1300 · Design Supplies	200.00	
1305 · Office Supplies	250.00	
1410 · Prepaid Advertising	500.00	
1420 · Prepaid Insurance	2,200.00	
1700 · Furniture	12,000.00	
1700 · Furniture:1750 · Accum. Dep., Furniture		100.00
1800 · Computers	3,600.00	
1800 · Computers:1850 · Accum. Dep., Computers		60.00
2010 · Accounts Payable		6,250.00
2020 · Notes Payable		7,000.00
2030 · Interest Payable		50.00
3010 · Kristin Raina, Capital		50,000.00
3020 · Kristin Raina, Drawings	400.00	
4010 · Design Services		4,740.00
4020 · Decorating Services		2,500.00
6020 · Accounting Expense	300.00	
6050 · Advertising Expense	100.00	
6175 · Deprec. Exp., Furniture	100.00	
6185 · Deprec. Exp., Computers	60.00	
6200 · Insurance Expense	200.00	
6300 · Janitorial Expenses	125.00	
6325 · Office Supplies Expense	150.00	
6400 · Rent Expense	800.00	
6450 · Telephone Expense	275.00	
6500 · Utilities Expense	450.00	
7000 · Interest Expense	50.00	
TOTAL	**70,700.00**	**70,700.00**

10. Close the report.

Compare the effect of the adjusting journal entries on the account balances by comparing the Trial Balance (figure 4–7) to the Adjusted Trial Balance (figure 4–14).

FINANCIAL REPORTS

The financial reports consist of the income statement and the balance sheet. Companies must prepare financial statements at least once a year, but they can be prepared more frequently, such as quarterly or monthly.

Profit & Loss Standard Report (Income Statement)

The income statement, known as the *Profit & Loss* report in QuickBooks Pro, can be displayed and printed in a variety of formats. The *Profit & Loss* report displays revenue and expenses for a specified period of time. The *Profit & Loss* report can also be displayed in a comparative format. A detailed *Profit & Loss* report can be produced that lists all transactions affecting a particular item on the report.

To view and print a year-to-date *Profit & Loss Standard* report—
1. Click Reports, and then click Company & Financial.
2. At the Company & Financial submenu, click Profit & Loss Standard.
3. At the *From* and *To* fields, choose *01/01/2004* and *02/29/2004* and then click Refresh on the command line. The report for the period will be displayed.
4. To print the report, click the Print on the command line.
5. At the Print Reports dialog box, check the settings, then click Print. Your printout should resemble figure 4–15.

FIGURE 4-15
Profit & Loss Standard Report

EX4 [Your Name] Kristin Raina Interior Designs
Profit & Loss
January through February 2004

		Jan - Feb 04
Accrual Basis	Ordinary Income/Expense	
	Income	
	4010 · Design Services	4,740.00
	4020 · Decorating Services	2,500.00
	Total Income	7,240.00
	Expense	
	6020 · Accounting Expense	300.00
	6050 · Advertising Expense	100.00
	6175 · Deprec. Exp., Furniture	100.00
	6185 · Deprec. Exp., Computers	60.00
	6200 · Insurance Expense	200.00
	6300 · Janitorial Expenses	125.00
	6325 · Office Supplies Expense	150.00
	6400 · Rent Expense	800.00
	6450 · Telephone Expense	275.00
	6500 · Utilities Expense	450.00
	Total Expense	2,560.00
	Net Ordinary Income	4,680.00
	Other Income/Expense	
	Other Expense	
	7000 · Interest Expense	50.00
	Total Other Expense	50.00
	Net Other Income	-50.00
	Net Income	**4,630.00**

6. Close the report.

Balance Sheet Standard Report

In QuickBooks Pro, the *Balance Sheet* report, which shows the assets, liabilities, and equity balances as of a certain date, may be displayed in a standard, summary, or comparative format. In addition, a detailed report, showing all transactions affecting balance sheet accounts, can be produced.

To display and print a *Balance Sheet Standard* report—
1. Click Reports, and then click Company & Financial.
2. At the Company & Financial submenu, click Balance Sheet Standard.
3. In the *As of* field, choose *02/29/2004* and then click Refresh on the command line. The balance sheet in standard format is displayed.
4. To print the report, click the Print button on the command line.
5. At the Print Reports dialog box, check the settings, then click Print. (See figure 4–16.)

FIGURE 4-16
Balance Sheet Standard Report

EX4 [Your Name] Kristin Raina Interior Designs
Balance Sheet
As of February 29, 2004

Accrual Basis

	Feb 29, 04
ASSETS	
Current Assets	
Checking/Savings	
1010 · Cash - Operating	47,400.00
Total Checking/Savings	47,400.00
Accounts Receivable	
1200 · Accounts Receivable	1,540.00
Total Accounts Receivable	1,540.00
Other Current Assets	
1300 · Design Supplies	200.00
1305 · Office Supplies	250.00
1410 · Prepaid Advertising	500.00
1420 · Prepaid Insurance	2,200.00
Total Other Current Assets	3,150.00
Total Current Assets	52,090.00
Fixed Assets	
1700 · Furniture	
1750 · Accum. Dep., Furniture	-100.00
1700 · Furniture - Other	12,000.00
Total 1700 · Furniture	11,900.00
1800 · Computers	
1850 · Accum. Dep., Computers	-60.00
1800 · Computers - Other	3,600.00
Total 1800 · Computers	3,540.00
Total Fixed Assets	15,440.00
TOTAL ASSETS	67,530.00
LIABILITIES & EQUITY	
Liabilities	
Current Liabilities	
Accounts Payable	
2010 · Accounts Payable	6,250.00
Total Accounts Payable	6,250.00
Other Current Liabilities	
2020 · Notes Payable	7,000.00
2030 · Interest Payable	50.00
Total Other Current Liabilities	7,050.00
Total Current Liabilities	13,300.00
Total Liabilities	13,300.00
Equity	
3010 · Kristin Raina, Capital	50,000.00
3020 · Kristin Raina, Drawings	-400.00
Net Income	4,630.00
Total Equity	54,230.00
TOTAL LIABILITIES & EQUITY	67,530.00

Notice that the amount of accumulated depreciation is deducted from the asset account.
6. Close the report.

REGISTERS

Because QuickBooks Pro is designed for the non-accountant, it includes an alternative method for reviewing daily activity by using *registers*. Registers are available for any balance sheet account, that is, any asset, liability, or equity account. They are not available for income and expense accounts.

The registers format is similar to that of a personal checkbook, but the information displayed in the registers is similar to the information displayed in the general ledger.

To view a register—
1. Click Lists, and then click Chart of Accounts.
2. In the Chart of Accounts window, double-click the *1010 Cash – Operating* account. The 1010 Cash – Operating register appears. (See figure 4–17.)

FIGURE 4-17
Cash – Operating Register

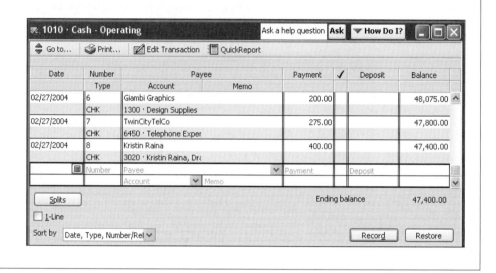

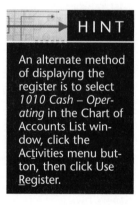

HINT

An alternate method of displaying the register is to select *1010 Cash – Operating* in the Chart of Accounts List window, click the Activities menu button, then click Use Register.

Transactions that were entered in any of the other windows that affected the 1010 Cash – Operating account are also displayed here. Scroll through the transactions and compare them to the 1010 Cash – Operating account in the general ledger (figure 4–12). You can use the register to correct any activity already recorded by drilling down to the source of the activity.

To drill down using the register—
1. At the 1010 Cash – Operating register, choose the *February 23, Cone and Clemens Associates* transaction by double-clicking. The Bill Payments (Check) window appears. (See figure 4–18.)

FIGURE 4-18
Bill Payments (Check)
Window

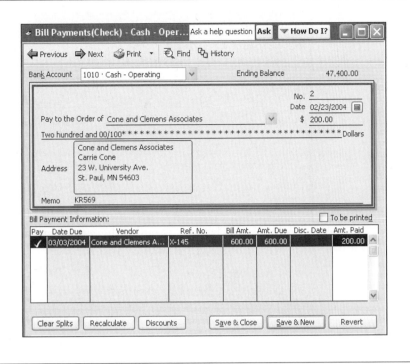

This transaction was originally recorded in the Pay Bills window. Recall that after saving a transaction in the Pay Bills window, it cannot subsequently be edited in that window. However, the Write Checks window will show all payments, both those entered through the Pay Bills window and those entered in the Write Checks window. So even though this transaction was initially recorded in the Pay Bills window, you can drill down to the Bill Payments (Check) window and correct any errors if necessary.

2. Close all the windows.

Registers are only available for balance sheet accounts. For income statement accounts, that is, income and expenses, a register is not available but an *Account QuickReport* is available that displays all of the activity to the account, again similar to the general ledger information.

HINT

An alternative method of drilling down from the register to the activity window is to select the transaction in the register and click on Edit Transaction in the register.

To view an income *Account QuickReport*—
1. Click <u>L</u>ists, and then click Chart of <u>A</u>ccounts.
2. At the Chart of Accounts list window, double-click *4020 Decorating Services*.
3. At the *From* and *To* fields, choose *02/01/2004* and *02/29/2004* and then click Refre<u>s</u>h on the command line. The *Account QuickReport* is displayed, listing all of the activity to this account during the time period chosen. (See figure 4–19.)

FIGURE 4-19
Account QuickReport

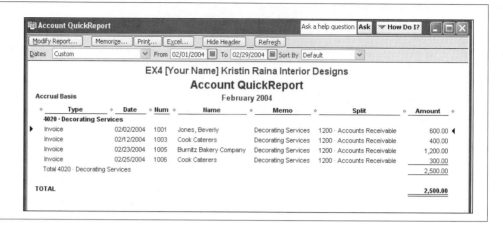

From this report, as with others, you can drill down to the window where the original activity was recorded.

4. Close the report.
5. Close the Chart of Accounts window.

INTERNET
Resources

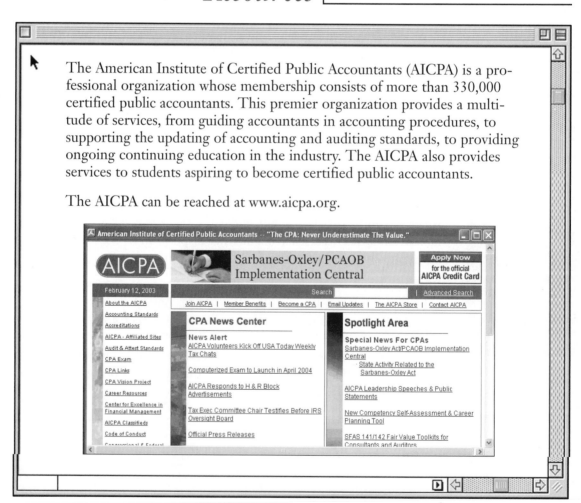

The American Institute of Certified Public Accountants (AICPA) is a professional organization whose membership consists of more than 330,000 certified public accountants. This premier organization provides a multitude of services, from guiding accountants in accounting procedures, to supporting the updating of accounting and auditing standards, to providing ongoing continuing education in the industry. The AICPA also provides services to students aspiring to become certified public accountants.

The AICPA can be reached at www.aicpa.org.

P R O G R E S S
Check

PROCEDURE REVIEW

To add an account—
1. Click <u>L</u>ists, and then click Chart of <u>A</u>ccounts.
2. At the Chart of Accounts window, click the <u>A</u>ccount menu button.
3. At the Account menu, click <u>N</u>ew.
4. Enter the background data for the account.
5. Click OK.
6. Close the Chart of Accounts window.

To delete an account—
1. Click <u>L</u>ists, and then click Chart of <u>A</u>ccounts.
2. At the Chart of Accounts window, select the account you wish to delete.
3. Click the <u>A</u>ccount menu button.
4. At the Account menu, click <u>D</u>elete.
5. Click OK at the warning.
6. Close the Chart of Accounts window.

You cannot delete an account that has a balance or has been used in a transaction during the current period.

To edit an account—
1. Click <u>L</u>ists, and then click Chart of <u>A</u>ccounts.
2. At the Chart of Accounts window, select the account you wish to edit.
3. Click the <u>A</u>ccount menu button.
4. At the Account menu, click <u>E</u>dit.
5. Change the appropriate information.
6. Click OK.
7. Close the Chart of Accounts window.

To record a journal entry—
1. Click <u>C</u>ompany, and then click Make <u>J</u>ournal Entry.
2. Enter the date in the *Date* field.
3. In the *Entry No.* field, key in the original journal entry number, if necessary, thereafter QuickBooks Pro will assign the Entry Nos. in sequence.
4. In the first line of the *Account* field, click once to access the drop-down list of accounts and choose the account to debit.
5. Enter the amount to debit in the *Debit* field.
6. Move to the second line in the *Account* field, and from the drop-down list of accounts, choose the account to credit.
7. Enter the amount to credit in the *Credit* field, if necessary.
8. In the *Memo* field, key in a brief explanation (optional).
9. Click S<u>a</u>ve & Close.

To view and print accounting reports from the <u>R</u>eports menu—
1. Click <u>R</u>eports, and then click <u>A</u>ccountant & Taxes.
2. At the Accountant & Taxes submenu, choose a report.
3. Indicate the appropriate dates for the report.
4. Click Prin<u>t</u> on the command line.
5. At the Print Reports dialog box, review the settings, then click Print.
6. Close the report.

To view and print financial reports from the <u>R</u>eports menu—
1. Click <u>R</u>eports, and then click Company & <u>F</u>inancial.
2. At the Company & Financial submenu, choose a financial report.
3. Indicate the appropriate dates for the report.
4. Click Prin<u>t</u> on the command line.
5. At the Print Reports dialog box, review the settings, then click Print.
6. Close the report.

To view and print a register or *Account QuickReport* from the <u>L</u>ists menu—
1. Click <u>L</u>ists, and then click Chart of <u>A</u>ccounts.
2. Double-click the account for which you want the register or *Account QuickReport*.
3. For the *Account QuickReport* indicate the date.
4. Click Prin<u>t</u> on the command line.
5. At the Print Reports dialog box, review the settings, then click Print.
6. Close the report.

KEY CONCEPTS

Select the letter of the item that best matches each definition.

a. General Journal Entry window   f. Registers
b. Filters   g. <u>H</u>eader/Footer
c. *Profit & Loss* report   h. *Trial Balance* report
d. *General Ledger* report   i. Adjusting journal entries
e. Chart of Accounts   j. Balance Sheet

_____ 1. Recorded periodically so financial statements can be prepared according to accounting rules.
_____ 2. The report that shows assets, liabilities, and equity balances at a specified date.
_____ 3. The list of accounts a company uses in business.
_____ 4. The tab in the Modify Report dialog box that is used to identify fields of information to be displayed in a report.
_____ 5. The report that lists the activity increases, decreases, and balances for each account.
_____ 6. Similar to a manual accounting system and allows for the recording of a debit entry, a credit entry, and an explanation.
_____ 7. The report that displays the revenue and expenses for a specified period of time.
_____ 8. The tab in the Modify Report dialog box that is used to change the heading on a report.

_____ 9. The format is similar to that of a checkbook and can be used to view the activities for any balance sheet account.

_____ 10. A report that displays all accounts and their debit or credit balance.

PROCEDURE CHECK

1. The manager has requested a list of all accounts the company uses. Which is the best report to print to provide this information and how would you obtain it?
2. The manager wants to know the balance in each of a business's accounts. Which is the best report to print to provide this information and how would you obtain it?
3. Explain why there aren't any default accounts in the General Journal Entry window.
4. Which report provides the information on the revenue and expenses of a company and how would you obtain the report? If you wanted to change the title of this report to Income Statement, how would you do it?
5. Which report provides the information on the assets, liabilities, and equity of the company and how would you obtain the report?
6. Explain the purpose of adjusting journal entries. Compare and contrast recording adjusting journal entries in a manual accounting system and QuickBooks Pro.

CASE PROBLEMS

CASE PROBLEM 1

On April 1, 2004, Lynn Garcia began her business, called Lynn's Music Studio. All of the daily activities for the month of April, including entering and paying bills, writing checks, recording of sales, both cash and on account, collection of receivables, and depositing receipts, have been recorded. It is the end of the first month of business and adjusting journal entries need to be recorded and the financial statements need to be printed. You will record the adjusting journal entries for April 30 using the information provided below. The company file includes the beginning information for Lynn's Music Studio along with the transactions recorded in chapters 2 and 3.

1. Open the company file CH4 Lynn's Music Studio.QBW.
2. Make a backup copy of the company file LMS4 [Your Name] Lynn's Music Studio.
3. Restore the backup copy of the company file. In both the Restore From and Restore To windows use the file name LMS4 [Your Name] Lynn's Music Studio.
4. Change the company name to LMS4 [Your Name] Lynn's Music Studio.
5. Add the following accounts to the Chart of Accounts List:

Type:	**Expense**
Number:	**6300**
Name:	**Music Supplies Expense**

Type:	**Expense**
Number:	**6325**
Name:	**Office Supplies Expense**

Delete the following account:
Advertising Expense

6. Display and print the *Trial Balance* Report prior to preparing the adjusting journal entries. (April 1, 2004 – April 30, 2004)
7. Use the information below to prepare adjusting journal entries. Record each adjusting journal entry separately and use April 30, 2004, for the date.
   a. The prepaid insurance represents a one-year policy. Record insurance expense for one month. Refer to the trial balance to determine the amount in the Prepaid Insurance account. For the Entry No., use AJE1.
   b. Monthly depreciation on the assets: $60 for the Music Instruments, $40 for the Furniture, and $35 for the Computer. Record each depreciation expense as a separate adjusting journal entry.
   c. The music supplies on hand total $430. Compare to the amount in the Music Supplies account to determine how much of the music supplies has been used and record the music supplies expense.
   d. The office supplies on hand total $300. Compare to the amount in the Office Supplies account to determine how much of the office supplies has been used and record the office supplies expense.
   e. The interest on the note payable for one month is $15. Record the interest expense. Add to the Chart of Accounts List, the Interest Payable account, Other Current Liability, number 2030.
8. Display and print the following reports for April 30, 2004:
   a. *Journal* report for only the adjusting journal entries. (April 30, 2004 – April 30, 2004)
   b. *Adjusted Trial Balance*. Change the name in the header of the report. (April 1, 2004 – April 30, 2004)
   c. *Profit & Loss Standard* (April 1, 2004 – April 30, 2004)
   d. *Balance Sheet Standard* (April 30, 2004)

CASE PROBLEM 2

On June 1, 2004, Olivia Chen began her business, which she named Olivia's Web Solutions. All of the daily activities for the month of June, including entering and paying bills, writing checks, recording sales, both cash and on account, collection of receivables, and depositing receipts, have been recorded. It is the end of the first month of business and adjusting journal entries need to be recorded and the financial statements need to be printed. You will record the adjusting journal entries for June 30 using the information provided below. The company file includes the beginning information for Olivia's Web Solutions along with the transactions recorded in chapters 2 and 3.

1. Open the company file CH4 Olivia's Web Solutions.QBW.
2. Make a backup copy of the company file OWS4 [Your Name] Olivia's Web Solutions.

3. Restore the backup copy of the company file. In both the Restore From and Restore To windows use the file name OWS4 [Your Name] Olivia's Web Solutions.

4. Change the company name to OWS4 [Your Name] Olivia's Web Solutions.

5. Add the following accounts to the Chart of Accounts List:

Type:	**Expense**
Number:	**6300**
Name:	**Computer Supplies Expense**

Type:	**Expense**
Number:	**6325**
Name:	**Office Supplies Expense**

Delete the following account:
Repair Expense

6. Display and print the *Trial Balance* report prior to preparing the adjusting journal entries. (June 1, 2004 – June 30, 2004)

7. Use the information below to prepare adjusting journal entries. Record each adjusting journal entry separately and use June 30, 2004, for the date.
   a. The prepaid insurance represents a one-year policy. Record insurance expense for one month. Refer to the trial balance to determine the amount in the Prepaid Insurance account. For the Entry No., use AJE1.
   b. The prepaid advertising represents a six-month contract. Record the advertising expense for one month.
   c. Monthly depreciation on the assets: $75 for the Computer, $50 for the Furniture, and $100 for the Software. Record each depreciation expense as a separate adjusting journal entry.
   d. The computer supplies on hand total $350. Compare to the amount in the Computer Supplies account to determine how much of the computer supplies has been used and record the computer supplies expense.
   e. The office supplies on hand total $325. Compare to the amount in the Office Supplies account to determine how much of the office supplies has been used and record the office supplies expense.
   f. The interest on the note payable for one month is $25. Record the interest expense. Add to the Chart of Accounts List the Interest Payable account, Other Current Liability, number 2030.

8. Display and print the following reports for June 30, 2004:
   a. *Journal* report for only the adjusting journal entries. (June 30, 2004 – June 30, 2004)
   b. *Adjusted Trial Balance.* Change the name in the header of the report. (June 1, 2004 – June 30, 2004)
   c. *Profit & Loss Standard* (June 1, 2004 – June 30, 2004)
   d. *Balance Sheet Standard* (June 30, 2004)

CHAPTER

5

INVENTORY

Receive Items, Sell Items, Process Sales Discounts, Adjust Quantity/ Value on Hand, and Pay Sales Tax

CHAPTER OBJECTIVES

- Identify the two inventory systems

- Update the Items List

- Record purchases of inventory items in the Enter Bills and Write Checks windows

- Identify transactions requiring sales tax

- Process sales discounts

- Record adjustments to inventory items in the Adjust Quantity/Value on Hand window

- Record payment of sales tax in the Pay Sales Tax window

- Display and print inventory-related reports

INTRODUCTION

inventory Merchandise that is sold to customers for a profit.

QuickBooks Pro allows you to track inventory transactions. Inventory is ready-made merchandise that is sold to customers for a profit. Before you can enter inventory transactions, you must establish a file for each inventory item. Inventory item files are included in the *Item List* (Lists).

Once you establish an inventory item file, transactions for the item (Activities) can be entered in the Enter Bills, Write Checks, Create Invoices, Enter Sales Receipts, and *Adjust Quantity/Value on Hand* activity windows in much the same manner as was done in prior chapters. Every time the company receives merchandise for resale, sells merchandise, or adjusts the inventory because of loss or damage, QuickBooks Pro will record that information in the Item List. This allows you to accurately determine inventory quantity, value, and profit on sales. In addition, QuickBooks Pro will automatically change balance sheet and income statement accounts based on the inventory information on the Item List (Reports).

In this chapter, our sample company, Kristin Raina Interior Designs, begins to purchase and sell decorative accessories to clients in addition to providing design and decorating services. This means that Kristin Raina must now be concerned with keeping an inventory.

QUICKBOOKS PRO VERSUS MANUAL ACCOUNTING: INVENTORY TRANSACTIONS

As discussed in previous chapters, in a manual accounting system, purchases on account are recorded in a purchases journal, while sales on account are recorded in a sales journal. This is true whether the purchase or sale is for services or for merchandise. Cash transactions are recorded in the cash receipts or cash payments journals, again for both inventory and non-inventory items.

In QuickBooks Pro, the Item List serves as an inventory subsidiary ledger for the company. The List includes all items the company sells, both inventory and service items. Relevant information for each inventory item, such as name/number, type, description, cost, sales price, and related general ledger accounts, is entered at the time the item file is created and updated as necessary.

When the company purchases an inventory item from a vendor on account, the transaction is recorded in the Enter Bills activity window in much the same manner as non-inventory purchases were recorded. When the inventory items are sold on account, the invoice will be recorded in the Create Invoices activity window in a manner similar to that done for other revenues. When you enter these transactions, QuickBooks Pro updates the Chart of Accounts List (general ledger) and at the same time updates each vendor and customer file. In addition, it updates the Item List to reflect the purchase and sale of the inventory items. Cash purchases of inventory items are recorded in the Write Checks activity window, while cash sales of inventory are recorded in the Enter Sales Receipts activity window. Changes in inventory not due to a sale or purchase are recorded in the Adjust Quantity/Value on Hand window. In all instances where inventory items are purchased, sold, or adjusted, the Item List is updated to reflect the new inventory quantity and value.

ACCOUNTING FOR INVENTORY TRANSACTIONS

There are two types of inventory systems: periodic and perpetual. Under the periodic inventory system, separate records are *not* maintained for inventory items and no attempt is made to adjust the inventory account for purchases and sales. Instead, inventory is counted periodically to determine inventory quantity, value, cost of goods sold, and gross profit. The periodic system is often used by businesses that sell high-volume, low-cost goods, for which keeping individual inventory records is not practical.

Under the perpetual inventory system, accounting records are maintained that continuously show the current inventory quantity and value. When inventory is purchased, the inventory (asset) account is increased. When inventory is sold, the inventory account is reduced. In addition, the cost of goods sold is simultaneously computed in order to arrive at gross profit. Prior to the availability of low-cost computer hardware and software, only businesses with low-volume, high-cost goods used the perpetual system.

QuickBooks Pro, like almost all general ledger accounting software programs, utilizes the perpetual system because it allows the user to know the current inventory quantity and value at any given moment and also calculates the cost of goods sold and gross profit after each sale without the need for a periodic physical inventory count.

periodic inventory system Values the inventory periodically based on a physical count of the merchandise; usually done once a year.

perpetual inventory system Values the inventory after every purchase and sale of inventory items.

CHAPTER PROBLEM

In this chapter, you will track inventory transactions for Kristin Raina Interior Designs, which has decided to begin selling decorative inventory items in addition to providing decorating and design services. Information for inventory items has been entered in the Item List. This information along with the March 1, 2004, beginning balances is contained in the company file CH5 Kristin Raina Interior Designs.

Begin by opening the company file—
1. Open QuickBooks Pro.
2. At the *No Company Open* window, click on the Open an existing company button or click File, and then click Open Company.
3. At the Open a Company dialog box in the Look in text box, choose the *QuickBooks Pro* subfolder, or the subfolder containing the company files.
4. Select the company, *CH5 Kristin Raina Interior Designs.QBW* and click Open.
5. If the Company Navigator window appears, click the X to close it.

Next, make a backup copy of the company file—
1. Click File, then click Back Up.
2. In the QuickBooks Backup dialog box, the Disk option should be selected.
3. In the Filename text box, key **EX5 [Your Name] Kristin Raina Interior Designs**.
4. Next to the Location text box, click the Browse button.
5. At the Back Up Company to dialog box, in the Save in text box, choose your subfolder, a network directory designated by your instructor, or a floppy drive.
6. Click Save.
7. In the QuickBooks Backup dialog box, click OK.
8. At the *Your data has been backed up successfully* message, click OK.

Now restore the backup copy of the company file—

1. Click File, and then click Restore.
2. At the Restore Company Backup dialog box, in the Get Company Backup From section, the Disk option should be selected.
3. Click the Browse button.
4. At the Restore From dialog box, in the Look in text box, choose the location where you saved your backup copy.
5. Select the company file *EX5 [Your Name] Kristin Raina Interior Designs Company.QBB* and click Open.
6. At the Restore Company Backup dialog box, in the Restore Company Backup To section, click the Browse button.
7. At the Restore To dialog box, in the Save in text box, choose the sub-folder where you will be opening and working on your copies of the company files.
8. In the File name text box, key **EX5 [Your Name] Kristin Raina Interior Designs** and click Save.
9. In the Restore Company Backup dialog box, click Restore.
10. At the *Your data has been restored successfully* message, click OK.
11. If the Company Navigator window appears, click the X to close it.

The backup copy has been restored, but the company name still reads CH5 Kristin Raina Interior Designs.

Change the company name—

1. Click Company, and then click Company Information.
2. Change the company name to **EX5 [Your Name] Kristin Raina Interior Designs**.
3. Click OK.

LISTS: THE ITEM LIST

Recall from chapter 1 that the second level of operation in QuickBooks Pro is to record background information on Lists. The Item List contains a file for each type of service or inventory item sold by the company. If the item sold is an inventory product, QuickBooks Pro calls this an *inventory part* as opposed to a service item. You should enter the information for each inventory item in the Item List prior to recording transactions. This will make the Activities function run more smoothly. However, if you inadvertently omit an item, you can add that item during the Activities level of operation with a minimum of disruption.

The Item List contains important information on each product, such as type of item; number; descriptions; cost; general ledger posting accounts for inventory asset; cost of goods sold; sales; preferred vendor; and sales tax status. All products or services sold by the company should be included in the Item List. Periodically, these files will need to be updated as products are added, discontinued, or background information changes.

Kristin Raina has entered information for various inventory items in the Item List.

To review the Item List—

1. Click Reports, and then click List.
2. At the List submenu, click Item Listing. The *Item Listing* report appears. (See figure 5–1.)

FIGURE 5-1
Item Listing

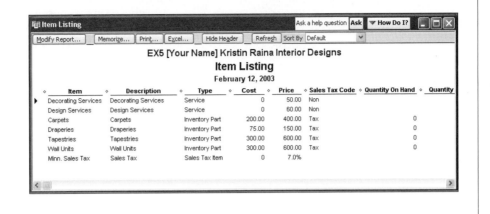

To view a specific inventory item file—
1. Place the mouse over the item name *Carpets*, and double-click. The inventory item file will appear in Edit Item mode. (See figure 5–2.)

FIGURE 5-2
Edit Item Window

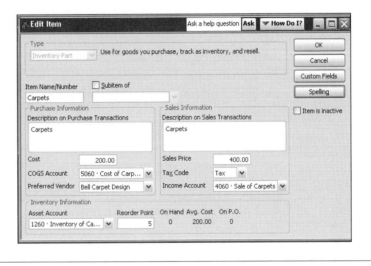

Note the following fields in this window:

TYPE	If this is an inventory item, select *Inventory Part*. Other selections include *Service* for service revenue items, *Non-inventory Part* for products sold that are not maintained in inventory, and *Other Charge*.
ITEM NAME/NUMBER	Used to assign an identifying name or number to each item.
SUBITEM OF	Used if item is a component of another item, such as in a construction or manufacturing company.

DESCRIPTION ON PURCHASE TRANSACTIONS/ DESCRIPTION ON SALES TRANSACTIONS	Used to enter a description of the item for purchase or sales activity windows.
COST	Used to enter the typical unit cost for the item. This amount will appear in the purchase activity window as the default cost amount. Can override as needed.
COGS ACCOUNT	Lists the default general ledger posting account for cost of goods sold when the item is sold. Can override this account as needed.
SALES PRICE	This is the default unit-selling price that will appear in sales activity windows. Can override this entry as needed.
TAX CODE	Used to indicate if the item is taxable or non-taxable for sales tax purposes
INCOME ACCOUNT	This is the default general ledger posting account for revenue when the item is sold. Can override this account as needed.
ASSET ACCOUNT	This is the default general ledger posting account for the inventory balance sheet account when items are purchased. Can override this entry as needed.

2. Close the Edit Item window.
3. Close the *Item Listing* report.

The Item List needs to be revised periodically when new inventory items need to be added, inventory items not used in the business need to be deleted, or when modifications need to be made as a result of inventory items changes. These adjustments to the inventory item files are referred to as updating the Item List.

FIGURE 5-3
Item Menu

ADDING AN ITEM
The company has decided to sell a line of modern lamps to its clients and needs to add this inventory item to the Item List.

To add an item—
1. Click Lists, and then click Item List.
2. At the Item List window, click the Item menu button. The Item menu appears. (See figure 5–3.)
3. At the Item menu, click New. The New Item window appears. (See figure 5–4.)

FIGURE 5-4
New Item Window

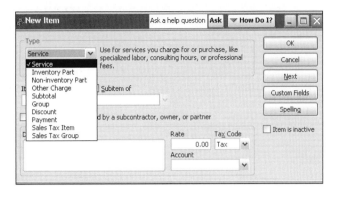

4. At the Type drop-down list, click *Inventory Part*.
5. Complete the balance of the window with the information provided below.

Item Name/Number:	**Lamps**
Description on Purchase/Sales Transactions:	**Lamps**
Cost:	**100**
COGS Account:	**5070 Cost of Lamps Sold**
Preferred Vendor:	**Lumiare Lighting Company**
Sales Price:	**200**
*Ta*x *Code:*	**Tax – Taxable Sale**
Income Account:	**4070 Sale of Lamps**
Asset Account:	**1270 Inventory of Lamps**
Reorder Point:	**5**

Your screen should look like figure 5–5.

FIGURE 5-5
New Item Window –
Complete

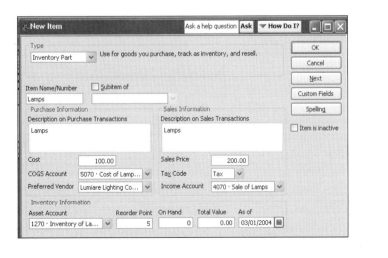

6. If the information is correct, click OK.
7. Close the Item List window.

DELETING AN ITEM

Kristin Raina wishes to delete Tapestries from the Item List because the company has decided not to sell this product.

To delete an item—
1. Click Lists, and then click Item List.
2. At the Item List, select *Tapestries* but do not open the file. (See figure 5–6.)

FIGURE 5-6
Item List – Tapestries Selected

HINT

If you delete the wrong item, click Edit and then Undo Delete Item immediately after deleting the item. If you do not do this immediately, you will not be able to undo the deletion.

3. Click the Item menu button. At the Item menu, click Delete.
4. A warning screen will appear. Click OK. The Item file will be deleted.
5. Close the Item List window.

You cannot delete an item with a balance or an item that has been part of a transaction for the period.

EDITING AN ITEM

Kristin Raina needs to edit the file for Draperies because the unit cost has increased to $125 and the sales price to $250.

To edit an item file—
1. Click Lists, and then click Item List.
2. Double-click the *Draperies* Item file. This will open the file in Edit mode. (See figure 5–7.)

FIGURE 5-7
Edit Item Window – Draperies

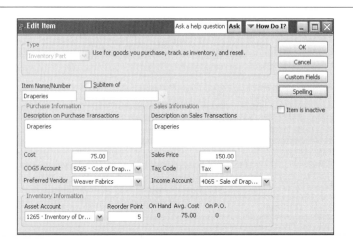

3. At the *Cost* and *Sales Price* fields delete the current information and enter the new amounts shown in figure 5–8.

FIGURE 5-8
Edit Item Window –
Draperies – Updated

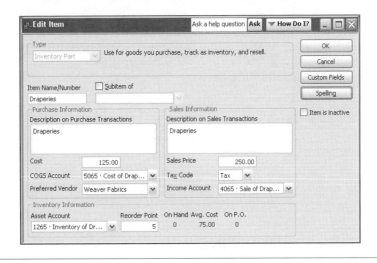

4. If the information is correct, click OK and close the Item List window.

PRACTICE *exercise*

Add the following item:

Type:	**Inventory Part**
Item Name/Number:	**Mirrors**
Description on Purchase/Sales Transactions:	**Decorative Mirror**
Cost:	**150**
COGS Account:	**5075 Cost of Mirrors Sold**
Preferred Vendor:	**Ace Glass Works**
Sales Price:	**300**
Tax Code:	**Tax – Taxable Sale**
Income Account:	**4075 Sale of Mirrors**
Asset Account:	**1275 Inventory of Mirrors**
Reorder Point:	**5**

Delete the following item:
Wall Units

QuickCheck: The updated Item List appears in figure 5–9.

FIGURE 5-9
Updated Item List

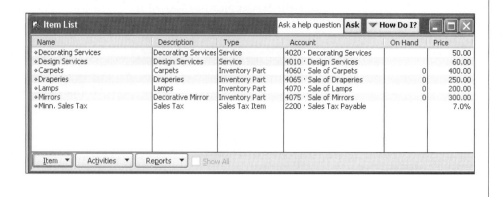

ACTIVITIES: PURCHASING INVENTORY

Recall from chapter 1 that the third level of operation in QuickBooks Pro is Activities, during which you record the daily business activities. Activities identified as purchases of inventory items on account are recorded in the Enter Bills window. Activities identified as purchases of inventory items for cash are recorded in the Write Checks window.

RECORDING INVENTORY PURCHASES USING THE ENTER BILLS WINDOW

In chapter 2, you used the Enter Bills activity window when goods and services were purchased on account from a vendor. There are two tabs in the Enter Bills window: Expenses and Items. When you chose Enter Bills from the Vendors pull-down menu, the Enter Bills window opens with the Expenses tab as the active tab. When a company wishes to use the inventory feature, the Vendors pull-down menu offers an additional choice of Receive Items and Enter Bill. When you click Receive Items and Enter Bill, the Enter Bills window is opened, but the Items tab is the active tab. In the Enter Bills window, the Items tab is similar to the Expenses tab but provides for additional fields that relate to inventory. In addition, you will find buttons that can be used when purchase orders are utilized in the purchase of inventory.

In some instances, items will be received before the vendor forwards a bill. If this occurs, a different procedure is employed to record the transactions. However, for this chapter, it is assumed that a bill from the vendor accompanies the receipt of the inventory item and that you will record the transaction in the Enter Bills window – Items tab by clicking Vendor and then Receive Items and Enter Bill. (See figure 5–10.)

FIGURE 5-10
*Enter Bills Window
with Items Tab*

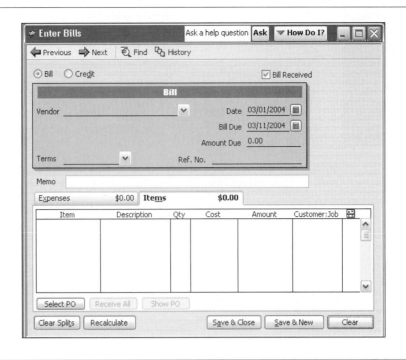

The Enter Bills window-Items tab contains the following new fields:

ITEM	Click the inventory item purchased from the drop-down list. Once an item is chosen the *Description* and unit *Cost* fields will automatically be filled based on information in the Item file.
QTY	Enter the quantity purchased. QuickBooks Pro multiplies the quantity purchased by the unit cost to arrive at the Amount and Amount Due figures.

Notice that a field for the general ledger accounts is not displayed. Recall that when you entered items in the Item List, the general ledger accounts for the purchase (inventory asset account) and sale (income account and COGS account) of inventory items were indicated. QuickBooks Pro uses the information in the Item List and the information entered in the Enter Bills window to adjust the correct accounts automatically.

The Enter Bills window - Items tab is designed for purchases of inventory items on account. The default accounts are the Inventory asset account and the Accounts Payable account. QuickBooks Pro uses the information on the Item List to correctly record the amount and account for the inventory asset. The transaction is recorded as follows:

		Inventory		XXX		
		Accounts Payable			XXX	

HINT

If you click Enter Bills instead of Receive Items and Enter Bill, simply click the Items tab in the Enter Bills window.

RECORDING A PURCHASE AND RECEIPT OF AN INVENTORY ITEM ON ACCOUNT

On March 1, 2004, Kristin Raina purchases and receives 10 mirrors from Ace Glass Works at a cost of $150 each, their Invoice No. K-588. The bill is due March 31, 2004, terms Net 30 Days.

To record a purchase and receipt of inventory items on account—

1. Click Vendors, and then click Receive Items and Enter Bill.
2. At the Vendor drop-down list, click *Ace Glass Works*.
3. Complete the *Date*, *Bill Due*, *Ref. No.*, and *Terms* fields in the same way as you would for non-inventory purchases. Make sure the Items tab is the active tab. (See figure 5–11.)

FIGURE 5-11
Enter Bills Window –
Partially Complete

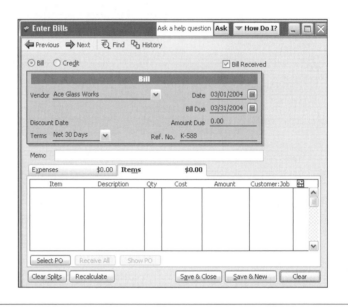

4. At the Item drop-down list, click *Mirrors*. The *Description* and *Cost* fields will fill automatically.
5. At the *Qty* field, key **10** and move to the next field. The *Amount* and *Amount Due* fields will be completed automatically. (See figure 5–12.)

FIGURE 5-12
Enter Bills Window –
Completed

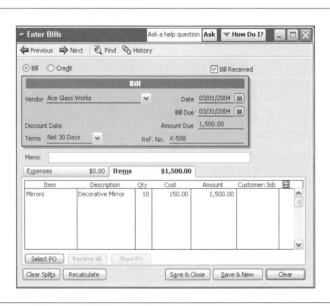

6. If all data is correct, click S<u>a</u>ve & Close.

ACCOUNTING
concept

For a purchase of inventory on account, the general ledger posting is as follows:

1275 Mirror Inventory		2010 Accts Payable	
Dr	Cr	Dr	Cr
1,500			1,500

In addition, the Vendor File (sub-ledger) for Ace Glass Works will reflect the new liability.

Ace Glass Works	
Dr	Cr
	1,500

In addition to the general ledger and vendor file changes, this transaction will update the item file for Mirrors to reflect a quantity of 10 on hand with an inventory value of $1,500.

RECORDING INVENTORY PURCHASES USING THE WRITE CHECKS WINDOW

Like the Enter Bills window, the Write Checks window has an E<u>x</u>penses tab and an Ite<u>m</u>s tab. For purchase of inventory items for cash, you switch to the Ite<u>m</u>s tab after opening the Write Checks window. The fields to enter information for inventory items in the Write Checks window Ite<u>m</u>s tab are similar to those in the Enter Bills window - Ite<u>m</u>s tab.

The Write Checks window - Ite<u>m</u>s tab is designed for purchases of inventory items for cash. The default accounts are the Inventory asset account and the Cash account. QuickBooks Pro uses the information on the Item List to correctly record the amount and account for the inventory asset. The transaction is recorded as follows:

		Inventory	XXX	
		Cash		XXX

RECORDING A PURCHASE AND RECEIPT OF AN INVENTORY ITEM FOR CASH

On March 2, 2004, Kristin Raina purchases and receives 16 lamps from Lumiare Lighting Company at a cost of $100 each, their Invoice No. 6844. Paid with Check No. 9.

1. Click <u>B</u>anking, and then click <u>W</u>rite Checks.
2. At the Write Checks window make sure Ban<u>k</u> Account *1010 Cash– Operating* is displayed, the check No. is *9*, and the To be printe<u>d</u> box is not checked.
3. At the *Date* field, choose *03/02/2004*.
4. At the Pay to the Order drop-down list, click *Lumiare Lighting Company*.
5. Click the Ite<u>m</u>s tab.
6. At the Items drop-down list, click *Lamps*.
7. At the *Qty* field, key **16** and move to the next field. QuickBooks Pro will complete the *Amount* fields. (See figure 5–13.)
8. Click S<u>a</u>ve & Close.

FIGURE 5-13
Write Checks Window –
Completed

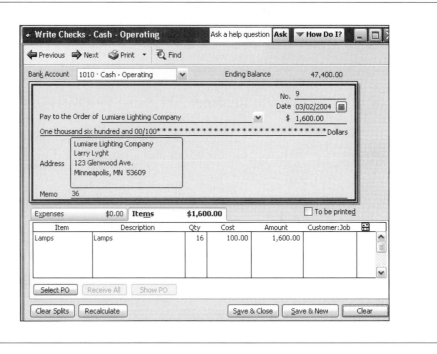

ACCOUNTING
c o n c e p t

For a cash payment for the purchase of inventory the general ledger posting will be as follows:

1270 Lamps Inventory		1010 Cash – Operating	
Dr	Cr	Dr	Cr
1,600			1,600

In addition, the item file for Lamps will be updated to reflect the new purchase.

P R A C T I C E *e x e r c i s e*

Record the following transactions in the Enter Bills or Write Checks window:

MAR. 5   Purchased and received 10 carpets from Bell Carpet Design at a cost of $200 each, their Invoice No. 12-5585. The bill is due April 4, 2004. *QuickCheck:* $2000

MAR. 12   Purchased and received 12 sets of draperies from Weaver Fabrics at a cost of $125 each. Pay immediately with Check No. 10. *QuickCheck:* $1500

SALES TAX

sales tax An amount charged on the sale of merchandise, usually a percentage of the sales price. It is collected by the company as part of the sale and later remitted to the appropriate government agency.

When a company sells a product to a customer, it will usually be required to collect sales tax on the sale. The sales tax amount charged is added to the invoice price of the product. For example, a customer purchases an item with a retail price of $1,000 and the applicable sales tax rate is 6%. The retailer will add $60 to the invoice and collect $1,060 from the customer. At a later date, the retailer will remit the tax collected from customers to the appropriate state sales tax collection agency. Rules for applying and collecting sales tax are complex and beyond the scope of this text. However, QuickBooks Pro, like most general ledger software programs, is equipped to track sales-taxable transactions and to facilitate the collection and payment of taxes due.

In this chapter, Kristin Raina Interior Designs will be selling decorative accessories to her customers. All sales of these products are subject to a sales tax charge of 7%, which is added to the invoice total. The tax will be payable to the Minnesota Department of Revenue at the end of each month. Sales tax will not be collected on services (decorating and design) in this text because services generally are not subject to sales tax. Note, however, that in some communities services also are subject to sales tax.

As you know from chapter 3, a sale on account is recorded in the Create Invoices window and a sale for cash is recorded in the Enter Sales Receipts window. The default account in the Create Invoices window is a debit to Accounts Receivable, and the default account in the Enter Sales Receipts window is a debit to Cash. When sales tax is charged on the sale of an item, a default Sales Tax Payable account is credited in both the Create Invoices and Enter Sales Receipts windows. The sale of taxable products for either cash or on account results in the following general ledger posting:

		Accounts Receivable/Cash	XXX	
		Sales		XXX
		Sales Tax Payable		XXX

ACTIVITIES: SALE OF INVENTORY

Activities identified as sales of inventory items on account are recorded in the Create Invoices window. Activities identified as sales of inventory items for cash are recorded in the Enter Sales Receipts window. Activities recorded in these windows are similar to those in chapter 3, but additional fields in the window are used that relate to inventory.

INVENTORY SALES ON ACCOUNT IN THE CREATE INVOICES WINDOW
When you record the sale of inventory items in the Create Invoices window, you use a template to access the additional fields needed for inventory items. In chapter 3, for the sale of services, you used the Intuit Service Invoice Template. For the sale of inventory items on account, you use the Intuit Product Invoice Template.

The Create Invoices window - Intuit Product Invoice is designed for the sale of inventory items on account. The default accounts are Accounts Receivable, Cost of Goods Sold, Inventory, Sales Tax Payable, and Sales. QuickBooks Pro uses the inventory Item List to determine the correct amount and account for the Cost of Goods Sold, Inventory, and Sales accounts. If an item is marked as taxable, QuickBooks Pro uses the Item List to determine the correct amount of sales tax to be recorded in the Sales Tax Payable account. The transaction is recorded as follows:

		Accounts Receivable	XXX			
		Cost of Goods Sold	XXX			
		Inventory			XXX	
		Sales Tax Payable			XXX	
		Sales			XXX	

RECORDING A SALE OF AN INVENTORY ITEM ON ACCOUNT

On March 15, 2004, Kristin Raina sells the following items to Jennie Guthrie on account, Invoice No. 1008. Terms 2/10, Net 30 Days:

2 lamps	$ 400.00
3 carpets	1,200.00
1 mirror	300.00
total sale of merchandise	$ 1,900.00
sales tax (0.07 x $1,900)	133.00
decorating services (8 hours)	400.00
total sale on account	$ 2,433.00

To record a sale of inventory on account—

1. Click Customers, and then click Create Invoices.
2. At the Customer:Job drop-down list, click *Guthrie, Jennie*.
3. At the Template drop-down list, click *Intuit Product Invoice*. Additional fields for inventory item information appear.
4. Enter the information listed above for the *Date* and *Invoice #* fields.
5. At the Terms drop-down list, click *2/10, Net 30 Days*.
6. At the *Quantity* field, key **2**.
7. Click the *Item Code* field and, at the Item Code drop-down list, click *Lamps*. QuickBooks Pro will automatically fill the *Description*, *Price Each*, *Amount*, and *Tax* fields. (See figure 5–14.)

FIGURE 5-14
Create Invoices Window – Partially Complete

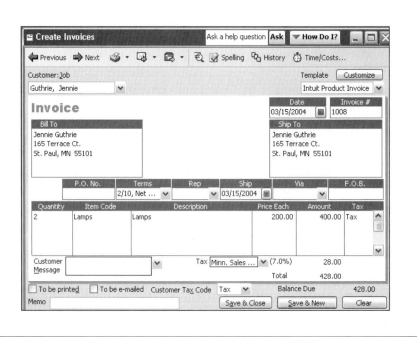

Note that the word *Tax* should appear in the Tax field for taxable items and *Non* should appear for the non-taxable service item. If the correct coding for tax does not appear, use the drop-down list in the field to indicate the correct tax code.

8. Move to the second line of the *Quantity* field and key **3**.
9. At the Item Code drop-down list, click *Carpets*. QuickBooks Pro will fill the *Description, Price Each, Amount,* and *Tax* fields.
10. Move to the third line of the *Quantity* field and key **1**.
11. At the Item Code drop-down list, click *Mirrors*. QuickBooks Pro will fill the remaining fields.
12. Move to the fourth line of the *Quantity* field and key **8**.
13. At the Item Code drop-down list, click *Decorating Services*. QuickBooks Pro will fill the remaining fields. Note that the tax field indicates Non because Decorating Services are not subject to sales tax.
14. Click the arrow at the Tax drop-down list and click *Minn. Sales Tax,* if necessary. (See figure 5–15.)

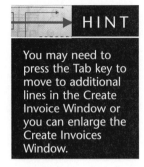

HINT

You may need to press the Tab key to move to additional lines in the Create Invoice Window or you can enlarge the Create Invoices Window.

FIGURE 5-15
Create Invoices
Window – Completed

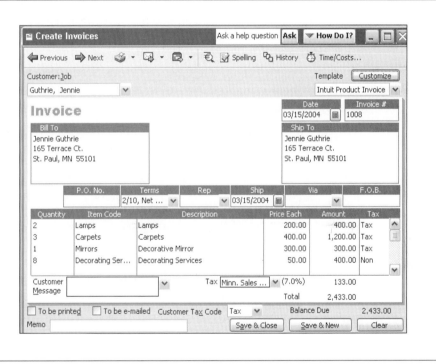

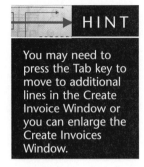

HINT

If you miss an item, click Edit and then Insert Line. If you wish to erase a line, click Edit and then Delete Line.

15. If the information is correct, click Save & Close.

For a sale of inventory products on account, the general ledger posting is as follows:

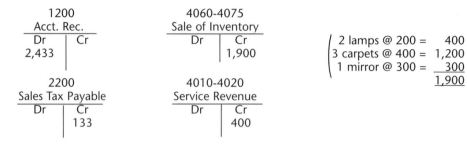

1200 Acct. Rec.			4060-4075 Sale of Inventory	
Dr	Cr		Dr	Cr
2,433				1,900

2200 Sales Tax Payable			4010-4020 Service Revenue	
Dr	Cr		Dr	Cr
	133			400

2 lamps @ 200 = 400
3 carpets @ 400 = 1,200
1 mirror @ 300 = 300
1,900

The cost of the inventory sold and resulting decline in the inventory is recorded as follows:

5060-5075 Cost of Goods Sold			1260-1275 Inventory	
Dr	Cr		Dr	Cr
950				950

2 lamps @ 100 = 200
3 carpets @ 200 = 600
1 mirror @ 150 = 150
950

INVENTORY SALES FOR CASH IN THE ENTER SALES RECEIPTS WINDOW

The Enter Sales Receipts window is designed for cash received for both the sale of services and the sale of inventory items for cash. Once an inventory item is chosen, QuickBooks Pro uses the information from the Item List to correctly record the Cost of Goods Sold, Inventory, and Sales accounts. If an item is marked as taxable, QuickBooks Pro uses the Item List to determine the correct amount of sales tax to be recorded in the Sales Tax Payable account. The transaction is recorded as follows:

	Cash		XXX	
	Cost of Goods Sold		XXX	
	Inventory			XXX
	Sales Tax Payable			XXX
	Sales			XXX

RECORDING A SALE OF AN INVENTORY ITEM FOR CASH

On March 22, 2004, Kristin Raina sells the following items to Beverly Jones, Invoice No. 1009, receiving payment immediately. Her Check No. 5477.

1 carpet	$ 400.00
2 draperies	500.00
total sale of merchandise	$ 900.00
sales tax (0.07 x $900)	63.00
decorating services (4 hrs)	200.00
Total sale for cash	$ 1,163.00

To record a sale of inventory for Cash—

1. Click C<u>u</u>stomers, and then click Enter <u>S</u>ales Receipts.
2. At the Customer:Job drop-down list, click *Jones, Beverly.*

3. Choose the appropriate date and key **1009** in the *Sale No.* field.
4. At the Payment method drop-down list, click *Check* and key **5477** in the *Check No.* field. The To be printe_d box should not be checked. The Group with other undeposited funds option should be selected, as should Tax from the Customer Ta_x Code drop down list.
5. Complete the balance of the window for each item in the same manner as you would in the Create Invoices window. (See figure 5–16.)

FIGURE 5-16
Enter Cash Sales
Window – Complete

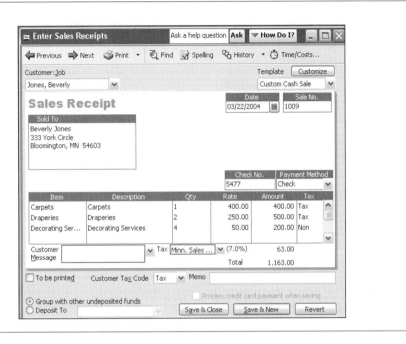

6. If all information is correct, click S_ave & Close.

HINT

If you miss an item, click _Insert Line from the _Edit menu; if you wish to erase a line click Delete L_ine from the _Edit menu.

ACCOUNTING
concept

For a sale of inventory products for cash, the general ledger posting is as follows:

1010		4060-4075			
Cash-Operating		Sale of Inventory		1 carpet @ 400 =	400
Dr	Cr	Dr	Cr	2 draperies @250 =	500
1,163			900		900

2200 Sales Tax Payable		4010-4020 Service Revenue	
Dr	Cr	Dr	Cr
	63		200

The cost of the inventory sold and resulting decline in the inventory is recorded as follows:

5060-5075		1260-1275			
Cost of Goods Sold		Inventory		1 carpet @ 200 =	200
Dr	Cr	Dr	Cr	2 draperies @125 =	250
450			450		450

PRACTICE *exercise*

Record the transactions in the Create Invoices or Enter Sales Receipts window:

MAR. 26   Sold the following on account to Hamilton Hotels, Invoice No. 1010, Terms 2/10, Net 30 Days:

2 mirrors	$ 600.00
2 carpets	800.00
total sale of merchandise	$ 1,400.00
sales tax (.07 x $1,400)	98.00
decorating services (6 hrs)	300.00
Total sale on account	$ 1,798.00

MAR. 29   Sold the following for cash to Franco Films Co., Invoice No. 1011, their Check No. 1361:

4 lamps	$ 800.00
2 draperies	500.00
total sale of merchandise	$ 1,300.00
sales tax (.07 x $1,300)	91.00
design services (4 hrs)	240.00
Total sale for cash	$ 1,631.00

SALES DISCOUNTS

 **Sales discounts** are offered to customers to encourage early payment of outstanding invoices. Generally, companies provide for a 1% or 2% reduction of the invoice amount if the payment is made within 10 days of the invoice date.

sales discount A reduction in the selling price if the invoice payment is made shortly after the invoice date.

On March 23, 2004, Kristin Raina receives full payment from Jennie Guthrie of Invoice No. 1008, her check No. 2453, less the appropriate discount.

To record a receipt of payment within the discount period—
1. Click Customers, and then click Receive Payments.
2. At the Received From drop-down list, click *Guthrie, Jennie*. The open invoice in the full amount for Jennie Guthrie displays.
3. At the *Date* field, choose *03/23/2004*.
4. Place a ✓ (check mark) in the Show discount and credit information box. (See figure 5–17.)

FIGURE 5-17
Receive Payments Window –
Jennie Guthrie

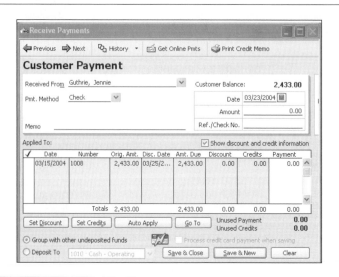

5. Select the invoice by clicking in the ✓ column next to the open invoice. A warning message appears.
6. Click OK, and then click the Set Discount button. This will display the Discount and Credits window.

   This window will display information concerning the selected invoice including the date the discount is available. The window will compute the default discount amount based on information contained in the customer file.

7. At the Discount Account drop-down list, click *4100 Sales Discounts*. (See figure 5–18.)

FIGURE 5-18
Discount and Credits Window

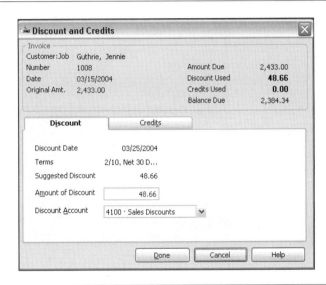

8. Click Done to accept the discount calculation. You will be returned to the Receive Payments window with the Amount Due recalculated based on the discount. (See figure 5–19.)

FIGURE 5-19
Receive Payments Window

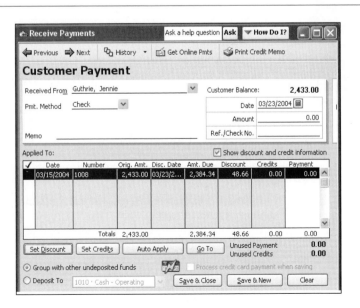

9. At the *Amount* field, key **2384.34**.
10. Enter the payment method and check number.
11. At the ✓ field, place a check mark next to the selected invoice, if necessary.
12. Click the Group with other undeposited funds option, if necessary. (See figure 5–20.)

FIGURE 5-20

Receive Payments Window – Complete

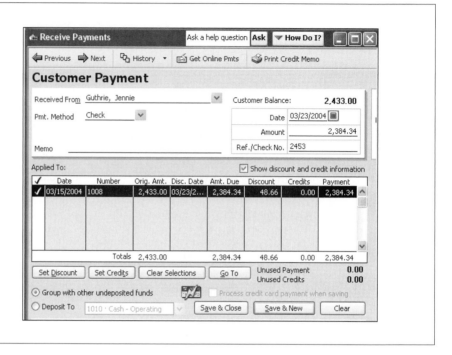

13. If the information is correct, click S*a*ve & Close.

Record the following transaction in the Receive Payments window:

HINT

If you make an error on the payment, you can correct changes and resave, or click Edit and then Delete Payment and start over.

ACCOUNTING
concept

For a collection of an accounts receivable with a sales discount, the general ledger posting is as follows:

1010 Cash-Operating			1200 Accts Receivable			4100 Sales Discounts	
Dr	Cr		Dr	Cr		Dr	Cr
2384.34			Bill 2433	Coll 2433		48.66	
			Bal 0				

In addition, the Customer File (subledger) for Jennie Guthrie will reflect the new collection.

P R A C T I C E *exercise*

MAR. 30   Received full payment from Hamilton Hotels for Invoice
No. 1010, their check No. 6555, less applicable discount.
QuickCheck: $1762.04

THE ADJUST QUANTITY/VALUE ON HAND WINDOW

In QuickBooks Pro, you use the Adjust Quantity/Value on Hand activity
window to record changes in the inventory from events other than a purchase or sale. If inventory items are lost, stolen, damaged, or spoiled, the
resulting change in the inventory quantity and/or value will be recorded in
this window as an **inventory adjustment**. The reduction is considered a
loss/expense with a corresponding reduction in the inventory asset account.
The account that will be used to record the reduction to inventory is the
Inventory Adjustment account. This account is a cost of goods sold account
and will be included in the cost of goods sold section of the income
statement.

inventory adjustment
An amount recorded in
an expense or loss
account to reflect the
reduction of inventory
value and/or quantity
due to loss, theft, or
damage.

Activities identified as adjustments to inventory are recorded in the Adjust
Quantity/Value on Hand window. All transactions entered in this window
result in a debit to the Inventory Adjustment account and a credit to the
appropriate inventory asset account. QuickBooks Pro records the transaction as follows:

		Inventory Adjustment (Loss/Expense)		XXX			
		Inventory (Asset)				XXX	

On March 30, Kristin Raina discovers that a mirror is damaged and cannot be returned to the manufacturer.

To record an inventory adjustment—
1. Click Vendors, and then click Inventory Activities.
2. At the Inventory Activities submenu, click Adjust Quantity/Value on
   Hand.
3. At the Adjustment Date drop-down list, choose *03/30/2004*.
   (See figure 5–21).

FIGURE 5-21

Adjust Quantity/Value on Hand Window

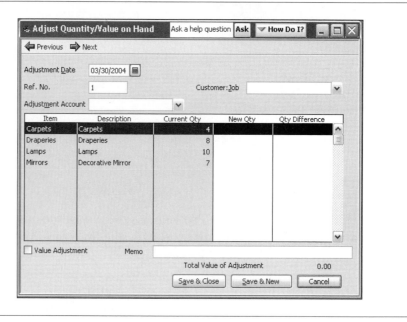

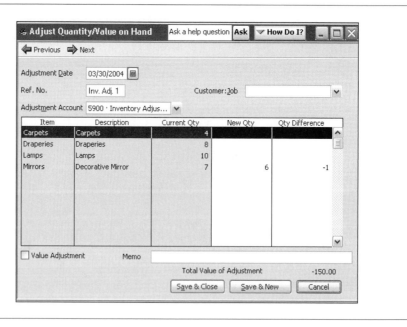

HINT

After entering Adjustment Account, if the Ref. No. changes, go back and correct it.

4. At the *Ref. No.* field, key **Inv. Adj. 1**.
5. At the Adjustment Account drop-down list, click *5900 – Inventory Adjustment*. If the Income or Expense expected window appears, click OK.
6. At the *New Qty* field on the Mirrors line, key **6**.

   When you move to the next field, QuickBooks Pro fills the *Qty Difference* field and enters the Total Value of Adjustment amount. (See figure 5–22.)

7. Place a ✓ in the Value Adjustment box. The amounts in the *Current Value* and *New Value* fields for all inventory items will be displayed. (See figure 5–23.)

FIGURE 5-23

*Adjust Quantity/Value
on Hand Window –
Completed for Value
Adjustment*

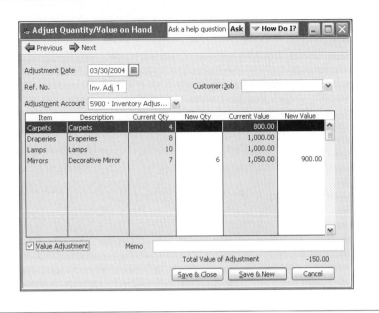

HINT

If you make an error in this window, click Edit and then Delete Inventory Adjustment and redo the transaction.

8. If the information is correct, click Save & Close.

If the inventory adjustment was a result of a change in value only, without a change in quantity, the Value Adjustment box should be checked before the adjustment is entered. This allows you to adjust the value without changing the quantity.

ACCOUNTING
concept

For an adjustment to inventory, the general ledger posting is as follows:

5900 Invent. Adj.			1275 Inv. of Mirrors	
Dr	Cr		Dr	Cr
150			Prev. Bal. 1,050	Adj. 150
			Bal 900	

In addition, the Item File (subledger) for Mirrors will reflect the new balance.

ACTIVITIES: THE PAY SALES TAX WINDOW

In QuickBooks Pro, the Pay Sales Tax window is used to record the remittance of sales tax charged to customers to the proper tax agency. QuickBooks Pro uses the default accounts Sales Tax Payable and Cash.

The Pay Sales Tax window is designed for Activities identified as payment of sales tax charged to customers. The default accounts are Sales Tax Payable and Cash. QuickBooks Pro records the transaction as follows:

				Sales Tax Payable				XXX					
				Cash							XXX		

At the conclusion of each month, Kristin Raina remits the sales tax collected from customers to the appropriate state agency.

To pay the sales tax collected—
1. Click Vendors, and then click Sales Tax.
2. At the Sales Tax submenu, click Pay Sales Tax. (See Figure 5-24.)

FIGURE 5-24
Pay Sales Tax Window

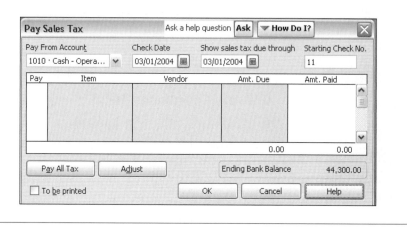

3. At the *Check Date* field, choose *03/31/2004*. Make sure the *1010 Cash – Operating* account is selected in the *Pay From Account* field and the To be printed box is not checked.
4. At the *Show sales tax due through* field, choose *03/31/2004*.
5. Click the Pay All Tax button to select the liability. The sales tax liabilities to date will be displayed.
6. At the *Pay* field, place a check mark, if necessary. (See figure 5–25.)

FIGURE 5-25
Pay Sales Tax Window – Liabilities Displayed

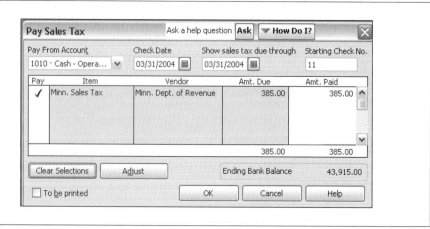

7. If the information is correct, click OK. The liability is now paid.

ACCOUNTING
concept

For a payment of sales tax, the general ledger posting is as follows:

1010 Cash-Operating		2200 Sales Tax Payable	
Dr	Cr	Dr	Cr
	Pmt. 385	Pmt. 385	385
			Bal 0

ACTIVITIES: MAKE DEPOSITS

Recall from chapter 3 that Kristin Raina Interior Designs deposits all funds collected from customers at the end of the month. Before reviewing the reports for the month, the deposits should be recorded.

PRACTICE *exercise*

Record the following transaction in the Make Deposits window:

MAR. 31   Deposit all undeposited funds to the Cash – Operating account. *QuickCheck:* $6940.38

REPORTS: INVENTORY ITEMS AND FINANCIAL REPORTS

Recall from chapter 1 that Reports, the fourth level of operation, reflect the activities recorded in the various Lists and Activities windows. Inventory activities entered in the various windows flow into the reports, many of which should be displayed and printed at the end of the month.

INVENTORY REPORTS FROM THE REPORTS MENU
Inventory reports, such as the *Inventory Valuation Detail* report, *Inventory Stock Status by Item* report, and the *Purchases by Item Detail* report help the company track and manage its inventory.

Inventory Valuation Detail Report
The *Inventory Valuation Detail* report displays the transactions affecting each inventory item along with the quantity and value on hand for each.

To view and print the *Inventory Valuation Detail* report—
1. Click Reports, and then click Inventory.
2. At the Inventory submenu, click Inventory Valuation Detail.
3. At the *From* and *To* fields, choose *03/01/2004* and *03/31/2004*, and then click Refresh on the command line. The report for the period will be displayed.
4. To print the report, click Print on the command line.
5. At the Print Report dialog box, check the settings, and then click Print. Your printout should look like figure 5–26.

FIGURE 5-26
*Inventory Valuation
Detail Report*

EX5 [Your Name] Kristin Raina Interior Designs
Inventory Valuation Detail
March 2004

Type	Date	Name	Num	Qty	Cost	On Hand	Avg Cost	Asset Value
Inventory								
Carpets								
Bill	03/05/2004	Bell Carpet Design	12-5585	10	2,000.00	10	200.00	2,000.00
Invoice	03/15/2004	Guthrie, Jennie	1008	-3		7	200.00	1,400.00
Sales Receipt	03/22/2004	Jones, Beverly	1009	-1		6	200.00	1,200.00
Invoice	03/26/2004	Hamilton Hotels	1010	-2		4	200.00	800.00
Total Carpets						4.00		800.00
Draperies								
Check	03/12/2004	Weaver Fabrics	10	12	1,500.00	12	125.00	1,500.00
Sales Receipt	03/22/2004	Jones, Beverly	1009	-2		10	125.00	1,250.00
Sales Receipt	03/29/2004	Franco Films Co.	1011	-2		8	125.00	1,000.00
Total Draperies						8.00		1,000.00
Lamps								
Check	03/02/2004	Lumiare Lighting Company	9	16	1,600.00	16	100.00	1,600.00
Invoice	03/15/2004	Guthrie, Jennie	1008	-2		14	100.00	1,400.00
Sales Receipt	03/29/2004	Franco Films Co.	1011	-4		10	100.00	1,000.00
Total Lamps						10.00		1,000.00
Mirrors								
Bill	03/01/2004	Ace Glass Works	K-588	10	1,500.00	10	150.00	1,500.00
Invoice	03/15/2004	Guthrie, Jennie	1008	-1		9	150.00	1,350.00
Invoice	03/26/2004	Hamilton Hotels	1010	-2		7	150.00	1,050.00
Inventory Adjust	03/30/2004		Inv. Adj. 1	-1		6	150.00	900.00
Total Mirrors						6.00		900.00
Total Inventory						28.00		3,700.00
TOTAL						**28.00**		**3,700.00**

6. Close the report.

Inventory Stock Status by Item Report

The *Inventory Stock Status by Item* report displays the on-hand status of each inventory item. The report indicates whether an item should be ordered based upon on-hand quantity and the reorder amount.

To view and print the *Inventory Stock Status by Item* report—
1. Click <u>R</u>eports, and then click <u>I</u>nventory.
2. At the Inventory submenu, click Inventory <u>S</u>tock Status by Item.
3. At the *From* and *To* fields, choose *03/01/2004* and *03/31/2004*, and then click Refre<u>s</u>h on the command line. The report for the period will be displayed. (See figure 5–27.)

FIGURE 5-27
*Inventory Stock Status
by Item Report*

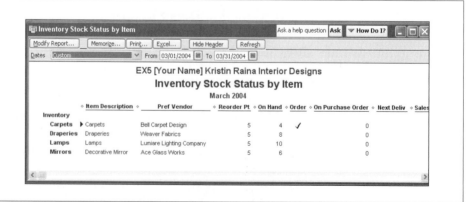

4. To print the report, click Prin<u>t</u>, check the settings, then click Print.
5. Close the report.

Purchases by Item Detail Report

The *Purchases by Item Detail* report displays all purchase information for each inventory item. The report shows vendor name, cost per unit, quantity purchased, and the total cost.

To view and print the *Purchases by Item Detail* report—
1. Click Reports, and then click Purchases.
2. At the Purchases submenu, click Purchases by Item Detail.
3. At the *From* and *To* fields, choose *03/01/2004* and *03/31/2004*, and then click Refresh on the command line. The report for the period will be displayed.
4. To print the report, click Print, check the settings, and then click Print. Your printout should look like figure 5–28.

FIGURE 5-28

Purchases by Item Detail Report

				EX5 [Your Name] Kristin Raina Interior Designs				
				Purchases by Item Detail				
				March 2004				
Accrual Basis								
Type	Date	Num	Memo	Source Name	Qty	Cost Price	Amount	Balance
Inventory								
Carpets								
Bill	03/05/2004	12-5585	Carpets	Bell Carpet Design	10	200.00	2,000.00	2,000.00
Total Carpets							2,000.00	2,000.00
Draperies								
Check	03/12/2004	10	Draperies	Weaver Fabrics	12	125.00	1,500.00	1,500.00
Total Draperies							1,500.00	1,500.00
Lamps								
Check	03/02/2004	9	Lamps	Lumiare Lighting Company	16	100.00	1,600.00	1,600.00
Total Lamps							1,600.00	1,600.00
Mirrors								
Bill	03/01/2004	K-588	Decorative Mirror	Ace Glass Works	10	150.00	1,500.00	1,500.00
Total Mirrors							1,500.00	1,500.00
Total Inventory							6,600.00	6,600.00
TOTAL							**6,600.00**	**6,600.00**

This report, like several of those reviewed in prior chapters, allows you to drill down to view the source transaction. Kristin Raina wishes to see the detail of the purchase of carpets on March 5, 2004.

To drill down to the purchase transaction of carpets—
1. Place the mouse pointer over the carpet purchase transaction until the zoom glass appears.
2. Double-click on the transaction. The Enter Bills window for this transaction displays.
3. Close the Enter Bills window and the report.

INVENTORY REPORTS FROM THE LISTS MENU

QuickBooks Pro allows you to view and print several inventory reports from the Lists windows. Once a list is accessed, a report list is available that is accessed by clicking the Reports menu button in the List window.

The *Sales by Item Detail* report shows sales of all inventory items both on account and for cash.

To view and print an Item List report such as *Sales by Item Detail*—
1. Click Lists, and then click Item List.
2. At the Item List window, click the Reports menu button.

3. At the Reports menu, click <u>R</u>eports on All Items.
4. At the Reports on all Items submenu, click <u>S</u>ales Reports.
5. At the Sales Reports submenu, click By I<u>t</u>em Detail.
6. At the *From* and *To* fields, choose *03/01/2004* and *03/31/2004*, and then click Refre<u>s</u>h on the command line. The report for the period will be displayed.
7. To print the report, click Prin<u>t</u>, check the settings, and then click Print. Your printout should look like figure 5–29.

FIGURE 5-29
Sales by Item Detail Report

EX5 [Your Name] Kristin Raina Interior Designs
Sales by Item Detail
March 2004

Accrual Basis

Type	Date	Num	Memo	Name	Qty	Sales Price	Amount	Balance
Inventory								
Carpets								
Invoice	03/15/2004	1008	Carpets	Guthrie, Jennie	3	400.00	1,200.00	1,200.00
Sales Receipt	03/22/2004	1009	Carpets	Jones, Beverly	1	400.00	400.00	1,600.00
Invoice	03/26/2004	1010	Carpets	Hamilton Hotels	2	400.00	800.00	2,400.00
Total Carpets							2,400.00	2,400.00
Draperies								
Sales Receipt	03/22/2004	1009	Draperies	Jones, Beverly	2	250.00	500.00	500.00
Sales Receipt	03/29/2004	1011	Draperies	Franco Films Co.	2	250.00	500.00	1,000.00
Total Draperies							1,000.00	1,000.00
Lamps								
Invoice	03/15/2004	1008	Lamps	Guthrie, Jennie	2	200.00	400.00	400.00
Sales Receipt	03/29/2004	1011	Lamps	Franco Films Co.	4	200.00	800.00	1,200.00
Total Lamps							1,200.00	1,200.00
Mirrors								
Invoice	03/15/2004	1008	Decorative Mirror	Guthrie, Jennie	1	300.00	300.00	300.00
Invoice	03/26/2004	1010	Decorative Mirror	Hamilton Hotels	2	300.00	600.00	900.00
Total Mirrors							900.00	900.00
Total Inventory							5,500.00	5,500.00
Service								
Decorating Services								
Invoice	03/15/2004	1008	Decorating Services	Guthrie, Jennie	8	50.00	400.00	400.00
Sales Receipt	03/22/2004	1009	Decorating Services	Jones, Beverly	4	50.00	200.00	600.00
Invoice	03/26/2004	1010	Decorating Services	Hamilton Hotels	6	50.00	300.00	900.00
Total Decorating Services							900.00	900.00
Design Services								
Sales Receipt	03/29/2004	1011	Design Services	Franco Films Co.	4	60.00	240.00	240.00
Total Design Services							240.00	240.00
Total Service							1,140.00	1,140.00
TOTAL							**6,640.00**	**6,640.00**

8. Close the report.

In addition to the *Sales* reports, *Purchase, Inventory, Item,* and *Price* reports can be viewed from the Reports menu of the Item List.

P R A C T I C E *exercise*

1. From the <u>I</u>nventory Reports menu, view and print the *Inventory St<u>o</u>ck Status by Vendor* report.

2. From the Item List window, view and print the *Item P<u>r</u>ofitability* report (from the <u>R</u>eports on All Items – Project submenu).

At the end of each month, the *Journal, Income Statement* (or *Profit & Loss*), and *Balance Sheet* reports should be viewed and printed. Your printouts should look like figures 5–30, 5–31, and 5–32, respectively.

FIGURE 5-30

Journal Report
March 1, 2004 – March 31, 2004

EX5 [Your Name] Kristin Raina Interior Designs
Journal
March 2004

Trans #	Type	Date	Num	Name	Memo	Account	Debit	Credit
39	Bill	03/01/2004	K-588	Ace Glass Works		2010 · Accounts Payable		1,500.00
				Ace Glass Works	Decorative Mirror	1275 · Inventory of Mirrors	1,500.00	
							1,500.00	1,500.00
40	Check	03/02/2004	9	Lumiare Lighting Company	36	1010 · Cash - Operating		1,600.00
				Lumiare Lighting Company	Lamps	1270 · Inventory of Lamps	1,600.00	
							1,600.00	1,600.00
41	Bill	03/05/2004	12-5585	Bell Carpet Design		2010 · Accounts Payable		2,000.00
				Bell Carpet Design	Carpets	1260 · Inventory of Carpets	2,000.00	
							2,000.00	2,000.00
42	Check	03/12/2004	10	Weaver Fabrics	9878	1010 · Cash - Operating		1,500.00
				Weaver Fabrics	Draperies	1265 · Inventory of Draperies	1,500.00	
							1,500.00	1,500.00
43	Invoice	03/15/2004	1008	Guthrie, Jennie		1200 · Accounts Receivable	2,433.00	
				Guthrie, Jennie	Lamps	4070 · Sale of Lamps		400.00
				Guthrie, Jennie	Lamps	1270 · Inventory of Lamps		200.00
				Guthrie, Jennie	Lamps	5070 · Cost of Lamps Sold	200.00	
				Guthrie, Jennie	Carpets	4060 · Sale of Carpets		1,200.00
				Guthrie, Jennie	Carpets	1260 · Inventory of Carpets		600.00
				Guthrie, Jennie	Carpets	5060 · Cost of Carpets Sold	600.00	
				Guthrie, Jennie	Decorative Mirror	4075 · Sale of Mirrors		300.00
				Guthrie, Jennie	Decorative Mirror	1275 · Inventory of Mirrors		150.00
				Guthrie, Jennie	Decorative Mirror	5075 · Cost of Mirrors Sold	150.00	
				Guthrie, Jennie	Decorating Services	4020 · Decorating Services		400.00
				Minn. Dept. of Revenue	Sales Tax	2200 · Sales Tax Payable		133.00
							3,383.00	3,383.00
44	Sales Receipt	03/22/2004	1009	Jones, Beverly		1250 · Undeposited Funds	1,163.00	
				Jones, Beverly	Carpets	4060 · Sale of Carpets		400.00
				Jones, Beverly	Carpets	1260 · Inventory of Carpets		200.00
				Jones, Beverly	Carpets	5060 · Cost of Carpets Sold	200.00	
				Jones, Beverly	Draperies	4065 · Sale of Draperies		500.00
				Jones, Beverly	Draperies	1265 · Inventory of Draperies		250.00
				Jones, Beverly	Draperies	5065 · Cost of Draperies Sold	250.00	
				Jones, Beverly	Decorating Services	4020 · Decorating Services		200.00
				Minn. Dept. of Revenue	Sales Tax	2200 · Sales Tax Payable		63.00
							1,613.00	1,613.00
45	Invoice	03/26/2004	1010	Hamilton Hotels		1200 · Accounts Receivable	1,798.00	
				Hamilton Hotels	Decorative Mirror	4075 · Sale of Mirrors		600.00
				Hamilton Hotels	Decorative Mirror	1275 · Inventory of Mirrors		300.00
				Hamilton Hotels	Decorative Mirror	5075 · Cost of Mirrors Sold	300.00	
				Hamilton Hotels	Carpets	4060 · Sale of Carpets		800.00
				Hamilton Hotels	Carpets	1260 · Inventory of Carpets		400.00
				Hamilton Hotels	Carpets	5060 · Cost of Carpets Sold	400.00	
				Hamilton Hotels	Decorating Services	4020 · Decorating Services		300.00
				Minn. Dept. of Revenue	Sales Tax	2200 · Sales Tax Payable		98.00
							2,498.00	2,498.00
46	Sales Receipt	03/29/2004	1011	Franco Films Co.		1250 · Undeposited Funds	1,631.00	
				Franco Films Co.	Lamps	4070 · Sale of Lamps		800.00
				Franco Films Co.	Lamps	1270 · Inventory of Lamps		400.00
				Franco Films Co.	Lamps	5070 · Cost of Lamps Sold	400.00	
				Franco Films Co.	Draperies	4065 · Sale of Draperies		500.00
				Franco Films Co.	Draperies	1265 · Inventory of Draperies		250.00
				Franco Films Co.	Draperies	5065 · Cost of Draperies Sold	250.00	
				Franco Films Co.	Design Services	4010 · Design Services		240.00
				Minn. Dept. of Revenue	Sales Tax	2200 · Sales Tax Payable		91.00
							2,281.00	2,281.00
47	Payment	03/23/2004	2453	Guthrie, Jennie		1250 · Undeposited Funds	2,384.34	
				Guthrie, Jennie		1200 · Accounts Receivable		2,384.34
				Guthrie, Jennie		1200 · Accounts Receivable		48.66
				Guthrie, Jennie		4100 · Sales Discounts	48.66	
							2,433.00	2,433.00
48	Payment	03/30/2004	6555	Hamilton Hotels		1250 · Undeposited Funds	1,762.04	
				Hamilton Hotels		1200 · Accounts Receivable		1,762.04
				Hamilton Hotels		1200 · Accounts Receivable		35.96
				Hamilton Hotels		4100 · Sales Discounts	35.96	
							1,798.00	1,798.00
49	Inventory Adjust	03/30/2004	Inv. Adj. 1			5900 · Inventory Adjustment	150.00	
					Mirrors Inventory Adjustment	1275 · Inventory of Mirrors		150.00
							150.00	150.00
50	Sales Tax Payment	03/31/2004	11	Minn. Dept. of Revenue		1010 · Cash - Operating		385.00
				Minn. Dept. of Revenue		2200 · Sales Tax Payable	385.00	
							385.00	385.00
51	Deposit	03/31/2004			Deposit	1010 · Cash - Operating	6,940.38	
				Jones, Beverly	Deposit	1250 · Undeposited Funds		1,163.00
				Guthrie, Jennie	Deposit	1250 · Undeposited Funds		2,384.34
				Franco Films Co.	Deposit	1250 · Undeposited Funds		1,631.00
				Hamilton Hotels	Deposit	1250 · Undeposited Funds		1,762.04
							6,940.38	6,940.38
TOTAL							**28,081.38**	**28,081.38**

EX5 [Your Name] Kristin Raina Interior Designs
Profit & Loss
January through March 2004

Accrual Basis

	Jan - Mar 04
Ordinary Income/Expense	
Income	
4010 · Design Services	4,980.00
4020 · Decorating Services	3,400.00
4060 · Sale of Carpets	2,400.00
4065 · Sale of Draperies	1,000.00
4070 · Sale of Lamps	1,200.00
4075 · Sale of Mirrors	900.00
4100 · Sales Discounts	-84.62
Total Income	13,795.38
Cost of Goods Sold	
5060 · Cost of Carpets Sold	1,200.00
5065 · Cost of Draperies Sold	500.00
5070 · Cost of Lamps Sold	600.00
5075 · Cost of Mirrors Sold	450.00
5900 · Inventory Adjustment	150.00
Total COGS	2,900.00
Gross Profit	10,895.38
Expense	
6020 · Accounting Expense	300.00
6050 · Advertising Expense	100.00
6175 · Deprec. Exp., Furniture	100.00
6185 · Deprec. Exp., Computers	60.00
6200 · Insurance Expense	200.00
6300 · Janitorial Expenses	125.00
6325 · Office Supplies Expense	150.00
6400 · Rent Expense	800.00
6450 · Telephone Expense	275.00
6500 · Utilities Expense	450.00
Total Expense	2,560.00
Net Ordinary Income	8,335.38
Other Income/Expense	
Other Expense	
7000 · Interest Expense	50.00
Total Other Expense	50.00
Net Other Income	-50.00
Net Income	**8,285.38**

EX5 [Your Name] Kristin Raina Interior Designs
Balance Sheet
As of March 31, 2004

Accrual Basis

	Mar 31, 04
ASSETS	
Current Assets	
Checking/Savings	
1010 · Cash - Operating	50,855.38
Total Checking/Savings	50,855.38
Accounts Receivable	
1200 · Accounts Receivable	1,540.00
Total Accounts Receivable	1,540.00
Other Current Assets	
1260 · Inventory of Carpets	800.00
1265 · Inventory of Draperies	1,000.00
1270 · Inventory of Lamps	1,000.00
1275 · Inventory of Mirrors	900.00
1300 · Design Supplies	200.00
1305 · Office Supplies	250.00
1410 · Prepaid Advertising	500.00
1420 · Prepaid Insurance	2,200.00
Total Other Current Assets	6,850.00
Total Current Assets	59,245.38
Fixed Assets	
1700 · Furniture	
1750 · Accum. Dep., Furniture	-100.00
1700 · Furniture - Other	12,000.00
Total 1700 · Furniture	11,900.00
1800 · Computers	
1850 · Accum. Dep., Computers	-60.00
1800 · Computers - Other	3,600.00
Total 1800 · Computers	3,540.00
Total Fixed Assets	15,440.00
TOTAL ASSETS	**74,685.38**
LIABILITIES & EQUITY	
Liabilities	
Current Liabilities	
Accounts Payable	
2010 · Accounts Payable	9,750.00
Total Accounts Payable	9,750.00
Other Current Liabilities	
2020 · Notes Payable	7,000.00
2030 · Interest Payable	50.00
Total Other Current Liabilities	7,050.00
Total Current Liabilities	16,800.00
Total Liabilities	16,800.00
Equity	
3010 · Kristin Raina, Capital	50,000.00
3020 · Kristin Raina, Drawings	-400.00
Net Income	8,285.38
Total Equity	57,885.38
TOTAL LIABILITIES & EQUITY	**74,685.38**

CPAnet is a Web site resource to help accountants take part in an online community, gain access to online resources, and improve client services. The site has over 800 links to accounting-related Web sites. The site gives access to newsletters, state accounting societies' Web sites, and Big Four accounting firm Web sites, among numerous other useful links.

The site can be reached at www.cpanet.com.

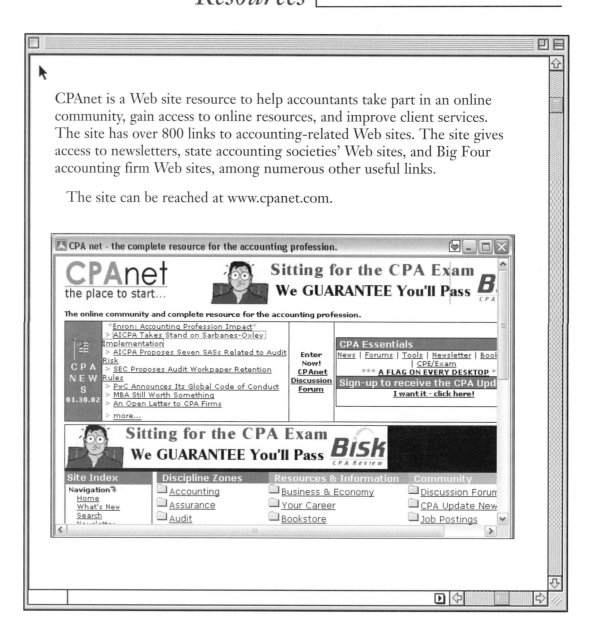

PROGRESS
Check

PROCEDURE REVIEW

To add an item—
1. Click Lists, and then Item List.
2. At the Item List window, click the Item menu button.
3. At the Item menu, click New.
4. Enter the background data for the item.
5. Click OK.
6. Close the Item List window.

To delete an item—
1. Click Lists, and then click Item List.
2. At the Item List window, select the item you wish to delete.
3. Click the Item menu button.
4. At the Item menu, click Delete.
5. Click OK at the warning.
6. Close the Item List window.
   You cannot delete an item that has a balance or is used in a transaction.

To edit an item—
1. Click Lists, and then click Item List.
2. At the Item List window, select the item you wish to edit.
3. Click the Item menu button.
4. At the Item menu, click Edit.
5. Change the appropriate information.
6. Click OK.
7. Close the Item List window.

To record a purchase and receipt of an inventory item on account—
1. Click Vendors, and then click Receive Items and Enter Bill.
2. At the Vendor drop-down list, click the vendor name.
3. Enter data into the *Date*, *Bill Due*, *Ref. No.*, and *Terms* fields in the usual manner.
4. Click the item from the Item drop-down list.
5. Enter the quantity; the *Amount* and *Amount Due* fields will fill automatically.
6. Click Save & Close.

To record a purchase and receipt of an inventory item for cash—
1. Click Banking, and then click Write Checks.
2. At the Write Checks window, click the appropriate bank account.
3. Enter the check date in the *Date* field.
4. Click the payee from the Pay to the Order of drop-down list.
5. Click the Items tab.
6. Click the item from the Item drop-down list.

7. Enter the quantity; the *Amount* field will fill automatically.
8. Click S<u>a</u>ve & Close.

To record a sale of inventory on account—
1. Click C<u>u</u>stomers, and then click Create <u>I</u>nvoices.
2. At the Customer:Job drop-down list, click the customer name.
3. At the Template drop-down list, click *Intuit Product Invoice*.
4. Enter data into the *Date*, *Invoice #*, and *Terms* fields in the usual manner.
5. Enter the quantity.
6. Click the item from the Item drop-down list; the *Description*, *Price Each*, and *Amount* field will fill automatically.
7. At the Tax drop-down list, click the applicable sales tax.
8. Click S<u>a</u>ve & Close.

To enter a cash sale of inventory—
1. Click C<u>u</u>stomers, and then click Enter <u>S</u>ales Receipt.
2. At the Customer:Job drop-down list, click the customer name.
3. Enter the date, invoice number, payment method, and check number.
4. Complete the balance of the window in the same manner as a sale on account.
5. Click S<u>a</u>ve & Close.

To record a receipt of payment within the discount period—
1. Click C<u>u</u>stomers, and then click Receive Pa<u>y</u>ments.
2. At the Received Fro<u>m</u> drop-down list, click the customer name.
3. Enter the payment date in the *Date* field.
4. Select the invoice by clicking in the ✓ column next to the open invoice.
5. Click OK at the warning and then click the Set <u>D</u>iscount button.
6. At the Discount <u>A</u>ccount drop-down list, click the Sales discount GL account.
7. Click <u>D</u>one to accept the discount calculation.
8. Enter the amount, the payment method, and check number.
9. At the ✓ field, place a check mark next to the selected invoice, if necessary.
10. Click the Group with other undeposited funds button.
11. Click S<u>a</u>ve & Close.

To record an inventory adjustment—
1. Click Vend<u>o</u>rs, and then click <u>I</u>nventory Activities.
2. At the Inventory Activities menu, click Adjust <u>Q</u>uantity/Value on Hand.
3. Enter data into the *Date* and *Ref. No.* fields.
4. At the Adjust<u>m</u>ent Account drop-down list, click *Inventory Adjustment*.
5. Enter the new quantity on the line for the item to be adjusted.
6. Place a ✓ in the Value Adjustment box.
7. Click S<u>a</u>ve & Close.

To pay sales tax—
1. Click Vend<u>o</u>rs, and then click Sales Ta<u>x</u>.

2. At the Sales Tax submenu, click Pay Sales Tax
3. Enter the payment date.
4. Click the Cash account.
5. Enter the correct date in the *Show sales tax due through* field.
6. Click the Pay All Tax button.
7. Place a check mark in the *Pay* field.
8. Click OK.

To view and print inventory reports from the Reports menu—
1. Click Reports, and then click Inventory.
2. At the Inventory submenu, choose a report.
3. Indicate the appropriate dates for the report.
4. Click Print on the command line.
5. At the Print Reports dialog box, review the settings, then click Print.
6. Close the report.

To view and print vendor reports from the Lists menu—
1. Click Lists, and then click Item List.
2. Click the Reports menu button.
3. Click Reports on All Items.
4. From the submenu, click a category.
5. From the second submenu, click a report.
6. Indicate the appropriate dates for the report.
7. Click Print on the command line.
8. At the Print Reports dialog box, review the settings, then click Print.
9. Close the report.

KEY CONCEPTS

Select the letter of the item that best matches each definition.

a. Enter Bills window-Items tab
b. Adjust Quantity/Value on Hand activity window
c. Item List
d. Sales discounts
e. *Purchases by Item Detail* report
f. Sales tax
g. Pay Sales Tax window
h. *Inventory Valuation Detail* report
i. *Sales by Item Detail* report
j. *Inventory Stock Status by Item* report

_____ 1. Report that displays all transactions affecting each inventory item.
_____ 2. Reduction of invoice amount due when customer pays by a specific date.
_____ 3. Window used to record purchases and receipt of inventory items.
_____ 4. Window used to adjust quantity or value of inventory as a result of damage or loss.
_____ 5. Contains a file of all inventory items.
_____ 6. Window used to remit sales tax collected from customers to the appropriate state tax agency.
_____ 7. Report that displays each purchase transaction for inventory items.

_____ 8. Report that displays the on-hand status of every inventory item.

_____ 9. Report from the Item List that show sales information for each inventory item.

_____ 10. Tax collected by a retailer from a customer on sales of goods.

PROCEDURE CHECK

1. Your company will be selling a new product. Describe the steps that must be taken to add the new item to the system.
2. Explain the difference between using Enter Bills or Receive Items and Enter Bills from the Vendors pull-down menu.
3. Which QuickBooks Pro report(s) would you use to view the sales and purchases of specific inventory items?
4. At year-end, you wish to confirm the quantity on hand for each inventory item. How would you use QuickBooks Pro reports to determine the quantity and value of the ending inventory?
5. Your company wishes to view the profitability of each inventory item. How could you use QuickBooks Pro to develop this information?

6. Discuss the advantages of using a computerized accounting system to maintain a perpetual inventory system.

CASE PROBLEMS

CASE PROBLEM 1

On April 1, 2004, Lynn Garcia began her business, called Lynn's Music Studio. In the first month of business, Lynn set up the music studio, provided guitar and piano lessons, and recorded month-end activity. In May, the second month of business, Lynn decides to purchase and sell inventory items of guitars, keyboards, music stands, and sheet music. For customers that purchase merchandise inventory, the terms of payment are 2/10, Net 30 Days. For illustration purposes, assume a 7% sales tax is charged on the sale of all inventory items. The company file includes the information for Lynn's Music Studio as of May 1, 2004.

1. Open the company file CH5 Lynn's Music Studio.QBW.
2. Make a backup copy of the company file LMS5 [Your Name] Lynn's Music Studio.
3. Restore the backup copy of the company file. In both the Restore From and Restore To windows use the file name: LMS5 [Your Name] Lynn's Music Studio.
4. Change the Company Name to LMS5 [Your Name] Lynn's Music Studio.
5. Add the following inventory items to the Item List:

Type:	**Inventory Part**
Item Name/Number:	**Keyboards**
Description on	
Purchase/Sales Transactions:	**Keyboards**
Cost:	**75**

COGS Account:	**5065 Cost of Keyboards Sold**
Preferred Vendor:	**Katie's Keyboards**
Sales Price:	**150**
Tax Code:	**Tax – Taxable Sales**
Income Account:	**4065 Sale of Keyboards**
Asset Account:	**1265 Inventory of Keyboards**
Reorder Point:	**10**

Type:	**Inventory Part**
Item Name/Number:	**Sheet Music**
Description on	
Purchase/Sales Transactions:	**Sheet Music**
Cost:	**3**
COGS Account:	**5075 Cost of Sheet Music Sold**
Preferred Vendor:	**Strings, Sheets, & Such**
Sales Price:	**6**
Tax Code:	**Tax – Taxable Sales**
Income Account:	**4075 Sale of Sheet Music**
Asset Account:	**1275 Inventory of Sheet Music**
Reorder Point:	**50**

Delete the following inventory item:
   Harmonicas

6. Using the appropriate window, record the following transactions for May:

May 3	Purchased 30 guitars on account from Music Instruments, Inc., at $50 each, their Invoice No. GU75998.
May 3	Purchased 30 keyboards on account from Katie's Keyboards at $75 each, their Invoice No. 10089-30.
May 3	Purchased 30 music stands from Melody Music Equipment at $20 each, paid immediately, Check No. 9. Do not print check.
May 3	Purchased 300 sheets of music of various themes from Strings, Sheets, & Such at $3 each, paid immediately, Check No. 10. Do not print check.
May 4	Sold 15 guitars for $100 each, 15 keyboards for $150 each, and 15 music stands for $40 each to Jefferson High School, Invoice No. 2012, terms 2/10, Net 30 Days. In addition, provided 15 hours of guitar lessons and 10 hours of piano lessons.
May 4	Sold 10 keyboards for $150 each to Highland School, Invoice No. 2013, terms 2/10, Net 30 Days. In addition, provided 12 hours of piano lessons.
May 7	Received full payment from Jefferson High School for Invoice 2009, Check No. 30531.
May 10	Record the weekly cash sales of sheet music, 75 sheets at

	$6 each, Sale No. 2014. Leave the *Customer:Job* field blank.
May 11	Sold 3 guitars, for $100 each, 3 keyboards for $150 each, and 3 music stands for $40 each to Mulligan Residence, Invoice No. 2015, terms 2/10, Net 30 Days. In addition, provided 5 hours of guitar lessons and 7 hours of piano lessons.
May 11	Received full payment net of discount from Jefferson High School for Invoice No. 2012, Check No. 30711.
May 14	Received full payment net of discount from Highland School, Check No. 76115.
May 17	Purchased 20 keyboards on account from Katie's Keyboard Company at $75 each, their Invoice No. 10758-20.
May 17	Purchased 10 music stands from Melody Music Equipment at $20 each, paid immediately, Check No. 11. Do not print check.
May 17	Record the weekly cash sales of sheet music, 100 sheets at $6 each, Sale No. 2016.
May 21	Sold 5 guitars for $100 each, 5 keyboards for $150 each, and 5 music stands to Twin Lakes Elementary, Invoice No. 2017, terms 2/10, Net 30 Days. In addition, provided 8 hours of guitar lessons and 5 hours of piano lessons.
May 24	Received a payment of $830 from Twin Lakes Elementary for Invoices 2004 and 2011, Check No. 7266.
May 24	Record the weekly cash sales of sheet music, 115 sheets at $6 each, Sale No. 2018.
May 24	Purchased 300 sheets of music of various themes from Strings, Sheets, & Such at $3 each, paid immediately, Check No. 12. Do not print check.
May 25	Received full payment net of discount from Twin Lakes Elementary for Invoice No. 2017, Check No. 7384.
May 25	Paid in full Music Instruments, Inc. (Check No. 13). Do not print check.
May 25	Paid in full Katie's Keyboard Company, Invoice No. 10089-30 (Check No. 14). Do not print check.
May 31	Record the weekly cash sales of sheet music, 145 sheets at $6 each, Invoice No. 2019.
May 31	Upon reviewing the inventory, Lynn discovers that one guitar is damaged, through no fault of the manufacturer, and cannot be sold. Adjust the inventory on hand to remove the one guitar from the inventory. Inv. Adj. 1.
May 31	Remit all sales taxes collected to the Commonwealth of Pennsylvania, Check No. 15.
May 31	Deposit all undeposited funds to the Cash – Operating account.

7. Display and print the following reports for May 1, 2004, to May 31, 2004:
    a. *Inventory Valuation Detail*
    b. *Inventory Stock Status by Item*
    c. *Purchases by Item Detail*
    d. *Sales by Item Detail*
    e. *Journal*
    f. *Profit & Loss Standard* (for the period April 1, 2004 – May 31, 2004)
    g. *Balance Sheet Standard*

CASE PROBLEM 2

On June 1, 2004, Olivia Chen began her business, which she named Olivia's Web Solutions. In the first month of business, Olivia set up the office, provided Web page design and Internet consulting services, and recorded month-end activity. In July, the second month of business, Olivia decides to purchase and sell inventory items of computer hardware and software. For customers that purchase merchandise inventory, the terms of payment are 2/10, Net 30 Days. For illustration purposes, assume an 8% sales tax is charged on the sale of all inventory items. The company file includes the information for Olivia's Web Solutions as of July 1, 2004.

1. Open the company file CH5 Olivia's Web Solutions.QBW.
2. Make a backup copy of the company file OWS5 [Your Name] Olivia's Web Solutions.
3. Restore the backup copy of the company file. In both the Restore From and Restore To windows use the file name: OWS5 [Your Name] Olivia's Web Solutions.
4. Change the Company Name to OWS5 [Your Name] Olivia's Web Solutions.
5. Add the following inventory items to the Item List:

Type:	**Inventory Part**
Item Name/Number:	**Scanners**
Description on	
Purchase/Sales Transactions:	**Scanners**
Cost:	**300**
COGS Account:	**5065 Cost of Scanners Sold**
Preferred Vendor:	**Scanntronix**
Sales Price:	**600**
Tax Code:	**Tax – Taxable Sales**
Income Account:	**4065 Sale of Scanners**
Asset Account:	**1265 Inventory of Scanners**
Reorder Point:	**5**
Type:	**Inventory Part**
Item Name/Number:	**Desktop Publishing Software**
Description on	
Purchase/Sales Transactions:	**Desktop Publishing Software**

Cost:	**100**
COGS Account:	**5075 Cost of Desktop Pub. Soft. Sold**
Preferred Vendor:	**Textpro Software, Inc.**
Sales Price:	**200**
Tax Code:	**Tax – Taxable Sales**
Income Account:	**4075 Sale of Desktop Pub. Soft.**
Asset Account:	**1275 Inventory of Desktop Pub. Soft.**
Reorder Point:	**5**

Delete the following inventory item:
Printers

6. Using the appropriate window, record the following transactions for July:

Jul. 2　　Purchased 10 computers on account from Computec Computers, at $1,000 each, their Invoice No. 068788.

Jul. 2　　Purchased 20 scanners on account from Scanntronix at $300 each, their Invoice No. 10089-30.

Jul. 2　　Purchased 10 desktop publishing software packages from Textpro Software, Inc. at $100 each, paid immediately, Check No. 9. Do not print check.

Jul. 2　　Purchased 20 HTML software packages from InterSoft Development Co. at $75 each, paid immediately, Check No. 10. Do not print check.

Jul. 5　　Sold 3 computers for $2,000 each, 2 scanners for $600 each, and 1 desktop publishing software package for $200 on account to Long Island Water Works, Invoice No. 1011, terms 2/10, Net 30 Days. In addition, provided 10 hours of Internet consulting services.

Jul. 6　　Sold 2 computers on account to Miguel's Restaurant, Invoice No. 1012, terms 2/10, Net 30 Days. In addition, provided 8 hours of Web page design services.

Jul. 9　　Sold 1 scanner for $600 and 1 desktop publishing software package for $200 to the Singh family, Invoice No. 1013. Received payment immediately, their Check No. 901.

Jul. 12　　Sold 1 computer for $2,000, 2 scanners for $600 each, and 1 HMTL software package for $150 on account to Breathe Easy, Invoice No. 1014, Net 30 Days. In addition, provided 12 hours of Internet consulting services.

Jul. 13　　Received full payment net of discount from Long Island Water Works for Invoice No. 1011, Check No. 125671.

Jul. 16　　Purchased 5 computers on account from Computec Computers at $1,000 each, their Invoice No. 072445.

Jul. 16	Purchased 5 desktop publishing software packages from Textpro Software, Inc. at $100 each, paid immediately, Check No. 11. Do not print check.
Jul. 19	Sold 1 computer for $2,000 and 1 desktop publishing software package for $200 to the Schneider Family, Invoice No. 1015. Received payment immediately, their Check No. 899.
Jul. 20	Sold 3 computers for $ 2,000 each, 3 scanners for $600 each, and 2 desktop publishing software packages to South Shore School District, Invoice No. 1016, terms 2/10, Net 30 Days. In addition, provided 16 hours of Web page design services.
Jul. 26	Received full payment, no discount, from Miguel's Restaurant, for Invoice No. 1012, Check No. 4110.
Jul. 27	Received full payment, no discount, from Breathe Easy for Invoices Nos. 1006 (remaining balance) and 1014, Check No. 1874.
Jul. 30	Purchased 5 computers on account from Computec Computers at $1,000 each, their Invoice No. 073111.
Jul. 30	Paid in full Computec Computers Invoice No. 068788, (Check No. 12). Do not print check.
Jul. 30	Paid in full Scanntronix, Invoice No. 10089-30, (Check No. 13). Do not print check.
Jul. 30	Upon reviewing the inventory, Olivia discovers one HTML software package was damaged, through no fault of the manufacturer, and cannot be sold. Adjust the inventory on hand to remove the one HTML software package from the inventory. Inv. Adj. 1
Jul. 30	Remit all sales taxes collected to New York State, Check No. 14.
Jul. 30	Deposit all undeposited funds to the Cash Operating account.

7. Display and print the following reports for July 1, 2004, to July 31, 2004:
   a. *Inventory Valuation Detail*
   b. *Inventory Stock Status by Item*
   c. *Purchases by Item Detail*
   d. *Sales by Item Detail*
   e. *Journal*
   f. *Profit & Loss Standard* (for the period June 1, 2004 – July 31, 2004)
   g. *Balance Sheet Standard*

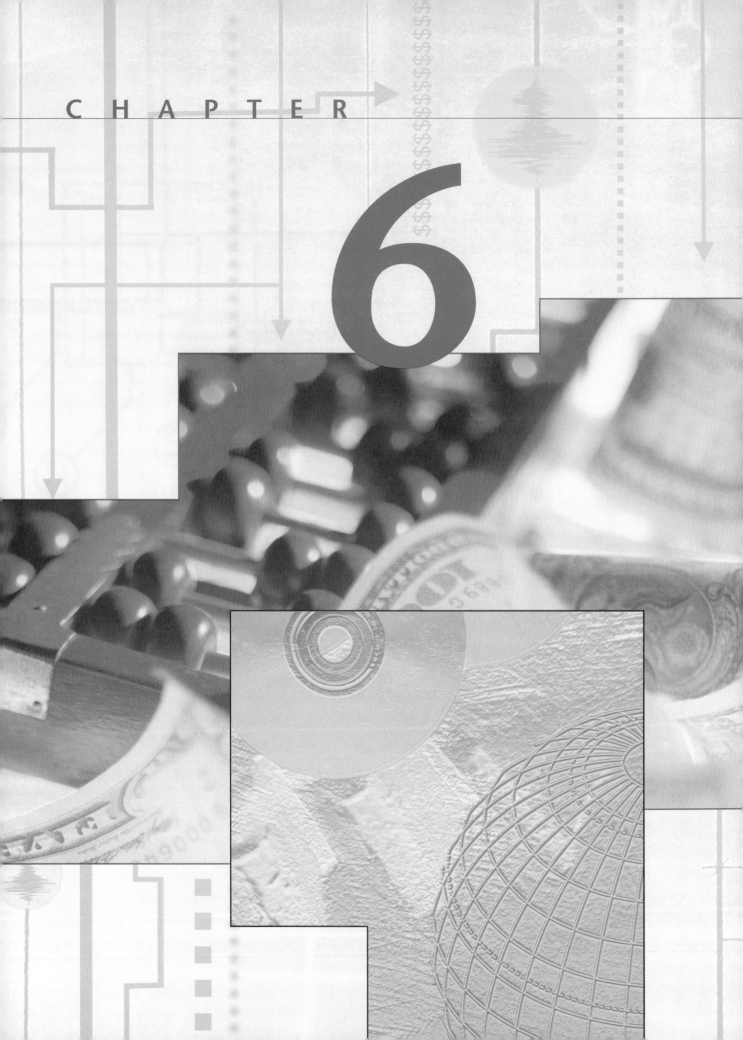

CHAPTER

6

NEW COMPANY SETUP—Part I
EasyStep Interview

- Create a new company file

- Set up the new company file using the EasyStep Interview window

- Display and print reports after using the EasyStep Interview window

- Review information recorded in the EasyStep Interview window and make any necessary corrections

INTRODUCTION

In this chapter you will begin learning how to create a new company file in QuickBooks Pro. As you know, the four levels of operation for QuickBooks Pro are New Company Setup, Lists, Activities, and Reports. In chapters 2 through 5, you learned and used the Lists, Activities, and Reports levels for both a service company and a merchandise company. You will now learn the first level of operations for QuickBooks Pro—New Company Setup.

QuickBooks Pro includes an *EasyStep Interview* window that is designed to guide you in creating and setting up a new company file. When you use the EasyStep Interview window, New Company Setup becomes a two-part process. The first part of the process involves entering information in the EasyStep Interview window. The second part allows you to take the information set up in the EasyStep Interview window, customize it according to your company's preferences, and prepare the company file for the accrual basis of accounting.

In this chapter, you will be using the EasyStep Interview window to create and set up a new company file for our sample company, Kristin Raina Interior Designs. Assume that Kristin Raina Interior Designs was recording accounting activities using a manual accounting system and has decided to convert the company's accounting records to QuickBooks Pro.

QUICKBOOKS PRO VERSUS MANUAL ACCOUNTING: NEW COMPANY SETUP

In a manual accounting system, a company's records are set up by creating the Chart of Accounts and the general ledger. The Chart of Accounts is the list of accounts (assets, liabilities, equity, revenues, and expenses) the company intends to use. The general ledger is the book of all accounts with the beginning balance for each. If desired, subsidiary ledgers are also created and beginning balances recorded. The subsidiary ledgers typically include accounts receivable and accounts payable. If the perpetual inventory system is used, an inventory subsidiary ledger would also be created.

In QuickBooks Pro, a company's records are set up by creating a new company file and establishing the Chart of Accounts List. As the accounts are set up, the opening balances are entered, from which QuickBooks Pro simultaneously sets up the general ledger. The Customer:Job List and Vendor List are set up; these lists are equivalent to the accounts receivable and accounts payable subsidiary ledgers. The Item List is set up, which is equivalent to an inventory subsidiary ledger, but in QuickBooks Pro the Item List also includes service revenue items and sales tax items in addition to inventory items.

In this chapter, you will use the EasyStep Interview window to create and set up a new company file. As you enter information in the EasyStep Interview window, the accounts with opening balances will be set up on the Chart of Accounts List. In addition, as you enter inventory items, customers, and vendors with opening balances, the Item List, Customer:Job List, and Vendor List will be set up.

CHAPTER PROBLEM

In this chapter, there is no company to open from the company files. Instead you will create and set up the company file for Kristin Raina Interior Designs.

Assume that Kristin Raina began operating her interior design business in January 2004 and has maintained accounting records with a manual accounting system for January through March. Effective April 1, 2004, Kristin Raina has decided to convert the company's accounting records to QuickBooks Pro using EasyStep Interview.

To create a new company file—
1. Open QuickBooks Pro.
2. At the *No Company Open* window, click on the Create a new company button or click File, and then click New Company. The EasyStep Interview window appears. (See figure 6–1.)

FIGURE 6-1
EasyStep Interview Window

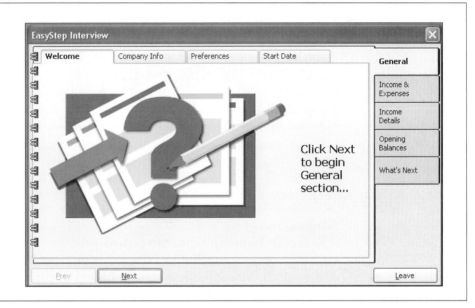

NEW COMPANY
SETUP: **EASYSTEP INTERVIEW**

In New Company Setup, the first level of operation in QuickBooks Pro, you will enter the information needed to create and set up a company file for Kristin Raina Interior Designs using the EasyStep Interview window.

The EasyStep Interview window is designed to guide you through the steps needed to create and set up a new company file. (EasyStep Interview is not the only way to create a company file in QuickBooks Pro; an alternative method is covered in chapter 8.)

The EasyStep Interview window includes five side tabs labeled General, Income & Expenses, Income Details, Opening Balances, and What's Next. When the window is first opened, the first side tab, General, is the active tab. Along the top of the window are four top tabs labeled Welcome, Company Info, Preferences, and Start Date. The top tabs displayed in figure 6–1 relate to the General side tab on the right. As the side tabs are changed, the top tabs will change accordingly.

For each top tab, there are a number of pages of information. As you click Next, the next page for each top tab is displayed. When all the pages for a top tab are finished, a check mark is placed on the top tab indicating that you completed the tab and QuickBooks Pro automatically moves to the first page of the next top tab. After all the top tabs are completed, QuickBooks Pro automatically moves to the next side tab on the right.

The EasyStep Interview window is organized based on the sections displayed on the side tabs. On the General tab, general company information is entered, company preferences are established, and a start date is identified. On the Income & Expenses tab, the income and expense accounts are created. On the Income Details tab, the service items and inventory items are set up. On the Opening Balances tab, the customers, vendors, and additional general ledger accounts (assets and liabilities) with opening balances are created.

At any time, you can click the Leave button to leave the EasyStep Interview window. However, although you may leave the EasyStep Interview window at any time, it is advisable not to leave before saving the company file, which is done in the Company Info top tab, and until the Preferences top tab is complete. If you leave the window before saving the company file, all information will be lost. If you leave the window before completing the Preferences top tab, QuickBooks Pro automatically assumes certain default settings that cannot be changed or reversed. If you cannot complete the EasyStep Interview in one sitting, at least complete the General tab before leaving the EasyStep Interview.

If you leave EasyStep Interview, you can return to it by clicking File and then EasyStep Interview. Whenever you return to EasyStep Interview, you return to the same page where you left off as long as the company file has been saved.

General Tab

The General side tab is used to record some basic background information about the company including company name, tax identification numbers, and so on. In addition, the company file preferences are established in this section. The company information can later be edited by clicking Company and then Company Information. The preferences can be edited by clicking Edit and then Preferences. Although most preferences can be subsequently changed, there are some that cannot be changed.

Welcome

1. At the Welcome top tab of the EasyStep Interview, click Next.
2. Read each page in the Welcome tab and click Next until the Welcome section is complete.
3. Click Next to move to the Company Info top tab.

You will see on one page in the Welcome section a button to Skip Interview. An alternative method of New Company Setup is to skip most of the EasyStep Interview window. This alternative method is covered in a later chapter. (Chapter 8.)

The Welcome tab is completed. A check mark is placed next to the Welcome top tab and you are moved to the Company Info top tab.

HINT

If you want to activate the Next button using the keyboard, press Alt + N.

Company Info

To enter company information—

1. On the Company Info tab, read the General: Company Information page and click <u>N</u>ext.
2. At the Your company name page, key the company name **CH6 [Your Name] Kristin Raina Interior Designs** in the *Company Name* field.

   When you tab to the *Legal name* field, the same name is automatically filled in. The legal name is the name that will be used on tax forms. If the company name and legal name are not the same you can make any necessary changes. (See figure 6–2.)

FIGURE 6-2
Company Info – Your Company Name Page

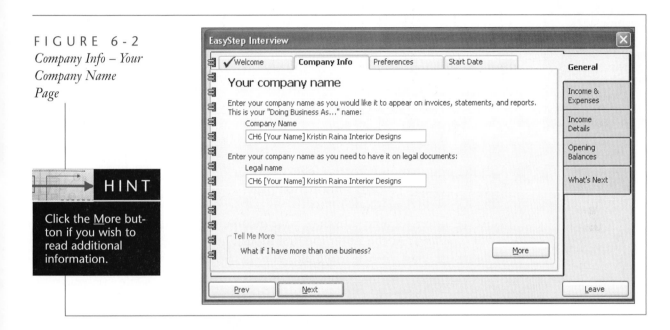

HINT

Click the <u>M</u>ore button if you wish to read additional information.

3. Since the company name and legal name are the same, click <u>N</u>ext.
4. At the Your company information page key in or click the following information:

Address:	**25 NE Johnson Street**
City:	**Minneapolis**
State:	**MN**
Zip:	**53402**
Phone #:	**651-555-1000**
FAX#:	**651-555-2000**
Email:	**KRID@emcp.net**

(See figure 6-3.)

FIGURE 6-3
Company Info – Your Company Information Page

HINT

If you key the letter **M** in the state field, the first state that begins with *M (MA)* is displayed. To choose *MN*, keep pressing the M key. You will scroll through all states beginning with M. An alternative is to click the drop-down arrow to display the list of states.

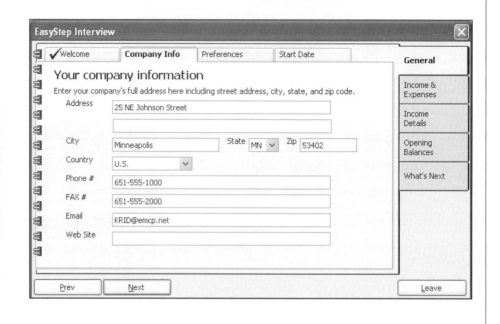

5. If the information is correct, click <u>N</u>ext.
6. At the Other company information page, at the *Enter the federal tax ID number* field, key **33-4777781**.
7. At the Enter the first month of your income tax year drop-down list, click *January*. At the Enter the first month in your fiscal year drop-down list, click *January*. (See figure 6–4.)

FIGURE 6-4
Company Info – Other Company Information Page

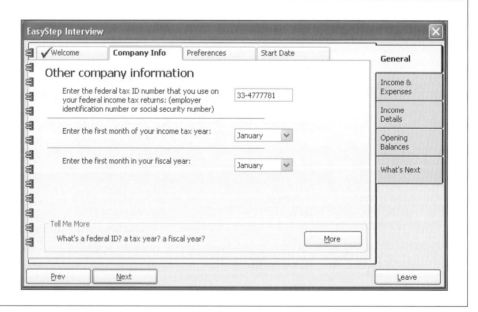

8. If the information is correct, click <u>N</u>ext.
9. At the Your company income tax form page, accept the default *<Other/None>* by clicking <u>N</u>ext.

10. If a Tax Form window appears, click OK.
11. At the Select your type of business page, scroll down the Industry list and click *Other*. (See figure 6–5.)

FIGURE 6-5
*Company Info –
Select Your Type of
Business Page*

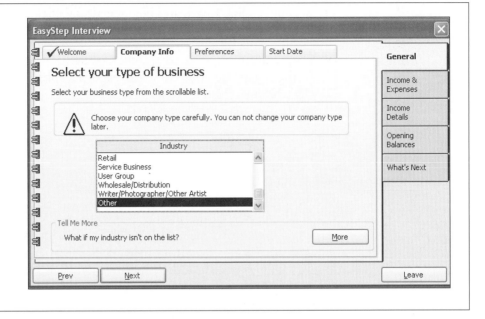

12. If the information is correct, click Next.
13. Read the Setup tips for your business page, then click Next.
14. Read the We're ready to create your company file now page, and click Next. The Save As dialog box appears.
15. Choose your subfolder in the Save in text box, and accept the file name *CH6 [Your Name] Kristin Raina Interior Designs.QBW*.
16. If the information is correct, click Save. The new company file has been created and saved.
17. At the Your income and expense accounts page, click *No, I'd like to create my own*. (See figure 6–6.)

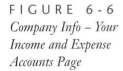

HINT

In the File name text box, use the arrow keys to scroll through the entire name.

FIGURE 6-6
*Company Info – Your
Income and Expense
Accounts Page*

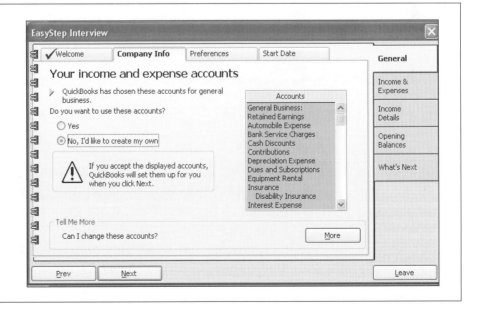

If you were to click *Yes* at this window, QuickBooks Pro would create a Chart of Accounts for you. If you click *Yes* and then click Next, you would not be able to return to the page using the Prev button and reverse your choice. If you inadvertently click *Yes* and create a Chart of Accounts, click Leave and begin again by clicking File and then New. In the Save As dialog box, replace the previous file.

18. If the information is correct, click Next.
19. At the Accessing your company page, accept the default 0 (zero), and click Next.
20. At the Company Info completed page, click Next.

The Company Info tab is completed. A check mark is placed next to the Company Info top tab and you are moved to the Preferences top tab.

Preferences

To enter preferences—

1. Read the What are preferences? page and click Next.
2. At the Inventory page, click *Yes* and then click Next.
3. At the Enabling Inventory page, click *Yes* and then click Next.
4. At the Sales tax page, click *Yes* and then click Next.
5. At the Single or multiple sales tax rates? page, click *I collect single tax rate paid to single tax agency* and then click Next.
6. At the Sales tax information page, key in the following information:

HINT

For the sales tax rate, you only have to key **7** and move to the next field and 7.0% is displayed.

short name for sales tax:	**Minn. Sales Tax**
sales tax description:	**Sales Tax**
sales tax rate:	7
government agency:	**Minn. Dept. of Revenue**

(See figure 6–7.)

FIGURE 6-7
Preferences – Sales Tax Information Page

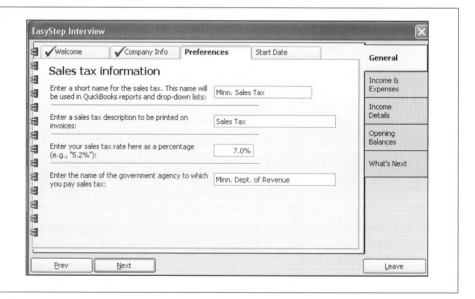

7. If the information is correct, click Next.
8. At the Your invoice format page, click *Product* and then click Next.

Recall in chapter 5 that in the Create Invoices window you used the Product Invoice template to record the sale of inventory items. By choosing Product in the EasyStep Interview window, you are choosing the Product Invoice as the default template for the Create Invoices window. If you do not choose Product Invoice here, the Create Invoices window will display the Service Invoice form by default. You can easily change the invoice in the *Template* field of the Create Invoices window.

9. At the Using QuickBooks for Payroll page, click *No*. (See figure 6–8.)

FIGURE 6-8

*Preferences – Using
QuickBooks for
Payroll Page*

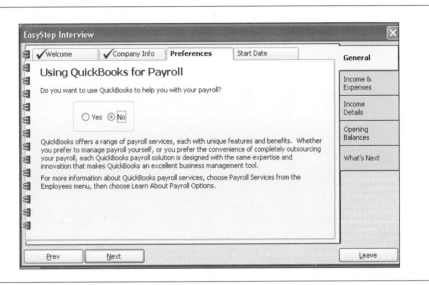

Regardless of whether you click Yes or No for using QuickBooks Pro for payroll, the software automatically creates a Payroll Liabilities account and a Payroll Expenses account. You will not be able to delete either of these accounts but you may mark them as Inactive accounts so that they do not appear in the Chart of Accounts.

10. If the information is correct, click Next.

At this point, the company file has been saved, the choice to create your own Chart of Accounts has been made, and the payroll option has been turned off. It is now safe to use the Leave button at any time from this point on. If you do leave the EasyStep Interview at this point, the new company file is opened. The Getting Started and Company Navigator windows, along with the Open Windows List all appear. You can close these windows by clicking the X in each window. At the Closing the Open Window List message, place a check mark in the box to the left of Do not display this message in the future and click Yes. To remove the Icon bar, click on View and then click Icon Bar.

To reopen the EasyStep Interview window, click File and then EasyStep Interview. When you reopen the EasyStep Interview window, you will return to the page you last had opened.

11. At the Estimates, Time tracking, and Tracking segments of your business with "classes" pages, click *No* and click Next at each page.
12. At the Two ways to handle bills and payments page, click *Enter the bills first and then enter the payments later.*

13. If the information is correct, click <u>N</u>ext.
14. At the Reminders list page, click *When I ask for it*, and then click <u>N</u>ext.
15. At the Preferences completed! page, click <u>N</u>ext.

The Preferences tab is completed. A check mark is placed next to the Preferences top tab and you are moved to the Start Date top tab.

Start Date
The Start Date top tab is used to identify the date the company began to use QuickBooks Pro. For our sample company Kristin Raina Interior Designs, the fiscal start date is January 1, 2004. The QuickBooks Pro start date is April 1. You will enter the balances as of April 1, which represent January 1 – March 31 activities, in the new company file as part of the New Company Setup.

1. Read the pages Understanding your QuickBooks start date and Information for your start date, and click <u>N</u>ext at each page.
2. At the Choose your QuickBooks start date page, choose *04/01/2004*. (See figure 6–9.)

(See figure 6–9.)

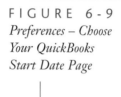

F I G U R E 6 - 9
Preferences – Choose Your QuickBooks Start Date Page

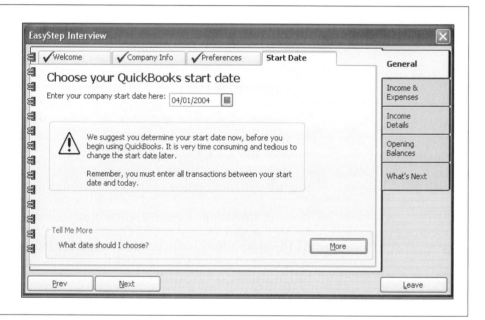

3. If the information is correct, click <u>N</u>ext. The Start Date tab is completed and a check mark is placed on the Start Date top tab.
4. At the General section completed! page, click <u>N</u>ext.

The General tab is completed. A check mark is placed next to the General side tab and you are moved to the Income & Expenses side tab.

INCOME & EXPENSES TAB
The Income & Expenses tab is used to record the income and expense accounts that you will use in this company file. These are accounts that will be added to the Chart of Accounts List and can later be edited, if necessary, using the procedures to edit an account. When you move to the Income &

Expenses side tab, the top tabs are changed to Income Accts and Expense Accts.

Income Accts

On the Income Accts top tab, the steps to add an income account are equivalent to adding a new income account to the Chart of Accounts List. In the EasyStep Interview window only account names, not account numbers, are entered. You will add the account numbers later when customizing the Chart of Accounts List. Kristin Raina Interior Designs has two service revenue accounts and four sale of inventory accounts.

To add income accounts—
1. Read each income accounts page and click Next until you come to the Adding an income account page.
2. At the Adding an income account page, in the *Account Name* field, key **Design Services**. Leave the *Tax Line* field as *<Unassigned>*. (See figure 6–10.)

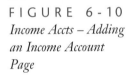

FIGURE 6-10
Income Accts – Adding an Income Account Page

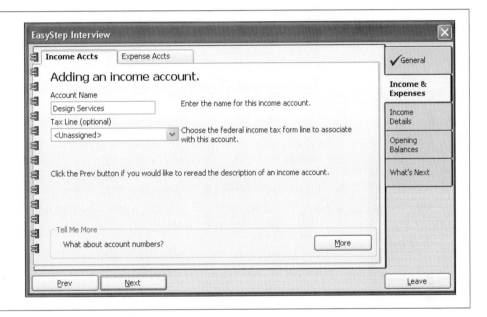

3. If the information is correct, click Next. The Add another income account page appears.

The first income account, *Design Services*, is listed in the Income Accounts box.

4. The default setting is to add another account. Accept the default *Yes* and click Next.
5. Add the remaining income accounts listed below in the same manner as in steps 2 through 4 above.

Decorating Services	**Sale of Lamps**
Sale of Carpets	**Sale of Mirrors**
Sale of Draperies	

As you add accounts, they will be listed alphabetically. When the account numbers are added later, the accounts will be listed numerically.

6. After adding the last account, *Sale of Mirrors*, click *No* at the Add another income account page. (See figure 6–11.)

FIGURE 6-11
Income Accts – Add Another Income Account Page – Completed

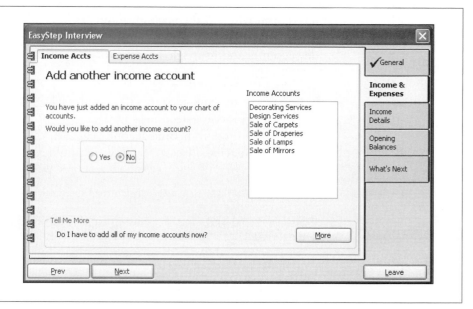

7. If the information is correct, click <u>N</u>ext.
8. At the Income accounts completed page, click <u>N</u>ext.

The Income Accts tab is completed. A check mark is placed next to the Income Accts top tab and you are moved to the Expense Accts top tab.

Expense Accts
On the Expense Accts top tab, the steps to add an expense account are equivalent to adding a new expense account to the Chart of Accounts List. Any expenses added in this section are labeled an Expense account type in the Chart of Accounts List. As with the income accounts, account numbers are not entered at this time but will be added when you customize the Chart of Accounts List. Kristin Raina Interior Designs has 10 expense accounts.

To add expense accounts—

1. Read the Expense Accounts, More details on expense accounts, and More details on subaccounts pages, clicking <u>N</u>ext after each, until you come to the Here are your expense accounts page.

   Notice one account, Payroll Expenses, is listed. QuickBooks Pro creates this account by default.

2. Click <u>N</u>ext. At the Adding an expense account page, in the *Account Name* field, key **Accounting Expense**. Leave the *Tax Line* field as *<Unassigned>*. (See figure 6–12.)

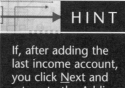

HINT

If, after adding the last income account, you click <u>N</u>ext and return to the Adding an income account page, click <u>P</u>rev to return to the Here are your income accounts page and then click *No*.

FIGURE 6-12
Expense Accts –
Adding an Expense
Account Page

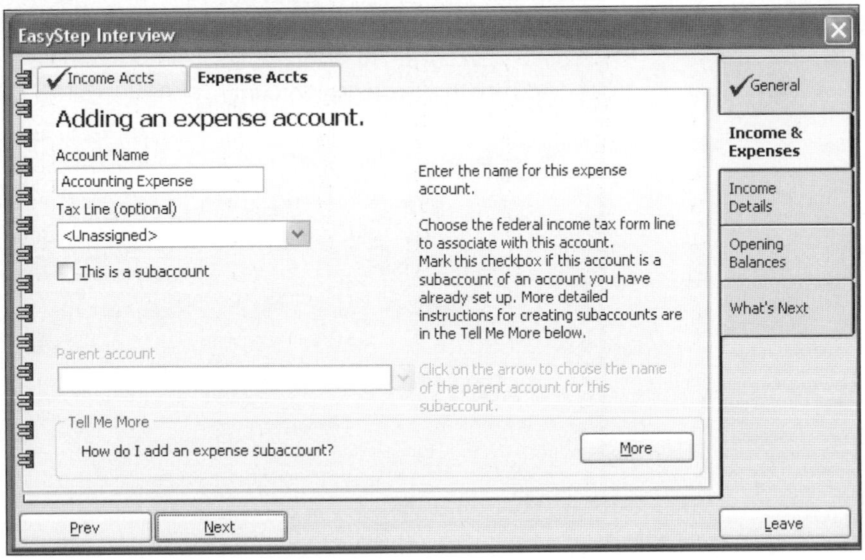

3. If the information is correct, click Next. The Add another expense account? page appears.

   The expense account, *Accounting Expense*, is now listed in the Expense Accounts box above Payroll Expenses.

4. The default setting is to add another account. Accept the default *Yes* and click Next. The Adding an expense account page appears.

5. Add the remaining expense accounts listed below in the same manner as in steps 2 through 4 above.

   > **Advertising Expense**
   > **Deprec. Exp., Furniture**
   > **Deprec. Exp., Computers**
   > **Insurance Expense**
   > **Janitorial Expense**
   > **Office Supplies Expense**
   > **Rent Expense**
   > **Telephone Expense**
   > **Utilities Expense**

   Use care when entering expense accounts. If you make a mistake here, it cannot be corrected in the EasyStep Interview window but must be corrected later when reviewing the Chart of Accounts List.

6. After adding the last expense account, *Utilities Expense*, at the Add another expense account? page, click *No*. (See figure 6–13.)

FIGURE 6-13
*Expense Accts – Add
Another Expense Account
Page - Completed*

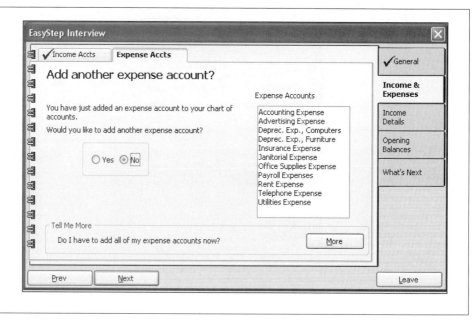

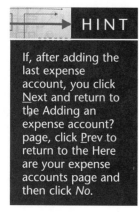

HINT

If, after adding the last expense account, you click <u>N</u>ext and return to the Adding an expense account? page, click <u>P</u>rev to return to the Here are your expense accounts page and then click *No*.

7. If the information is correct, click <u>N</u>ext. The Expense Accts tab is completed and a check mark is placed next to the Expense Accts top tab.
8. At the Expense accounts completed! page, click <u>N</u>ext.

The Income & Expenses tab is completed. A check mark is placed next to the Income & Expenses side tab and you are moved to the Income Details side tab.

INCOME DETAILS TAB

The Income Details side tab is used to identify service items, non-inventory part items, and inventory part items. The service items and non-inventory part items are identified in the Items top tab; the inventory part items are identified on the Inventory top tab. Kristin Raina Interior Designs provides two service items and four inventory items.

Introduction

1. Read the introduction pages.
2. Accept the defaults, and click <u>N</u>ext after each page until the Introduction tab is completed and you move to the Items top tab.

Items

On the Items top tab, the steps to enter the service items are equivalent to adding a new service item to the Item List.

To enter the service items—

1. Read the Income Details: Items page and click <u>N</u>ext.
2. At the Service Items page click *Yes* and then click <u>N</u>ext.
3. At the Service Item: Name page, in both the *Item Name* and *Sales Description* fields, key **Design Services**.
4. In the *Sales Price* field, key **60**. For this company, services are not taxable items, so leave the Taxable Item check box unchecked. (See figure 6–14.)

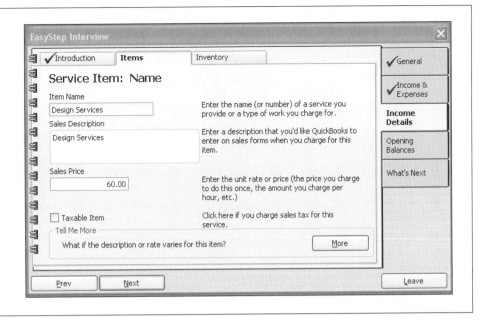

FIGURE 6-14
*Items – Service Item:
Name Page*

5. If the information is correct, click <u>N</u>ext.
6. At the Service Item: Income account page, in the *Income Account* field, click *Design Services* from the drop-down list.
7. If the information is correct, click <u>N</u>ext.
8. At the Subcontracted expenses page, click *No* and click <u>N</u>ext.
9. At the Set up another service item page, click *Yes* and click <u>N</u>ext.
10. Add the *Decorating Services* item in the same manner as in steps 3 through 8. Decorating Services are charged at $50 per hour.
11. At the Set up another service item page, click *No* and click <u>N</u>ext.
12. At the Non-inventory Parts page and Other Charges page, click *No* and then click <u>N</u>ext.
13. At the Items completed! page, click <u>N</u>ext.

The Items tab is completed. A check mark is placed next to the Items top tab and you are moved to the Inventory top tab.

Inventory
On the Inventory top tab, the steps to enter the inventory items are equivalent to adding an inventory part to the Item List.

To enter the inventory items—
1. Read the Income Details: Inventory page and click <u>N</u>ext.
2. At the Adding an inventory item page, click *Yes* and then click <u>N</u>ext.
3. At the Inventory Item: Sales Information page, key the following information:

Item Name:	**Carpets**
Sales Description:	**Carpets**
Sales Price:	**400**
Taxable Item:	**✓ (taxable)**

(See figure 6–15.)

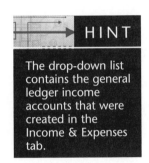

HINT

The drop-down list contains the general ledger income accounts that were created in the Income & Expenses tab.

HINT

The Items tab is used to record service items and non-inventory part items; the Inventory tab is used to record inventory part items.

FIGURE 6-15
Inventory – Inventory Item:
Sales Information Page

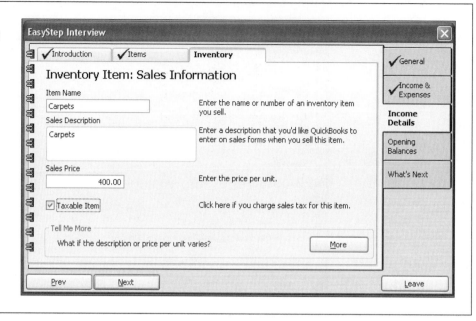

4. If the information is correct, click <u>N</u>ext.
5. At the Inventory Item: Income Account page, click *Sale of Carpets* from the drop-down list.
6. If the information is correct, click <u>N</u>ext.
7. At the Inventory Item: Purchase Information page, key the following information:

Purchase Description:	**Carpets**
Cost:	**200**

(See figure 6–16.)

FIGURE 6-16
Inventory – Inventory Item:
Purchase Information Page

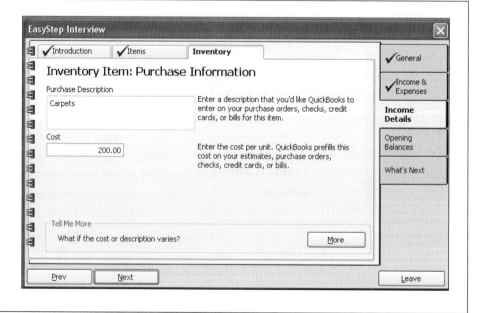

8. If the information is correct, click <u>N</u>ext.
9. At the Inventory Item: Inventory Information page, key the following information:

Reorder Point:	**5**
Qty on Hand:	**4**

When you move to the Total value as of 4/01/2004, the total value of 800.00 is automatically completed based on the quantity on hand and the cost indicated in the purchase information window. (See figure 6–17.)

FIGURE 6-17

Inventory – Inventory Item: Inventory Information Page

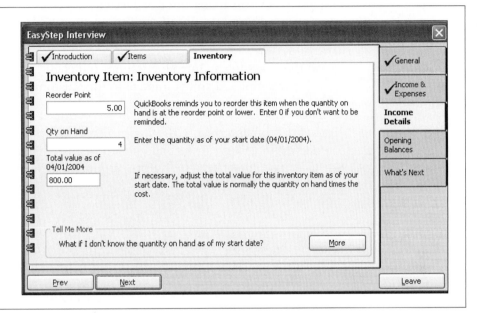

10. If the information is correct, click <u>N</u>ext.
11. At the Set up another inventory item, click *Yes* and then <u>N</u>ext.
12. Enter the remaining inventory items listed below in the same manner as in steps 3 through 10. All inventory items are taxable.

Item Name, Sales and Purchase Description	Sales Price	Income Account	Cost	Reorder Point	Qty on Hand	Total Value
Draperies	$250.00	Sale of Draperies	$125.00	5	8	$1,000.00
Lamps	200.00	Sale of Lamps	100.00	5	10	1,000.00
Mirrors	300.00	Sale of Mirrors	150.00	5	6	900.00

ACCOUNTING
c o n c e p t

Inventory Asset		Open. Bal. Equity	
Dr	Cr	Dr	Cr
Carpets 800			800
Draperies 1,000			1,000
Lamps 1,000			1,000
Mirrors 900			900
Bal 3,700			3,700

13. After entering all inventory items, at the Set up another inventory item page, click *No* and then click <u>N</u>ext. The Inventory tab is completed and a check mark is placed next to the Inventory top tab.
14. At the Inventory completed! page, click <u>N</u>ext.

The Income Details tab is completed. A check mark is placed on the Income Details side tab and you are moved to the Opening Balances side tab.

OPENING BALANCES TAB

The Opening Balances side tab is used to create and enter the beginning balances for customers, vendors, and accounts. Only customers, vendors, and accounts with beginning balances are entered at this time. Customers, vendors, and accounts without a balance are entered as part of updating Lists after completing the EasyStep Interview. In addition, only the customer and vendor names are entered in this section. Additional background information, such as address, telephone number, and so on, is added as part of updating Vendor and Customer:Job Lists after completing the EasyStep Interview. Kristin Raina Interior Designs has two customers and seven vendors with balances.

Introduction

Read the pages in the Introduction tab and click Next until the Introduction top tab is completed and you move to the Customers top tab.

Customers

At the Customers top tab, the steps to enter customers with opening balances are similar to those of adding a new customer to the Customer:Job List, but not all background information is entered at this time.

To enter Customers with opening balances—
1. Read the Opening Balances: Customers page and click Next.
2. At the Enter customers page, click *Yes* and then Next.
3. At the Customer job tracking page, click *No* and then click Next.
4. At the Adding customer page, in the *Customer Name* field, key **Burnitz Bakery Company**.
5. At the *Balance due on start date* field, key **600**. (See figure 6–18.)

FIGURE 6-18
Customers – Adding Customer Page

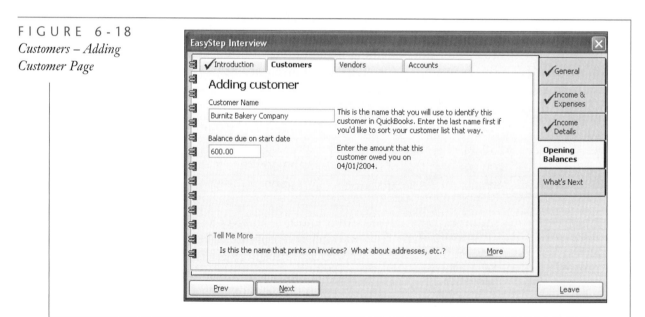

6. If the information is correct, click Next. The Adding another customer page appears. Burnitz Bakery Company is listed in the Customer:Jobs list.
7. At Would you like to add another customer now? click *Yes* and click Next.

8. Add the remaining customer listed below in the same manner as steps 4 through 6.

Franco Films Co.   **940**

9. After entering this customer, click *No* at the Adding another customer page. (See figure 6–19.)

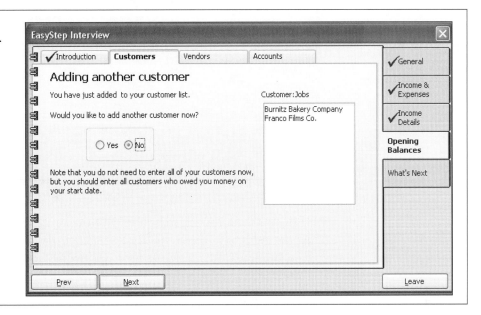

FIGURE 6-19
Customers – Adding Another Customer Page – Completed

10. If the information is correct, click <u>N</u>ext. The Customers tab is completed and a check mark is placed next to the Customers top tab.
11. At the Customers completed! page, click <u>N</u>ext. You are moved to the Vendors top tab.

ACCOUNTING
concept

Accounts Receivable		Uncategorized Income	
Dr	Cr	Dr	Cr
600			600
940			940
Bal 1,540			1,540 Bal

Vendors

On the Vendors top tab, the steps to enter vendors with opening balances are similar to those of adding a new vendor to the Vendor List, but not all background information is entered at this time.

To enter vendors with opening balances—
1. Read the Opening Balances: Vendors page and click <u>N</u>ext.
2. At the Adding Vendors with open balances page, click *Yes* and then click <u>N</u>ext.
3. At the Adding Vendor page in the *Vendor Name* field, key **Ace Glass Works**.
4. At the *Balance due on start date* field, key **1500**. (See figure 6–20.)

FIGURE 6-20
Vendors – Adding Vendor Page

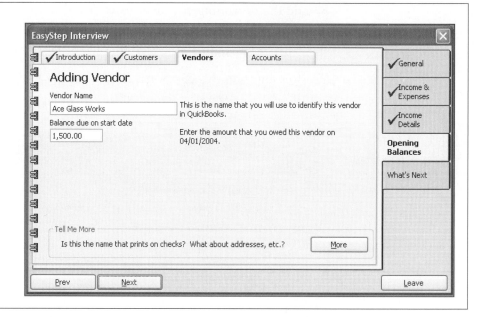

5. If the information is correct, click <u>N</u>ext.
6. At the Adding another vendor page, click *Yes* and then click <u>N</u>ext.
7. Add the remaining vendors listed below in the same manner as steps 3 through 5.

Bell Carpet Design	**2,000**
Cone and Clemens Associates	**400**
Galeway Computers	**2,600**
Midwest Mutual Insurance Co.	**2,400**
Minneapolis Electric & Gas Co.	**450**
Williams Office Supply Company	**400**

8. After the last vendor is added, at the Adding another vendor page click *No* and then click <u>N</u>ext. The Vendors tab is completed and a check mark is placed next to the Vendors top tab.
9. At the Vendors completed! page, click <u>N</u>ext. You are moved to the Accounts top tab.

ACCOUNTING
c o n c e p t

Uncategorized Expenses		Accounts Payable	
Dr	Cr	Dr	Cr
1,500			1,500
2,000			2,000
400			400
2,600			2,600
2,400			2,400
450			450
400			400
Bal 9,750			9,750 Bal

Accounts

Up to this point, QuickBooks Pro has created income and expense general ledger accounts as part of the EasyStep Interview process. In addition, QuickBooks Pro automatically creates the Accounts Receivable, Inventory Asset, Accounts Payable, Payroll Liabilities, Sales Tax Payable, and Opening Bal. Equity accounts based on information entered in the EasyStep Interview window.

On the Accounts top tab, the steps to add accounts with opening balances are equivalent to those of adding a new account to the Chart of Accounts List. At this time, you will add the remaining accounts with opening balances. Kristin Raina Interior Designs has 11 accounts with balances. The liabilities accounts are entered first, followed by current assets, and finally fixed assets.

To add accounts with opening balances—

1. Read the Opening Balances: Accounts page, and click <u>N</u>ext.
2. At the Credit card accounts and Adding line of credit pages, click *No* and then <u>N</u>ext.
3. At the Loans and Notes Payable page, click *Yes* and then click <u>N</u>ext.
4. At the Adding a loan (liability) account page, key **Notes Payable** in the *Name* field.
5. In the *Unpaid Balance on 04/01/2004* field, key **7000**. This is not a long-term liability. (See figure 6–21.)

FIGURE 6-21
Accounts – Adding a Loan (Liability) Account Page

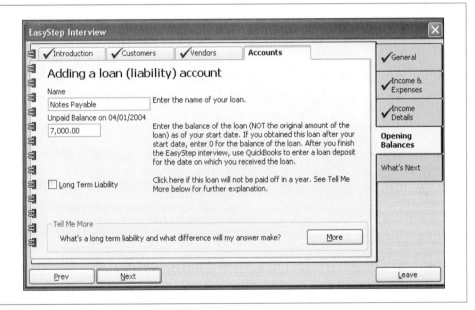

6. If the information is correct, click <u>N</u>ext.

   The Adding another loan page appears. The accounts listed are labeled Other Liabilities type accounts in the Chart of Accounts List. The Sales Tax Payable account was created by QuickBooks Pro when information about Sales Tax was entered on the General tab – Preferences tab. QuickBooks Pro creates the Payroll Liabilities account by default.

7. At the Adding another loan page, click *Yes* and then click <u>N</u>ext.

8. Add **Interest Payable** with an unpaid balance of **150** and then click <u>N</u>ext.
9. At the Adding another loan page, click *No*. (See figure 6–22.)

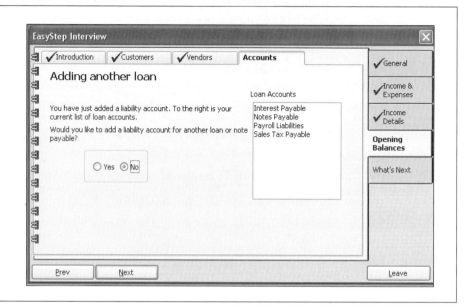

10. If the information is correct, click <u>N</u>ext.

ACCOUNTING
  c o n c e p t

Notes Payable		Interest Payable		Open. Bal. Equity	
Dr	Cr	Dr	Cr	Dr	Cr
	7,000		150	7,000	
				150	

11. At the Bank accounts page, click *Yes* and then click <u>N</u>ext.
12. At the Adding a bank account page, in the *Name* field, key **Cash – Operating**.
13. Click <u>N</u>ext.
14. At the Last statement date and balance page, in the *Statement Ending Date* field, choose *04/01/2004*.
15. At the *Statement Ending Balance* field, key **50855.38**. (See figure 6–23.)

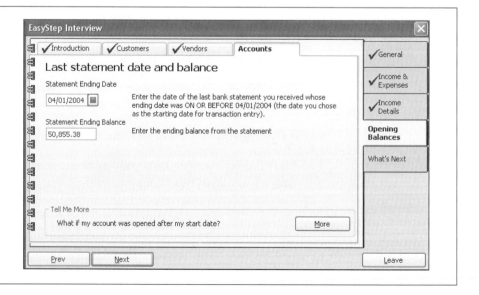

16. If the information is correct, click Next.
17. At the Adding another bank account page, click *No* and then click Next.
18. Read the Introduction to assets page and click Next.
19. At the Asset accounts page, click *Yes* and then click Next.
20. At the Adding an asset account page, key the following information:

Name:	**Design Supplies**
Type:	**Other Current Asset**
Asset value on 04/01/2004:	**200**

(See figure 6–24.)

Accounts – Adding an Asset Account Page

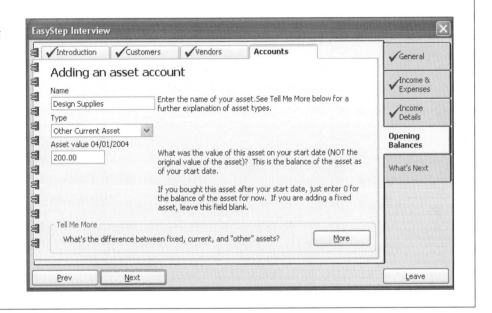

21. If the information is correct, click Next.
22. At the Adding another asset page, click *Yes*.
23. Click Next and add the remaining other current asset accounts listed below in the same manner as steps 20 through 21.

Office Supplies	**250**
Prepaid Advertising	**400**
Prepaid Insurance	**2,200**

HINT

The Accounts Receivable account was created when customers were entered. The Inventory Asset account was created when inventory part items were entered.

ACCOUNTING
concept

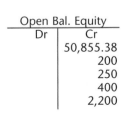

Cash - Operating		Design Supplies		Office Supplies		Prepaid Advertising	
Dr	Cr	Dr	Cr	Dr	Cr	Dr	Cr
50,855.38		200		250		400	

Prepaid Insurance		Open Bal. Equity	
Dr	Cr	Dr	Cr
2,200			50,855.38
			200
			250
			400
			2,200

24. At the Adding another asset page, click *Yes* and then click <u>N</u>ext.
25. Add the asset account Furniture. Change the account type to *Fixed Asset*. The asset value field becomes dim, or inactive. (See figure 6–25.)

FIGURE 6-25

Accounts – Adding an Asset Account Page – Fixed Asset

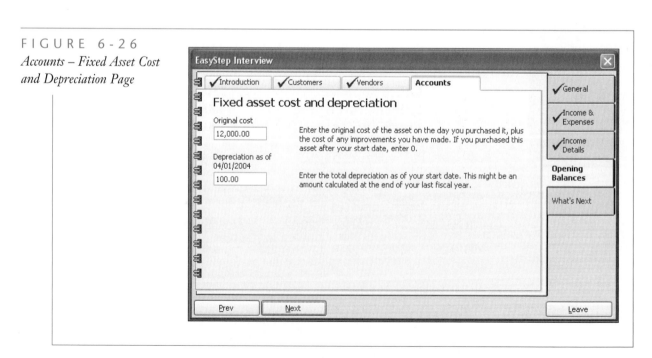

26. If the information is correct, click <u>N</u>ext.
27. At the question Do you track depreciation for this fixed asset?, click *Yes* and then click <u>N</u>ext.
28. At the Fixed asset cost and depreciation page, in the *Original cost* field, key **12000**.
29. In the *Depreciation as of 4/01/2004* field, key **100**. (See figure 6–26.)

FIGURE 6-26

Accounts – Fixed Asset Cost and Depreciation Page

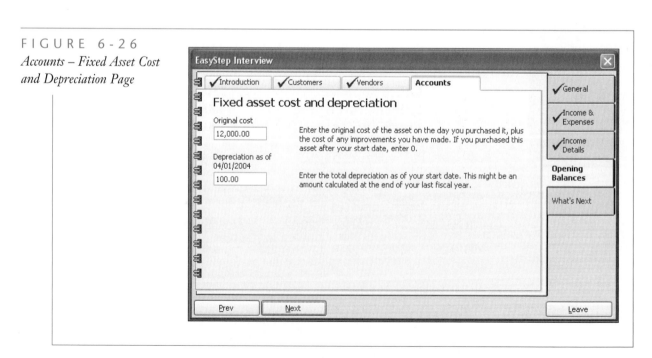

30. If the information is correct, click <u>N</u>ext.
31. At the Adding another asset page, click *Yes* and then click <u>N</u>ext.
32. Add the computer accounts listed below in the same manner as steps 25 through 30.

> | | |
> |---|---|
> | *Computers (Original cost)* | **3,600** |
> | *Depreciation as of 4/01/2004* | **60** |

33. After all the assets are entered, at the Adding another asset page, click *No*. (See figure 6–27.)

FIGURE 6-27
Accounts – Adding Another Asset Account Page – Completed

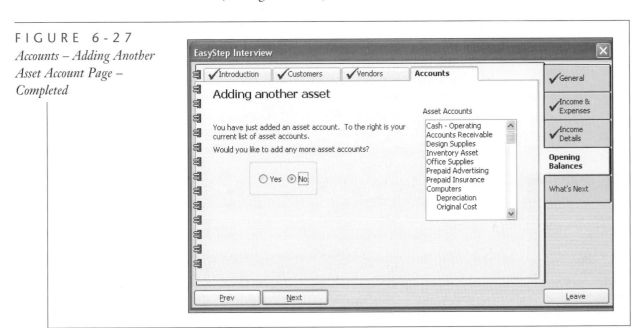

The Furniture accounts are listed below the Computer accounts. Use the scroll arrow to review all accounts.

ACCOUNTING
c o n c e p t

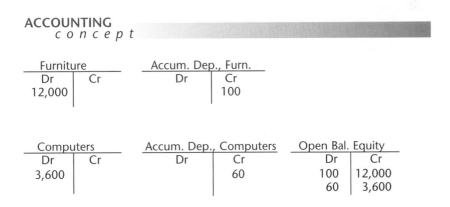

Furniture		Accum. Dep., Furn.	
Dr	Cr	Dr	Cr
12,000			100

Computers		Accum. Dep., Computers		Open Bal. Equity	
Dr	Cr	Dr	Cr	Dr	Cr
3,600			60	100	12,000
				60	3,600

34. If the information is correct, click <u>N</u>ext.
35. Read the pages on equity and click <u>N</u>ext at each page. The Accounts tab is completed and a check mark is placed next to the Accounts top tab.
36. At the Accounts completed! page, click <u>N</u>ext.

The Opening Balances tab is complete. A check mark is placed next to the Opening Balances side tab and you are moved to the What's Next side tab.

WHAT'S NEXT TAB

The What's Next side tab provides you with information and steps recommended to complete the company file setup.

1. Read the pages in the What's Next tab and click <u>N</u>ext until you come to the Finishing Up top tab. The What's Next tab is completed and a check mark is placed next to the What's Next side tab.
2. Read the Finishing Up tab. The Finishing Up tab is completed. A check mark is placed next to the Finishing Up top tab.
3. Click <u>L</u>eave. If you have not previously clicked the Leave button, the Getting Started and Company Navigator windows, the Open Windows List, and the Icon Bar all appear.
4. You can close the Getting Started, Company Navigator windows and the Open Windows List by clicking the X in each window. At the Closing the Open Window List message, place a check mark in the box to the left of Do not display this message in the future and click <u>Y</u>es. To remove the Icon bar, click on <u>V</u>iew and then click <u>I</u>con Bar.

Upon completing the EasyStep Interview window, you need to review and edit the information before continuing on to Part II of New Company Setup.

REVIEWING AND EDITING EASYSTEP INTERVIEW INFORMATION

Upon completing the EasyStep Interview, you need to review certain reports to view how QuickBooks Pro has recorded the information based on the EasyStep Interview and to determine if any errors, such as misspellings or wrong amounts, were entered and need to be corrected. Only errors in entering information in the EasyStep Interview are corrected at this time. You will make other changes as part of customizing the company file in Part II of New Company Setup (chapter 7).

CHART OF ACCOUNTS LIST

Reviewing the Chart of Accounts List allows you to see the accounts set up as part of the EasyStep Interview.

To view and print the Chart of Accounts List—

1. Click <u>R</u>eports, and then click <u>L</u>ist.
2. At the List submenu, click <u>A</u>ccount Listing.
3. To print the Chart of Accounts List, click Prin<u>t</u>.
4. At the Print Reports dialog box, check the settings, then click Print. If you receive a message about Printing Features, place a check mark in the box to the left of Do not display this message in the future and click <u>N</u>o. Your printout should look like figure 6–28.

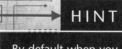

FIGURE 6-28
Account Listing

CH6 [Your Name] Kristin Raina Interior Designs
Account Listing
April 1, 2004

Account	Type	Balance Total	Description	Tax Line
Cash - Operating	Bank	50,855.38		<Unassigned>
Accounts Receivable	Accounts Receivable	1,540.00		<Unassigned>
Design Supplies	Other Current Asset	200.00		<Unassigned>
Inventory Asset	Other Current Asset	3,700.00		<Unassigned>
Office Supplies	Other Current Asset	250.00		<Unassigned>
Prepaid Advertising	Other Current Asset	400.00		<Unassigned>
Prepaid Insurance	Other Current Asset	2,200.00		<Unassigned>
Computers	Fixed Asset	3,540.00		<Unassigned>
Computers:Depreciation	Fixed Asset	-60.00		<Unassigned>
Computers:Original Cost	Fixed Asset	3,600.00		<Unassigned>
Furniture	Fixed Asset	11,900.00		<Unassigned>
Furniture:Depreciation	Fixed Asset	-100.00		<Unassigned>
Furniture:Original Cost	Fixed Asset	12,000.00		<Unassigned>
Accounts Payable	Accounts Payable	9,750.00		<Unassigned>
Interest Payable	Other Current Liability	150.00		<Unassigned>
Notes Payable	Other Current Liability	7,000.00		<Unassigned>
Payroll Liabilities	Other Current Liability	0.00		<Unassigned>
Sales Tax Payable	Other Current Liability	0.00		<Unassigned>
Opening Bal Equity	Equity	65,895.38		<Unassigned>
Retained Earnings	Equity			<Unassigned>
Decorating Services	Income			<Unassigned>
Design Services	Income			<Unassigned>
Sale of Carpets	Income			<Unassigned>
Sale of Draperies	Income			<Unassigned>
Sale of Lamps	Income			<Unassigned>
Sale of Mirrors	Income			<Unassigned>
Uncategorized Income	Income			<Unassigned>
Cost of Goods Sold	Cost of Goods Sold			<Unassigned>
Accounting Expense	Expense			<Unassigned>
Advertising Expense	Expense			<Unassigned>
Deprec. Exp., Computers	Expense			<Unassigned>
Deprec. Exp., Furniture	Expense			<Unassigned>
Insurance Expense	Expense			<Unassigned>
Janitorial Expense	Expense			<Unassigned>
Office Supplies Expense	Expense			<Unassigned>
Payroll Expenses	Expense			<Unassigned>
Rent Expense	Expense			<Unassigned>
Telephone Expense	Expense			<Unassigned>
Uncategorized Expenses	Expense			<Unassigned>
Utilities Expense	Expense			<Unassigned>

Upon reviewing the Account Listing, observe the following:

a. There is only one Inventory asset account.
b. There are two equity accounts, Opening Bal Equity and Retained Earnings.
c. There are three accounts for each fixed asset.
d. There is only one Cost of Goods Sold account.
e. There is an Uncategorized Income account.
f. There is an Uncategorized Expenses account.

5. Close the report. If you receive a message about Memorize Report, place a check mark in the box to the left of Do not display this message in the future and click <u>N</u>o.

Correcting Errors

If you misspelled an account name, or you omitted an account, you can correct the errors by clicking <u>L</u>ists and then Chart of <u>A</u>ccounts, and then adding, deleting, or editing the account as illustrated in chapter 4. (At this point, correct only errors you may have made; do not add additional new accounts. You will add new accounts in Part II of New Company Setup.)

If the balance in the Accounts Receivable is incorrect, then you did not enter the correct balance when you added the customers in EasyStep Interview. If you did not enter a balance for a customer, go to the Customer:Job List from the Lists menu, and delete the customer. Then create a new customer file with the correct balance. If you entered the customer with an incorrect balance, correct it later when viewing the Journal report. Similarly, if the balance in the Accounts Payable is incorrect, then you did not enter the correct balance when you added the vendors in the Easy Step Interview. If you did not enter a balance for a vendor, go to the Vendor List from the Lists menu, and delete the vendor. Then create a new vendor file with the correct balance. If you entered the vendor with an incorrect balance, correct it later when viewing the Journal report.

TRIAL BALANCE

Reviewing the Trial Balance will allow you to see the balances in the accounts you created as part of the EasyStep Interview.

To view and print the Trial Balance—

1. Click Reports, and then click Accountant & Taxes.
2. At the Accountant & Taxes menu, click Trial Balance.
3. In the *From* and *To* fields, choose *04/01/2004* and then click Refresh. (See figure 6–29.)

FIGURE 6-29
Trial Balance April 1, 2004 (after EasyStep Interview)

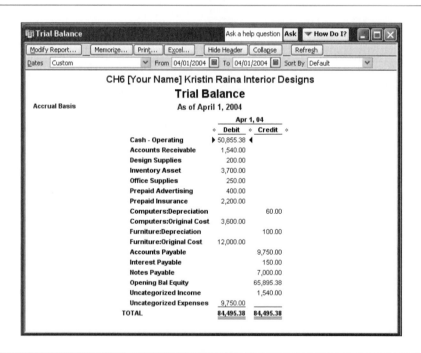

4. To print the Trial Balance, click Print.
5. At the Print Reports dialog box, check the settings, then click Print.

Upon reviewing the Trial Balance, observe the following:

a. There is a balance in the Uncategorized Income account.

This balance was created by QuickBooks Pro each time you entered a customer balance in the EasyStep Interview window. Therefore, the Accounts Receivable equals the Uncategorized Income.

b. There is a balance in the Uncategorized Expenses account.

This balance was created by QuickBooks Pro each time you entered a vendor balance in the EasyStep Interview window. Therefore, the Accounts Payable equals the Uncategorized Expenses.

6. Close the report.

Figure 6–30 shows the Trial Balance from EX5 [Your Name] Kristin Raina Interior Designs. It reflects the activities of January 1 – March 31, 2004, which were recorded in chapters 2 through 5. Compare the trial balance of April 1, 2004 (figure 6–29) to the trial balance of March 31, 2004 (figure 6–30).

FIGURE 6-30
Trial Balance March 31, 2004 (from Chapter 5)

EX5 [Your Name] Kristin Raina Interior Designs
Trial Balance
As of March 31, 2004

Accrual Basis

	Mar 31, 04	
	Debit	Credit
1010 · Cash - Operating	50,855.38	
1200 · Accounts Receivable	1,540.00	
1250 · Undeposited Funds	0.00	
1260 · Inventory of Carpets	800.00	
1265 · Inventory of Draperies	1,000.00	
1270 · Inventory of Lamps	1,000.00	
1275 · Inventory of Mirrors	900.00	
1300 · Design Supplies	200.00	
1305 · Office Supplies	250.00	
1410 · Prepaid Advertising	500.00	
1420 · Prepaid Insurance	2,200.00	
1700 · Furniture	12,000.00	
1700 · Furniture:1750 · Accum. Dep., Furniture		100.00
1800 · Computers	3,600.00	
1800 · Computers:1850 · Accum. Dep., Computers		60.00
2010 · Accounts Payable		9,750.00
2020 · Notes Payable		7,000.00
2030 · Interest Payable		50.00
2200 · Sales Tax Payable	0.00	
3010 · Kristin Raina, Capital		50,000.00
3020 · Kristin Raina, Drawings	400.00	
4010 · Design Services		4,980.00
4020 · Decorating Services		3,400.00
4060 · Sale of Carpets		2,400.00
4065 · Sale of Draperies		1,000.00
4070 · Sale of Lamps		1,200.00
4075 · Sale of Mirrors		900.00
4100 · Sales Discounts	84.62	
5060 · Cost of Carpets Sold	1,200.00	
5065 · Cost of Draperies Sold	500.00	
5070 · Cost of Lamps Sold	600.00	
5075 · Cost of Mirrors Sold	450.00	
5900 · Inventory Adjustment	150.00	
6020 · Accounting Expense	300.00	
6050 · Advertising Expense	100.00	
6175 · Deprec. Exp., Furniture	100.00	
6185 · Deprec. Exp., Computers	60.00	
6200 · Insurance Expense	200.00	
6300 · Janitorial Expenses	125.00	
6325 · Office Supplies Expense	150.00	
6400 · Rent Expense	800.00	
6450 · Telephone Expense	275.00	
6500 · Utilities Expense	450.00	
7000 · Interest Expense	50.00	
TOTAL	**80,840.00**	**80,840.00**

Upon comparing the two trial balances, observe the following:
a. There are more accounts and amounts on the March 31, 2004, trial balance than the April 1, 2004, trial balance.
b. There are four inventory accounts, not one.
c. There are subaccounts in the fixed assets accounts.
d. There are two equity accounts, capital and drawings.
e. There are four cost of goods sold accounts.
f. There are balances in the income and expense accounts.
g. There are no Uncategorized Income and Uncategorized Expenses accounts.

Although EasyStep Interview guides you in creating a new company file, it does not completely enter all the information for a company. Upon completion of New Company Setup — Part II (chapter 7), the trial balance of April 1 will be the same as the trial balance of March 31.

JOURNAL REPORT

As information is recorded in the EasyStep Interview window, behind the scenes QuickBooks Pro records the beginning information in general journal format. QuickBooks Pro automatically assigns a number in sequence to each entry made in the General Journal. This is a feature that may be turned off or may be edited.

To view and print the *Journal* report—
1. Click Reports, and then click Accountant & Taxes.
2. At the Accountant & Taxes menu, click Journal.
3. In the *From* and *To* fields, choose *04/01/2004*, and then click Refresh.
4. Click Print.
5. At the Print Reports dialog box, check the settings, then click Print. Your printout should look like figure 6–31.

Review the journal entries. They can be categorized four ways—

1. For items that are debit entries to asset accounts, excluding accounts receivable, the corresponding credit entry was to the Opening Bal Equity account.
2. For items that are credit entries to liabilities accounts, excluding accounts payable, the corresponding debit entry was to the Opening Bal Equity account.
3. For entries that are debits to Accounts Receivable, the corresponding credit is to Uncategorized Income.
4. For entries that are credits to Accounts Payable, the corresponding debit is to Uncategorized Expenses.

If you determine an error in this report, you can drill down to the original source, as seen in prior chapters. The original source you drill down to is based on the transaction type. The transaction types are the same as seen in prior chapters:

Transaction Type	Original Source Window
Bill (chapter 2)	Enter Bills
Invoice (chapter 3)	Create Invoices
Deposit (chapter 3)	Make Deposits
General Journal (chapter 4)	Registers/General Journal Entry
Inventory Adjustment (chapter 5)	Adjust Quantity/Value on Hand

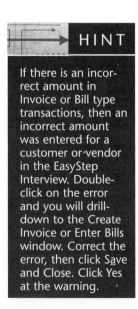

HINT

If there is an incorrect amount in Invoice or Bill type transactions, then an incorrect amount was entered for a customer or vendor in the EasyStep Interview. Double-click on the error and you will drill-down to the Create Invoice or Enter Bills window. Correct the error, then click Save and Close. Click Yes at the warning.

FIGURE 6-31

Journal Report

CH6 [Your Name] Kristin Raina Interior Designs
Journal
April 1, 2004

Trans #	Type	Date	Num	Name	Memo	Account	Debit	Credit
1	Inventory Adjust	04/01/2004			Carpets Opening balance	Opening Bal Equity		800.00
					Carpets Opening balance	Inventory Asset	800.00	
							800.00	800.00
2	Inventory Adjust	04/01/2004			Draperies Opening balance	Opening Bal Equity		1,000.00
					Draperies Opening balance	Inventory Asset	1,000.00	
							1,000.00	1,000.00
3	Inventory Adjust	04/01/2004			Lamps Opening balance	Opening Bal Equity		1,000.00
					Lamps Opening balance	Inventory Asset	1,000.00	
							1,000.00	1,000.00
4	Inventory Adjust	04/01/2004			Mirrors Opening balance	Opening Bal Equity		900.00
					Mirrors Opening balance	Inventory Asset	900.00	
							900.00	900.00
5	Invoice	04/01/2004		Burnitz Bakery Company	Opening balance	Accounts Receivable	600.00	
				Burnitz Bakery Company	Opening balance	Uncategorized Income		600.00
							600.00	600.00
6	Invoice	04/01/2004		Franco Films Co.	Opening balance	Accounts Receivable	940.00	
				Franco Films Co.	Opening balance	Uncategorized Income		940.00
							940.00	940.00
7	Bill	04/01/2004		Ace Glass Works	Opening balance	Accounts Payable		1,500.00
				Ace Glass Works	Opening balance	Uncategorized Expenses	1,500.00	
							1,500.00	1,500.00
8	Bill	04/01/2004		Bell Carpet Design	Opening balance	Accounts Payable		2,000.00
				Bell Carpet Design	Opening balance	Uncategorized Expenses	2,000.00	
							2,000.00	2,000.00
9	Bill	04/01/2004		Cone and Clemens Associates	Opening balance	Accounts Payable		400.00
				Cone and Clemens Associates	Opening balance	Uncategorized Expenses	400.00	
							400.00	400.00
10	Bill	04/01/2004		Galeway Computers	Opening balance	Accounts Payable		2,600.00
				Galeway Computers	Opening balance	Uncategorized Expenses	2,600.00	
							2,600.00	2,600.00
11	Bill	04/01/2004		Midwest Mutual Insurance Co.	Opening balance	Accounts Payable		2,400.00
				Midwest Mutual Insurance Co.	Opening balance	Uncategorized Expenses	2,400.00	
							2,400.00	2,400.00
12	Bill	04/01/2004		Minneapolis Electric & Gas Co.	Opening balance	Accounts Payable		450.00
				Minneapolis Electric & Gas Co.	Opening balance	Uncategorized Expenses	450.00	
							450.00	450.00
13	Bill	04/01/2004		Williams Office Supply Company	Opening balance	Accounts Payable		400.00
				Williams Office Supply Company	Opening balance	Uncategorized Expenses	400.00	
							400.00	400.00
14	General Journal	04/01/2004	1		Account Opening Balance	Notes Payable		7,000.00
					Account Opening Balance	Opening Bal Equity	7,000.00	
							7,000.00	7,000.00
15	General Journal	04/01/2004	2		Account Opening Balance	Interest Payable		150.00
					Account Opening Balance	Opening Bal Equity	150.00	
							150.00	150.00
16	Deposit	04/01/2004			Account Opening Balance	Cash - Operating	50,855.38	
					Account Opening Balance	Opening Bal Equity		50,855.38
							50,855.38	50,855.38
17	Deposit	04/01/2004			Account Opening Balance	Design Supplies	200.00	
					Account Opening Balance	Opening Bal Equity		200.00
							200.00	200.00
18	Deposit	04/01/2004			Account Opening Balance	Office Supplies	250.00	
					Account Opening Balance	Opening Bal Equity		250.00
							250.00	250.00
19	Deposit	04/01/2004			Account Opening Balance	Prepaid Advertising	400.00	
					Account Opening Balance	Opening Bal Equity		400.00
							400.00	400.00
20	Deposit	04/01/2004			Account Opening Balance	Prepaid Insurance	2,200.00	
					Account Opening Balance	Opening Bal Equity		2,200.00
							2,200.00	2,200.00
21	General Journal	04/01/2004	3		Account Opening Balance	Original Cost	12,000.00	
					Account Opening Balance	Opening Bal Equity		12,000.00
							12,000.00	12,000.00
22	General Journal	04/01/2004	4		Account Opening Balance	Depreciation		100.00
					Account Opening Balance	Opening Bal Equity	100.00	
							100.00	100.00
23	General Journal	04/01/2004	5		Account Opening Balance	Original Cost	3,600.00	
					Account Opening Balance	Opening Bal Equity		3,600.00
							3,600.00	3,600.00
24	General Journal	04/01/2004	6		Account Opening Balance	Depreciation		60.00
					Account Opening Balance	Opening Bal Equity	60.00	
							60.00	60.00
TOTAL							**91,805.38**	**91,805.38**

In chapter 3, you used the Make Deposits window only for depositing undeposited cash receipts. As part of the EasyStep Interview window, however, QuickBooks Pro records all bank and other current asset accounts, excluding inventory and accounts receivable, in the Make Deposits window.

For example, assume when comparing the two trial balances you notice that on the March 31, 2004, trial balance the correct prepaid advertising account balance is $500, not the $400 shown in the April 1, 2004, trial balance. Upon reviewing the *Journal* report you wish to correct the error:

Errors in the Deposits Window

To correct an error recorded as a Deposit transaction type—

1. In the *Journal* report, double-click the transaction that records the prepaid advertising account. QuickBooks Pro drills down to the Make Deposits window. (See figure 6–32.)

FIGURE 6-32
Make Deposits Window

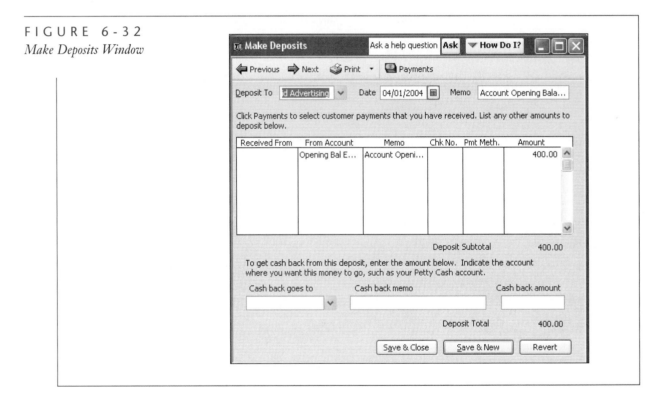

2. In the *Amount* field, change the amount to **500** and then move to the next field. (See figure 6–33.)

FIGURE 6-33
Make Deposits Window –
Corrected

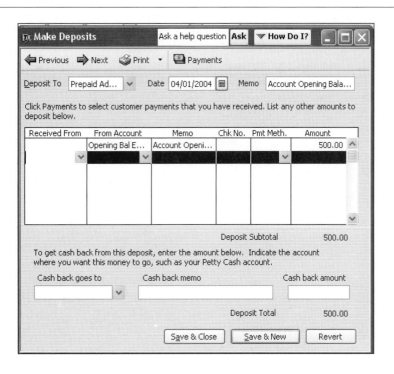

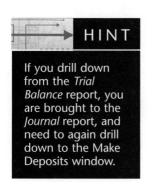

HINT

If you drill down from the *Trial Balance* report, you are brought to the *Journal* report, and need to again drill down to the Make Deposits window.

3. If the information is correct, click Save & Close.
4. Click Yes at the warning. If a message appears about refreshing the report, place a check mark in the Do not ask again box and click Yes. The amount is corrected immediately in the *Journal* report.

Errors in the General Journal

In chapter 4 you learned that QuickBooks Pro maintains a register for all asset, liability, and equity accounts. It does not maintain registers for income or expense accounts. The registers provide an alternative method for recording transactions instead of using the Activities windows.

If you drill down a General Journal transaction type from the *Journal* report, you will not drill down to the General Journal Entry window; instead you will drill down to the register.

For example, assume that, when comparing the trial balances, you also noticed that the Interest Payable balance was $50, not $150.

To correct an error recorded as a General Journal type—
1. In the *Journal* report, double-click the transaction that recorded the interest payable account. You are drilled down to the Interest Payable register window. (See figure 6–34.)

FIGURE 6-34
Interest Payable Register Window

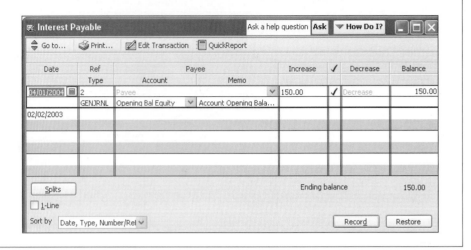

You may correct the amount of the error in the Interest Payable register by changing the amount in the increase column to **50**. The balance column changes when you click Reco<u>r</u>d. As an alternative, you can click the Edit Transaction button and you are further drilled down to the General Journal Entry window.

2. In the Interest Payable register, click Edit Transaction. You are drilled down to the General Journal Entry window. At the Assigning Numbers to Journal Entries message, place a check mark in the box to the left of Do not display this message in the future and click OK.
3. Change the amount in both the credit and debit columns to **50**. (See figure 6–35.)

FIGURE 6-35
General Journal Entry Window – Corrected

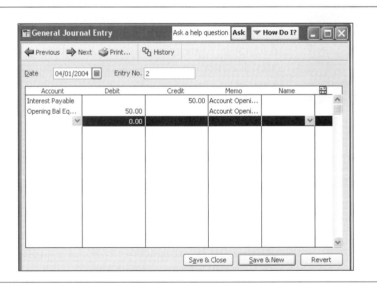

4. If the information is correct, click S<u>a</u>ve & Close.
5. At the warning, click <u>Y</u>es. You are returned to the Interest Payable register and the amount and balance are corrected.
6. Close the Interest Payable register. The amount is corrected immediately in the *Journal* report.
7. Close the report.

If you double-click any asset, liability, or equity account in the Chart of Accounts List window, you will drill down to the appropriate register. Some people prefer to record all activity in registers instead of activities windows.

Another way to correct errors in the *Journal* report that are labeled as general journal transaction types is to click Company and then Make Journal Entry. You will enter the General Journal Entry window directly instead of drilling down to the register first. When you enter the General Journal Entry window, click the Previous arrow until the entry with the error is displayed, make any necessary corrections, and then save the entry.

ACCOUNTING
concept

The effect of correcting the errors is as follows:

Prepaid Advertising			Interest Payable			Open Bal. Equity	
Dr	Cr		Dr	Cr		Dr	Cr
400				150			100
Adj 100			Adj 100				100
Bal 500				Bal 50			

PROFIT & LOSS STANDARD (INCOME STATEMENT) REPORT
To view and print the *Profit & Loss Standard* report—
1. Click Reports, and then click Company & Financial.
2. At the Company & Financial menu, click Profit & Loss Standard.
3. In the *From* and *To* fields, choose *04/01/2004* and then click Refresh. (See figure 6–36.)

FIGURE 6-36
Profit & Loss Standard Report (after EasyStep Interview)

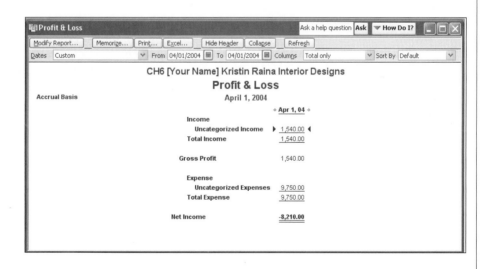

4. To print the *Profit & Loss* standard report, click Print.
5. At the Print Reports dialog box, check the settings, then click Print.
6. Close the report.

At this point in the setup process, the *Profit & Loss Standard* report only lists Uncategorized Income and Uncategorized Expenses. As you recall, these amounts are offsetting amounts of the Accounts Receivable and Accounts Payable accounts. Therefore, this is not a proper representation of the income and expenses of this company and will have to be adjusted in Part II of New Company Setup.

BALANCE SHEET STANDARD REPORT

To display the *Balance Sheet Standard* report—
1. Click Reports, and then click Company & Financial.
2. At the Company & Financial submenu, click Balance Sheet Standard.
3. In the *As of* field, choose *04/01/2004*, and then click Refresh.
4. To print the balance sheet, click Print.
5. At the Print Reports dialog box, check the settings, then click Print. (See figure 6–37.)

   A review of the balance sheet indicates the following:
   a. The fixed assets are not summarized in the same format as previous chapters.
   b. The equity section does not reflect a capital and drawings account.
   c. The net income is incorrect.
6. Close the report.

Using the EasyStep Interview window is only part of the New Company Setup process. It is then necessary to customize the new company file according to your company's preferences and prepare the company file for the accrual basis of accounting. This second part of New Company Setup is covered in the next chapter.

BACKING UP THE NEW COMPANY FILE

You should make a backup copy of the new company file in the event there is damage to the file or the computer. Using the procedures used in previous chapters, make a backup copy of the new company file. Back up the file to your subfolder and/or a floppy and use the name EX6 [Your Name] Kristin Raina Interior Designs. Restore the backup copy and change the company name to EX6 [Your Name] Kristin Raina Interior Designs.

FIGURE 6-37
Balance Sheet Standard Report (after EasyStep Interview)

CH6 [Your Name] Kristin Raina Interior Designs
Balance Sheet
Accrual Basis **As of April 1, 2004**

	Apr 1, 04
ASSETS	
Current Assets	
Checking/Savings	
Cash - Operating	50,855.38
Total Checking/Savings	50,855.38
Accounts Receivable	
Accounts Receivable	1,540.00
Total Accounts Receivable	1,540.00
Other Current Assets	
Design Supplies	200.00
Inventory Asset	3,700.00
Office Supplies	250.00
Prepaid Advertising	500.00
Prepaid Insurance	2,200.00
Total Other Current Assets	6,850.00
Total Current Assets	59,245.38
Fixed Assets	
Computers	
Depreciation	-60.00
Original Cost	3,600.00
Total Computers	3,540.00
Furniture	
Depreciation	-100.00
Original Cost	12,000.00
Total Furniture	11,900.00
Total Fixed Assets	15,440.00
TOTAL ASSETS	**74,685.38**
LIABILITIES & EQUITY	
Liabilities	
Current Liabilities	
Accounts Payable	
Accounts Payable	9,750.00
Total Accounts Payable	9,750.00
Other Current Liabilities	
Interest Payable	50.00
Notes Payable	7,000.00
Total Other Current Liabilities	7,050.00
Total Current Liabilities	16,800.00
Total Liabilities	16,800.00
Equity	
Opening Bal Equity	66,095.38
Net Income	-8,210.00
Total Equity	57,885.38
TOTAL LIABILITIES & EQUITY	**74,685.38**

PROGRESS *Check*

PROCEDURE REVIEW

To create and set up a new company file using the EasyStep Interview window—

1. At the *No Company Open* window, click on the Create a new company button or click File, and then click New Company. The EasyStep Interview window appears.
2. At the EasyStep Interview Window, read and complete each of the tabs listed below. Click Next after each page is completed.
   - General Tab
     - Welcome
     - Company Info
     - Preferences
     - Start Date
   - Income & Expenses Tab
     - Income Accts
     - Expense Accts
   - Income Details Tab
     - Introduction
     - Items
     - Inventory
   - Opening Balances Tab
     - Introduction
     - Customers
     - Vendors
     - Accounts
   - What's Next
     - What's Next
     - Finishing Up

To leave the EasyStep Interview window—
   Click the Leave button.

   You should not Leave EasyStep Interview window until the General side tab is complete.

To reenter EasyStep Interview window—
   Click File, and then click EasyStep Interview.
You are returned to the page you were last using.

To view and print accounting reports from the Reports menu—
1. Click Reports, and then click Accountant & Taxes.
2. At the Accountant & Taxes submenu, choose a report.
3. Indicate the start date and end date for the report.
4. Click Print on the command line.
5. At the Print Reports dialog box, review the settings, then click Print.
6. Close the report.

To view and print financial reports from the <u>R</u>eports menu—
1. Click <u>R</u>eports, and then click Company & <u>F</u>inancial.
2. At the Company & Financial submenu, choose a financial report.
3. Indicate the start date and end date for the report.
4. Click Prin<u>t</u> on the command line.
5. At the Print Reports dialog box, review the settings, then click Print.
6. Close the report.

To correct an error recorded as a Deposit transaction type in the *Journal* report—
1. In the *Journal* report, double-click the transaction with the error. You are drilled down to the Make Deposits window.
2. In the amount column, change the amount to the correct amount and move to the next field.
3. If the information is correct, click S<u>a</u>ve & Close.
4. Click <u>Y</u>es at the warning. The amount is corrected immediately in the *Journal* report.
5. Close the *Journal* report.

To correct an error recorded as a General Journal type in the *Journal* report—
1. In the *Journal* report, double-click the transaction with the error. You are drilled down to the register window.
2. In the register click, click Edit Transaction. You are drilled down to the General Journal Entry window.
3. Correct the error.
4. If the information is correct, click S<u>a</u>ve & Close.
5. At the warning, click <u>Y</u>es. You are returned to the register and the amount and balance are corrected.
6. Close the register. The amount is corrected immediately in the *Journal* report.
7. Close the *Journal* report.

KEY CONCEPTS

Select the letter of the item that best matches each definition.

a. Uncategorized Expenses
b. Items tab
c. EasyStep Interview
d. Company Info tab
e. Inventory tab
f. Income Accts tab
g. Registers
h. Customers tab
i. Accounts tab
j. Uncategorized Income

_____ 1. Window where a new company file is created.
_____ 2. Account created by QuickBooks Pro as an offsetting amount for Accounts Receivable.
_____ 3. Tab used to record company name and identification numbers and to choose the Chart of Accounts.
_____ 4. Tab used to record revenue accounts.
_____ 5. Alternative window that can be used to record activities or correct asset, liability, or equity account information.

_____ 6. Tab used to record the customers with beginning balances.
_____ 7. Tab used to record service revenue items.
_____ 8. Tab used to record fixed assets accounts.
_____ 9. Tab used to record inventory items.
_____10. Account created by QuickBooks Pro as an offsetting amount of Accounts Payable.

PROCEDURE CHECK

1. What is New Company Setup? What is one method of New Company Setup?
2. If you are using the EasyStep Interview window, at what point is it safe to leave the window and why?
3. If you leave the EasyStep Interview window, how can you reenter the window? At what point would you be when you returned to the window?
4. You are reviewing the new company file you created using QuickBooks Pro EasyStep Interview window and you see an account called Uncategorized Income and another account called Uncategorized Expenses on the trial balance. What are these accounts?
5. When you are reviewing the *Journal* report, you notice you recorded $1,200 in the Prepaid Insurance account but you should have recorded $2,200. Explain how you would correct this error.

6. Your manager is just learning QuickBooks Pro. He has asked you to explain what EasyStep Interview means. Provide the manager with a written explanation of the EasyStep Interview. In your explanation, explain what is included in the EasyStep Interview window.

CASE PROBLEMS

CASE PROBLEM 1

On April 1, 2004, Lynn Garcia began her business, called Lynn's Music Studio. In the first month of business, Lynn set up the music studio, provided guitar and piano lessons, and recorded month-end activity. In May, the second month of business, Lynn started purchasing and selling inventory items of guitars, keyboards, music stands, and sheet music. In April and May, Lynn was recording the financial activities using a manual accounting system. On June 1, 2004, Lynn decides to switch her accounting method to QuickBooks Pro. Lynn has organized the information about the company but has hired you to convert the accounting records to QuickBooks Pro.

1. Use the information below to create the company file and record the information for the company in the EasyStep Interview window. Where no specific information is given, accept the EasyStep Interview window default setting.

Company Name: **CH6 [Your Name] Lynn's Music Studio**
Address: **228 Pearl Street**
Scranton, PA 18501

Phone #:	**570-555-0400**
FAX #:	**570-555-0500**
E-mail:	**LYNN@emcp.net**
Federal tax ID:	**45-6123789**
First month of tax year:	**January**
First month of fiscal year:	**April**
Types of business:	**Other**
Save As:	**CH6 [Your Name] Lynn's Music Studio**

Create your own accounts.
Maintain inventory.

Sales Tax:	**PA Sales Tax, Sales Tax, 7%, PA Dept. of Revenue**

You will not use payroll, estimates, time-tracking, or tracking segments.
Enter bills first and payments later.

Start date:	**06/01/2004**
Income accounts:	**Piano Lessons**
	Guitar Lessons
	Sale of Guitars
	Sale of Keyboards
	Sale of Music Stands
	Sale of Sheet Music
Expense accounts:	**Dep. Exp., Music Instruments**
	Dep. Exp., Furniture
	Dep. Exp., Computers
	Instrument Tuning
	Insurance Expense
	Music Supplies Expense
	Office Supplies Expense
	Rent Expense
	Telephone Expense
	Utilities Expense
Service items:	
(not performed by subcontractor)	
	Guitar Lessons, $30 per hour
	Piano Lessons, $35 per hour

There are no non-inventory part items or other charges.
Inventory part items (all inventory part items are taxable):

Item and Description	Sales Price	Cost	Reorder	Qty on Hand
Guitars	**$100**	**$50**	**10**	**6**
Keyboards	**150**	**75**	**10**	**17**
Music Stands	**40**	**20**	**10**	**17**
Sheet Music	**6**	**3**	**50**	**165**

Customers with outstanding balances:

Douglaston Senior Center	175.00
Mulligan Residence	1,575.90

Vendors with outstanding balances:

Computer Town	2,000.00
Katie's Keyboards	1,500.00
Mills Family Furniture	1,500.00
Mutual Insurance Company	1,200.00
Paper, Clips, and More	350.00

Do not set up credit cards or lines of credit.
Accounts with balances:

Other Current Liabilities:	
Notes Payable	2,000.00
Interest Payable	150.00
Bank Account:	
Cash – Operating (6/1/04)	14,615.18
Other Current Assets:	
Music Supplies	430.00
Office Supplies	300.00
Prepaid Insurance	1,100.00
Fixed Assets:	
Music Instruments: Original Cost	4,000.00
Music Instruments: Depreciation	60.00
Furniture: Original Cost	2,500.00
Furniture: Depreciation	40.00
Computers: Original Cost	3,000.00
Computers: Depreciation	35.00

2. Display and print the following reports for June 1, 2004, to June 1, 2004:
   a. *Journal*
   b. *Trial Balance*
   c. *Profit & Loss standard*
   d. *Balance Sheet standard*
   e. *Item Listing*
   f. *Customer Contact List*
   g. *Vendor Contact List*

3. Make a backup copy of the new company file. Use the name LMS6 [Your Name] Lynn's Music Studio. Restore the backup copy and change the company name.

CASE PROBLEM 2

On June 1, 2004, Olivia Chen began her business, called Olivia's Web Solutions. In the first month of business, Olivia set up the office, provided Web page design and Internet consulting services, and recorded month-end activity. In July, the second month of business, Olivia began to purchase and sell inventory items of computer hardware and software. In June and July,

Olivia was recording the financial activities using a manual accounting system. On August 1, 2004, Olivia decides to switch her accounting method to QuickBooks Pro. Olivia has organized the information about the company but has hired you to convert the accounting records to QuickBooks Pro.

1. Use the information below to create the company file and record the information for the company in the EasyStep Interview window. Where no specific information is given, accept the EasyStep Interview window default setting.

Company Name:	**CH6 [Your Name] Olivia's Web Solutions**
Address:	**547 Miller Place**
	Westport, NY 11858
Phone #:	**516-555-5000**
FAX #:	**516-555-6000**
E-mail:	**LIV@emcp.net**
Federal tax ID:	**55-5656566**
First month of tax year:	**January**
First month of fiscal year:	**June**
Types of business:	**Other**
Save As:	**CH6 [Your Name] Olivia's Web Solutions**

Create your own accounts.
You will maintain inventory.

Sales Tax:	**NY Sales Tax, Sales Tax, 8%, NYS Tax Dept.**

You will not use payroll, estimates, time-tracking, or tracking segments.
Enter bills first and payment later.

Start date:	**08/01/2004**

Income accounts:	**Web Page Design Fees**
	Internet Consulting Fees
	Sale of Computers
	Sale of Scanners
	Sale of HTML Software
	Sale of Desktop Pub. Software

Expense accounts:	**Advertising Expense**
	Dep. Exp., Computers
	Dep. Exp., Furniture
	Dep. Exp., Software
	Insurance Expense
	Computer Supplies Expense
	Office Supplies Expense
	Online Service Expense
	Rent Expense
	Telephone Expense
	Utility Expense

Service items (not performed by subcontractors):
> **Internet Consulting Services, $100 per hour**
> **Web Page Design Services, $125 per hour**

There are no non-inventory part items or other charges.

Inventory part items (all inventory part items are taxable):

Item and Description	Sales Price	Cost	Reorder	Qty on Hand
Computers	$2000	$1000	3	10
Desktop Pub. Software	200	100	5	10
HTML Software	150	75	5	18
Scanners	600	300	5	12

Customers with outstanding balances:

Artie's Auto Repair	800.00
Schneider Family	1,000.00
Sehorn & Smith, Attorneys	800.00
South Shore School District	12,056.00
Thrifty Stores	1,500.00

Vendors with outstanding balances:

Chrbet Advertising	1,200.00
Computec Computers	10,000.00
Eastel	350.00
Lewis Furniture Co.	1,700.00
Netsoft Development Co.	1,600.00
Office Plus	375.00

Do not set up credit cards or lines of credit.

Accounts with balances:

Other Current Liabilities:	
Notes Payable	2,500.00
Interest Payable	75.00
Bank Account:	
Cash – Operating (8/1/04)	24,489.16
Other Current Assets:	
Computer Supplies	350.00
Office Supplies	325.00
Prepaid Advertising	1,000.00
Prepaid Insurance	1,650.00
Fixed Assets:	
Computers: Original Cost	5,000.00
Computers: Depreciation	75.00
Furniture: Original Cost	3,200.00
Furniture: Depreciation	50.00
Software: Original Cost	3,600.00
Software: Depreciation	100.00

2. Display and print the following reports for August 1, 2004 to August 1, 2004:
   a. *Journal*
   b. *Trial Balance*
   c. *Profit & Loss standard*
   d. *Balance Sheet standard*
   e. *Item Listing*
   f. *Customer Contact List*
   g. *Vendor Contact List*

3. Make a backup copy of the new company file. Use the name OWS6 [Your Name] Olivia's Web Design. Restore the backup copy and change the company name.

CHAPTER

7

NEW COMPANY SETUP—Part II

Customize, Update, and Prepare for the Accrual Basis of Accounting

CHAPTER OBJECTIVES

- Customize the Chart of Accounts and Item Lists

- Update the Chart of Accounts, Customer:Job, and Vendor Lists

- Adjust the new company file to follow the accrual basis of accounting

- Display and print accounting, financial, and Lists reports

- Identify system default accounts created by QuickBooks Pro

INTRODUCTION

As you learned in chapter 1, the first level of operation for QuickBooks Pro is New Company Setup. In chapter 6, you learned one method of setting up a new company: the QuickBooks Pro EasyStep Interview window. When you use the EasyStep Interview window, New Company Setup is a two-part process. The first part is creating the new company file and setting up the Chart of Accounts, Items, Customer:Job, and Vendor Lists with opening balances. This part of the process was covered in chapter 6.

The second part of the process is to use the information set up in the EasyStep Interview window to customize the new company file according to your company's preferences; update the Lists with more complete background information; to include those Lists without beginning balances; and prepare the company file for the accrual basis of accounting by recording three adjusting journal entries. In this chapter you will learn this second part of the process, using the sample company, Kristin Raina Interior Designs, that you began in chapter 6.

CHAPTER PROBLEM

In chapter 6, you created and set up a new company file for Kristin Raina Interior Designs using the EasyStep Interview window. At the end of chapter 6, you reviewed the EasyStep Interview information by viewing several reports and corrected any input errors you may have made.

When reviewing the reports at the end of chapter 6, you could see that EasyStep Interview set up the Chart of Accounts, Items, Customer:Job, and Vendor Lists. However, several areas of the company file need to be revised to customize it and prepare it for the accrual basis of accounting. In this chapter, you will customize and update the file's Lists, and then record three adjusting journal entries to prepare the company file for the accrual basis of accounting.

Using the steps similar to those you used in chapters 1 through 5, begin by opening the company file CH7 Kristin Raina Interior Designs.QBW. Make a backup copy of the file using the file name EX7 [Your Name] Kristin Raina Interior Designs, and then restore the backup copy. Before proceeding with the chapter problem, change the company name in the file to EX7 [Your Name] Kristin Raina Interior Designs.

NEW COMPANY SETUP: CUSTOMIZING THE NEW COMPANY FILE

At the end of chapter 6, you reviewed the *Account Listing*, *Trial Balance*, *Journal*, *Profit & Loss*, and *Balance Sheet* reports after completing the EasyStep Interview window. In addition, you compared the *Trial Balance* report that resulted from completing the EasyStep Interview window to the *Trial Balance* at the end of chapter 5, which represented several months of activities for our sample company. You observed that there were differences in account names (such as Opening Bal Equity), that accounts were missing (such as several inventory and cost of goods sold accounts), that QuickBooks Pro created accounts (such as the uncategorized accounts), and so on. You now need to change account names, add accounts, and reclassify inventory items to additional new inventory accounts to organize the financial information into a more desirable format. This is referred to as customizing the new company file.

You will do most of the customizing in the Chart of Accounts List. Revisions to the Chart of Accounts will flow through to the presentations on the trial balance and the financial statements. You may also need to make some changes in the Item List.

CUSTOMIZING THE CHART OF ACCOUNTS LIST

You will customize the Chart of Accounts for Kristin Raina by adding account numbers, revising some account names, adding new accounts, editing parent and subaccount classifications, and deleting accounts no longer needed after customizing.

Adding Account Numbers

Open the Chart of Accounts List, select any account, click the Account menu button, and then click Edit to view the account. Notice there is no account number field. By default, QuickBooks Pro does not use account numbers. Close the Edit Account and Chart of Accounts windows. To add account numbers to the Chart of Accounts List, you must activate the account numbers option in the Preferences window.

To activate the account numbers options—
1. Click Edit, and then click Preferences. The Preferences window appears.
2. Along the left frame of the Preferences window, click the *Accounting* icon.
3. Click the Company Preferences tab.
4. At the *Account Numbers* field, place a ✓ in Use account numbers to turn on the account numbers option. (See figure 7–1.)

FIGURE 7-1
Preferences Window – Accounting – Company Preferences Tab

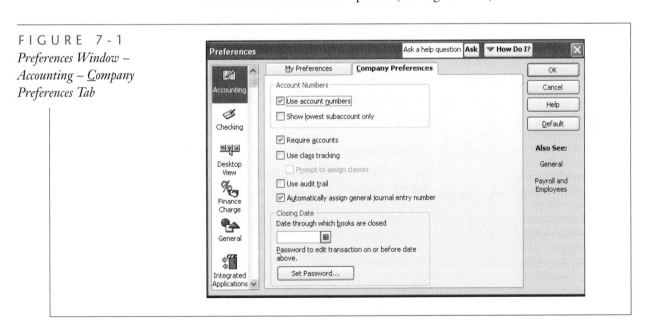

5. If the information is correct, click OK. The *Account Number* field now appears in the Edit Account and New Account windows.

When you activate the account numbers option, QuickBooks Pro assigns account numbers to certain accounts. You can change or delete these numbers. Open the company file's Chart of Accounts List and edit each account to add or change the account numbers and edit the account names as listed below:

HINT

To edit an account in the Chart of Accounts List window, select the account, then click the Edit button. Do not double-click the account.

Number	Name	New/Edited Number	Edited Name
	Cash – Operating	1010	
1200	Accounts Receivable		
1120	Inventory Asset	1260	Inventory of Carpets
	Design Supplies	1300	
	Office Supplies	1305	
	Prepaid Advertising	1410	
	Prepaid Insurance	1420	
	(Furniture) Original Cost	1700	Furniture (cost)
	(Furniture) Depreciation	1750	Accum. Dep., Furniture

(For the Furniture account with a balance of $11,900, do not enter an account number or change the name; it will later have a zero balance and be deleted.)

	(Computers) Original Cost	1800	Computers (cost)
	(Computers) Depreciation	1850	Accum. Dep., Computers

(For the Computers account with a balance of $3,540, do not enter an account number or change the name; it will later have a zero balance and be deleted.)

Number	Name	New/Edited Number	Edited Name
2000	Accounts Payable	2010	
	Notes Payable	2020	
	Interest Payable	2030	
2200	Sales Tax Payable		
3000	Opening Bal Equity	3010	Kristin Raina, Capital
	Design Services	4010	
	Decorating Services	4020	
	Sale of Carpets	4060	
	Sale of Draperies	4065	
	Sale of Lamps	4070	
	Sale of Mirrors	4075	
5000	Cost of Goods Sold	5060	Cost of Carpets Sold
	Accounting Expense	6020	
	Advertising Expense	6050	
	Deprec. Exp., Furniture	6175	
	Deprec. Exp., Computers	6185	
	Insurance Expense	6200	
	Janitorial Expense	6300	
	Office Supplies Expense	6325	
	Rent Expense	6400	
	Telephone Expense	6450	
	Utilities Expense	6500	

Adding New Accounts

In the Chart of Accounts window, create the following new accounts:

Type	Number	Name	Opening Balance
Other Current Asset	1265	Inventory of Draperies	
Other Current Asset	1270	Inventory of Lamps	
Other Current Asset	1275	Inventory of Mirrors	
Equity	3020	Kristin Raina, Drawings	-400 04/01/04
Income	4100	Sales Discounts	
Cost of Goods Sold	5065	Cost of Draperies Sold	
Cost of Goods Sold	5070	Cost of Lamps Sold	
Cost of Goods Sold	5075	Cost of Mirrors Sold	
Cost of Goods Sold	5900	Inventory Adjustment	
Other Expense	7000	Interest Expense	

At this point, you can only enter beginning balances for asset, liability, and equity accounts. You already recorded the inventory balances in the EasyStep Interview window, but now need to reclassify them to the new inventory accounts. You will enter the balances in the income and expense accounts later by way of a journal entry.

ACCOUNTING
concept

The effect of adding a balance in the Drawings account is as follows:

3020 Kristin Raina, Drawings		3010 Kristin Raina, Capital (Open Bal. Equity)	
Dr	Cr	Dr	Cr
400			400

Updating Subaccounts

As part of the EasyStep Interview process, QuickBooks Pro created a parent account for each fixed asset, with two subaccounts, one for the original cost and one for accumulated depreciation. You just renamed and assigned a number to the original cost account and the accumulated depreciation account. You will now make the original cost account the parent account and the accumulated depreciation account will be a subaccount of the cost account. After you do this, the fixed asset parent account created by QuickBooks Pro will have a zero balance and can be deleted.

1. Open the Edit Account window for account 1700 Furniture (cost).
2. Remove the check mark next to <u>S</u>ubaccount of.
3. Click OK.
4. Open the Edit Account window for account 1750 Accum. Dep., Furniture.
5. From the <u>S</u>ubaccount of drop-down list, click 1700 Furniture (cost).
6. Click OK.
7. Remove the checkmark next to <u>S</u>ubaccount of for the 1800 - Computers account, and then click OK.
8. For account 1850 Accum. Dep., Computers, change the subaccount to 1800 Computers (cost) and click OK. The Chart of Accounts List for fixed assets should look like figure 7–2.

FIGURE 7-2

Chart of Accounts List for Fixed Assets

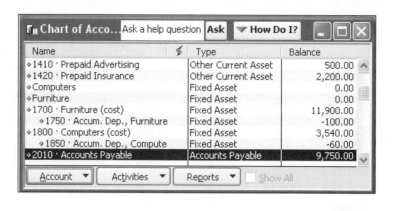

Deleting Unnecessary Accounts

After the new accounts are created, and the fixed assets subaccounts revised, there now remain some accounts created by QuickBooks Pro in the EasyStep Interview that are no longer needed and can be deleted.

Delete the following accounts:

	Furniture	the account with no number, now has a 0 balance
	Computers	the account with no number, now has a 0 balance
3900	Retained Earnings	

By default QuickBooks Pro creates a Payroll Liabilities and Payroll Expenses accounts even though the payroll feature was turned off. Since we do not need these accounts, they will be marked as inactive.

To mark an account as inactive.

1. At the Chart of Accounts List window, select the Payroll Liabilities account.
2. Click the Account button, then click on Make Inactive. The Payroll Liabilities account is no longer displayed in the Chart of Accounts List.
3. Select the Payroll Expenses account.
4. Click the Account button, then click on Make Inactive.

   To see Inactive accounts listed on the Chart of Accounts List, place a check mark in the box to the left of Show All. You will see the Inactive accounts with an X next to the account name. To hide the accounts, remove the check mark from the Show All box.

5. Close the Chart of Accounts List window.

CUSTOMIZING INVENTORY ITEMS

When a company indicates in the EasyStep Interview window that it will maintain inventory records, QuickBooks Pro automatically creates an Inventory Asset account and a Cost of Goods Sold account. As part of the EasyStep Interview, QuickBooks Pro recorded all inventory items in the one Inventory Asset account, and the one Cost of Goods Sold account was identified for each inventory part in the Item List.

When you customized the Chart of Accounts, you renamed the Inventory Asset account created by QuickBooks Pro to Inventory of Carpets. In addition, you created three more inventory accounts for Draperies, Lamps, and Mirrors. You renamed the Cost of Goods Sold account, created by QuickBooks Pro, as Cost of Carpets Sold, and created three additional cost of goods sold accounts for Draperies, Lamps, and Mirrors.

After the Chart of Accounts List is customized, you can then customize the Inventory Items List to identify the correct Inventory asset and Cost of Goods Sold account for each inventory item. As you do this, you must make sure the revenue account for each inventory item is correct, because a separate revenue account was identified with each inventory item in the EasyStep Interview window.

To customize the inventory part items—
1. Click Lists, and then click Item List.
2. At the Item List window, double-click the first inventory part item, *Carpets*. The Edit Item window for Carpets appears. The information displayed is based on information entered for inventory items during the EasyStep Interview process.
3. Verify or correct the accounts as necessary based on the following information:

Field	Number	Name
COGS Account	5060	Cost of Carpets Sold
Income Account	4060	Sale of Carpets
Asset Account	1260	Inventory of Carpets

(See figure 7–3.)

FIGURE 7-3
Edit Item – Carpets

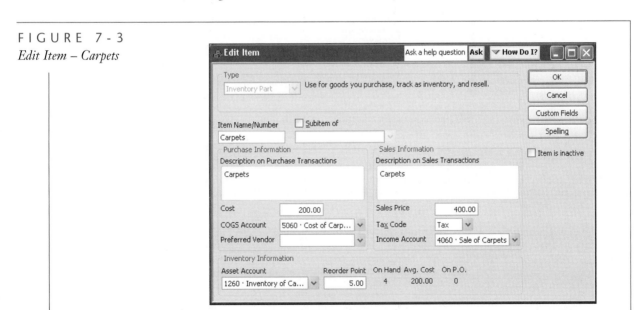

4. If the information is correct, click OK.

5. Verify and correct the Item List for the Draperies, Lamps, and Mirrors inventory part items using the information listed below:

Item	Cost of Goods Sold	Income	Asset
Draperies	5065	4065	1265
Lamps	5070	4070	1270
Mirrors	5075	4075	1275

6. After completing the customizing of the accounts and inventory items, review the trial balance for 04/01/2004. It should look like figure 7–4.

FIGURE 7-4
Trial Balance after Customizing the Accounts and Inventory Items

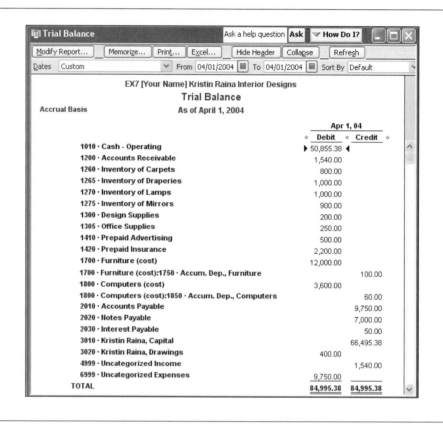

ACCOUNTING concept

The effect of renaming the Inventory Asset account to Inventory of Carpets and of customizing the Item List is as follows:

1260 Inventory of Carpets (Inventory Asset)		1265 Inventory of Draperies		1270 Inventory of Lamps		1275 Inventory of Mirrors	
Dr	Cr	Dr	Cr	Dr	Cr	Dr	Cr
3,700		1,000		1,000		900	
	1,000						
	1,000						
	900						
Bal 800							

SETTING UP PAYMENT TERMS

In QuickBooks Pro a list with payment terms is established that can be accessed in customer files, vendor files, and activities windows when needed. As seen in prior chapters, payment terms such as Net 30 Days, 2/10 Net 30

Days, and so on, can be identified in both the customer and vendor files if they relate to a particular customer or vendor. Before you update the Vendor and Customer Lists as part of the customization process, you need to set up the list of payment terms. You do this using the Lists menu.

To set up payment terms—
1. Click Lists, and then click Customer & Vendor Profile Lists.
2. At the Customer & Vendor Profile Lists submenu, click Terms List. The Terms List window appears.
3. At the Terms List window, click the Terms button.
4. At the Terms menu, click New. The New Terms window appears.
5. In the *Terms* field, key **Net 30 Days**.
6. In the *Net due in days* field, key **30**. (See figure 7–5.)

FIGURE 7-5
New Terms Window –
Net 30 Days – Completed

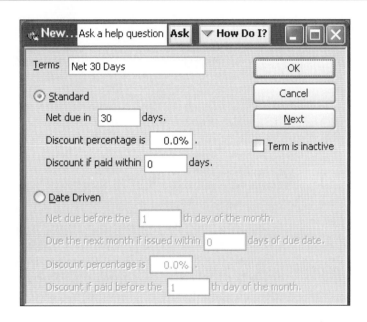

7. If the information is correct, click Next.
8. Enter the terms listed below using the steps 4 through 7 again:
   Net 10 Days
   Net 15 Days

9. At the New Terms window, in the *Terms* field, key **2/10, Net 30 Days**.
10. In the *Net due in days* field, key **30**.
11. In the *Discount percentage is* field, key **2**.
12. In the *Discount if paid within days* field, key **10**. (See figure 7–6.)

FIGURE 7-6
New Terms Window – 2/10,
Net 30 Days – Completed

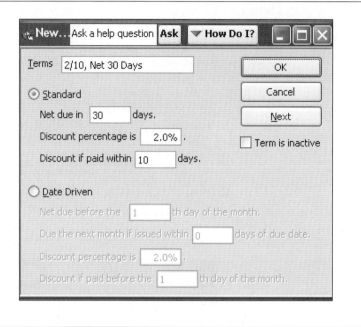

13. If the information is correct, click OK.
14. Close the Terms List window.

LISTS: UPDATING LISTS

As part of the EasyStep Interview process, general ledger accounts, as well as customer files and vendor files were set up. However, only accounts, customer files, and vendor files with beginning balances were set up. In addition, you could only indicate the name of the customer and vendor, without any other background information. After you have customized the company file, you can add any desired general ledger accounts, customer files, and vendor files without beginning balances to the Lists. In addition, you can update background information on customers and vendors with beginning balances.

UPDATING THE CHART OF ACCOUNTS LIST

Add the following account, which has a zero balance, to the Chart of Accounts List:

Type	Number	Name
Other Current Asset	1250	Undeposited Funds

UPDATING THE CUSTOMER:JOB LIST

At this point, update the Customer:Job List to include all customers, even those with a zero balance, and to include background information for the customer files created as part of the EasyStep Interview.

HINT

In the event you need to add any items with a zero balance to the Item List, you would do it at this time.

Adding Customer Files with Zero Balances

The customer files you created in the EasyStep Interview process included only customers with an outstanding balance. Listed in table 7–1 are the customers of Kristin Raina Interior Designs that do not have outstanding balances. Using the procedures learned in chapter 3 for adding a new customer, add the customers listed in table 7–1.

Adding Background Information to Customer Files

When you created customer files in the EasyStep Interview process you could only include the customer name and outstanding balance. Using the procedures learned in chapter 3 for editing a customer file, add the background information listed in table 7–2 for the appropriate customers.

TABLE 7-1

Customers with Zero Balances

Customer/Company Name	Name/Contact	Address	Phone/Fax	Terms	Account No.
Alomar Company	Oliver Alomar	1001 Oak Lake Ave. Minneapolis, MN 55401	612-555-5757 612-555-5858	Net 30 Days	O1535
Benitez Bagel Barn	Belinda Benitez	148 46th Ave. N Plymouth, MN 53406	612-555-1233 612-555-1234	Net 30 Days	B0250
Cook Caterers	Stephen Cook	275 Oak Lake Ave. Minneapolis, MN 55401	612-555-7896 612-555-7599	Net 30 Days	C0360
Guthrie, Jennie	Jennie Guthrie	165 Terrace Ct. St. Paul, MN 55101	651-555-1515	2/10, Net 30 Days	O1565
Hamilton Hotels	Hilda Hamilton	1000 York Ave. St. Paul, MN 55101	651-555-1050 651-555-1060	2/10, Net 30 Days	H0830
Jones, Beverly	Beverly Jones	333 York Circle Bloomington, MN 54603	612-555-7778	Net 30 Days	J1013
Ordonez, Maria	Maria Ordonez	210 NE Lowry Ave. Minneapolis, MN 54204	612-555-9999 612-555-9998	Net 30 Days	O1545
Piazza Pizza Palace	Mikey Piazza	360 Border Ave. N Minneapolis, MN 55401	612-555-9000 612-555-9800	Net 30 Days	P1650

TABLE 7-2

Background Information for Customers with an Outstanding Balance

Customer/Company Name	Name/Contact	Address	Phone/Fax	Terms	Account No.
Burnitz Bakery Co.	Barry Burnitz	18 N Grand Ave. Minneapolis, MN 55403	612-555-2240 612-555-2241	Net 30 Days	R1825
Franco Films Co.	Fred Franco	100 Pleasant Ave. S Minneapolis, MN 55409	612-555-4566 612-555-4567	Net 30 Days	F0660

UPDATING THE VENDOR LIST

At this point, you update the Vendor List so that it includes all vendors, even those with a zero balance, and add any background information needed for the vendor files.

Adding Vendor Files with Zero Balances

Using the EasyStep Interview process, you could only create vendor files for vendors with an outstanding balance. Vendors for Kristin Raina Interior

Designs that do not have outstanding balances are listed in table 7–3. Using the procedures learned in chapter 2 for adding a new vendor, add the vendors listed in table 7–3.

Adding Background Information to Vendor Files with Balances

The vendor files you created in the EasyStep Interview process only included the vendor name and outstanding balance. Using the procedures learned in chapter 2 for editing a vendor file, edit the vendor files listed in table 7–4 to include all background information for the vendors with an outstanding balance.

TABLE 7-3

Vendors with Zero Balances

Vendor/Company Name	Name/Contact	Address	Phone/Fax	Account No.	Terms
Darren Tapestry	Donna Darren	10 W Larpenteur Ave. Minneapolis, MN 52604	612-555-2221 612-555-2222	2365	Net 30 Days
Giambi Graphics	Gregg Giambi	56 Amity Way Bloomington, MN 53608	612-555-0002 612-555-0003	33-2221	Net 30 Days
Jeter Janitorial Services	Jason Jeter	233 Lilac Rd. Minneapolis, MN 54302 `	612-555-4444 612-555-4445	555-32	Net 30 Days
Kristin Raina					
Lumiare Lighting Company	Larry Lyght	123 Glenwood Ave. Minneapolis, MN 53609	612-555-4790 612-555-4795	36	Net 30 Days
Nordic Realty	Jack Marx	23 N. 12th Street Minneapolis, MN 53604	612-555-3232 612-555-3233	55-1212	Net 10 Days
TwinCity Tel Co.	Terry Ameche	3223 River Dr. St. Paul, MN 53908	651-555-6667 651-555-6668	666-6667	Net 30 Days
Weaver Fabrics	Jon Weaver	355 W 70th Street Minneapolis, MN 53604	612-555-8777 612-555-8778	9878	Net 30 Days
[Your Name] Accounting Services	Your Name	One Main Plaza St. Paul, MN 53602	612-555-2222 612-555-2223	99-2001-XX	Net 30 Days

TABLE 7-4

Background Information for Vendors with an Outstanding Balance

Vendor/Company Name	Name/Contact	Address	Phone/Fax	Account No.	Terms
Ace Glass Works	Archie Ace	25 SE Como Ave. Minneapolis, MN 53602	612-555-9812 612-555-6813	1245	Net 30 Days
Bell Carpet Design	Bill Bell	55 North Main Ave. St. Paul, MN 54603	651-555-8823 651-555-8824	66-87874	Net 30 Days
Cone and Clemens Associates	Carrie Cone	23 W. University Ave. St. Paul, MN 54603	651-555-8855 651-555-8856	KR569	Net 30 Days
Galeway Computers	Roger Rivera	33 Route 10 Springfield, MA 24105	617-555-4747 617-555-4748	2455-897	Net 30 Days
Midwest Mutual Insurance Co.	Jack Mills	3566 Broadway Chicago, IL 58303	805-555-4545 805-555-4546	54778784	Net 30 Days
Minneapolis Electric & Gas Co.	Jack Watts	150 Douglas Ave. St. Paul, MN 55303	651-555-4949 651-555-4950	2001-23657	Net 30 Days
Williams Office Supply Company	Bernard Williams	15 Grand Ave. S. Minneapolis, MN 55404	612-555-2240 612-555-2241	55-8988	Net 30 Days

ADJUSTING FOR THE ACCRUAL BASIS OF ACCOUNTING

You have now created the company file (Part I) and customized it by updating the Chart of Accounts and Item Lists, adding accounts, vendor files, and customer files with zero balances, and adding background information for vendors and customers with outstanding balances (Part II). The next step is to prepare the company file for the **accrual basis of accounting,** which requires the recording of revenues when earned and expenses when incurred.

During the EasyStep Interview process, QuickBooks Pro set up an Uncategorized Income account, which is the offset to the Accounts Receivable accounts that you set up. It also set up an Uncategorized Expenses account, which is the offset to the Accounts Payable accounts that you set up. These uncategorized accounts do not reflect the actual revenues and expenses of the company. In addition, the EasyStep Interview window is not designed to record the beginning balances in the revenue and expense accounts. Therefore, the revenues and expenses for the company have not yet been recorded.

To prepare the company file for the accrual basis of accounting, you must make three journal entries in the General Journal Entry window. The first two journal entries are referred to as **reversing entries.** The first journal entry reverses the Uncategorized Income account created by QuickBooks Pro. The second journal entry reverses the Uncategorized Expenses account created by QuickBooks Pro. The third journal entry records all the balances for the revenue and expense accounts as of April 1, 2004.

accrual basis of accounting Accounting method that requires the recording of revenue when it is earned and the recording of expenses when they are incurred.

reversing entries Entries recorded in the general journal to offset a balance in an account.

REVERSING THE UNCATEGORIZED INCOME ACCOUNT

Recall in the *Journal* report shown in figure 6–31 that there were two journal entries recorded that debited Accounts Receivable and credited Uncategorized Income for two customers as follows:

Burnitz Bakery Company	$ 600
Franco Films Co.	940
	$1,540

The debit entries to the Accounts Receivable account are correct and should stay in that account. However, the credits to the Uncategorized Income account need to be reversed. You can do this by debiting account 4999 Uncategorized Income for the total of $1,540, and crediting account 3010 Kristin Raina, Capital (formerly the Opening Bal Equity account) for $1,540.

To reverse the Uncategorized Income account—
1. Click Company, and then click Make Journal Entry.
2. At the General Journal Entry window, choose the date, *04/01/2004*, and at the *Entry No.* field, accept Entry No. 8.
3. Debit account *4999 Uncategorized Income* for 1,540, and credit account *3010 Kristin Raina, Capital* for 1,540. (See figure 7–7.)

HINT

Remember that as part of customizing the Chart of Accounts, you changed the account Opening Bal Equity, created by QuickBooks Pro, to account 3010 Kristin Raina, Capital.

FIGURE 7-7
*General Journal Entry
Window – Reverse
Uncategorized Income*

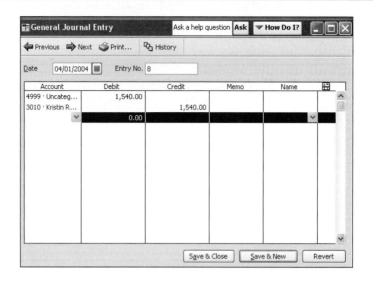

4. If the information is correct, click Save & New.

ACCOUNTING
concept

4999 Uncategorized Income		3010 Kristin Raina, Capital	
Dr	Cr	Dr	Cr
1,540	1,540		1,540
	Bal 0		

REVERSING THE UNCATEGORIZED EXPENSES ACCOUNT

In the Journal Report of figure 6–31, there were seven journal entries recorded that credited Accounts Payable and debited Uncategorized Expenses for seven vendor balances as follows:

Ace Glass Works	$1,500
Bell Carpet Design	2,000
Cone and Clemens Associates	400
Galeway Computers	2,600
Midwest Mutual Insurance	2,400
Minneapolis Electric & Gas	450
Williams Office Supply Company	400
	$9,750

The credit entries to the Accounts Payable account are correct and should stay in that account. However, the debits to the Uncategorized Expenses need to be reversed. You can do this by crediting account 6999 Uncategorized Expenses for the total of $9,750 and debiting account 3010 Kristin Raina Capital for $9,750.

To reverse the Uncategorized Expenses account—
1. At the General Journal Entry window, choose the date of *04/01/2004*, and at the *Entry No.* field, accept Entry No. 9.
2. Debit account *3010 Kristin Raina, Capital* for 9,750, and credit account *6999 Uncategorized Expenses* for 9,750. (See figure 7–8.)

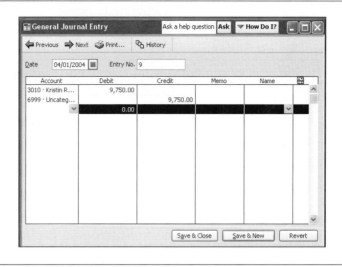

3. If the information is correct, click Save & New.

ACCOUNTING
concept

6999 Uncategorized Expenses		3010 Kristin Raina, Capital	
Dr	Cr	Dr	Cr
9,750	9,750 Adj	9,750	
Bal 0			

RECORDING REVENUES AND EXPENSES

The final step in preparing the company file for the accrual basis of accounting is to record all the balances for the revenue and expense accounts as of April 1, 2004. This will be one large, compound journal entry you will make in the General Journal Entry window to record all the revenues and expenses balances for Kristin Raina Interior Designs.

To record the revenue and expenses in the General Journal Entry window—

1. At the General Journal Entry window, choose the date of *04/01/2004*, and at *Entry No.* field, accept Entry No. 10.
2. *Debit* the accounts and amounts listed below—

HINT

Maximize the General Journal Entry window while recording the journal entry so that you can more easily see all of the entries.

HINT

You can key in the account number for each account or use the drop-down list. Keying in the amount in the correct column will delete any amounts QuickBooks Pro is anticipating that may not be correct.

Account		Debit
4100	Sales Discounts	$84.62
5060	Cost of Carpets Sold	1,200
5065	Cost of Draperies Sold	500
5070	Cost of Lamps Sold	600
5075	Cost of Mirrors Sold	450
5900	Inventory Adjustment	150
6020	Accounting Expense	300
6050	Advertising Expense	100
6175	Deprec. Exp., Furniture	100
6185	Deprec. Exp., Computers	60
6200	Insurance Expense	200
6300	Janitorial Expense	125
6325	Office Supplies Expense	150
6400	Rent Expense	800

6450	Telephone Expense	275
6500	Utilities Expense	450
7000	Interest Expense	50

As you are recording this information, notice how QuickBooks Pro is creating a balancing amount after each entry. After entering all the debits, there should be a balance amount of 5,594.62 in the credit column.

3. *Credit* accounts and amounts listed below—

Account		Credit
4010	Design Services	$4980
4020	Decorating Services	3400
4060	Sale of Carpets	2400
4065	Sale of Draperies	1000
4070	Sale of Lamps	1200
4075	Sale of Mirrors	900

After entering all the credits, there should be a balance amount of 8,285.38 in the debit column.

4. For the balancing amount of 8,285.38, debit the account 3010 Kristin Raina, Capital. (See figure 7–9.)

FIGURE 7-9
General Journal Entry Window – Record Revenue and Expenses

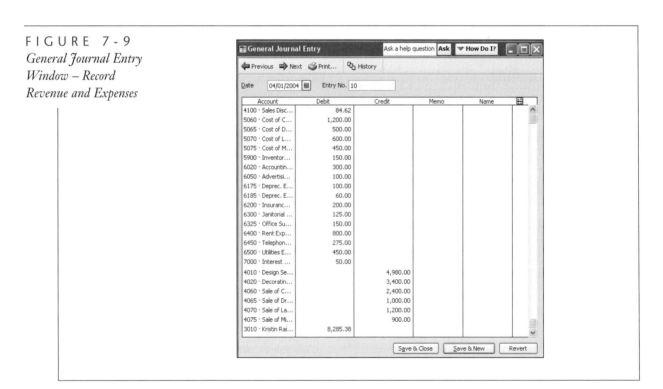

5. If the information is correct, click S*a*ve & Close.

3010 Kristin Raina, Capital

Dr	Cr
8285.38	

4010-4020 Service Revenue			4060-4075 Sale of Inventory			4100 Sales Discounts	
Dr	Cr		Dr	Cr		Dr	Cr
	Design	4,980		Carpets	2,400	84.62	
	Decor.	3,400		Draperies	1,000		
		8,380		Lamps	1,200		
				Mirrors	900		
					5,500		

5060-5075, 5900 Cost of Goods Sold			6020-6500 Expenses			7000 Interest Exp.	
Dr		Cr	Dr		Cr	Dr	Cr
Carpets	1,200		Accounting	300		50	
Draperies	500		Advertising	100			
Lamps	600		Dep. Exp.,				
Mirrors	450		Furniture	100			
Inv. Adj.	150		Dep. Exp.,				
Bal	2,900		Computers	60			
			Insurance	200			
			Janitorial	125			
			Office Supplies	150			
			Rent	800			
			Telephone	275			
			Utilities	450			
			Bal	2,560			

REPORTS: CUSTOMIZED NEW COMPANY FILE AND FINANCIAL REPORTS

Once you have completed the New Company Setup operation—going through the EasyStep Interview process (Part I); reviewing and correcting EasyStep Interview information; customizing the Chart of Accounts and Item Lists; updating the Chart of Accounts, Vendors, Customer:Jobs, and Item Lists; and adjusting the company file for the accrual basis of accounting (Part II)—you can display and print the accounting and financial reports for the new company file. You can also display and print the Lists.

ACCOUNTING REPORTS

The accounting reports in the new company file consist of the *Journal*, *General Ledger*, and *Trial Balance* reports.

Journal Report

Recall that you displayed and printed the *Journal* report after the EasyStep Interview process was completed (figure 6–31). Recording the Kristin Raina, Drawings account with a beginning balance of $400, and recording the three journal entries to adjust for the accrual basis of accounting created more journal entries. View and print all journal entries for April 1, 2004. Figure 7–10 displays only the additional four journal entries.

FIGURE 7-10
Additional Journal Entries

EX7 [Your Name] Kristin Raina Interior Designs
Journal
April 1, 2004

Trans #	Type	Date	Num	Name	Memo	Account	Debit	Credit
25	General Journal	04/01/2004	7		Account Opening Balance	3020 · Kristin Raina, Drawings	400.00	
					Account Opening Balance	3010 · Kristin Raina, Capital		400.00
							400.00	400.00
26	General Journal	04/01/2004	8			4999 · Uncategorized Income	1,540.00	
						3010 · Kristin Raina, Capital		1,540.00
							1,540.00	1,540.00
27	General Journal	04/01/2004	9			3010 · Kristin Raina, Capital	9,750.00	
						6999 · Uncategorized Expenses		9,750.00
							9,750.00	9,750.00
28	General Journal	04/01/2004	10			4100 · Sales Discounts	84.62	
						5060 · Cost of Carpets Sold	1,200.00	
						5065 · Cost of Draperies Sold	500.00	
						5070 · Cost of Lamps Sold	600.00	
						5075 · Cost of Mirrors Sold	450.00	
						5900 · Inventory Adjustment	150.00	
						6020 · Accounting Expense	300.00	
						6050 · Advertising Expense	100.00	
						6175 · Deprec. Exp., Furniture	100.00	
						6185 · Deprec. Exp., Computers	60.00	
						6200 · Insurance Expense	200.00	
						6300 · Janitorial Expense	125.00	
						6325 · Office Supplies Expense	150.00	
						6400 · Rent Expense	800.00	
						6450 · Telephone Expense	275.00	
						6500 · Utilities Expense	450.00	
						7000 · Interest Expense	50.00	
						4010 · Design Services		4,980.00
						4020 · Decorating Services		3,400.00
						4060 · Sale of Carpets		2,400.00
						4065 · Sale of Draperies		1,000.00
						4070 · Sale of Lamps		1,200.00
						4075 · Sale of Mirrors		900.00
						3010 · Kristin Raina, Capital	8,285.38	
							13,880.00	13,880.00
TOTAL							**117,375.38**	**117,375.38**

Trial Balance Report

Next, view and print the *Trial Balance* for April 1, 2004. It should look like figure 7–11. Compare the trial balance of April 1, 2004, to the trial balance of March 31, 2004, shown in figure 6–30. The trial balances should be the same.

   Note: The Trial Balance in figure 6-30 shows accounts with zero balances (Undeposited Funds and Sales Tax Payable). These accounts previously had activities posted to them that subsequently resulted in a zero balance. In the case of the Trial Balance in figure 7-11, these accounts are new accounts where activities have not yet been recorded. QuickBooks Pro does not display new accounts with zero balances—therefore these accounts are not displayed.

   QuickBooks Pro created the Uncategorized Income and Uncategorized Expenses accounts you see in figure 7-11 when you entered outstanding Accounts Receivable and Accounts Payable accounts in the EasyStep Interview window. The balances in these uncategorized accounts were subsequently reversed when the company file was prepared for the accrual basis of accounting. These accounts are no longer needed. They cannot be deleted, but they can be marked as Inactive so they do not appear in the reports.

FIGURE 7-11
Trial Balance

EX7 [Your Name] Kristin Raina Interior Designs
Trial Balance

Accrual Basis   **As of April 1, 2004**

	Apr 1, 04	
	Debit	**Credit**
1010 · Cash - Operating	50,855.38	
1200 · Accounts Receivable	1,540.00	
1260 · Inventory of Carpets	800.00	
1265 · Inventory of Draperies	1,000.00	
1270 · Inventory of Lamps	1,000.00	
1275 · Inventory of Mirrors	900.00	
1300 · Design Supplies	200.00	
1305 · Office Supplies	250.00	
1410 · Prepaid Advertising	500.00	
1420 · Prepaid Insurance	2,200.00	
1700 · Furniture (cost)	12,000.00	
1700 · Furniture (cost):1750 · Accum. Dep., Furniture		100.00
1800 · Computers (cost)	3,600.00	
1800 · Computers (cost):1850 · Accum. Dep., Computers		60.00
2010 · Accounts Payable		9,750.00
2020 · Notes Payable		7,000.00
2030 · Interest Payable		50.00
3010 · Kristin Raina, Capital		50,000.00
3020 · Kristin Raina, Drawings	400.00	
4010 · Design Services		4,980.00
4020 · Decorating Services		3,400.00
4060 · Sale of Carpets		2,400.00
4065 · Sale of Draperies		1,000.00
4070 · Sale of Lamps		1,200.00
4075 · Sale of Mirrors		900.00
4100 · Sales Discounts	84.62	
4999 · Uncategorized Income	0.00	
5060 · Cost of Carpets Sold	1,200.00	
5065 · Cost of Draperies Sold	500.00	
5070 · Cost of Lamps Sold	600.00	
5075 · Cost of Mirrors Sold	450.00	
5900 · Inventory Adjustment	150.00	
6020 · Accounting Expense	300.00	
6050 · Advertising Expense	100.00	
6175 · Deprec. Exp., Furniture	100.00	
6185 · Deprec. Exp., Computers	60.00	
6200 · Insurance Expense	200.00	
6300 · Janitorial Expense	125.00	
6325 · Office Supplies Expense	150.00	
6400 · Rent Expense	800.00	
6450 · Telephone Expense	275.00	
6500 · Utilities Expense	450.00	
6999 · Uncategorized Expenses	0.00	
7000 · Interest Expense	50.00	
TOTAL	**80,840.00**	**80,840.00**

FINANCIAL REPORTS

The financial reports consist of the *Profit & Loss* standard report (see figure 7–12) and the *Balance Sheet* standard report (see figure 7–13). You should print these reports once you have completed New Company Setup.

FIGURE 7-12
Profit & Loss Standard Report

EX7 [Your Name] Kristin Raina Interior Designs
Profit & Loss
April 1, 2004

Accrual Basis

	Apr 1, 04
Ordinary Income/Expense	
Income	
4010 · Design Services	4,980.00
4020 · Decorating Services	3,400.00
4060 · Sale of Carpets	2,400.00
4065 · Sale of Draperies	1,000.00
4070 · Sale of Lamps	1,200.00
4075 · Sale of Mirrors	900.00
4100 · Sales Discounts	-84.62
4999 · Uncategorized Income	0.00
Total Income	13,795.38
Cost of Goods Sold	
5060 · Cost of Carpets Sold	1,200.00
5065 · Cost of Draperies Sold	500.00
5070 · Cost of Lamps Sold	600.00
5075 · Cost of Mirrors Sold	450.00
5900 · Inventory Adjustment	150.00
Total COGS	2,900.00
Gross Profit	10,895.38
Expense	
6020 · Accounting Expense	300.00
6050 · Advertising Expense	100.00
6175 · Deprec. Exp., Furniture	100.00
6185 · Deprec. Exp., Computers	60.00
6200 · Insurance Expense	200.00
6300 · Janitorial Expense	125.00
6325 · Office Supplies Expense	150.00
6400 · Rent Expense	800.00
6450 · Telephone Expense	275.00
6500 · Utilities Expense	450.00
6999 · Uncategorized Expenses	0.00
Total Expense	2,560.00
Net Ordinary Income	8,335.38
Other Income/Expense	
Other Expense	
7000 · Interest Expense	50.00
Total Other Expense	50.00
Net Other Income	-50.00
Net Income	8,285.38

FIGURE 7-13
Balance Sheet
Standard Report

EX7 [Your Name] Kristin Raina Interior Designs
Balance Sheet
As of April 1, 2004

Accrual Basis

	Apr 1, 04
ASSETS	
Current Assets	
Checking/Savings	
1010 · Cash - Operating	50,855.38
Total Checking/Savings	50,855.38
Accounts Receivable	
1200 · Accounts Receivable	1,540.00
Total Accounts Receivable	1,540.00
Other Current Assets	
1260 · Inventory of Carpets	800.00
1265 · Inventory of Draperies	1,000.00
1270 · Inventory of Lamps	1,000.00
1275 · Inventory of Mirrors	900.00
1300 · Design Supplies	200.00
1305 · Office Supplies	250.00
1410 · Prepaid Advertising	500.00
1420 · Prepaid Insurance	2,200.00
Total Other Current Assets	6,850.00
Total Current Assets	59,245.38
Fixed Assets	
1700 · Furniture (cost)	
1750 · Accum. Dep., Furniture	-100.00
1700 · Furniture (cost) - Other	12,000.00
Total 1700 · Furniture (cost)	11,900.00
1800 · Computers (cost)	
1850 · Accum. Dep., Computers	-60.00
1800 · Computers (cost) - Other	3,600.00
Total 1800 · Computers (cost)	3,540.00
Total Fixed Assets	15,440.00
TOTAL ASSETS	74,685.38
LIABILITIES & EQUITY	
Liabilities	
Current Liabilities	
Accounts Payable	
2010 · Accounts Payable	9,750.00
Total Accounts Payable	9,750.00
Other Current Liabilities	
2020 · Notes Payable	7,000.00
2030 · Interest Payable	50.00
Total Other Current Liabilities	7,050.00
Total Current Liabilities	16,800.00
Total Liabilities	16,800.00
Equity	
3010 · Kristin Raina, Capital	50,000.00
3020 · Kristin Raina, Drawings	-400.00
Net Income	8,285.38
Total Equity	57,885.38
TOTAL LIABILITIES & EQUITY	74,685.38

Lists Reports

The Lists reports consist of the Chart of Accounts, Item, Customer:Job, and Vendor Lists. You should also print these reports once you have completed the New Company Setup, and they should look like figures 7–14 through 7–17.

FIGURE 7-14

Account Listing

EX7 [Your Name] Kristin Raina Interior Designs
Account Listing
April 1, 2004

Account	Type	Balance Total	Description	Accnt. #	Tax Line
1010 · Cash - Operating	Bank	50,855.38		1010	<Unassigned>
1200 · Accounts Receivable	Accounts Receivable	1,540.00		1200	<Unassigned>
1250 · Undeposited Funds	Other Current Asset	0.00		1250	<Unassigned>
1260 · Inventory of Carpets	Other Current Asset	800.00		1260	<Unassigned>
1265 · Inventory of Draperies	Other Current Asset	1,000.00		1265	<Unassigned>
1270 · Inventory of Lamps	Other Current Asset	1,000.00		1270	<Unassigned>
1275 · Inventory of Mirrors	Other Current Asset	900.00		1275	<Unassigned>
1300 · Design Supplies	Other Current Asset	200.00		1300	<Unassigned>
1305 · Office Supplies	Other Current Asset	250.00		1305	<Unassigned>
1410 · Prepaid Advertising	Other Current Asset	500.00		1410	<Unassigned>
1420 · Prepaid Insurance	Other Current Asset	2,200.00		1420	<Unassigned>
1700 · Furniture (cost)	Fixed Asset	11,900.00		1700	<Unassigned>
1700 · Furniture (cost):1750 · Accum. Dep., Furniture	Fixed Asset	-100.00		1750	<Unassigned>
1800 · Computers (cost)	Fixed Asset	3,540.00		1800	<Unassigned>
1800 · Computers (cost):1850 · Accum. Dep., Computers	Fixed Asset	-60.00		1850	<Unassigned>
2010 · Accounts Payable	Accounts Payable	9,750.00		2010	<Unassigned>
2020 · Notes Payable	Other Current Liability	7,000.00		2020	<Unassigned>
2030 · Interest Payable	Other Current Liability	50.00		2030	<Unassigned>
2200 · Sales Tax Payable	Other Current Liability	0.00		2200	<Unassigned>
3010 · Kristin Raina, Capital	Equity	50,000.00		3010	<Unassigned>
3020 · Kristin Raina, Drawings	Equity	-400.00		3020	<Unassigned>
3900 · Retained Earnings	Equity			3900	<Unassigned>
4010 · Design Services	Income			4010	<Unassigned>
4020 · Decorating Services	Income			4020	<Unassigned>
4060 · Sale of Carpets	Income			4060	<Unassigned>
4065 · Sale of Draperies	Income			4065	<Unassigned>
4070 · Sale of Lamps	Income			4070	<Unassigned>
4075 · Sale of Mirrors	Income			4075	<Unassigned>
4100 · Sales Discounts	Income			4100	<Unassigned>
4999 · Uncategorized Income	Income			4999	<Unassigned>
5060 · Cost of Carpets Sold	Cost of Goods Sold			5060	<Unassigned>
5065 · Cost of Draperies Sold	Cost of Goods Sold			5065	<Unassigned>
5070 · Cost of Lamps Sold	Cost of Goods Sold			5070	<Unassigned>
5075 · Cost of Mirrors Sold	Cost of Goods Sold			5075	<Unassigned>
5900 · Inventory Adjustment	Cost of Goods Sold			5900	<Unassigned>
6020 · Accounting Expense	Expense			6020	<Unassigned>
6050 · Advertising Expense	Expense			6050	<Unassigned>
6175 · Deprec. Exp., Furniture	Expense			6175	<Unassigned>
6185 · Deprec. Exp., Computers	Expense			6185	<Unassigned>
6200 · Insurance Expense	Expense			6200	<Unassigned>
6300 · Janitorial Expense	Expense			6300	<Unassigned>
6325 · Office Supplies Expense	Expense			6325	<Unassigned>
6400 · Rent Expense	Expense			6400	<Unassigned>
6450 · Telephone Expense	Expense			6450	<Unassigned>
6500 · Utilities Expense	Expense			6500	<Unassigned>
6560 · Payroll Expenses	Expense			6560	<Unassigned>
6999 · Uncategorized Expenses	Expense			6999	<Unassigned>
7000 · Interest Expense	Other Expense			7000	<Unassigned>

FIGURE 7-15
Item Listing

EX7 [Your Name] Kristin Raina Interior Designs
Item Listing
April 1, 2004

Item	Description	Type	Cost	Price	Sales Tax Code	Quantity On Hand	Reorder ...
Decorating Services	Decorating Services	Service	0	50.00	Non		
Design Services	Design Services	Service	0	60.00	Non		
Carpets	Carpets	Inventory Part	200.00	400.00	Tax	4	5.00
Draperies	Draperies	Inventory Part	125.00	250.00	Tax	8	5.00
Lamps	Lamps	Inventory Part	100.00	200.00	Tax	10	5.00
Mirrors	Mirrors	Inventory Part	150.00	300.00	Tax	6	5.00
Minn. Sales Tax	Sales Tax	Sales Tax Item	0.00	7%		0.00	0.00
Out of State	Out-of-state sale, exempt from sales tax	Sales Tax Item	0.00	0%		0.00	0.00

FIGURE 7-16
Customer Contact List

EX7 [Your Name] Kristin Raina Interior Designs
Customer Contact List
April 1, 2004

Customer	Bill to	Contact	Phone	Fax	Balance Total
Alomar Company	Alomar Company Oliver Alomar 1001 Oak Lake Ave. Minneaplis, MN 54204	Oliver Alomar	612-555-5757	612-555-5858	0.00
Benitez Bagel Barn	Benitez Bagel Barn Belinda Benitez 148 46th Ave. N Plymouth, MN 53406	Belinda Benitez	612-555-1233	612-555-1234	0.00
Burnitz Bakery Company	Burnitz Bakery Company Barry Burnitz 18 N Grand Ave. Minneapolis, MN 55403	Barry Burnitz	612-555-2240	612-555-2241	600.00
Cook Caterers	Cook Caterers Stephen Cook 275 Oak Lake Ave. Minneapolis, MN 55401	Stephen Cook			0.00
Franco Films Co.	Franco Films Co. Fred Franco 100 Pleasant Ave. S Minneapolis, MN 55409	Fred Franco	612-555-4566	612-555-4567	940.00
Guthrie, Jennie	Jennie Guthrie 165 Terrace Ct. St. Paul, MN 55101	Jennie Guthrie	651-555-1515		0.00
Hamilton Hotels	Hamilton Hotels Hilda Hamilton 1000 York Ave. St. Paul, MN 55101	Hilda Hamilton	651-555-1050	651-555-1060	0.00
Jones, Beverly	Beverly Jones 333 York Circle Bloomington, MN 54603	Beverly Jones	612-555-7778		0.00
Ordonez, Maria	Maria Ordonez 210 NE Lowry Ave. Minneapolis, MN 54204	Maria Ordonez			0.00
Piazza Pizza Palace	Piazza Pizza Palace Mikey Piazza 360 Border Ave. N Minneapolis, MN 55401	Mikey Piazza	612-555-9000	612-555-9800	0.00

FIGURE 7-17
Vendor Contact List

EX7 [Your Name] Kristin Raina Interior Designs
Vendor Contact List
April 1, 2004

Vendor	Account No.	Address	Contact	Phone	Fax	Balance ...
Ace Glass Works	1245	Ace Glass Works Archie Ace 25 SE Como Ave. Minneapolis, MN 53602	Archie Ace	612-555-9812	612-555-6813	1,500.00
Bell Carpet Design	66-87874	Bell Carpet Design Bill Bell 55 North Main Ave. St. Paul, MN 54603	Bill Bell	651-555-8823	651-555-8824	2,000.00
Cone and Clemens Associates	KR569	Cone and Clemens Associates Carrie Cone 23 W. University Ave. St. Paul, MN 54603	Carrie Cone	651-555-8855	651-555-8856	400.00
Darren Tapestry	2365	Darren Tapestry Donna Darren 10 W Larpenteur Ave. Minneapolis, MN 52604	Donna Darren	612-555-2221	612-555-2222	0.00
Galeway Computers	2455-897	Galeway Computers Roger Rivera 33 Route 10 Springfield, MA 24105	Roger Rivera	617-555-4747	617-555-4748	2,600.00
Giambi Graphics	33-2221	Giambi Graphics Gregg Giambi 56 Amity Way Bloomington, MN 53608	Gregg Giambi	612-555-0002	612-555-0003	0.00
Jeter Janitorial Services	555-32	Jeter Janitorial Services Jason Jeter 233 Lilac Rd. Minneapolis, MN 54302	Jason Jeter	612-555-4444	612-555-4445	0.00
Kristin Raina						0.00
Lumiare Lighting Company	36	Lumiare Lighting Company Larry Lyght 123 Glenwood Ave. Minneapolis, MN 53609	Larry Lyght	612-555-4790	612-555-4795	0.00
Midwest Mutual Insurance Co.	54778784	Midwest Mutual Insurance Co. Jack Mills 3566 Broadway Chicago, IL 58303	Jack Mills	805-555-4545	805-555-4546	2,400.00
Minn. Dept. of Revenue		Minn. Dept. of Revenue				0.00
Minneapolis Electric & Gas Co.	2001-23657	Minneapolis Electric & Gas Co. Jack Watts 150 Douglas Ave. St. Paul, MN 55303	Jack Watts	651-555-4949	651-555-4950	450.00
Nordic Realty	55-1212	Nordic Realty Jack Marx 23 N. 12th Street Minneapolis, MN 53604	Jack Marx	612-555-3232	612-555-3233	0.00
TwinCity Tel Co.	666-6667	Twin City Tel Co. Terry Ameche 3223 River Dr. St. Paul, MN 53908	Terry Ameche	651-555-6667	651-555-6668	0.00
Weaver Fabrics	9878	Weaver Fabrics Jon Weaver 355 W 70th Street Minneapolis, MN 53604	Jon Weaver	612-555-8777	612-555-8778	0.00
Williams Office Supply Company	55-8988	Williams Office Supply Company Bernard Williams 15 Grand Ave. S. Minneapolis, MN 55404	Bernard Williams	612-555-2240	612-555-2241	400.00
Your Name Accounting Services	99-2001-XX	Your Name Accounting Services Your Name One Main Plaza St. Paul, MN 53602	Your Name	612-555-2222	612-555-2223	0.00

BACKING UP THE NEW COMPANY FILE

In business, backup copies of the new company file would be made to floppies and stored in a safe location off the company premises before recording activities on the file. You are working with a backup copy of the file. At this time, you should make another backup copy of the file to a floppy disk.

Upon completion of the New Company Setup level of operation (Part I and Part II), viewing and printing Reports, and making a backup copy of the new company file, your accounting records are now ready for recording daily activities.

NEW COMPANY SETUP:

SYSTEM DEFAULT ACCOUNTS CREATED BY QUICKBOOKS PRO

As you saw in the prior chapters, QuickBooks Pro establishes default accounts for the windows and uses those accounts when recording the transaction in the general journal. QuickBooks Pro looks for the system default accounts in the Chart of Accounts List and, if it cannot find an account, it will create it. Some system default accounts you learned so far are Accounts Receivable, Accounts Payable, Sales Tax Payable, Inventory Asset, and Cost of Goods Sold.

When you set up a new company using the EasyStep Interview process, QuickBooks Pro creates the system default accounts for your company based on the information you enter in the EasyStep Interview windows. In system default accounts that QuickBooks Pro creates, the account type is shown as gray shaded, or dimmed. These are the account types QuickBooks Pro uses to locate system default accounts. You can change the account number and the account name for a system default account, but you cannot change the account type.

For instance, open the Chart of Accounts List and edit the Accounts Receivable account. Notice how the account type is dimmed. Now edit the account Inventory of Carpets. Again the account type is dimmed. Recall that this account was originally the Inventory Asset account. When customizing the Chart of Accounts List, you added the number 1260 and you changed the account name to Inventory of Carpets. Likewise, QuickBooks Pro created the Cost of Goods Sold account. Again you changed the account name and number, which QuickBooks Pro allows, but QuickBooks would not allow you to change the account type Cost of Goods Sold.

Whenever you add an inventory part item to the Item List, QuickBooks Pro will look for an Inventory Asset account and Cost of Goods Sold account. If QuickBooks Pro does not find the necessary accounts, it will create them. If you create the account yourself, QuickBooks Pro does not find the account because it doesn't look at the account number and name, but instead looks for the dimmed account type created by the software. For example, if you choose *Group with Undeposited Funds* in the Enter Cash Sales window, QuickBooks Pro will look for the Undeposited Funds account. If it cannot find the account it will create it.

Open the Chart of Accounts List and find account 1250 Undeposited Funds. Note that it was created when you updated the Chart of Accounts List. Open the Edit Account window and notice that the account type is Other Current Asset, but it is not dimmed. Now open the Enter Sales Receipts window. (Click No at the message.) When you open that window, even though you did not record a transaction, QuickBooks Pro is looking for the Undeposited Funds account but will not identify the account 1250 you created.

Close the Enter Sales Receipts window and look at the Chart of Accounts List again. QuickBooks Pro created an account called 1499 *Undeposited Funds. Edit this new account. Notice that the account type in the Edit Account window is dimmed. (See figure 7–18.)

FIGURE 7-18
New Account 1499
**Undeposited Funds*

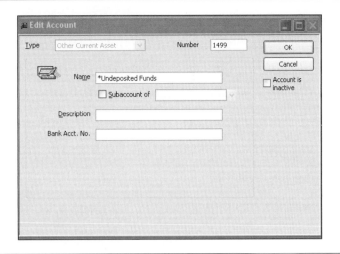

Because QuickBooks Pro cannot identify your account 1250, you should delete it. Then edit account 1499 *Undeposited Funds as follows:

1. Change the account number to 1250.
2. Remove the asterisk from the account name. (See figure 7–19.)

FIGURE 7-19
*Undeposited Funds
Account Edited*

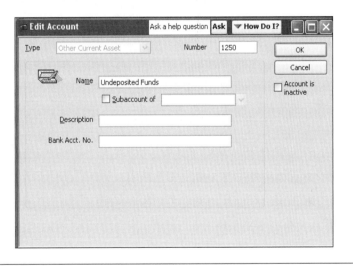

3. If the information is correct, click OK.

Reopen the Enter Sales Receipts window and close it. Review the Chart of Accounts List again. Notice that QuickBooks Pro did not create an Undeposited Funds account again because it found its own system default account, with the dimmed account type, even though you changed the account number and edited the name.

As can be seen in this example, QuickBooks Pro looks for certain default accounts. Even though you create accounts, QuickBooks Pro does not always recognize accounts you create, and subsequently will create its own accounts. An advantage to using the EasyStep Interview process is that QuickBooks Pro creates its own system default accounts that it will later recognize when transactions are recorded in the activities window. As a result, you do not have to go through the above process for most of the accounts.

P R O G R E S S
Check

PROCEDURE REVIEW

To activate the account numbers options—
1. Click Edit, and then click Preferences.
2. Along the left frame of the Preferences window, click the *Accounting* icon.
3. Click the Company Preferences tab.
4. At the *Account Numbers* field, place a ✓ in Use account numbers to turn on the account numbers option.
5. Click OK. The account numbers option is activated.

To edit the accounts on the Chart of Accounts List to add account numbers and change account name—
1. Click Lists, and then click Chart of Accounts.
2. Select the account to edit.
3. Click the Account button.
4. At the Account menu, click Edit.
5. Make any necessary changes to the account and click OK.

To add any new accounts not entered in the EasyStep Interview window—
1. Click Lists, and then click Chart of Accounts.
2. Click the Account button.
3. At the Account menu, click New.
4. At the New Account window, key in the information and click OK.

To update subaccounts—
1. Click Lists, and then click Chart of Accounts.
2. Select the account to edit.
3. Click the Account button.
4. At the Account menu, click Edit.
5. Make any necessary changes to the account and click OK.

To delete unnecessary accounts set up by QuickBooks Pro—
1. Click Lists, and then click Chart of Accounts.
2. Select the account to delete.
3. Click the Account button.
4. At the Account menu, click Delete, and then click OK.

To customize the Item List—
1. Click Lists, and then click Item List.
2. At the Item List window, double-click each item to display the Edit window for that item.
3. Review the Item information and make any necessary changes.
4. Click OK.

To set up payment terms—
1. Click Lists, and then click Customer & Vendor Profile Lists.
2. At the Customer & Vendor Profile Lists submenu, click Terms List.
3. At the Terms List window, click the Terms button.
4. At the Terms menu, click New.
5. In the New Terms window, key in the appropriate information.
6. Click Next or OK.

To update the Chart of Accounts List for accounts with zero balances—
1. Click Lists, and then click Chart of Accounts.
2. Click the Account button.
3. At the Account menu, click New.
4. At the New Account window, key in the information and click OK.

To update the Customer:Job List for customers with zero balances—
1. Click Lists, and then click Customer:Job List.
2. At the Customer:Job List window, click the Customer:Job menu button.
3. At the Customer:Job menu, click New.
4. Enter the background data for the vendor.
5. Click Next or OK.

To update the Customer:Job List with background information for customers with balances entered in the EasyStep Interview window—
1. Click Lists, and then click Customer:Job List.
2. At the Customer:Job List window, select the customer about whom you wish to add the background information.
3. Click the Customer:Job menu button.
4. At the Customer:Job menu, click Edit.
5. Change the appropriate information.
6. Click OK.
   You can also double-click the vendor name to enter the Edit window.

To update the Vendor List for vendors with zero balances—
1. Click Lists, and then click Vendor List.
2. At the Vendor List window, click the Vendor button.
3. At the Vendor menu, click New.
4. Enter the background data for the vendor.
5. Click Next or OK.

To update the Vendor List with background information for vendors with balances entered in the EasyStep Interview window—
1. Click Lists, and then click Vendor List.
2. At the Vendor List window, select the vendor about whom you wish to add the background information.
3. Click the Vendor button.
4. At the Vendor menu, click Edit.
5. Change the appropriate information.
6. Click OK.
   You can also double-click the vendor name to enter the Edit window.

To reverse the Uncategorized Income account—
1. Click Company, and then click Make Journal Entry.
2. Choose the date and check the entry in the *Entry No.* field.
3. Debit the Uncategorized Income account for the full amount in that account and credit the Capital account for the same amount.
4. Click Save & Close.

To reverse the Uncategorized Expenses account—
1. Click Company, and then click Make Journal Entry.
2. Choose the date and check the entry in the *Entry No.* field.
3. Debit the Capital account for the full amount in the Uncategorized Expenses account and credit the Uncategorized Expenses account for the same amount.
4. Click Save & Close.

To record the revenue and expenses in the General Journal Entry window—
1. Click Company, and then click Make Journal Entry.
2. Choose the date and check the entry in the *Entry No.* field.
3. Debit the Sales Discounts account and all of the expense accounts for the full amount of each of those accounts.
4. Credit all of the revenue accounts for the full amount of each of those accounts.
5. Debit (or credit) the Capital account for the balancing amount.
6. Click Save & Close.

To view and print accounting reports from the Reports menu—
1. Click Reports, and then click Accountant & Taxes.
2. At the Accountant & Taxes submenu, choose a report.
3. Indicate the start and end dates for the report.
4. Click Print on the command line.
5. At the Print Reports dialog box, review the settings, then click Print.
6. Close the report.

To view and print financial reports from the Reports menu—
1. Click Reports, and then click Company & Financial.
2. At the Company & Financial submenu, choose a financial report.
3. Indicate the start and end dates for the report.
4. Click Print on the command line.
5. At the Print Reports dialog box, review the settings, then click Print.
6. Close the report.

To view and print Lists from the Reports menu—
1. Click Reports, and then click List.
2. At the List submenu, choose a report.
3. Click Print on the command line.
4. At the Print Reports dialog box, review the settings, then click Print.
5. Close the report.

KEY CONCEPTS

Select the letter of the item that best matches each definition.

a. System default accounts
b. Journal entry
c. Account numbers
d. Uncategorized
e. Customizing the Chart of Accounts List
f. Inventory Asset and Cost of Goods Sold

g. <u>L</u>ists – Customer & Vendor Profile <u>L</u>ists — <u>T</u>erms
h. New Company Setup – Part II
i. <u>E</u>dit – Preferences
j. Dimmed account type

_____ 1. The way QuickBooks Pro recognizes system default accounts.
_____ 2. A personal preference in a company to identify accounts; must be activated in the Preferences window.
_____ 3. Menu choice used to set up payment terms.
_____ 4. Only way to enter the dollar value opening balance of revenue and expense accounts.
_____ 5. Uses EasyStep Interview information to customize and update the new company file and prepare for the accrual basis of accounting.
_____ 6. Accounts created by QuickBooks Pro to be used in the windows and journal entries.
_____ 7. Menu choice used to make account numbers active.
_____ 8. Adding and changing account numbers and names.
_____ 9. Accounts created by QuickBooks Pro that are reversed by a journal entry to a zero balance.
_____ 10. System default accounts QuickBooks Pro looks for when an inventory part item is set up.

PROCEDURE CHECK

1. You have switched your company accounting records to QuickBooks Pro using the EasyStep Interview window. What steps would you take to customize the Chart of Accounts List created by QuickBooks Pro?
2. You have switched your company accounting records to QuickBooks Pro using the EasyStep Interview window. What would you do to customize the Item List created by QuickBooks Pro?
3. How and why would you adjust the Uncategorized Income and Uncategorized Expenses accounts?
4. You are reviewing the new company file you created using QuickBooks Pro and you notice that there are no balances in the revenue and expense accounts. Why is this and how would you correct it?
5. How does QuickBooks Pro identify system default accounts?
6. You had previously provided your manager with an explanation of the EasyStep Interview window. Continue with your explanation by describing the additional procedures necessary to complete the New Company Setup after completing the EasyStep Interview window. Provide an advantage of using the EasyStep Interview.

CASE PROBLEMS

CASE PROBLEM 1

On April 1, 2004, Lynn Garcia began her business, called Lynn's Music Studio. In April and May, Lynn was recording the financial activities using a manual accounting system. On June 1, 2004, Lynn decided to switch her accounting method to QuickBooks Pro. Lynn has organized the information about the company and completed the EasyStep Interview window, but has hired you to complete the New Company Setup process.

1. Open the company file: CH7 Lynn's Music Studio.QBW.
2. Make a backup copy of the company file: LMS7 [Your Name] Lynn's Music Studio.
3. Restore the backup copy of the company file. In both the Restore From and Restore To windows use the file name LMS7 [Your Name] Lynn's Music Studio.
4. Change the company name to LMS7 [Your Name] Lynn's Music Studio.
5. Activate the account numbers option. Use the information below to customize the Chart of Accounts List:

Number	Name	Edited Number or Name
	Cash – Operating	1010
1200	Accounts Receivable	
1120	Inventory Asset	change to 1260 Inventory of Guitars
	Music Supplies	1300
	Office Supplies	1305
	Prepaid Insurance	1420
	(Music Instruments) Original Cost	change to 1700 Music Instruments (cost)
	(Music Instruments) Depreciation	change to 1750 Accum. Dep., Music Instruments

(For the Music Instruments account with a balance of $3,940, do not enter an account number or change the name; it will later have a zero balance and be deleted.)

(Furniture) Original Cost	change the account to 1800 Furniture (cost)
(Furniture) Depreciation	change to 1850 Accum. Dep., Furniture

(For the Furniture account with a balance of $2,460, do not enter an account number or change the name; it will later have a zero balance and be deleted.)

(Computers) Original Cost	change to 1900 Computers (cost)
(Computers) Depreciation	change to 1950 Accum. Dep., Computers

(For the Computers account with a balance of $2,965, do not enter an account number or change the name; it will later have a zero balance and be deleted.)

2000	Accounts Payable	2010	
	Notes Payable	2020	
	Interest Payable	2030	
2200	Sales Tax Payable		
3000	Opening Bal Equity	change to 3010 Lynn Garcia, Capital	
	Piano Lessons	4010	
	Guitar Lessons	4020	
	Sale of Guitars	4060	
	Sale of Keyboards	4065	
	Sale of Music Stands	4070	
	Sale of Sheet Music	4075	
5000	Cost of Goods Sold	change to 5060 Cost of Guitars Sold	
	Dep. Exp., Music Instruments	6075	
	Dep. Exp., Furniture	6085	
	Dep. Exp., Computers	6095	
	Instrument Tuning	6150	
	Insurance Expense	6200	
	Music Supplies Expense	6300	
	Office Supplies Expense	6325	
	Rent Expense	6400	
	Telephone Expense	6450	
	Utilities Expense	6500	

Create the following new accounts:

Type	Number	Name	Beginning Balance
Other Current Asset	1250	Undeposited Funds	
Other Current Asset	1265	Inventory of Keyboards	
Other Current Asset	1270	Inventory of Music Stands	
Other Current Asset	1275	Inventory of Sheet Music	
Equity	3020	Lynn Garcia, Drawings	−1,000 06/01/04
Income	4100	Sales Discounts	
Cost of Goods Sold	5065	Cost of Keyboards Sold	
Cost of Goods Sold	5070	Cost of Music Stands Sold	
Cost of Goods Sold	5075	Cost of Sheet Music Sold	
Cost of Goods Sold	5900	Inventory Adjustment	
Other Expense	7000	Interest Expense	

Edit the following subaccounts:
  a. Remove the subaccounts from accounts 1700 Music Instruments (cost), 1800 Furniture (cost), and 1900 Computers (cost).
  b. Change the subaccounts for the Accumulated Depreciation account to the subaccounts listed below:
    1750 Accum. Dep., Music Instruments subaccount of 1700
    1850 Accum. Dep., Furniture subaccount of 1800
    1950 Accum. Dep., Computers subaccount of 1900

Delete the following accounts:
Furniture
Music Instruments
Computers
Retained Earnings

6. Use the information below to customize the Item List for the inventory part items:

	Cost of Goods Sold	Income	Asset
Guitars	5060	4060	1260
Keyboards	5065	4065	1265
Music Stands	5070	4070	1270
Sheet Music	5075	4075	1275

7. Correct the amount in the Interest Payable account to $15.
8. Set up the following payment terms:
Net 30 Days
Net 15 Days
Net 10 Days
2/10, Net 30 Days

9. Edit existing customers to include background information and add the customers with zero balance listed in Table LMS – Customers.
10. Edit existing vendors to include background information and add the vendors with zero balance as listed in Table LMS – Vendors.

TABLE LMS CUSTOMERS

Customer/Company Name	Name/Contact	Address	Phone/Fax	Terms	Balance
Douglaston Senior Center	Herbie Richardson	574 S Beech Street Scranton, PA 18506	570-555-7748 570-555-8800	Net 30 Days	175.00*
Highland School	Asst. Principal Office	115 Forrest Street Waymart, PA 18472	570-555-6963 570-555-6970	2/10, Net 30 Days	
Jefferson High School	Music Department	500 Apple Street Dunmore, PA 18512	570-555-9600 570-555-9700	2/10, Net 30 Days	
Mulligan Residence	Adam Smith	299 Hickory Lane Scranton, PA 18504	570-555-3325 570-555-3500	2/10, Net 30 Days	1575.90*
Musical Youth Group	Dana Thompson	550 Marion Lane Scranton, PA 18504	570-555-6642 570-555-6700	Net 30 Days	
Patel Family	Ari Patel	574 Kenwood Drive Dickson City, PA 18519	570-555-1132	Net 30 Days	
Patterson Family	Jonathan Patterson	650 Memory Lane Dickson City, PA 18519	570-555-6321	Net 30 Days	
Schroeder Family	Betty Schroeder	98 Belmont Rd. Carbondale, PA 18407	570-555-1897	Net 30 Days	
Twin Lakes Elementary	Miss Brooks	515 Hobson Street Honesdale, PA 18431	570-555-4474 570-555-4485	2/10, Net 30 Days	

*Customers with balances were recorded as part of the EasyStep Interview process; you need only edit these customers, not create new files for them.

TABLE LMS- VENDORS

Vendor/Company Name	Name/Contact	Address	Phone/Fax	Terms	Balance
Computer Town	Customer Service	1000 Carbondale Highway Scranton, PA 18502	570-555-1500 570-555-1550	Net 30 Days	2000.00*
Katie's Keyboards	Katie Shea	158 Clay Road Scranton, PA 18505	570-555-7777 570-555-8888	Net 30 Days	1500.00*
Lynn Garcia					
Melody Music Equipment	Melody Arhmand	780 Roselyn Ave. Scranton, PA 18505	570-555-1120 570-555-1125	Net 30 Days	
Mills Family Furniture	Edna Mills	150 Amelia Street Scranton, PA 18503	570-555-7144 570-555-7200	Net 30 Days	1500.00*
Music Instruments, Inc.	Matilda Molloy	25 Monroe Ave. Scranton, PA 18505	570-555-9630 570-555-9635	Net 30 Days	
Mutual Insurance Company	Bob Maxwell	1 Main Street Honesdale, PA 18431	570-555-5600 570-555-5900	Net 30 Days	1200.00*
Paper, Clips, and More	Justin Daves	157 Waymart Lane Waymart, PA 18472	570-555-8558 570-555-5555	Net 30 Days	350.00*
Pioneer Phone	Customer Service	1000 Route 6 Carbondale, PA 18407	570-555-6000 570-555-6500	Net 15 Days	
Steamtown Electric	Customer Service	150 Vine Lane Scranton, PA 18501	570-555-2500 570-555-3000	Net 15 Days	
Strings, Sheets, & Such	Manuela Perez	250 Lincoln St. Scranton, PA 18505	570-555-3636 570-555-3700	Net 15 Days	
Tune Tones	Tony Tune	500 Monroe Ave. Dunmore, PA 18512	570-555-1111 570-555-2222	Net 30 Days	
Viewhill Realty	Matt Snyder	100 Commerce Blvd. Scranton, PA 18501	570-555-1000 570-555-1200	Net 15 Days	

*Vendors with balances were recorded as part of the EasyStep Interview process; you need only edit these vendors, not create new files for them.

11. Make three journal entries on June 1, 2004 (accept the default Entry Nos.):
    a. Reverse the Uncategorized Income account.
    b. Reverse the Uncategorized Expenses account.
    c. Record the revenue and expenses listed below:

Account		Debit
4100	Sales Discounts	188.92
5060	Cost of Guitars Sold	1,150.00
5065	Cost of Keyboards Sold	2,475.00
5070	Cost of Music Stands Sold	460.00
5075	Cost of Sheet Music Sold	1,305.00
5900	Inventory Adjustment	50.00
6075	Dep. Exp., Music Instruments	60.00
6085	Dep. Exp., Furniture	40.00
6095	Dep. Exp., Computers	35.00
6150	Instrument Tuning	100.00
6200	Insurance Expense	100.00
6300	Music Supplies Expense	70.00
6325	Office Supplies Expense	50.00
6400	Rent Expense	600.00

6450	Telephone Expense	50.00
6500	Utilities Expense	70.00
7000	Interest Expense	15.00

Account		Credit
4010	Piano Lessons	3,535.00
4020	Guitar Lessons	2,910.00
4060	Sale of Guitars	2,300.00
4065	Sale of Keyboards	4,950.00
4070	Sale of Music Stands	920.00
4075	Sale of Sheet Music	2,610.00

12. Display and print the following reports for June 1, 2004, to June 1, 2004:
    a. *Journal*
    b. *Trial Balance*
    c. *Profit & Loss standard*
    d. *Balance Sheet standard*
    e. *Item Listing*
    f. *Customer Contact List*
    g. *Vendor Contact List*

13. Open and close the Enter Sales Receipts window. Review the Chart of Accounts List. If QuickBooks Pro created an Undeposited Funds account, change it to account 1250 Undeposited Funds.

CASE PROBLEM 2

On June 1, 2004, Olivia Chen began her business, called Olivia's Web Solutions. In June and July, Olivia recorded her financial activities using a manual accounting system. On August 1, 2004, Olivia decided to switch her accounting method to QuickBooks Pro. Olivia has organized the information about the company and completed the EasyStep Interview window, but has hired you to complete the New Company Setup process.

1. Open the company file: CH7 Olivia's Web Solutions.QBW.
2. Make a backup copy of the company file OWS7 [Your Name] Olivia's Web Solutions.
3. Restore the backup copy of the company file. In both the Restore From and Restore To windows use the file name OWS7 [Your Name] Olivia's Web Solutions.
4. Change the company name to OWS7 [Your Name] Olivia's Web Solutions.
5. Activate the account numbers feature. Use the information below to customize the Chart of Accounts List:

Number	Name	Edited Number/Name
	Cash – Operating	1010
1200	Accounts Receivable	
1120	Inventory Asset	change to 1260 Inventory of Computers
	Computer Supplies	1300
	Office Supplies	1305

| | Prepaid Advertising | 1410 |
| | Prepaid Insurance | 1420 |

| | (Computers) Original Cost | change to 1700 Computers (cost) |
| | (Computers) Depreciation | change to 1750 Accum. Dep., Computers |

(For the Computers account with a balance of $4,925, do not enter an account number or change the name; it will later have a zero balance and be deleted.)

| | (Furniture) Original Cost | change to 1800 Furniture (cost) |
| | (Furniture) Depreciation | change to 1850 Accum. Dep., Furniture |

(For the Furniture account with a balance of $3,150, do not enter an account number or change the name; it will later have a zero balance and be deleted.)

| | (Software) Original Cost | change to 1900 Software (cost) |
| | (Software) Depreciation | change to 1950 Accum. Dep., Software |

(For the Software account with a balance of $3,500, do not enter an account number or change the name; it will later have a zero balance and be deleted.)

2000	Accounts Payable	2010
	Notes Payable	2020
	Interest Payable	2030
2200	Sales Tax Payable	
	Opening Bal Equity	change to 3010 Olivia Chen, Capital
	Web Page Design Fees	4010
	Internet Consulting Fees	4020
	Sale of Computers	4060
	Sale of Scanners	4065
	Sale of HTML Software	4070
	Sale of Desktop Pub. Software	4075
5000	Cost of Goods Sold	change to 5060 Cost of Computers Sold
	Advertising Expense	6050
	Dep. Exp., Computers	6075
	Dep. Exp., Furniture	6085
	Dep. Exp., Software	6095
	Insurance Expense	6100
	Computer Supplies Expense	6300
	Office Supplies Expense	6325
	Online Service Expense	6350
	Rent Expense	6400
	Telephone Expense	6450
	Utility Expense	6500

Create the following new accounts:

Type	Number	Name	Beginning Balance
Other Current Asset	1250	Undeposited Funds	
Other Current Asset	1265	Inventory of Scanners	
Other Current Asset	1270	Inventory of HTML Software	
Other Current Asset	1275	Inventory of Desktop Pub. Soft.	
Equity	3020	Olivia Chen, Drawings	−500 08/01/04
Income	4100	Sales Discounts	
Cost of Goods Sold	5065	Cost of Scanners Sold	
Cost of Goods Sold	5070	Cost of HTML Software Sold	
Cost of Goods Sold	5075	Cost of Desktop Pub. Soft. Sold	
Cost of Goods Sold	5900	Inventory Adjustment	
Other Expense	7000	Interest Expense	

Edit the following subaccounts:
   a. Remove the subaccounts for accounts 1700 Computers (cost), 1800 Furniture (cost), and 1900 Software (cost).
   b. Change the subaccounts of the Accumulated Depreciation accounts to the subaccounts listed below:
   1750 Accum. Dep., Computers subaccount of 1700
   1850 Accum. Dep., Furniture subaccount of 1800
   1950 Accum. Dep., Software subaccount of 1900

Delete the following accounts:
   Computers
   Furniture
   Software
   Retained Earnings

6. Use the information below to customize the Item List for the inventory part items:

	Cost of Goods Sold	Income	Asset
Computers	5060	4060	1260
Scanners	5065	4065	1265
HTML Software	5070	4070	1270
Desktop Pub. Soft.	5075	4075	1275

7. Correct the amount in the Interest Payable account to $25.
8. Set up the following payment terms:
   Net 30 Days
   Net 15 Days
   2/10, Net 30 Days

9. Edit existing customers to include background information and add the customers with zero balance listed in Table OWS – Customers.
10. Edit existing vendors to include background information and add the vendors with zero balance as listed in Table OWS – Vendors.

OWS - CUSTOMERS

Customer/Company Name	Name/Contact	Address	Phone/Fax	Terms	Balance
Artie's Auto Repair	Leon Artie	32 W. 11th Street New Hyde Park, NY 11523	516-555-1221 516-555-1231	Net 30 Days	800.00*
Breathe Easy A/C Contractors	Allen Scott	556 Atlantic Ave. Freeport, NY 11634	516-555-6868 516-555-6869	Net 30 Days	
Long Island Water Works	Customer Service	87-54 Bayview Ave. Glen Cove, NY 11563	516-555-4747 516-555-4748	2/10, Net 30 Days	
Miguel's Restaurant	Miguel Perez	30 Willis Ave. Roslyn, NY 11541	516-555-3236 516-555-3237	2/10, Net 30 Days	
Schneider Family	Johnny Schneider	363 Farmers Rd. Syosset, NY 11547	516-555-8989 516-555-8990	Net 15 Days	1,000.00*
Sehorn & Smith Attorneys	Jerry Sehorn	510 Fifth Ave. New York, NY 10022	212-555-3339 212-555-3338	Net 30 Days	800.00*
Singh Family	David Singh	363 Marathon Parkway Little Neck, NY 11566	718-555-3233 718-555-3239	Net 15 Days	
South Shore School District	Joseph Porter	3666 Ocean Ave. South Beach, NY 11365	516-555-4545 516-555-4546	2/10, Net 30 Days	12,056.00*
Thrifty Stores	William Way	23 Boston Ave. Bronx, NY 11693	718-555-2445 718-555-2446	Net 30 Days	1,500.00*

*Customers with balances were recorded as part of the EasyStep Interview process; you need only edit these customers, not create new files for them.

OWS- VENDORS

Vendor/Company Name	Name/Contact	Address	Phone/Fax	Terms	Balance
ARC Management	Alvin R. Clinton	668 Lakeville Ave. Garden City, NY 11678	516-555-6363 516-555-6364	Net 30 Days	
Chrbet Advertising	Chris Chrbet	201 E. 10th Street New York, NY 10012	212-555-8777 212-555-8778	Net 30 Days	1,200.00*
Comet Computer Supplies	Customer Service	657 Motor Parkway Center Island, NY 11488	631-555-4444 631-555-4455	Net 15 Days	
Computec Computers	Customer Service	3631 Gate Blvd. Greenboro, NC 27407	705-555-6564 705-555-6563	Net 30 Days	10,000.00*
Eastel	Customer Service	655 Fifth Ave. New York, NY 10012	212-555-6565 212-555-6566	Net 30 Days	350.00*
Eastern Mutual Insurance	Customer Service	55 Broadway Room 55 New York, NY 10001	212-555-6363 212-555-6364	Net 30 Days	
InterSoft Development Co.	Customer Service	556 Route 347 Hauppauge, NY 11654	631-555-3634 631-555-3635	Net 30 Days	
Lewis Furniture Co.	Manny Lewis	1225 Route 110 Farmingdale, NY 11898	631-555-6161 631-555-6162	Net 30 Days	1,700.00*
LI Power Company	Customer Service	5444 Northern Blvd. Plainview, NY 11544	516-555-8888 516-555-8889	Net 15 Days	
Martin Computer Repairs	Ken Martin	366 N. Franklin St. Garden City, NY 11568	516-555-7777 516-555-7778	Net 30 Days	
Netsoft Development Co.	Customer Service	684 Mountain View Rd. Portland, OR 68774	974-555-7873 974-555-7874	Net 30 Days	1,600.00*
NYS Tax Department					
Office Plus	Customer Service	45 Jericho Tpke. Jericho, NY 11654	516-555-3214 516-555-3213	Net 30 Days	375.00*
Olivia Chen					
Scanntronix	Customer Service	2554 Bedford Rd. Boston, MA 02164	617-555-8778 617-555-8776	Net 30 Days	
Systems Service	Jeremy Jones	36 Sunrise Lane Hempstead, NY 11004	516-555-2525 516-555-2526	Net 30 Days	
Textpro Software, Inc.	Customer Service	877 Route 5 Ft. Lauderdale, FL 70089	615-555-4545 615-555-4546	Net 30 Days	

*Vendors with balances were recorded as part of the EasyStep Interview process; you need only edit these vendors, not create new files for them.

11. Make three journal entries on August 1, 2004 (accept the default entry Nos.):
   a. Reverse the Uncategorized Income account.
   b. Reverse the Uncategorized Expenses account.
   c. Record the revenue and expenses listed below:

Account		Debit
4100	Sales Discounts	179.84
5060	Cost of Computers Sold	10,000.00
5065	Cost of Scanners Sold	2,400.00
5070	Cost of HTML Software Sold	75.00
5075	Cost of Desktop Pub. Soft. Sold	500.00
5900	Inventory Adjustment	75.00
6050	Advertising Expense	200.00
6075	Dep. Exp., Computers	75.00
6085	Dep. Exp., Furniture	50.00
6095	Dep. Exp., Software	100.00
6100	Insurance Expense	150.00
6300	Computer Supplies Expense	250.00
6325	Office Supplies Expense	50.00
6350	Online Service Expense	150.00
6400	Rent Expense	800.00
6450	Telephone Expense	350.00
6500	Utility Expense	125.00
7000	Interest Expense	25.00

Account		Credit
4010	Web Page Design Fees	9,750.00
4020	Internet Consulting Fees	6,600.00
4060	Sale of Computers	20,000.00
4065	Sale of Scanners	4,800.00
4070	Sale of HTML Software	150.00
4075	Sale of Desktop Pub. Software	1,000.00

12. Display and print the following reports for August 1, 2004, to August 1, 2004:

   a. *Journal*
   b. *Trial Balance*
   c. *Profit & Loss standard*
   d. *Balance Sheet standard*
   e. *Item Listing*
   f. *Customer Contact List*
   g. *Vendor Contact List*

13. Open and close the Enter Sales Receipts window. Review the Chart of Accounts List. If QuickBooks Pro created an Undeposited Funds account, edit it to be account 1250 Undeposited Funds.

8

NEW COMPANY SETUP—
an ALTERNATIVE

Skip EasyStep Interview

CHAPTER OBJECTIVES

- Create a new company file without using EasyStep Interview

- Establish preferences

- Set up payment terms

- Update the Chart of Accounts, Customer:Job, and Vendor Lists

- Customize system default accounts in the Chart of Accounts List

- Enter opening balances

- Reverse accounts QuickBooks Pro creates that are not used in the accrual basis of accounting

- Display and print accounting, financial, and Lists reports

INTRODUCTION

In this chapter you will learn an alternative method for creating a new company file in QuickBooks Pro. As you know, the four levels of operation for QuickBooks Pro are New Company Setup, Lists, Activities, and Reports. In chapters 2 through 5, the Lists, Activities, and Reports levels were presented for both a service company and a merchandise company. In those chapters, you opened an existing company file, updated the Lists, recorded Activities in the various windows, and viewed and printed Reports.

The New Company Setup level of operations was presented using the QuickBooks Pro EasyStep Interview in chapter 6. As you saw, when you use the EasyStep Interview process, you have to make several modifications to customize the company file, update the Lists, and prepare the company file for the accrual basis of accounting; these modifications were illustrated in chapter 7. In this chapter, you will learn how to conduct New Company Setup without using EasyStep Interview. With this method, you skip most of the EasyStep Interview windows and instead use many of the procedures you learned earlier for updating the Lists to set up the new company file.

In this chapter, you will again create and set up a new company file for our sample company, Kristin Raina Interior Designs. It is assumed that Kristin Raina Interior Designs was recording accounting activities using a manual accounting system and has decided to convert the company's accounting records to QuickBooks Pro.

QUICKBOOKS PRO VERSUS MANUAL ACCOUNTING: NEW COMPANY SETUP

In a manual accounting system, a company's records are set up by creating the Chart of Accounts and creating a general ledger. The general ledger is the book of each account with the beginning balance for each account. If subsidiary ledgers, such as accounts receivable and accounts payable, are to be used, they would be set up and beginning balances recorded. If a perpetual inventory system is used, an inventory subsidiary ledger would also be created.

In QuickBooks Pro, a company's records are set up by creating a new company file and establishing the Chart of Accounts List. Customer:Job and Vendor Lists, which are the equivalent to the accounts receivable and accounts payable subsidiary ledgers, and the Item List, which is equivalent to an inventory subsidiary ledger, but which also includes service revenue items and sales tax items in addition to inventory items, are then set up. Opening balances are entered, from which QuickBooks Pro simultaneously creates the general ledger.

When you set up a new company file without using the EasyStep Interview, you must first identify certain company preferences. After that, you use the Lists windows to continue with the setup of the new company file. Entering information in the Lists is similar to creating a Chart of Accounts, general ledger, and subsidiary ledgers in a manual accounting system. Finally, there are three journal entries you need to make to complete the New Company Setup. One journal entry records the opening balances in the accounts that were not included when you set up the Lists; the other two journal entries reverse accounts QuickBooks Pro sets up during New Company Setup that are not used in the accrual basis of accounting.

CHAPTER PROBLEM

In this chapter, there is no prepared company file to open. Instead, you will create and set up the company file for Kristin Raina Interior Designs.

Assume that Kristin Raina began the Interior Design business in January 2004 and has maintained accounting records with a manual accounting system for January through March. Effective April 1, 2004, Kristin Raina has decided to convert the company's accounting records to QuickBooks Pro, and has asked you to create a company file in QuickBooks. You have decided to skip the EasyStep Interview window in creating the file.

To create a new company file—

1. Open QuickBooks Pro.
2. Click <u>F</u>ile, and then click <u>N</u>ew Company. The EasyStep Interview window appears. (See figure 8–1.)

F I G U R E   8 - 1
EasyStep Interview Window

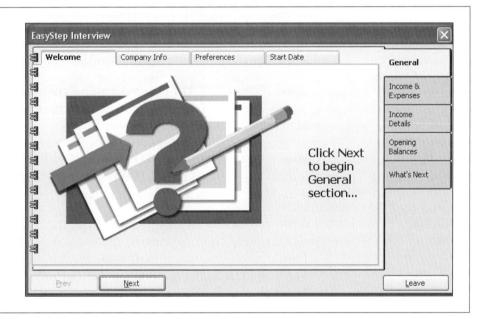

| NEW COMPANY SETUP: | **SKIPPING EASYSTEP INTERVIEW**

The EasyStep Interview window is designed to guide you through the steps to create and set up a new company file. If you are not going to use EasyStep Interview, you still need to go through a couple of pages of the EasyStep Interview window until you come to the choice to skip EasyStep Interview.

1. At the Welcome tab of the EasyStep Interview, click <u>N</u>ext.
2. Read the next page in the Welcome tab and click <u>N</u>ext again.
3. At the Setting up a new QuickBooks company page, click the <u>S</u>kip Interview button. (See figure 8–2.) The Creating New Company window appears.

FIGURE 8-2
*Setting Up a
New QuickBooks
Company Page*

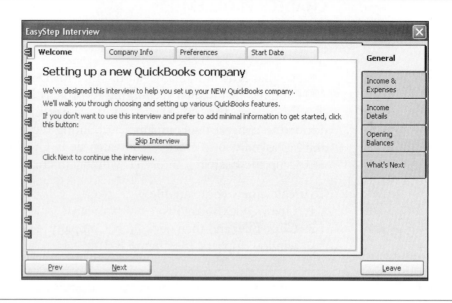

4. At the Creating New Company window, key the following information:

Company Name:	**CH8 [Your Name] Kristin Raina Interior Designs**
Legal Name:	**CH8 [Your Name] Kristin Raina Interior Designs**
Address:	**25 NE Johnson Street**
	Minneapolis, MN 53402
Phone #:	**651-555-1000**
FAX #:	**651-555-2000**
E-mail:	**KRID@emcp.net**

When you move to the *Legal Name* field, the company name is automatically filled in. The legal name is the name that will be used on tax forms. If the company name and legal name are not the same, any necessary changes can be made. For our sample company, the names are the same. When you are finished, your screen should look like figure 8–3.

FIGURE 8-3
*Creating New Company
Window – Complete*

5. If the information is correct, click <u>N</u>ext. The Creating New Company window appears.

6. In the Creating New Company window, click *(No Type)* and accept *(No Accounts)*. See figure 8-4.

FIGURE 8-4
Creating New Company Window

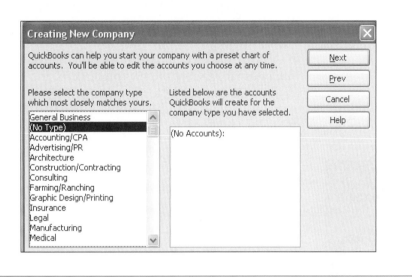

7. Click <u>N</u>ext. The Filename for New Company dialog box appears.

8. Change the Save <u>i</u>n text box to your subfolder.

9. Accept the file name *CH8 [Your Name] Kristin Raina Interior Designs. QBW.*

10. If the information is correct, click <u>S</u>ave.

11. At the Industry-specific Documentation message, click <u>N</u>o. The company file has been created and saved.

12. The Getting Started and Company Navigator windows, along with the Open Windows List all appear. You can close these windows by clicking the X in each window. At the Closing the Open Window List message, place a check mark in the box to the left of Do not display this message in the future and click <u>Y</u>es. To remove the Icon bar, click on <u>V</u>iew and then click <u>I</u>con Bar.

HINT

In the File <u>n</u>ame text box, use the arrow keys to scroll through the entire name.

To continue the New Company Setup, you must take the following steps: establish Preferences and Payment Terms; set up the Chart of Accounts List; set up the Item, Customer:Job, and Vendor Lists with beginning balances; enter opening balances in accounts by journal entry; and record two journal entries to offset two accounts created by QuickBooks Pro that are not used in the accrual basis of accounting.

ESTABLISHING PREFERENCES AND PAYMENT TERMS

When you use the EasyStep Interview window, QuickBooks Pro asks questions, and based on your responses establishes preferences for your company. If you skip EasyStep Interview, then you must establish the preferences for the new company file yourself. The preferences are necessary in order for you to have access to certain windows or fields of information.

You set these preferences in the Preferences window. Along the left side of the window are 18 icons that represent the different categories of features. For each category there is a <u>M</u>y Preferences tab and a <u>C</u>ompany Preferences tab. The <u>C</u>ompany Preferences tab is used for most preferences when setting up a new company file. The <u>M</u>y Preferences tab records the preferences for each individual user. After the Preferences are established, the Payment Terms are set up.

You will use the Preferences window to activate the *Account Numbers* field in the Chart of Accounts List window, activate the inventory feature, activate sales tax, disable the payroll feature, and disable the Reminders window for the new company file.

ACCOUNT NUMBERS

Since QuickBooks Pro by default does not use account numbers, you must activate the account numbers option to add them.

HINT

Scroll down the left side of the Preferences window to see all of the icons.

To activate the account numbers option—

1. Click <u>E</u>dit, and then click Preferences. The Preferences window appears.
2. Along the left side of the Preferences window, click the *Accounting* icon.
3. Click the <u>C</u>ompany Preferences tab.
4. At the *Account Numbers* field, place a ✓ in the Use account <u>n</u>umbers check box to turn on the account numbers option. (See figure 8–5.)

FIGURE 8-5
*Preferences Window –
Accounting – <u>C</u>ompany
Preferences Tab*

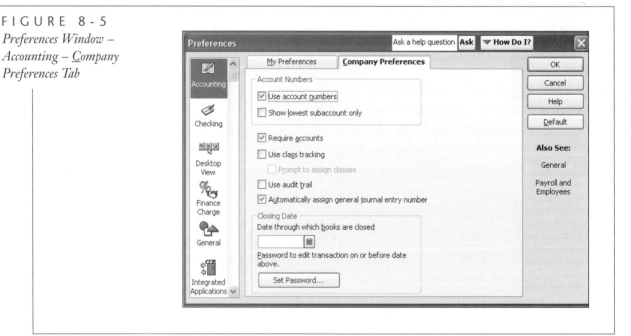

5. If the information is correct, click OK. The *Account Number* field now appears in the Edit Account and New Account windows.

INVENTORY

QuickBooks Pro provides you with the ability to maintain inventory records, but the inventory feature must be activated.

To activate the inventory feature—
1. Click Edit, and then click Preferences. The Preferences window appears.
2. Along the left frame of the Preferences window, click the *Purchases & Vendors* icon.
3. Click the Company Preferences tab.
4. At the *Purchase Orders and Inventory* section, place a ✓ in the Inventory and purchase orders are active check box to turn on the inventory feature. (See figure 8–6.)

FIGURE 8-6

Preferences Window –
Purchases & Vendors –
Company Preferences Tab

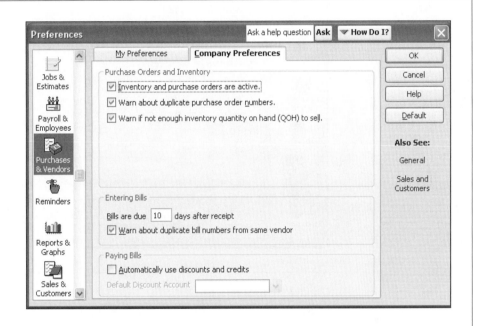

5. If the information is correct, click OK. The inventory feature is now activated and fields of information relevant to inventory will now appear in the windows.

SALES TAX

QuickBooks Pro also provides you with the ability to charge and maintain sales tax information, but the sales tax feature must be activated.

To activate the sales tax feature—

1. Click Edit, and then click Preferences.
2. Along the left frame of the Preferences window, click the *Sales Tax* icon.
3. Click the Company Preferences tab.
4. At the *Do You Charge Sales Tax?* section, click Yes.

The other fields of information that were dimmed now become activated. You must complete the *Most common sales tax* field. (See figure 8–7.)

FIGURE 8-7
Preferences Window –
Sales Tax – Company
Preferences Tab

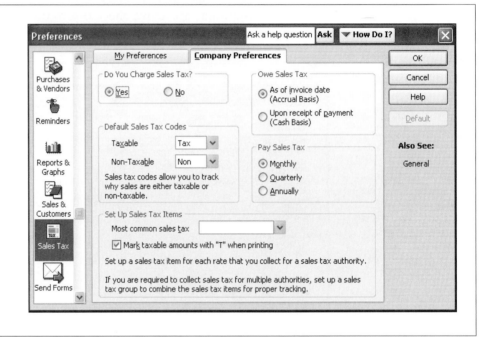

5. Move to the *Most common sales tax* field and click the drop-down arrow.

Because this is a new company, there is no information regarding sales tax. You will add it in this window.

6. Click *<Add New>*.

The New Item window appears. This allows you to add sales tax to the item list.

7. Key the sales tax item information listed below:

Type:	**Sales Tax Item**
Tax Name:	**Minn. Sales Tax**
Description:	**Sales Tax**
Tax Rate (%):	**7**

8. Move to the *Tax Agency* field and click the drop-down arrow. Again, because this is a new company file, vendors have not yet been entered into the file.

9. At the Tax Agency drop-down list, click *<Add New>*. The New Vendor window appears.

10. In the *Vendor Name* and *Company Name* fields, key **Minn. Dept. of Revenue** and move to the next field. (See figure 8–8.)

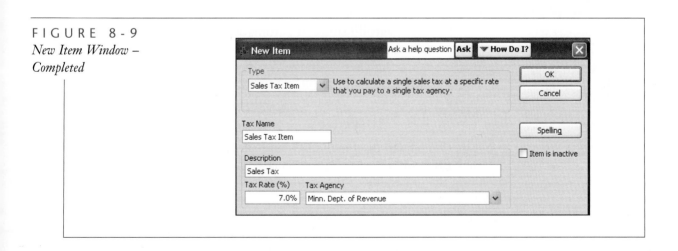

11. If the information is correct, click OK. The New Item window is complete. (See figure 8–9.)

12. If the information is correct, click OK. The Preferences window for Sales Tax is complete. (See figure 8–10.)

FIGURE 8-10
Preferences Window – Sales Tax – Completed

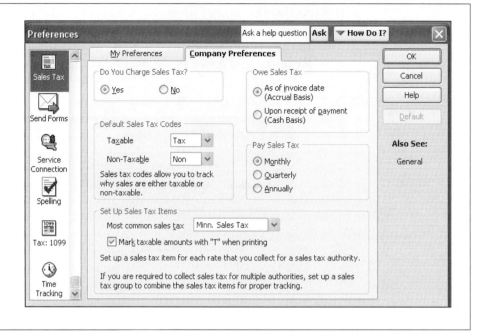

13. If the information is correct, click OK.

    The Updating Sales Tax dialog box appears. In this dialog box, QuickBooks Pro is inquiring if all existing customers and all non-inventory and inventory parts should be made taxable. (See figure 8–11.)

14. Click OK. The sales tax item is established.

FIGURE 8-11
Updating Sales Tax Dialog Box

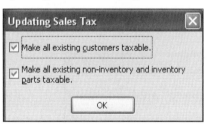

PAYROLL

When you create a new company file, QuickBooks Pro assumes you will be using the Payroll feature and by default activates it. When QuickBooks Pro activated the payroll feature, it automatically created a Payroll Liabilities account and Payroll Expenses account in the Chart of Accounts List. It also created a Payroll Item List. Our sample company, Kristin Raina Interior Designs, has not yet utilized the payroll feature and does not need it activated.

To disable the payroll feature—
1. Click Edit, and then click Preferences.
2. Along the left frame of the Preferences window, click the *Payroll & Employees* icon.
3. Click the Company Preferences tab.
4. At the *QuickBooks Payroll Features* section, click *No payroll*.
5. If the information is correct, click OK.

Even though you have disabled the payroll feature, the Payroll Liabilities account and the Payroll Expenses account will still appear on the Chart of Accounts List. In addition, the Employee List will appear on the List menu. However, QuickBooks Pro will remove the Payroll Item List from the Lists menu.

PAYMENT TERMS

In QuickBooks Pro you can establish a list with payment terms that can be accessed in customer files, vendor files, and activities windows when needed. As seen in prior chapters, payment terms such as Net 30 Days, 2/10 Net 30 Days, and so on can be identified in both the customer and vendor files if they relate to a particular customer or vendor.

Before updating the Vendor and Customer Lists in your new company file, you need to set up the list of payment terms. You do this using the Lists menu.

To set up the payment terms—

1. Click Lists, and then click Customer & Vendor Profile Lists.
2. At the Customer & Vendor Profile Lists submenu, click Terms List. The Terms List window appears.
3. At the Terms List window, click the Terms button.
4. At the Terms menu, click New. The New Terms window appears.
5. In the *Terms* field, key **Net 30 Days.**
6. In the *Net due in days* field, key **30.** (See figure 8–12.)

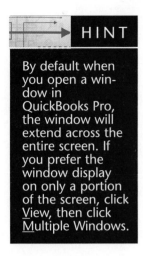
FIGURE 8-12
New Terms Window – Net 30 Days – Completed

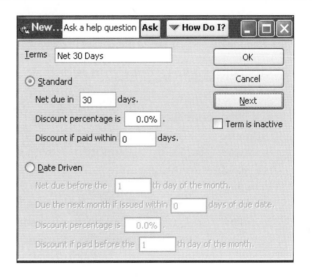

7. If the information is correct, click Next.
8. Enter the terms listed below using the same steps as 5 through 7 above:

Net 10 Days
Net 15 Days

9. At the New Terms window in the *Terms* field, key **2/10, Net 30 Days.**
10. In the *Net due in days* field, key **30.**
11. In the *Discount percentage is* field, key **2.**
12. In the *Discount if paid within days* field, key **10.** (See figure 8–13.)

FIGURE 8-13
*New Terms Window – 2/10,
Net 30 Days – Completed*

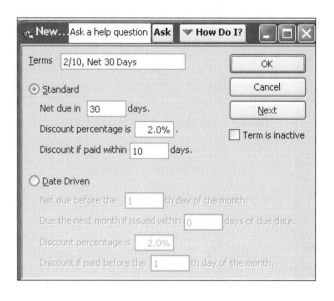

13. If the information is correct, click OK.
14. Close the Terms List window.

SYSTEM DEFAULT ACCOUNTS

As you saw in prior chapters, QuickBooks Pro establishes default accounts and uses those accounts when recording transactions in the general journal. QuickBooks Pro looks for these system default accounts in the Chart of Accounts List, and if it cannot find an account it will create one. Some system default accounts you learned so far are Accounts Receivable, Accounts Payable, Sales Tax Payable, Inventory Asset, and Cost of Goods Sold.

When you established some of the company preferences in your new company file, QuickBooks Pro created some of the system default accounts. Open the Chart of Accounts List window and review the List. When you create a new company file but skip EasyStep Interview, QuickBooks Pro assumes by default that you will be using the payroll feature and automatically creates a Payroll Liabilities account and a Payroll Expenses account. Even though you subsequently turned off the payroll feature in the Preferences window, once payroll accounts are created in QuickBooks Pro, you cannot delete them.

In addition, once you turned on the account numbers feature, QuickBooks Pro assigned the account numbers 2100 to the Payroll Liabilities account and 6560 to the Payroll Expenses account. When you turned on the sales tax feature, QuickBooks Pro automatically created the account 2200 Sales Tax Payable. Because payroll has not yet been covered, you will not be using the payroll accounts at this time. You can make them inactive and they will not be displayed in the reports. However, you will need to use the Sales Tax Payable account.

HINT

You can enter the opening balances when you create a new account in the Chart of Accounts List for assets, liabilities, and equity accounts as part of the EasyStep Interview process, or you can enter account balances by journal entry.

To mark an account as inactive:

1. At the Chart of Accounts List window, select the Payroll Liabilities account.
2. Click the Account button, then click on Make Inactive. The Payroll Liabilities account is no longer displayed in the Chart of Accounts List.
3. Select the Payroll Expenses account.
4. Click the Account button, then click on Make Inactive.

   To see Inactive accounts listed on the Chart of Accounts List, place a check mark in the box to the left of Show All. You will see the Inactive accounts with an X next to the account name. To hide the accounts, remove the check mark from the Show All box.

5. Close the Chart of Accounts List window.

QuickBooks Pro usually identifies a system default account by graying, or dimming, the account type. In the Chart of Accounts List window, edit the Sales Tax Payable account. Notice the account type is dimmed.

The Lists you have learned about so far consist of the Chart of Accounts, Items, Vendor, and Customer:Job Lists. If you use EasyStep Interview, QuickBooks Pro begins to set up the Lists for you. Since you are not using EasyStep Interview in this chapter, the next step is for you to set up the Lists.

LISTS: UPDATING LISTS

When you established some of the preferences for the new company file, QuickBooks Pro began to set up some of the Lists. You must now finish the setup of the Lists using the procedures to add, edit, and delete accounts, items, vendors, or customers that you learned in prior chapters. As you set up the Lists, QuickBooks Pro will create additional system default accounts.

UPDATING THE CHART OF ACCOUNTS LIST

As noted above, QuickBooks Pro has already created some accounts in the new company file. However, there are many additional accounts that must be added to the Chart of Accounts List for Kristin Raina Interior Designs. Most of these accounts have opening balances. You can enter these opening balances by general journal entry.

You add accounts to the Chart of Accounts Lists using the Chart of Accounts window as illustrated in prior chapters.

To add a new account—

1. Click Lists, and then click Chart of Accounts.
2. At the Chart of Accounts window, click the Account button.
3. At the Account menu, click New.
4. At the New Account window, enter the following information:

Type:	**Bank**
Number:	**1010**
Name:	**Cash – Operating**

Your screen should look like figure 8–14.

FIGURE 8-14
New Account Window

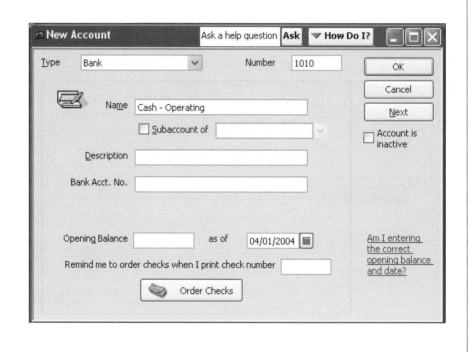

HINT

In the *Type* field, instead of looking for the type in the drop-down list, key the first letter of the type name.

5. If the information is correct, click Next. The New Account window is displayed with the fields cleared for the next account.
6. Using the information in table 8–1, key in all of the accounts.

TABLE 8-1

Chart of Accounts List

Type	Number	Name
Accounts Receivable	1200	Accounts Receivable
Other Current Asset	1250	Undeposited Funds
Other Current Asset	1265	Inventory of Draperies
Other Current Asset	1270	Inventory of Lamps
Other Current Asset	1275	Inventory of Mirrors
Other Current Asset	1300	Design Supplies
Other Current Asset	1305	Office Supplies
Other Current Asset	1410	Prepaid Advertising
Other Current Asset	1420	Prepaid Insurance
Fixed Asset	1700	Furniture
Fixed Asset	1750	Accum. Dep., Furniture subaccount of 1700
Fixed Asset	1800	Computers
Fixed Asset	1850	Accum. Dep., Computers subaccount of 1800
Accounts Payable	2010	Accounts Payable
Other Current Liability	2020	Notes Payable
Other Current Liability	2030	Interest Payable
Equity	3020	Kristin Raina, Drawings
Income	4010	Design Services
Income	4020	Decorating Services
Income	4060	Sale of Carpets
Income	4065	Sale of Draperies
Income	4070	Sale of Lamps
Income	4075	Sale of Mirrors
Income	4100	Sales Discounts
Cost of Goods Sold	5065	Cost of Draperies Sold
Cost of Goods Sold	5070	Cost of Lamps Sold
Cost of Goods Sold	5075	Cost of Mirrors Sold
Cost of Goods Sold	5900	Inventory Adjustment
Expense	6020	Accounting Expense
Expense	6050	Advertising Expense
Expense	6175	Deprec. Exp., Furniture
Expense	6185	Deprec. Exp., Computers
Expense	6200	Insurance Expense
Expense	6300	Janitorial Expense
Expense	6325	Office Supplies Expense
Expense	6400	Rent Expense
Expense	6450	Telephone Expense
Expense	6500	Utilities Expense
Other Expense	7000	Interest Expense

UPDATING THE ITEM LIST

In QuickBooks Pro, the Item List stores information about the service items sold, the inventory part items sold, and the sales tax. As transactions are recorded in the Activities windows, QuickBooks Pro uses information in the Item List to record the transaction to the correct accounts.

Open and review the Item List. Notice that QuickBooks Pro recorded the sales tax item when the sales tax feature was activated in the Preferences window. The Item List needs to be updated to include the service items and inventory part items that describe the services and inventory that Kristin Raina Interior Design provides or stocks in order to conduct business. These items are added to the Item List using the Item List window as illustrated in prior chapters.

To add a service item—

1. Click Lists, and then click Item List.
2. At the Item List window, click the Item button.
3. At the Item menu, click New. The New Item window appears.
4. At the *Type* field, click *Service*.
5. At the *Item Name/Number* and *Description* fields, key **Design Services**.
6. At the *Rate* field, key **60**.
7. At the *Tax Code* field, click Non for Non-Taxable Sales.
8. At the *Account* field, click *4010 Design Services*. Your screen should look like figure 8–15.

FIGURE 8-15
New Item Window

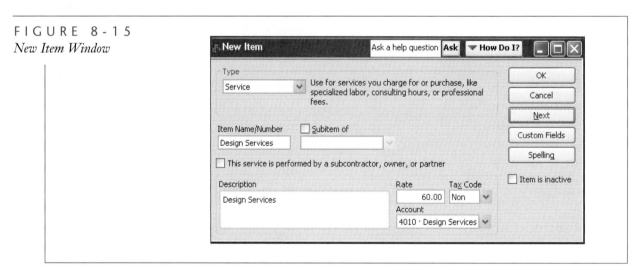

9. If the information is correct, click Next.
10. Enter the information listed below for the next service item:

Type:	**Service**
Item Name/Number:	**Decorating Services**
Description:	**Decorating Services**
Rate:	**50**
Tax Code:	**Non**
Account:	**4020 Decorating Services**

11. Click Next and in the *Type* field, click *Inventory Part*.
12. Close the New Item window. At the Save window, click No, and then close the Item List window.

When you selected the Inventory Part type, QuickBooks Pro immediately looked for an inventory asset account and a cost of goods sold account. Even though you created those accounts in the Chart of Accounts List, QuickBooks Pro could not locate them because it is looking for its own accounts with the dimmed account type. If you open the Chart of Accounts List you will see an 1120 Inventory Asset account and a 5000 Cost of Goods Sold account are listed. Edit each of those accounts and notice the account type is dimmed.

You can create as many inventory asset and cost of goods sold accounts as you like and use any name and number for them, but you must have at least one inventory asset and one cost of goods sold account with the dimmed account type. If you do not, every time you choose an inventory part in the New Item window, QuickBooks Pro will create these accounts on its own. Once QuickBooks Pro creates these accounts, you can revise their names and numbers using the Edit Account window, but you cannot change the account type.

For Kristin Raina Interior Designs, change the 1120 Inventory Asset account created by QuickBooks Pro to 1260 Inventory of Carpets, and change the 5000 Cost of Goods Sold account to 5060 Cost of Carpets Sold.

To edit the accounts created by QuickBooks Pro—
1. In the Chart of Accounts List window, select (highlight) account *1120 Inventory Asset.*
2. Click the Account button, and then, from the Account menu, click Edit.
3. Change the account number from *1120* to *1260.*
4. Change the account name from *Inventory Asset* to *Inventory of Carpets.* (See figure 8–16.)

FIGURE 8-16
Edit Account Window –
Inventory of Carpets

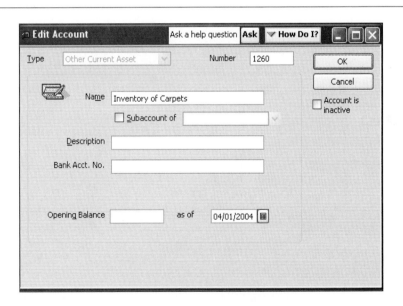

5. If the information is correct, click OK.
6. Using the same procedures as in steps 1 through 5, change account 5000 Cost of Goods Sold to account 5060 Cost of Carpets Sold.

7. If the information is correct, click OK and close the Chart of Accounts List window.

You added all other inventory and cost of goods sold accounts when you updated the Chart of Accounts List. You can now continue adding inventory part items to the Item List and use the inventory and cost of goods sold accounts you edited or previously added.

To add inventory part items—
1. Click Lists, then Item List, and then click New on the Item menu.
2. At the *Type* field, click *Inventory Part*.
3. Enter the information listed below for the carpets inventory:

HINT

In the account fields, you can key in the account number instead of using the drop-down list.

Item Name/Number:	**Carpets**
Description on Purchase and	
Sales Transactions:	**Carpets**
Cost:	**200**
COGS Account:	**5060 Cost of Carpets Sold**
Sales Price:	**400**
Tax Code:	**Tax Taxable Sales**
Income Account:	**4060 Sale of Carpets**
Asset Account:	**1260 Inventory of Carpets**
Reorder Point:	**5**
On Hand:	**4**
As of:	**04/01/2004**

The amount of 800.00 in the *Total Value* field is computed automatically based on cost times quantity on hand. (See figure 8–17.)

FIGURE 8-17
New Item Window –
Inventory Part

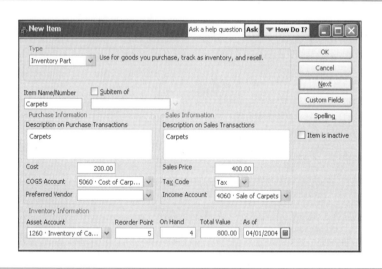

4. If the information is correct, click Next. The New Item window is displayed with the fields cleared for the next item.
5. Using the information in table 8–2, key in the rest of the inventory part items. All inventory part items are taxable and the reorder point is 5. Be sure to have the date as of 04/01/2004 on each item.
6. Close the New Item and Item List windows.

TABLE 8-2
Inventory Part Items

Item Name, Purchase and Sales Description	Cost	COGS Acct	Sales Price	Income Acct	Asset Acct	Reorder Point	On Hand	Total Value
Draperies	$125	5065	$250	4065	1265	5	8	$1,000
Lamps	100	5070	200	4070	1270	5	10	1,000
Mirrors	150	5075	300	4075	1275	5	6	900

ACCOUNTING *concept*

1260 Inventory of Carpets		1265 Inventory of Draperies		1270 Inventory of Lamps		1275 Inventory of Mirrors		3000 Open Bal Equity	
Dr	Cr	Dr	Cr	Dr	Cr	Dr	Cr	Dr	Cr
800		1,000		1,000		900			800
									1,000
									1,000
									900

UPDATING THE CUSTOMER:JOB LIST

The Customer:Job List records the information for all customers with whom the company does business. You can update the Customer:Job List using the procedures learned in chapter 3 to add a new customer. The only additional step you need to take is to enter outstanding balances that some of these customers have when recording the new customer file.

When you add a customer, QuickBooks Pro looks for an accounts receivable account type. The Accounts Receivable account was created using accounts receivable as the account type. Even though in this case the account type is not dimmed, QuickBooks Pro does recognize the accounts receivable account type and does not create a new account.

Kristin Raina has ten customers. Two of the customers have an outstanding balance.

To add a customer with an outstanding balance—
1. Click Lists, and then click Customer:Job List.
2. At the Customer:Job List window, click the Customer:Job button.
3. At the Customer:Job menu, click New. The New Customer window appears.
4. At the *Customer Name* field, key **Burnitz Bakery Company**.
5. Move to the *Opening Balance* field and key **600.**
6. Move to the *as of* field and choose *04/01/2004*.
7. Enter the information listed below on the Address Info tab:

Company Name:	**Burnitz Bakery Company**
First Name:	**Barry**
Last Name:	**Burnitz**
Address:	**18 N. Grand Ave.**
	Minneapolis, MN 55403
Contact:	**Barry Burnitz**
Phone:	**612-555-2240**
FAX:	**612-555-2241**

(See figure 8–18.)

HINT

On the A̲ddress Info tab, after completing the *Address Bill To* field, click Copy to fill in the *Ship to* field.

8. On the Additional Info tab, at the *Terms* drop-down list, click *Net 30 Days*.
9. On the *Payment Info* tab, at the Account No. field, key **R1825.**

FIGURE 8-18
New Customer Window –
Address Info Tab

HINT

If you inadvertently do not enter the opening balance, delete the customer and re-enter the customer with the balance and the correct date.

ACCOUNTING
concept

1200 Accounts Receivable		4999 Uncategorized Income	
Dr	Cr	Dr	Cr
600			600
940			940
Bal 1,540			Bal 1,540

TABLE 8-3
Customers

10. If the information is correct, click <u>N</u>ext. The New Customer window appears with the fields cleared for the next customer.

11. Using the information in table 8–3, key in the information for all of the customers. Be sure to have the date as of 04/01/2004 for the customer with the opening balance.

Customer/ Company Name	Name/Contact	Address	Phone/Fax	Terms	Account No.	Balance
Alomar Company	Oliver Alomar	1001 Oak Lake Ave. Minneapolis, MN 55401	612-555-5757 612-555-5858	Net 30 Days	O1535	
Benitez Bagel Barn	Belinda Benitez	148 46th Ave. N Plymouth, MN 53406	612-555-1233 612-555-1234	Net 30 Days	B0250	
Cook Caterers	Stephen Cook	275 Oak Lake Ave. Minneapolis, MN 55401	612-555-7896 612-555-7599	Net 30 Days	C0360	
Franco Films Co.	Fred Franco	100 Pleasant Ave. S. Minneapolis, MN 55409	612-555-4566 612-555-4567	Net 30 Days	F0660	$940
Guthrie, Jennie	Jennie Guthrie	165 Terrace Ct. St. Paul, MN 55101	615-555-1515	2/10, Net 30 Days	O1565	
Hamilton Hotels	Hilda Hamilton	1000 York Ave. St. Paul, MN 55101	615-555-1050 615-555-1060	2/10, Net 30 Days	H0830	
Jones, Beverly	Beverly Jones	333 York Circle Bloomington, MN 54603	612-555-7778	Net 30 Days	J1013	
Ordonez, Maria	Maria Ordonez	210 NE Lowry Ave. Minneapolis, MN 54204	612-555-9999 612-555-9998	Net 30 Days	O1545	
Piazza Pizza Palace	Mikey Piazza	360 Border Ave. N Minneapolis, MN 55401	612-555-9000 612-555-9800	Net 30 Days	P1650	

UPDATING THE VENDOR LIST

The Vendor List records the information for all vendors with whom the company does business. Open and review the Vendor List. QuickBooks Pro added one vendor, Minn. Dept. of Revenue, when you set up the sales tax item. All other vendors need to be added to the Vendor List.

The Vendor List is updated using procedures learned in chapter 2 to add a new vendor. The only additional step you need to take is to enter outstanding balances for some of these vendors when recording the new vendor file.

When you add a vendor, QuickBooks Pro looks for an Accounts Payable account. Since the Accounts Payable account was created using accounts payable as the account type, QuickBooks Pro recognizes the account type accounts payable and does not create a new account, even though the account type is not dimmed.

Kristin Raina has seventeen vendors. Seven of the vendors have an outstanding balance.

To add a vendor with an outstanding balance—
1. Click Lists, and then click Vendor List.
2. At the Vendor List window, click the Vendor menu button.
3. At the Vendor menu, click New. The New Vendor window appears.
4. At the *Vendor Name* field, key **Ace Glass Works**.
5. At the *Opening Balance* field, key **1500.**
6. At the *as of* field, choose *04/01/2004.*
7. Enter the information listed below:

ADDRESS INFO

Company Name:	**Ace Glass Works**
First Name:	**Archie**
Last Name:	**Ace**
Address:	**25 SE Como Ave.**
	Minneapolis, MN 53602
Contact:	**Archie Ace**
Phone:	**612-555-9812**
FAX:	**612-555-6813**

ADDITIONAL INFO

Account No.:	**1245**
Terms:	**Net 30 Days**

(See figure 8–19.)

FIGURE 8-19
New Vendor Window –
Additional Info Tab

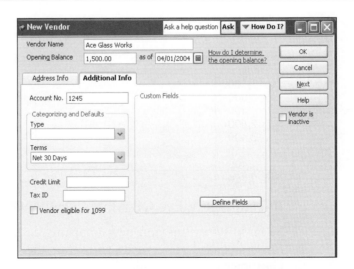

8. If the information is correct, click <u>N</u>ext. The New Vendor window is displayed with the fields cleared for the next vendor.
9. Using the information in table 8–4, key in all of the vendors. Be sure to have the date as of 04/01/2004 for the vendors with the opening balance.

T A B L E 8 - 4
Vendors

Vendor/Company Name	Name/Contact	Address	Phone/Fax	Account No.	Terms	Balance
Bell Carpet Design	Bill Bell	55 North Main Ave. St. Paul, MN 54603	651-555-8823 651-555-8824	66-87874	Net 30 Days	$2,000
Cone and Clemens Associates	Carrie Cone	23 W. University Ave. St. Paul, MN 54603	651-555-8855 651-555-8856	KR569	Net 30 Days	400
Darren Tapestry	Donna Darren	10 W. Larpenteur Ave. Minneapolis, MN 52604	612-555-2221 612-555-2222	2365	Net 30 Days	
Galeway Computers	Roger Rivera	33 Route 10 Springfield, MA 24105	617-555-4747 617-555-4748	2455-897	Net 30 Days	2,600
Giambi Graphics	Gregg Giambi	56 Amity Way Bloomington, MN 53608	612-555-0002 612-555-0003	33-2221	Net 30 Days	
Jeter Janitorial Services	Jason Jeter	233 Lilac Rd. Minneapolis, MN 54302	612-555-4444 612-555-4445	555-32	Net 30 Days	
Kristin Raina	Kristin Raina					
Lumiare Lighting Company	Larry Lyght	123 Glenwood Ave. Minneapolis, MN 53609	612-555-4790 612-555-4795	36	Net 30 Days	
Midwest Mutual Insurance Co.	Mike Mills	3566 Broadway Chicago, IL 58303	805-555-4545 805-555-4546	54778784	Net 30 Days	2,400
Minneapolis Electric & Gas Co.	Jack Watts	150 Douglas Ave. St. Paul, MN 55303	651-555-4949 651-555-4950	2001-23657	Net 30 Days	450
Nordic Realty	Melanie Marx	23 N. 12th Street Minneapolis, MN 53604	612-555-3232 612-555-3233	55-1212	Net 10 Days	
TwinCity Tel Co.	Terry Ameche	3223 River Dr. St. Paul, MN 53908	651-555-6667 651-555-6668	666-6667	Net 30 Days	
Williams Office Supply Company	Bernard Williams	15 Grand Ave. S Minneapolis, MN 55404	612-555-2240 612-555-2241	55-8988	Net 30 Days	400
Weaver Fabrics	Jon Weaver	355 W. 70th Street Minneapolis, MN 53604	612-555-8777 612-555-8778	9878	Net 30 Days	
[Your Name] Accounting Services	Your Name	One Main Plaza St. Paul, MN 53602	612-555-2222 612-555-2223	99-2001-XX	Net 30 Days	

HINT

If you forget to enter the opening balance, delete the vendor and reenter the vendor along with the balance and the correct date.

ACCOUNTING
concept

6999 Uncategorized Expenses		2010 Accounts Payable	
Dr	Cr	Dr	Cr
1,500			1,500
2,000			2,000
400			400
2,600			2,600
2,400			2,400
450			450
400			400
Bal 9,750			Bal 9,750

INTERIM REVIEW OF NEW COMPANY SETUP

So far in setting up your new company file, you have created the company file, established preferences, and set up the Chart of Accounts, Item, Customer:Job, and Vendor Lists.

As you added the inventory items, customers, and vendors, with balances to the Lists, behind the scenes QuickBooks Pro recorded the information in general journal format and updated the appropriate account balances. Now display the *Journal*, *Profit & Loss Standard*, and *Balance Sheet Standard* reports to see the activity taking place behind the scenes up to this point.

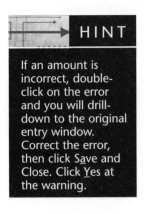

HINT

If an amount is incorrect, double-click on the error and you will drill-down to the original entry window. Correct the error, then click Save and Close. Click Yes at the warning.

JOURNAL REPORT

To view and print the Journal Report—

1. Click Reports, and then click Accountants & Taxes.
2. At the Accountants & Taxes submenu, click Journal.
3. In the *From* and *To* fields, choose *04/01/2004*, then click Refresh.
4. To print the *Journal* report, click Print. If you receive a message about Printing Features, place a check mark in the box to the left of Do not display this message in the future and click No.
5. At the Print Reports dialog box, check the settings, and then click Print. Your printout should look like figure 8–20.

FIGURE 8-20

Journal Report

CH8 [Your Name] Kristin Raina Interior Designs
Journal
April 1, 2004

Trans #	Type	Date	Num	Name	Memo	Account	Debit	Credit
1	Inventory Adjust	04/01/2004			Carpets Opening balance	3000 · Opening Bal Equity		800.00
					Carpets Opening balance	1260 · Inventory of Carpets	800.00	
							800.00	800.00
2	Inventory Adjust	04/01/2004			Draperies Opening balance	3000 · Opening Bal Equity		1,000.00
					Draperies Opening balance	1265 · Inventory of Draperies	1,000.00	
							1,000.00	1,000.00
3	Inventory Adjust	04/01/2004			Lamps Opening balance	3000 · Opening Bal Equity		1,000.00
					Lamps Opening balance	1270 · Inventory of Lamps	1,000.00	
							1,000.00	1,000.00
4	Inventory Adjust	04/01/2004			Mirrors Opening balance	3000 · Opening Bal Equity		900.00
					Mirrors Opening balance	1275 · Inventory of Mirrors	900.00	
							900.00	900.00
5	Invoice	04/01/2004		Burnitz Bakery Company	Opening balance	1200 · Accounts Receivable	600.00	
				Burnitz Bakery Company	Opening balance	4999 · Uncategorized Income		600.00
							600.00	600.00
6	Invoice	04/01/2004		Franco Films Co.	Opening balance	1200 · Accounts Receivable	940.00	
				Franco Films Co.	Opening balance	4999 · Uncategorized Income		940.00
							940.00	940.00
7	Bill	04/01/2004		Ace Glass Works	Opening balance	2010 · Accounts Payable		1,500.00
				Ace Glass Works	Opening balance	6999 · Uncategorized Expens...	1,500.00	
							1,500.00	1,500.00
8	Bill	04/01/2004		Bell Carpet Design	Opening balance	2010 · Accounts Payable		2,000.00
				Bell Carpet Design	Opening balance	6999 · Uncategorized Expens...	2,000.00	
							2,000.00	2,000.00
9	Bill	04/01/2004		Cone and Clemens Ass...	Opening balance	2010 · Accounts Payable		400.00
				Cone and Clemens Ass...	Opening balance	6999 · Uncategorized Expens...	400.00	
							400.00	400.00
10	Bill	04/01/2004		Galeway Computers	Opening balance	2010 · Accounts Payable		2,600.00
				Galeway Computers	Opening balance	6999 · Uncategorized Expens...	2,600.00	
							2,600.00	2,600.00
11	Bill	04/01/2004		Midwest Mutual Insuran...	Opening balance	2010 · Accounts Payable		2,400.00
				Midwest Mutual Insuran...	Opening balance	6999 · Uncategorized Expens...	2,400.00	
							2,400.00	2,400.00
12	Bill	04/01/2004		Minneapolis Electric & ...	Opening balance	2010 · Accounts Payable		450.00
				Minneapolis Electric & ...	Opening balance	6999 · Uncategorized Expens...	450.00	
							450.00	450.00
13	Bill	04/01/2004		Williams Office Supply	Opening balance	2010 · Accounts Payable		400.00
				Williams Office Supply	Opening balance	6999 · Uncategorized Expens...	400.00	
							400.00	400.00
TOTAL							**14,990.00**	**14,990.00**

Review the journal entries. They can be categorized as follows:

    a. For items that are debit entries to the inventory accounts, the corresponding credit entry is to the Opening Bal Equity account.

    b. For entries that are debits to Accounts Receivable, the corresponding credit is to Uncategorized Income.

    c. For entries that are credits to Accounts Payable, the corresponding debit is to Uncategorized Expenses.

6. Close the report. If you receive a message about Memorize Report, place a check mark in the box to the left of Do not display this message in the future and click No.

PROFIT & LOSS STANDARD (INCOME STATEMENT) REPORT

To view and print the *Profit & Loss Standard* report:

1. Click Reports, and then click Company & Financial.
2. At the Company & Financial menu, click Profit & Loss Standard.
3. In the *From* and *To* fields, choose *04/01/2004*, and then click Refresh. (See figure 8–21.)

FIGURE 8-21
*Profit & Loss
Standard Report*

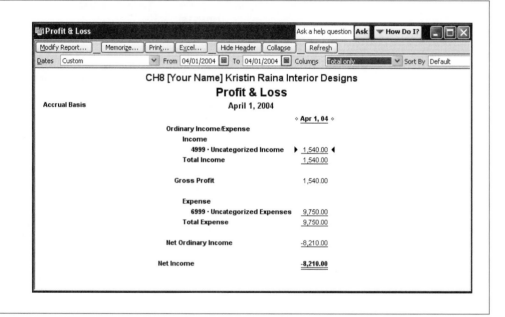

4. To print the *Profit & Loss Standard* report, click Print.
5. At the Print Reports dialog box, check the settings, and then click Print.
6. Close the report.

The *Profit & Loss Standard* report indicates only Uncategorized Income and Uncategorized Expenses. These amounts are offsetting amounts of the Accounts Receivable and Accounts Payable accounts. This is not a proper representation of the income and expenses of this company.

BALANCE SHEET STANDARD REPORT

To display the *Balance Sheet Standard* report—

1. Click Reports, and then click Company & Financial.
2. At the Company & Financial submenu, click Balance Sheet Standard.

3. In the *As of* field, choose *04/01/2004*, and then click Refresh.
4. To print the *Balance Sheet Standard* report, click Print.
5. At the Print Reports dialog box, check the settings, and then click Print. Your printout should look like figure 8–22.

FIGURE 8-22
*Balance Sheet
Standard Report*

CH8 [Your Name] Kristin Raina Interior Designs
Balance Sheet
As of April 1, 2004

Accrual Basis

	Apr 1, 04
ASSETS	
Current Assets	
Accounts Receivable	
1200 · Accounts Receivable	1,540.00
Total Accounts Receivable	1,540.00
Other Current Assets	
1260 · Inventory of Carpets	800.00
1265 · Inventory of Draperies	1,000.00
1270 · Inventory of Lamps	1,000.00
1275 · Inventory of Mirrors	900.00
Total Other Current Assets	3,700.00
Total Current Assets	5,240.00
TOTAL ASSETS	5,240.00
LIABILITIES & EQUITY	
Liabilities	
Current Liabilities	
Accounts Payable	
2010 · Accounts Payable	9,750.00
Total Accounts Payable	9,750.00
Total Current Liabilities	9,750.00
Total Liabilities	9,750.00
Equity	
3000 · Opening Bal Equity	3,700.00
Net Income	-8,210.00
Total Equity	-4,510.00
TOTAL LIABILITIES & EQUITY	5,240.00

A review of the balance sheet indicates the following:
a. The only assets recorded so far are accounts receivable and inventory.
b. The only liabilities recorded so far are the accounts payable.
c. The balance in the Opening Bal Equity account is the same as the total inventory.
d. The net income is incorrect as seen in the Income Statement.
6. Close the report.

CUSTOMIZING THE SYSTEM DEFAULT ACCOUNTS IN THE CHART OF ACCOUNTS

As was stated earlier, when you establish preferences and update the Lists, QuickBooks Pro creates certain system default accounts. You can customize these system default accounts in the Chart of Accounts List.

In setting up the new company file, you saw examples of how QuickBooks Pro created accounts. For instance, when you selected inventory part in the Item List window, QuickBooks Pro created an inventory asset account and a cost of goods sold account. As you can see in the *Journal* report, QuickBooks Pro created an Opening Bal Equity account which it used as a balancing account to record the inventory item parts.

You already customized the inventory asset and cost of goods sold accounts when you updated the Lists. You will now customize the Opening Bal Equity account created by QuickBooks Pro.

When QuickBooks Pro created the Opening Bal Equity account it assigned the Equity account type, which is shown as dimmed. You will now customize this account so that it becomes the 3010 Kristin Raina, Capital account using the Edit command in the Chart of Accounts List window.

To edit the equity account—
1. Click Lists, and then Chart of Accounts List.
2. Select (highlight) *3000 Opening Bal Equity*.
3. Click the Account button and click Edit.
4. At the Edit Account window, change the account number to *3010*.
5. At the *Name* field, change the name to *Kristin Raina, Capital*. (See figure 8–23.)

FIGURE 8-23
Edit Account Window –
Kristin Raina, Capital

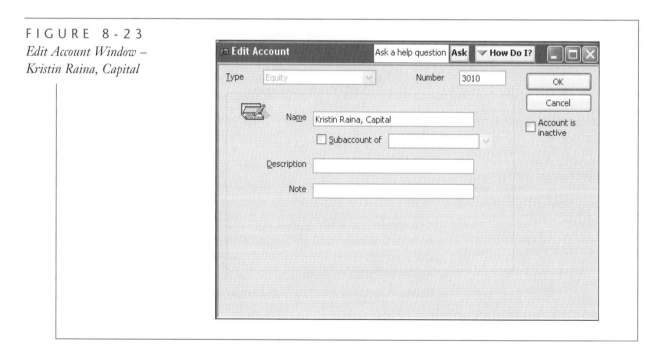

6. If the information is correct, click OK.

QuickBooks Pro creates system default accounts not only when you establish preferences and update Lists, but also when you open certain Activity windows. An example of this is the Undeposited Funds account. Even though you created this account in the Chart of Accounts List, QuickBooks Pro cannot identify this account as a system default account because it looks for the dimmed account type, not the account number or name. Therefore, you must allow QuickBooks Pro to create the system default account. Then you can customize it.

Look at the Chart of Accounts List and notice the 1250 Undeposited Funds account created as part of the process of updating the Chart of Accounts List. Open the Edit Account window and notice the account type is Other Current Asset, but it is not dimmed. Close the Edit Account window. Now open the Enter Sales Receipts window. (Click <u>N</u>o at the message.) When you open that window, even though you did not record a transaction, QuickBooks Pro is looking for the Undeposited Funds account but will not identify the 1250 Undeposited Funds account you created.

Close the Enter Sales Receipts window and look at the Chart of Accounts List again. QuickBooks Pro created the account 1499 *Undeposited Funds. Edit this new account. Notice the account type is dimmed. (See figure 8–24.)

FIGURE 8-24
*1499 *Undeposited Funds Account Created by QuickBooks Pro*

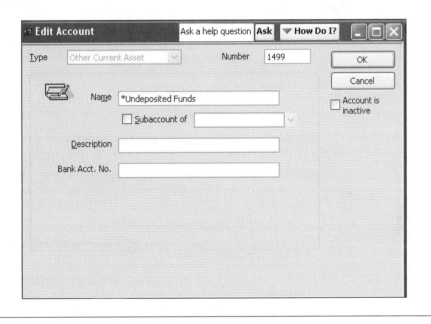

HINT

QuickBooks Pro uses any account number not already in use. An asterisk before an account name means QuickBooks Pro created the account.

Since QuickBooks Pro cannot identify your 1250 account, you should delete it. After you delete the 1250 account, edit account 1499 *Undeposited Funds as follows:

1. Change the account number to *1250*.
2. Remove the asterisk from the account name. (See figure 8–25.)

FIGURE 8-25
*Undeposited Funds
Account Edited*

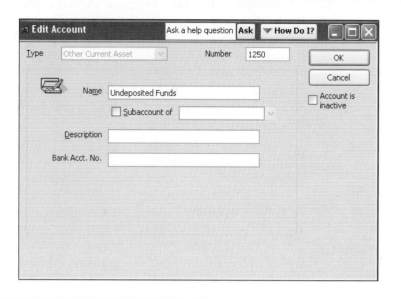

3. If the information is correct, click OK.

Reopen the Enter Sales Receipts window and then close it. Review the Chart of Accounts List again. Notice, QuickBooks Pro did not create an Undeposited Funds account again because it found its own system default account, with the dimmed account type, even though you changed the account number and edited the name.

ENTERING OPENING BALANCES AND REVERSING UNCATEGORIZED ACCOUNTS

You have now created the new company file, established preferences, updated the Lists, and customized the Chart of Accounts for the system default accounts. Now you must enter the remaining opening balances and prepare the company file for the **accrual basis of accounting,** which requires the recording of revenues when earned and expenses when incurred.

accrual basis of accounting An accounting method that requires the recording of revenue when it is earned and the recording of expenses when they are incurred.

Recall that you entered the opening balances for the Inventory Asset, Accounts Receivable, and Accounts Payable accounts when you set up and updated the Lists. When you set up the Chart of Accounts List, you could have entered the opening balances for assets (excluding Accounts Receivable), liabilities (excluding Accounts Payable), and equity accounts at that time also. If you entered the opening balances in the Chart of Accounts, the effect would have been the same as using EasyStep Interview. In this chapter, however, you will enter the opening balances as a general journal entry. This is an important function to know, because for revenue and expense accounts, you can use neither EasyStep Interview nor the Chart of Accounts window to enter beginning balances. You must use general journal entries.

As you saw in the *Journal* report (figure 8–20), every time an Accounts Receivable account was recorded, a corresponding Uncategorized Income account was recorded, and every time an Accounts Payable account was recorded, a corresponding Uncategorized Expenses account was recorded.

reversing entries
Entries recorded in the general journal to offset a balance in an account.

The Uncategorized Income and Uncategorized Expenses accounts are not used in an accrual basis of accounting and therefore must be reversed to eliminate them. You do this by using reversing entries.

ENTERING OPENING BALANCES

You will enter all opening balances for Kristin Raina Interior Designs, excluding inventory, accounts receivable, and accounts payable, as one large compound journal entry.

To enter opening balances in the General Journal Entry window—

1. Click Company, and then click Make Journal Entry. At the Assigning Numbers to Journal Entries message, place a check mark in the box to the left of Do not display this message in the future and click OK. The General Journal Entry window appears.
2. At the *Date* field, choose *04/01/2004*.
3. At the *Entry No.* field, accept the default Entry No.
4. Enter the following accounts and amounts as debits:

HINT

You can key in the account number for each account, or use the drop-down list.

HINT

Maximize the General Journal Entry window while recording journal entries so that you can see all the entries.

Number	Name	Balance
1010	Cash – Operating	$50,855.38
1300	Design Supplies	200.00
1305	Office Supplies	250.00
1410	Prepaid Advertising	500.00
1420	Prepaid Insurance	2,200.00
1700	Furniture	12,000.00
1800	Computers	3,600.00
3020	Kristin Raina, Drawings	400.00
4100	Sales Discounts	84.62
5060	Cost of Carpets Sold	1,200.00
5065	Cost of Draperies Sold	500.00
5070	Cost of Lamps Sold	600.00
5075	Cost of Mirrors Sold	450.00
5900	Inventory Adjustment	150.00
6020	Accounting Expense	300.00
6050	Advertising Expense	100.00
6175	Deprec. Exp., Furniture	100.00
6185	Deprec. Exp., Computers	60.00
6200	Insurance Expense	200.00
6300	Janitorial Expense	125.00
6325	Office Supplies Expense	150.00
6400	Rent Expense	800.00
6450	Telephone Expense	275.00
6500	Utilities Expense	450.00
7000	Interest Expense	50.00

QuickCheck: $75,600

5. Enter the following accounts and amounts as credits:

Number	Name	Balance
1750	Accum. Dep., Furniture	$ 100
1850	Accum. Dep., Computers	60
2020	Notes Payable	7,000
2030	Interest Payable	50
4010	Design Services	4,980
4020	Decorating Services	3,400
4060	Sale of Carpets	2,400
4065	Sale of Draperies	1,000
4070	Sale of Lamps	1,200
4075	Sale of Mirrors	900

QuickCheck: $54,510

6. Record the credit balance of $54,510 as a credit to account 3010 Kristin Raina, Capital.
7. Click <u>S</u>ave & New.

ACCOUNTING
c o n c e p t

The effect of recording the opening balances is as follows:

1010-1800 Assets

Dr		Cr
Cash	50,855.38	
Design Supplies	200.00	
Office Supplies	250.00	
Prepaid Advertising	500.00	
Prepaid Insurance	2,200.00	
Furniture	12,000.00	
Computers	3,600.00	
	69,605.38	

1750-1850 Accum. Dep.

Dr	Cr
	100
	60

2020-2030 Payables

Dr	Cr
	7,000 Notes
	50 Interest

3020 Kristin Raina, Drawings

Dr	Cr
400	

3010 Kristin Raina, Capital

Dr	Cr
	54,510

4010-4020 Service Revenue

Dr	Cr
	Design 4,980
	Decor. 3,400
	8,380

4060-4075 Sale of Inventory

Dr	Cr	
	Carpets	2,400
	Draperies	1,000
	Lamps	1,200
	Mirrors	900
		5,500

4100 Sales Discounts

Dr	Cr
84.62	

5060-5075,5900 Cost of Goods Sold

Dr		Cr
Carpets	1,200	
Draperies	500	
Lamps	600	
Mirrors	450	
Inv. Adj.	150	
	2,900	

6020-6500 Expenses

Dr		Cr
Accounting	300	
Advertising	100	
Dep. Exp., Furniture	100	
Dep. Exp., Computers	60	
Insurance	200	
Janitorial	125	
Office Supplies	150	
Rent	800	
Telephone	275	
Utilities	450	
Bal	2,560	

7000 Interest Exp.

Dr	Cr
50	

REVERSING UNCATEGORIZED INCOME

Recall that in the *Journal* report of figure 8–20, there are two journal entries recorded that debit the Accounts Receivable and credit Uncategorized Income for two customers as follows:

Burnitz Bakery Company	$ 600
Franco Films Co.	940
	$1,540

The debit entries to the Accounts Receivable account are correct and will stay in that account. The credits to the Uncategorized Income account will be reversed by debiting Uncategorized Income for the total of $1,540, and crediting the account 3010 Kristin Raina, Capital (formerly the Opening Bal Equity account) for $1,540.

To reverse the Uncategorized Revenue account—
1. At the General Journal Entry window, choose the date, *04/01/2004*, and at the *Entry No.* field, accept Entry No. 2.
2. At the General Journal Entry window, debit account 4999 Uncategorized Income for 1,540, and credit account 3010 Kristin Raina, Capital for 1,540.
3. If the information is correct, click <u>S</u>ave & New.

ACCOUNTING
concept

4999 Uncategorized Income				3010 Kristin Raina, Capital		
Dr		Cr			Dr	Cr
Adj 1,540		1,540				1,540
	0	Bal 0				

REVERSING THE UNCATEGORIZED EXPENSES ACCOUNT

In the *Journal* report shown in figure 8–20, there are seven journal entries that credit Accounts Payable and debit Uncategorized Expenses for seven vendor balances as follows:

Ace Glass Works	$1,500
Bell Carpet Design	2,000
Cone and Clemens Associates	400
Galeway Computers	2,600
Midwest Mutual Insurance Co.	2,400
Minneapolis Electric & Gas Co.	450
Williams Office Supply Company	400
	$9,750

The credit entries to the Accounts Payable account are correct and will stay in that account. The debits to the Uncategorized Expenses, however, have to be reversed by crediting Uncategorized Expenses for the total of $9,750, and debiting the 3010 Kristin Raina, Capital account for $9,750.

To reverse the Uncategorized Expenses account—
1. At the General Journal Entry window, choose the date *04/01/2004*, and at the *Entry No.* field, accept Entry No. 3.
2. Debit account 3010 Kristin Raina, Capital for 9,750, and credit account 6999 Uncategorized Expenses for 9,750.

HINT

As part of customizing the Chart of Accounts, the account Opening Bal Equity, created by QuickBooks Pro, was changed to 3010 Kristin Raina, Capital.

3. If the information is correct, click S<u>a</u>ve & Close.

ACCOUNTING
concept

6999 Uncategorized Expenses			3010 Kristin Raina, Capital	
Dr	Cr		Dr	Cr
9,750	Adj 9,750		9,750	
0				

REPORTS: NEW COMPANY FILE AND FINANCIAL REPORTS

HINT

To display only the last three journal entries in the *Journal* report, click the <u>M</u>odify Report button. Then click the <u>F</u>ilters tab. In the *Filter* field, click *Transaction Type*. In the *Account* field, click *Journal*.

Upon completing the New Company Setup, you should display and print the accounting and financial reports and the Lists.

ACCOUNTING REPORTS

The accounting reports you need to print and review consist of the *Journal* and the *Trial Balance*.

Journal Report

You displayed and printed the *Journal* report after the initial company setup was completed (figure 8–20). After recording the opening balances and reversing the Uncategorized Revenue and Uncategorized Expenses accounts, three more journal entries have been added to the *Journal* report. You can view and print all of the journal entries for April 1, 2004. Figure 8–26 displays only the additional three journal entries.

FIGURE 8-26
Additional Journal Entries

CH8 [Your Name] Kristin Raina Interior Designs
Journal
April 1, 2004

Trans #	Type	Date	Num	Name	Memo	Account	Debit	Credit
14	General Journal	04/01/2004	1			1010 · Cash - Operating	50,855.38	
						1300 · Design Supplies	200.00	
						1305 · Office Supplies	250.00	
						1410 · Prepaid Advertising	500.00	
						1420 · Prepaid Insurance	2,200.00	
						1700 · Furniture	12,000.00	
						1800 · Computers	3,600.00	
						3020 · Kristin Raina, Drawings	400.00	
						4100 · Sales Discounts	84.62	
						5060 · Cost of Carpets Sold	1,200.00	
						5065 · Cost of Draperies Sold	500.00	
						5070 · Cost of Lamps Sold	600.00	
						5075 · Cost of Mirrors Sold	450.00	
						5900 · Inventory Adjustment	150.00	
						6020 · Accounting Expense	300.00	
						6050 · Advertising Expense	100.00	
						6175 · Deprec. Exp., Furniture	100.00	
						6185 · Deprec. Exp., Computers	60.00	
						6200 · Insurance Expense	200.00	
						6300 · Janitorial Expense	125.00	
						6325 · Office Supplies Expense	150.00	
						6400 · Rent Expense	800.00	
						6450 · Telephone Expense	275.00	
						6500 · Utilities Expense	450.00	
						7000 · Interest Expense	50.00	
						1750 · Accum. Dep., Furniture		100.00
						1850 · Accum. Dep., Computers		60.00
						2020 · Notes Payable		7,000.00
						2030 · Interest Payable		50.00
						4010 · Design Services		4,980.00
						4020 · Decorating Services		3,400.00
						4060 · Sale of Carpets		2,400.00
						4065 · Sale of Draperies		1,000.00
						4070 · Sale of Lamps		1,200.00
						4075 · Sale of Mirrors		900.00
						3010 · Kristin Raina, Capital		54,510.00
							75,600.00	75,600.00
15	General Journal	04/01/2004	2			4999 · Uncategorized Income	1,540.00	
						3010 · Kristin Raina, Capital		1,540.00
							1,540.00	1,540.00
16	General Journal	04/01/2004	3			3010 · Kristin Raina, Capital	9,750.00	
						6999 · Uncategorized Expenses		9,750.00
							9,750.00	9,750.00
TOTAL							**86,890.00**	**86,890.00**

Trial Balance Report

Next, view and print the *Trial Balance* report for April 1, 2004. (It should look like figure 8–27.) The accounts and balances on this trial balance should match the trial balance of March 31, 2004, after transactions were recorded in chapters 2 through 5.

FIGURE 8-27
Trial Balance Report

CH8 [Your Name] Kristin Raina Interior Designs
Trial Balance

Accrual Basis

As of April 1, 2004

	Apr 1, 04	
	Debit	Credit
1010 · Cash - Operating	50,855.38	
1200 · Accounts Receivable	1,540.00	
1260 · Inventory of Carpets	800.00	
1265 · Inventory of Draperies	1,000.00	
1270 · Inventory of Lamps	1,000.00	
1275 · Inventory of Mirrors	900.00	
1300 · Design Supplies	200.00	
1305 · Office Supplies	250.00	
1410 · Prepaid Advertising	500.00	
1420 · Prepaid Insurance	2,200.00	
1700 · Furniture	12,000.00	
1700 · Furniture:1750 · Accum. Dep., Furniture		100.00
1800 · Computers	3,600.00	
1800 · Computers:1850 · Accum. Dep., Computers		60.00
2010 · Accounts Payable		9,750.00
2020 · Notes Payable		7,000.00
2030 · Interest Payable		50.00
3010 · Kristin Raina, Capital		50,000.00
3020 · Kristin Raina, Drawings	400.00	
4010 · Design Services		4,980.00
4020 · Decorating Services		3,400.00
4060 · Sale of Carpets		2,400.00
4065 · Sale of Draperies		1,000.00
4070 · Sale of Lamps		1,200.00
4075 · Sale of Mirrors		900.00
4100 · Sales Discounts	84.62	
4999 · Uncategorized Income	0.00	
5060 · Cost of Carpets Sold	1,200.00	
5065 · Cost of Draperies Sold	500.00	
5070 · Cost of Lamps Sold	600.00	
5075 · Cost of Mirrors Sold	450.00	
5900 · Inventory Adjustment	150.00	
6020 · Accounting Expense	300.00	
6050 · Advertising Expense	100.00	
6175 · Deprec. Exp., Furniture	100.00	
6185 · Deprec. Exp., Computers	60.00	
6200 · Insurance Expense	200.00	
6300 · Janitorial Expense	125.00	
6325 · Office Supplies Expense	150.00	
6400 · Rent Expense	800.00	
6450 · Telephone Expense	275.00	
6500 · Utilities Expense	450.00	
6999 · Uncategorized Expenses	0.00	
7000 · Interest Expense	50.00	
TOTAL	80,840.00	80,840.00

The financial reports consist of the *Profit & Loss Standard* report (see figure 8–28) and the *Balance Sheet Standard* report (see figure 8–29). Upon completion of the New Company Setup, these reports should be the same as the financial reports printed at the end of chapter 5.

FIGURE 8-28
Profit & Loss Standard Report

CH8 [Your Name] Kristin Raina Interior Designs
Profit & Loss

Accrual Basis   **April 1, 2004**

	Apr 1, 04
Ordinary Income/Expense	
Income	
4010 · Design Services	4,980.00
4020 · Decorating Services	3,400.00
4060 · Sale of Carpets	2,400.00
4065 · Sale of Draperies	1,000.00
4070 · Sale of Lamps	1,200.00
4075 · Sale of Mirrors	900.00
4100 · Sales Discounts	-84.62
4999 · Uncategorized Income	0.00
Total Income	13,795.38
Cost of Goods Sold	
5060 · Cost of Carpets Sold	1,200.00
5065 · Cost of Draperies Sold	500.00
5070 · Cost of Lamps Sold	600.00
5075 · Cost of Mirrors Sold	450.00
5900 · Inventory Adjustment	150.00
Total COGS	2,900.00
Gross Profit	10,895.38
Expense	
6020 · Accounting Expense	300.00
6050 · Advertising Expense	100.00
6175 · Deprec. Exp., Furniture	100.00
6185 · Deprec. Exp., Computers	60.00
6200 · Insurance Expense	200.00
6300 · Janitorial Expense	125.00
6325 · Office Supplies Expense	150.00
6400 · Rent Expense	800.00
6450 · Telephone Expense	275.00
6500 · Utilities Expense	450.00
6999 · Uncategorized Expenses	0.00
Total Expense	2,560.00
Net Ordinary Income	8,335.38
Other Income/Expense	
Other Expense	
7000 · Interest Expense	50.00
Total Other Expense	50.00
Net Other Income	-50.00
Net Income	**8,285.38**

FIGURE 8-29
Balance Sheet
Standard Report

CH8 [Your Name] Kristin Raina Interior Designs
Balance Sheet
As of April 1, 2004

Accrual Basis

	Apr 1, 04
ASSETS	
Current Assets	
Checking/Savings	
1010 · Cash - Operating	50,855.38
Total Checking/Savings	50,855.38
Accounts Receivable	
1200 · Accounts Receivable	1,540.00
Total Accounts Receivable	1,540.00
Other Current Assets	
1260 · Inventory of Carpets	800.00
1265 · Inventory of Draperies	1,000.00
1270 · Inventory of Lamps	1,000.00
1275 · Inventory of Mirrors	900.00
1300 · Design Supplies	200.00
1305 · Office Supplies	250.00
1410 · Prepaid Advertising	500.00
1420 · Prepaid Insurance	2,200.00
Total Other Current Assets	6,850.00
Total Current Assets	59,245.38
Fixed Assets	
1700 · Furniture	
1750 · Accum. Dep., Furniture	-100.00
1700 · Furniture - Other	12,000.00
Total 1700 · Furniture	11,900.00
1800 · Computers	
1850 · Accum. Dep., Computers	-60.00
1800 · Computers - Other	3,600.00
Total 1800 · Computers	3,540.00
Total Fixed Assets	15,440.00
TOTAL ASSETS	74,685.38
LIABILITIES & EQUITY	
Liabilities	
Current Liabilities	
Accounts Payable	
2010 · Accounts Payable	9,750.00
Total Accounts Payable	9,750.00
Other Current Liabilities	
2020 · Notes Payable	7,000.00
2030 · Interest Payable	50.00
Total Other Current Liabilities	7,050.00
Total Current Liabilities	16,800.00
Total Liabilities	16,800.00
Equity	
3010 · Kristin Raina, Capital	50,000.00
3020 · Kristin Raina, Drawings	-400.00
Net Income	8,285.38
Total Equity	57,885.38
TOTAL LIABILITIES & EQUITY	74,685.38

LISTS REPORTS

The Lists reports consist of the Chart of Accounts, Item, Customer:Job, and Vendor Lists. Upon completion of the New Company Setup, these reports should be printed and reviewed. See figures 8–30 through 8–33 for examples of what the Lists should look like.

FIGURE 8-30

Account Listing

CH8 [Your Name] Kristin Raina Interior Designs
Account Listing
April 1, 2004

Account	Type	Balance Total	Description	Accnt. #	Tax Line
1010 · Cash - Operating	Bank	50,855.38		1010	<Unassigned>
1200 · Accounts Receivable	Accounts Receivable	1,540.00		1200	<Unassigned>
1250 · Undeposited Funds	Other Current Asset	0.00		1250	<Unassigned>
1260 · Inventory of Carpets	Other Current Asset	800.00		1260	<Unassigned>
1265 · Inventory of Draperies	Other Current Asset	1,000.00		1265	<Unassigned>
1270 · Inventory of Lamps	Other Current Asset	1,000.00		1270	<Unassigned>
1275 · Inventory of Mirrors	Other Current Asset	900.00		1275	<Unassigned>
1300 · Design Supplies	Other Current Asset	200.00		1300	<Unassigned>
1305 · Office Supplies	Other Current Asset	250.00		1305	<Unassigned>
1410 · Prepaid Advertising	Other Current Asset	500.00		1410	<Unassigned>
1420 · Prepaid Insurance	Other Current Asset	2,200.00		1420	<Unassigned>
1700 · Furniture	Fixed Asset	11,900.00		1700	<Unassigned>
1700 · Furniture:1750 · Accum. Dep., Furniture	Fixed Asset	-100.00		1750	<Unassigned>
1800 · Computers	Fixed Asset	3,540.00		1800	<Unassigned>
1800 · Computers:1850 · Accum. Dep., Computers	Fixed Asset	-60.00		1850	<Unassigned>
2010 · Accounts Payable	Accounts Payable	9,750.00		2010	<Unassigned>
2020 · Notes Payable	Other Current Liability	7,000.00		2020	<Unassigned>
2030 · Interest Payable	Other Current Liability	50.00		2030	<Unassigned>
2100 · Payroll Liabilities	Other Current Liability	0.00		2100	<Unassigned>
2200 · Sales Tax Payable	Other Current Liability	0.00		2200	<Unassigned>
3010 · Kristin Raina, Capital	Equity	50,000.00		3010	<Unassigned>
3020 · Kristin Raina, Drawings	Equity	-400.00		3020	<Unassigned>
3900 · Retained Earnings	Equity			3900	<Unassigned>
4010 · Design Services	Income			4010	<Unassigned>
4020 · Decorating Services	Income			4020	<Unassigned>
4060 · Sale of Carpets	Income			4060	<Unassigned>
4065 · Sale of Draperies	Income			4065	<Unassigned>
4070 · Sale of Lamps	Income			4070	<Unassigned>
4075 · Sale of Mirrors	Income			4075	<Unassigned>
4100 · Sales Discounts	Income			4100	<Unassigned>
4999 · Uncategorized Income	Income			4999	<Unassigned>
5060 · Cost of Carpets Sold	Cost of Goods Sold			5060	<Unassigned>
5065 · Cost of Draperies Sold	Cost of Goods Sold			5065	<Unassigned>
5070 · Cost of Lamps Sold	Cost of Goods Sold			5070	<Unassigned>
5075 · Cost of Mirrors Sold	Cost of Goods Sold			5075	<Unassigned>
5900 · Inventory Adjustment	Cost of Goods Sold			5900	<Unassigned>
6020 · Accounting Expense	Expense			6020	<Unassigned>
6050 · Advertising Expense	Expense			6050	<Unassigned>
6175 · Deprec. Exp., Furniture	Expense			6175	<Unassigned>
6185 · Deprec. Exp., Computers	Expense			6185	<Unassigned>
6200 · Insurance Expense	Expense			6200	<Unassigned>
6300 · Janitorial Expense	Expense			6300	<Unassigned>
6325 · Office Supplies Expense	Expense			6325	<Unassigned>
6400 · Rent Expense	Expense			6400	<Unassigned>
6450 · Telephone Expense	Expense			6450	<Unassigned>
6500 · Utilities Expense	Expense			6500	<Unassigned>
6560 · Payroll Expenses	Expense			6560	<Unassigned>
6999 · Uncategorized Expenses	Expense			6999	<Unassigned>
7000 · Interest Expense	Other Expense			7000	<Unassigned>

CH8 [Your Name] Kristin Raina Interior Designs
Item Listing
April 1, 2004

Item	Description	Type	Cost	Price	Sales Tax Code	Quantity On Hand	Reorder Point
Decorating Services	Decorating Services	Service	0	50.00	Non		
Design Services	Design Services	Service	0	60.00	Non		
Carpets	Carpets	Inventory Part	200.00	400.00	Tax	4	5
Draperies	Draperies	Inventory Part	125.00	250.00	Tax	8	5
Lamps	Lamps	Inventory Part	100.00	200.00	Tax	10	5
Mirrors	Mirrors	Inventory Part	150.00	300.00	Tax	6	5
Minn. Sales Tax	Sales Tax	Sales Tax Item	0	7%			

CH8 [Your Name] Kristin Raina Interior Designs
Customer Contact List
April 1, 2004

Customer	Bill to	Contact	Phone	Fax	Balance Total
Alomar Company	Alomar Company Oliver Alomar 1001 Oak Lake Ave. Minneapolis, MN 55401	Oliver Alomar	612-555-5757	612-555-5858	0.00
Benitez Bagel Barn	Benitez Bagel Barn Belinda Benitez 148 46th Ave. N Plymouth, MN 53406	Belinda Benitez	612-555-1233	612-555-1234	0.00
Burnitz Bakery Company	Burnitz Bakery Company Barry Burnitz 18 N. Grand Ave. Minneapolis, MN 55403	Barry Burnitz	612-555-2240	612-555-2241	600.00
Cook Caterers	Cook Caterers Stephen Cook 275 Oak Lake Ave. Minneapolis, MN 55401	Stephen Cook	612-555-7896	612-555-7599	940.00
Franco Films Co.	Franco Films Co. Fred Franco 100 Pleasant Ave. S Minneapolis, MN 55409	Fred Franco	612-555-4566		940.00
Guthrie, Jennie	Jennie Guthrie 165 Terrace Ct. St. Paul, MN 55101	Jennie Guthrie	612-555-1515		0.00
Hamilton Hotels	Hamilton Hotels Hilda Hamilton 1000 York Ave. St. Paul, MN 55101	Hilda Hamilton	615-555-1050	615-555-1060	0.00
Jones, Beverly	Beverly Jones 333 York Circle Bloomington, MN 54603	Beverly Jones	612-555-7778		0.00
Ordonez, Maria	Maria Ordonez 210 NE Lowry Ave. Minneapolis, MN 54204	Maria Ordonez	612-555-9999	612-555-9998	0.00
Piazza Pizza Palace	Piazza Pizza Palace Mikey Piazza 360 Border Ave. N Minneapolis, MN 55401	Mikey Piazza	612-555-9000	612-555-9800	0.00

CH8 [Your Name] Kristin Raina Interior Designs
Vendor Contact List
April 1, 2004

Vendor	Account No.	Address	Contact	Phone	Fax	Balance Total
Ace Glass Works	1245	Ace Glass Works Archie Ace 25 SE Como Ave. Minneapolis, MN 53602	Archie Ace	612-555-9812	612-555-6813	1,500.00
Bell Carpet Design	66-87874	Bell Carpet Design Bill Bell 55 North Main Ave. St. Paul, MN 54603	Bill Bell	651-555-8823	651-555-8824	2,000.00
Cone and Clemens Associates	KR569	Cone and Clemens Associates Carrie Cone 23 W. University Ave. St. Paul, MN 54603	Carrie Cone	651-555-8855	651-555-8856	400.00
Darren Tapestry	2365	Darren Tapestry Donna Darren 10 W. Larpenteur Ave. Minneapolis, MN 52604	Donna Darren	612-555-2221	612-555-2222	0.00
Galeway Computers	2455-897	Galeway Computers Roger Rivera 33 Route 10 Springfield, MA 24105	Roger Rivera	617-555-4747	617-555-4748	2,600.00
Giambi Graphics	33-2221	Giambi Graphics Gregg Giambi 56 Amity Way Bloomington, MN 53608	Gregg Giambi	612-555-0002	612-555-0003	0.00
Jeter Janitorial Services	555-32	Jeter Janitorial Services Jason Jeter 233 Lilac Rd. Minneapolis, MN 54302	Jason Jeter	612-555-4444	612-555-4445	0.00
Kristin Raina						0.00
Lumiare Lighting Company	36	Lumiare Lighting Company Larry Lyght 123 Glenwood Ave. Minneapolis, MN 53609	Larry Lyght	612-555-4790	612-555-4795	0.00
Midwest Mutual Insurance Co.	54778784	Midwest Mutual Insurance Co. Mike Mills 3566 Chicago, IL 58303	Mike Mills	805-555-4545	805-555-4546	2,400.00
Minn. Dept. of Revenue		Minn. Dept. of Revenue				0.00
Minneapolis Electric & Gas Co.	2001-23657	Minneapolis Electric & Gas Co. Jack Watts 150 Douglas Ave. St. Paul, MN 55303	Jack Watts	651-555-4949	651-555-4950	450.00
Nordic Realty	55-1212	Nordic Realty Melanie Marx 23 N. 12th Street Minneapolis, MN 53604	Melanie Marx	612-555-3232	612-555-3233	0.00
TwinCity Tel Co.	666-6667	TwinCity Tel Co. Terry Ameche 3223 River Dr. St. Paul, MN 53908	Terry Ameche	651-555-6667	651-555-6668	0.00
Weaver Fabrics	9878	Weaver Fabrics Jon Weaver 355 W. 70th Street Minneapolis, MN 53604	Jon Weaver	612-555-8777	612-555-8778	0.00
Williams Office Supply	55-8988	Williams Office Supply Bernard Williams 15 Grand Ave. S Minneapolis, MN 55404	Bernard Williams	612-555-2240	612-555-2241	400.00
Your Name Accounting Services	99-2001-XX	Your Name Accounting Services Your Name One Main Plaza St. Paul, MN 53602	Your Name	612-555-2222	612-555-2223	0.00

HYBRID METHOD OF NEW COMPANY SETUP

You have now learned two methods of New Company Setup. One method utilizes the EasyStep Interview window, the other does not. It is not necessary to use one method exclusive of the other. Once you have learned the procedures for each method, you can use both methods in setting up a company file. For example, maybe you wish to use the EasyStep Interview to set up the Chart of Accounts, allowing QuickBooks Pro to set up the system default accounts, but you opt to set up the Accounts Receivable by directly entering all of the information for a customer in the Customer:Job List window at one time. QuickBooks Pro accepts either method of New Company Setup and can accept a combination of both methods.

BACKING UP THE NEW COMPANY FILE

You should make a backup copy of the new company file in the event there is damage to the file or the computer. Using the procedures learned in previous chapters, make a backup copy of the new company file to your subfolder and/or a floppy and name it EX8 [Your Name] Kristin Raina Interior Designs. Restore the backup copy and change the company name to EX8 [Your Name] Kristin Raina Interior Designs.

Upon completion of the New Company Setup level of operation, updating the Lists, viewing and printing Reports, and making a backup copy of the new company file, your accounting records are now ready for recording daily activities. Activities would be recorded in the new company file using the procedures illustrated in the prior chapters.

PROCEDURE REVIEW

To create a new company file—
1. Click <u>F</u>ile, and then click <u>N</u>ew Company.
2. At the EasyStep Interview window, click <u>N</u>ext until you come to the page with the <u>S</u>kip Interview button.
3. Click <u>S</u>kip Interview.
4. At the Creating New Company window, enter the company information, and then click <u>N</u>ext.
5. At the Creating New Company window, click *No Type* and accept *No Accounts* by clicking <u>N</u>ext.
6. Save the new company file to your subfolder, and then click <u>S</u>ave.
7. At the Industry specific Documentation window, click <u>N</u>o.
8. The company file is created and saved. You enter QuickBooks Pro with the new company file open. Close the QuickBooks Navigator window.

To activate the account numbers option—
1. Click <u>E</u>dit, and then click Preferences.
2. Along the left frame of the Preferences window, click the *Accounting* icon.
3. Click the <u>C</u>ompany Preferences tab.
4. At the *Account Numbers* section, place a ✓ in the Use account <u>n</u>umbers to turn on the account numbers option.
5. Click OK. The account numbers option is activated.

To activate the inventory feature—
1. Click <u>E</u>dit, and then click Preferences.
2. Along the left frame of the Preferences window, click the *Purchases & Vendors* icon.
3. Click the <u>C</u>ompany Preferences tab.
4. At the *Purchase Orders and Inventory* section, place a ✓ in the <u>I</u>nventory and purchase orders are active to turn on the inventory feature.
5. Click OK.

To activate the sales tax feature—
1. Click <u>E</u>dit, and then click Preferences.
2. Along the left frame of the Preferences window, click the *Sales Tax* icon.
3. Click the <u>C</u>ompany Preferences tab.
4. At the *Do You Charge Sales Tax?* section, click <u>Y</u>es.
5. Move to the *Most common sales <u>t</u>ax* field and click the drop-down arrow.
6. Click < *Add New* >.
7. Key in the sales tax item information.
8. Move to the *Tax Agency* field and click the drop-down arrow.
9. At the Tax Agency drop-down list, click < *Add New* >.
10. Enter the appropriate vendor information, and then click OK.

11. Click OK at the completed New Item window, and then click OK at the Preferences window.
12. At the Updating Sales Tax dialog box, click OK.

To disable the payroll feature—
1. Click Edit, and then click Preferences.
2. Along the left frame of the Preferences window, click the *Payroll & Employees* icon.
3. Click the Company Preferences tab.
4. At the *QuickBooks Payroll Features* section, click *No Payroll*.
5. Click OK.

To set up payment terms—
1. Click Lists, and then click Customer & Vendor Profile Lists.
2. At the Customer & Vendor Profile Lists submenu, click Terms List.
3. At the Terms List window, click the Terms menu button.
4. At the Terms menu, click New.
5. At the New Terms window, key the appropriate information.
6. Click Next or OK.

To update the Chart of Accounts List—
1. Click Lists, and then click Chart of Accounts.
2. Click the Account menu button.
3. At the Account menu, click New.
4. At the New Account window, key the information, and then click Next or OK.

To update the Item List—
1. Click Lists, and then click Item List.
2. At the Item List window, click the Item menu button.
3. At the Item menu, click New.
4. At the New Item window, key the information, and then click Next or OK.

To edit the accounts created by QuickBooks Pro—
1. In the Chart of Accounts List window, select (highlight) the account created by QuickBooks Pro.
2. Click the Account menu button, and then from the Account menu, click Edit.
3. Change the account number and name to your preference.
4. Click OK.

To update the Customer:Job List—
1. Click Lists, and then click Customer:Job List.
2. At the Customer:Job List window, click the Customer:Job menu button.
3. At the Customer:Job menu, click New.
4. Enter the background data for the customer including the opening balance, if any, and the correct date.
5. Click Next or OK.

To update the Vendor List—
1. Click Lists, and then click Vendor List.
2. At the Vendor List window, click the Vendor menu button.
3. At the Vendor menu, click New.
4. Enter the background data for the vendor including the opening balance, if any, and the correct date.
5. Click Next or OK.

To enter opening balances in the General Journal Entry window—
1. Click Company, and then click Make Journal Entry.
2. Choose the date and make or accept an entry in the *Entry No.* field.
3. Enter the accounts and amounts to be debited.
4. Enter the accounts and amounts to be credited.
5. Record the balancing amount as a credit (or debit) to the capital account.
6. Click Save & Close.

To reverse the Uncategorized Revenue account—
1. Click Company, and then click Make Journal Entry.
2. Choose the date and make or accept an entry in the *Entry No.* field.
3. Debit the Uncategorized Income account for the full amount in that account and credit the Capital account for the same amount.
4. Click Save & Close.

To reverse the Uncategorized Expenses account—
1. Click Company, and then click Make Journal Entry.
2. Choose the date and make or accept an entry in the *Entry No.* field.
3. Debit the Capital account for the full amount in the Uncategorized Expenses account and credit the Uncategorized Expenses account for the same amount.
4. Click Save & Close.

To view and print accounting reports from the Reports menu—
1. Click Reports, and then click Accountants & Taxes.
2. At the Accountants & Taxes submenu, choose a report.
3. Indicate the start and end dates for the report.
4. Click Print on the command line.
5. At the Print Reports dialog box, review the settings, and then click Print.
6. Close the report.

To view and print financial reports from the Reports menu—
1. Click Reports, and then click Company & Financial.
2. At the Company & Financial submenu, choose a financial report.
3. Indicate the start and end dates for the report.
4. Click Print on the command line.
5. At the Print Reports dialog box, review the settings, and then click Print.
6. Close the report.

To view and print Lists from the Reports menu—
1. Click Reports, and then click List.
2. At the List submenu, choose a report.
3. Click Print on the command line.
4. At the Print Reports dialog box, review the settings, and then click Print.
5. Close the report.

KEY CONCEPTS

Select the letter of the item that best matches each definition.

a. Most common sales tax
b. Inactive
c. Uncategorized Income
d. Preferences – Accounting
e. Inventory Asset and Cost of Goods Sold
f. Preferences – Purchases & Vendors
g. Skip EasyStep Interview
h. System default accounts
i. Uncategorized Expenses
j. Customer & Vendor Profile Lists

_____ 1. An alternative method of New Company Setup.
_____ 2. Accounts automatically created by QuickBooks Pro when you choose an inventory item part in the New Item window.
_____ 3. An option you can choose so accounts not in use are not displayed in the reports.
_____ 4. Window used to activate account numbers.
_____ 5. Accounts automatically created by QuickBooks Pro.
_____ 6. Account created by QuickBooks Pro as an offsetting amount of Accounts Receivable.
_____ 7. Window used to activate the inventory feature.
_____ 8. Submenu used to open the Terms List window.
_____ 9. Field that must be completed to activate the sales tax feature.
_____10. Account created by QuickBooks Pro as an offsetting amount of Accounts Payable.

PROCEDURE CHECK

1. You are setting up a new company file and you wish to use the Skip EasyStep Interview method. Which preferences should be established before recording data?
2. When you first choose inventory part item in the New Item window of the Item List, which two accounts does QuickBooks Pro look for on the Chart of Accounts List? Can you customize these accounts? If so, explain how.
3. What is the Open Bal Equity account? Can you customize this account? If so, explain how.
4. If you set up a new company file using the Skip EasyStep Interview method, how are the accounts receivables and accounts payables recorded?
5. If you set up a new company file using the Skip EasyStep Interview method, which journal entries would you normally record to complete the New Company Setup process?

6. Your manager is just learning QuickBooks Pro. He asked you if it is necessary to use the EasyStep Interview window for New Company Setup. Provide the manager with a written explanation of how he could set up the new company file using the Skip EasyStep Interview window.

CASE PROBLEMS

CASE PROBLEM 1

On April 1, 2004, Lynn Garcia began her business, called Lynn's Music Studio. In the first month of business, Lynn set up the music studio, provided guitar and piano lessons, and recorded month-end activity. In May, the second month of business, Lynn started purchasing and selling inventory items of guitars, keyboards, music stands, and sheet music. In April and May, Lynn was recording the financial activities using a manual accounting system. On June 1, 2004, Lynn decides to switch her accounting method to QuickBooks Pro. Lynn has organized the information about the company, but has hired you to convert the accounting records to QuickBooks Pro.

1. Use the information below to create and set up the company file using the Skip EasyStep Interview method:

Company Name:	**CH8 [Your Name] Lynn's Music Studio**
Legal Name:	**CH8 [Your Name] Lynn's Music Studio**
Address:	**228 Pearl Street**
	Scranton, PA 18501
Phone #:	**570-555-0400**
FAX #:	**570-555-0500**
E-mail:	**LYNN@emcp.net**
First month in fiscal year:	**April 2004**
First month in tax year:	**January 2004**

2. Activate the account numbers, inventory, and sales tax features. For sales tax, use the following information:

Type:	**Sales Tax Item**
Tax Name:	**PA Sales Tax**
Description:	**Sales Tax**
Tax Rate (%):	**7**
Tax Agency:	**PA Dept. of Revenue**

3. Disable the Payroll.
4. Set up the following payment terms:

Net 30 Days	Net 10 Days
Net 15 Days	2/10, Net 30 Days

5. Use the information in table LMS – Accounts to update the Chart of Accounts List.

TABLE LMS – Accounts

Type	Number	Name
Bank	1010	Cash – Operating
Accounts Receivable	1200	Accounts Receivable
Other Current Asset	1265	Inventory of Keyboards
Other Current Asset	1270	Inventory of Music Stands
Other Current Asset	1275	Inventory of Sheet Music
Other Current Asset	1300	Music Supplies
Other Current Asset	1305	Office Supplies
Other Current Asset	1410	Prepaid Advertising
Other Current Asset	1420	Prepaid Insurance
Fixed Asset	1700	Music Instruments
Fixed Asset	1750	Accum. Dep., Music Instruments (subaccount of 1700)
Fixed Asset	1800	Furniture
Fixed Asset	1850	Accum. Dep., Furniture (subaccount of 1800)
Fixed Asset	1900	Computers
Fixed Asset	1950	Accum. Dep., Computers (subaccount of 1900)
Accounts Payable	2010	Accounts Payable
Other Current Liability	2020	Notes Payable
Other Current Liability	2030	Interest Payable
Equity	3020	Lynn Garcia, Drawings
Income	4010	Piano Lessons
Income	4020	Guitar Lessons
Income	4060	Sale of Guitars
Income	4065	Sale of Keyboards
Income	4070	Sale of Music Stands
Income	4075	Sale of Sheet Music
Income	4100	Sales Discounts
Cost of Goods Sold	5065	Cost of Keyboards Sold
Cost of Goods Sold	5070	Cost of Music Stands Sold
Cost of Goods Sold	5075	Cost of Sheet Music Sold
Cost of Goods Sold	5900	Inventory Adjustment
Expense	6075	Deprec. Exp., Music Instruments
Expense	6085	Deprec. Exp., Furniture
Expense	6095	Deprec. Exp., Computers
Expense	6150	Instrument Tuning
Expense	6200	Insurance Expense
Expense	6300	Music Supplies Expense
Expense	6325	Office Supplies Expense
Expense	6400	Rent Expense
Expense	6450	Telephone Expense
Expense	6500	Utilities Expense
Other Expense	7000	Interest Expense

6. Open the Item List window, open the New Item window, select *Inventory Part*, and then close the windows. Open the Enter Sales Receipts window, and then close the window.

7. Customize the following accounts in the Chart of Accounts List window:

Account		Change to	
1120	Inventory Asset	1260	Inventory of Guitars
1499	*Undeposited Funds	1250	Undeposited Funds
3000	Opening Balance Equity	3010	Lynn Garcia, Capital
5000	Cost of Goods Sold	5060	Cost of Guitars Sold

8. Use the information in table LMS – Inventory Items to update the Item List. For the inventory part items, be sure to use the date June 1, 2004.

TABLE LMS – Inventory Items

Item Name, Purchase and Sales Description	Cost	COGS Acct	Sales Price	Income Acct	Asset Acct	Reorder Point	On Hand	Total Value
Service Items (nontaxable):								
Guitar Lessons			$ 30	4020				
Piano Lessons			35	4010				
Inventory Part Items (taxable):								
Guitars	$50	5060	100	4060	1260	10	6	$ 300
Keyboards	75	5065	150	4065	1265	10	17	1,275
Music Stands	20	5070	40	4070	1270	10	17	340
Sheet Music	3	5075	6	4075	1275	50	165	495

9. Use the information in table LMS – Customers to update the Customer:Job List.

TABLE LMS – Customers

Customer/Company Name	Name/Contact	Address	Phone/Fax	Terms	Balance
Douglaston Senior Center	Herbie Richardson	574 S Beech Street Scranton, PA 18506	570-555-7748 570-555-8900	Net 30 Days	175.00
Highland School	Asst. Principal Office	115 Forrest Street Waymart, PA 18472	570-555-6963 570-555-6970	2/10, Net 30 Days	
Jefferson High School	Music Department	500 Apple Street Dunmore, PA 18512	570-555-9600 570-555-9700	2/10, Net 30 Days	
Mulligan Residence	Adam Smith	299 Hickory Lane Scranton, PA 18504	570-555-3325 570-555-3500	2/10, Net 30 Days	1575.90
Musical Youth Group	Dana Thompson	550 Marion Lane Scranton, PA 18504	570-555-6642 570-555-6700	Net 30 Days	
Patel Family	Ari Patel	574 Kenwood Drive Dickson City, PA 18519	570-555-1132	Net 30 Days	
Patterson Family	Jonathan Patterson	650 Memory Lane Dickson City, PA 18519	570-555-6321	Net 30 Days	
Schroeder Family	Betty Schroeder	98 Belmont Rd. Carbondale, PA 18407	570-555-1897	Net 30 Days	
Twin Lakes Elementary	Miss Brooks	515 Hobson Street Honesdale, PA 18431	570-555-4474 570-555-4485	2/10, Net 30 Days	

10. Use the information in table LMS – Vendors to update the Vendor List.

TABLE LMS – Vendors

Vendor/Company Name	Name/Contact	Address	Phone/Fax	Terms	Balance
Computer Town	Customer Service	1000 Carbondale Highway Scranton, PA 18502	570-555-1500 570-555-1550	Net 30 Days	2000.00
Katie's Keyboards	Katie Shea	158 Clay Road Scranton, PA 18505	570-555-7777 570-555-8888	Net 30 Days	1500.00
Lynn Garcia					
Melody Music Equipment	Melody Arhmand	780 Roselyn Ave. Scranton, PA 18505	570-555-1120 570-555-1125	Net 30 Days	
Mills Family Furniture	Edna Mills	150 Amelia Street Scranton, PA 18503	570-555-7144 570-555-7200	Net 30 Days	1500.00
Music Instruments, Inc.	Matilda Molloy	25 Monroe Ave. Scranton, PA 18505	570-555-9630 570-555-9635	Net 30 Days	
Mutual Insurance Company	Bob Maxwell	1 Main Street Honesdale, PA 18431	570-555-5600 570-555-5900	Net 30 Days	1200.00
Paper, Clips, and More	Justin Daves	157 Waymart Lane Waymart, PA 18472	570-555-8558 570-555-5555	Net 30 Days	350.00
Pioneer Phone	Customer Service	1000 Route 6 Carbondale, PA 18407	570-555-6000 570-555-6500	Net 15 Days	
Steamtown Electric	Customer Service	150 Vine Lane Scranton, PA 18501	570-555-2500 570-555-3000	Net 15 Days	
Strings, Sheets, & Such	Manuela Perez	250 Lincoln St. Scranton, PA 18505	570-555-3636 570-555-3700	Net 30 Days	
Tune Tones	Tony Tune	500 Monroe Ave. Dunmore, PA 18512	570-555-1111 570-555-2222	Net 30 Days	
Viewhill Realty	Matt Snyder	100 Commerce Blvd. Scranton, PA 18501	570-555-1000 570-555-1200	Net 15 Days	

11. Make three journal entries on June 1, 2004 (accept the default Entry Nos.):
    a. Enter the opening balances listed below. Accept Entry No. 1.
       Enter the following accounts and amounts as debits:

Number	Name	Balance
1010	Cash – Operating	$14,615.18
1300	Music Supplies	430.00
1305	Office Supplies	300.00
1420	Prepaid Insurance	1,100.00
1700	Music Instruments	4,000.00
1800	Furniture	2,500.00
1900	Computers	3,000.00
3020	Lynn Garcia, Drawings	1,000.00
4100	Sales Discounts	188.92
5060	Cost of Guitars Sold	1,150.00
5065	Cost of Keyboards Sold	2,475.00
5070	Cost of Music Stands Sold	460.00

5075	Cost of Sheet Music Sold	1,305.00
5900	Inventory Adjustment	50.00
6075	Deprec. Exp., Music Instruments	60.00
6085	Deprec. Exp., Furniture	40.00
6095	Deprec. Exp., Computers	35.00
6150	Instrument Tuning	100.00
6200	Insurance Expense	100.00
6300	Music Supplies Expense	70.00
6325	Office Supplies Expense	50.00
6400	Rent Expense	600.00
6450	Telephone Expense	50.00
6500	Utilities Expense	70.00
7000	Interest Expense	15.00

Enter the following accounts and amounts as credits:

Number	Name	Balance
1750	Accum. Dep., Music Instruments	$ 60.00
1850	Accum. Dep., Furniture	40.00
1950	Accum. Dep., Computers	35.00
2020	Notes Payable	2,000.00
2030	Interest Payable	15.00
4010	Piano Lessons	3,535.00
4020	Guitar Lessons	2,910.00
4060	Sale of Guitars	2,300.00
4065	Sale of Keyboards	4,950.00
4070	Sale of Music Stands	920.00
4075	Sale of Sheet Music	2,610.00

    b. Make a journal entry to reverse the Uncategorized Income account.
    c. Make a journal entry to reverse the Uncategorized Expenses account.

12. Display and print the following reports for June 1, 2004:

    a. *Journal*
    b. *Trial Balance*
    c. *Profit & Loss Standard*
    d. *Balance Sheet Standard*
    e. *Item Listing*
    f. *Customer Contact List*
    g. *Vendor Contact List*

13. Make a backup copy of the new company file. Use the name LMS8 [Your Name] Lynn's Music Studio. Restore the backup copy and change the company name to LMS8 [Your Name] Lynn's Music Studio.

CASE PROBLEM 2

On June 1, 2004, Olivia Chen began her business, called Olivia's Web Solutions. In the first month of business, Olivia set up the office, provided Web page design and Internet consulting services, and recorded month-end activity. In July, the second month of business, Olivia began to purchase and sell inventory items of computer hardware and software. In June and July, Olivia was recording the financial activities using a manual accounting system. On August 1, 2004, Olivia decides to switch her accounting method to QuickBooks Pro. Olivia has organized the information about the company, but has hired you to convert the accounting records to QuickBooks Pro.

1. Use the information below to create and set up the company file using the Skip EasyStep Interview method:

Company Name:	**CH8 [Your Name] Olivia's Web Solutions**
Legal Name:	**CH8 [Your Name] Olivia's Web Solutions**
Address:	**547 Miller Place**
	Westport, NY 11858
Phone #:	**516-555-5000**
FAX #:	**516-555-6000**
E-mail:	**LIV@emcp.net**
First month in fiscal year:	**June**
First month in tax year:	**January**

2. Activate the account numbers, inventory, and sales tax features. For sales tax, use the following information:

Type:	**Sales Tax Item**
Tax Name:	**NYS Sales Tax**
Description:	**Sales Tax**
Tax Rate (%):	**8**
Tax Agency:	**NYS Tax Dept.**

3. Disable the Payroll.
4. Set up the following payment terms:

   Net 30 Days
   Net 15 Days
   Net 10 Days
   2/10, Net 30 Days

5. Use the information in table OWS – Accounts to update the Chart of Accounts List.

TABLE OWS – Accounts

Type	Number	Name
Bank	1010	Cash – Operating
Accounts Receivable	1200	Accounts Receivable
Other Current Asset	1265	Inventory of Scanners
Other Current Asset	1270	Inventory of HTML Software
Other Current Asset	1275	Inventory of Desktop Pub. Soft.
Other Current Asset	1300	Computer Supplies
Other Current Asset	1305	Office Supplies
Other Current Asset	1410	Prepaid Advertising
Other Current Asset	1420	Prepaid Insurance
Fixed Asset	1700	Computers
Fixed Asset	1750	Accum. Dep., Computers (subaccount of 1700)
Fixed Asset	1800	Furniture
Fixed Asset	1850	Accum. Dep., Furniture (subaccount of 1800)
Fixed Asset	1900	Software
Fixed Asset	1950	Accum. Dep., Software (subaccount of 1900)
Accounts Payable	2010	Accounts Payable
Other Current Liability	2020	Notes Payable
Other Current Liability	2030	Interest Payable
Equity	3020	Olivia Chen, Drawings
Income	4010	Web Page Design Fees
Income	4020	Internet Consulting Fees
Income	4060	Sale of Computers
Income	4065	Sale of Scanners
Income	4070	Sale of HTML Software
Income	4075	Sale of Desktop Pub. Software
Income	4100	Sales Discounts
Cost of Goods Sold	5065	Cost of Scanners Sold
Cost of Goods Sold	5070	Cost of HTML Software Sold
Cost of Goods Sold	5075	Cost of Desktop Pub. Soft. Sold
Cost of Goods Sold	5900	Inventory Adjustment
Expense	6050	Advertising Expense
Expense	6075	Deprec. Exp., Computers
Expense	6085	Deprec. Exp., Furniture
Expense	6095	Deprec. Exp., Software
Expense	6100	Insurance Expense
Expense	6300	Computers Supplies Expense
Expense	6325	Office Supplies Expense
Expense	6350	Online Service Expense
Expense	6400	Rent Expense
Expense	6450	Telephone Expense
Expense	6500	Utility Expense
Other Expense	7000	Interest Expense

6. Open the Item List window, open the New Item window, select *Inventory Part*, and then close the windows. Open the Enter Sales Receipts window, and then close the window.

7. Customize the following accounts in the Chart of Accounts List window:

	Account		Change to
1120	Inventory Asset	1260	Inventory of Computers
1499	*Undeposited Funds	1250	Undeposited Funds
3000	Opening Balance Equity	3010	Olivia Chen, Capital
5000	Cost of Goods Sold	5060	Cost of Computers Sold

8. Use the information in table OWS – Inventory Items to update the Item List. For the inventory part items, be sure to use the date August 1, 2004.

TABLE OWS – Inventory Items

Item Name, Purchase and Sales Description	Cost	COGS Acct	Sales Price	Income Acct	Asset Acct	Reorder Point	On Hand	Total Value
Service Items (nontaxable):								
Internet Consulting Services			$ 100	4020				
Web Page Design Services			125	4010				
Inventory Part Items (taxable):								
Computers	$1,000	5060	2,000	4060	1260	3	10	$10,000
Scanners	300	5065	600	4065	1265	5	12	3,600
HTML Software	75	5070	150	4070	1270	5	18	1,350
Desktop Pub. Software	100	5075	200	4075	1275	5	10	1,000

9. Use the information in table OWS – Customers to update the Customer:Job List.

TABLE OWS - Customers

Customer/Company Name	Name/Contact	Address	Phone/Fax	Terms	Balance
Artie's Auto Repair	Leon Artie	32 W. 11th Street New Hyde Park, NY 11523	516-555-1221 516-555-1231	Net 30 Days	800.00
Breathe Easy A/C Contractors	Allen Scott	556 Atlantic Ave. Freeport, NY 11634	516-555-6868 516-555-6869	Net 30 Days	
Long Island Water Works	Customer Service	87-54 Bayview Ave. Glen Cove, NY 11563	516-555-4747 516-555-4748	2/10, Net 30 Days	
Miguel's Restaurant	Miguel Perez	30 Willis Ave. Roslyn, NY 11541	516-555-3236 516-555-3237	2/10, Net 30 Days	
Schneider Family	Johnny Schneider	363 Farmers Rd. Syosset, NY 11547	516-555-8989 516-555-8990	Net 15 Days	1,000.00
Sehorn & Smith Attorneys	Jerry Sehorn	510 Fifth Ave. New York, NY 10022	212-555-3339 212-555-3338	Net 30 Days	800.00
Singh Family	David Singh	363 Marathon Parkway Little Neck, NY 11566	718-555-3233 718-555-3239	Net 15 Days	
South Shore School District	Joseph Porter	3666 Ocean Ave. South Beach, NY 11365	516-555-4545 516-555-4546	2/10, Net 30 Days	12,056.00
Thrifty Stores	William Way	23 Boston Ave. Bronx, NY 11693	718-555-2445 718-555-2446	Net 30 Days	1,500.00

10. Use the information in table OWS – Vendors to update the Vendor List.

TABLE OWS – Vendors

Vendor/Company Name	Name/Contact	Address	Phone/Fax	Terms	Balance
ARC Management	Alvin R. Clinton	668 Lakeville Ave. Garden City, NY 11678	516-555-6363 516-555-6364	Net 30 Days	
Chrbet Advertising	Chris Chrbet	201 E. 10th Street New York, NY 10012	212-555-8777 212-555-8778	Net 30 Days	1,200.00
Comet Computer Supplies	Customer Service	657 Motor Parkway Center Island, NY 11488	631-555-4444 631-555-4455	Net 15 Days	
Computec Computers	Customer Service	3631 Gate Blvd. Greenboro, NC 27407	705-555-6564 702-555-6563	Net 30 Days	10,000.00
Eastel	Customer Service	655 Fifth Ave. New York, NY 10012	212-555-6565 212-555-6566	Net 30 Days	350.00
Eastern Mutual Insurance	Customer Service	55 Broadway Room 55 New York, NY 10001	212-555-6363 212-555-6364	Net 30 Days	
InterSoft Development Co.	Customer Service	556 Route 347 Hauppauge, NY 11654	631-555-3634 631-555-3635	Net 30 Days	
Lewis Furniture Co.	Manny Lewis	1225 Route 110 Farmingdale, NY 11898	631-555-6161 631-555-6162	Net 30 Days	1,700.00
LI Power Company	Customer Service	5444 Northern Blvd. Plainview, NY 11544	516-555-8888 516-555-8889	Net 15 Days	
Martin Computer Repairs	Ken Martin	366 N. Franklin St. Garden City, NY 11568	516-555-7777 516-555-7778	Net 30 Days	
Netsoft Development Co.	Customer Service	684 Mountain View Rd. Portland, OR 68774	974-555-7873 974-555-7874	Net 30 Days	1,600.00
Office Plus	Customer Service	45 Jericho Tpke. Jericho, NY 11654	516-555-3214 516-555-3213	Net 30 Days	375.00
Olivia Chen					
Scanntronix	Customer Service	2554 Bedford Rd. Boston, MA 02164	617-555-8778 617-555-8776	Net 30 Days	
Systems Service	Jeremy Jones	36 Sunrise Lane Hempstead, NY 11004	516-555-2525 516-555-2526	Net 30 Days	
Textpro Software, Inc.	Customer Service	877 Route 5 Ft. Lauderdale, FL 70089	615-555-4545 615-555-4546	Net 30 Days	

11. Make three journal entries on August 1, 2004 (accept the default Entry Nos.):

    a. Enter the opening balances listed below.

Enter the following accounts and amounts as debits:

Number	Name	Balance
1010	Cash – Operating	$24,489.16
1300	Computer Supplies	350.00
1305	Office Supplies	325.00
1410	Prepaid Advertising	1,000.00
1420	Prepaid Insurance	1,650.00
1700	Computers	5,000.00
1800	Furniture	3,200.00
1900	Software	3,600.00
3020	Olivia Chen, Drawings	500.00
4100	Sales Discounts	179.84

5060	Cost of Computers Sold	10,000.00
5065	Cost of Scanners Sold	2,400.00
5070	Cost of HTML Software Sold	75.00
5075	Cost of Desktop Pub. Soft. Sold	500.00
5900	Inventory Adjustment	75.00
6050	Advertising Expense	200.00
6075	Deprec. Exp., Computers	75.00
6085	Deprec. Exp., Furniture	50.00
6095	Deprec. Exp., Software	100.00
6100	Insurance Expense	150.00
6300	Computer Supplies Expense	250.00
6325	Office Supplies Expense	50.00
6350	Online Service Expense	150.00
6400	Rent Expense	800.00
6450	Telephone Expense	350.00
6500	Utility Expense	125.00
7000	Interest Expense	25.00

Enter the following accounts and amounts as credits:

Number	Name	Balance
1750	Accum. Dep., Computers	$ 75.00
1850	Accum. Dep., Furniture	50.00
1950	Accum. Dep., Software	100.00
2020	Notes Payable	2,500.00
2030	Interest Payable	25.00
4010	Web Page Design Fees	9,750.00
4020	Internet Consulting Fees	6,600.00
4060	Sale of Computers	20,000.00
4065	Sale of Scanners	4,800.00
4070	Sale of HTML Software	150.00
4075	Sale of Desktop Pub. Software	1,000.00

    b. Make a journal entry to reverse the Uncategorized Income account.
    c. Make a journal entry to reverse the Uncategorized Expenses account.

12. Display and print the following reports for August 1, 2004:

    a. *Journal*
    b. *Trial Balance*
    c. *Profit & Loss Standard*
    d. *Balance Sheet Standard*
    e. *Item Listing*
    f. *Customer Contact List*
    g. *Vendor Contact List*

13. Make a backup copy of the new company file. Use the name OWS8 [Your Name] Olivia's Web Solutions. Restore the backup copy and change the company name to OWS8 [Your Name] Olivia's Web Solutions.

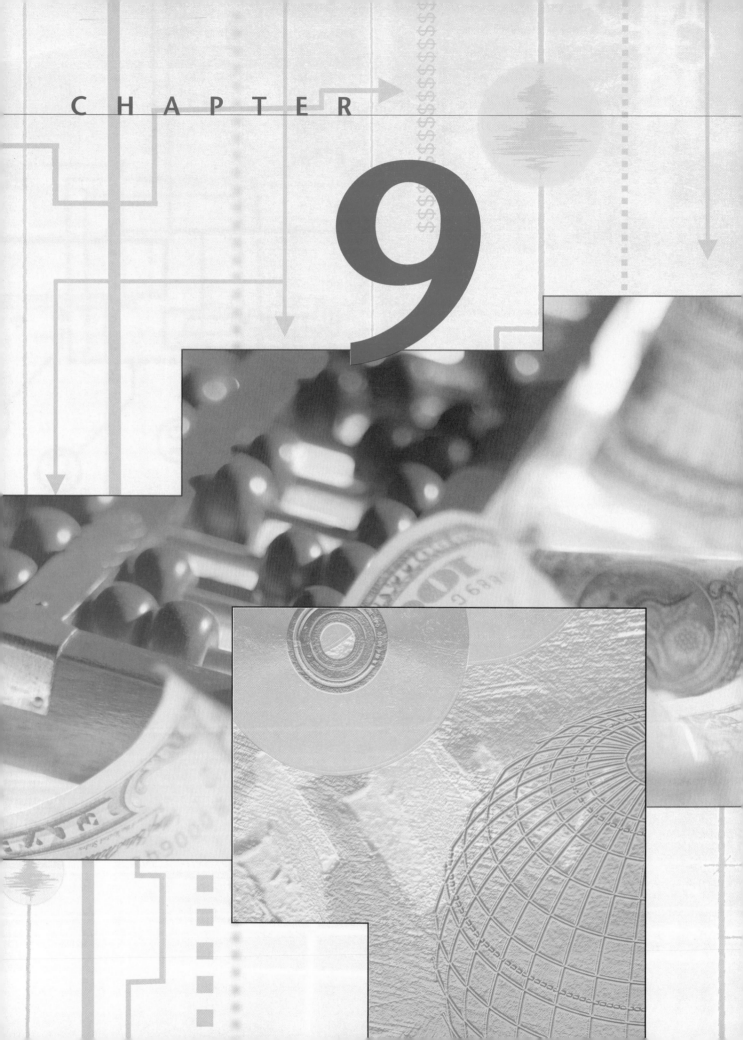

CHAPTER

9

PAYROLL SETUP and PROCESSING

Pay Employees, Pay Payroll Liabilities, and Process Payroll Forms

CHAPTER OBJECTIVES

- Review payroll terminology and accounting

- Set up payroll

- Update the Chart of Accounts List for payroll

- Update the Payroll Item List

- Update the Employee List

- Record payroll in the Pay Employees windows

- Record payments of payroll taxes in the Pay Liabilities window

- Display and print payroll-related reports

INTRODUCTION

employee Someone hired by the company who will receive salary or wages on a regular basis.

QuickBooks Pro allows you to process payroll and track payroll information for your company's **employees.** You can establish a file for each employee and then process payroll transactions. These employee files comprise the *Employee List*. In addition, a file for each type of payroll item, such as the income, payroll tax, or payroll deduction, needs to be established. These payroll items comprise the *Payroll Item List*.

Once you have established an employee file, you can enter transactions for payroll (Activities) in the *Pay Employees* and *Pay Liabilities* windows. Every time your company processes payroll for employees in the activities windows, QuickBooks Pro simultaneously updates the information in the Employee List. In addition, QuickBooks Pro changes balance sheet and income statement accounts based upon payroll transactions entered in the payroll activities windows.

In this chapter, our sample company, Kristin Raina Interior Designs, will hire and pay two employees beginning April 1, 2004. Kristin Raina will have to establish an employee file for each employee in the Employee List and enter the appropriate payroll items in the Payroll Item List prior to recording payroll transactions.

QUICKBOOKS PRO VERSUS MANUAL ACCOUNTING: PAYROLL

payroll journal (register) A journal used to calculate payroll and record payroll entries for each employee.

In a manual accounting system, employee pay transactions are usually recorded in a **Payroll Journal** or **Register.** The employee's gross pay, tax withholding, and other payroll deductions are calculated in the journal using the employee's background information (pay rate, marital status, state of residency, and so on) along with the applicable tax schedules. Payroll checks and tax remittance checks are usually recorded in the Cash Payments Journal.

In QuickBooks Pro, the Employee List contains background information for each employee, such as name, address, Social Security number, pay rate, and applicable tax deductions. The Payroll Item List contains a file for all payroll items such as taxes and withholdings affecting the pay computation for the company.

When the company processes payroll, the transactions are recorded in the Pay Employees window. QuickBooks Pro uses the information entered in the Employee List along with the items on the Payroll Item List applicable to the employee to determine gross pay, payroll deductions, and net pay in the Pay Employees window.

When payroll tax liabilities are paid, the Pay Liabilities window is used to record the transaction. These transactions update the Chart of Accounts List (general ledger) while at the same time updating the employee's file.

In both manual and computerized systems, payroll reports will be generated and forwarded periodically to the appropriate federal and state tax authorities. In QuickBooks Pro, these payroll forms are prepared using the Process Payroll Forms window.

PAYROLL DEFINITIONS AND TERMS

Whether payroll is processed manually or with a software package, the laws, procedures, filing requirements, definitions, and terminology remain the same. The following is a brief review of the steps to process payroll and some of the more common payroll definitions.

EMPLOYEE PAYROLL INFORMATION

In order to properly determine an employee's gross pay, tax withholding, deductions, and net pay, and to meet federal and state record keeping requirements, the employer needs specific information about the employee. This information includes, but is not limited to—

- Name
- Address
- Social Security number
- Marital status
- Gross pay amount or hourly rate
- Tax withholding allowances
- Voluntary deductions (pensions, 401K, insurance, and so on)

The employer uses this information along with the applicable tax rates to compute the employee's paycheck and track the employee's pay information.

GROSS PAY

gross pay Total earnings for an employee for a specific pay period before deductions.

Gross pay is the total earnings for the employee for a specific pay period before any deductions. Compensation can be in the form of a salary, hourly wages, tips, commissions, bonus, and overtime earned during a pay period. If the employee is paid based upon an annual salary, the annual figure is divided over the number of pay periods in the year. Gross pay for hourly workers is determined based on the number of hours worked during the pay period multiplied by the employee's hourly pay rate. The gross pay will be subject to payroll taxes, for both the employer and employee.

FICA TAX (SOCIAL SECURITY) AND MEDICARE TAX

The Federal Insurance Contribution Act (FICA) tax, also known as Social Security, is a tax imposed on both the employer and employee at a rate for each of 6.2% of the first $87,000 (year 2003) of wages for each employee. Medicare tax is also imposed on both the employer and the employee at a rate for each of 1.45%—there is no wage ceiling for the Medicare tax. The employer periodically remits both the employer and employee portion of the tax to the federal government.

FEDERAL INCOME TAX (FIT)

Employers are required to withhold from each employee's pay the appropriate amount of federal income tax (FIT). The Internal Revenue Service publishes tables and instructions in order to assist employers in determining the proper withholding amount for each employee. The withholding amount is determined based upon the employee's gross pay, marital status, and exemption allowances claimed. The employer periodically forwards the tax withheld to the federal government along with the Social Security and Medicare taxes.

STATE INCOME TAX (SIT)

Many states impose an income tax and require employers to withhold the tax from the employees' pay, in a manner similar to that used for FIT. The employer will remit this tax periodically to the appropriate state taxing authority. Some local governments (city, county) may also impose income taxes. Rules for withholding local taxes for local governments are similar to those used by federal and state governments.

FEDERAL UNEMPLOYMENT INSURANCE TAX (FUTA)

The Federal Unemployment Insurance (FUTA) tax is imposed on the employer only. The tax is used to fund unemployment insurance programs administered by the federal government. The effective rate of the tax is .8% (.008) of the first $7,000 of each employee's wages.

STATE UNEMPLOYMENT INSURANCE (SUI)

In addition to paying the FUTA tax, employers are required by all states to contribute to a state unemployment insurance (SUI) fund. Rates and regulations vary from state to state. However, most states impose the tax only on the employer. The rates can vary from 1% to 8% based upon the employer's location and unemployment experience, and the taxable amount will vary from state to state.

STATE DISABILITY INSURANCE (SDI)

Most states require employers to purchase an insurance policy, sometimes called state disability insurance (SDI), that will compensate employees if they are unable to work for an extended period due to illness or injury. Some states allow employers to withhold a small amount from each employee's pay to defray the employer's insurance premium cost.

COMPANY DEDUCTIONS

Many employers will sponsor various fringe benefit programs and deduct amounts from employee's pay to fund or offset the costs of the benefits. Programs such as 401K plans, medical and dental insurance, pension and profit sharing plans, long-term disability, life insurance, and so on may be partially funded by a deduction made by the company from an employee's paycheck.

NET PAY

net pay Total earnings for an employee minus all employee deductions.

Net pay is the amount of the employee's gross pay less all employee deductions. As anyone who has worked knows, net pay is only a fraction of the gross pay earned.

INTERNAL REVENUE SERVICE (IRS)

The Internal Revenue Service (IRS) is the tax-collecting agency of the federal government. The IRS is responsible for collecting the FICA tax, Medicare tax, FIT, and the FUTA tax.

ACCOUNTING FOR PAYROLL TRANSACTIONS

When a company generates a paycheck, the transaction affects a number of expense and liability accounts.

The employee's gross pay is an expense the company records at the payroll date. Additional expenses for the company include the various taxes imposed on the employer including, but not limited to, Social Security Tax (FICA), Medicare Tax, Federal Unemployment Insurance (FUTA), and State Unemployment Insurance (SUI) recorded in the appropriate expense accounts at the payroll date.

The employee, at a minimum, will have amounts for FICA, Medicare, federal income tax, and state income tax (if applicable) deducted from his or her paycheck by the employer. These withheld taxes, along with the taxes imposed on the employer, are recorded as liabilities on the books of the company because the company is responsible for remitting these taxes to the appropriate governmental tax-collecting agency at a later date.

The gross pay less the employee deductions results in a net payroll check to the employee. The following example illustrates the effect one paycheck has on the general ledger:

Company A has one employee who earns an annual salary of $48,000 per year. The company pays its employees semimonthly, on the 15th and last day of the month. Therefore, there are 24 pay periods in the year. Consequently, our employee will earn $2,000 of salary income for each pay period. The employee is subject to FICA (6.2% of $2,000 = $124); Medicare tax (1.45% of $2,000 = $29); FIT ($300); and SIT ($100); with a resulting net pay of $1,447. The employer is also subject to the matching FICA tax and Medicare tax along with FUTA (.8% of $2,000 = $16) and SUI (3% of $2,000 = $60). The journal entry to record the employee's earnings, deductions, and net pay is as follows:

Salaries Expense	2 0 0 0			
Social Security/Medicare Tax Payable			1 5 3	
($124 + $29)				
FIT Payable			3 0 0	
SIT Payable			1 0 0	
Cash – Payroll			1 4 4 7	

Many companies use a separate checking account for payroll transactions. Periodically, funds are transferred into this account from the operating account. Having a separate checking account helps track payroll transactions.

In addition, the journal entry of the employer's payroll tax expenses is recorded on the paycheck date as follows:

Social Security/Medicare Tax Expense	1 5 3			
FUTA Expense (.008 X $2,000)	1 6			
SUI Expense (.03 X $2,000)	6 0			
Social Security/Medicare Tax Payable			1 5 3	
FUTA Payable			1 6	
SUI Payable			6 0	

When the company remits the employer and employee taxes to the federal and local governments, it records several journal entries. Payment for the employer and employee Social Security tax and Medicare tax, the employee federal withholding, and the FUTA tax will be forwarded to the federal government. The journal entry is as follows:

	Social Security/Medicare Tax Payable	3 0 6			
	($153 + $153)				
	FIT Payable	3 0 0			
	FUTA Payable	1 6			
	Cash – Payroll			6 2 2	

Payment for the state withholding tax and the SUI is usually made with one check payable to the state taxing authority responsible for these taxes. In some states, two checks have to be sent because two different tax agencies are responsible.

	SIT Payable	1 0 0			
	SUI Payable	6 0			
	Cash – Payroll			1 6 0	

As you can see, the journal entries for the foregoing transactions can be complex since a number of general ledger accounts are affected. In addition, federal and state payroll and compliance laws are detailed and burdensome, with costly penalties for noncompliance. As a result, payroll accounting is a time-consuming process that can result in costly errors and omissions.

Prior to the availability of low-cost, off-the-shelf accounting software, most small companies either processed payroll manually or utilized outside computerized payroll services that charged per check. With the coming of QuickBooks Pro and other general ledger software packages, small companies can now process payroll; determine gross pay, tax expenses, and tax liabilities; and prepare employee paychecks and payroll data in compliance with federal and state payroll regulations.

CHAPTER PROBLEM

In this chapter, Kristin Raina Interior Designs will hire two employees and begin to process payroll during the month of April 2004. You will enter information for each employee in the Employee List. The April 1 beginning balances for the company are contained in the company file CH9 Kristin Raina Interior Designs.

Before you begin the chapter, open the company file CH9 Kristin Raina Interior Designs.QBW. Make a backup copy of the file, name it **EX9 [Your Name] Kristin Raina Interior Designs**, and then restore the file. Finally, change the company name in the file to **EX9 [Your Name] Kristin Raina Interior Designs**.

PAYROLL SETUP

If you set up a new company file by skipping the EasyStep Interview window, QuickBooks Pro automatically activates the payroll feature. However, if you set up a new company file using the EasyStep Interview window, you have the choice of disabling the payroll feature. In this company file, the payroll feature was disabled and needs to be activated in the Preferences window on the Edit menu.

To activate the QuickBooks Pro payroll feature—

1. Click Edit, and then click Preferences.
2. Along the left frame of the Preferences window, click the *Payroll & Employees* icon.
3. Click the Company Preferences tab. If the payroll processing feature is not activated, the No payroll button is selected.
4. Click the Full payroll features button. (See figure 9–1)

FIGURE 9-1
*Preferences Window –
Payroll & Employees –
Company
Preferences Tab*

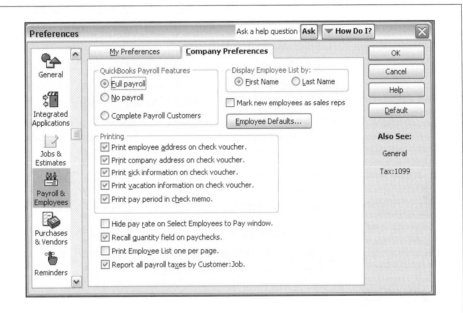

5. Accept the defaults and click OK.

Like most computerized accounting packages, QuickBooks Pro offers payroll services. If the company has subscribed to one of the QuickBooks Pro payroll services, taxes imposed on employers and employee withholdings for taxes are automatically computed based upon the data in the employee's file along with tax table information provided by the QuickBooks Pro tax service. If the company has not subscribed to a QuickBooks Pro tax service, then you must enter tax information manually.

Once you have activated the Payroll feature, QuickBooks Pro automatically establishes a Payroll Item List with several standard payroll items on it. In addition, QuickBooks Pro creates two default general ledger accounts: Payroll Liabilities and Payroll Expenses. These default settings may need to be modified based upon your company's background information and general ledger.

PRACTICE *exercise*

Open and review the Chart of Accounts List. Find the accounts QuickBooks Pro created when you turned on the payroll feature (*2100 Payroll Liabilities* and *6560 Payroll Expenses*). Open each account in the *Edit* mode and notice the account type for both is dimmed.

Recall that when QuickBooks Pro creates an account and dims the account type, this indicates that the account is a system default account. The account number and name can be edited, but not the account type. QuickBooks Pro looks for system default accounts when items are added to the Lists and activities are recorded in the windows.

LISTS: UPDATING THE CHART OF ACCOUNTS FOR PAYROLL

When the payroll feature is activated, QuickBooks Pro establishes one default general ledger liability posting account for *all* payroll-related liabilities and one expense account for *all* payroll expenses. Left unchanged, all payroll liabilities (FIT, SIT, Social Security, Medicare, and so on) are posted to the one liability account. Similarly, employee salary expense and all employer payroll tax expenses (Social Security, Medicare, FUTA, SUI, and so on) are posted to a single expense account. However, a company usually posts salary expense, each type of employer payroll tax expense, and each type of liability to separate general ledger accounts. Therefore, you must update the Chart of Accounts List to create separate payroll liabilities and expense accounts.

ADDING PAYROLL ACCOUNTS

Using the procedures reviewed in chapter 4, add the payroll accounts listed below to the Chart of Accounts List.

HINT

To add an account, click the Account button in the Chart of Accounts List window, and then click New.

Other Current Liability account type:

2110	Social Sec/Medicare Tax Payable	Subaccount of 2100 Payroll Liabilities
2115	FIT Payable	Subaccount of 2100 Payroll Liabilities
2120	SIT Payable	Subaccount of 2100 Payroll Liabilities
2125	FUTA Payable	Subaccount of 2100 Payroll Liabilities
2130	SUI Payable	Subaccount of 2100 Payroll Liabilities

Expense account type:

HINT

Use Edit from the Account menu in the Chart of Accounts List window to correct any errors.

6565	Salaries and Wages Expense	Subaccount of 6560 Payroll Expenses
6610	Social Sec/Medicare Tax Expense	Subaccount of 6560 Payroll Expenses
6625	FUTA Expense	Subaccount of 6560 Payroll Expenses
6630	SUI Expense	Subaccount of 6560 Payroll Expenses

QuickCheck: The updated Account Listing appears in figure 9–2.

FIGURE 9-2

Updated Account Listing

EX9 [Your Name] Kristin Raina Interior Designs
Account Listing
April 1, 2004

Account	Type	Balance Total	Accnt. #	Tax Line
1010 · Cash - Operating	Bank	43,355.38	1010	<Unassigned>
1020 · Cash - Payroll	Bank	7,500.00	1020	<Unassigned>
1200 · Accounts Receivable	Accounts Receivable	1,540.00	1200	<Unassigned>
1250 · Undeposited Funds	Other Current Asset	0.00	1250	<Unassigned>
1260 · Inventory of Carpets	Other Current Asset	800.00	1260	<Unassigned>
1265 · Inventory of Draperies	Other Current Asset	1,000.00	1265	<Unassigned>
1270 · Inventory of Lamps	Other Current Asset	1,000.00	1270	<Unassigned>
1275 · Inventory of Mirrors	Other Current Asset	900.00	1275	<Unassigned>
1300 · Design Supplies	Other Current Asset	200.00	1300	<Unassigned>
1305 · Office Supplies	Other Current Asset	250.00	1305	<Unassigned>
1410 · Prepaid Advertising	Other Current Asset	500.00	1410	<Unassigned>
1420 · Prepaid Insurance	Other Current Asset	2,200.00	1420	<Unassigned>
1700 · Furniture	Fixed Asset	11,900.00	1700	<Unassigned>
1700 · Furniture:1750 · Accum. Dep., Furniture	Fixed Asset	-100.00	1750	<Unassigned>
1800 · Computers	Fixed Asset	3,540.00	1800	<Unassigned>
1800 · Computers:1850 · Accum. Dep., Computers	Fixed Asset	-60.00	1850	<Unassigned>
2010 · Accounts Payable	Accounts Payable	9,750.00	2010	<Unassigned>
2020 · Notes Payable	Other Current Liability	7,000.00	2020	<Unassigned>
2030 · Interest Payable	Other Current Liability	50.00	2030	<Unassigned>
2100 · Payroll Liabilities	Other Current Liability	0.00	2100	<Unassigned>
2100 · Payroll Liabilities:2110 · Social Sec/Medicare Tax Payable	Other Current Liability	0.00	2110	<Unassigned>
2100 · Payroll Liabilities:2115 · FIT Payable	Other Current Liability	0.00	2115	<Unassigned>
2100 · Payroll Liabilities:2125 · FUTA Payable	Other Current Liability	0.00	2125	<Unassigned>
2100 · Payroll Liabilities:2130 · SUI Payable	Other Current Liability	0.00	2130	<Unassigned>
2200 · Sales Tax Payable	Other Current Liability	0.00	2200	<Unassigned>
3010 · Kristin Raina, Capital	Equity	50,000.00	3010	<Unassigned>
3020 · Kristin Raina, Drawings	Equity	-400.00	3020	<Unassigned>
3900 · Retained Earnings	Equity		3900	<Unassigned>
4010 · Design Services	Income		4010	<Unassigned>
4020 · Decorating Services	Income		4020	<Unassigned>
4060 · Sale of Carpets	Income		4060	<Unassigned>
4065 · Sale of Draperies	Income		4065	<Unassigned>
4070 · Sale of Lamps	Income		4070	<Unassigned>
4075 · Sale of Mirrors	Income		4075	<Unassigned>
4100 · Sales Discounts	Income		4100	<Unassigned>
5060 · Cost of Carpets Sold	Cost of Goods Sold		5060	<Unassigned>
5065 · Cost of Draperies Sold	Cost of Goods Sold		5065	<Unassigned>
5070 · Cost of Lamps Sold	Cost of Goods Sold		5070	<Unassigned>
5075 · Cost of Mirrors Sold	Cost of Goods Sold		5075	<Unassigned>
5900 · Inventory Adjustment	Cost of Goods Sold		5900	<Unassigned>
6020 · Accounting Expense	Expense		6020	<Unassigned>
6050 · Advertising Expense	Expense		6050	<Unassigned>
6175 · Deprec. Exp., Furniture	Expense		6175	<Unassigned>
6185 · Deprec. Exp., Computers	Expense		6185	<Unassigned>
6200 · Insurance Expense	Expense		6200	<Unassigned>
6300 · Janitorial Expenses	Expense		6300	<Unassigned>
6325 · Office Supplies Expense	Expense		6325	<Unassigned>
6400 · Rent Expense	Expense		6400	<Unassigned>
6450 · Telephone Expense	Expense		6450	<Unassigned>
6500 · Utilities Expense	Expense		6500	<Unassigned>
6560 · Payroll Expenses	Expense		6560	<Unassigned>
6560 · Payroll Expenses:6565 · Salaries and Wages Expense	Expense		6565	<Unassigned>
6560 · Payroll Expenses:6610 · Social Sec/Medicare Tax Expense	Expense		6610	<Unassigned>
6560 · Payroll Expenses:6625 · FUTA Expense	Expense		6625	<Unassigned>
6560 · Payroll Expenses:6630 · SUI Expense	Expense		6630	<Unassigned>
7000 · Interest Expense	Other Expense		7000	<Unassigned>

THE PAYROLL ITEM LIST

Once you have activated the payroll feature, QuickBooks Pro automatically sets up a Payroll Item List. The Payroll Item List contains an item for each type of payroll item that affects the company's employees. QuickBooks Pro automatically creates several standard payroll items including Social Security Company (FICA tax), Medicare Company (Medicare tax), federal withholding, and so on. Typically, you must modify the Payroll Item List based upon your company's geographic location, company deductions, and pay policies.

As you know, the second level of operation in QuickBooks Pro is to update the background information in the Lists. In prior chapters, you added, deleted, or edited vendor, customer, inventory items, and accounts files in order to keep each List current for your company. Now you will be updating the Payroll Item List to match the payroll information unique to your company.

To review the Payroll Item List created by QuickBooks Pro, click Lists, and then click Payroll Item List. Click No at the QuickBooks help menu. The Payroll Item List displays. (See figure 9–3).

FIGURE 9-3
Payroll Item List

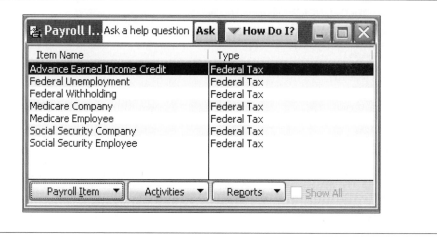

Notice that the payroll items initially created by QuickBooks Pro are the ones generally applicable to all payroll situations, such as Social Security, Medicare tax, Federal Withholding tax, Federal Unemployment tax, and so on.

To view a specific payroll item, such as Federal Withholding—
1. Double-click *Federal Withholding*. The Edit payroll item (Federal Withholding) window appears. (See figure 9–4.)

HINT

Use the scroll arrow to view additional payroll items not in view. Depending on the upgrades in your copy of QuickBooks Pro, you may have different items on the Payroll Item List.

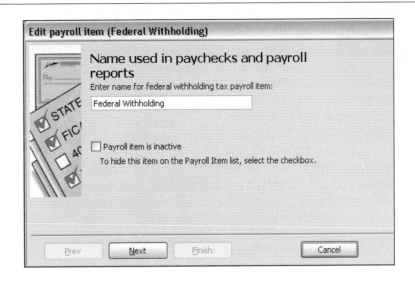

This window displays the name used in paychecks and payroll reports. The Edit payroll item window for each payroll item file displays several pages of information that are displayed each time you click <u>N</u>ext.

2. Click <u>N</u>ext, and the Agency for employee-paid liability page appears. (See figure 9–5.)

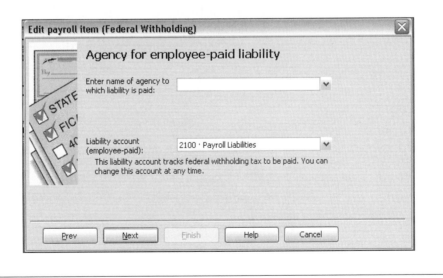

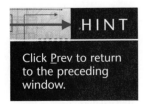

HINT

Click <u>P</u>rev to return to the preceding window.

This page displays the government agency to which payment should be forwarded and also shows the general ledger account for the tax liability. Remember, federal income tax withheld from the employees' paycheck is counted as a liability to the employer that at some point in time must be paid to the appropriate tax agency. The Edit payroll item (Federal Withholding) window – Agency for employee-paid liability page identifies that agency.

HINT

Depending on the upgrades included in your copy of QuickBooks Pro, there may be an additional page for pension items. If so, accept the defaults by clicking <u>N</u>ext or <u>F</u>inish.

3. Click <u>N</u>ext to move to the next page, Taxable compensation. This page indicates all items subject to federal income tax withholdings.
4. Accept the default by clicking <u>F</u>inish. You are returned to the Payroll Item List window.
5. Close the Payroll Item List.

ADDING A PAYROLL ITEM

In QuickBooks Pro there are two methods for adding a payroll item, the Easy Setup and the Custom Setup. The Easy Setup method is used for items such as salary and hourly wages. The Custom Setup method is used for both salary and wages along with the related payroll taxes and deductions. The Custom Setup method will be used in this text. In Custom Setup, the steps to set up the Payroll Items of salary and wages are slightly different than the steps to set up the Payroll Items of payroll withholdings and employer payroll taxes.

Adding a Salary and Wage Payroll Item

Kristin Raina wishes to add Salary to the Payroll Item List.

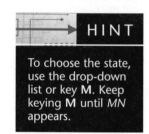

HINT

To choose the state, use the drop-down list or key **M**. Keep keying **M** until *MN* appears.

To add Salary to the Payroll Item List—
1. Click <u>L</u>ists, and then click Payroll Item <u>L</u>ist. Click <u>N</u>o at the QuickBooks help menu.

   (The Payroll Item List was not a choice on the <u>L</u>ists menu in prior chapters because the Payroll feature was not activated.)

2. At the Payroll Item List window, click the Payroll <u>I</u>tem menu button.
3. At the Payroll Item menu, click New. The Add a new payroll item window with the Select setup method page appears. For each payroll item listed at the Payroll item type page, there are several pages of information that are displayed as you click <u>N</u>ext. (See figure 9-6.)

FIGURE 9-6
Add New Payroll Item
Window – Select Setup
Method Page

4. At the Select setup method page, click the <u>C</u>ustom Setup option, and then click <u>N</u>ext. The Payroll item type page appears.

This second page in the Add new payroll item window lists the types of payroll items you can create.

5. At the Payroll item type list, click *Wage (Hourly, Salary, Commission, Bonus)*. (See figure 9-7.)

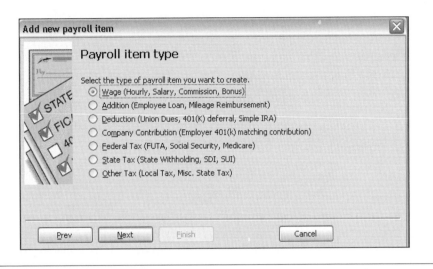

6. If the information is correct, click Next. The Wages page appears.
7. Choose the *Salary Wages* option. (See figure 9-8.)

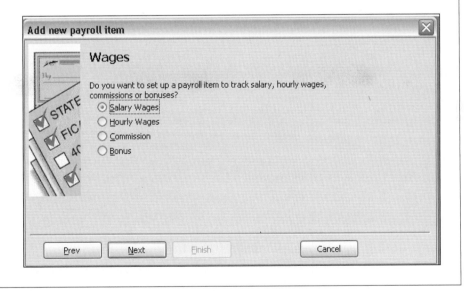

8. If the information is correct, click Next. The next page lets you indicate the type of pay: regular, sick, or vacation.
9. Choose *Regular Pay*. (See figure 9-9.)

FIGURE 9-9
Add New Payroll Item (Salary) Window – Wages Page

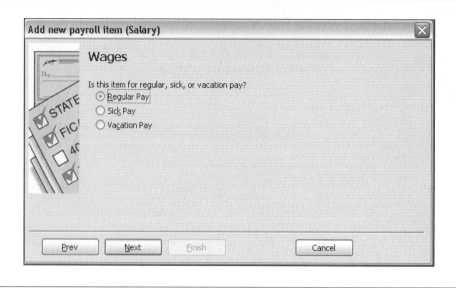

10. If the information is correct click <u>N</u>ext. The next page that appears assigns a name for the item on paychecks and reports.
11. At the *Enter name for salary item* field, key **Salary** and then click <u>N</u>ext. The next page that appears records the general ledger account for Salary expense.
12. At the *Enter the account for tracking this expense* field, click *6565 Salaries and Wages* from the drop-down list. (See figure 9-10.)

FIGURE 9-10
Add New Payroll Item (Salary:Salary) Window – Expense Account Page

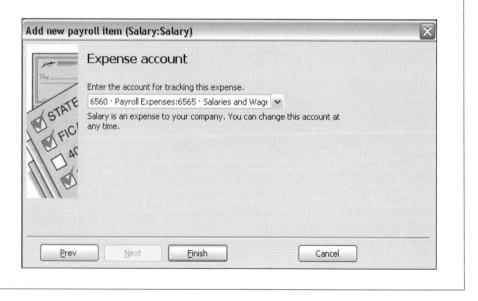

13. If the information is correct, click <u>F</u>inish. You are returned to the Payroll Item List window with the new item included. (See figure 9-11.)

FIGURE 9-11
*Payroll Item List Window
with New Payroll Item*

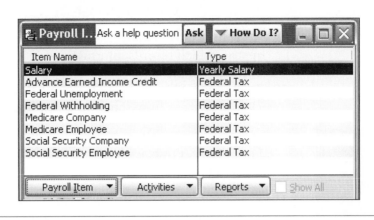

14. Close the Payroll Item List.

Adding a Payroll Withholding Payroll Item

Kristin Raina wishes to add Minnesota state income tax to the Payroll Item List.

To add Minnesota state income tax to the Payroll Item List—

1. Click <u>L</u>ists, and then click Payroll Item List. Click <u>N</u>o at the QuickBooks help window, if it appears.
2. At the Payroll Item List window, click the Payroll <u>I</u>tem menu button.
3. At the Payroll Item menu, click New. The Add a new payroll item window with the Select setup method page appears.
4. At the Select a setup method page, click the <u>C</u>ustom Setup option, and then click <u>N</u>ext. The Payroll item type page appears.
5. At the Payroll item type list, click *State Tax (State Withholding, SDI, SUI)* and then click <u>N</u>ext. The State tax page appears.
6. At the Enter the state drop-down list, click *MN*.
7. At the *Select the type of tax you want to create* field, click *State Withholding*. (See figure 9–12.)

FIGURE 9-12
*Add New Payroll Item
Window – State Tax Page*

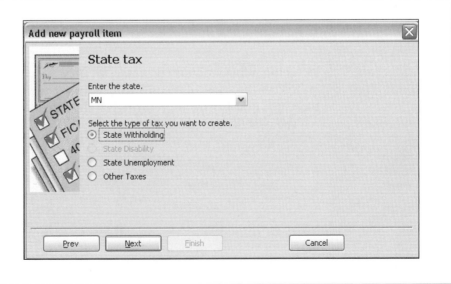

8. If the information is correct, click <u>N</u>ext.

The next page appears which assigns a name for the tax for paycheck and payroll reporting purposes.

9. Accept the default name assigned and click <u>N</u>ext. The next page appears which records information for tax vendors and general ledger posting accounts.

10. At the *Enter name of agency to which liability is paid* field, click *Minn. Dept. of Revenue* from the drop-down list.

Since the company will be writing a check to this government agency, QuickBooks Pro considers it a vendor of the company and adds it to the Vendor List.

11. At the *Enter the number that identifies you to agency* field, key **33-477781**.

12. At the *Liability account (employee-paid)* field, click *2120 SIT Payable*. Both the parent account, *2100 Payroll Liabilities*, and the subaccount, *2120 SIT Payable*, are displayed. (See figure 9–13.)

HINT

This is the same ID number you used in the Company Information window and entered in New Company Setup.

FIGURE 9-13

Add New Payroll Item (MN-State Withholding Tax) Window – Agency for Employee-paid Liability Page

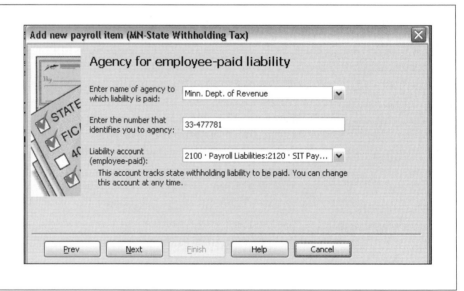

13. If the information is correct, click <u>N</u>ext. The next page appears which shows the types of income subject to the tax.

14. Click <u>F</u>inish. You are returned to the Payroll Item List window with the new tax included. (See figure 9–14.)

FIGURE 9-14

Payroll Item List Window with New Payroll Item

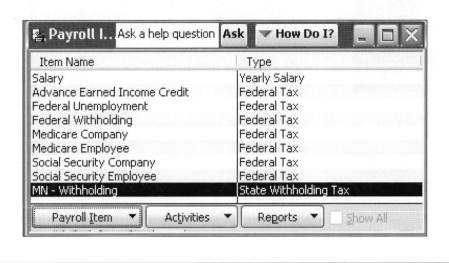

EDITING A PAYROLL ITEM

Kristin Raina wishes to enter the vendor for Social Security Company tax payments. She also wants to change the general ledger posting accounts for the expense and the liability on the Payroll Item List.

To edit the Social Security Company payroll item file—

1. Open the Payroll Item List, if necessary, and choose the *Social Security Company* payroll item file by double-clicking. The file is opened in Edit mode. (See figure 9–15.)

HINT

An alternative method is to select (highlight) the payroll item, click the Payroll Item button, and then click Edit.

FIGURE 9-15

Edit Payroll Item (Social Security Taxes) Window – Name Used in Paychecks and Payroll Reports Page

HINT

If the vendor is not on the Vendor List, click < *Add New* > to add the new vendor.

2. Accept the defaults and click <u>N</u>ext. The Liability agency page appears.
3. At the *Enter name of agency to which liability is paid* field, click *Internal Revenue Service* from the drop-down list.
4. At both *Liability account* fields, click *2110 Social Sec/Medicare Tax Payable*. (See figure 9–16.)

FIGURE 9-16

Edit Payroll Item (Social Security Taxes) Window – Liability Agency Page

5. If the information is correct, click <u>N</u>ext. The Expense account page appears.

   Only the employer's portion of Social Security and Medicare are considered an expense for the company. The portion withheld from the employee's paycheck is not.

6. At the *Enter the account for tracking this expense* field, click *6610 Social Sec/Medicare Tax Expense*. (See figure 9–17.)

FIGURE 9-17

Edit Payroll Item (Social Security Taxes) Window – Expense Account Page

7. If the information is correct, click <u>N</u>ext. The Company and employee tax rates page appears displaying the current tax rates.
8. Click <u>N</u>ext to accept. The Taxable compensation page appears.
9. Accept the default settings by clicking <u>F</u>inish. You will be returned to the Payroll Item List with all changes saved.

PRACTICE *exercise*

Add the following new payroll items:

MINNESOTA STATE UNEMPLOYMENT (SUI)

Type:	**State Tax (State Withholding, SDI, SUI)**
State:	**MN; State Unemployment**
Name:	**MN-Unemployment Company**
Agency:	**Minn. Dept. of Revenue**
ID Number:	**ER-12343**
Liability Account:	**2130 SUI Payable**
Expense Account:	**6630 SUI Expense**
Rate:	**4% each quarter**

HOURLY WAGES

Type:	**<u>W</u>age (Hourly, Salary, Commission, Bonus)**
Wages:	**<u>H</u>ourly Wages, <u>R</u>egular Pay**
Name:	**Hourly Wages**
Expense Account:	**6565 Salaries and Wages Expense**

Edit each of the payroll items listed below. For each item:

- accept the name listed
- choose the Internal Revenue Service as the agency to which the liability will be paid
- select the liability and expense accounts indicated below
- accept all tax rates
- accept all taxable compensation default.

Payroll Item	Liability Account	Expense Account
Federal Withholding	2115 FIT Payable	
Federal Unemployment	2125 FUTA Payable	6625 FUTA Expense
Medicare Company	2110 Social Sec/ Medicare Tax Payable	6610 Social Sec/ Medicare Tax Expense
Medicare Employee	2110 Social Sec/ Medicare Tax Payable	6610 Social Sec/ Medicare Tax Expense
Social Security Employee	2110 Social Sec/ Medicare Tax Payable	6610 Social Sec/ Medicare Tax Expense

You will notice that when you edit the company portion of the tax (for example, Medicare Company) the employee portion of the tax is also edited. If you edit the employee portion first, then the company portion would be similarly edited.

QuickCheck: The updated Payroll Item List appears in figure 9–18.

FIGURE 9-18
Updated Payroll Item List

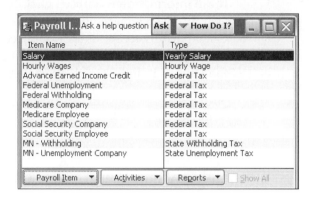

LISTS: THE EMPLOYEE LIST

The Employee List contains a file for each employee of the company. Information such as name, address, Social Security number, hire date, pay rate, and applicable payroll taxes are indicated for each employee. QuickBooks Pro uses the information contained in each employee's file, along with the information in the Payroll Item List, to calculate the employee's gross pay, deductions, and net paycheck.

Like all other Lists in QuickBooks Pro, the Employee List needs to be updated as new employees are hired, employees leave the company, or information about an employee changes and needs to be revised.

Kristin Raina has hired two employees, Harry Renee and Richard Henderson, beginning April 1, 2004. Since our sample company did not previously have employees, the only updating to the Employee List at this time is to add the new employees.

To add an employee—

1. Click Lists, and then click Employee List. Click No at the QuickBooks help window, if it appears.
2. At the Employee List window, click the Employee menu button.
3. At the Employee menu, click New. The New Employee window appears. At the Change tabs field, click on the drop-down arrow. (See figure 9–19.)

FIGURE 9-19
New Employee Window

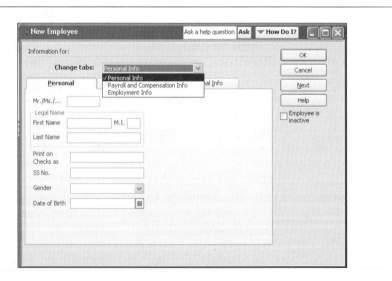

The New Employee window has three sets of information tabs: Personal Info, Payroll and Compensation Info, and Employment Info. The Personal Information tabs are the initial display.

4. Enter the information listed below on the Personal tab.

First Name:	**Harry**
Last Name:	**Renee**
Print on Checks as:	**Harry Renee**
SS No.:	**112-55-9999**
Gender:	**Male**
Date of Birth:	**2/17/48**

(See figure 9-20.)

FIGURE 9-20
New Employee Window –
Personal Tab – Completed

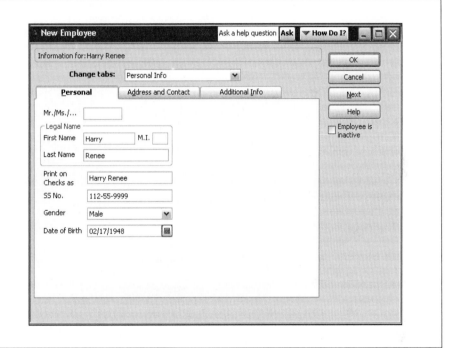

5. Click the *Address and Contact* tab. Enter the information listed below.

Address:	**323 S. Main Ave.**
	St. Paul, MN 54120
Phone:	**651-555-3311**
Cellular:	**651-555-0001**

(See figure 9-21.)

FIGURE 9-21

*New Employee Window –
Address and Contact Tab
Completed*

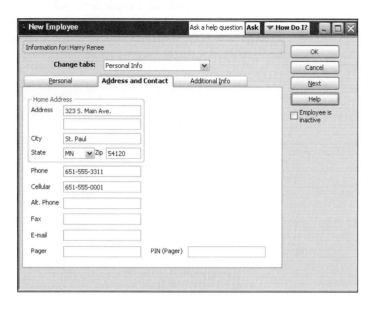

6. At the Change tabs field, choose Payroll and Compensation Info from the drop-down list. The Payroll Info tab appears.
7. In the *Earnings – Item Name* field, click *Salary* from the drop-down list.
8. In the *Hourly/Annual Rate* field, key **24000**.
9. In the *Pay Period* field, click *Semimonthly* from the drop-down list. (See figure 9–22.)

FIGURE 9-22

*New Employee Window –
Payroll Info Tab –
Partially Completed*

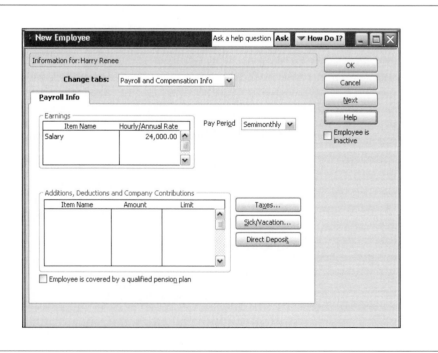

10. Click the Ta**x**es button. The Taxes for Harry Renee window appears.
11. At the **F**ederal tab, at the *Filing Status* field, accept *Single* and at the *Allowances* field, key **1**. Accept the *Subject to* defaults. (See figure 9–23.)

FIGURE 9-23
Taxes for Harry Renee Window – Federal Tab

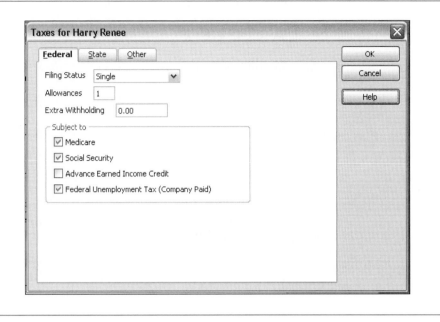

12. Click the **S**tate tab. In the *State Worked* and *State Subject to Withholding* sections, click *MN*. When you move to the next field, additional fields appear.
13. Accept *Single* in the *Filing Status* field, and in the allowances field, key **1**. (See figure 9–24.)

FIGURE 9-24
Taxes for Harry Renee Window – State Tab

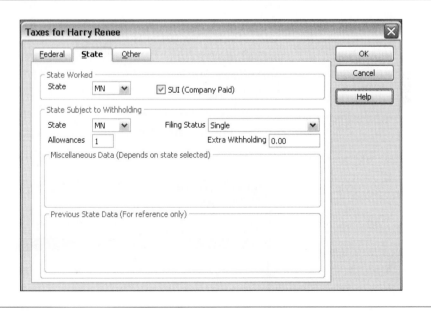

14. If the information is correct, click OK.

   If the QuickBooks Information window appears, read the information and then click OK. Press **Ctrl + Delete** to remove the tax added by the program.

PAYROLL SETUP AND PROCESSING | 337

15. Click OK to close the window. At the QuickBooks for Windows question box, click <u>N</u>o. You are returned to the <u>P</u>ayroll Info tab.
16. Click OK. The New Employee: Payroll Info (Other) window appears.
17. Click <u>L</u>eave As Is.

PRACTICE *exercise*

Add the following employee:

<u>P</u>ERSONAL INFO TAB:

   <u>P</u>ERSONAL TAB

First Name:	**Richard**
Last Name:	**Henderson**
Print on Checks as:	**Richard Henderson**
SS No.:	**333-44-5555**
Gender:	**Male**
Date of Birth:	**8/1/75**

   A<u>D</u>DRESS AND CONTACT TAB:

Address:	**23 Ashland Rd.**
	St. Paul, MN 54120
Phone:	**651-555-6868**
Cellular:	**651-555-2541**

PAYROLL AND COMPENSATION INFO TAB:

   PAYROLL INFO TAB:

Earnings-Item Name:	**Hourly Wages**
Hourly/Annual Rate:	**20**
Pay Peri<u>o</u>d:	**Semimonthly**

   TA<u>X</u>ES:

Federal Filing Status:	**Married**
Federal Allowances:	**2**
State Worked/Subject to Withholding	**MN**
Subject to SUI?:	**✔**
State Filing Status:	**Married**
State Allowances:	**2**
Not Subject to Local Taxes	

QuickCheck: The updated Employee List appears in figure 9–25.

FIGURE 9-25
Updated Employee List

THE PAY EMPLOYEES WINDOWS

You use the Pay Employees windows to calculate gross pay, taxes, and net payroll for employees, a daily business activity that is part of the third order of operations in QuickBooks Pro. As in a manual accounting system, when you process payroll through the Pay Employees window, a number of general ledger accounts are affected by the transaction.

As illustrated earlier in the chapter, it is common in a manual accounting system to record payroll using two journal entries. One journal entry records the salaries/wages expense, the employees' withholdings as liabilities, and the net pay. The second journal entry usually records the employer's related tax expense and related liabilities.

In QuickBooks Pro the transaction is recorded as one compound journal entry instead of two separate journal entries. The transaction is recorded as follows:

Salaries Expense (Gross pay)	XXX			
Social Security/Medicare Tax Expense	XXX			
FUTA Expense	XXX			
SUI Expense	XXX			
Social Security/Medicare Tax Payable			XXX	
Federal Withholding Tax Payable			XXX	
State Withholding Tax Payable			XXX	
FUTA Payable			XXX	
SUI Payable			XXX	
Cash – Payroll			XXX	

At the same time you record the transaction, QuickBooks Pro updates the Employee List and payroll reports to reflect pay earned to date and taxes withheld.

There are two Pay Employees windows: Select Employees To Pay and Preview Paycheck. The Select Employees To Pay window is used to select the employee(s) to be paid at the current pay date. (See figure 9–26.)

FIGURE 9-26
Select Employees To Pay Window

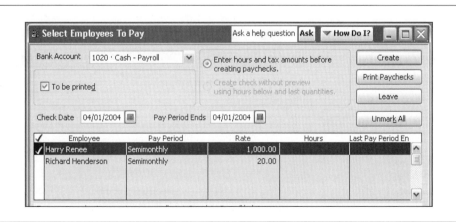

Once an employee(s) is selected, you move to the Preview Paycheck window. (See figure 9–27.)

FIGURE 9-27
Preview Paycheck Window

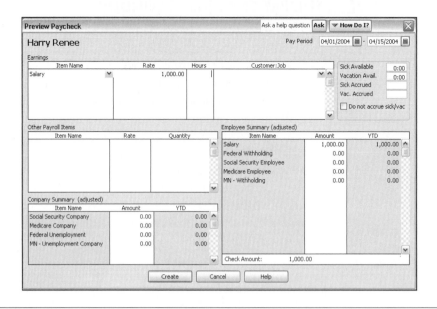

The Preview Paycheck window allows you to enter pay and tax information both for company-imposed taxes and employee deductions. If the company has subscribed to a QuickBooks Pro payroll service, tax figures for the company and the employee also would be calculated and displayed automatically in this window. If you do not subscribe to a service, which is assumed in this text, you simply key in the amounts for the taxes.

In order to manually enter payroll withholdings and taxes, that option must be selected from the QuickBooks payroll options choices.

To enter payroll withholdings and taxes manually-
1. Click Emplo*y*ees, then click *P*ay Employees, and then click OK at the QuickBooks Payroll Service message. The Payroll Setup window within the Payroll Setup page appears. (See figure 9-28.)

FIGURE 9-28
Payroll Setup Window –
Payroll Setup Page

2. With option *1 – Choose a payroll option* selected, click Continue. The Choose a Payroll Option page appears.
3. At the Choose a Payroll Option page, scroll to the bottom of the page. Next to *If you don't want to use an Intuit Payroll Service, you can still use Quickbooks to prepare your payroll.*, click the *Learn More* link.
4. At the Payroll Setup page, scroll down the window until you see the *I choose to manually calculate payroll taxes* button. (See figure 9-29.)

FIGURE 9-29
Payroll Setup Window

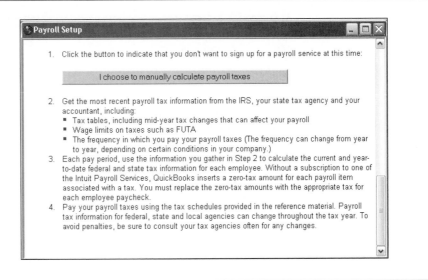

5. Click the button *I choose to manually calculate payroll taxes*. You return to the original Payroll Setup window. Click Finish Later. You will now be able to pay employees.

HINT

Click the X in the upper right corner to close the QuickBooks Payroll Services window. Clicking OK will place you in the Sign Up for Payroll Services window.

PAYING AN EMPLOYEE

On April 15, 2004, Kristin Raina will pay the company's two employees. Harry Renee will be paid first. When Harry Renee was entered on the Employee List, an annual salary of $24,000 was entered and the semimonthly pay period was indicated. Semimonthly pay periods result in 24 paychecks per year. Based on this information, QuickBooks Pro determines that Harry Renee is to be paid $1,000 ($24,000/24 pay periods) per pay period.

To pay an employee—

1. Click Employees, and then click Pay Employees. Click No at the QuickBooks help window, if it appears.

   The Pay Employees window appears inquiring about year-to-date adjustments for the employees. Since our two employees are new, there are not any year-to-date balances and no adjustment is necessary.

2. At the Pay Employees adjustments window, click OK. The Select Employees To Pay window appears.
3. At the *Bank Account* field, click *1020 Cash – Payroll*.
4. Make sure the To be printe_d_ check box is not checked.
5. At the First Check Number box, key **1**.
6. At the *Check Date* and *Pay Period Ends* fields, choose *04/15/2004*.
7. Select Harry Renee by placing a ✓ next to the name. (See figure 9–30.)

FIGURE 9-30
*Select Employees to Pay
Window – Completed*

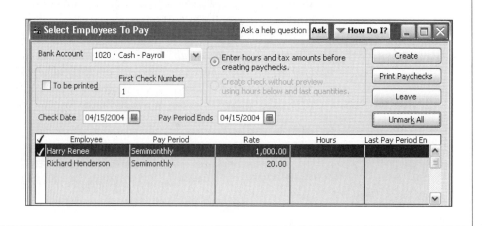

8. If the information is correct, click Create.
9. A warning appears that your tax table is outdated. Click Continue. You will move to the Preview Paycheck window.
10. Make sure the *Item Name* field lists *Salary*, the *Rate* field shows *1,000*, and the *Pay Period* fields display *04/01/2004* and *04/15/2004*.
11. Move to the Company Summary (adjusted) section.

    In the Company Summary (adjusted) section, you enter the employer's payroll-related tax expenses. When you key information in this section, use the mouse or Tab key to move to each field, not the Enter key. If you press the Enter key, QuickBooks Pro assumes the pay information is complete and exits you out of this window and will not let you reenter it.

12. Key the employer's taxes in the Company Summary (adjusted) section as listed below:

Social Security Company:	**62.00**
Medicare Company:	**14.50**
Federal Unemployment:	**8.00**
MN – Unemployment Company:	**40.00**

13. Move to the Employee Summary (adjusted) section.

    In the Employee Summary (adjusted) section, you enter the amount of taxes withheld from the employee's paycheck. As in the Company Summary (adjusted) section, use the mouse or Tab key to move to each field; do not press Enter. You do not have to precede the amount with a minus sign; QuickBooks Pro automatically enters the minus sign before each amount.

14. Key the employee's taxes in the Employee Summary (adjusted) section as listed below:

Federal Withholding:	**120.00**
Social Security Employee:	**62.00**
Medicare Employee:	**14.50**
MN – Withholding:	**46.00**

After entering all of the taxes, the Check Amount total should display as *757.50*. (See figure 9–31.)

FIGURE 9-31
*Preview Paycheck
Window – Completed*

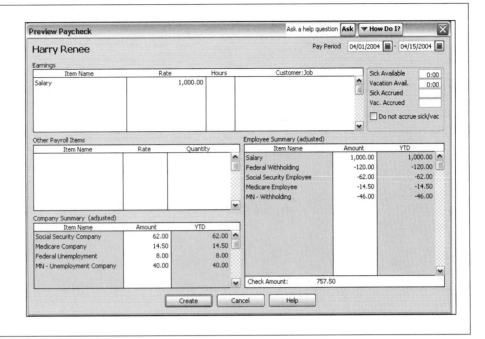

15. If the information is correct, click Create. You are returned to the Select Employees to Pay window.
16. At the Select Employees To Pay window, click Leave.

ACCOUNTING
concept

For the processing of a paycheck the general ledger posting is as follows:
(The taxes payable accounts consist of both the employee and employer taxes;
er represents the employer's share and *ee* represents the employee's share.)

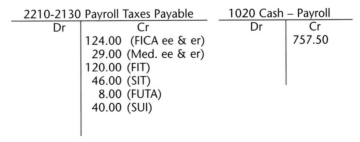

6565 Salary and Wages Expense	
Dr	Cr
1,000	

6610-6630 Employer Payroll Tax Expense	
Dr	Cr
(FICA er) 62.00	
(Med. er) 14.50	
(FUTA) 8.00	
(SUI) 40.00	

2210-2130 Payroll Taxes Payable		1020 Cash – Payroll	
Dr	Cr	Dr	Cr
	124.00 (FICA ee & er)		757.50
	29.00 (Med. ee & er)		
	120.00 (FIT)		
	46.00 (SIT)		
	8.00 (FUTA)		
	40.00 (SUI)		

CORRECTING AN ERROR IN A PAYCHECK

If you discover an error in a paycheck after you have created the check, you cannot correct the error in the Preview Paycheck window. You will have to use the Paycheck – Cash – Payroll window to edit or, if necessary, delete the paycheck and start over.

To correct a paycheck—

1. Click Banking, and then click Write Checks.
2. At the Bank Account drop-down list, click *1020 Cash – Payroll*. At the Setting Default Accounts message, place a check mark in the box to the left of Do not display this message in the future and click OK.
3. Click the Previous button until you arrive at the check for Harry Renee. (See figure 9–32.)

FIGURE 9-32
Paycheck – Cash –
Payroll Window

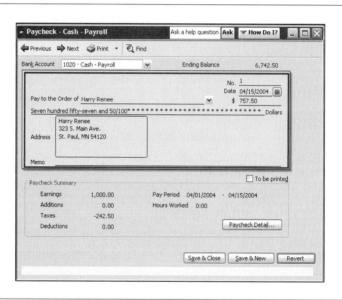

4. Click the Paycheck Detail button. The Review Paycheck window appears. This window is the same as the Preview Paycheck window. (See figure 9–33.)

FIGURE 9-33
Review Paycheck Window

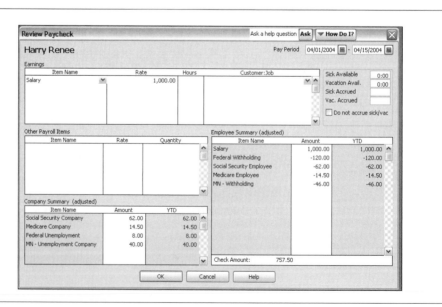

In this window you can correct any errors, and then click OK. You are returned to the Paycheck – Cash – Payroll window.

5. If the information is correct, click Save & Close.

As an alternative to correcting any errors, you can delete the entire paycheck. Use Write Checks from the Banking menu, select the Cash – Payroll account, and then click Previous until the paycheck is displayed as in steps 1 through 3 above. Then use the Edit menu to delete or void the paycheck.

PRACTICE *exercise*

Process the pay for Richard Henderson for the pay period ending April 15, 2004, in the Pay Employees windows using the information listed below.

Richard Henderson's pay information:

Item Name:	**Hourly Wages**
Rate:	**20**
Hours:	**80**

Richard is an hourly employee. You must key the actual number of hours he has worked in the *Hours* field. QuickBooks Pro then computes the gross pay by multiplying his hourly pay rate (previously entered in the Employee List and displayed in this window) by the number of hours worked for this pay period.

COMPANY TAXES:

Social Security Company:	**99.20**
Medicare Company:	**23.20**
Federal Unemployment:	**12.80**
MN – Unemployment Company:	**64.00**

EMPLOYEE TAXES:

Federal Withholding:	**120.00**
Social Security Employee:	**99.20**
Medicare Employee:	**23.20**
MN – Withholding:	**54.00**

QuickCheck: The Check Amount should be $1,303.60.

ADDITIONAL PAYROLL JOURNAL ENTRIES

For pay date April 30, 2004, the following is the pay information for Kristin Raina's two employees for the pay period April 16 to April 30, 2004. Record the payroll for April 30, 2004, in the Pay Employees window using the information listed on the next page for each employee.

Harry Renee's pay information—

Check Number:	**3**
Item Name:	**Salary**
Rate:	**1,000**
Company Taxes:	
Social Security Company:	**62.00**
Medicare Company:	**14.50**
Federal Unemployment:	**8.00**
MN – Unemployment Company:	**40.00**
Employee Taxes:	
Federal Withholding:	**120.00**
Social Security Employee:	**62.00**
Medicare Employee:	**14.50**
MN – Withholding:	**46.00**

QuickCheck: Check Amount $757.50.

Richard Henderson's pay information—

Check Number:	**4**
Item Name:	**Hourly Wages**
Rate:	**20**
Hours:	**88**
Company Taxes:	
Social Security Company:	**109.12**
Medicare Company:	**25.52**
Federal Unemployment:	**14.08**
MN – Unemployment Company:	**70.40**
Employee Taxes	
Federal Withholding:	**132.00**
Social Security Employee:	**109.12**
Medicare Employee:	**25.52**
MN – Withholding:	**61.00**

QuickCheck: Check Amount $1,432.36.

ACTIVITIES: THE PAY LIABILITIES WINDOW

Activities identified as paying employees were recorded in the Pay Employees window. Subsequently, Activities identified as paying payroll liabilities are then recorded in the *Pay Liabilities* window. As you process paychecks in the Pay Employees windows, QuickBooks Pro tracks all payroll liabilities as they accumulate from each paycheck. The Pay Liabilities window then displays all payroll liabilities existing at a specified date and allows you to pay each to its appropriate tax-collecting agency.

The Pay Liabilities window is designed for the payment of federal and local payroll tax liabilities. The default accounts are the various payroll tax liability accounts that have been credited during the payroll processing in the Pay Employees window. Once a liability is selected for payment, the transaction is recorded as follows:

		Payroll Tax Payable	XXX		
		Cash – Payroll			XXX

The QuickBooks Pro Pay Liabilities window appears in figure 9–34.

FIGURE 9-34
Pay Liabilities Window

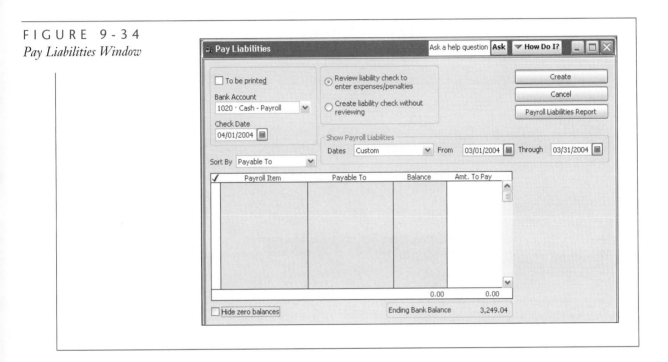

Once you enter the period of time, QuickBooks Pro displays all payroll tax liabilities accrued during that period that remain unpaid. Because of this, you can pay all liabilities payable to a given taxing authority with a single check.

On April 30, 2004, Kristin Raina wishes to remit the federal employer and employee payroll taxes owed to the Internal Revenue Service for the April payroll. The company and employee FICA, the company and employee Medicare tax, the employee's FIT, and the employer's FUTA tax are all to be remitted to the federal government (IRS).

To pay federal payroll tax liabilities—
1. Click Employees, and then click Process Payroll Liabilities.
2. At the Process Payroll Liabilities submenu, click Pay Payroll Liabilities.

3. At the Select Date Range For Liabilities dialog box, choose from *04/01/2004* through *04/30/2004*, and then click OK. The Pay Liabilities window is displayed, showing all payroll tax liabilities accumulated during the selected period. The company can pay the entire liability or only a portion as needed.

4. Make sure the To be printed box is unchecked, the Review liability check to enter expenses/penalties option is selected, and the correct date range appears.

5. At the Bank Account drop-down list, click *1020 Cash – Payroll*.

6. At the Check Date box, choose *04/30/2004*.

7. Place a check next to the liabilities listed below which are all payable to the Internal Revenue Service:

> *Federal Unemployment*
> *Federal Withholding*
> *Medicare Company*
> *Medicare Employee*
> *Social Security Company*
> *Social Security Employee*

The Amt. To Pay column should total $1,354.96. (See figure 9–35.)

FIGURE 9-35
*Pay Liabilities
Window – Completed*

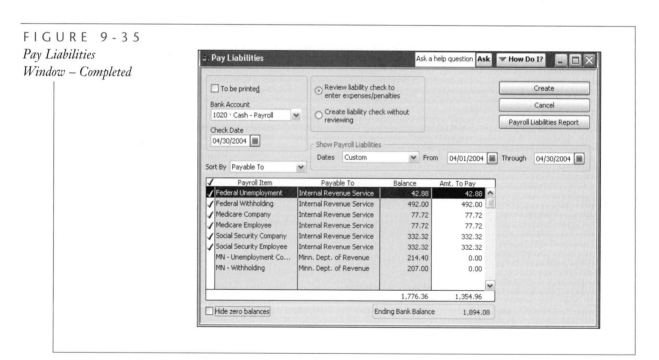

8. If all of the information is correct, click Create. The Liability Check – Cash – Payroll window will be displayed. (See figure 9–36.)

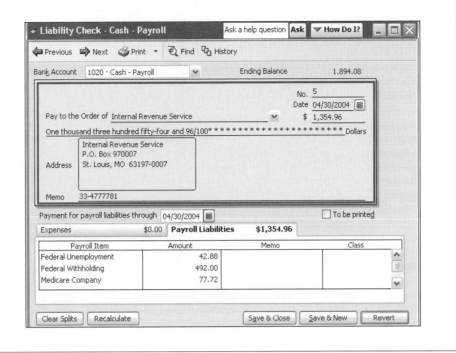

9. If the information on the check is correct, click S̲ave & Close.

Like other Write Check windows in QuickBooks Pro, even though a check is not printed, the liability is paid and a check is recorded in the system.

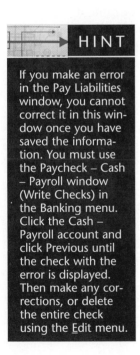

ACCOUNTING
concept

For a payment of payroll liability the general ledger posting is as follows:

2110 Social Security/MedicareTaxes Payable

Dr	Cr
Pmt 820.08	820.08
	Bal 0

2115 FIT Payable

Dr	Cr
Pmt 492.00	492.00
	Bal 0

2125 FUTA Payable

Dr	Cr
Pmt 42.88	42.88
	Bal 0

1020 Cash in Bank – Payroll

Dr	Cr
	1,354.96

P R A C T I C E   *exercise*

Pay the payroll tax liabilities for MN – Unemployment Company and MN Withholding.

QuickCheck: Amount due and to pay $421.40.

REPORTS: PAYROLL AND FINANCIAL REPORTS

Reports, the fourth level of operation in QuickBooks Pro, allows you to display and print a number of payroll reports, both for internal payroll management, and for government and payroll tax compliance.

The payroll management reports provide the company with valuable information concerning payroll costs, such as gross pay; payroll liabilities and withholding; and employer payroll taxes.

The government compliance reports (Forms 941, W-2, and 940) are replications of the federal form 941, which is filed quarterly, and the federal forms W-2 and 940, which are filed annually. QuickBooks Pro does not generate state compliance reports, but payroll management reports can provide information needed to complete state and local compliance reports that the company may be required to submit.

PAYROLL MANAGEMENT REPORTS

The following reports are available in QuickBooks Pro to assist the company in managing and tracking the payroll process. These reports are accessed from the Employees and Payroll submenu of the Reports menu. They are not required by law and therefore are not forwarded to a government agency. However, information contained in these reports is sometimes used to complete government-mandated payroll reports, especially at the state or local level.

Payroll Summary Report

The *Payroll Summary* report lists the earnings, deductions, and employer payroll taxes for each employee for a specified period of time.

To view and print the *Payroll Summary* Report—
1. Click Reports, and then click Employees & Payroll.
2. At the Employees & Payroll submenu, click Payroll Summary.
3. At the *From* and *To* fields, choose *04/01/2004* to *04/30/2004*, and then click Refresh. The report will be displayed for the period.
4. To print the report, click Print from the command line, check the settings in the Print Reports dialog box, and then click Print. Your report should look like figure 9–37.

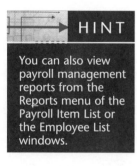

HINT

You can also view payroll management reports from the Reports menu of the Payroll Item List or the Employee List windows.

FIGURE 9-37
Payroll Summary Report

EX9 [Your Name] Kristin Raina Interior Designs
Payroll Summary
April 2004

	Harry Renee 112-55-9999			Richard Henderson 333-44-5...			TOTAL		
	Hours	Rate	Apr 04	Hours	Rate	Apr 04	Hours	Rate	Apr 04
Employee Wages, Taxes and Adjustments									
Gross Pay									
Salary			2,000.00			0.00			2,000.00
Hourly Wages			0.00	168	20.00	3,360.00	168.00		3,360.00
Total Gross Pay			2,000.00			3,360.00			5,360.00
Adjusted Gross Pay			2,000.00			3,360.00			5,360.00
Taxes Withheld									
Federal Withholding			-240.00			-252.00			-492.00
Medicare Employee			-29.00			-48.72			-77.72
Social Security Employee			-124.00			-208.32			-332.32
MN - Withholding			-92.00			-115.00			-207.00
Total Taxes Withheld			-485.00			-624.04			-1,109.04
Net Pay			1,515.00			2,735.96			4,250.96
Employer Taxes and Contributions									
Federal Unemployment			16.00			26.88			42.88
Medicare Company			29.00			48.72			77.72
Social Security Company			124.00			208.32			332.32
MN - Unemployment Company			80.00			134.40			214.40
Total Employer Taxes and Contributions			249.00			418.32			667.32

5. Close the report.

Payroll Liability Balances Report

The *Payroll Liabilities* report lists all payroll liabilities owed and unpaid for a specified period of time. If liabilities have been accrued and paid, a zero will appear for that liability.

To view and print the *Payroll Liability Balances* Report—

1. Click Reports, and then click Employees & Payroll.
2. At the Employees & Payroll submenu, click Payroll Liability Balances.
3. At the *From* and *To* fields, choose *04/01/2004* to *04/30/2004*, and then click Refresh. The report will be displayed for the period. (See figure 9–38.)

FIGURE 9-38
Payroll Liability Balances

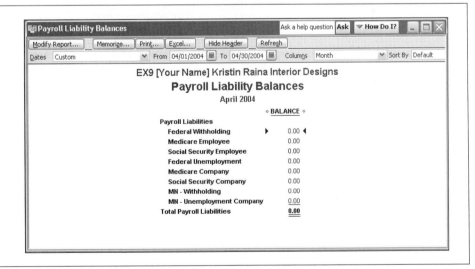

4. To print the report, click Print from the command line, check the settings in the Print Reports dialog box, and then click Print.
5. Close the report.

Payroll Transaction Detail Report

The *Payroll Transaction Detail* report provides detailed information for each payroll transaction (paychecks and payroll liability payments) recorded during the period. Information such as employee salary per paycheck, tax withholding, net pay, employer paid taxes, and taxes remitted are presented in this report.

To view and print the *Payroll Transaction Detail* report—

1. Click Reports, and then click Employees & Payroll.
2. At the Employees & Payroll submenu, click Payroll Transaction Detail.
3. At the *To* and *From* fields, choose *04/01/2004* and *04/30/2004*, and then click Refresh. The report will display all payroll transactions recorded during the specified period.
4. To print the report, click Print from the command line, check the settings in the Print Reports dialog box, and then click Print. (See figure 9–39.)

FIGURE 9-39
Payroll Transaction Detail Report

EX9 [Your Name] Kristin Raina Interior Designs
Payroll Transaction Detail
April 2004

Date	Num	Type	Source Name	Payroll Item	Wage Base	Amount
04/15/2004	1	Paycheck	Harry Renee	Salary	0.00	1,000.00
			Harry Renee	Federal Withholding	1,000.00	-120.00
			Harry Renee	Social Security Company	1,000.00	62.00
			Harry Renee	Social Security Company	1,000.00	-62.00
			Harry Renee	Social Security Employee	1,000.00	-62.00
			Harry Renee	Medicare Company	1,000.00	14.50
			Harry Renee	Medicare Company	1,000.00	-14.50
			Harry Renee	Medicare Employee	1,000.00	-14.50
			Harry Renee	Federal Unemployment	1,000.00	8.00
			Harry Renee	Federal Unemployment	1,000.00	-8.00
			Harry Renee	MN - Withholding	1,000.00	-46.00
			Harry Renee	MN - Unemployment Company	1,000.00	40.00
			Harry Renee	MN - Unemployment Company	1,000.00	-40.00
						757.50
04/15/2004	2	Paycheck	Richard Henderson	Hourly Wages	0.00	1,600.00
			Richard Henderson	Federal Withholding	1,600.00	-120.00
			Richard Henderson	Social Security Company	1,600.00	99.20
			Richard Henderson	Social Security Company	1,600.00	-99.20
			Richard Henderson	Social Security Employee	1,600.00	-99.20
			Richard Henderson	Medicare Company	1,600.00	23.20
			Richard Henderson	Medicare Company	1,600.00	-23.20
			Richard Henderson	Medicare Employee	1,600.00	-23.20
			Richard Henderson	Federal Unemployment	1,600.00	12.80
			Richard Henderson	Federal Unemployment	1,600.00	-12.80
			Richard Henderson	MN - Withholding	1,600.00	-54.00
			Richard Henderson	MN - Unemployment Company	1,600.00	64.00
			Richard Henderson	MN - Unemployment Company	1,600.00	-64.00
						1,303.60
04/30/2004	3	Paycheck	Harry Renee	Salary	0.00	1,000.00
			Harry Renee	Federal Withholding	1,000.00	-120.00
			Harry Renee	Social Security Company	1,000.00	62.00
			Harry Renee	Social Security Company	1,000.00	-62.00
			Harry Renee	Social Security Employee	1,000.00	-62.00
			Harry Renee	Medicare Company	1,000.00	14.50
			Harry Renee	Medicare Company	1,000.00	-14.50
			Harry Renee	Medicare Employee	1,000.00	-14.50
			Harry Renee	Federal Unemployment	1,000.00	8.00
			Harry Renee	Federal Unemployment	1,000.00	-8.00
			Harry Renee	MN - Withholding	1,000.00	-46.00
			Harry Renee	MN - Unemployment Company	1,000.00	40.00
			Harry Renee	MN - Unemployment Company	1,000.00	-40.00
						757.50
04/30/2004	4	Paycheck	Richard Henderson	Hourly Wages	0.00	1,760.00
			Richard Henderson	Federal Withholding	1,760.00	-132.00
			Richard Henderson	Social Security Company	1,760.00	109.12
			Richard Henderson	Social Security Company	1,760.00	-109.12
			Richard Henderson	Social Security Employee	1,760.00	-109.12
			Richard Henderson	Medicare Company	1,760.00	25.52
			Richard Henderson	Medicare Company	1,760.00	-25.52
			Richard Henderson	Medicare Employee	1,760.00	-25.52
			Richard Henderson	Federal Unemployment	1,760.00	14.08
			Richard Henderson	Federal Unemployment	1,760.00	-14.08
			Richard Henderson	MN - Withholding	1,760.00	-61.00
			Richard Henderson	MN - Unemployment Company	1,760.00	70.40
			Richard Henderson	MN - Unemployment Company	1,760.00	-70.40
						1,432.36
04/30/2004	5	Liability Check	Internal Revenue Service	Federal Unemployment		42.88
			Internal Revenue Service	Federal Withholding		492.00
			Internal Revenue Service	Medicare Company		77.72
			Internal Revenue Service	Medicare Employee		77.72
			Internal Revenue Service	Social Security Company		332.32
			Internal Revenue Service	Social Security Employee		332.32
						1,354.96
04/30/2004	6	Liability Check	Minn. Dept. of Revenue	MN - Unemployment Company		214.40
			Minn. Dept. of Revenue	MN - Withholding		207.00
						421.40
TOTAL						6,027.32

5. Close the report.

Employee State Taxes Detail Report

As previously mentioned, QuickBooks Pro does not prepare state compliance reports. However, the *Employee State Taxes Detail* report provides most, if not all, of the information most states will require a company to submit on a periodic basis.

Information such as type of state tax, amount of income subject to tax, and amount of each tax will be displayed in this report.

To view and print the *Employee State Taxes Detail* report—
1. Click Reports, and then click Employees & Payroll.
2. At the Employees & Payroll submenu, click Employee State Taxes Detail.
3. Since most states require quarterly filings, at the *To* and *From* fields, choose *04/01/2004* and *06/30/2004*, and then click Refresh. The report will be displayed for the period. (See figure 9–40.)

FIGURE 9-40
Employee State Taxes Detail Report

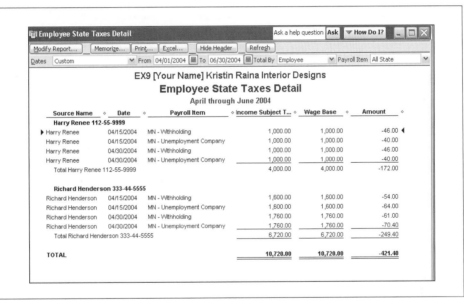

4. To print the report, click Print from the command line, check the settings in the Print Reports dialog box, and then click Print.
5. Close the report.

HINT

Remember that the drill-down feature is available if the zoom glass appears.

PAYROLL GOVERNMENT COMPLIANCE REPORTS

The Employees menu contains the basic government compliance reports all companies with payroll are required to file with the federal government (IRS).

Form 941

Form 941 – Employer's Quarterly Federal Tax Return is forwarded to the Internal Revenue Service quarterly. This report summarizes the total wages paid to all employees for the quarter, along with the federal tax withheld and employer's and employee's Social Security and Medicare tax liabilities.

To view and print the Form 941—

1. At the Employees menu, click Process Payroll Forms.
2. At the Select Payroll Form dialog box, click *Form 941* and *Schedule B* and click OK.
3. At the Form 941/Schedule B window, click the *New Form 941/Schedule B* option and enter *06/30/2004* as the quarter ending date. You are entering 06/30/2004, as the date as Form 941 is filed for each calendar quarter. (See figure 9–41.)

FIGURE 9-41
Form 941/Schedule B Window

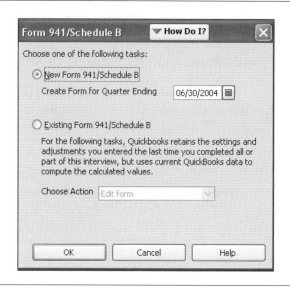

4. If the information is correct, click OK.
5. At the next Form 941/Schedule B window, at the Enter state code drop-down list, click *MN*, at the *Date quarter ended* field, choose *06/30/2004*, and then click Next several times
6. At the Line 15 and 16 page, choose the Monthly depositor option in the Deposit Schedule section. (See figure 9-42.)

FIGURE 9-42
Form 941/Schedule B Window – Monthly Depositor Page

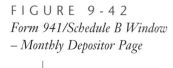

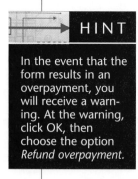

HINT

In the event that the form results in an overpayment, you will receive a warning. At the warning, click OK, then choose the option *Refund overpayment*.

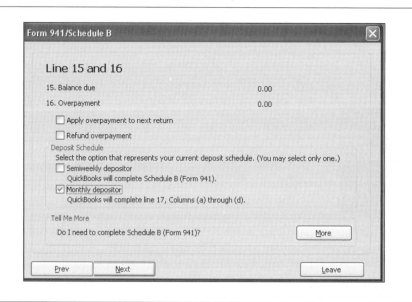

7. Click Next until you arrive at the You have completed your quarterly federal tax form(s) window. (See figure 9-43.)

FIGURE 9-43

*Form 941/Schedule B
Window – You Have
Completed Your Quarterly
Federal Tax Form(s) Page*

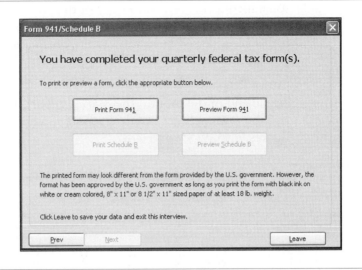

8. Click Preview Form 9**4**1. The Form Preview window is displayed.
   (See figure 9–44.)

FIGURE 9-44

Form 941 – Displayed

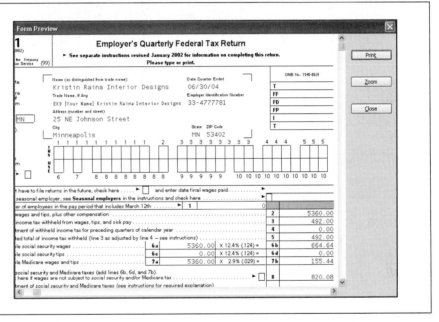

9. To print the form, click Prin**t**, or to close the Form Preview page, click
   Close, and then click **L**eave to exit the Form 941 window.

Form 940

Form 940 – Employer's Annual Federal Unemployment (FUTA) Tax Return is
filed annually with the Internal Revenue Service. This form computes the
FUTA tax liability for the company for the year and reconciles the amount
to the tax payments made by the company toward the tax during the year.
The Form 940 report is accessed from the Employ**e**es menu using similar
steps to those you used to access Form 941.

Form W-2

Form W-2 – Wage and Tax Statement is prepared annually and furnished to
the employee. This report totals the employee's earnings and tax withholding for the year. The employee uses this form to complete his or her per-

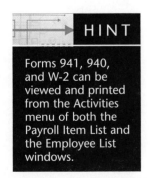

HINT

Forms 941, 940,
and W-2 can be
viewed and printed
from the Activities
menu of both the
Payroll Item List and
the Employee List
windows.

sonal income tax return. A copy of this form is also forwarded to the federal government to be reconciled with the quarterly Form 941 filings. The W-2 forms are accessed from the Employees menu using similar steps to those you used to access Form 941.

OTHER REPORTS

At the end of the month, the *Journal* report, *Profit & Loss Standard* report, and the *Balance Sheet Standard* report should be displayed and printed. See figures 9–45, 9–46, and 9–47.

FIGURE 9-45
Journal Report
April 1, 2004 – April 30, 2004

EX9 [Your Name] Kristin Raina Interior Designs
Journal
April 2004

Trans #	Type	Date	Num	Name	Memo	Account	Debit	Credit
52	General Journal	04/01/2004				1020 · Cash - Payroll	7,500.00	
						1010 · Cash - Operating		7,500.00
							7,500.00	7,500.00
53	Paycheck	04/15/2004	1	Harry Renee		1020 · Cash - Payroll		757.50
				Harry Renee		6565 · Salaries and Wages Expense	1,000.00	
				Harry Renee		2115 · FIT Payable		120.00
				Harry Renee		6610 · Social Sec/Medicare Tax Expense	62.00	
				Harry Renee		2110 · Social Sec/Medicare Tax Payable		62.00
				Harry Renee		2110 · Social Sec/Medicare Tax Payable		62.00
				Harry Renee		6610 · Social Sec/Medicare Tax Expense	14.50	
				Harry Renee		2110 · Social Sec/Medicare Tax Payable		14.50
				Harry Renee		2110 · Social Sec/Medicare Tax Payable		14.50
				Harry Renee		6625 · FUTA Expense	8.00	
				Harry Renee		2125 · FUTA Payable		8.00
				Harry Renee		2120 · SIT Payable		46.00
				Harry Renee		6630 · SUI Expense	40.00	
				Harry Renee		2130 · SUI Payable		40.00
							1,124.50	1,124.50
54	Paycheck	04/15/2004	2	Richard Henderson		1020 · Cash - Payroll		1,303.60
				Richard Henderson		6565 · Salaries and Wages Expense	1,600.00	
				Richard Henderson		2115 · FIT Payable		120.00
				Richard Henderson		6610 · Social Sec/Medicare Tax Expense	99.20	
				Richard Henderson		2110 · Social Sec/Medicare Tax Payable		99.20
				Richard Henderson		2110 · Social Sec/Medicare Tax Payable		99.20
				Richard Henderson		6610 · Social Sec/Medicare Tax Expense	23.20	
				Richard Henderson		2110 · Social Sec/Medicare Tax Payable		23.20
				Richard Henderson		2110 · Social Sec/Medicare Tax Payable		23.20
				Richard Henderson		6625 · FUTA Expense	12.80	
				Richard Henderson		2125 · FUTA Payable		12.80
				Richard Henderson		2120 · SIT Payable		54.00
				Richard Henderson		6630 · SUI Expense	64.00	
				Richard Henderson		2130 · SUI Payable		64.00
							1,799.20	1,799.20
55	Paycheck	04/30/2004	3	Harry Renee		1020 · Cash - Payroll		757.50
				Harry Renee		6565 · Salaries and Wages Expense	1,000.00	
				Harry Renee		2115 · FIT Payable		120.00
				Harry Renee		6610 · Social Sec/Medicare Tax Expense	62.00	
				Harry Renee		2110 · Social Sec/Medicare Tax Payable		62.00
				Harry Renee		2110 · Social Sec/Medicare Tax Payable		62.00
				Harry Renee		6610 · Social Sec/Medicare Tax Expense	14.50	
				Harry Renee		2110 · Social Sec/Medicare Tax Payable		14.50
				Harry Renee		2110 · Social Sec/Medicare Tax Payable		14.50
				Harry Renee		6625 · FUTA Expense	8.00	
				Harry Renee		2125 · FUTA Payable		8.00
				Harry Renee		2120 · SIT Payable		46.00
				Harry Renee		6630 · SUI Expense	40.00	
				Harry Renee		2130 · SUI Payable		40.00
							1,124.50	1,124.50
56	Paycheck	04/30/2004	4	Richard Henderson		1020 · Cash - Payroll		1,432.36
				Richard Henderson		6565 · Salaries and Wages Expense	1,760.00	
				Richard Henderson		2115 · FIT Payable		132.00
				Richard Henderson		6610 · Social Sec/Medicare Tax Expense	109.12	
				Richard Henderson		2110 · Social Sec/Medicare Tax Payable		109.12
				Richard Henderson		2110 · Social Sec/Medicare Tax Payable		109.12
				Richard Henderson		6610 · Social Sec/Medicare Tax Expense	25.52	
				Richard Henderson		2110 · Social Sec/Medicare Tax Payable		25.52
				Richard Henderson		2110 · Social Sec/Medicare Tax Payable		25.52
				Richard Henderson		6625 · FUTA Expense	14.08	
				Richard Henderson		2125 · FUTA Payable		14.08
				Richard Henderson		2120 · SIT Payable		61.00
				Richard Henderson		6630 · SUI Expense	70.40	
				Richard Henderson		2130 · SUI Payable		70.40
							1,979.12	1,979.12
57	Liability Check	04/30/2004	5	Internal Revenue S...	33-4777781	1020 · Cash - Payroll		1,354.96
				Internal Revenue S...	33-4777781	2125 · FUTA Payable	42.88	
				Internal Revenue S...	33-4777781	2115 · FIT Payable	492.00	
				Internal Revenue S...	33-4777781	2110 · Social Sec/Medicare Tax Payable	77.72	
				Internal Revenue S...	33-4777781	2110 · Social Sec/Medicare Tax Payable	77.72	
				Internal Revenue S...	33-4777781	2110 · Social Sec/Medicare Tax Payable	332.32	
				Internal Revenue S...	33-4777781	2110 · Social Sec/Medicare Tax Payable	332.32	
							1,354.96	1,354.96
58	Liability Check	04/30/2004	6	Minn. Dept. of Rev...	ER-12343, 33-477781	1020 · Cash - Payroll		421.40
				Minn. Dept. of Rev...	ER-12343, 33-477781	2130 · SUI Payable	214.40	
				Minn. Dept. of Rev...	ER-12343, 33-477781	2120 · SIT Payable	207.00	
							421.40	421.40
TOTAL							**15,303.68**	**15,303.68**

FIGURE 9-46

Profit & Loss Standard Report
January 1, 2004 – April 30, 2004

EX9 [Your Name] Kristin Raina Interior Designs
Profit & Loss
January through April 2004

Accrual Basis

	Jan - Apr 04
Ordinary Income/Expense	
Income	
4010 · Design Services	4,980.00
4020 · Decorating Services	3,400.00
4060 · Sale of Carpets	2,400.00
4065 · Sale of Draperies	1,000.00
4070 · Sale of Lamps	1,200.00
4075 · Sale of Mirrors	900.00
4100 · Sales Discounts	-84.62
Total Income	13,795.38
Cost of Goods Sold	
5060 · Cost of Carpets Sold	1,200.00
5065 · Cost of Draperies Sold	500.00
5070 · Cost of Lamps Sold	600.00
5075 · Cost of Mirrors Sold	450.00
5900 · Inventory Adjustment	150.00
Total COGS	2,900.00
Gross Profit	10,895.38
Expense	
6020 · Accounting Expense	300.00
6050 · Advertising Expense	100.00
6175 · Deprec. Exp., Furniture	100.00
6185 · Deprec. Exp., Computers	60.00
6200 · Insurance Expense	200.00
6300 · Janitorial Expenses	125.00
6325 · Office Supplies Expense	150.00
6400 · Rent Expense	800.00
6450 · Telephone Expense	275.00
6500 · Utilities Expense	450.00
6560 · Payroll Expenses	
6565 · Salaries and Wages Expense	5,360.00
6610 · Social Sec/Medicare Tax Expense	410.04
6625 · FUTA Expense	42.88
6630 · SUI Expense	214.40
Total 6560 · Payroll Expenses	6,027.32
Total Expense	8,587.32
Net Ordinary Income	2,308.06
Other Income/Expense	
Other Expense	
7000 · Interest Expense	50.00
Total Other Expense	50.00
Net Other Income	-50.00
Net Income	2,258.06

EX9 [Your Name] Kristin Raina Interior Designs
Balance Sheet
As of April 30, 2004

Accrual Basis

	Apr 30, 04
ASSETS	
Current Assets	
Checking/Savings	
1010 · Cash - Operating	43,355.38
1020 · Cash - Payroll	1,472.68
Total Checking/Savings	44,828.06
Accounts Receivable	
1200 · Accounts Receivable	1,540.00
Total Accounts Receivable	1,540.00
Other Current Assets	
1260 · Inventory of Carpets	800.00
1265 · Inventory of Draperies	1,000.00
1270 · Inventory of Lamps	1,000.00
1275 · Inventory of Mirrors	900.00
1300 · Design Supplies	200.00
1305 · Office Supplies	250.00
1410 · Prepaid Advertising	500.00
1420 · Prepaid Insurance	2,200.00
Total Other Current Assets	6,850.00
Total Current Assets	53,218.06
Fixed Assets	
1700 · Furniture	
1750 · Accum. Dep., Furniture	-100.00
1700 · Furniture - Other	12,000.00
Total 1700 · Furniture	11,900.00
1800 · Computers	
1850 · Accum. Dep., Computers	-60.00
1800 · Computers - Other	3,600.00
Total 1800 · Computers	3,540.00
Total Fixed Assets	15,440.00
TOTAL ASSETS	**68,658.06**
LIABILITIES & EQUITY	
Liabilities	
Current Liabilities	
Accounts Payable	
2010 · Accounts Payable	9,750.00
Total Accounts Payable	9,750.00
Other Current Liabilities	
2020 · Notes Payable	7,000.00
2030 · Interest Payable	50.00
Total Other Current Liabilities	7,050.00
Total Current Liabilities	16,800.00
Total Liabilities	16,800.00
Equity	
3010 · Kristin Raina, Capital	50,000.00
3020 · Kristin Raina, Drawings	-400.00
Net Income	2,258.06
Total Equity	51,858.06
TOTAL LIABILITIES & EQUITY	**68,658.06**

I N T E R N E T
Resources

Over the past several years, The Internal Revenue Service (IRS) has made a determined effort not only to enforce the tax laws, but also to assist taxpayers and businesses to comply with them. To that end, the IRS has made increasing use of the Internet to disseminate tax assistance. The IRS Web site is located at www.irs.ustreas.gov.

Publication 15, known as *Circular E*, the *Employer's Tax Guide*, is a publication designed to assist employers in complying with federal tax laws and filing requirements for payroll processing. To view this publication online—

1. Go to the IRS Web site at www.irs.ustreas.gov.
2. Scroll down the window and click *Businesses* under the Contents heading.
3. Click *Forms and Publications* under the Resources heading.
4. Scroll down and click *Publications Online* from the Forms and Publications list.
5. Click *Publication 15, Circular E, Employer's Tax Guide*.

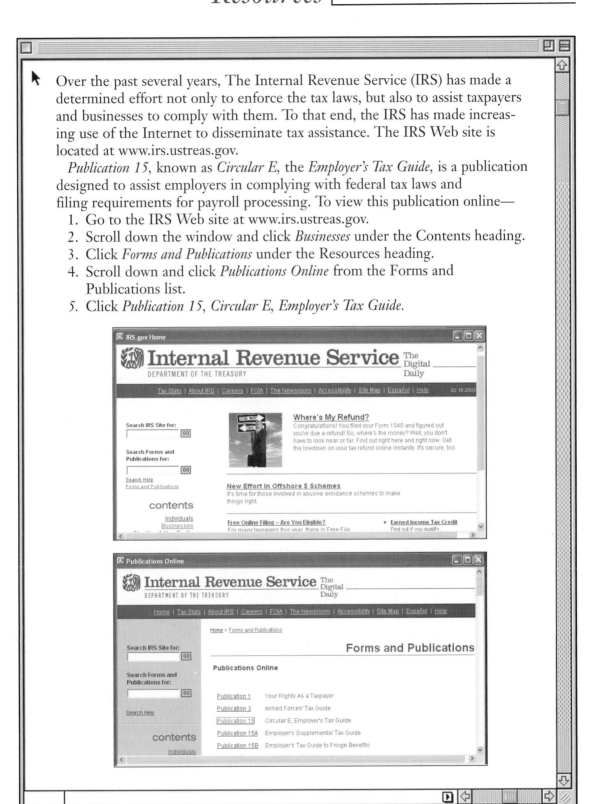

P R O G R E S S
Check

PROCEDURE REVIEW

To activate QuickBooks Pro payroll feature—
1. Click Edit, and then click Preferences.
2. Along the left frame of the Preferences window, click the *Payroll & Employees* icon.
3. Click the Company Preferences tab.
4. Click the Full payroll features option.
5. Accept the defaults.
6. Click OK.

To add a salary and wages payroll item—
1. Click Lists, and then click Payroll Item List. Click No at the QuickBooks help menu.
2. At the Payroll Item List window, click the Payroll Item menu button.
3. At the Payroll Item menu, click New.
4. At the Select setup method page, click the Custom Setup option, and then click Next.
5. At the Payroll item type list, click *Wage (Hourly, Salary, Commission, Bonus)* and click Next.
6. Choose the *Salary Wages* or *Hourly Wages* option and click Next.
7. Choose *Regular Pay* and click Next.
8. At the Enter name for salary item field, key **Salary** or **Hourly Wages** and then click Next.
9. At the Expenses window, choose the expense account to track this item and click Finish.
10. Close the Payroll Item List.

To add a withholding and tax payroll item—
1. Click Lists, and then click Payroll Item List. Click No at the QuickBooks help menu.
2. At the Payroll Item List page, click the Payroll Item menu button.
3. At the Payroll Item menu, click New.
4. At the Select setup method page, click the Custom Setup option, and then click Next.
5. At the Payroll item type list, choose the applicable tax and click Next.
6. At the Enter name tax withholding field, accept the default and click Next.
7. At the Enter name of agency page, click the tax agency from the drop-down list.
8. Key the tax ID number.
9. At the Liability account field page, choose the balance sheet liability account for the tax and click Next.
10. The next window shows which types of income are subject to tax. Click Finish to accept.
11. Close the Payroll Item List.

To add an employee—
1. Click Lists, and then click Employee List.
2. At the Employee List window, click the Employee menu button. At the Employee menu, click New.
3. Enter the information on the Personal tab.
4. Click the *Address and Contact* tab. Enter the information.
5. At the *Change tabs* field, choose Payroll and Compensation Info from the drop-down list.
6. At the Payroll Info tab enter the information for the *Item Name*, *Hourly/Annual Rate*, and *Pay Period* fields.
7. Click Taxes. The Taxes window will be displayed.
8. At the Federal tab, enter the information for federal withholding tax.
9. Click the State tab and enter the state withholding tax information.
10. Click OK. If the Information window appears, click OK to close it and Ctrl + Delete to remove the tax added by the program.
11. Click OK.
12. At the question box, click No.
13. Click OK.
14. Click Leave As Is.
15. Close the Employee List.

To pay an employee—
1. Click Employees, and then click Pay Employees.
2. Click OK at the Enter Pay Adjustments window. The Select Employees To Pay window appears.
3. At the *Bank Account* field, click *1020 Cash – Payroll*.
4. Make sure the To be printed check box is not checked.
5. Enter the correct dates in the *Check Date* and *Pay Period Ends* fields.
6. Select the employee to be paid by placing a ✓ next to the name.
7. Click Create and then click Continue at the warning window. You will move to the Preview Paycheck Window.
8. Enter the needed information in the Earnings section.
9. At the Company Summary (adjusted) section, enter the company tax information.
10. At the Employee Summary (adjusted) section, enter the employee taxes.
11. If the information is correct, click Create.
12. At the Select Employees To Pay window, click Create.

To enter payroll withholdings and taxes manually—
1. Click Employees, then click Pay Employees, and then click OK at the QuickBooks Payroll Service message.
2. At the Payroll Setup Steps window, with option *1 – Choose a payroll option* selected, click Continue.
3. At the Choose a Payroll Option window, scroll to the bottom of the window. Next to *If you don't want to use an Intuit Payroll Service you can still use Quickbooks to prepare your payroll.*, click the *Learn More* link.
4. At the Payroll Setup page, scroll down the window until you see the *I choose to manually calculate payroll taxes* button and click the button.
5. You return to the original Payroll Setup window. Click Finish Later. You will now be able to pay employees.

To pay payroll liabilities—

1. Click Employees, and then click Process Payroll Liabilities.
2. At the Process Payroll Liabilities submenu, click Pay Payroll Liabilities.
3. At the *Select Date Range For Liabilities* dialog box, choose the date range and click OK.
4. Make sure the To be printed box is unchecked, the Review liability check button is selected, and the correct date range appears.
5. At the Bank Account drop-down list, click *1020 Cash – Payroll*.
6. Enter the payment date.
7. Place a check next to the liabilities you wish to pay.
8. If all of the information is correct, click Create. The liability check will be displayed.
9. If the information on the check is correct, click Save & Close.

To view and print reports from the Reports menu—

1. At the Reports menu, click Employees & Payroll.
2. At the Employees & Payroll submenu, click a report.
3. Indicate the appropriate dates.
4. Click Print from the command line.
5. At the Print Reports dialog box, review the settings, and then click Print.
6. Close the report.

To view and print reports from the Employees menu—

1. Click Employees, and then click Process Payroll Forms.
2. At the Select Payroll Form window, choose a payroll form, then click OK.
3. At the Form window, click New and enter the quarter ending date.
4. If the information is correct, click OK.
5. At the next window, at the Enter state code drop-down list, click the state code, and then click Next.
6. Click Next several times. At the Line 15 and 16 page, choose the Monthly depositor option in the Deposit Schedule section.
7. Click Next until you arrive at the Print or Preview Form window.
8. Click Print to print the form.
9. Click Leave to exit.

KEY CONCEPTS

Select the letter of the item that best matches each definition.

    a. Pay Employee window
    b. Social Security Tax, Medicare Tax, FUTA, and SUI
    c. Employee List
    d. Payroll Item List
    e. Social Security Tax, Medicare Tax, Federal Withholding, and State Withholding
    f. *Payroll Summary* report
    g. Form 941
    h. *Employee State Taxes Detail* report
    i. *Payroll Liability Balances* report
    j. Pay Liabilities window

_____ 1. Payroll taxes imposed on the employer.

_____ 2. Quarterly payroll report forwarded to the Internal Revenue Service.

_____ 3. Window used to record processing of employee pay.

_____ 4. Payroll taxes imposed on the employee and collected by the employer.

_____ 5. Contains a file for each type of payroll item that affects the payroll computation.

_____ 6. Report that lists all payroll liabilities unpaid as of a specified date.

_____ 7. Contains a file with each employee's payroll background information.

_____ 8. Report that displays information concerning state taxes imposed on the employer and employee.

_____ 9. Window used to pay payroll liabilities accumulated when pay is processed.

_____ 10. Report that displays the earnings, deductions, and employer payroll taxes for each employee.

PROCEDURE CHECK

1. You have decided to utilize the payroll feature of QuickBooks Pro. How do you activate the payroll feature in an existing company file?

2. Your company plans to convert from a manual payroll process to a computerized payroll processing system. What information must be assembled before you could process the first payroll check?

3. Describe the steps to set up a withholding and tax payroll item.

4. Your company has hired a new employee. Describe the steps to add this employee to the Employee List.

5. Your company's management wishes to have a report of the amount of each local payroll tax the company is subject to. How would you use QuickBooks Pro to gather this information?

6. Your company's newly hired college intern has just received her first paycheck. She is disappointed that her net check is only a fraction of what she thought she was earning. Prepare a brief memo, describing the taxes that must be withheld from her check.

CASE PROBLEMS

CASE PROBLEM 1

In June, the third month of business for Lynn's Music Studio, Lynn Garcia has decided to hire two employees. One employee will be the Studio Manager, who will be paid a salary. The other employee, an assistant instructor, will be paid on an hourly basis. The company file includes information for Lynn's Music Studio as of June 1, 2004.

1. Open the company file CH9 Lynn's Music Studio.QBW.

2. Make a backup copy of the company file LMS9 [Your Name] Lynn's Music Studio.

3. Restore the backup copy of the company file. In both the Restore From and Restore To windows, use the file name LMS9 [Your Name] Lynn's Music Studio.

4. Change the company name to LMS9 [Your Name] Lynn's Music Studio.
5. Set up the payroll feature for Lynn's Music Studio.
6. Add the following accounts to the Chart of Accounts List:

2110	Social Sec/Medicare Tax Payable	Subaccount of 2100 Payroll Liabilities
2115	FIT Payable	Subaccount of 2100 Payroll Liabilities
2120	SIT Payable	Subaccount of 2100 Payroll Liabilities
2125	FUTA Payable	Subaccount of 2100 Payroll Liabilities
2130	SUI Payable	Subaccount of 2100 Payroll Liabilities
6565	Salaries and Wages Expense	Subaccount of 6560 Payroll Expenses
6611	Social Sec/Medicare Tax Expense	Subaccount of 6560 Payroll Expenses
6625	FUTA Expense	Subaccount of 6560 Payroll Expenses
6630	SUI Expense	Subaccount of 6560 Payroll Expenses

7. Add the following payroll items:

Salary

Type:	**Wage (Hourly, Salary, Commission, Bonus)**
Wages:	**Salary Wages, Regular Pay**
Name:	**Salary**
Expense account:	**6565 Salaries and Wages Expense**

Wages

Type:	**Wage (Hourly, Salary, Commission, Bonus)**
Wages:	**Hourly Wages, Regular Pay**
Name:	**Hourly Wages**
Expense account:	**6565 Salaries and Wages Expense**

State Tax (State Withholding)

State:	**PA**
Type of Tax:	**State Withholding**
Name Used in Paychecks:	**PA – Withholding**
Agency for Liabilities:	**PA Dept. of Revenue**
Identifying Number:	**45-6123789**
Liability Account:	**2120 SIT Payable**
Taxable Compensation:	**Accept defaults**

State Tax (SUI)

State:	**PA**
Type of Tax:	**State Unemployment**
Name Used on Paychecks:	**PA – Unemployment Company**

Agency for Liabilities:	**PA Dept. of Revenue**
Identifying Number:	**ER-76558**
Liability Account:	**2130 SUI Payable**
Expense Account:	**6630 SUI Expense**
Company Tax Rate:	**4% each quarter**
Taxable Compensation:	**Accept defaults**

8. Edit each of the payroll items listed below. For each item—
   - accept the name listed
   - choose the Internal Revenue Service as the agency to which the liability will be paid
   - select the liability and expense accounts indicated below
   - accept all tax rates
   - accept all taxable compensation defaults

Payroll Item	Liability Account	Expense Account
Federal Unemployment	2125 FUTA Payable	6625 FUTA Expense
Federal Withholding	2115 FIT Payable	
Medicare Company	2110 Social Sec/ Medicare Tax Payable	6611 Social Sec/ Medicare Tax Expense
Medicare Employee	2110 Social Sec/ Medicare Tax Payable	6611 Social Sec/ Medicare Tax Expense
Social Security Company	2110 Social Sec/ Medicare Tax Payable	6611 Social Sec/ Medicare Tax Expense
Social Security Employee	2110 Social Sec/ Medicare Tax Payable	6611 Social Sec/ Medicare Tax Expense

9. Add the following employees:

First Name:	**Wei**
Last Name:	**Chan**
Print on Checks as:	**Wei Chan**
SS No.:	**159-89-2527**
Gender:	**Female**
Date of Birth:	**3/23/80**
Address:	**417 Willow Street**
	Scranton, PA 18505
Phone:	**570-555-3980**
Cellular:	**570-555-9898**
Item Name:	**Salary**
Hourly/Annual Rate:	**$18,000**
Pay Period:	**Semimonthly**
Federal Filing Status:	**Married**
Federal Allowances:	**1**
State Worked/Subject to Withholding:	**PA**
Subject to SUI?:	**Yes**
State Filing Status:	**Withhold**
State Allowances:	**1**
Not Subject to Local Taxes	

First Name:		**Michelle**
Last Name:		**Auletta**
Print on Checks as:		**Michelle Auletta**
SS No.:		**291-08-7433**
Gender:		**Female**
Date of Birth:		**8/9/55**
Address:		**23 Grand Ave.**
		Scranton, PA 18505
Phone:		**570-555-4872**
Cellular:		**570-555-4949**
Item Name:		**Hourly Wages**
Hourly/Annual Rate:		**12**
Pay Period:		**Semimonthly**
Federal Filing Status:		**Single**
Federal Allowances:		**1**
State Worked/Subject to Withholding:		**PA**
Subject to SUI?:		**Yes**
State Filing Status:		**Withhold**
State Allowances:		**1**
Not Subject to Local Taxes		

10. Process pay for June 15, 2004 using the following information:

Check No.:	**1**	
Check Date:	**06/15/2004**	
Pay Period Ends:	**06/15/2004**	
Employee:	**Michelle Auletta**	
Item Name:	**Hourly Wages**	
Rate:	**12**	
Hours:	**30**	
Company Taxes:		
Social Security Company:		22.32
Medicare Company:		5.22
Federal Unemployment:		2.88
PA – Unemployment Company:		14.40
Employee Taxes:		
Federal Withholding:		32.40
Social Security Employee:		22.32
Medicare Employee:		5.22
PA – Withholding:		10.80

Check No.:	**2**	
Check Date:	**06/15/2004**	
Pay Period Ends:	**06/15/2004**	
Employee:	**Wei Chun**	
Item Name:	**Salary**	
Rate:	**750.00**	
Company Taxes:		
Social Security Company:		46.50
Medicare Company:		10.88
Federal Unemployment:		6.00
PA – Unemployment Company:		30.00

Employee Taxes:
  Federal Withholding: **82.50**
  Social Security Employee: **46.50**
  Medicare Employee: **10.88**
  PA – Withholding: **22.50**

11. Process pay for June 30, 2004 using the following information:

Check No.:   **3**
Check Date: **06/30/2004**
Pay Period Ends: **06/30/2004**
Employee: **Michelle Auletta**
Item Name: **Hourly Wages**
Rate: **12**
Hours: **45**
Company Taxes:
  Social Security Company: **33.48**
  Medicare Company: **7.83**
  Federal Unemployment: **4.32**
  PA – Unemployment Company: **21.60**
Employee Taxes:
  Federal Withholding: **48.60**
  Social Security Employee: **33.48**
  Medicare Employee: **7.83**
  PA – Withholding: **16.20**

Check No.:   **4**
Check Date: **06/30/2004**
Pay Period Ends: **06/30/2004**
Employee: **Wei Chan**
Item Name: **Salary**
Rate: **750.00**
Company Taxes:
  Social Security Company   **46.50**
  Medicare Company   **10.88**
  Federal Unemployment   **6.00**
  PA – Unemployment Company **30.00**
Employee Taxes:
  Federal Withholding   **82.50**
  Social Security Employee   **46.50**
  Medicare Employee   **10.88**
  PA – Withholding   **22.50**

12. June 30, 2004, pay all payroll tax liabilities owed to the Internal Revenue Service for the period June 1, 2004 to June 30, 2004, Check No. 5.

13. Display and print the following reports for June 1, 2004 to June 30, 2004:

 a. *Payroll Summary*   d. *Employee State Taxes Detail*
 b. *Payroll Transaction Detail*   e. *Form 941* (Quarter ended
 c. *Journal*   June 30, 2004)

CASE PROBLEM 2

In August, the third month of business for Olivia's Web Solutions, Olivia Chen has decided to hire two employees. One employee will be a Web page designer, who will be paid hourly. The other employee, an administrative assistant, will be paid on a salary. The company file includes information for Olivia's Web Solutions as of August 1, 2004.

1. Open the company file: CH9 Olivia's Web Solutions.QBW.
2. Make a backup copy of the company file OWS9 [Your Name] Olivia's Web Solutions.
3. Restore the backup copy of the company file. In both the Restore From and Restore To windows use the file name OWS9 [Your Name] Olivia's Web Solutions.
4. Change the company name to OWS9 [Your Name] Olivia's Web Solutions.
5. Set up the payroll feature for Olivia's Web Solutions.
6. Add the following accounts to the Chart of Accounts List:

2110	Social Sec/Medicare Tax Payable	Subaccount of 2100 Payroll Liabilities
2115	FIT Payable	Subaccount of 2100 Payroll Liabilities
2120	SIT Payable	Subaccount of 2100 Payroll Liabilities
2125	FUTA Payable	Subaccount of 2100 Payroll Liabilities
2130	SUI Payable	Subaccount of 2100 Payroll Liabilities
6565	Salaries and Wages Expense	Subaccount of 6560 Payroll Expenses
6611	Social Sec/Medicare Tax Expense	Subaccount of 6560 Payroll Expenses
6625	FUTA Expense	Subaccount of 6560 Payroll Expenses
6630	SUI Expense	Subaccount of 6560 Payroll Expenses

7. Add the following payroll items:

Salary

Type:	**Wage (Hourly, Salary, Commission, Bonus)**
Wages:	**Salary Wages, Regular Pay**
Name:	**Salary**
Expense account:	**6565 Salaries and Wages Expense**

Wages

Type:	**Wage (Hourly, Salary, Commission, Bonus)**
Wages:	**Hourly Wages, Regular Pay**
Name:	**Hourly Wages**
Expense account:	**6565 Salaries and Wages Expense**

State Tax (State Withholding)

State:	**NY**
Type of Tax:	**State Withholding**
Name Used on Paychecks:	**NY – Withholding**
Agency for Liabilities:	**NYS Tax Department**

Identifying Number:	**55-5656566**
Liability Account:	**2120 SIT Payable**
Taxable Compensation:	**Accept defaults**

State Tax (SUI)

State:	**NY**
Type of Tax:	**State Unemployment**
Name Used on Paychecks:	**NY – Unemployment Company**
Agency for Liabilities:	**NYS Tax Department**
Identifying Number:	**ER-4877**
Liability Account:	**2130 SUI Payable**
Expense Account:	**6630 SUI Expense**
Company Tax Rate:	**4% each quarter**
Taxable Compensation:	**Accept defaults**

8. Edit each of the payroll items listed below. For each item—
   - accept the name listed
   - choose the Internal Revenue Service as the agency to which the liability will be paid
   - select the liability and expense accounts indicated below
   - accept all tax rates
   - accept all taxable compensation default

Payroll Item	Liability Account	Expense Account
Federal Unemployment	2125 FUTA Payable	6625 FUTA Expense
Federal Withholding	2115 FIT Payable	
Medicare Company	2110 Social Sec/ Medicare Tax Payable	6611 Social Sec/ Medicare Tax Expense
Medicare Employee	2110 Social Sec/ Medicare Tax Payable	6611 Social Sec/ Medicare Tax Expense
Social Security Company	2110 Social Sec/ Medicare Tax Payable	6611 Social Sec/ Medicare Tax Expense
Social Security Employee	2110 Social Sec/ Medicare Tax Payable	6611 Social Sec/ Medicare Tax Expense

9. Add the following employees:

First Name:	**Fiona**
Last Name:	**Ferguson**
Print on Checks as:	**Fiona Ferguson**
SS No.:	**449-99-3333**
Gender:	**Female**
Date of Birth:	**8/8/81**
Address:	**23 E. 14th Street**
	Westport, NY 11858
Phone:	**631-555-1020**
Cellular:	**631-555-3814**
Item Name:	**Salary**
Hourly/Annual Rate:	**19,200**
Pay Period:	**Semimonthly**
Federal Filing Status:	**Single**
Federal Allowances:	**1**
State Worked/Subject to Withholding:	**NY**
Subject to SUI?:	**Yes**

State Filing Status:	**Single**
State Allowances:	**1**
Not Subject to Local Taxes	(press Ctrl + Delete 4 times to remove taxes)
First Name:	**Gary**
Last Name:	**Glenn**
Print on Checks as:	**Gary Glenn**
SS No.:	**101-55-3333**
Gender:	**Male**
Date of Birth:	**12/23/75**
Address:	**1050 York Ave.**
	Westport, NY 11858
Phone:	**631-555-5447**
Cellular:	**631-555-7111**
Item Name:	**Hourly Wages**
Hourly/Annual Rate:	**25**
Pay Period:	**Semimonthly**
Federal Filing Status:	**Married**
Federal Allowances:	**2**
State Worked/Subject to Withholding:	**NY**
Subject to SUI?:	**Yes**
State Filing Status:	**Married**
State Allowances:	**2**
Not Subject to Local Taxes	(press Ctrl + Delete 4 times to remove taxes)

10. Process pay for August 15, 2004 using the following information:

Check No.:	**1**
Check Date:	**08/15/2004**
Pay Period Ends:	**08/15/2004**
Employee:	**Fiona Ferguson**
Item Name:	**Salary**
Rate:	**800**

Company Taxes:

Social Security Company:	**49.60**
Medicare Company:	**11.60**
Federal Unemployment:	**6.40**
NY – Unemployment Company:	**32.00**

Employee Taxes:

Federal Withholding:	**110.00**
Social Security Employee:	**49.60**
Medicare Employee:	**11.60**
NY – Withholding:	**40.00**

Check No.:	**2**
Check Date	**08/15/2004**
Pay Period Ends:	**08/15/2004**
Employee:	**Gary Glenn**
Item Name:	**Hourly Wages**
Rate:	**25**
Hours:	**80**

Company Taxes:

Social Security Company:	**124.00**

Medicare Company:		**29.00**
Federal Unemployment:		**16.00**
NY – Unemployment Company:		**80.00**
Employee Taxes:		
Federal Withholding:		**360.00**
Social Security Employee:		**124.00**
Medicare Employee:		**29.00**
NY – Withholding:		**98.00**

11. Process pay for August 31, 2004 using the following information:

Check No.:	**3**
Check Date:	**08/15/2004**
Pay Period Ends:	**08/31/2004**
Employee:	**Fiona Ferguson**
Item Name:	**Salary**
Rate:	**800**
Company Taxes:	
Social Security Company:	**49.60**
Medicare Company:	**11.60**
Federal Unemployment:	**6.40**
NY – Unemployment Company:	**32.00**
Employee Taxes	
Federal Withholding:	**110.00**
Social Security Employee:	**49.60**
Medicare Employee:	**11.60**
NY – Withholding:	**40.00**

Check No.:	**4**
Check Date:	**08/31/2004**
Pay Period Ends:	**08/31/2004**
Employee:	**Gary Glenn**
Item Name:	**Hourly Wages**
Rate:	**25**
Hours:	**88**
Company Taxes:	
Social Security Company:	**136.40**
Medicare Company:	**31.90**
Federal Unemployment:	**17.60**
NY – Unemployment Company:	**88.00**
Employee Taxes:	
Federal Withholding:	**400.00**
Social Security Employee:	**136.40**
Medicare Employee:	**31.90**
NY – Withholding:	**105.00**

12. August 31, 2004, pay all payroll tax liabilities owed to the Internal Revenue Service for the period August 1, 2004 to August 31, 2004, Check No. 5.

13. Display and print the following reports for August 1, 2004 to August 31, 2004:

a. *Payroll Summary*

b. *Payroll Transaction Detail*

c. *Journal*

d. *Employee State Taxes Detail*

e. *Form 941* (Quarter ended September 30, 2004)

CHAPTER

10

BANKING

Transfer Funds, Reconcile Accounts, and Enter Credit Card Charges

CHAPTER OBJECTIVES

- Transfer funds between accounts using the Transfer Funds between Accounts window

- Reconcile cash accounts using the Reconcile window

- Enter credit card charges using the Enter Credit Card Charges window

- Pay credit card charges using the Write Checks window

- Display and print banking-related reports

INTRODUCTION

An integral part of operating any business is effectively managing cash. This usually involves maintaining cash in one or more bank accounts. In addition, it involves transferring funds among the bank accounts, reconciling account balances, and utilizing credit cards for business purchases and making credit card payments. QuickBooks Pro allows you to transfer funds from one bank account to another, process the month-end bank reconciliation, and enter and pay credit card charges.

Many companies have more than one checking account. The regular checking account, commonly known as the operating account, is used for paying bills and collecting and depositing receivables and other funds. Usually a company maintains a separate checking account solely for payroll transactions. Periodically, funds from the operating checking account will be transferred to the payroll checking account in order to pay employees and payroll taxes.

As a business grows in complexity, the need for special purpose accounts grows correspondingly. For example, many companies have interest bearing money market accounts that are designed to hold excess funds temporarily. These funds earn interest until they are needed for an operating activity, at which time they are transferred to a checking account.

tranfer funds The movement of money from one account to another account.

Companies can **transfer funds** as needed among the different accounts, often via online banking connections. With QuickBooks Pro, you can use the *Transfer Funds Between Accounts* window to record and monitor the transfer of funds between accounts.

Companies typically receive a statement from the bank at the end of the month detailing the activity the bank has recorded in the company's checking account, along with a month-end balance. Often, this balance does not agree with the company's records. The differences are usually due to transactions that the bank has recorded in the account of which the company is unaware. **Bank reconciliation** is a procedure used to determine the correct cash balance by accounting for these differences and ensuring that they are not a result of errors, either on the part of the bank or the company, or of theft of funds. In addition, if the bank makes changes to the company's account, the company will have to record transactions in the general ledger accounts to reflect these changes. In QuickBooks Pro, the *Reconcile* window is used to reconcile the balance per the bank statement to the balance per the accounting records.

bank reconciliation Procedure used to determine the correct cash balance in an account by comparing the activity recorded in the account to the activity recorded on the bank statement.

credit card charges Expenditures charged to a credit card to be paid at a later date.

Many companies now utilize credit cards to pay bills. These **credit card charges** allow the company to track expenses of a specific nature, such as travel and entertainment expenses, and defer payment of expenses as needed. In QuickBooks Pro, the *Enter Credit Card Charges* window is used to record credit card expenditures.

In this chapter, our sample company, Kristin Raina Interior Designs, will transfer funds between accounts, process bank reconciliations, and use a credit card to pay for expenses.

QUICKBOOKS PRO VERSUS MANUAL ACCOUNTING: BANKING

Banking activities in both manual and computerized accounting systems require a company to record transfers of funds among bank accounts, reconcile each bank account balance to the company's balances, and track charges and payments by credit card.

TRANSFER FUNDS

In a manual accounting system, when funds are transferred to or from one cash account to another, the transaction can be handled in several ways. Transfers from the company's operating account can be recorded in the cash payments journal or the general journal. If the cash payments journal is used for transfers out of the cash accounts, the cash receipts journal will be used for transfers into the cash accounts. Similarly, if the general journal is used to record the transfer out of the cash accounts, it also will be used to record the transfers into the cash accounts. A cash payments journal procedure is used when a check is drawn from a cash account in order to accomplish the transfer. If the transfer is accomplished via a bank credit and debit memo or phone transfer, the general journal procedure is used.

In QuickBooks Pro, transfers among bank accounts, if not done by check, are recorded in the Transfer Funds Between Accounts activity window. This window indicates the cash accounts involved in the transfer and the amount of the transfer.

BANK RECONCILIATION

reconciling items Differences between the bank statement and the company's records that have to be reconciled in order to have the cash balance in the company's accounting records agree with the balance in its bank statement.

deposit in transit A deposit recorded on the company's books, usually at the end of the month, yet deposited too late to be on the current month's bank statement.

outstanding check A check written and recorded by the company that has not yet been paid by the bank.

The steps to completing a bank reconciliation in QuickBooks Pro are similar to those in a manual accounting system. The company receives a statement from the bank detailing the activity in the account for the month. The statement shows the deposits (or other additions) to the account along with the checks that have cleared (were paid by) the bank. If the account has earned interest, it is added to the balance by the bank. If the bank has charged any fees, called service charges, they will be deducted from the account. Other items that may appear are NSF (Non Sufficient Funds) checks, credit memos (additions), or debit memos (subtractions). The bank statement is compared to the company's accounting records and any differences identified. Generally, these differences, called **reconciling items,** fall into three categories: timing differences, such as **deposits in transit** or **outstanding checks;** omissions, such as the interest recorded by the bank not yet recorded by the company; or errors by either party. The first two are normal differences that are expected as part of the reconciliation process. If all timing differences and omissions are accounted for, and there are no errors, the adjusted bank balances will agree with the adjusted balance for the company's books. The account is then said to be reconciled. However, if there is an error, a difference will remain until the source of the mistake is found.

In QuickBooks Pro, the bank reconciliation procedure is carried out using the Reconcile window. Once a cash account is identified, the window displays all activity to the account, including deposits or other additions (debits), and checks or other reductions (credits). This information is compared to the bank statement in order to reconcile the account.

CREDIT CARD CHARGES

In a manual accounting system, a credit card charge is usually recorded when the bill is paid by the company or tracked as part of accounts payable. This often results in expenses being recorded in periods after they are actually incurred. In QuickBooks Pro, a credit card charge can be recorded immediately when it is incurred using the Enter Credit Card Charges window. The program also tracks the resulting credit card liability, which will be paid at a later date separate from accounts payable. This ensures that assets and/or expenses are recorded in the proper time period and the credit card liability is tracked.

CHAPTER PROBLEM

In this chapter, Kristin Raina Interior Designs will transfer funds among the company's bank accounts, prepare a reconciliation of the cash accounts, and enter credit card transactions. The balances as of April 30, 2004, are contained in the company file CH10 Kristin Raina Interior Designs. Open that file, make a backup copy, name it **EX10 [Your Name] Kristin Raina Interior Designs**, restore the backup copy, and change the company name to **EX10 [Your Name] Kristin Raina Interior Designs**.

LISTS: UPDATING THE CHART OF ACCOUNTS LIST

Kristin Raina has decided to open and fund a money market cash account because the bank offers a higher rate of interest on money market funds than it offers on a Cash – Operating account. Typically a company will have a separate general ledger account for each bank account to facilitate the bank reconciliation process. Kristin Raina needs to add an additional cash account and add accounts that reflect the adjustments resulting from the bank reconciliation. In addition, Kristin will begin using a credit card to pay for travel-related expenses, so accounts must be added for this additional expense and liability. You will need to update Kristin Raina's Chart of Accounts List to include these new accounts necessary for the additional banking procedures.

Follow the procedures presented in chapter 4 to add the following accounts:

Type	Number	Name
Bank	1050	Cash – Money Market
Credit Card	2015	American Travel Card
Expense	6100	Bank Service Charges
Expense	6475	Travel Expense
Other Income	6900	Interest Income

The revised Account Listing appears in figure 10–1.

FIGURE 10-1
Updated Account Listing

EX10 [Your Name] Kristin Raina Interior Designs
Account Listing
April 30, 2004

Account	Type	Balance Total	Accnt. #	Tax Line
1010 · Cash - Operating	Bank	43,355.38	1010	<Unassigned>
1020 · Cash - Payroll	Bank	1,472.68	1020	<Unassigned>
1050 · Cash - Money Market	Bank	0.00	1050	<Unassigned>
1200 · Accounts Receivable	Accounts Receivable	1,540.00	1200	<Unassigned>
1250 · Undeposited Funds	Other Current Asset	0.00	1250	<Unassigned>
1260 · Inventory of Carpets	Other Current Asset	800.00	1260	<Unassigned>
1265 · Inventory of Draperies	Other Current Asset	1,000.00	1265	<Unassigned>
1270 · Inventory of Lamps	Other Current Asset	1,000.00	1270	<Unassigned>
1275 · Inventory of Mirrors	Other Current Asset	900.00	1275	<Unassigned>
1300 · Design Supplies	Other Current Asset	200.00	1300	<Unassigned>
1305 · Office Supplies	Other Current Asset	250.00	1305	<Unassigned>
1410 · Prepaid Advertising	Other Current Asset	500.00	1410	<Unassigned>
1420 · Prepaid Insurance	Other Current Asset	2,200.00	1420	<Unassigned>
1700 · Furniture	Fixed Asset	11,900.00	1700	<Unassigned>
1700 · Furniture:1750 · Accum. Dep., Furniture	Fixed Asset	-100.00	1750	<Unassigned>
1800 · Computers	Fixed Asset	3,540.00	1800	<Unassigned>
1800 · Computers:1850 · Accum. Dep., Computers	Fixed Asset	-60.00	1850	<Unassigned>
2010 · Accounts Payable	Accounts Payable	9,750.00	2010	<Unassigned>
2015 · American Travel Card	Credit Card	0.00	2015	<Unassigned>
2020 · Notes Payable	Other Current Liability	7,000.00	2020	<Unassigned>
2030 · Interest Payable	Other Current Liability	50.00	2030	<Unassigned>
2100 · Payroll Liabilities	Other Current Liability	0.00	2100	<Unassigned>
2100 · Payroll Liabilities:2110 · Social Sec/Medicare Tax Payable	Other Current Liability	0.00	2110	<Unassigned>
2100 · Payroll Liabilities:2115 · FIT Payable	Other Current Liability	0.00	2115	<Unassigned>
2100 · Payroll Liabilities:2120 · SIT Payable	Other Current Liability	0.00	2120	<Unassigned>
2100 · Payroll Liabilities:2125 · FUTA Payable	Other Current Liability	0.00	2125	<Unassigned>
2100 · Payroll Liabilities:2130 · SUI Payable	Other Current Liability	0.00	2130	<Unassigned>
2200 · Sales Tax Payable	Other Current Liability	0.00	2200	<Unassigned>
3010 · Kristin Raina, Capital	Equity	50,000.00	3010	<Unassigned>
3020 · Kristin Raina, Drawings	Equity	-400.00	3020	<Unassigned>
3900 · Retained Earnings	Equity		3900	<Unassigned>
4010 · Design Services	Income		4010	<Unassigned>
4020 · Decorating Services	Income		4020	<Unassigned>
4060 · Sale of Carpets	Income		4060	<Unassigned>
4065 · Sale of Draperies	Income		4065	<Unassigned>
4070 · Sale of Lamps	Income		4070	<Unassigned>
4075 · Sale of Mirrors	Income		4075	<Unassigned>
4100 · Sales Discounts	Income		4100	<Unassigned>
5060 · Cost of Carpets Sold	Cost of Goods Sold		5060	<Unassigned>
5065 · Cost of Draperies Sold	Cost of Goods Sold		5065	<Unassigned>
5070 · Cost of Lamps Sold	Cost of Goods Sold		5070	<Unassigned>
5075 · Cost of Mirrors Sold	Cost of Goods Sold		5075	<Unassigned>
5900 · Inventory Adjustment	Cost of Goods Sold		5900	<Unassigned>
6020 · Accounting Expense	Expense		6020	<Unassigned>
6050 · Advertising Expense	Expense		6050	<Unassigned>
6100 · Bank Service Charges	Expense		6100	<Unassigned>
6175 · Deprec. Exp., Furniture	Expense		6175	<Unassigned>
6185 · Deprec. Exp., Computers	Expense		6185	<Unassigned>
6200 · Insurance Expense	Expense		6200	<Unassigned>
6300 · Janitorial Expenses	Expense		6300	<Unassigned>
6325 · Office Supplies Expense	Expense		6325	<Unassigned>
6400 · Rent Expense	Expense		6400	<Unassigned>
6450 · Telephone Expense	Expense		6450	<Unassigned>
6475 · Travel Expense	Expense		6475	<Unassigned>
6500 · Utilities Expense	Expense		6500	<Unassigned>
6560 · Payroll Expenses	Expense		6560	<Unassigned>
6560 · Payroll Expenses:6565 · Salaries and Wages Expense	Expense		6565	<Unassigned>
6560 · Payroll Expenses:6610 · Social Sec/Medicare Tax Expense	Expense		6610	<Unassigned>
6560 · Payroll Expenses:6625 · FUTA Expense	Expense		6625	<Unassigned>
6560 · Payroll Expenses:6630 · SUI Expense	Expense		6630	<Unassigned>
6900 · Interest Income	Other Income		6900	<Unassigned>
7000 · Interest Expense	Other Expense		7000	<Unassigned>

As you know, the third level of operations in QuickBooks Pro is to record the daily transactions of the business. In QuickBooks Pro, you use the Transfer Funds Between Accounts window (or Transfer Funds window, for short) to record the movement of funds among the cash accounts of the business. If you transfer funds by writing a check from one cash account to be deposited into another cash account, you can use the Write Checks window. However, when you transfer funds via bank memo, telephone, or online services, you use the Transfer Funds window to record the transaction. In this window, since there are no default accounts, you identify the source (transferor) cash account and the receiving account (transferee), and the amount to be transferred. The transaction is recorded as follows:

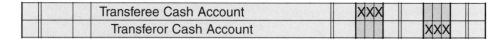

| | | | Transferee Cash Account | XXX | | |
| | | | Transferor Cash Account | | | XXX |

The QuickBooks Pro Transfer Funds window appears in figure 10–2.

FIGURE 10-2
Transfer Funds Between
Accounts Window

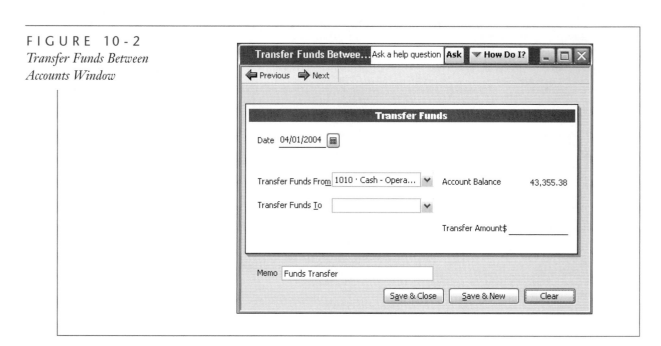

This window allows you to identify the source (transferor) cash account, the receiving (transferee) account, and the amount to be transferred. It also displays the current balance of the source account, thus preventing you from overdrawing from it. The Previous and Next arrows, and the Save & Close, Save & New, and Clear buttons all have the same function in this window as in other Activity windows.

On April 30, 2004, Kristin Raina wants you to transfer $7,000 from the company's Cash – Operating account to its Cash – Payroll account in order to have sufficient funds in that account to pay May's payroll and payroll tax liabilities.

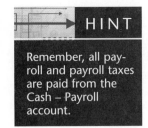

To transfer funds—
1. Click Banking, and then click Transfer Funds.
2. At the *Date* field, choose *04/30/2004*.
3. At the Transfer Funds From drop-down list, click *1010 Cash – Operating*. The balance in the account is displayed.
4. At the Transfer Funds To drop-down list, click *1020 Cash – Payroll*.
5. At the *Transfer Amount* field, key **7000**. (See figure 10–3).

FIGURE 10-3
Transfer Funds Between Accounts Window – Complete

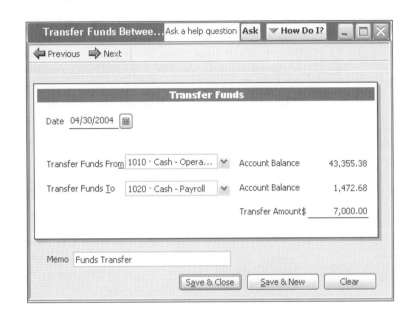

6. If the information is correct, click Save & New.

ACCOUNTING
concept

For a transfer of funds between accounts the general ledger posting is as follows:

1010 Cash – Operating			1020 Cash – Payroll		
Dr		Cr		Dr	Cr
Bal	43,355.38	Trf	7,000	Bal	1,472.68	
				Trf	7,000.00	
Bal	36,355.38			Bal	8,472.68	

PRACTICE *exercise*

On April 30, 2004, transfer $10,000 from the Cash – Operating account to the Cash – Money Market account.

In QuickBooks Pro, Activities identified as bank reconciliation are processed in the Reconcile windows. The reconciliation procedure in QuickBooks Pro accomplishes two purposes. First, it ensures that the company's cash records are correct and agree with that of the bank. Second, transactions missing from the company's records that are discovered during the reconciling process can be recorded at this time.

The Reconcile windows display all additions to a given account, such as deposits and transfers in; and all reductions to the account, such as checks written and transfers out. Using these windows, you can compare the information for each account with the bank statement for that account. You can indicate the transactions that have cleared the bank by placing a check next to the transaction, and add transactions recorded on the bank statement that are not yet on the company's books.

As part of the reconciling process, you may need to make adjustments to the cash account. For example, the bank may have deducted service charges from the company's bank account during the course of the month. This deduction is reflected on the bank statement, but has not yet been recorded in the company's records. The same holds true for any interest income earned on the company's bank account. While performing the bank reconciliation in the Reconcile windows, you have the opportunity to identify and record these transactions and adjust the company's accounts accordingly.

When you add service charges, the default accounts are the Bank Service Charges account and the Cash account. QuickBooks Pro records the transaction as follows:

	Bank Service Charges (expense)		XXX		
	Cash				XXX

When you record interest income, the default accounts are the Cash account and the Interest Income account. QuickBooks Pro records the transaction as follows:

	Cash		XXX		
	Interest Income				XXX

If the bank records an NSF from a customer, QuickBooks Pro does not automatically record the transaction. Instead, you must record the transaction in the Create Invoices window to reestablish the accounts receivable for this customer and deduct the cash that was never actually collected.

Recall that the system default account in the Create Invoices window is a debit to Accounts Receivable. When you select an item, usually a service or inventory part item, the appropriate revenue account is credited. If you are using QuickBooks Pro to reconcile accounts, you create an item for NSFs in the Item List. When you establish an NSF item, you will identify the default account as Cash. When you record an NSF in the Create Invoices window, the Accounts Receivable is debited for the amount of the NSF still due the company and the corresponding credit, based on the NSF item, will be to Cash.

The QuickBooks Pro Reconcile window consists of two parts. The first window, called the Begin Reconciliation window, allows you to select a bank account to reconcile, add transactions such as service charges and interest income, and enter the bank statement balance. (See figure 10-4.)

FIGURE 10-4
Begin Reconciliation
Window

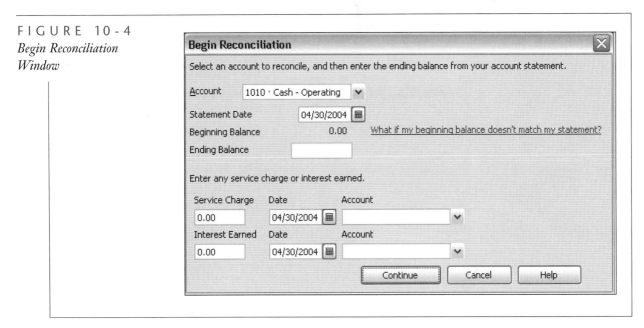

Special note should be made of the following fields:

ACCOUNT	QuickBooks Pro allows you to reconcile all cash accounts set up by the company. Once you select an account from the drop-down list, all activity for that account only is displayed.
BEGINNING BALANCE	Indicates the opening balance for the bank statement. If this is the first time you are reconciling the account, the figure will be zero. **Do not edit this number.**
ENDING BALANCE	Used to enter the ending balance appearing on the bank statement.
SERVICE CHARGE	Used to enter the amount of the service charges appearing on the bank statement. You also indicate the account the service charge will be charged to here. When you click Reconcile Now in the Reconcile window, QuickBooks Pro automatically posts the expense and reduces the cash account.
INTEREST EARNED	Used to enter the amount of interest shown on the bank statement along with the appropriate income account for interest. When you click Reconcile Now, QuickBooks Pro automatically posts the increase to both Cash and Interest Income.

Once the information is entered in the first window, the second window called the Reconcile window will be used to indicate which transactions recorded on the company's books have cleared the bank. Once all cleared or missing transactions have been accounted for the difference amount should be zero.

FIGURE 10-5
Reconcile Window

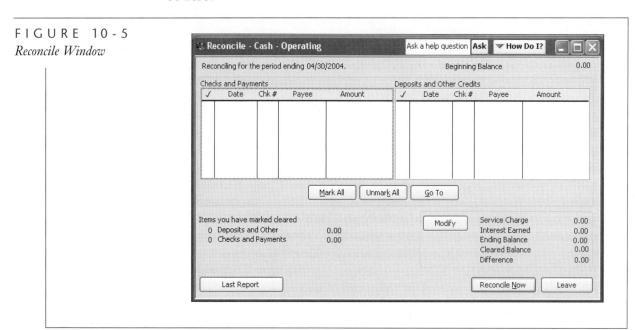

Special note should be made of the following fields:

DIFFERENCE	If all reconciling items are accounted for, the difference will be zero. If after completing the reconciliation process a difference remains, it is probably due to an error, either on the part of the bank or the company. You must identify the error and correct it before completing the reconciliation.
RECONCILE NOW	Click this button if the Difference amount is zero. The account is now reconciled and a *Reconciliation* report can be printed.

On April 30, 2004, Kristin Raina receives the bank statement for the Cash – Operating account from her bank. After a review of the bank statement, you determine the following:

1. The cash balance per the bank statement is $20,675.
2. The cash balance per the books is $ 26,355.38.

   You can review the Chart of Accounts List, the trial balance, or the general ledger for the Cash – Operating account to determine the balance on the books.

3. The bank charged the account $35 for bank service charges.
4. The bank credited the account for $10 of interest income.
5. All deposits, except the deposit of March 31, 2004, have cleared the bank.

6. All checks and payments, except Check Nos. 10 and 11, have cleared the bank.
7. A check for $600 from Burnitz Bakery Company, included in the deposit of February 28, 2001, was returned as NSF. The bank deducted the amount from the bank statement.

HINT

Do not edit the Opening Balance figure.

To reconcile the Cash – Operating account with the bank statement—
1. Click <u>B</u>anking, and then click Reconci<u>l</u>e. The Begin Reconciliation window appears.
2. At the <u>A</u>ccount drop-down list, click *1010 Cash – Operating*.
3. At the *Statement Date* field, choose *April 30, 2004*.
4. At the *Ending Balance* field, key **20,675**.
5. At the *Service Charge* field, key **35**.
6. At the *Date* field, choose *April 30, 2004*.
7. At the Account drop-down list, click *6100 Bank Service Charges*.
8. At the *Interest Earned* field, key **10**.
9. At the *Date* field, choose *April 30, 2004*.
10. At the Account drop-down list, click *6900 Interest Income*. (See figure 10-6)

FIGURE 10-6
Begin Reconciliation Window – Completed

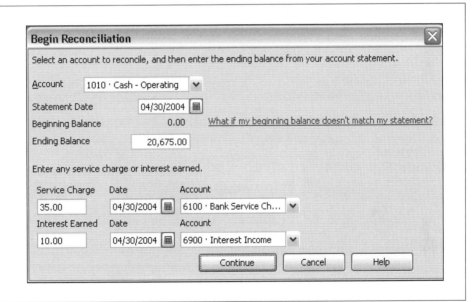

11. If the information is correct, click Continue. The Reconcile – Cash – Operating window appears. The activity for that account will be displayed.

12. Place a ✓ next to all of the deposits, except the deposit of March 31, to indicate that all have cleared. (See figure 10–7.)

FIGURE 10-7

Reconcile – Cash –
Operating Window with
Cleared Deposits

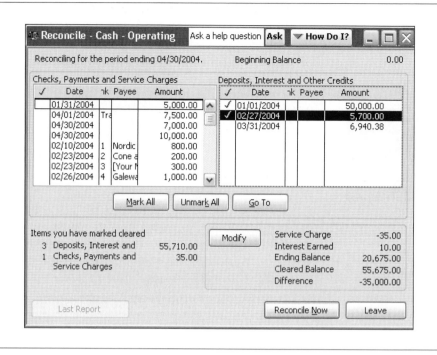

13. Place a ✓ next to all checks and payments except Check Nos. 10 and 11 since they have not cleared the bank. The Difference is now ⁻600.00, the amount of the NSF. (See figure 10–8.)

FIGURE 10-8

Reconcile Window with
Cleared Checks and
Payments

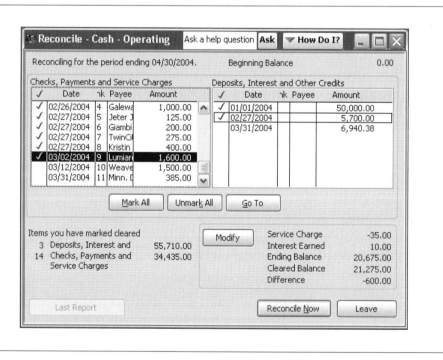

14. Click the deposit of 02/27/2004 to select it, and then click Go To. The Make Deposits window displays listing the checks that were included in the deposit of February 27. Notice the $600 check from Burnitz Bakery Company is included in the deposit. (See figure 10–9.)

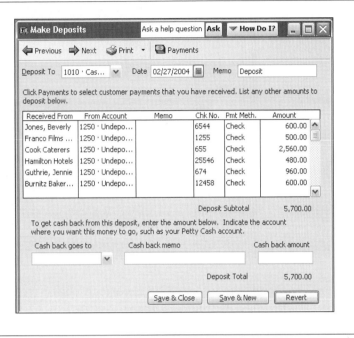

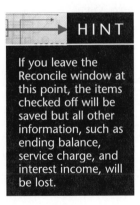

When this deposit was made on February 27, the bank recorded the total deposit and increased the bank balance by $5,700. When the Burnitz Bakery Company check was returned due to non-sufficient funds, the bank then deducted the $600 from the bank balance. To reconcile with the bank account, the $600 must be deducted from the Cash – Operating account.

15. Close the Make Deposits window. If the ✓ was removed from the February 27 deposit, click the deposit to replace the check mark.
16. With the Reconcile window open, on the Main menu click Customers, and then click Create Invoices.
17. In the Create Invoices window, enter the following information:

Customer:Job	**Burnitz Bakery Company**
Date	**04/30/2004**
Invoice #	**NSF1**
Item Code	**NSF**
Amount	**600**
Tax	**Non**

(See figure 10–10.)

FIGURE 10-10
Create Invoices Window

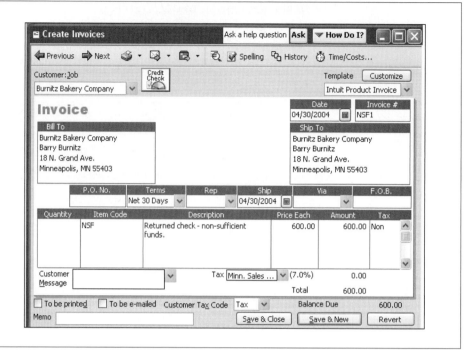

18. If the information is correct, click S<u>a</u>ve & Close. You are returned to the Reconcile window.
19. Scroll in the Checks and Payments section until you locate the $600 adjustment to the Cash account for the NSF check.
20. Place a ✓ next to the 600 NSF. The difference is now zero. (See figure 10–11.)

FIGURE 10-11
Reconcile – Cash – Operating Window Completed

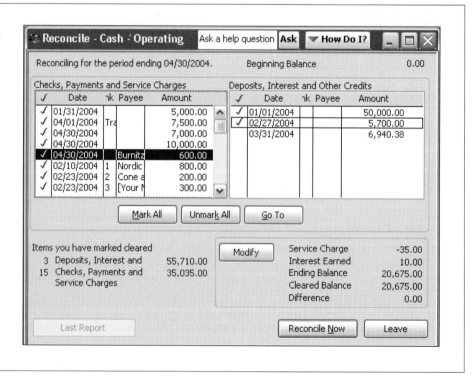

21. If the information is correct, click Reconcile <u>N</u>ow. At the Information message, click OK. The account is now reconciled and the missing transactions for service charges and interest are now posted to the appropriate accounts.

22. At the Select Reconciliation Detail Report dialog box, click D<u>e</u>tail, and then click <u>P</u>rint.

23. At the Print Lists dialog box, choose the Po<u>r</u>trait orientation and click Print. The report will be printed, and it should look like figure 10–12.

FIGURE 10-12

Reconciliation Detail Report – Cash – Operating Account

EX10 [Your Name] Kristin Raina Interior Designs
Reconciliation Detail
1010 · Cash - Operating, Period Ending 04/30/2004

Type	Date	Num	Name	Clr	Amount	Balance
Beginning Balance						0.00
Cleared Transactions						
Checks and Payments - 15 items						
General Journal	01/01/2004			X	-5,000.00	-5,000.00
Bill Pmt -Check	02/10/2004	1	Nordic Realty	X	-800.00	-5,800.00
Bill Pmt -Check	02/23/2004	2	Cone and Clemens ...	X	-200.00	-6,000.00
Bill Pmt -Check	02/25/2004	3	[Your Name] Accou...	X	-300.00	-6,300.00
Bill Pmt -Check	02/26/2004	4	Galeway Computers	X	-1,000.00	-7,300.00
Check	02/27/2004	7	TwinCityTelCo	X	-275.00	-7,575.00
Check	02/27/2004	6	Giambi Graphics	X	-200.00	-7,775.00
Check	02/27/2004	5	Jeter Janitorial Serv...	X	-125.00	-7,900.00
Check	02/27/2004	8	Kristin Raina	X	-400.00	-8,300.00
Check	03/02/2004	9	Lumiare Lighting Co...	X	-1,600.00	-9,900.00
General Journal	04/01/2004			X	-7,500.00	-17,400.00
Invoice	04/30/2004	NSF1	Burnitz Bakery Com...	X	-600.00	-18,000.00
Check	04/30/2004			X	-35.00	-18,035.00
Transfer	04/30/2004			X	-7,000.00	-25,035.00
Transfer	04/30/2004			X	-10,000.00	-35,035.00
Total Checks and Payments					-35,035.00	-35,035.00
Deposits and Credits - 3 items						
General Journal	01/01/2004			X	50,000.00	50,000.00
Deposit	02/27/2004			X	5,700.00	55,700.00
Deposit	04/30/2004			X	10.00	55,710.00
Total Deposits and Credits					55,710.00	55,710.00
Total Cleared Transactions					20,675.00	20,675.00
Cleared Balance					20,675.00	20,675.00
Uncleared Transactions						
Checks and Payments - 2 items						
Check	03/12/2004	10	Weaver Fabrics		-1,500.00	-1,500.00
Sales Tax Payment	03/31/2004	11	Minn. Dept. of Reve...		-385.00	-1,885.00
Total Checks and Payments					-1,885.00	-1,885.00
Deposits and Credits - 1 item						
Deposit	03/31/2004				6,940.38	6,940.38
Total Deposits and Credits					6,940.38	6,940.38
Total Uncleared Transactions					5,055.38	5,055.38
Register Balance as of 04/30/2004					25,730.38	25,730.38
Ending Balance					**25,730.38**	**25,730.38**

You should print the report immediately. The *Reconciliation* report is available from the <u>R</u>eports menu. However, this option is only available until you do the next reconciliation.

For a bank reconciliation, the postings to the general ledger are as follows:

Cash – Operating				Accounts Receivable	
Dr	Cr			Dr	Cr
26,355.38	600 NSF			600	
Int. Inc 10.00	35 S.C.				
Bal 25,730.38					

Bank Service Charges				Interest Income	
Dr	Cr			Dr	Cr
35.00					10.00

Adjusted Bank Statement Balance:

Ending Balance		$20,675.00
Deposit-in-transit		6,940.38
Outstanding Checks:		
No. 10	1,500.00	
No. 11	385.00	(1,885.00)
		$25,730.38

In addition, the customer file for Burnitz Bakery Company will reflect the increased asset amount:

Burnitz Bakery Company	
Dr	Cr
600	

PRACTICE *exercise*

Reconcile the company's Cash – Payroll account. The following information relates to this account:

1. The cash figure per the bank statement is $3,224.04 as of 4/30/04.
2. The bank charged the account $25 for bank service charges.
3. No interest was earned on this account.
4. The deposit of $7,000 on April 30, 2004, did not clear the bank statement.
5. Check Nos. 5 and 6 did not clear the bank.

QuickCheck: See the bank reconciliation report in figure 10–13.

FIGURE 10-13
*Reconciliation Detail
Report – Cash – Payroll
Account*

EX10 [Your Name] Kristin Raina Interior Designs
Reconciliation Detail
1020 · Cash - Payroll, Period Ending 04/30/2004

Type	Date	Num	Name	Clr	Amount	Balance
Beginning Balance						0.00
Cleared Transactions						
Checks and Payments - 5 items						
Paycheck	04/15/2004	2	Richard Henderson	X	-1,303.60	-1,303.60
Paycheck	04/15/2004	1	Harry Renee	X	-757.50	-2,061.10
Paycheck	04/30/2004	4	Richard Henderson	X	-1,432.36	-3,493.46
Check	04/30/2004			X	-25.00	-3,518.46
Paycheck	04/30/2004	3	Harry Renee	X	-757.50	-4,275.96
Total Checks and Payments					-4,275.96	-4,275.96
Deposits and Credits - 1 item						
General Journal	04/01/2004			X	7,500.00	7,500.00
Total Deposits and Credits					7,500.00	7,500.00
Total Cleared Transactions					3,224.04	3,224.04
Cleared Balance					3,224.04	3,224.04
Uncleared Transactions						
Checks and Payments - 2 items						
Liability Check	04/30/2004	5	Internal Revenue S...		-1,354.96	-1,354.96
Liability Check	04/30/2004	6	Minn. Dept. of Reve...		-421.40	-1,776.36
Total Checks and Payments					-1,776.36	-1,776.36
Deposits and Credits - 1 item						
Transfer	04/30/2004				7,000.00	7,000.00
Total Deposits and Credits					7,000.00	7,000.00
Total Uncleared Transactions					5,223.64	5,223.64
Register Balance as of 04/30/2004					8,447.68	8,447.68
Ending Balance					8,447.68	8,447.68

ACTIVITIES: THE ENTER CREDIT CARD CHARGES WINDOW

Activities identified as credit card purchases of goods or services are recorded in the Enter Credit Card Charges window. When a credit card is used to purchase goods, the asset purchased or expense incurred is recorded as if the goods were purchased with cash or on account. The purchase creates a liability in the form of a credit card balance that will be paid at a later date. The default account is a Credit Card Liability account. Since the liability is not posted to the Accounts Payable account, Accounts Payable is not used to track the credit card liability. The transaction is recorded as follows:

			Asset/Expense		XXX			
			Credit Card Liability				XXX	

When the credit card bill is paid, the credit card liability is reduced by a cash payment. The default accounts are the Credit Card Liability account and the Cash account. The journal entry is as follows:

			Credit Card Liability		XXX		
			Cash – Operating			XXX	

The QuickBooks Pro Enter Credit Card Charges window appears in figure 10–14.

FIGURE 10-14
Enter Credit Card Charges Window

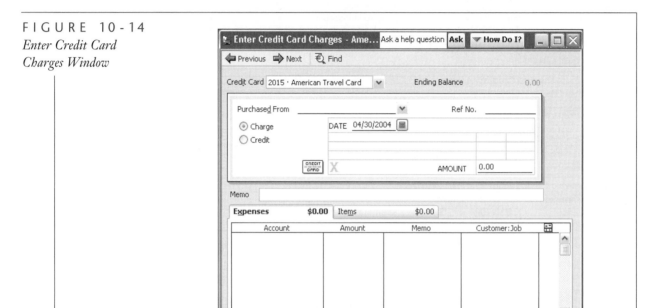

The procedures for this window are very similar to those of the Enter Bills and Write Checks windows. Make special note of the following fields:

CREDIT CARD	QuickBooks Pro allows you to track the activity of more than one credit card. Choose the credit card for the current transaction from the drop-down list.
PURCHASED FROM	Used to choose the vendor that the item or expense was purchased from in the same manner as the Enter Bills window.
CHARGE/CREDIT	If this is a purchase, click *Charge*. If you are processing a vendor credit, click *Credit*. A charge will increase the liability; a credit will reduce the liability.

ENTERING A CREDIT CARD CHARGE

On May 1, 2004, Kristin Raina travels to a decorator's convention being held in Las Vegas, Nevada. She spends three days attending meetings and conferences. The travel expense for the trip is $600, which is paid with a credit card on May 4. The Ref No. is 47887.

To enter a credit card charge—
1. Click Banking, and then click Enter Credit Card Charges.
2. At the Credit Card drop-down list, accept *2015 American Travel Card*.
3. At the Purchased From drop-down list, click *American Travel*.
4. At the *Ref No.* field, key **47887**.
5. Click the Charge button.
6. At the *Date* field, choose *05/04/2004*.
7. At the *Amount* field, key **600**.
8. At the *Account* field of the Expenses tab, click *6475 Travel Expense*. (See figure 10–15.)

FIGURE 10-15
Enter Credit Card Charges Window – Completed

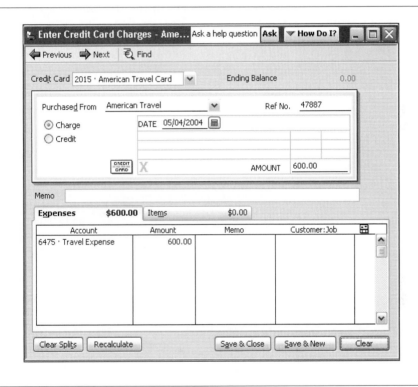

9. If the information is correct, click Save & New.

ACCOUNTING
concept

For a credit card charge for travel expense the general journal posting is as follows:

6475 Travel Expense		2015 Credit Card Liability	
Dr	Cr	Dr	Cr
600			600

PRACTICE exercise

On May 17, 2004, Kristin Raina traveled to St. Louis, Missouri to meet with a new client. The travel costs were $350, which were charged to American Travel Card, Ref No. 84441.

PAYING A CREDIT CARD CHARGE

On May 21, 2004, Kristin Raina wishes to pay the $600 credit card charge incurred on May 4, 2004, Check No. 12.

To pay a credit card charge—

1. Click Banking, and then click Write Checks.
2. At the *Bank Account* field, click *1010 Cash – Operating.* Make sure the No. field reads *12* and the To be printed box is not checked.
3. At the *Date* field, choose *05/21/2004.*
4. At the Pay to the Order of drop-down list, click *American Travel.*
5. At the *$* field, key **600**.
6. At the Expenses tab in the *Account* field, click *2015 American Travel Card.*

   Do not choose the 6475 Travel Expense account in the Expenses tab because that account has already been debited when the charges were recorded. When a credit card bill is paid, always choose the credit card liability account. (See figure 10–16.)

FIGURE 10-16
Write Checks Window – Completed

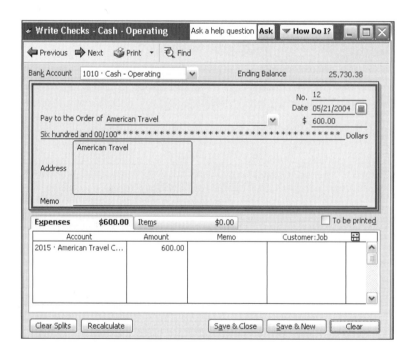

7. If the information is correct, click Save & New.

concept

For a payment of a credit card charge, the general ledger posting is as follows:

2015 Credit Card Liability			1010 Cash – Operating	
Dr	Cr		Dr	Cr
Pmt 600	600			600
	Bal 0			

PRACTICE *exercise*

On May 31, 2004, pay the remaining credit card balance to American Travel, $350, Check No. 13.

REPORTS: BANKING AND FINANCIAL REPORTS

As you know, in QuickBooks Pro, the fourth level of operation is to view and print reports. As we reviewed in prior chapters, reports for an activity can be accessed from both the Reports menu and the Lists menu.

BANKING REPORTS FROM THE REPORTS MENU

The *Reconciliation* report is printed as part of the reconciliation process. The company, in addition to the Reconciliation report, uses the following reports:

Deposit Detail Report

The *Deposit Detail* report displays the components of all deposits to each cash account for a specified period of time. The report will show the payee's name, amount of each payment, nature of payment, and date of payment and deposit. This report is helpful in tracing a collection from a customer to the actual bank deposit.

To view and print the *Deposit Detail* report—
  1. Click Reports, and then click Banking.
  2. From the Banking submenu, click Deposit Detail.
  3. At the *From* and *To* date fields, choose *02/01/2004* and *04/30/2004*.
  4. Click Refresh. The report for the period will be displayed.
  5. Print the report. (See figure 10–17.)

FIGURE 10-17
Deposit Detail Report

EX10 [Your Name] Kristin Raina Interior Designs
Deposit Detail
February through April 2004

Type	Num	Date	Name	Account	Amount
Deposit		02/27/2004		1010 · **Cash - Operating**	5,700.00
Payment	6544	02/20/2004	Jones, Beverly	1250 · Undeposited Funds	-600.00
Payment	1255	02/20/2004	Franco Films Co.	1250 · Undeposited Funds	-500.00
Payment	655	02/26/2004	Cook Caterers	1250 · Undeposited Funds	-2,560.00
Sales Receipt	1007	02/26/2004	Hamilton Hotels	1250 · Undeposited Funds	-480.00
Payment	674	02/27/2004	Guthrie, Jennie	1250 · Undeposited Funds	-960.00
Payment	12458	02/27/2004	Burnitz Bakery Company.	1250 · Undeposited Funds	-600.00
TOTAL					-5,700.00
Deposit		03/31/2004		1010 · **Cash - Operating**	6,940.38
Sales Receipt	1009	03/22/2004	Jones, Beverly	1250 · Undeposited Funds	-1,163.00
Payment	2453	03/23/2004	Guthrie, Jennie	1250 · Undeposited Funds	-2,384.34
Sales Receipt	1011	03/29/2004	Franco Films Co.	1250 · Undeposited Funds	-1,631.00
Payment	6555	03/30/2004	Hamilton Hotels	1250 · Undeposited Funds	-1,762.04
TOTAL					-6,940.38
General Journal		04/01/2004		1020 · **Cash - Payroll**	7,500.00
				1010 · Cash - Operating	-7,500.00
TOTAL					-7,500.00
Deposit		04/30/2004		1010 · **Cash - Operating**	10.00
				6900 · Interest Income	-10.00
TOTAL					-10.00

6. Close the report.

Missing Checks Report

The title of this report is somewhat misleading. The *Missing Checks* report actually displays detailed information for all checks written from a specified cash account. The report includes the check number, date written, payee, and purpose (type) of check. Since each check is listed, the report is helpful in finding missing or duplicate checks.

To view and print the Missing Checks report—
1. Click Reports, and then click Banking.
2. At the Banking submenu, click Missing Checks. The Missing Checks dialog box will appear. (See figure 10–18.)

FIGURE 10-18
Missing Checks Dialog Box

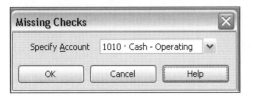

3. At the Specify <u>A</u>ccount drop-down list, click *1010 Cash – Operating*, and then click OK. The report will display all checks written since the account was opened.

4. Print the report. (See figure 10–19.)

FIGURE 10-19
Missing Checks Report

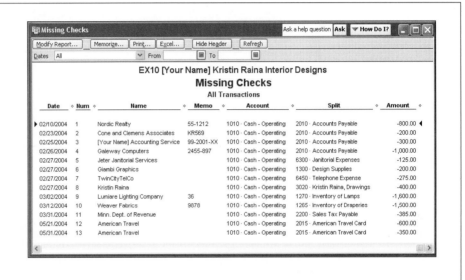

HINT

The report can be displayed for any cash account and for any time period specified.

5. Close the report.

BANKING REPORTS FROM THE LISTS MENU

QuickBooks Pro allows you to view and print banking reports from the Lists windows. Once you access a List, you can view a list of available reports by clicking the Reports button in the List window.

To view and print a QuickReport of the cash account—
1. Click <u>L</u>ists, and then click Chart of <u>A</u>ccounts.
2. Select (highlight) *1010 Cash – Operating*, but do not open the account.
3. Click the Reports button.
4. At the Reports menu, click *QuickReport: 1010 Cash – Operating*. The report will be displayed. (See figure 10–20.)

FIGURE 10-20

Account QuickReport:
1010 Cash – Operating

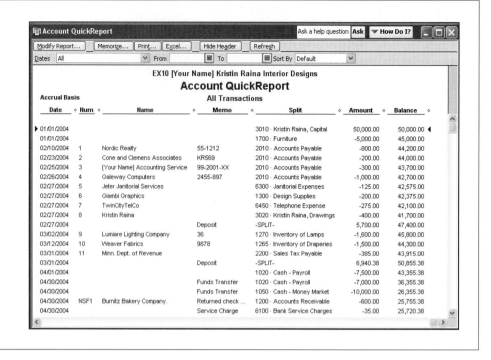

This report displays all of the activity affecting the account. The default setting is for all transactions for the fiscal year. However, you can set any period. If you scroll down the window, notice that the transactions for bank service charges and interest income have been included in the account activity.

5. Close the report.
6. Close the Chart of Accounts list.

OTHER REPORTS

In addition to the banking reports, there are other reports related to the company's banking that can be viewed and printed at the end of the month.

Transaction Detail by Account Report

An additional report that can be helpful in the reconciliation process is the *Transaction Detail by Account* report. This report will display, for the cash accounts, all checks written by the company and tell if the checks have cleared the bank. This report is similar to the *General Ledger* report.

To view and print the *Transaction Detail by Account* report—
1. Click Reports, and then click Accountant & Taxes.
2. From the Accountant & Taxes submenu, click Transaction Detail by Account.
3. At the *From* and *To* fields, choose *01/01/2004* and *05/31/2004*, and then click Refresh. The report for the period will be displayed. (See figure 10–21.)

FIGURE 10-21
Transaction Detail by Account Report

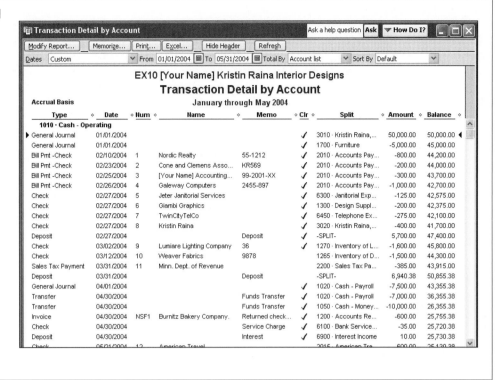

Notice that in the 1010 Cash – Operating account and the 1020 Cash – Payroll account the cleared items have a check in the *Clr* column indicating that they have cleared.

4. Close the report.

Month-End Reports

At the end of each month, the *Journal* report, the *Profit & Loss Standard* report, and the *Balance Sheet Standard* report should be viewed and printed. These reports are displayed in figures 10–22, 10–23, and 10–24.

EX10 [Your Name] Kristin Raina Interior Designs
Journal
April 30 through May 31, 2004

Trans #	Type	Date	Num	Name	Memo	Account	Debit	Credit
59	Transfer	04/30/2004			Funds Transfer	1010 · Cash - Operating		7,000.00
					Funds Transfer	1020 · Cash - Payroll	7,000.00	
							7,000.00	7,000.00
60	Transfer	04/30/2004			Funds Transfer	1010 · Cash - Operating		10,000.00
					Funds Transfer	1050 · Cash - Money Market	10,000.00	
							10,000.00	10,000.00
61	Invoice	04/30/2004	NSF1	Burnitz Bakery Company.		1200 · Accounts Receivable	600.00	
				Burnitz Bakery Company.	Returned check - non-...	1010 · Cash - Operating		600.00
				Minn. Dept. of Revenue	Sales Tax	2200 · Sales Tax Payable	0.00	
							600.00	600.00
62	Check	04/30/2004			Service Charge	1010 · Cash - Operating		35.00
					Service Charge	6100 · Bank Service Charges	35.00	
							35.00	35.00
63	Deposit	04/30/2004			Interest	1010 · Cash - Operating	10.00	
					Interest	6900 · Interest Income		10.00
							10.00	10.00
64	Check	04/30/2004			Service Charge	1020 · Cash - Payroll		25.00
					Service Charge	6100 · Bank Service Charges	25.00	
							25.00	25.00
65	Credit Card Charge	05/04/2004	47887	American Travel		2015 · American Travel Card		600.00
				American Travel		6475 · Travel Expense	600.00	
							600.00	600.00
66	Credit Card Charge	05/17/2004	84441	American Travel		2015 · American Travel Card		350.00
				American Travel		6475 · Travel Expense	350.00	
							350.00	350.00
67	Check	05/21/2004	12	American Travel		1010 · Cash - Operating		600.00
				American Travel		2015 · American Travel Card	600.00	
							600.00	600.00
68	Check	05/31/2004	13	American Travel		1010 · Cash - Operating		350.00
				American Travel		2015 · American Travel Card	350.00	
							350.00	350.00
TOTAL							**24,449.98**	**24,449.98**

1

EX10 [Your Name] Kristin Raina Interior Designs
Profit & Loss
January through May 2004

Accrual Basis

	Jan - May 04
Ordinary Income/Expense	
Income	
4010 · Design Services	4,980.00
4020 · Decorating Services	3,400.00
4060 · Sale of Carpets	2,400.00
4065 · Sale of Draperies	1,000.00
4070 · Sale of Lamps	1,200.00
4075 · Sale of Mirrors	900.00
4100 · Sales Discounts	-84.62
Total Income	13,795.38
Cost of Goods Sold	
5060 · Cost of Carpets Sold	1,200.00
5065 · Cost of Draperies Sold	500.00
5070 · Cost of Lamps Sold	600.00
5075 · Cost of Mirrors Sold	450.00
5900 · Inventory Adjustment	150.00
Total COGS	2,900.00
Gross Profit	10,895.38
Expense	
6020 · Accounting Expense	300.00
6050 · Advertising Expense	100.00
6100 · Bank Service Charges	60.00
6175 · Deprec. Exp., Furniture	100.00
6185 · Deprec. Exp., Computers	60.00
6200 · Insurance Expense	200.00
6300 · Janitorial Expenses	125.00
6325 · Office Supplies Expense	150.00
6400 · Rent Expense	800.00
6450 · Telephone Expense	275.00
6475 · Travel Expense	950.00
6500 · Utilities Expense	450.00
6560 · Payroll Expenses	
6565 · Salaries and Wages Expense	5,360.00
6610 · Social Sec/Medicare Tax Expense	410.04
6625 · FUTA Expense	42.88
6630 · SUI Expense	214.40
Total 6560 · Payroll Expenses	6,027.32
Total Expense	9,597.32
Net Ordinary Income	1,298.06
Other Income/Expense	
Other Income	
6900 · Interest Income	10.00
Total Other Income	10.00
Other Expense	
7000 · Interest Expense	50.00
Total Other Expense	50.00
Net Other Income	-40.00
Net Income	1,258.06

FIGURE 10-24
Balance Sheet Standard Report
May 31, 2004

EX10 [Your Name] Kristin Raina Interior Designs
Balance Sheet

Accrual Basis   **As of May 31, 2004**

	May 31, 04
ASSETS	
Current Assets	
Checking/Savings	
1010 · Cash - Operating	24,780.38
1020 · Cash - Payroll	8,447.68
1050 · Cash - Money Market	10,000.00
Total Checking/Savings	43,228.06
Accounts Receivable	
1200 · Accounts Receivable	2,140.00
Total Accounts Receivable	2,140.00
Other Current Assets	
1260 · Inventory of Carpets	800.00
1265 · Inventory of Draperies	1,000.00
1270 · Inventory of Lamps	1,000.00
1275 · Inventory of Mirrors	900.00
1300 · Design Supplies	200.00
1305 · Office Supplies	250.00
1410 · Prepaid Advertising	500.00
1420 · Prepaid Insurance	2,200.00
Total Other Current Assets	6,850.00
Total Current Assets	52,218.06
Fixed Assets	
1700 · Furniture	
1750 · Accum. Dep., Furniture	-100.00
1700 · Furniture - Other	12,000.00
Total 1700 · Furniture	11,900.00
1800 · Computers	
1850 · Accum. Dep., Computers	-60.00
1800 · Computers - Other	3,600.00
Total 1800 · Computers	3,540.00
Total Fixed Assets	15,440.00
TOTAL ASSETS	**67,658.06**
LIABILITIES & EQUITY	
Liabilities	
Current Liabilities	
Accounts Payable	
2010 · Accounts Payable	9,750.00
Total Accounts Payable	9,750.00
Other Current Liabilities	
2020 · Notes Payable	7,000.00
2030 · Interest Payable	50.00
Total Other Current Liabilities	7,050.00
Total Current Liabilities	16,800.00
Total Liabilities	16,800.00
Equity	
3010 · Kristin Raina, Capital	50,000.00
3020 · Kristin Raina, Drawings	-400.00
Net Income	1,258.06
Total Equity	50,858.06
TOTAL LIABILITIES & EQUITY	**67,658.06**

A bank reconciliation is part of an overall internal control process. A company uses an internal control process to safeguard its assets from fraud and theft.

A primary concern of the accounting process is to help businesses prevent fraud and theft. The Association of Certified Fraud Examiners, established in 1988, is a 25,000-member organization dedicated to educating qualified individuals to detect fraud and other white-collar crime. The organization conducts local seminars and classes, and publishes texts and newsletters dedicated to helping the accounting profession, and others involved in accounting, combat fraud. They maintain a Web site and a newsletter that is available free of charge. Their Web site address is www.cfenet.com.

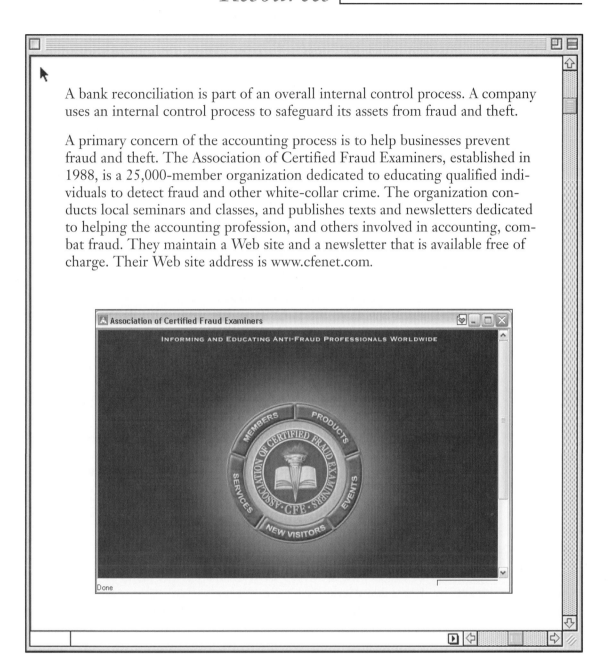

P R O G R E S S
Check

PROCEDURE REVIEW

To transfer funds between accounts—

1. Click Banking, and then click Transfer Funds.
2. At the *Date* field, enter the transfer date.
3. At the Transfer Funds From drop-down list, click the cash account from which the funds are transferring.
4. At the Transfer Funds To drop-down list, click the cash account to which the funds are transferring.
5. Enter the transfer amount in the *Transfer Amount* field.
6. Click Save & Close.

To reconcile a cash account—

1. Click Banking, and then click Reconcile.
2. At the Account drop-down list, click the account to reconcile.
3. Enter the date in the *Statement Date* field.
4. Enter the bank statement ending balance in the *Ending Balance* field.
5. Enter the bank service charges in the *Service Charge* field.
6. Enter the reconciliation date in the *Date* field.
7. Click the expense account for the service charges from the Account drop-down list.
8. Enter the interest income in the *Interest Earned* field.
9. Enter the reconciliation date in the *Date* field.
10. Click the revenue account for interest income at the Account drop-down list.
11. If the information is correct, click Continue. The Reconcile window appears. The activity for that account will be displayed.
12. Place a ✓ next to all deposits that have cleared the bank.
13. Place a ✓ next to checks and payments that have cleared the bank.
14. If there are any NSF checks, record them in the Create Invoices window while the Reconcile window is open.
15. In the Create Invoices window, click Save & Close and return to the Reconcile window.
16. Place a ✓ next to any NSF amounts in the *Checks and Payments* field.
17. Check to see if the *Difference* field reads zero.
18. If the information is complete, click Reconcile Now.
19. At the Select Reconciliation Detail Report dialog box, click Detail and then click Print.
20. At the Print dialog box, click Print.

To enter a credit card charge—

1. Click Banking, and then click Enter Credit Card Charges.
2. At the Credit Card drop-down list, click the appropriate credit card.
3. At the Purchased from drop-down list, click the credit card vendor name.

4. Enter the vendor reference number at the *Ref No.* field.
5. Click the Charge button.
6. Choose the charge date at the *Date* field.
7. Enter the charge amount at the *Amount* field.
8. At the *Account* field of the E<u>x</u>penses tab, click the account to be debited.
9. Click S<u>a</u>ve & Close.

To pay a credit card charge—
1. Click <u>B</u>anking, and then click <u>W</u>rite Checks.
2. At the *Ban<u>k</u> Account* field, click the appropriate cash account.
3. Choose the check date in the *Date* field.
4. Click the credit card vendor from the Pay to the Order of drop-down list.
5. At the *$* field, enter the amount of the check.
6. At the E<u>x</u>penses tab in the *Account* field, click the appropriate credit card liability account.
7. Click S<u>a</u>ve & Close.

To view and print banking reports from the <u>R</u>eports menu—
1. Click <u>R</u>eports, and then click Ban<u>k</u>ing.
2. At the Banking submenu, click a report.
3. Indicate the appropriate dates of the report.
4. Click Prin<u>t</u> on the command line.
5. Close the report.

To view and print banking reports from the <u>L</u>ists menu—
1. Click <u>L</u>ists, and then click Chart of <u>A</u>ccounts.
2. Highlight the appropriate cash account.
3. Click the Re<u>p</u>orts menu button.
4. Click a report.
5. Indicate the appropriate dates for the report, if necessary.
6. Click Prin<u>t</u> on the command line.
7. Close the report.

KEY CONCEPTS

Select the letter of the item that best matches each definition.

a. Bank reconciliation
b. *Missing Checks* report
c. Reconcile windows
d. Reconciling items
e. *Deposit Detail* report
f. Transfer Funds Between Accounts window
g. <u>B</u>anking menu
h. Enter Credit Card Charges window
i. Cleared checks
j. QuickReport

_____ 1. Menu that contains the <u>W</u>rite Checks, Reconci<u>l</u>e, and <u>T</u>ransfer Funds choices.

_____ 2. The procedure to account for all differences between the company's cash account record and the bank statement.

_____ 3. Report from the Chart of Accounts List window that displays all activity within an account.

_____ 4. Activity windows used to reconcile a cash account.

_____ 5. Activity window used to transfer funds among cash accounts.

_____ 6. Report that displays detailed information for each check written.

_____ 7. Activity window used to enter credit card charges.

_____ 8. Report from the Reports menu that displays details of each deposit for a specified period of time.

_____ 9. Items, such as deposits in transit, outstanding checks, bank charges, and interest income, that account for differences in cash between the company's books and the bank statement.

_____ 10. Checks written by the company that have cleared the bank.

PROCEDURE CHECK

1. Your company has four cash accounts. How would you use QuickBooks Pro to move funds from one account to another without having to write a check?

2. Your company wishes to verify the accuracy of the accounting records concerning its cash accounts. How would you use QuickBooks Pro to accomplish this?

3. What is an NSF and how is it treated?

4. Your company has given all sales personnel a company credit card for travel and entertainment expenses. How would you use QuickBooks Pro to record the sales force's expenses?

5. You wish to print a list of all checks written for the year. How would you use QuickBooks Pro to prepare this list?

6. Describe the steps to prepare a bank reconciliation that are common to both a manual accounting system and QuickBooks Pro.

CASE PROBLEMS

CASE PROBLEM 1

On June 30, 2004, Lynn's Music Studio will open a new bank account and transfer funds among the various cash accounts. At the end of June, after receiving the bank statement for the company's Cash – Operating account, Lynn Garcia will prepare a bank reconciliation. In addition, during the month of July, Lynn Garcia will begin using a credit card for travel and seminar expenses. The company file includes the information for Lynn's Music Studio as of June 30, 2004.

1. Open the company file CH10 Lynn's Music Studio.QBW.

2. Make a backup copy of the company file: LMS10 [Your Name] Lynn's Music Studio.

3. Restore the backup copy of the company file. In both the Restore From and Restore To windows, use the file name LMS10 [Your Name] Lynn's Music Studio.

4. Change the company name to LMS10 [Your Name] Lynn's Music Studio.
5. Add the following accounts:

Type	Number and Name
Bank	1050 Cash – Money Market
Credit Card	2015 Harmony Club Card
Expense	6060 Bank Service Charges
Expense	6475 Travel and Seminars
Other Income	6900 Interest Income

6. Using the Transfer Funds Between Accounts window, record the following transactions:

Jun. 30   Transfer $3,000 from the Cash – Operating account to the Cash – Payroll account.

Jun. 30   Transfer $6,000 from the Cash – Operating account to the Cash – Money Market account.

7. Using the Reconcile window, prepare a bank reconciliation for the Cash – Operating account as of June 30, 2004, based upon the information listed below. Remember, since this is the first reconciliation, the opening balance is zero.

   a. The cash figure per the bank statement is $5,464.78 as of June 30.
   b. The cash balance per the company's books is $2,615.18.
   c. The bank charged the account $20 for bank service charges.
   d. The bank credited the account $10 for interest income.
   e. All deposits cleared the bank.
   f. Check Nos. 14 and 15 did not clear the bank.
   g. A check from Mulligan Residence included in the April 30 deposit was returned NSF. (Non taxable.)

8. Print a bank reconciliation report using the full detail report choice. Statement closing date is June 30, 2004.
9. Using the Enter Credit Card Charges window, enter the following transaction:

Jul. 16   Charged $400 for travel and seminars expense to Harmony Club to attend an instructors' convention in Philadelphia, Inv. No. 2718.

10. Using the Write Checks window, enter the following transaction:

Jul. 27   Paid in full, $400, for the Harmony Club Card charge incurred on July 16, Check No. 16.

11. Display and print the following reports:

   a. *Deposit Detail* for April 1, 2004 to June 30, 2004
   b. *Missing Checks* for the Cash – Operating account
   c. *Journal* for June 30, 2004 to July 31, 2004

CASE PROBLEM 2

On August 31, 2004, Olivia's Web Solutions will open a new bank account and transfer funds among the various cash accounts. At the end of August, after receiving the bank statement for the company's Cash – Operating account, Olivia Chen will prepare a bank reconciliation. In addition, during the month of September, Olivia Chen will begin using a credit card for travel and entertainment expenses. The company file includes the information for Olivia's Web Solutions as of August 31, 2004.

1. Open the company file CH10 Olivia's Web Solutions.QBW.
2. Make a backup copy of the company file: OWS10 [Your Name] Olivia's Web Solutions.
3. Restore the backup copy of the company file. In both the Restore From and Restore To windows, use the file name OWS10 [Your Name] Olivia's Web Solutions.
4. Change the company name to OWS10 [Your Name] Olivia's Web Solutions.
5. Add the following accounts:

Type	Number and Name
Bank	1050 Cash – Money Market
Credit Card	2015 Travelers Express Card
Expense	6060 Bank Service Charges
Expense	6475 Travel & Entertainment
Other Income	6900 Interest Income

6. Using the Transfer Funds Between Accounts window, record the following transactions:

   Aug. 31   Transfer $6,000 from the Cash – Operating account to the Cash – Payroll account.

   Aug. 31   Transfer $4,000 from the Cash – Operating account to the Cash – Money Market account.

7. Using the Reconcile window, prepare a bank reconciliation for the Cash – Operating account as of August 31, 2004, based upon the information below. Remember, since this is the first reconciliation the opening balance is zero.

   a. The cash figure per the bank statement was $14,487.16 as of August 31.
   b. The cash balance per the company's books was $ 7,989.16.
   c. The bank charged the account $30 for bank service charges.
   d. The bank credited the account $20 for interest income.
   e. All deposits cleared the bank.
   f. Check Nos. 12 and 14 did not clear the bank.
   g. A check from Breathe Easy from the July 30 deposit was returned NSF. (Non taxable.)

8. Print a bank reconciliation report using the full detail report choice. Statement closing date is August 31, 2004.

9. Using the Enter Credit Card Charges window, enter the following transaction:

Sep. 15 Charged $750 for travel and entertainment expense to Travelers Express to attend a sales convention in Florida, Inv. No. 6554.

10. Using the Write Checks window, enter the following transaction:

Sep. 28 Paid $400 toward the Travelers Express credit card charge incurred on September 15, Check No. 15.

11. Display and print the following reports:

a. *Deposit Detail* for June 1, 2004 to August 31, 2004
b. *Missing Checks* for the Cash – Operating account
c. *Journal* for August 31, 2004 to September 30, 2004

CHAPTER

11

JOBS and TIME TRACKING

Record Job Income, Record Job Payroll Expenses, and Track Time for Employees and Jobs

CHAPTER OBJECTIVES

- Add a job to the Customer:Job List

- Record and allocate payroll incurred for a specific job in the Pay Employees window

- Record and allocate services rendered for a specific job in the Create Invoices window

- Set up Time Tracking

- Track employee time for each job using the Weekly Timesheet window

- Pay employees using Time Tracking data

- Create Invoices using Time Tracking data

- Display and print job and time tracking reports

INTRODUCTION

QuickBooks Pro allows you to allocate income and expenses for a specific job for a customer. A job is a project, assignment, or any identifiable segment of work for a customer. Identifying jobs allows the company to measure the profitability of individual customer projects or assignments. When you record revenue in windows such as the Create Invoices or Enter Sales Receipts windows, you can indicate the job for which the revenue was earned. When you record expenses such as payroll in the Pay Employees window, you can also allocate employee pay and payroll tax expenses to a job.

Most service businesses track employee hours as part of the invoicing process. Customers are billed, usually at an hourly rate, for services provided by various company personnel. This is called billable time or billable hours. Time tracking mechanisms can vary from a simple manual system using handwritten timesheets, to stand-alone time-and-billing software. The billable hours are used to allocate expenses to a job, determine the invoice to be billed for the job, and ultimately determine the profit (job revenue less job expenses) for the job.

To allocate the revenue and expenses to a specific job, you can maintain the details manually or you can utilize QuickBooks Pro's *Time Tracking* feature. When activated, this feature allows you to record time spent by company personnel for customers and specific jobs by entering data in the *Weekly Timesheet* window. This data is then used to allocate payroll expenses to those jobs and to bill customers for work done. (**Note:** *The Time Tracking feature is available only in QuickBooks Pro, not QuickBooks.*)

QUICKBOOKS PRO VERSUS MANUAL ACCOUNTING: JOBS AND TIME TRACKING

In a manual accounting system, when revenue is recorded in a sales or cash receipts journal, an additional step must be taken to identify the job earning the revenue and to record that revenue in a jobs subsidiary ledger. Similarly, when job expenses are recorded in the purchases, cash payments, or payroll journals, they also must be posted to the jobs subsidiary ledger. These steps must be taken in addition to the customer and vendor subsidiary ledger posting.

In QuickBooks Pro, the job file of the Customer:Job List serves as the jobs subsidiary ledger for the company. When it is desirable to track revenues and expenses for a particular job, that job is created as part of the customer's file of the Customer:Jobs List. Relevant information, such as job name, status, start date, and job description, is entered at the time the job file is created and is updated as necessary.

When the company earns revenue from the job, the revenue is recorded in much the same manner as previously recorded in the Create Invoices window or the Enter Sales Receipts window. However, when the revenue is identified with a particular job in each window, it is automatically allocated to the job while the transaction is recorded. These transactions simultaneously update the general ledger for the revenue earned, the customer file for the account receivable (in the Create Invoices window), and the job file for the job revenue. If employees work on a specific job, the Pay Employees window itself allows you to identify the time spent or salary expense related to the job.

In addition, QuickBooks Pro has a time tracking feature that is integrated into the existing accounting software. Time tracking is used to track the billable time allocated to the jobs. Billable time by job is recorded in the Weekly Timesheet window for each employee. This information is then carried to the Pay Employees window when payroll is processed, where the payroll expense is allocated to the identified jobs. This information is also used in the Create Invoices or Enter Sales Receipts windows to bill customers by job based on the billable time.

CHAPTER PROBLEM

In this chapter, our sample company Kristin Raina Interior Designs will track revenue and expenses for several jobs for a customer. As revenue is generated, you will identify the job earning the revenue and allocate the revenue to that job. You will also charge selected payroll to a specific job. Although not an employee, Kristin Raina also will track and allocate her time to specific jobs.

The time tracking feature is an optional feature; you can track revenue and expenses with or without using it. For the first half of the month, you will allocate revenues and expenses to jobs without using the time tracking feature. In the second half of the month, you will activate the time tracking feature that will be used to allocate revenues and expenses to jobs.

Beginning balances for May 1, 2004, are contained in company file CH11 Kristin Raina Interior Designs. Open that file, make a backup copy, name it **EX11 [Your Name] Kristin Raina Interior Designs**, restore the backup copy, and change the company name to **EX11 [Your Name] Kristin Raina Interior Designs**.

THE CUSTOMER:JOB LIST

As you know, the Customer:Job List contains a file for each customer with which the company does business. If there are specific jobs for a customer, or multiple jobs for that customer, you identify those jobs in the customer file. *A job must always be associated with a customer.* Once a job is added it will have its own file, separate but part of the customer's file. It carries over the customer information from the customer's file (name, address, telephone, and so on). In addition, the job file will contain important information such as job name, description, start and expected completion dates, and status of the job.

On May 1, 2004, Kristin Raina Interior Designs was awarded a contract to redesign the lobbies of the three hotels owned by Hamilton Hotels. Kristin Raina wishes to track the revenue and payroll expenses for each of the three jobs by utilizing the jobs feature of QuickBooks Pro.

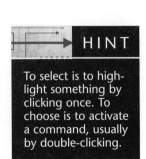

HINT

To select is to highlight something by clicking once. To choose is to activate a command, usually by double-clicking.

To add a job—
  1. Click Lists, and then click Customer:Job List.
  2. At the Customer:Job List window, select (highlight) *Hamilton Hotels*, but do not open the file. (See figure 11–1.)

FIGURE 11-1
*Hamilton Hotels
File Selected*

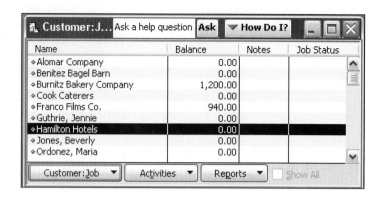

3. Click the Customer:Job button.
4. At the Customer:Job menu, click Add Job. The New Job window opens. Notice that the New Job window carries over information from the Hamilton Hotels file. (See figure 11–2.)

FIGURE 11-2
New Job Window

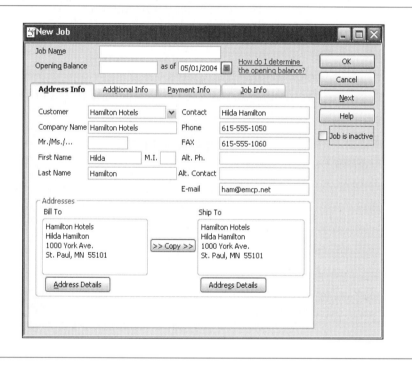

5. At the *Job Name* field, key **Lakeside Hotel**.
6. At the Job Info tab, choose or key the following data:

Job Status:	**Awarded**
Start Date:	**05/01/2004**
Projected End:	**08/31/2004**
Job Description:	**Lakeside Hotel Lobby Redesign**

(See figure 11–3.)

FIGURE 11-3

New Job Window –
Completed

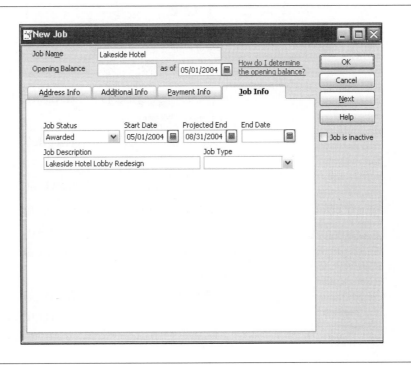

7. If the information is correct, click OK. You will be returned to the
    Customer:Job List. Notice that the Lakeside Hotel job is listed below
    the Hamilton Hotels file as a subfile. (See figure 11–4.)

FIGURE 11-4

Customer:Job List

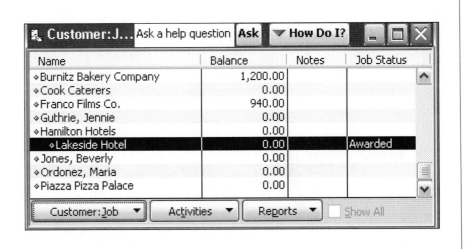

Add the following jobs:

Customer:	**Hamilton Hotels**
Job Name:	**Riverside Hotel**
Job Info:	
Job Status:	**Awarded**
Start Date:	**05/01/2004**
Projected End:	**08/31/2004**
Job Description:	**Riverside Hotel Lobby Redesign**
Customer:	**Hamilton Hotels**
Job Name:	**Mountainside Hotel**
Job Info:	
Job Status:	**Awarded**
Start Date:	**05/01/2004**
Projected End:	**08/31/2004**
Job Description:	**Mountainside Hotel Lobby Redesign**

HINT

If you click <u>N</u>ext instead of OK to save data, you will be moved to the next job with job information from the previous job carried over. The first job information is saved, but you will need to modify the job information carried over for the next job.

QuickCheck: The updated Customer:Job List appears in figure 11–5.

FIGURE 11-5
Updated Customer:Job List

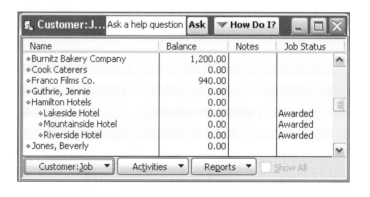

LISTS: THE ITEM LIST

Beginning this month, Kristin Raina will begin billing customers for design and decorating work done by both her and one of her employees. Recall that the rate for Design Services is $60 per hour and the rate for Decorating Services is $50 per hour. These rates apply to work done by Kristin Raina, the owner. The work done by the employee, Richard Henderson, will be billed at $40 per hour for both Design and Decorating Services.

Since the company will now bill customers at different rates depending on who is doing the work, separate items have to be set up for each rate. The Item List in the company file has been modified to reflect the foregoing changes. The Design Services item has been changed to Design Services – Owner. Decorating Services has been changed in a similar manner. A new item has been added: Decorating Services – Assistant, which reflects the services performed and billed for Richard Henderson with a rate of $40 per hour. (See figure 11–6.)

FIGURE 11-6
Item List

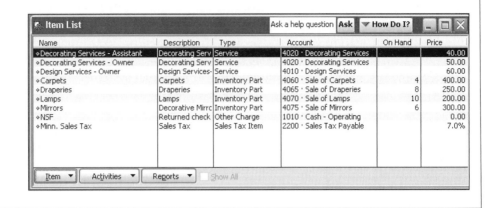

PRACTICE *exercise*

Using the procedures you learned in chapter 5, add the following item—

Type:	**Service**
Item Name/Number:	**Design Services – Assistant**
Description:	**Design Services – Assistant**
Rate:	**40**
Tax Code:	**Non-Taxable Sales**
Account:	**4010 Design Services**

QuickCheck: The updated Item List appears in figure 11–7.

FIGURE 11-7
Item List – Updated

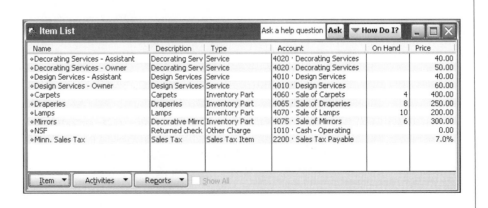

As you recall from chapter 9 on payroll, Kristin Raina has two employees, Harry Renee and Richard Henderson. Harry Renee is an administrative assistant whose time is not billable. Richard Henderson is a Design Assistant and, along with the owner Kristin Raina, provides design and decorating services to customers. Both Richard Henderson and Kristin Raina will be spending time working on the Hamilton Hotels project.

Kristin Raina wishes to charge the payroll expense to each project in order to measure the profitability of each project. For the first payroll in June, Kristin Raina has kept track of the hours spent on each job, by both Richard Henderson and herself, on a manual system.

On May 15, 2004, Kristin Raina pays Richard Henderson, who spent all of his time during the pay period working on the Hamilton Hotels jobs. He worked 25 hours at Lakeside Hotel, 35 hours at Mountainside Hotel, and 28 hours at Riverside Hotel for a total of 88 hours. In preparing the payroll for May 15, 2004, allocate the 88 hours he worked to the different jobs. This will allow you to keep track of the payroll costs by job.

To pay an employee and allocate to jobs—
1. Click Employees, and then click Pay Employees.
2. At the *Bank Account* field, click *1020 Cash – Payroll*. The To be printed check box should not be checked. The First Check Number should be 7.
3. At the *Check Date* and *Pay Period Ends* fields, choose *05/15/2004*.
4. Select *Richard Henderson* by placing a ✓ next to his name.
5. If the information is correct, click Create. Click Continue at the Warning window. You will move to the Preview Paycheck window.
6. Make sure the item name is *Hourly Wages*, the rate is *20*, and the pay period is *05/01/2004* to *05/15/2004*.
7. At the first line of the *Hours* column, key **25**.
8. At the Customer:Job drop-down list, click *Lakeside Hotel*. (See figure 11–8.)

FIGURE 11-8
Preview Paycheck Window

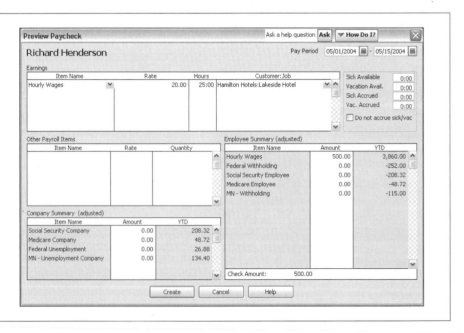

9. Move to the second line of the *Item Name* field and click *Hourly Wages* from the drop-down list.
10. At the *Hours* field, key **35**.
11. At the Customer:Job drop-down list, click *Mountainside Hotel*. Notice that there are now two hourly wages totals. (See figure 11–9.)

FIGURE 11-9
Preview Paycheck
Window

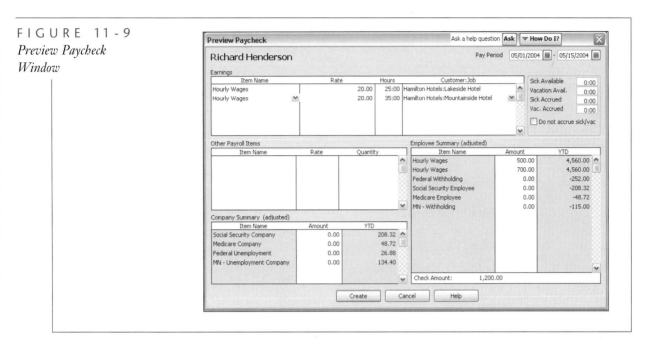

12. Move to the next line and complete the information for Riverside Hotel for 28 hours. Notice that there are three hourly wage amounts totaling $1,760 (88 hours @ $20 per hour). (See figure 11–10.)

FIGURE 11-10
Preview Paycheck
Window

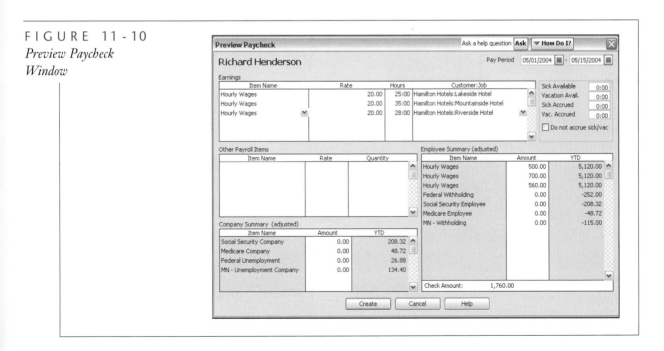

14. Complete the remainder of the window using the information listed below in the manner learned in chapter 9.

COMPANY TAXES:

Social Security Company	**109.12**
Medicare Company	**25.52**
Federal Unemployment	**14.08**
MN – Unemployment Company	**70.40**

EMPLOYEE TAXES:

Federal Withholding	**132.00**
Social Security Employee	**109.12**
Medicare Employee	**25.52**
MN – Withholding	**61.00**

QuickCheck: Check Amount $1,432.36.

(See figure 11–11.)

FIGURE 11-11
Preview Paycheck
Window – Complete

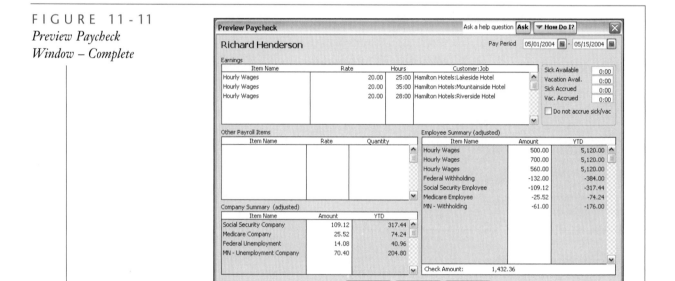

15. If the information is correct, click Create. You will be returned to the Select Employees To Pay window. Leave the window.

As a result of this transaction, payroll expense including the employer payroll tax expense is allocated to each job in proportion to the hours worked for each.

For the processing of a paycheck, the general ledger posting is as follows:
(The taxes payable accounts consist of both the employee and employer taxes;
er represents the employer's share, and *ee* represents the employee's share.)

6565 Salaries and Wages Expense	
Dr	Cr
(88 hrs. @ $20) 1,760	

6610-6630 Employer Payroll Tax Expense	
Dr	Cr
(FICA er) 109.12	
(Med. er) 25.52	
(FUTA) 14.08	
(SUI) 70.40	
Bal 219.12	

2210-2130 Payroll Taxes Payable		1020 Cash – Payroll	
Dr	Cr	Dr	Cr
	218.24 (FICA ee & er)		1,432.36
	51.04 (Med. ee & er)		
	132.00 (FIT)		
	61.00 (SIT)		
	14.08 (FUTA)		
	70.40 (SUI)		
	Bal 546.76		

In addition, the job files will keep track of the expenses as follows:

Lakeside		Mountainside		Riverside	
Dr	Cr	Dr	Cr	Dr	Cr
(25 hrs. @ $20) 500.00		(35 hrs. @ $20) 700.00		(28 hrs. @ $20) 560.00	
er taxes 62.25		er taxes 87.15		er taxes 69.72	
Bal 562.25		Bal 787.15		Bal 629.72	

Employer taxes are allocated to the jobs as follows:

Lakeside:	25/88 X 219.12 =	$62.25
Mountainside:	35/88 X 219.12 =	87.15
Riverside:	28/88 X 219.12 =	69.72
		$219.12

CREATING AN INVOICE FOR A JOB

In chapter 3, you learned how to create an invoice using the Create Invoices window. When invoices are prepared for specific jobs, the procedure will be similar but with one difference. At the Customer:Job drop-down list, you will select the *Job* rather than the Customer.

On May 15, 2004, Kristin Raina is preparing an invoice for the Lakeside Hotel job. During the period from May 1, 2004 to May 15, 2004, Kristin Raina and Richard Henderson spent the following time on Design Services for each job:

Job	Kristin Raina Hours	Richard Henderson Hours
Lakeside Hotel	15	25
Mountainside Hotel	5	35
Riverside Hotel	20	28

The hours for Richard are the same hours you used to record the payroll, which allocates the payroll expenses to each job. QuickBooks Pro now uses these hours to bill the customer for the job, which will record the revenue to each job.

Kristin Raina will now invoice the client for the work done on the Lakeside Hotel project by her and her staff, Invoice No. 1011.

To create an invoice for a job—
1. Click Customers, and then click Create Invoices.
2. At the Customer:Job drop-down list, click *Lakeside Hotel*. Although the Lakeside Hotel job is selected, the bill will be forwarded to Hamilton Hotels.
3. At the Template drop-down list, click *Intuit Service Invoice*.
4. At the *Date* field, choose the date *05/15/2004*, and at the *Invoice #* field, key **1011**. Accept the terms shown.
5. At the Item drop-down list, click *Design Services – Owner*.
6. At the *Qty* field, key **15**.
7. Move to the second line of the *Item* field and click *Design Services – Assistant* from the drop-down list.

Recall that when you process pay for the period, Richard Henderson, the design assistant, spent 25 hours on this project. Kristin Raina will invoice the customer for these hours at a rate of $40 per hour. At present this information is maintained manually. Later in the chapter, we will use the QuickBooks Pro Time Tracking feature to incorporate this information into the company file.

8. At the *Qty* field, key **25**. (See figure 11–12.)

FIGURE 11-12
*Create Invoices
Window – Completed*

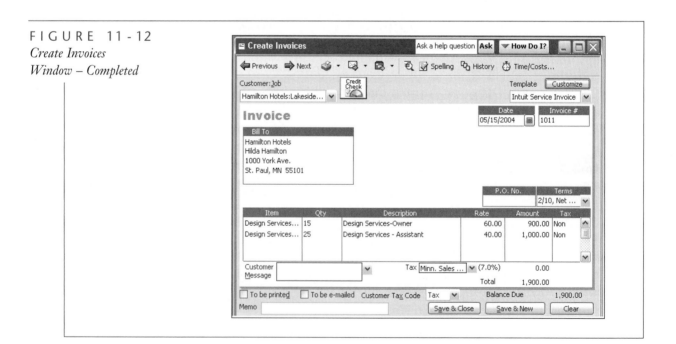

9. If the information is correct, click Save & New.

PRACTICE *exercise*

MAY 15   Create Invoice No. 1012 for Mountainside Hotel for work done from May 1, 2004 to May 15, 2004 based upon hours devoted to that job by Kristin Raina and Richard Henderson.

QuickCheck: Total Invoice $1,700.

MAY 15   Create Invoice No. 1013 for Riverside Hotel for work done from May 1, 2004 to May 15, 2004, based upon hours devoted to that job by Kristin Raina and Richard Henderson.

QuickCheck: Total Invoice $2,320.

ACCOUNTING *concept*

For design services provided on account, the general ledger postings are as follows:

1200 Accounts Receivable			4010 Design Services	
(Lakeside)	1,900			1,900
(Mountainside)	1,700			1,700
(Riverside)	2,320			2,320
Bal	5,920			Bal 5,920

The Hamilton Hotels customer file is updated for the three invoices. In addition, the job files are updated for the revenues as follows:

Lakeside		Mountainside		Riverside	
	1,900		1,700		2,320

SETTING UP TIME TRACKING

The Time Tracking feature of QuickBooks Pro allows you to track hours worked by both employees and owners. Tracking time means recording the hours worked by company personnel while identifying the customer or job for which they spend their working hours. Many companies maintain manual timesheets or timecards to record employee time. The QuickBooks Pro Time Tracking feature automates that process and enables you to use the resulting data in a number of ways. You can use it to bill clients by job for work done by the company's personnel, allocate income and expenses to jobs, and process payroll by job.

You set up the Time Tracking feature in the Preferences window. Once you have done that, the Weekly Timesheet window is available with which you input hourly and daily work activity for customers and/or jobs.

To set up Time Tracking—

1. Click Edit, and then click Preferences. The Preferences window appears.
2. Along the left frame of the Preferences window, click the *Time Tracking* icon. You may have to scroll down the frame to find it.
3. Click the Company Preferences tab.
4. At the Do You Track Time? section, click *Yes*. Accept *Monday* at the *First Day of Work Week* field. (See figure 11–13.)

FIGURE 11-13
Preferences Window –
Time Tracking –
Company Preferences Tab

5. If the information is correct, click OK.

ACTIVITIES: THE WEEKLY TIMESHEET WINDOW

In QuickBooks Pro, you can use the Weekly Timesheet window to enter the daily work activity of employees and owners on a weekly basis. Each employee or owner indicates the number of hours worked for a customer or job. You enter the daily hours along with the customer or job name and the type of service that is performed in the Weekly Timesheet window. This information does not in itself generate a transaction or journal entry. Instead, when you wish to invoice a customer for the work and to prepare the payroll for the employees, QuickBooks Pro uses the information in the Weekly Timesheet to automatically complete fields in the Create Invoices, Enter Sales Receipts and Pay Employee windows. The QuickBooks Pro Weekly Timesheet window appears in figure 11–14.

FIGURE 11-14
Weekly Timesheet Window

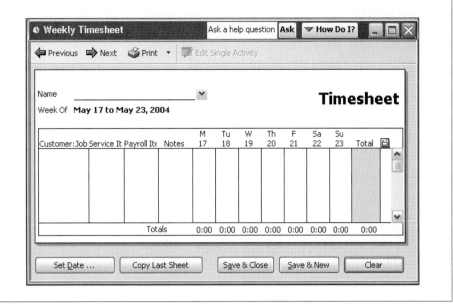

The Weekly Timesheet window allows you to select the name of the employee or owner doing the work, the type of service to be invoiced, the type of payroll item (salary or hourly pay), and the daily hours spent for each customer or job. Ideally, this information is entered daily by the employee/owner. However, in this chapter you will enter the data for an entire pay period at one time. The *Small Invoice* icon on the right side of the window indicates if the hours are billable ⊟ or non-billable ▨ . The hours for employees always default as billable. The hours for the owner default as non-billable. When recording data for the owner, just click the icon and it will change to billable.

Kristin Raina has been tracking time manually. Beginning May 16, she wants to utilize the Time Tracking feature and the Weekly Timesheet.

On May 31, 2004, Richard Henderson submitted the following time data for the period May 16, 2004 to May 31, 2004 for Design Services.

Job	Hours per Job for May by Date										
	17	18	19	20	21	24	25	26	27	28	31	Totals
Lakeside Hotel	2	2	2		3		2	4	2	2	2	21
Mountainside Hotel	3	4	4		1	4	2	2	4	4		28
Riverside Hotel	3	2	2	8	4	4	4	2	2	2	6	39

To enter time tracking in the Weekly Timesheet—
1. Click Employees, and then click Time Tracking.
2. At the Time Tracking submenu, click Use Weekly Timesheet.
3. At the Name drop-down list, click *Richard Henderson*. Click *Yes* at the Transfer Activities to Payroll window message box.
4. Click the Set Date button. The Set Date dialog box appears.
5. At the *New Date* field, choose *05/17/2004*. (See figure 11–15.)

FIGURE 11-15
Set Date Dialog Box

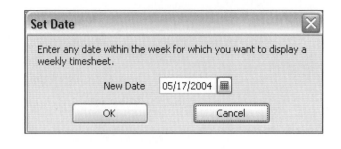

6. Click OK to return to the Weekly Timesheet window.
7. At the first line of the Customer:Job drop-down list, click *Lakeside Hotel*.
8. At the Service Item drop-down list, click *Design Services – Assistant*.
9. At the *Payroll Item* field, click *Hourly Wages*.
10. At the M 17 column, key **2**.
11. At the Tu 18 column, key **2**.
12. At the W 19 column, key **2**.
13. At the F 21 column, key **3**. Notice that the invoice icon correctly indicates billable. (See figure 11-16.)

FIGURE 11-16
Weekly Timesheet Window – Partially Complete

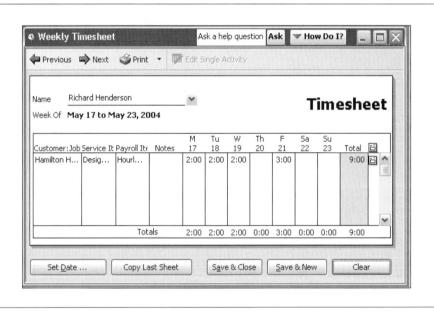

14. Move to the second line of the *Customer:Job* field and from the drop-down list, click *Mountainside Hotel*.
15. At the Service Item drop-down list, click *Design Services – Assistant*.
16. Accept the *Hourly Wages* default for *Payroll Item*.
17. Key the hours for the appropriate dates.
    (See figure 11–17.)

FIGURE 11-17

Weekly Timesheet
Window – Partially
Complete

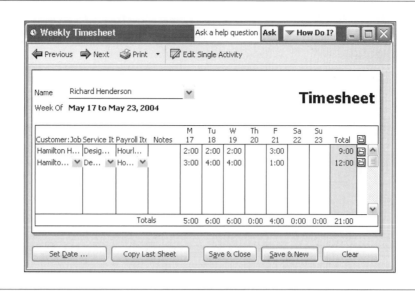

18. Move to the third line of the *Customer:Job* field and from the drop-down list, click *Riverside Hotel*.
19. Complete the balance of the line by repeating steps similar to steps 15 through 17. (See figure 11–18.)

FIGURE 11-18

Weekly Timesheet
Window – Completed

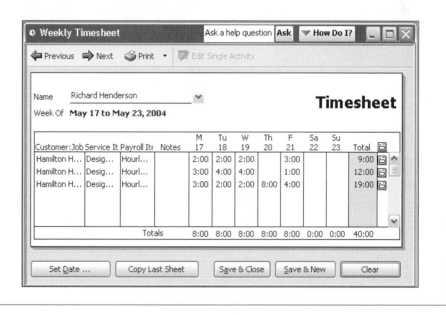

HINT

It is not necessary to enter zero where no work is indicated for a job.

20. If the information is correct, click the Next arrow. You will be moved to the next week.
21. Enter the information for May 24, 2004 to May 28, 2004, for all three jobs. (See figure 11–19.)

FIGURE   11-19

Weekly Timesheet
Window – Completed

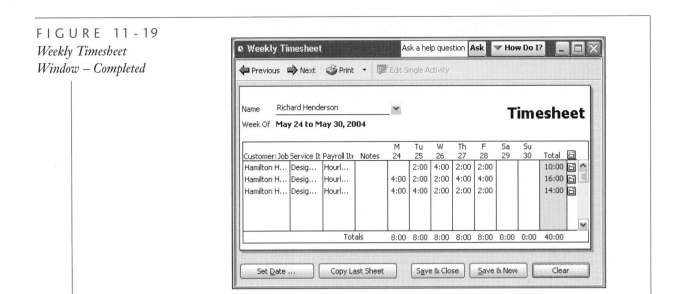

22. If the information is correct, click the <u>N</u>ext arrow. Repeat the process for Richard Henderson for May 31, 2004. (See figure 11–20.)

FIGURE   11-20

Weekly Timesheet
Window – Completed

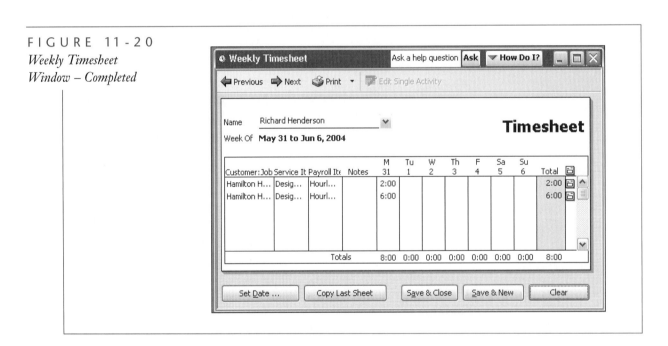

23. If the information is correct, click S<u>a</u>ve & Close.

The time records for Richard Henderson are now stored in the system for later use. When you bill Hamilton Hotels for the work done, QuickBooks Pro will retrieve this information to assist in calculating billable time as part of creating an invoice for the work. In addition, this information will be part of the payroll processing and job allocation procedures. Since the time is billable, this information will be needed to create invoices for this customer.

PRACTICE *exercise*

MAY 31 Kristin Raina submitted the following data for Design Services time spent on each project. Enter the above in the Weekly Timesheet window. By default, the invoice icon shows non-billable. You must click the icon for each line to make the hours billable.

Job — **Hours per Job for May by Date**

Job	17	18	19	20	21	24	25	26	27	28	31	Totals
Lakeside Hotel	2	1	2			4					2	11
Mountainside Hotel		1			1	1	3	2	2			10
Riverside Hotel	1		2	1	1	2	1	3	4	1	3	19

To review the data entered in the Weekly Timesheet, you can print the timesheets—

1. In the Weekly Timesheet, click Print. The Select Timesheets to Print dialog box appears.
2. In the *Dates* field, choose *05/17/2004* through *05/23/2004*, and then move to the next field. All personnel for whom time data have been entered are listed and selected.
3. Click OK. A timesheet is printed for each person for each week. One of the timesheets is shown in figure 11–21.
4. Close the Weekly Timesheet.

FIGURE 11-21

Timesheet

Timesheet

Name: Richard Henderson

May 17 to May 23, 2004

Customer:Job	Service Item	Payroll Item	Notes	M	Tu	W	Th	F	Sa	Su	Total	Bill*
Hamilton Hotels:Lakeside Hotel	Design Services - Assistant	Hourly Wages		2:00	2:00	2:00		3:00			9:00	B
Hamilton Hotels:Mountainside Hotel	Design Services - Assistant	Hourly Wages		3:00	4:00	4:00		1:00			12:00	B
Hamilton Hotels:Riverside Hotel	Design Services - Assistant	Hourly Wages		3:00	2:00	2:00	8:00	4:00			19:00	B
			Totals	8:00	8:00	8:00	8:00	8:00	0:00	0:00	40:00	

Signature _____

*Billing State: B=Billable, N=Not Billable, D=Billed

Review the timesheets to make sure the hours are correct and the correct service item is listed. The data on these timesheets will flow through to the Pay Employees and Create Invoices windows. If there is an error, the payroll and invoices generated will be incorrect. Once you have recorded payroll and invoices, any subsequent changes you make to the timesheets will *not* flow through to correct them.

ACTIVITIES: PAYING AN EMPLOYEE AND ALLOCATING PAYROLL EXPENSE TO A JOB

On May 15, 2004, when Kristin Raina processed the pay for Richard Henderson, the hours spent for each job were manually entered in the Review Paycheck window. This was necessary because the QuickBooks Pro Time Tracking feature had not yet been set up. Now the Time Tracking feature has been set up and daily work activity has been entered into the Weekly Timesheet window. This information can now be utilized to assist in the payroll process and to allocate employee payroll costs to specific customer jobs.

On May 31, 2004, Kristin Raina will process the pay for Richard Henderson, who worked on all three jobs during the pay period.

To pay an employee and allocate payroll costs using Time Tracking—
1. Click Employees, and then click Pay Employees.
2. At the *Bank Account* field, click *1020 Cash – Payroll*. The To be printed check box should not be checked, and the *First Check Number* field should read *8*.
3. At the *Check Date* and *Pay Period Ends* fields, choose *05/31/2004*.
4. Select *Richard Henderson* by placing a ✓ next to the name.
5. After all information is entered, click Create, and then click Continue at the Warning window. You will move to the Preview Paycheck window. Notice that QuickBooks Pro has filled the data for the hours worked on each job and the pay amount automatically. (See figure 11–22.)

FIGURE 11-22
Preview Paycheck Window – Partially Complete

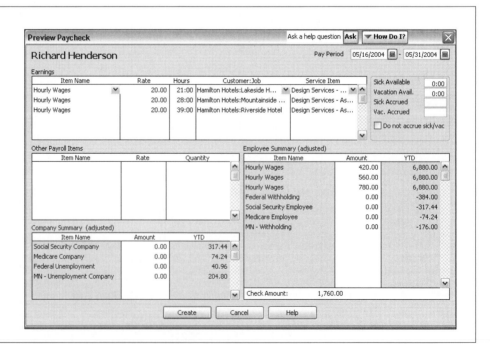

6. Complete the tax information using the information below using the procedures you learned in chapter 9.

COMPANY TAXES:

Social Security Company	**109.12**
Medicare Company	**25.52**
Federal Unemployment	**14.08**
MN – Unemployment Company	**70.40**

EMPLOYEE TAXES:

Federal Withholding	**132.00**
Social Security Employee	**109.12**
Medicare Employee	**25.52**
MN – Withholding	**61.00**

QuickCheck: Check Amount $1,432.36.

(See figure 11–23.)

FIGURE 11-23
*Preview Paycheck
Window – Completed*

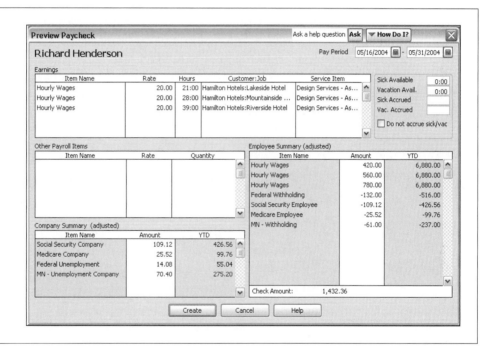

7. If there is an error in the Preview Paycheck window, close the Pay Employees window. Open the Time Worksheet, choose the employee, and set the date. Use the Previous and Next buttons to display the data for each week. Correct any errors, save the corrections, close the Time Worksheet, and then return to the Pay Employees window to continue with processing the payroll.
8. If the information is correct, click Create. When you return to the Select Employees To Pay window, click Leave.

As a result of this transaction, all payroll expenses for Richard Henderson (including employer payroll taxes) have been allocated to each job based upon the hours entered in the Weekly Timesheet window.

CREATING AN INVOICE WITH TIME TRACKING

You have entered the daily work information for Kristin Raina and Richard Henderson in the Weekly Timesheet window. When you processed the payroll for Richard Henderson, QuickBooks Pro used the information from the Weekly Timesheet window to total the hours spent on each job and to allocate the payroll expense accordingly. QuickBooks Pro also uses the timesheet data to bill customers for services rendered and to allocate revenue earned to each job.

On May 31, 2004, Kristin Raina will bill Hamilton Hotels for work done by the company personnel from May 17, 2004 to May 31, 2004 for each job at the rates established in the Item List for Design Services, Invoice Nos. 1014, 1015, and 1016.

To create an invoice using Time Tracking—
1. Click Customers, and then click Create Invoices.
2. At the Customer:Job drop-down list, click *Lakeside Hotel*.
3. At the *Date* field, choose *05/31/2004*.
4. Make sure the invoice number is 1014 and the Template reads *Intuit Service Invoice*. Accept the terms indicated in the *Terms* field.
5. At the top of the window, click the Time/Costs clock. The Choose Billable Time and Costs window appears. (See figure 11–24.)

FIGURE 11-24
Choose Billable Time and Costs Window

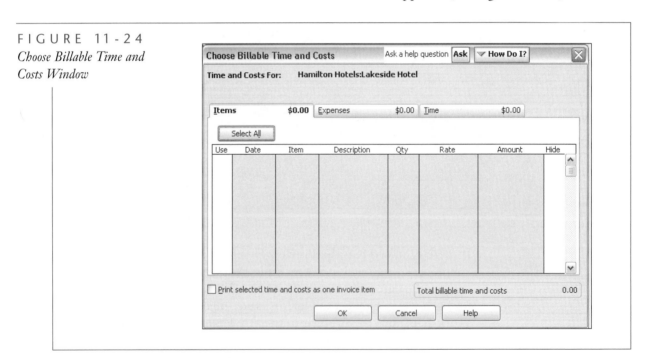

6. Click the Time tab. The hours spent by both Kristin Raina and Richard Henderson on the Lakeside Hotel project are displayed. (See figure 11–25.)

FIGURE 11-25

*Choose Billable Time and
Costs Window – Time Tab*

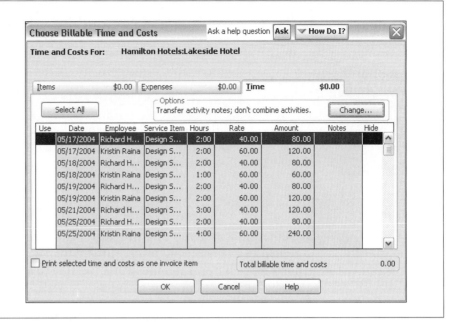

HINT

You will need to
scroll down to view
all of the daily
activity.

7. Click Select All. A ✓ will be placed next to all items listed.
8. Click OK, and then click OK at the Invoicing for Vendor Time window. You will be returned to the Create Invoices window with all billable hours entered at the appropriate rate and time.(See figure 11–26.)

FIGURE 11-26

*Create Invoices
Window – Completed*

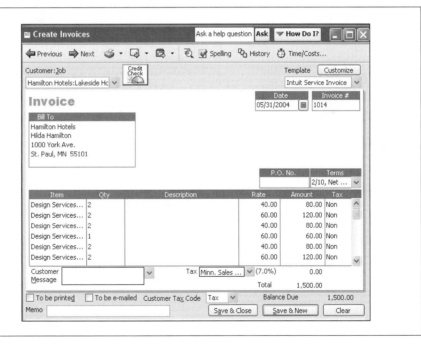

9. If the information is correct, click Save & New.

As a result of this transaction, $1,500 of Design Services revenue has been earned by the Lakeside Hotel job and will be credited to that job file.

P R A C T I C E *exercise*

HINT

Use the Select All button on the <u>T</u>ime Tab to allocate all time to the job.

MAY 31   Bill Hamilton Hotels for all work done on the Mountainside Hotel job. Invoice No. 1015. Terms 2/10, Net 30.

QuickCheck: $1,720.

MAY 31   Bill Hamilton Hotels for all work done on the Riverside Hotel job. Invoice No. 1016. Terms 2/10, Net 30.

QuickCheck: $2,700.

REPORTS: JOB, TIME TRACKING, AND FINANCIAL REPORTS

Both the Job and Time Tracking features produce reports that companies find helpful in measuring job profit and managing employee time. The job reports focus on profitability, while the time tracking reports analyze time spent by each person or for each job.

JOB AND TIME TRACKING REPORTS FROM THE REPORTS MENU

Several reports can be accessed from the <u>R</u>eports menu that analyze information related to jobs. Two of these reports are the *Profit & Loss by Job* report and the *Time by Job Summary* report.

Profit & Loss by Job Report

The *Profit & Loss by Job* report provides information on the profitability of customer and job activity. The report shows the type of revenue earned and the expenses incurred for each job for a specified period of time.

To view and print the *Profit & Loss by Job* report—

1. Click <u>R</u>eports, and then click <u>J</u>obs & Time.
2. At the Jobs & Time submenu, click Profit & Loss by <u>J</u>ob.
3. At the *To* and *From* fields, choose *05/01/2004* and *05/31/2004*, and then click Refre<u>s</u>h. The report for the three jobs is displayed.
4. Print the report. (See figure 11–27.)
5. Close the Report.

FIGURE 11-27

Profit & Loss by Job Report

EX11 [Your Name] Kristin Raina Interior Designs
Profit & Loss by Job
May 2004

	Lakeside Hotel (Hamilton Hotels)	Mountainside Hotel (Hamilton Hotels)	Riverside Hotel (Hamilton Hotels)	Total Hamilton Hotels	TOTAL
Ordinary Income/Expense					
Income					
4010 · Design Services	3,400.00	3,420.00	5,020.00	11,840.00	11,840.00
Total Income	3,400.00	3,420.00	5,020.00	11,840.00	11,840.00
Gross Profit	3,400.00	3,420.00	5,020.00	11,840.00	11,840.00
Expense					
6560 · Payroll Expenses					
6565 · Salaries and Wages Expense	920.00	1,260.00	1,340.00	3,520.00	3,520.00
6610 · Social Sec/Medicare Tax Expense	70.38	96.39	102.51	269.28	269.28
6625 · FUTA Expense	7.36	10.08	10.72	28.16	28.16
6630 · SUI Expense	36.80	50.40	53.60	140.80	140.80
Total 6560 · Payroll Expenses	1,034.54	1,416.87	1,506.83	3,958.24	3,958.24
Total Expense	1,034.54	1,416.87	1,506.83	3,958.24	3,958.24
Net Ordinary Income	2,365.46	2,003.13	3,513.17	7,881.76	7,881.76
Net Income	2,365.46	2,003.13	3,513.17	7,881.76	7,881.76

Time by Job Summary Report

The *Time by Job Summary* report lists hours spent by job for a specified period of time. The report lists the job and the time each employee devoted to each.

To view and print the *Time by Job Summary* report—

1. Click Reports, and then click Jobs & Time.
2. At the Jobs & Time submenu, click Time by Job Summary.
3. At the *To* and *From* fields, choose *05/01/2004* and *05/31/2004*, and then click Refresh. The report will be displayed for the period. (See figure 11–28.)

FIGURE 11-28
Time by Job Summary Report

4. Print the report.
5. Close the Report.

OTHER REPORTS

At the end of the month the *Journal* report, *Profit & Loss Standard* report, and *Balance Sheet* report should be viewed and printed. The *Journal* report is displayed in figure 11–29, the *Profit & Loss Standard* report is displayed in figure 11-30, and the *Balance Sheet* report is shown in figure 11-31.

RECONCILIATION OF DATA TO REPORTS

As was seen in this chapter, income and expenses can be allocated to jobs either by entering data directly into the Create Invoices window and Payroll window, or by activating the Time Tracking feature and utilizing the Weekly Timesheet. When data is entered manually or into the Weekly Timesheet, QuickBooks Pro, behind the scenes, calculates the amounts per job that appear in the Create Invoice window, Payroll windows, Job files, and Job reports. To better understand some of the behind the scenes computations, refer to figure 11-32. This figure displays how the amounts are calculated by QuickBooks Pro.

Journal Report
May 1, 2004 – May 31, 2004

EX11 [Your Name] Kristin Raina Interior Designs
Journal
May 2004

Trans #	Type	Date	Num	Name	Memo	Account	Debit	Credit
69	Paycheck	05/15/2004	7	Richard Henderson		1020 · Cash - Payroll		1,432.36
				Hamilton Hotels:Lakeside Hotel		6565 · Salaries and Wages Expense	500.00	
				Hamilton Hotels:Mountainside Hotel		6565 · Salaries and Wages Expense	700.00	
				Hamilton Hotels:Riverside Hotel		6565 · Salaries and Wages Expense	560.00	
				Richard Henderson		2115 · FIT Payable		132.00
				Hamilton Hotels:Lakeside Hotel		6610 · Social Sec/Medicare Tax Expense	31.00	
				Hamilton Hotels:Mountainside Hotel		6610 · Social Sec/Medicare Tax Expense	43.40	
				Hamilton Hotels:Riverside Hotel		6610 · Social Sec/Medicare Tax Expense	34.72	
				Richard Henderson		2110 · Social Sec/Medicare Tax Payable		109.12
				Richard Henderson		2110 · Social Sec/Medicare Tax Payable		109.12
				Hamilton Hotels:Lakeside Hotel		6610 · Social Sec/Medicare Tax Expense	7.25	
				Hamilton Hotels:Mountainside Hotel		6610 · Social Sec/Medicare Tax Expense	10.15	
				Hamilton Hotels:Riverside Hotel		6610 · Social Sec/Medicare Tax Expense	8.12	
				Richard Henderson		2110 · Social Sec/Medicare Tax Payable		25.52
				Richard Henderson		2110 · Social Sec/Medicare Tax Payable		25.52
				Hamilton Hotels:Lakeside Hotel		6625 · FUTA Expense	4.00	
				Hamilton Hotels:Mountainside Hotel		6625 · FUTA Expense	5.60	
				Hamilton Hotels:Riverside Hotel		6625 · FUTA Expense	4.48	
				Richard Henderson		2125 · FUTA Payable		14.08
				Richard Henderson		2120 · SIT Payable		61.00
				Hamilton Hotels:Lakeside Hotel		6630 · SUI Expense	20.00	
				Hamilton Hotels:Mountainside Hotel		6630 · SUI Expense	28.00	
				Hamilton Hotels:Riverside Hotel		6630 · SUI Expense	22.40	
				Richard Henderson		2130 · SUI Payable		70.40
							1,979.12	1,979.12
70	Invoice	05/15/2004	1011	Hamilton Hotels:Lakeside Hotel		1200 · Accounts Receivable	1,900.00	
				Hamilton Hotels:Lakeside Hotel	Design Services - Owner	4010 · Design Services		900.00
				Hamilton Hotels:Lakeside Hotel	Design Services - Assistant	4010 · Design Services		1,000.00
				Minn. Dept. of Revenue	Sales Tax	2200 · Sales Tax Payable	0.00	
							1,900.00	1,900.00
71	Invoice	05/15/2004	1012	Hamilton Hotels:Mountainside Hotel		1200 · Accounts Receivable	1,700.00	
				Hamilton Hotels:Mountainside Hotel	Design Services - Owner	4010 · Design Services		300.00
				Hamilton Hotels:Mountainside Hotel	Design Services - Assistant	4010 · Design Services		1,400.00
				Minn. Dept. of Revenue	Sales Tax	2200 · Sales Tax Payable	0.00	
							1,700.00	1,700.00
72	Invoice	05/15/2004	1013	Hamilton Hotels:Riverside Hotel		1200 · Accounts Receivable	2,320.00	
				Hamilton Hotels:Riverside Hotel	Design Services - Owner	4010 · Design Services		1,200.00
				Hamilton Hotels:Riverside Hotel	Design Services - Assistant	4010 · Design Services		1,120.00
				Minn. Dept. of Revenue	Sales Tax	2200 · Sales Tax Payable	0.00	
							2,320.00	2,320.00
73	Paycheck	05/31/2004	8	Richard Henderson		1020 · Cash - Payroll		1,432.36
				Hamilton Hotels:Lakeside Hotel		6565 · Salaries and Wages Expense	420.00	
				Hamilton Hotels:Mountainside Hotel		6565 · Salaries and Wages Expense	560.00	
				Hamilton Hotels:Riverside Hotel		6565 · Salaries and Wages Expense	780.00	
				Richard Henderson		2115 · FIT Payable		132.00
				Hamilton Hotels:Lakeside Hotel		6610 · Social Sec/Medicare Tax Expense	26.04	
				Hamilton Hotels:Mountainside Hotel		6610 · Social Sec/Medicare Tax Expense	34.72	
				Hamilton Hotels:Riverside Hotel		6610 · Social Sec/Medicare Tax Expense	48.36	
				Richard Henderson		2110 · Social Sec/Medicare Tax Payable		109.12
				Richard Henderson		2110 · Social Sec/Medicare Tax Payable		109.12
				Hamilton Hotels:Lakeside Hotel		6610 · Social Sec/Medicare Tax Expense	6.09	
				Hamilton Hotels:Mountainside Hotel		6610 · Social Sec/Medicare Tax Expense	8.12	
				Hamilton Hotels:Riverside Hotel		6610 · Social Sec/Medicare Tax Expense	11.31	
				Richard Henderson		2110 · Social Sec/Medicare Tax Payable		25.52
				Richard Henderson		2110 · Social Sec/Medicare Tax Payable		25.52
				Hamilton Hotels:Lakeside Hotel		6625 · FUTA Expense	3.36	
				Hamilton Hotels:Mountainside Hotel		6625 · FUTA Expense	4.48	
				Hamilton Hotels:Riverside Hotel		6625 · FUTA Expense	6.24	
				Richard Henderson		2125 · FUTA Payable		14.08
				Richard Henderson		2120 · SIT Payable		61.00
				Hamilton Hotels:Lakeside Hotel		6630 · SUI Expense	16.80	
				Hamilton Hotels:Mountainside Hotel		6630 · SUI Expense	22.40	
				Hamilton Hotels:Riverside Hotel		6630 · SUI Expense	31.20	
				Richard Henderson		2130 · SUI Payable		70.40
							1,979.12	1,979.12
74	Invoice	05/31/2004	1014	Hamilton Hotels:Lakeside Hotel		1200 · Accounts Receivable	1,500.00	
				Hamilton Hotels:Lakeside Hotel		4010 · Design Services		80.00
				Hamilton Hotels:Lakeside Hotel		4010 · Design Services		120.00
				Hamilton Hotels:Lakeside Hotel		4010 · Design Services		80.00
				Hamilton Hotels:Lakeside Hotel		4010 · Design Services		60.00
				Hamilton Hotels:Lakeside Hotel		4010 · Design Services		80.00
				Hamilton Hotels:Lakeside Hotel		4010 · Design Services		120.00
				Hamilton Hotels:Lakeside Hotel		4010 · Design Services		120.00
				Hamilton Hotels:Lakeside Hotel		4010 · Design Services		80.00
				Hamilton Hotels:Lakeside Hotel		4010 · Design Services		240.00
				Hamilton Hotels:Lakeside Hotel		4010 · Design Services		160.00
				Hamilton Hotels:Lakeside Hotel		4010 · Design Services		80.00
				Hamilton Hotels:Lakeside Hotel		4010 · Design Services		80.00
				Hamilton Hotels:Lakeside Hotel		4010 · Design Services		80.00
				Hamilton Hotels:Lakeside Hotel		4010 · Design Services		120.00
				Minn. Dept. of Revenue	Sales Tax	2200 · Sales Tax Payable	0.00	
							1,500.00	1,500.00

continued

EX11 [Your Name] Kristin Raina Interior Designs
Journal
May 2004

Trans #	Type	Date	Num	Name	Memo	Account	Debit	Credit
75	Invoice	05/31/2004	1015	Hamilton Hotels:Mountainside Hotel		1200 · Accounts Receivable	1,720.00	
				Hamilton Hotels:Mountainside Hotel		4010 · Design Services		120.00
				Hamilton Hotels:Mountainside Hotel		4010 · Design Services		160.00
				Hamilton Hotels:Mountainside Hotel		4010 · Design Services		60.00
				Hamilton Hotels:Mountainside Hotel		4010 · Design Services		160.00
				Hamilton Hotels:Mountainside Hotel		4010 · Design Services		40.00
				Hamilton Hotels:Mountainside Hotel		4010 · Design Services		60.00
				Hamilton Hotels:Mountainside Hotel		4010 · Design Services		160.00
				Hamilton Hotels:Mountainside Hotel		4010 · Design Services		60.00
				Hamilton Hotels:Mountainside Hotel		4010 · Design Services		80.00
				Hamilton Hotels:Mountainside Hotel		4010 · Design Services		180.00
				Hamilton Hotels:Mountainside Hotel		4010 · Design Services		80.00
				Hamilton Hotels:Mountainside Hotel		4010 · Design Services		120.00
				Hamilton Hotels:Mountainside Hotel		4010 · Design Services		160.00
				Hamilton Hotels:Mountainside Hotel		4010 · Design Services		120.00
				Hamilton Hotels:Mountainside Hotel		4010 · Design Services		160.00
				Minn. Dept. of Revenue	Sales Tax	2200 · Sales Tax Payable	0.00	
							1,720.00	1,720.00
76	Invoice	05/31/2004	1016	Hamilton Hotels:Riverside Hotel		1200 · Accounts Receivable	2,700.00	
				Hamilton Hotels:Riverside Hotel		4010 · Design Services		120.00
				Hamilton Hotels:Riverside Hotel		4010 · Design Services		60.00
				Hamilton Hotels:Riverside Hotel		4010 · Design Services		80.00
				Hamilton Hotels:Riverside Hotel		4010 · Design Services		80.00
				Hamilton Hotels:Riverside Hotel		4010 · Design Services		120.00
				Hamilton Hotels:Riverside Hotel		4010 · Design Services		320.00
				Hamilton Hotels:Riverside Hotel		4010 · Design Services		60.00
				Hamilton Hotels:Riverside Hotel		4010 · Design Services		160.00
				Hamilton Hotels:Riverside Hotel		4010 · Design Services		60.00
				Hamilton Hotels:Riverside Hotel		4010 · Design Services		160.00
				Hamilton Hotels:Riverside Hotel		4010 · Design Services		120.00
				Hamilton Hotels:Riverside Hotel		4010 · Design Services		160.00
				Hamilton Hotels:Riverside Hotel		4010 · Design Services		60.00
				Hamilton Hotels:Riverside Hotel		4010 · Design Services		80.00
				Hamilton Hotels:Riverside Hotel		4010 · Design Services		180.00
				Hamilton Hotels:Riverside Hotel		4010 · Design Services		80.00
				Hamilton Hotels:Riverside Hotel		4010 · Design Services		240.00
				Hamilton Hotels:Riverside Hotel		4010 · Design Services		80.00
				Hamilton Hotels:Riverside Hotel		4010 · Design Services		60.00
				Hamilton Hotels:Riverside Hotel		4010 · Design Services		240.00
				Hamilton Hotels:Riverside Hotel		4010 · Design Services		180.00
				Minn. Dept. of Revenue	Sales Tax	2200 · Sales Tax Payable	0.00	
							2,700.00	2,700.00
TOTAL							17,698.24	17,698.24

FIGURE 11-30

Profit & Loss
Standard Report
May 1, 2004 – May 31, 2004

EX11 [Your Name] Kristin Raina Interior Designs
Profit & Loss
May 2004

Accrual Basis

	May 04
Ordinary Income/Expense	
Income	
4010 · Design Services	11,840.00
Total Income	11,840.00
Gross Profit	11,840.00
Expense	
6475 · Travel Expense	950.00
6560 · Payroll Expenses	
6565 · Salaries and Wages Expense	3,520.00
6610 · Social Sec/Medicare Tax Expense	269.28
6625 · FUTA Expense	28.16
6630 · SUI Expense	140.80
Total 6560 · Payroll Expenses	3,958.24
Total Expense	4,908.24
Net Ordinary Income	6,931.76
Net Income	**6,931.76**

FIGURE 11-31
Balance Sheet
Standard Report
May 31, 2004

EX11 [Your Name] Kristin Raina Interior Designs
Balance Sheet
Accrual Basis | As of May 31, 2004

	May 31, 04
ASSETS	
Current Assets	
Checking/Savings	
1010 · Cash - Operating	24,780.38
1020 · Cash - Payroll	5,582.96
1050 · Cash - Money Market	10,000.00
Total Checking/Savings	40,363.34
Accounts Receivable	
1200 · Accounts Receivable	13,980.00
Total Accounts Receivable	13,980.00
Other Current Assets	
1260 · Inventory of Carpets	800.00
1265 · Inventory of Draperies	1,000.00
1270 · Inventory of Lamps	1,000.00
1275 · Inventory of Mirrors	900.00
1300 · Design Supplies	200.00
1305 · Office Supplies	250.00
1410 · Prepaid Advertising	500.00
1420 · Prepaid Insurance	2,200.00
Total Other Current Assets	6,850.00
Total Current Assets	61,193.34
Fixed Assets	
1700 · Furniture	
1750 · Accum. Dep., Furniture	-100.00
1700 · Furniture - Other	12,000.00
Total 1700 · Furniture	11,900.00
1800 · Computers	
1850 · Accum. Dep., Computers	-60.00
1800 · Computers - Other	3,600.00
Total 1800 · Computers	3,540.00
Total Fixed Assets	15,440.00
TOTAL ASSETS	**76,633.34**
LIABILITIES & EQUITY	
Liabilities	
Current Liabilities	
Accounts Payable	
2010 · Accounts Payable	9,750.00
Total Accounts Payable	9,750.00
Other Current Liabilities	
2020 · Notes Payable	7,000.00
2030 · Interest Payable	50.00
2100 · Payroll Liabilities	
2110 · Social Sec/Medicare Tax Payable	538.56
2115 · FIT Payable	264.00
2120 · SIT Payable	122.00
2125 · FUTA Payable	28.16
2130 · SUI Payable	140.80
Total 2100 · Payroll Liabilities	1,093.52
Total Other Current Liabilities	8,143.52
Total Current Liabilities	17,893.52
Total Liabilities	17,893.52
Equity	
3010 · Kristin Raina, Capital	50,000.00
3020 · Kristin Raina, Drawings	-400.00
Net Income	9,139.82
Total Equity	58,739.82
TOTAL LIABILITIES & EQUITY	**76,633.34**

Reconciliation of Data to
Reports

RECONCILIATION OF DATA TO REPORTS

		Lakeside Hotel				Mountainside Hotel				Riverside Hotel		Total
Design Services:												
May 15, 2004 Kristin Raina	(15 x	$60) =	$900	(5 x	$60) =	$300	(20 x	$60) =	$1,200			$2,400
Richard Henderson	(25 x	$40) =	1,000	(35 x	$40) =	1,400	(28 x	$40) =	1,120			3,520
			$1,900			$1,700			$2,320			$5,920
May 31, 2004 Kristin Raina	(11 x	$60) =	$660	(10 x	$60) =	$600	(19 x	$60) =	1,140			$2,400
Richard Henderson	(21 x	$40) =	840	(28 x	$40) =	1,120	(39 x	$40) =	1,560			3,520
			$1,500			$1,720			$2,700			$5,920
Total Income			$3,400			$3,420			$5,020			$11,840
Payroll Expenses:												
May 15, 2004 Salaries Expense	(25 x	$20) =	500.00	(35 x	$20) =	700.00	(28 x	$20) =	560.00			$1,760.00
PR Tax Expense			$62.25			87.15			69.72			219.12
			562.25			787.15			629.72			$1,979.12
May 31, 2004 Salaries Expense	(21 x	$20) =	420.00	(28 x	$20) =	560.00	(39 x	$20) =	780.00			$1,760.00
PR Tax Expense			52.29			69.72			97.11			219.12
			472.29			629.72			877.11			$1,979.12
Total Expenses			1,034.54			1,416.87			1,506.83			3,958.24
Net Income			$2,365.46			$2,003.13			$3,513.17			$7,881.76

Allocation of Payroll Tax Expense:

Company Payroll Tax Expense:		Allocation of payroll tax expense based on hours to each job:				
May 15, 2004 Social Security Company	$109.12					
Medicare Company	25.52	Lakeside Hotel	(25 ÷	88) x	$219.12 =	$62.25
Federal Unemployment	14.08	Mountainside Hotel	(35 ÷	88) x	$219.12 =	87.15
MN - Unemployment Company	70.40	Riverside Hotel	(28 ÷	88) x	$219.12 =	69.72
	$219.12	Total				$219.12
May 31, 2004 Social Security Company	$109.12					
Medicare Company	25.52	Lakeside Hotel	(21 ÷	88) x	$219.12 =	$52.29
Federal Unemployment	14.08	Mountainside Hotel	(28 ÷	88) x	$219.12 =	$69.72
MN - Unemployment Company	70.40	Riverside Hotel	(39 ÷	88) x	$219.12 =	$97.11
	$219.12	Total				$219.12

The American Management Organization (AMA) is the largest organization in the United States dedicated to management training and development. This nonprofit organization conducts seminars, conferences, and in-house training to help professionals develop their business skills and improve their management practices.

One of their programs is "Operation Enterprise," which provides leadership and management training to high school and college students, and to other young adults in business. The programs focus on three areas: career development, career guidance, and career skills. Topics such as internship programs, writing, speaking, and presentation skill building, along with business ethics, are covered. Seminars range from one day to one week in length.

Further information on this and other AMA programs can be obtained at their Web site at www.amanet.org.

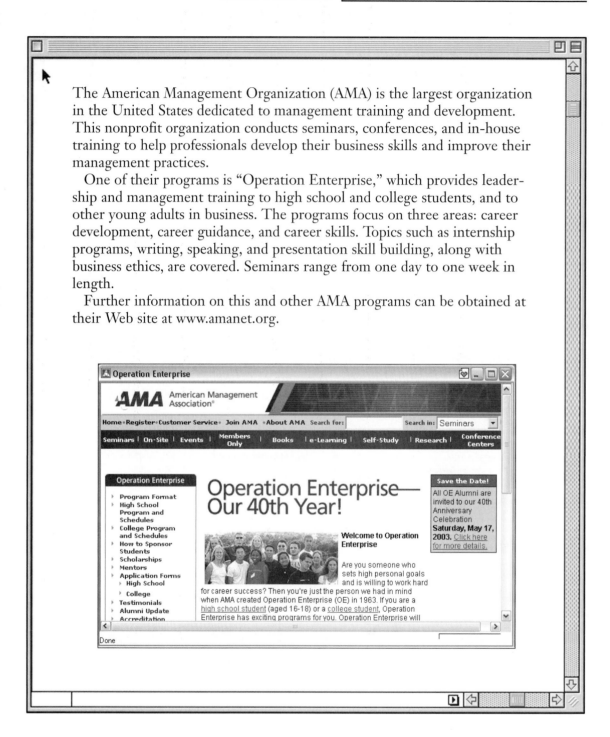

P R O G R E S S
Check

PROCEDURE REVIEW

To add a job—

1. Click <u>L</u>ists, and then click Customer:<u>J</u>ob List.
2. At the Customer:Job List window, select (highlight) the customer to which the job is associated, but do not open the file.
3. Click the Customer:Job menu button.
4. At the Customer:Job menu, click Add Job. The New Job window opens. The New Job window carries over information from the customer's file.
5. At the *Job Na<u>m</u>e* field, key the job name.
6. At the <u>J</u>ob Info tab, key the appropriate data in the following fields:
   > *Job Status*
   > *Start Date*
   > *Projected End*
   > *Job Description*

7. Click OK.

To allocate payroll expenses to a job (without the Time Tracking feature)—

1. Click Emplo<u>y</u>ees, and then click <u>P</u>ay Employees.
2. At the *Bank Account* field, click the appropriate cash account. The To be printe<u>d</u> check box should not be checked.
3. At the *First Check Number* field, key the paycheck number.
4. Enter the appropriate dates in the *Check Date* and *Pay Period Ends* fields.
5. Select the employee to be paid by placing a ✓ next to the name.
6. Click Create, and then click OK at the Warning window. You will move to the Preview Paycheck window.
7. Make sure the correct payroll item appears.
8. At the first line of the *Hours* column, key the hours for the first job.
9. At the Customer:<u>J</u>ob drop-down list, click the job.
10. Move to the second line of the *Item Name* column and click the payroll item from the drop-down list.
11. At the *Hours* field, key the hours for the second job.
12. At the Customer:<u>J</u>ob drop-down list, click the second job.
13. Repeat this procedure for all remaining jobs.
14. Complete the balance of the window in the manner explained in chapter 9 for company taxes and employee taxes.
15. Click Create. You are returned to the Select Employees To Pay window.
16. Select another employee and repeat the steps, or click Leave.

Creating an invoice for a job (without the Time Tracking feature)—
1. Click Customers, and then click Create Invoices.
2. At the Customer:Job drop-down list, click the job name.
3. At the Template drop-down list, click *Intuit Service Invoice*.
4. Enter the date and invoice number and accept the terms.
5. Click the appropriate items from the Item drop-down list.
6. Enter the quantity. The To be printed box should not be checked.
7. Click Save & Close.

Setting up Time Tracking—
1. Click Edit, and then click Preferences. The Preferences window appears.
2. Along the left frame of the Preferences window, click the *Time Tracking* icon. You will have to scroll down the frame to find it.
3. Click the Company Preferences tab.
4. At the *Do You Track Time?* field, click *Yes*. Accept *Monday* as the first day of the work week.
5. If the information is correct, click OK.

Entering Time Tracking data—
1. Click Employees, and then click Time Tracking.
2. At the Time Tracking submenu, click Use Weekly Timesheet.
3. At the Name drop-down list, click the employee name, and then click *Yes* at the Transfer Activities to Payroll window message box.
4. Click the Set Date button. The Set Date dialog box appears.
5. At the *New Date* field, choose the start date.
6. Click OK to return to the Weekly Timesheet window.
7. At the first line of the Customer:Job drop-down list, click the job name.
8. At the Service Item drop-down list, click the service item.
9. At the Payroll Item drop-down list, click the payroll item for this employee.
10. At the column for first day of work, key the hours for that job.
11. Continue entering the hours for that job for the period of time displayed.
12. Make sure the invoice icon shows as billable.
13. Move to the second line of the *Customer:Job* field and click the second job from the drop-down list.
14. Repeat the process for all successive jobs for this time period.
15. If the information is correct, click the Next arrow.
16. Repeat the process for the employee for the next week.
17. If this is the final period of work, click Save & Close.

Paying an employee and allocating time with Time Tracking—
1. Click Employees, and then click Pay Employees.
2. At the *Bank Account* field, click the appropriate cash account. The To be printed check box should not be checked.
3. At the *First Check Number* field, key the paycheck number.
4. Enter the dates in the *Check Date* and *Pay Period Ends* fields.

5. Select the employee to be paid by placing a ✓ next to the name.
6. Click Create, and then click OK at the Warning window. You will move to the Preview Paycheck window.
7. Notice that the data for the hours worked on each job and the pay amount have been filled automatically.
8. Complete the tax information in the usual manner.
9. If the information is correct, click Create. You are returned to the Select Employees To Pay window.
10. Select another employee and repeat the steps, or click Leave.

To create an invoice with Time Tracking—
1. Click Customers, and then click Create Invoices.
2. At the Customer:Job drop-down list, click the job name.
3. At the Template drop-down list, click *Intuit Service Invoice*.
4. Enter the date and invoice number and accept the terms.
5. At the top of the window, click the Time/Costs clock. The Choose Billable Time and Costs window appears.
6. Click the Time tab. The hours spent by all company employees for the job are displayed.
7. Click Select All. A ✓ will be placed next to all items listed.
8. Click OK, and then click OK at the Warning window. You will be returned to the Create Invoices window with all billable hours entered at the appropriate rate and time.
9. Click Save & Close.

To view and print the *Profit & Loss by Job* report—
1. Click Reports, and then click Jobs & Time.
2. At the Jobs & Time submenu, click Profit & Loss by Job.
3. Enter the report dates.
4. Print the report, and then close it.

To view and print the *Time by Job Summary* report—
1. Click Reports, and then click Jobs & Time.
2. At the Jobs & Time submenu, click Time by Job Summary.
3. Enter the dates of the report.
4. Print the report, and then close it.

KEY CONCEPTS

Select the letter of the item that best matches each definition.

a. Job	f. Weekly Timesheet window
b. Time Tracking	g. Job Profit
c. Customer:Job List	h. *Profit & Loss by Job* report
d. Job revenue	i. *Time by Job Summary* report
e. Time tab	j. Billable time

_____ 1. Tab on the Choose Billable Time and Costs window that lists billable hours worked a specific job.

_____ 2. List that contains a file for each customer job.

_____ 3. Report that displays the revenues, expenses, and net profit for each job for a specified period of time.

_____ 4. Time worked by company personnel that can be billed to customers.

_____ 5. Process by which a company maintains records of time worked by employees for various customers or jobs.

_____ 6. Job revenue less job expenses.

_____ 7. Report that displays employee time spent on each job.

_____ 8. Can be a project, assignment, or any identifiable segment of work for a customer.

_____ 9. Window where time worked by company personnel is entered.

_____ 10. Income earned for a particular job.

PROCEDURE CHECK

1. Your company is a construction contractor working on several projects for one customer. How would you use QuickBooks Pro to determine which jobs are making money?

2. Describe the steps to add a job to the Customer:Job List.

3. Your company wishes to keep a record of the time worked by company personnel in order to bill customers for service provided. How would you use QuickBooks Pro to track time information?

4. Upper management requests a report on the profit or loss on each project the company is currently working on. How would you use QuickBooks Pro to develop the information?

5. You wish to see how many hours the company's personnel are spending on each job. How would you use QuickBooks Pro to develop this information?

6. Explain why it is very important for a service business to keep accurate records of the time employees and others are spending for each job or customer.

CASE PROBLEMS

CASE PROBLEM 1

In July, the fourth month of business for Lynn's Music Studio, one of her clients, Highland School, has asked her to organize, coordinate, and supervise an eight-week intensive music program. All classes will be held at the schools, but will be offered to three levels of students: beginning, intermediate, and advanced. Highland School needs separate invoices each month for each level of students, so Lynn has decided that it is necessary to track income and expenses for each level. To aid in this process, she has decided to activate the Time Tracking feature of QuickBooks Pro so that the time spent by herself and one of her employees, Michelle Auletta, can be tracked and allocated to each level of student and then billed to the client Highland School. She has added two service items to the Item List for Michelle Auletta's billable time as an assistant. The company file includes information for Lynn's Music Studio as of July 1, 2004.

1. Open the company file: CH11 Lynn's Music Studio.QBW.
2. Make a backup copy of the company file: LMS11 [Your Name] Lynn's Music Studio.
3. Restore the backup copy of the company file. In both the Restore From and Restore To windows use the file name LMS11 [Your Name] Lynn's Music Studio.
4. Change the company name to LMS11 [Your Name] Lynn's Music Studio.
5. Set up the time tracking feature for Lynn's Music Studio. Monday is the first day of the work week.
6. Add the following jobs to the Customer:Job List:

Customer: **Highland School**

Job Name:	**Beginner Level**
Job Status:	**Awarded**
Start Date:	**07/05/2004**
Projected End:	**08/27/2004**
Job Description:	**Beginner Level Summer Program**

Job Name:	**Intermediate Level**
Job Status:	**Awarded**
Start Date:	**07/05/2004**
Projected End:	**08/27/2004**
Job Description:	**Intermediate Level Summer Program**

Job Name:	**Progressive Level**
Job Status:	**Awarded**
Start Date:	**07/05/2004**
Projected End:	**08/27/2004**
Job Description:	**Progressive Level Summer Program**

7. Enter the following hours worked in the Weekly Timesheet window: (Remember to click *Yes* at the Transfer Activities to Payroll window message box.)

Michelle Auletta: Piano Lessons – Assistant

Job	Hours per Job for July by Date									Totals
	5	6	7	8	9	12	13	14	15	
Beginner Level	2	2	2	2	2	2	2	2	2	18
Intermediate Level							2		2	4
Progressive Level			2					2		4

Lynn Garcia: Piano Lessons – Owner

Job	Hours per Job for July by Date									Totals
	5	6	7	8	9	12	13	14	15	
Beginner Level	2	2				2				6
Intermediate Level	2	2	2	2	2	2	2	2	2	18
Progressive Level	2	2	2	2	2	2	2	2	2	18

8. Process pay and allocate time for July 15, 2004, for Michelle Auletta:

Check No.:	**6**
Item Name:	**Hourly Wages**
Rate:	**12**
Company Taxes:	
Social Security Company	**19.34**
Medicare Company	**4.52**
Federal Unemployment	**2.50**
PA– Unemployment Company	**12.48**
Employee Taxes:	
Federal Withholding	**28.08**
Social Security Employee	**19.34**
Medicare Employee	**4.52**
PA– Withholding	**9.36**

9. Create the following invoices:

Jul. 15   Create invoice for Highland School Beginner Level piano lessons provided by Lynn Garcia and Michelle Auletta for the period July 2, 2004 to July 15, 2004. Invoice No. 2020. Terms 2/10, Net 30 Days.

Jul.15   Create invoice for Highland School Intermediate Level piano lessons provided by Lynn Garcia and Michelle Auletta for the period July 2, 2004 to July 15, 2004. Invoice No 2021. Terms 2/10, Net 30 Days.

Jul.15   Create invoice for Highland School Progressive Level piano lessons provided by Lynn Garcia and Michelle Auletta for the period July 2, 2004 to July 15, 2004. Invoice No. 2022. Terms 2/10, Net 30 Days.

10. Enter the following hours worked in the Weekly Timesheet window:

Michelle Auletta: Piano Lessons – Assistant

Job	Hours per Job for July by Date										Totals
	19	20	21	22	23	26	27	28	29	30	
Beginner Level	3	3	2	3	2	3	2	2	2	2	24
Intermediate Level	3		3			3		3			12
Progressive Level		2		2	2		3		3	2	14

Lynn Garcia: Piano Lessons – Owner

Job	Hours per Job for July by Date										Totals
	19	20	21	22	23	26	27	28	29	30	
Beginner Level	2			2						2	6
Intermediate Level	2	2	2	2	2	2	2		2	2	18
Progressive Level	2	3	2	2	2	3	2	2	2	2	22

11. Process pay and allocate time for July 31, 2004, for Michelle Auletta:

Check No.:	**7**
Item Name:	**Hourly Wages**
Rate:	**12**
Company Taxes:	
Social Security Company	**37.20**
Medicare Company	**8.70**
Federal Unemployment	**4.80**
PA– Unemployment Company	**24.00**
Employee Taxes:	
Federal Withholding	**54.00**
Social Security Employee	**37.20**
Medicare Employee	**8.70**
PA– Withholding	**18.00**

12. Create the following invoices:

Jul. 31   Create invoice for Highland School Beginner Level piano lessons provided by Lynn Garcia and Michelle Auletta for the period July 16, 2004 to July 31, 2004. Invoice No. 2023. Terms Net 30 Days.

Jul. 31   Create invoice for Highland School Intermediate Level piano lessons provided by Lynn Garcia and Michelle Auletta for the period July 16, 2004 to July 31, 2004. Invoice No. 2024. Terms Net 30 Days.

Jul. 31   Create invoice for Highland School Progressive Level piano lessons provided by Lynn Garcia and Michelle Auletta for the period July 16, 2004 to July 31, 2004. Invoice No. 2025. Terms Net 30 Days.

13. Display and print the following reports for July 1, 2004 to July 31, 2004:

a. *Profit & Loss by Job*
b. *Time by Job Summary*

CASE PROBLEM 2

In September, the fourth month of business for Olivia's Web Solutions, one of her customers, Thrifty Stores, has decided to expand to three stores, each one of which will need its own Web page design services since they carry different products. Olivia Chen has decided that it is necessary to track income and expenses for each store. In addition, she wishes to activate the Time Tracking feature of QuickBooks Pro so that the time spent by herself and one of her employees, Gary Glenn, can be tracked and allocated to each job and then billed to the customer. She has added two service items to the Item List for Gary Glenn's billable time as an assistant. The company file includes information for Olivia's Web Solutions as of September 1, 2004.

1. Open the company file: CH11 Olivia's Web Solutions.QBW.
2. Make a backup copy of the company file: OWS11 [Your Name] Olivia's Web Solutions.
3. Restore the backup copy of the company file. In both the Restore From and Restore To windows use the file name OWS11 [Your Name] Olivia's Web Solutions.
4. Change the company name to OWS11 [Your Name] Olivia's Web Solutions.
5. Set up the Time Tracking feature for Olivia's Web Solutions. Monday is the first day of the work week.
6. Add the following jobs to Customer:Job List:

   Customer: **Thrifty Stores**

Job Name:	**Queens Store**
Job Status:	**Awarded**
Start Date:	**09/01/2004**
Projected End:	**10/31/2004**
Job Description:	**Thrifty Queens Store Web Page Design**

Job Name:	**Brooklyn Store**
Job Status:	**Awarded**
Start Date:	**09/01/2004**
Projected End:	**10/31/2004**
Job Description:	**Thrifty Brooklyn Store Web Page Design**

Job Name:	**Bronx Store**
Job Status:	**Awarded**
Start Date:	**09/01/2004**
Projected End:	**10/31/2004**
Job Description:	**Thrifty Bronx Store Web Page Design**

7. Enter the following hours worked in the Weekly Timesheet window: (Remember to click *Yes* at the Transfer Activities to Payroll window message box.)

Gary Glenn: Web Page Design – Assistant

Job	Hours per Job for September by Date											
	1	2	3	6	7	8	9	10	13	14	15	Totals
Bronx Store	2	3	1		5	2	4		1	2	2	22
Brooklyn Store		1	4	4	3	2	1	6	4	6		31
Queens Store	2	4	3	4		4	3	2	3		2	27

Olivia Chen: Web Page Design – Owner

Job	Hours per Job for September by Date											
	1	2	3	6	7	8	9	10	13	14	15	Totals
Bronx Store		2		2	2	2	1	4	2			15
Brooklyn Store		1	2		3		1		2	4	2	15
Queens Store	2	1	1	2		1		2	3		2	14

8. Process pay and allocate time for September 15, 2004, for Gary Glenn:

Check No.:	**6**
Item Name:	**Hourly Wages**
Rate:	**25**

Company Taxes:

Social Security Company	**124.00**
Medicare Company	**29.00**
Federal Unemployment	**16.00**
NY – Unemployment Company	**80.00**

Employee Taxes:

Federal Withholding	**360.00**
Social Security Employee	**124.00**
Medicare Employee	**29.00**
NY – Withholding	**98.00**

9. Create the following invoices:

Sep. 15   Create invoice for Web Page Design Services for Thrifty Bronx Store for services provided by Olivia Chen and Gary Glenn for period September 1, 2004 to September 15, 2004. Invoice No. 1017. Terms Net 30 Days.

Sep. 15   Create invoice for Web Page Design Services for Thrifty Brooklyn Store for services provided by Olivia Chen and Gary Glenn for period September 1, 2004 to September 15, 2004. Invoice No. 1018. Terms Net 30 Days.

Sep. 15   Create invoice for Web Page Design Services for Thrifty Queens Store for services provided by Olivia Chen and Gary Glenn for period September 1, 2004 to September 15, 2004. Invoice No. 1019. Terms Net 30 Days.

10. Enter the following hours worked in the Weekly Timesheet window:

Gary Glenn: Web Page Design – Assistant
(Remember to click *Yes* at the Transfer Activities to Payroll window message box.)

Job	Hours per Job for September by Date									
	20	21	22	23	24	27	28	29	30	Totals
Bronx Store	4	3	6	4	2		1	2	3	25
Brooklyn Store	2	3	1	2	4	6	5	5	5	33
Queens Store	3	3	1	3	3	3	3	2	1	22

Olivia Chen: Web Page Design – Owner

Job	Hours per Job for September by Date									
	20	21	22	23	24	27	28	29	30	Totals
Bronx Store	1	2	5	2	3	4		2	2	21
Brooklyn Store	2	2	2	2	2		4		2	16
Queens Store	4	3		3	1	4	2	1	1	19

11. Process pay and allocate time for September 30, 2004, for Gary Glenn:

Check No.:	**7**
Item Name:	**Hourly Wages**
Rate:	**25**
Company Taxes:	
Social Security Company	**124.00**
Medicare Company	**29.00**
Federal Unemployment	**16.00**
NY – Unemployment Company	**80.00**
Employee Taxes:	
Federal Withholding	**360.00**
Social Security Employee	**124.00**
Medicare Employee	**29.00**
NY – Withholding	**98.00**

12. Create the following invoices:

Sep. 30   Create invoice for Web Page Design Services for Thrifty Bronx Store for services provided by Olivia Chen and Gary Glenn for the period September 16, 2004 to September 30, 2004. Invoice No. 1020. Terms Net 30 Days.

Sep. 30   Create invoice for Web Page Design Services for Thrifty Brooklyn Store for services provided by Olivia Chen and Gary Glenn for the period September 16, 2004 to September 30, 2004. Invoice No. 1021. Terms Net 30 Days.

Sep. 30   Create invoice for Web Page Design Services for Thrifty Queens Store for services provided by Olivia Chen and Gary Glenn for the period September 16, 2004 to September 30, 2004. Invoice No. 1022. Terms Net 30 Days.

13. Display and print the following reports for September 1, 2004 to September 30, 2004:

a. *Profit & Loss by Job*
b. *Time by Job Summary*

CHAPTER

12

CUSTOMIZING YOUR COMPANY FILE

Reports, Graphs, Subaccounts, Invoices, Letters, and Memorized Transactions

CHAPTER OBJECTIVES

- Customize the appearance of reports using the Modify Report button and Collapse/Expand buttons

- Memorize a customized report

- Export a report into Microsoft Excel

- Change report default settings

- View and print a graph

- Change subaccount default settings

- Customize an activity window display

- Customize and print an invoice

- Prepare and view a QuickBooks Letter in Microsoft Word

- Memorize a transaction

- View fiscal year closing

INTRODUCTION

At this point, you should have a good understanding of operating QuickBooks Pro in order to create and set up a new company file, set up and update the Lists, record transactions in the Activities windows, and view and print a variety of management, accounting, and financial reports.

In this final chapter, you will learn how to customize reports, export a report to Microsoft Excel, change report default settings, view and print graphs, change subaccount default settings, customize the Create Invoices window and related printed invoices, prepare a QuickBooks Letter in Microsoft Word, and memorize transactions.

CHAPTER PROBLEM

Begin by opening the company file CH12 Kristin Raina Interior Designs.QBW. Make a backup copy, and name it **EX12 [Your Name] Kristin Raina Interior Designs**. Restore the backup copy, and then change the company name to **EX12 [Your Name] Kristin Raina Interior Designs**.

CUSTOMIZING THE APPEARANCE OF REPORTS

As you have seen, QuickBooks Pro contains a large variety of pre-established management, accounting, and financial reports, many of which you have displayed and printed throughout this text.

When you display a report, there is a row of buttons, called the *command line*, along the top of the report. These buttons can be used to change the presentation of the report, memorize settings in a report, and export a report into an Excel spreadsheet. In prior chapters, you displayed and printed reports using the pre-established settings, with the exception of chapter 4 where you modified the report using the Filters and Header/Footer tabs of the Modify Report button. In this chapter, you will use the remaining buttons on the command line.

MODIFY REPORT BUTTON

The Modify Report button is used to adjust the appearance of the report. The Modify Report dialog box consists of four tabs: Display, Filters, Header/Footer, and Fonts & Numbers. A report can be modified to add or delete fields of information displayed in a report (Display tab); to filter (select) which categories of information should be included in a report (Filters tab); indicate which information should be displayed in the headers or footers (Header/Footer tab); and indicate the fonts and formats of the numbers in the reports (Fonts & Numbers tab).

MODIFY REPORT – DISPLAY TAB

Open the *Account Listing* report. (See figure 12–1.)

FIGURE 12-1

Account Listing Report

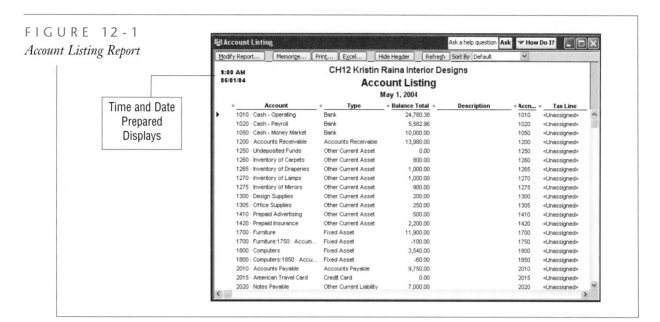

Time and Date
Prepared
Displays

To Modify a report using the <u>D</u>isplay tab—

1. In the *Account Listing* report, click <u>M</u>odify Report on the command line. The Modify Report dialog box appears.

    In the Modify Report dialog box, the default tab is <u>D</u>isplay. The <u>D</u>isplay tab is used to indicate the fields of information that can be displayed in the columns in a report. Any column title that is checked is displayed.

    When adding new accounts to the Chart of Accounts, you did not utilize the *Description* field, therefore this field of information is blank. In the *Tax Line* field, all accounts are marked unassigned. Since you do not need the information in these two fields, you can remove the fields.

2. Remove the check marks from the field titles *Description* and *Tax Line*. (See figure 12–2.)

FIGURE 12-2

Modify Report – <u>D</u>isplay tab

3. If the information is correct, click OK. The report is revised to exclude those two fields of information.
4. Widen the *Account* name column to display the entire account name. (See figure 12–3.)

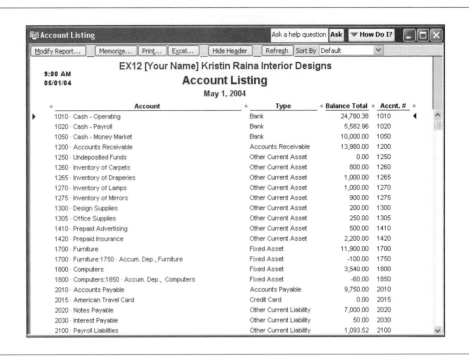

MODIFY REPORT – HEADER/FOOTER TAB

The Header/Footer tab is used to establish the presentation of the headers (including titles) and footers (including page numbers) to be displayed in a report. Two items in the heading of a report you can format is the Date Prepared and Time Prepared items. You may have noticed when reports are displayed, by default, the date and time the report is prepared always displays in the upper left corner. The *Date Prepared* and *Time Prepared* fields are where you tell the software to display the current date and time on each report. By default this field is activated, which tells the software to display the current date and time as maintained by your computer.

If you print reports often, it is useful to have the date and time you print a report listed to avoid confusion among the many printouts. But there may be times you do not want the date or time displayed on the report. The printouts reproduced in this text did not include a current date or time because the *Date Prepared* and *Time Prepared* fields defaults were disabled.

To disable or change the format of the *Date Prepared* and *Time Prepared* fields and change a title in a report—

1. In the *Account Listing* report, click Modify Report on the command line. The Modify Report dialog box appears.
2. In the Modify Report dialog box, click the Header/Footer tab. The Header/Footer tab appears.
3. Click the Date Prepared drop-down list. You can use this drop-down list to change the format of the date.
4. To not display a date at all, remove the check mark from the box to the left of the *Date Prepared* field.
5. To not display the time at all, remove the check mark from the box to the left of the *Time Prepared* field.

In the Header/Footer dialog box, you can also change or remove the company name, title, subtitle, and footer information of the report.

6. In the *Subtitle* field, delete the date provided and key **May 31, 2004**. (See figure 12–4.)

FIGURE 12-4
Modify Report –
Header/Footer Tab

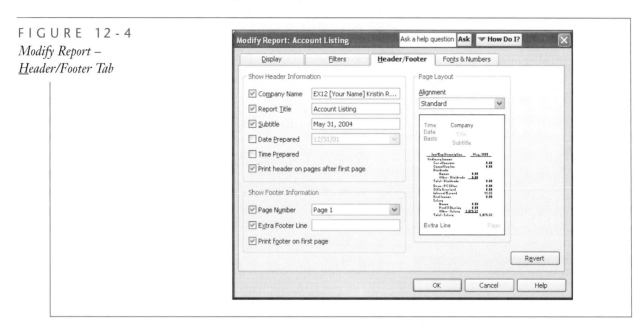

7. If the information is correct, click OK. You are returned to the *Account Listing* report. The Date Prepared and Time Prepared items have been removed and the subtitle has been changed. (See figure 12–5.)

FIGURE 12-5
Account Listing Report
– Customized and
Header Modified

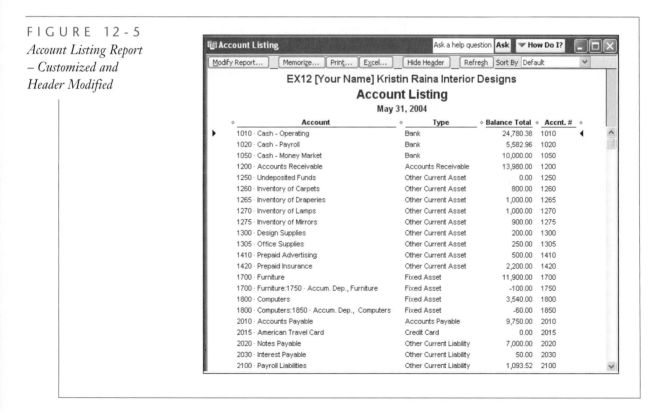

MEMORIZE BUTTON

The changes you just made to the report remain in place as long as the report is displayed. But as soon as you close the report, those changes are lost. When you reopen the report, the original default settings again display. Instead of having to change the settings each time you open the report, you can save the changes to a report by using the Memorize button.

To memorize the settings for a report—

1. With the *Account Listing* report open, the *Description* and *Tax Line* fields removed, and the heading format changed, click Memorize on the command line.
2. In the Memorize Report dialog box, key **Account Listing – Custom**. (See figure 12–6.)

FIGURE 12-6
Memorize Report Dialog Box

3. If the information is correct, click OK.
4. Close the *Account Listing* report.

Reopen the *Account Listing* report. Notice that all of the original default settings are used to display the report. Close the *Account Listing* report. If you wish to see the memorized report, you must open the memorized report.

To open a memorized report—

1. Click <u>R</u>eports, and then click Memori<u>z</u>ed Reports.

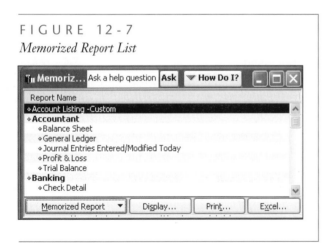

FIGURE 12-7
Memorized Report List

2. At the Memorized Reports submenu, click on Memorized Report <u>L</u>ist. The Memorized Reports List appears. (See figure 12-7.)

The first report on the list is the Account Listing – Custom memorized report. The other reports listed are the same reports that can be accessed from the <u>R</u>eports menu or from the Re<u>p</u>orts button in the Lists window but QuickBooks Pro has organized them into groups for easy retrieval.

3. Double-click the report *Account Listing – Custom.*

The *Account Listing* report displays with all changes intact. If you make any changes to a memorized report, they will only be stored while the report is displayed. If you wish to memorize the new changes, you must click Memorize. At that time you will be given a choice to replace the memorized report with the new changes, or create an additional memorized report.

4. Close the report and then close the Memorized Report List.

COLLAPSE/EXPAND BUTTON

Open the *Balance Sheet* standard report for June 30, 2004. Notice the Date Prepared and Time Prepared items appear in the report window. Remove the Date Prepared and Time Prepared items using the Modify Report button (Header/Footer tab) on the command line. Scroll down until the fixed assets section appears in the screen, as seen in figure 12–8.

FIGURE 12-8

Balance Sheet Standard Report – Expanded

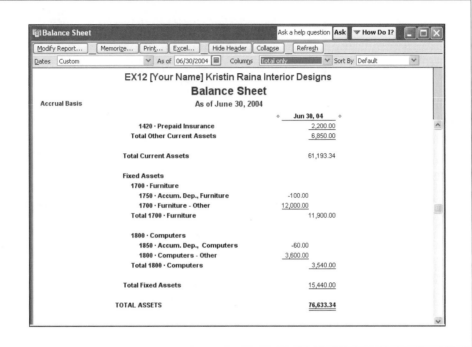

Recall that in the fixed assets section, the fixed asset account is the parent account and the related accumulated depreciation account is a subaccount of the fixed asset. On the *Balance Sheet Standard* report, the amounts for each account are indented to the left of the dollar value column, and the net of the two accounts are listed on the right in the dollar value column. This format is referred to as *expanded*. As an alternative, you can *collapse* the numbers, which will display only the net amount for each fixed asset account in the dollar value column.

To collapse and expand the numbers in a report—

1. In the *Balance Sheet Standard* report, click Collapse on the command line. Scroll down until the fixed assets again display. Only the net amount for each fixed asset displays. (See figure 12–9.)

2. To expand the numbers, click Expand on the command line. The report returns to the original presentation.

FIGURE 12-9
*Balance Sheet Standard
Report – Collapsed*

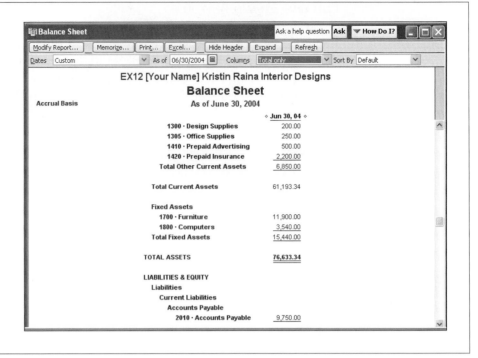

EXCEL BUTTON

QuickBooks Pro allows you to export the reports to a Microsoft Excel spreadsheet where you can incorporate the report into other Excel files you may have or create a new spreadsheet. You can then utilize Excel to further customize the report. Excel must be installed on your computer to export the report. (**Note:** *Exporting to Excel is available only with QuickBooks Pro, not with QuickBooks.*)

To export a report to Excel—

1. With the *Balance Sheet Standard* report (expanded) displayed, click Excel on the command line.

   The Export Report to Excel dialog box appears. You have a choice to export the data into a new spreadsheet or to export it into an existing spreadsheet.

2. Accept the default to send the report to a new spreadsheet by clicking OK.

   Excel is opened and a spreadsheet is prepared with the *Balance Sheet* standard report exported into the spreadsheet. (See figure 12–10.)

FIGURE 12-10
*Balance Sheet Standard Report
Exported to Microsoft Excel*

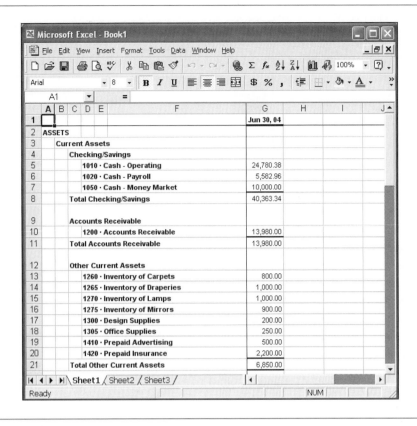

If you are familiar with operating Excel, you may revise the report according to your preferences.

3. Close Excel by clicking the Close (X) button. If asked to save changes, click No. Then close the *Balance Sheet Standard* report.

SETTING UP REPORTS

You saw that each time you display a report, you can modify the display using the Modify Report (Display, Filters, Header/Footer tabs) and Collapse/Expand buttons. You also saw that these changes are only temporary. To save the changes, you can memorize the report. Or, as an alternative, you can change the default settings of *all* reports using the Preferences window. For example, you can change the Date Prepared and Time Prepared items default setting.

To turn off or change the Date Prepared and Time Prepared items default settings—
1. Click Edit, and then click Preferences.
2. Along the left frame of the Preferences window, click the *Reports & Graphs* icon. By default the My Preferences tab is displayed. Read the choices on the My Preferences tab.
3. Click Company Preferences. Read the choices on the Company Preferences tab. (See figure 12–11.)

FIGURE 12-11

Reports & Graphs –
Company Preferences Tab

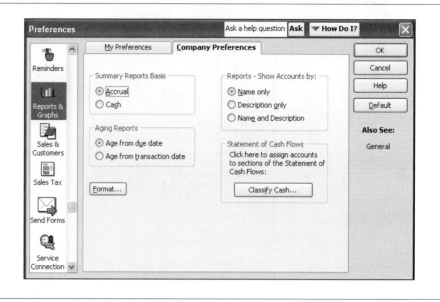

4. Click <u>F</u>ormat. The Report Format Preferences dialog box appears which consists of two tabs: <u>H</u>eader/Footer and Fo<u>n</u>ts & Numbers.
5. Click the <u>H</u>eader/Footer tab, if necessary. You can change default formats or disable any field of information in all reports on this tab.
6. To disable the Date Prepared item, remove the check mark from the box to the left of the *Date <u>P</u>repared* field.
7. To disable the Time Prepared item, remove the check mark from the box to the left of the *Time P<u>r</u>epared* field. (See figure 12–12.)

FIGURE 12-12

Report Format Preferences
Dialog Box – <u>H</u>eader/Footer Tab
– Date <u>P</u>repared and Time
P<u>r</u>epared Fields Disabled

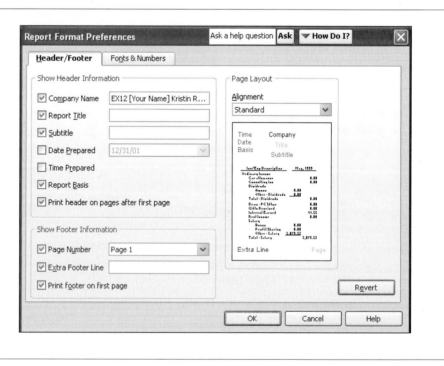

8. Click OK at the Report Format Preferences dialog box. You are returned to the Preferences window.
9. Click OK.

The steps you used to disable the Date Prepared and Time Prepared items using the Preferences window are the same steps taken when you disabled the Date Prepared and Time Prepared items while a report was opened. By changing the setting of the Date Prepared and Time Prepared items in the Preferences window, you changed the default setting. Now, each time you open any report, the date and time prepared will no longer display. However, if you wish to see the date or time prepared in an individual report, you can activate it for the specific report.

GRAPHS

QuickBooks Pro allows you to display financial information in graph format. Graph presentations are available for the *Income and Expenses, Net Worth, Accounts Receivable, Sales,* and *Accounts Payable* reports.

To view the Income and Expense graph—
1. Click <u>R</u>eports, and then click Company & <u>F</u>inancial.
2. At the Company & Financial submenu, click Income & Expense <u>G</u>raph.
3. Click Da<u>t</u>es.
4. At the Change Graph Dates dialog box, choose from *01/01/2004* to *05/31/2004,* and then click OK. The Income and Expense graph for that period of time displays. (See figure 12–13.)

FIGURE 12-13
Income and Expense Graph

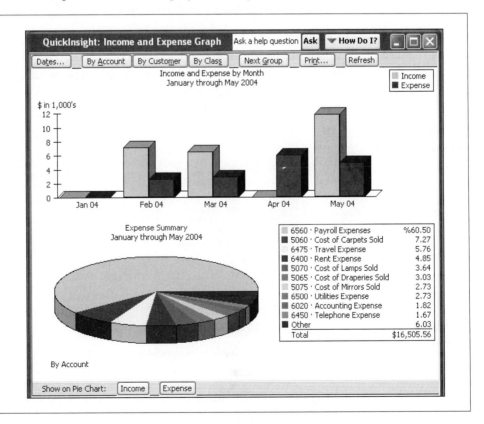

The column chart displays a comparative analysis of income and expenses. The pie chart, by default, displays the expense analysis.

5. To display the income analysis as a pie chart, click Income. The pie chart changes to display the income analysis.
6. Close the graph.

All graphs are displayed in the same manner. The graphs that are available can be accessed using the <u>R</u>eports menu on the Main Menu bar or the Reports button in the List windows.

SUBACCOUNTS PRESENTATION

As you know, accounts in the Chart of Accounts can be denoted as subaccounts. When an account is a subaccount, the account it is a subaccount of is referred to as the parent account. Accounts are marked as subaccounts for the primary purpose of showing a subtotal or net amount of the parent account on the financial statements. This was illustrated with fixed assets where the accumulated depreciation account (subaccount) was deducted from the fixed asset (parent) to show the net book value of the asset account on the *Balance Sheet*.

When you have a parent and related subaccount in the Chart of Accounts, by default, QuickBooks Pro displays the parent account first, followed by the subaccount. However, sometimes when you are reviewing the *Account Listing*, or choosing an account in an activity window, the default listing of first the parent account, followed by the subaccount is sometimes cumbersome. Therefore, you can change the default settings to simplify the presentation of the parent and subaccounts.

CHART OF ACCOUNTS LIST WINDOW PRESENTATION
Open the Chart of Accounts List window. Scroll down to the fixed asset section. Look at the accumulated depreciation accounts. These subaccounts are indented under the parent accounts. This is referred to as the hierarchical view. (See figure 12–14.)

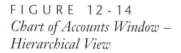
FIGURE 12-14
Chart of Accounts Window –
Hierarchical View

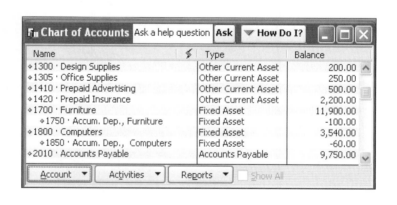

If you do not like the subaccounts indented, you can change the format to list all accounts aligned to the left of the window. This is called the *flat view*.

To change to flat or hierarchical view—
1. In the Chart of Accounts window, click the <u>A</u>ccount menu button. Notice that Hierarchical View is checked.
2. Click Flat View.
3. Scroll down the Chart of Accounts window until the fixed assets again display. The subaccounts are no longer indented, but are left aligned in the window. (See figure 12–15.)

FIGURE 12-15
Chart of Accounts Window – Flat View

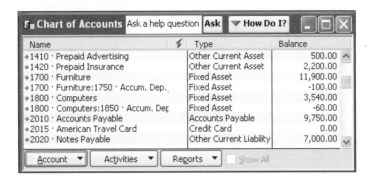

4. Click the <u>A</u>ccount button and then click Hierarchical View. The presentation changes to again indent the subaccounts.
5. Close the window.

The change in view settings in the Chart of Accounts window affects only this window.

REPORTS AND ACTIVITIES WINDOWS PRESENTATION

Review the subaccounts listed in the *Account Listing* in figures 12–1 and 12–3. Notice that the subaccounts 1750 and 1850, the accumulated depreciation accounts, are listed next to the parent account.

Open the General Journal Entry window and in the *Account* field on the first line click the account *1750 Accum. Dep. – Furniture*. In this field, the parent account is listed first. Because the field is small, you see only the parent account, not the subaccount. (See figure 12–16.) Close the General Journal Entry window.

FIGURE 12-16
General Journal Entry Window – Subaccount Selected – Parent Account Displays

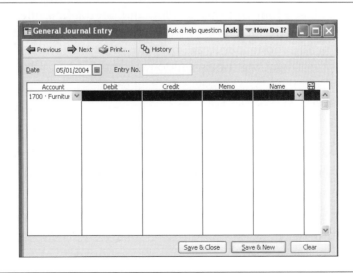

In both the reports and the activity windows, the default setting is to display the subaccounts after the parent account. This default setting can be changed in the Preferences window.

To change the default setting of subaccounts—
1. Click Edit, and then click Preferences.
2. Along the left frame of the Preferences window, click the *Accounting* icon.
3. Click Company Preferences.
4. In the *Account Numbers* section, place a check mark in the box next to Show lowest subaccount only. (See figure 12–17.)

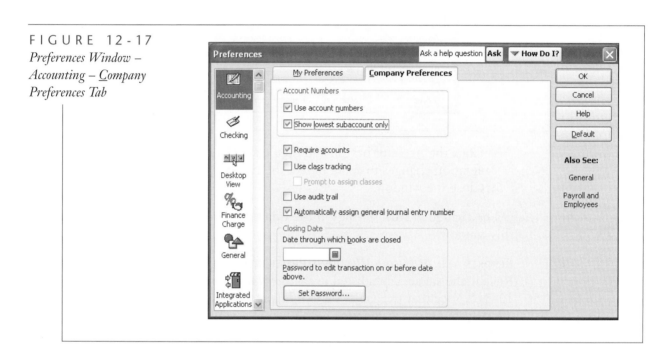

5. If the information is correct, click OK.

To see the effect of this default setting change, first reopen the General Journal Entry window and, on the first line of the *Account* field, click the account *1750 Accum. Dep., Furniture*. Notice now that the parent account is no longer listed, only the subaccount. (See figure 12–18.) Close the General Journal Entry window.

FIGURE 12-18
*General Journal Entry
Window – Subaccount
Selected – Subaccount
Displays*

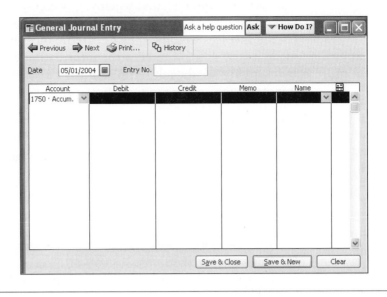

Now view the *Account Listing* report. The subaccounts are listed on a line separate from the parent account. (See figure 12–19.) This default change is also applied to any memorized reports.

FIGURE 12-19
*Account Listing –
Subaccounts Listed on
Separate Line*

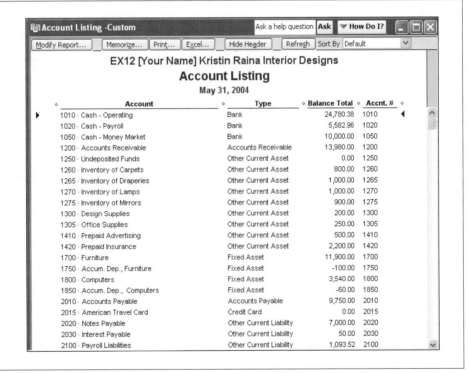

CUSTOMIZING WINDOWS AND PRINTED DOCUMENTS

In all chapters, the activity window displayed was based on default settings. QuickBooks Pro allows you to change the default settings of a window and also of a document that can be printed as a result of data entered in a window.

Recall in chapter 11 that when you used time tracking, the data you entered in the Weekly Time Sheet window was carried forward to the Create Invoices window. The Create Invoices window displayed by default made it very difficult to view the information carried over to that window. By changing the default settings in the Create Invoices window, more of the important information can be displayed.

To view the default settings and print an invoice—

1. Click Customers, and then click Create Invoices.
2. Click the Previous button to display Invoice No. 1016. (See figure 12–20.)

FIGURE 12-20
Create Invoices Window –
Invoice No. 1016

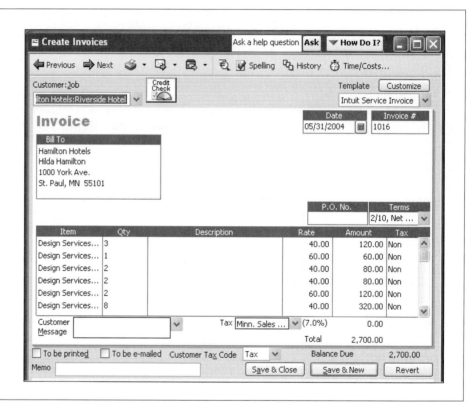

3. To print the invoice for this customer, click the Print icon.
4. At the Print One Invoice dialog box, accept the defaults and click Print. At the warning, click OK. The invoice printed should look like figure 12–21.

EX12 [Your Name] Kristin Raina Interior
Design
25 NE Johnson Street
Minneapolis, MN 53402

Invoice

Date	Invoice #
05/31/2004	1016

Bill To
Hamilton Hotels Hilda Hamilton 1000 York Ave. St. Paul, MN 55101

P.O. No.	Terms	Project
	2/10, Net 30 Days	Riverside Hotel

Item	Qty	Description	Rate	Amount
Design Services - ...	3		40.00	120.00
Design Services - ...	1		60.00	60.00
Design Services - ...	2		40.00	80.00
Design Services - ...	2		40.00	80.00
Design Services - ...	2		60.00	120.00
Design Services - ...	8		40.00	320.00
Design Services - ...	1		60.00	60.00
Design Services - ...	4		40.00	160.00
Design Services - ...	1		60.00	60.00
Design Services - ...	4		40.00	160.00
Design Services - ...	2		60.00	120.00
Design Services - ...	4		40.00	160.00
Design Services - ...	1		60.00	60.00
Design Services - ...	2		40.00	80.00
Design Services - ...	3		60.00	180.00
Design Services - ...	2		40.00	80.00
Design Services - ...	4		60.00	240.00
Design Services - ...	2		40.00	80.00
Design Services - ...	1		60.00	60.00
Design Services - ...	6		40.00	240.00
Design Services - ...	3		60.00	180.00
		Sales Tax	7.00%	0.00

Total	$2,700.00

In both the Create Invoices window and the invoice itself, it is very difficult to view the detail information. Notice that on the invoice, part of the company name is cut off. This is not an invoice you would want to send to a customer. You can customize both the window and the invoice so that all detailed information is adequately displayed. In addition, you can widen the company name field so the entire company name is presented. These changes are made in the Template.

To customize the Create Invoices window and a printed invoice—

1. With the Create Invoices window open and Invoice No. 1016 displayed, click the drop-down arrow in the *Template* field.

   The choices previously used, *Intuit Product Invoice* and *Intuit Service Invoice*, are listed. These are pre-established invoices provided by QuickBooks Pro. You can create your own invoices using the Customize choice.

2. Click *Customize.*

   The Customize Template dialog box appears. (See figure 12–22.) You can edit an Intuit pre-established invoice, or you can use one of Intuit's pre-established invoices and customize it to your personal preferences. It is better not to edit existing invoices in case you ever need them.

FIGURE 12-22
Customize Template Dialog Box

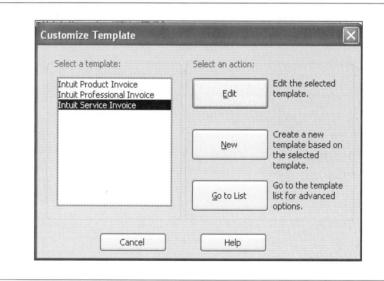

3. Select *Intuit Service Invoice*, and then click <u>N</u>ew. You will create your own invoice using the Service Invoice template as a guideline.
4. At the Customize Invoice dialog box, click the <u>C</u>olumns tab.

   The <u>C</u>olumns tab lists the pre-established settings for the service invoice. Since nothing was listed in the *Description* field, we will remove this column from both the window and the invoice, which will allow more room for the columns where data is displayed.

5. Remove the check marks from the two boxes to the right of the *Description* field. The first box applies to the *Screen*—the Create Invoices window. The second box applies to the invoice to be printed. (See figure 12–23.)

FIGURE 12-23
Customize Invoice Dialog Box

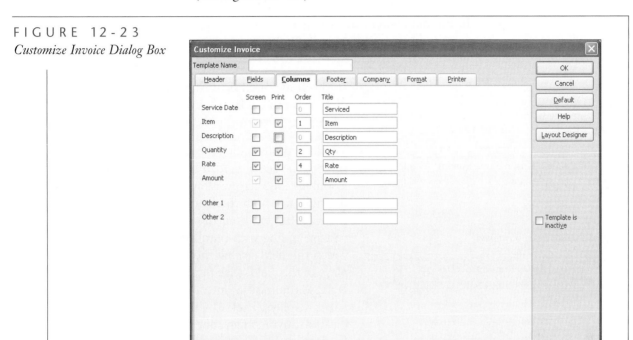

6. Click Layout Designer. The Layout Designer – Custom Invoice window appears. (See figure 12–24.)

FIGURE 12-24
Layout Designer – Custom Invoice Window

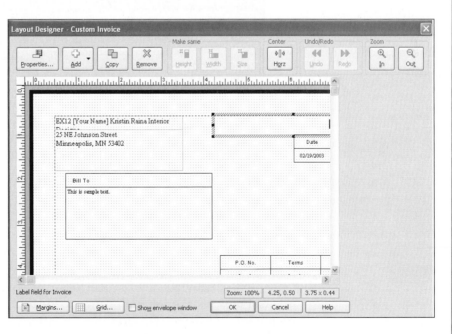

The Layout Designer window indicates the space allotted to each field of information in the invoice. You can widen the field where the company information is displayed to allow more room for the company name.

7. In the field where the company name *EX12 [Your Name] Kristin Raina Interior Designs* is displayed, click once to make it the active field. A box appears around the field. (See figure 12–25.)

In the active field box, there are small black handles. You can click and drag these handles to change the size of the field.

8. With the mouse, click the middle black handle on the right of the active field. The mouse pointer turns into a double-sided arrow. Drag the double-sided arrow to the right to widen the field. Watch above the field on the ruler as you drag the mouse pointer. Drag until you are in line with number 4 on the ruler. This will widen the field so that the entire company name displays in this field. (See figure 12–26.)

9. Release the mouse button. If the entire company name displays, click OK in the Layout Designer Custom Invoice window. You are returned to the Customize Invoice window. Now you must assign a name to the new invoice template you created.

10. In the *Template Name* field, key **Job Invoice**, and then click OK.

You are returned to the Create Invoices window. The *Form Template* field displays the new format created, *Job Invoice*. (See figure 12–27.)

FIGURE 12-25
Company Name Selected as Active Field

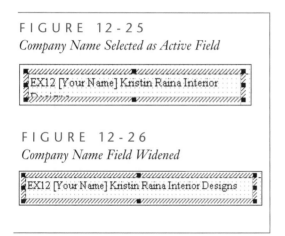

FIGURE 12-26
Company Name Field Widened

FIGURE 12-27
Create Invoices Window – Job Invoice Template

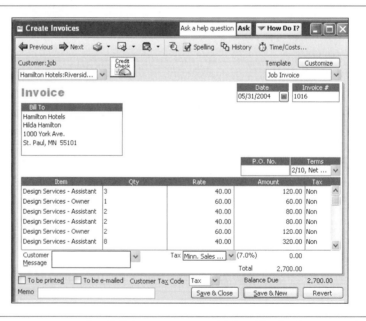

You can now see the full item name and identify the hours and rate for each item. But the actual dates these hours were worked are not shown on the template. You will now edit the Job Invoice you created to indicate the dates on which services were provided.

11. At the *Template* field, click *Customize*.
12. At the Customize Template dialog box, *Job Invoice* should be selected. Click <u>E</u>dit. You will edit the Job Invoice you just created.
13. At the Customize Invoice dialog box, click the <u>C</u>olumns tab.
14. On the Service Date line, place a check mark in both boxes, *Screen* and *Print*. QuickBooks Pro automatically assigns an order number of 4. (See figure 12–28.)

FIGURE 12-28
Customize Invoice Dialog Box –
Columns Tab – Service Date

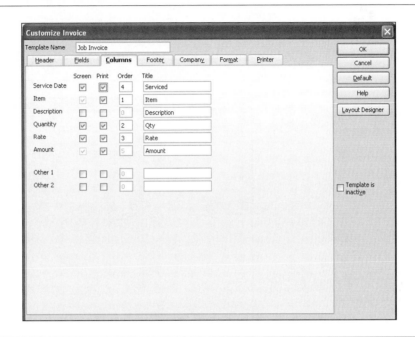

15. If the information is correct, click OK. You are returned to the Create Invoices window showing Job Invoice with the *Serviced* field added. (See figure 12–29.)

FIGURE 12-29
Create Invoices Window – Job
Invoice – Service Dates Added

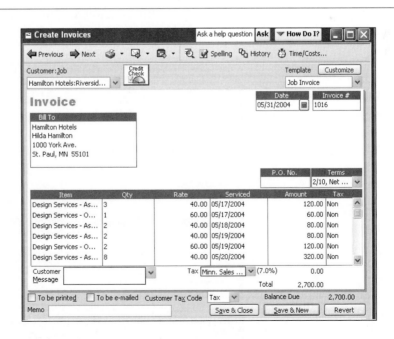

Upon reviewing the Create Invoices window, you realize the order of data fields should be different.

16. At the *Template* field, click *Customize*.
17. At the Customize Template dialog box, *Job Invoice* should be selected. Click *E*dit.
18. At the Customize Invoice dialog box, click the *C*olumns tab.
19. Change the order of the data fields as follows:

Service Date:	**2**	*Quantity:*	**3**
Item:	**1**	*Rate:*	**4**

The Amount order is automatically changed to 5. (See figure 12–30.)

FIGURE 12-30

Customize Invoice Dialog Box –
Columns Tab – Order

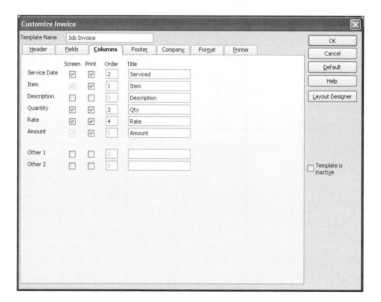

20. If the information is correct, click OK. You are returned to the Create Invoices window with the updated Job Invoice data displayed. (See figure 12–31.)

FIGURE 12-31

Create Invoices Window – Job
Invoice – Updated Order

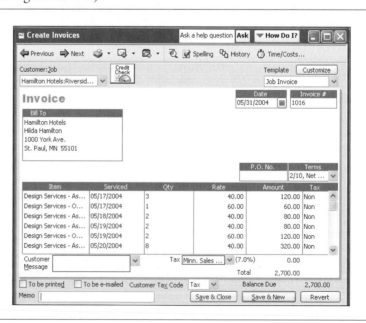

21. If the information is correct, click the Print icon. At the Print One Invoice dialog box, click Print. The invoice is printed using the custom-designed Job Invoice format. (See figure 12–32.)

FIGURE 12-32
Invoice No. 1016 –
Job Invoice Format

EX12 [Your Name] Kristin Raina Interior Designs
25 NE Johnson Street
Minneapolis, MN 53402

Invoice

Date	Invoice #
05/31/2004	1016

Bill To

Hamilton Hotels
Hilda Hamilton
1000 York Ave.
St. Paul, MN 55101

P.O. No.	Terms	Project
	2/10, Net 30 Days	Riverside Hotel

Item	Serviced	Qty	Rate	Amount
Design Services - Assistant	05/17/2004	3	40.00	120.00
Design Services - Owner	05/17/2004	1	60.00	60.00
Design Services - Assistant	05/18/2004	2	40.00	80.00
Design Services - Assistant	05/19/2004	2	40.00	80.00
Design Services - Owner	05/19/2004	2	60.00	120.00
Design Services - Assistant	05/20/2004	8	40.00	320.00
Design Services - Owner	05/20/2004	1	60.00	60.00
Design Services - Assistant	05/21/2004	4	40.00	160.00
Design Services - Owner	05/21/2004	1	60.00	60.00
Design Services - Assistant	05/24/2004	4	40.00	160.00
Design Services - Owner	05/24/2004	2	60.00	120.00
Design Services - Assistant	05/25/2004	4	40.00	160.00
Design Services - Owner	05/25/2004	1	60.00	60.00
Design Services - Assistant	05/26/2004	2	40.00	80.00
Design Services - Owner	05/26/2004	3	60.00	180.00
Design Services - Assistant	05/27/2004	2	40.00	80.00
Design Services - Owner	05/27/2004	4	60.00	240.00
Design Services - Assistant	05/28/2004	2	40.00	80.00
Design Services - Owner	05/28/2004	1	60.00	60.00
Design Services - Assistant	05/31/2004	6	40.00	240.00
Design Services - Owner	05/31/2004	3	60.00	180.00
			7.00%	0.00

Total $2,700.00

22. If the information is correct, click S<u>a</u>ve & Close. Click <u>Y</u>es at the warning.

After creating this new format for an invoice, you could review the other invoices in the Create Invoices window that used time tracking and apply the new Job Invoice format to those invoices.

QUICKBOOKS LETTERS

QuickBooks Pro provides preformatted letters that may be used in certain business circumstances. **(Note:** *QuickBooks Letters is available only in QuickBooks Pro, not QuickBooks.)* You can use these letters as they are, or customize them based on your personal preferences. You must have Microsoft Word on your computer to use this feature.

Kristin Raina wants to send a letter to Burnitz Bakery Company regarding the check that was returned NSF with the April 30 bank statement. She will use QuickBooks Pro Letters to do this.

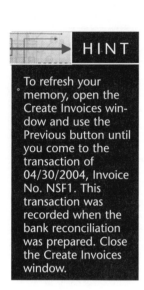

HINT

To refresh your memory, open the Create Invoices window and use the Previous button until you come to the transaction of 04/30/2004, Invoice No. NSF1. This transaction was recorded when the bank reconciliation was prepared. Close the Create Invoices window.

To prepare a business letter using QuickBooks Pro Letters—

1. Click <u>C</u>ompany, and then click Write <u>L</u>etters.

   If you see the Find QuickBooks Letters message box, click Cop<u>y</u>.

2. Click *Prepare <u>A</u>nother Type of Letter*, and then click <u>N</u>ext.
3. At the Select a Letter to Use page, click *Bounced check*, and then click <u>N</u>ext.
4. At the Choose Who You Want to Write to page, click <u>C</u>lear All to remove all of the check marks from the customer names.
5. Click *Burnitz Bakery Company* to select that customer, and then click <u>N</u>ext.
6. At the Enter What You Want at the End of the Letter page, enter the following data:

Name:	**[Your Name]**
Title:	**Assistant Accountant**

   (See figure 12–33.)

FIGURE 12-33
Write Letters Window

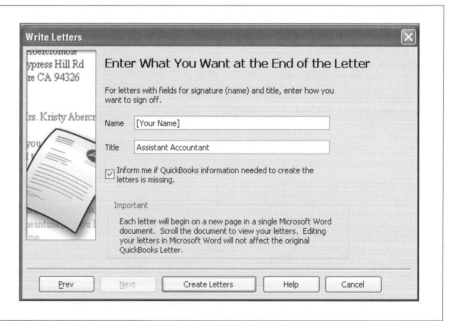

7. If the information is correct, click Create Letters. Click OK at the warning. Microsoft Word opens and the bounced check letter displays with your company name and customer name included. (See figure 12–34.)

FIGURE 12-34
QuickBooks Pro Bounced Check Letter Exported to Word

EX12 [Your Name] Kristin Raina Interior Designs
25 NE Johnson Street
Minneapolis, MN 53402

May 1, 2004

Burnitz Bakery Company
Barry Burnitz
18 N. Grand Ave.
Minneapolis, MN 55403

Dear Barry Burnitz,

Your recent payment has been returned for insufficient funds. To keep your account with us in good standing, we ask that you send a money order or cashier's check for the amount due within three days.

If the returned check is due to a bank error, please contact us with verification from the bank. In the case of a bank error, we do let customers simply send a replacement check.

Please handle this matter promptly, as a delay may affect your account with us. If you have questions about this letter, please contact me.

Sincerely,

[Your Name]
Assistant Accountant
EX12 [Your Name] Kristin Raina Interior Designs

8. Close Word. Do not save the letter.

MEMORIZED TRANSACTIONS

Many routine business activities are repeated often at daily, weekly, and monthly intervals. QuickBooks Pro allows you to *memorize* repetitive transactions. Once a transaction is memorized, you can recall the transaction at the appropriate time to record it, or you can have QuickBooks Pro automatically record the transaction on certain dates.

An example of a transaction that could be memorized is the monthly rent Kristin Raina Interior Designs pays for its space.

On June 1, 2004, Kristin Raina Interior Designs is ready to pay the monthly rent of $800 to Nordic Realty. Since this is a routine bill, Kristin Raina decides to have you set it up as a memorized transaction. To memorize a transaction, you first enter the data for the transaction as a regular transaction, and then, before saving it, you set it up as a memorized transaction.

To set up and memorize a transaction—

1. Click <u>B</u>anking, and then click <u>W</u>rite Checks.
2. Enter the following data for the rent expense as previously learned:

Bank Account:	**1010 – Cash – Operating**
No.:	**14**
Date:	**06/01/2004**
Pay to the Order of:	**Nordic Realty**
Amount:	**800**
Account:	**Rent Expense**

(See figure 12–35.)

FIGURE 12-35
Write Checks Window –
Rent Expense

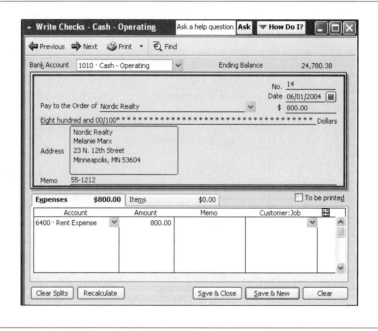

3. If the information is correct, click <u>E</u>dit on the Main Menu bar, and then click <u>M</u>emorize Check. The Memorize Transaction dialog box appears.
4. In the *How Often* field, click *Monthly*.
5. In the *Ne<u>x</u>t Date* field, click *07/01/2004*. (See figure 12–36.)

FIGURE 12-36
Memorize Transaction
Dialog Box

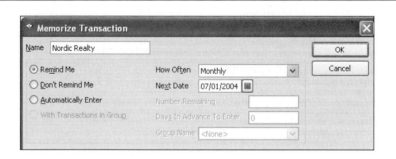

6. If the information is correct, click OK. The transaction is memorized.
7. At the Write Checks window, click S<u>a</u>ve & Close.

Assume it is now July 1, 2004, and time to pay the rent for July. You can recall the memorized transaction.

To recall a memorized transaction—
1. Click Lists, and then click Memorized Transaction List. The Memorized Transaction List window appears. (See figure 12–37.)

FIGURE 12-37
Memorized Transaction List Window

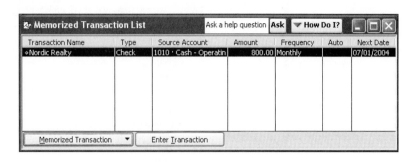

2. To recall the transaction, click Enter Transaction.

   The Write Checks window appears with the correct date and the next check number automatically entered.

3. Do not record the transaction at this time. Close the Write Checks window. Click No at the warning.
4. Close the Memorized Transaction List window.

FISCAL YEAR CLOSING

fiscal year The 12-month financial reporting year of the company. It can be the calendar year or any other 12-month period.

In a manual accounting system, and most other computerized accounting software packages, the books are closed on **fiscal year** end. When the books are closed, the temporary accounts, usually revenues, expenses, and some equity accounts, are brought to a zero balance and the net income for the year is transferred into a capital or retained earnings equity account for the next year. After the books are closed, pre-closing balances in the temporary accounts are no longer accessible.

QuickBooks Pro does not require you to close the books on fiscal year end. However, QuickBooks Pro automatically creates a Retained Earnings account and at the start of a new fiscal year automatically transfers the net income for the previous fiscal year into it. In addition, at the beginning of the new fiscal year, all revenue and expense accounts will begin with a zero balance so the net income for the new fiscal year can be accumulated.

When the new company file was created for Kristin Raina Interior Designs, the fiscal year was designated as beginning on January 1, 2004. When you move to the new fiscal year, January 1, 2005, QuickBooks Pro transfers the net income for 2004 into a new equity account called Retained Earnings. For example, look at the *Profit & Loss Standard* report for the period 01/01/2004 to 06/30/2004. There is a net income of $8,339.82. (See figure 12–38.)

FIGURE 12-38
Profit & Loss Standard Report
January 1, 2004 –
June 30, 2004

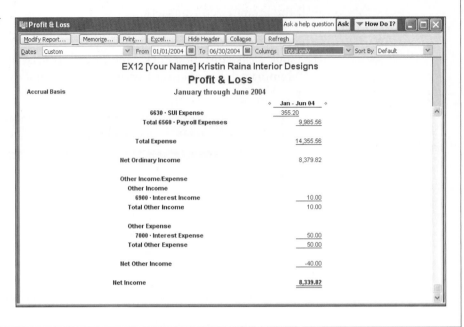

The net income is carried over to the *Balance Sheet* standard report as shown in figure 12–39.

FIGURE 12-39
Balance Sheet Standard Report
June 30, 2004

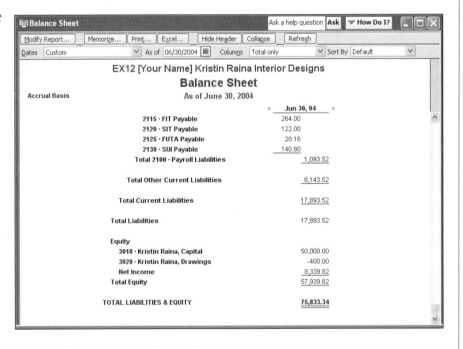

Assuming no other activity for the year 2004, look at the *Balance Sheet* standard report for the first day of the new fiscal year, January 1, 2005. Notice there is no longer a line for net income, but the $8,339.82 has been transferred into the new Retained Earnings account. (See figure 12–40.)

FIGURE 12-40
Balance Sheet Standard Report January 1, 2005

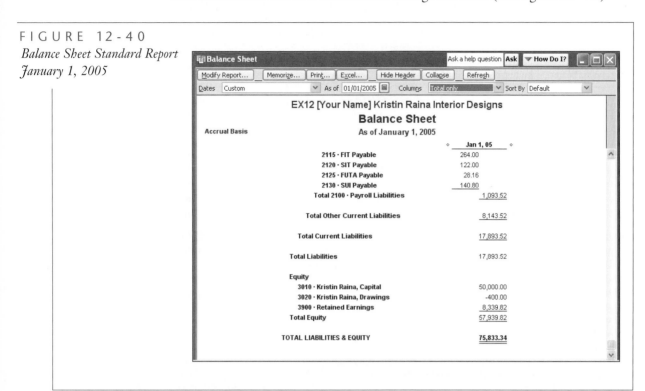

In addition, the revenue and expenses all begin with a zero balance for the start of the new fiscal year. Since there are no revenues or expenses on January 1, 2005, there is no income. (See figure 12–41.)

FIGURE 12-41
Profit & Loss Standard Report January 1, 2005

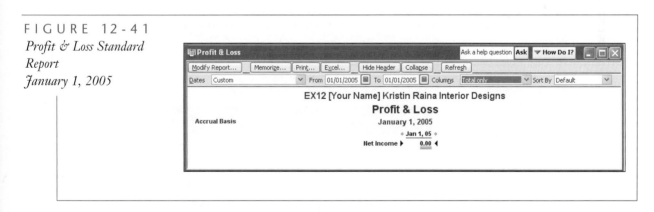

At this point, if you wanted to close the Drawings account, you would have to record an adjusting journal entry in the General Journal Entry window.

Because QuickBooks does not actually close the books, you still have access to all records for prior years. As a precaution, however, you can protect the data for a fiscal year by restricting access to the records so no changes can be made after fiscal year end.

INTERNET *Resources*

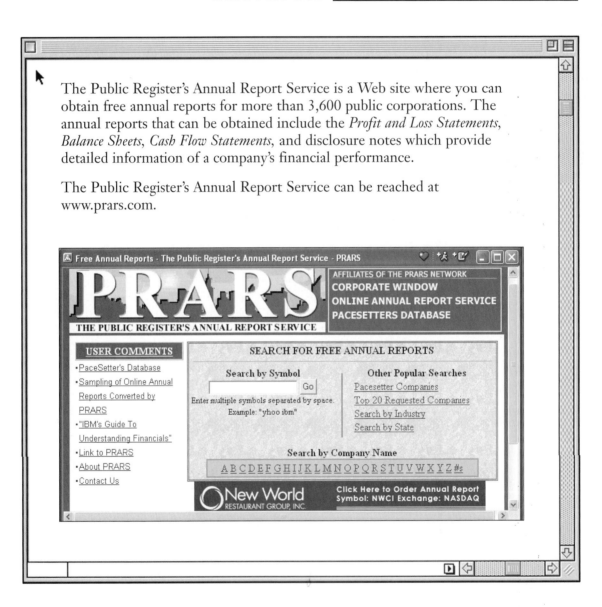

The Public Register's Annual Report Service is a Web site where you can obtain free annual reports for more than 3,600 public corporations. The annual reports that can be obtained include the *Profit and Loss Statements*, *Balance Sheets*, *Cash Flow Statements*, and disclosure notes which provide detailed information of a company's financial performance.

The Public Register's Annual Report Service can be reached at www.prars.com.

P R O G R E S S *Check*

PROCEDURE REVIEW

To modify a report using the Display tab—
1. Open the report, and then click Modify Report.
2. In the Modify Report dialog box, the default tab is Display.
3. Place or remove the check marks from the field titles you wish to add or hide, and then click OK.

To disable or change the format of the Date Prepared and Time Prepared items, and to change a title in a report—
1. Open the report, and then click Modify Report on the command line.
2. In the Modify Report dialog box, click the Header/Footer tab.
3. Remove the check mark from the box to the left of Date Prepared and Time Prepared.
4. In the *Subtitle* field, delete the date provided and key the new subtitle.
5. Click OK at the Modify Report dialog box.

To memorize the settings for a report—
1. Open the report and make the desired changes.
2. Click Memorize.
3. At the Memorize Report dialog box, key the new report name.
4. Click OK.

To open a memorized report—
1. Click Reports, and then click Memorized Reports.
2. At the Memorized Reports submenu, click on Memorized Report List. The Memorized Reports List appears.
3. In the Memorized Reports List, double-click the desired report. The memorized report displays.

To collapse and expand the numbers in a report—
1. Open the report, and then click Collapse. Any account that has subaccounts is collapsed into one amount.
2. To expand the numbers, click Expand. The report returns to the original presentation.

To export a report to Excel—
1. Open the report, and then click Excel.
2. Accept the default to send the report to a new spreadsheet by clicking OK. Excel is opened and a spreadsheet is prepared using the report.
3. If you are familiar with operating Excel, you may revise the report according to your preferences.
4. Close Excel by clicking the Close (X) button.

To disable or change the Date Prepared and Time Prepared items default settings—
1. Click Edit, and then click Preferences.
2. Along the left frame of the Preferences window, click the *Reports & Graphs* icon. By default the My Preferences tab is displayed.
3. Click Company Preferences. Read the choices on the Company Preferences tab and make any desired changes.

4. Click Format.
5. Click the Header/Footer tab. You can change the default formats or disable any field of information for all reports in this dialog box.
6. To disable the Date Prepared item, remove the check mark from the box to the left of Date Prepared.
7. To disable the Time Prepared item, remove the check mark from the box to the left of the Time Prepared field.
8. Click OK at the Report Format Preferences dialog box. You are returned to the Preferences window.
9. Click OK.

To view a graph—
1. Use the Reports menu from the Main Menu bar, or the Reports button in a List window, to choose a graph.
2. Click Dates.
3. Choose the dates, and then click OK. The graph for that period of time displays.
4. To display the income as a pie chart, click Income. The pie chart changes to display the income analysis.
5. Close the graph.

To change to flat or hierarchical view in the Chart of Accounts List window—
1. In the Chart of Accounts window, click the Account button. By default, the Hierarchical View is checked.
2. Click Flat View. The subaccounts are no longer indented, but are left aligned in the window.
3. Click the Account button and then click Hierarchical View. The presentation changes to indent the subaccounts.
4. Close the window.

To change the default setting of subaccounts—
1. Click Edit, and then click Preferences.
2. Along the left frame of the Preferences window, click the *Accounting* icon.
3. Click Company Preferences.
4. In the *Account Numbers* section, place a check mark in the box next to Show lowest subaccount only.
5. Click OK.

To customize the Create Invoices window and a printed invoice—
1. With the Create Invoices window open, click *Customize* in the Template drop-down list.
2. With *Intuit Service Invoice* selected, click New.
3. At the Customize Invoice dialog box, click the Columns tab.
4. Add or delete check marks for the different fields of information.
5. Change the order of the fields, if necessary.
6. Click Layout Designer.
7. Select a field and click and drag to change the size or location of the field.
8. Click OK in the Layout Designer window.
9. In the Customize Invoice window, in the *Template Name* field, key the name of the new invoice.
10. Click OK.

To prepare a business letter using QuickBooks Pro Letters—
1. Click Company, and then click Write Letters.
2. Click the option *Prepare Another Type of Letter*, and then click Next.
3. At the Select a Letter to Use page, select a letter, and then click Next.
4. At the Choose Who You Want to Write to page, click *Clear All* to remove all of the check marks from the customer names.
5. Select the desired name, and then click Next.
6. At the Enter What You Want at the End of the Letter page, enter the appropriate data.
7. If the information is correct, click Create Letters. Click OK at the warning. Microsoft Word opens and the chosen letter displays with your company name and customer name included.
8. Save and print the letter, and then close Word.

To set up and memorize a transaction—
1. Record a transaction as usual in a window, but do not click Save.
2. Click Edit, and then click Memorize Check.
3. In the *How Often* field, click *Monthly*.
4. In the *Next Date* field, choose the date to start the memorized transaction.
5. Click OK. The transaction is memorized.
6. At the activity window, click Save & Close.

To recall a memorized transaction—
1. Click Lists, and then click Memorized Transaction List.
2. At the Memorized Transaction List window, select the transaction you wish to record, and then click Enter Transaction.
3. The activity window appears with the correct date and other information automatically entered. You may make changes if necessary, or if the information is correct, save the transaction.
4. If you wish to record the transaction, click Save & Close.
5. Close the Memorized Transaction List window.

KEY CONCEPTS

Select the letter of the item that best matches each definition.

a. Excel button
b. Customize Invoice dialog box - Columns Tab
c. Header/Footer tab
d. Memorize Check on Edit menu
e. Layout Designer dialog box
f. Display tab
g. Memorize button on command line
h. Write Letters
i. Customize on Template
j. Collapse/Expand button

_____ 1. Used to choose fields of information and order of appearance in the Create Invoices window and on a printed invoice.

_____ 2. Command choice to utilize pre-formatted business letters available in QuickBooks Pro.

_____ 3. Button used to save the changes made to the settings in a report.

_____ 4. Used to customize a pre-established invoice in QuickBooks Pro.

_____ 5. Buttons used to list all numbers in a report in one column, or to separate the subaccounts into the left column of a report.

_____ 6. Command used to save a routine transaction so you can recall it for later use.

_____ 7. Tab used to add or delete the fields of information displayed in each column in a report.

_____ 8. Shows the space allotted to each field of information in the invoice.

_____ 9. Button used to export a report into a spreadsheet.

_____10. Tab used to establish the headers and footers to be displayed in a report.

PROCEDURE CHECK

1. You change the columns of information displayed in the Customer Contact List every time you display it. What steps could you take to eliminate this repetitive formatting each time you view the List?

2. The *Date Prepared* field has been disabled on all reports. How can you activate this feature on all reports?

3. You wish to display a graph representing the sales for the first quarter of the year. How can you use QuickBooks Pro to accomplish this?

4. In the activity windows, when you choose an account with a subaccount, only the parent account displays in the account field. How can you modify this display of account names?

5. The first of each month you write a check for $100 for the liability insurance premium. How can you use QuickBooks Pro to simplify this monthly process?

6. Your manager is new to QuickBooks Pro and has just used the Time Tracking feature. However, when the data was transferred into the Create Invoices window, he found it difficult to read the information in the window. Explain to the manager how QuickBooks Pro can be utilized to display the information in a more meaningful presentation.

CASE PROBLEMS

CASE PROBLEM 1

Lynn's Music Studio recorded the income earned on the Highland Schools jobs earned for the month of July 2004 in the Create Invoices window, but she has not yet sent the invoices to the school. It is now August 1, 2004, and she is ready to send the invoices for the first half of July but wishes to present the detail in a more desirable format. You have been requested to prepare a job invoice format and print them for Invoices Nos. 2020, 2021, and 2022.

1. Open the company file: CH12 Lynn's Music Studio.QBW.

2. Make a backup copy of the company file: LMS12 [Your Name] Lynn's Music Studio.

3. Restore the backup copy of the company file. In both the Restore From and Restore To windows use the file name LMS12 [Your Name] Lynn's Music Studio.

4. Change the company name to LMS12 [Your Name] Lynn's Music Studio.

5. Open the Create Invoices window and display Invoice No. 2020.

6. Create a Job Invoice, based on the Intuit Service Invoice, using the following information:
   a. Delete the *Description* column.
   b. Add the *Service Date* column.

c. Put the invoice columns in the following order:

Item:	1
Service Date:	2
Quantity:	3
Rate:	4
Amount:	5

   d. Save the new invoice as Job Invoice.

7. Print Invoice No. 2020, and then save the invoice.
8. Open Invoice No. 2021, change it to the Job Invoice format, print the invoice, and then save the change.
9. Open Invoice No. 2022, change it to the Job Invoice format, print the invoice, and then save the change.

CASE PROBLEM 2

Olivia's Web Solutions recorded the income earned on the Thrifty Stores jobs earned for the month of September 2004 in the Create Invoices window, but she has not yet sent the invoices to the store. It is now October 1, 2004, and she is ready to send the invoices for the first half of September but wishes to present the detail in a more desirable format. You have been requested to prepare a job invoice format and print them for Invoice Nos. 1017, 1018, and 1019.

1. Open the company file: CH12 Olivia's Web Solutions.QBW.
2. Make a backup copy of the company file: OWS12 [Your Name] Olivia's Web Solutions.
3. Restore the backup copy of the company file. In both the Restore From and Restore To windows use the file name OWS12 [Your Name] Olivia's Web Solutions.
4. Change the company name to OWS12 [Your Name] Olivia's Web Solutions.
5. Open the Create Invoices window and display Invoice No. 1017.
6. Create a Job Invoice, based on the Intuit Service Invoice, using the following information:
   a. Delete the *Description* column.
   b. Add the *Service Date* column.
   c. Put the invoice columns in the following order:

Item:	1
Service Date:	2
Quantity:	3
Rate:	4
Amount:	5

   d. Save the new invoice as Job Invoice.

7. Print Invoice No. 1017, and then save the invoice.
8. Open Invoice No. 1018, change it to the Job Invoice format, print the invoice, and then save the change.
9. Open Invoice No. 1019, change it to the Job Invoice format, print the invoice, and then save the change.

APPENDICES

Manual Accounting versus QuickBooks Pro

Manual Accounting System	QuickBooks Pro
Accounts Payable Subsidiary Ledger	Vendor List
Purchases Journal	Enter Bills window
Cash Payments Journal	Pay Bills window Write Checks window
Accounts Receivable Subsidiary Ledger	Customer:Job List
Sales Journal	Create Invoices window
Cash Receipts Journal	Receive Payments window Enter Sales Receipts window
General Ledger	General Ledger
General Journal	Journal Report General Journal Entry window
Inventory Subsidiary Ledger	Item List (inventory part items)
Payroll Journal or Register	Pay Employees windows
Jobs Subsidiary Ledger	Customer:Job List

APPENDIX B

Summary of Journal Report "Types"

Type	Activity Window	System Default Account	
	Debit	Credit	
Bill	Enter Bills		Accounts Payable
Credit	Enter Bills	Accounts Payable	
Bill Pmt – Check	Pay Bills	Accounts Payable	Cash
Check	Write Checks		Cash
Invoice	Create Invoices	Accounts Receivable	
Payment	Receive Payments	Cash	Accounts Receivable
Sales Receipt	Enter Sales Receipts	Undeposited Funds	
Deposit	Make Deposits	Cash	Undeposited Funds
General Journal	General Journal Entry		
Inventory Adjust	Adjust Quantity/Value on Hand		
Sales Tax Payment	Pay Sales Tax	Sales Tax Payable	Cash
Paycheck	Pay Employees	Salaries and Wages Expense Payroll Tax Expenses	Payroll Liabilities Cash – Payroll
Liability Check	Pay Payroll Liabilities	Payroll Liabilities	Cash – Payroll
Transfer	Transfer Funds Between Accounts		
Credit Card Charge	Enter Credit Card Charges		Credit Card Liability

INDEX